CENTRE OF THE CREATIVE UNIVERSE: LIVERPOOL & THE AVANT-GARDE

Edited by
Christoph Grunenberg
& Robert Knifton

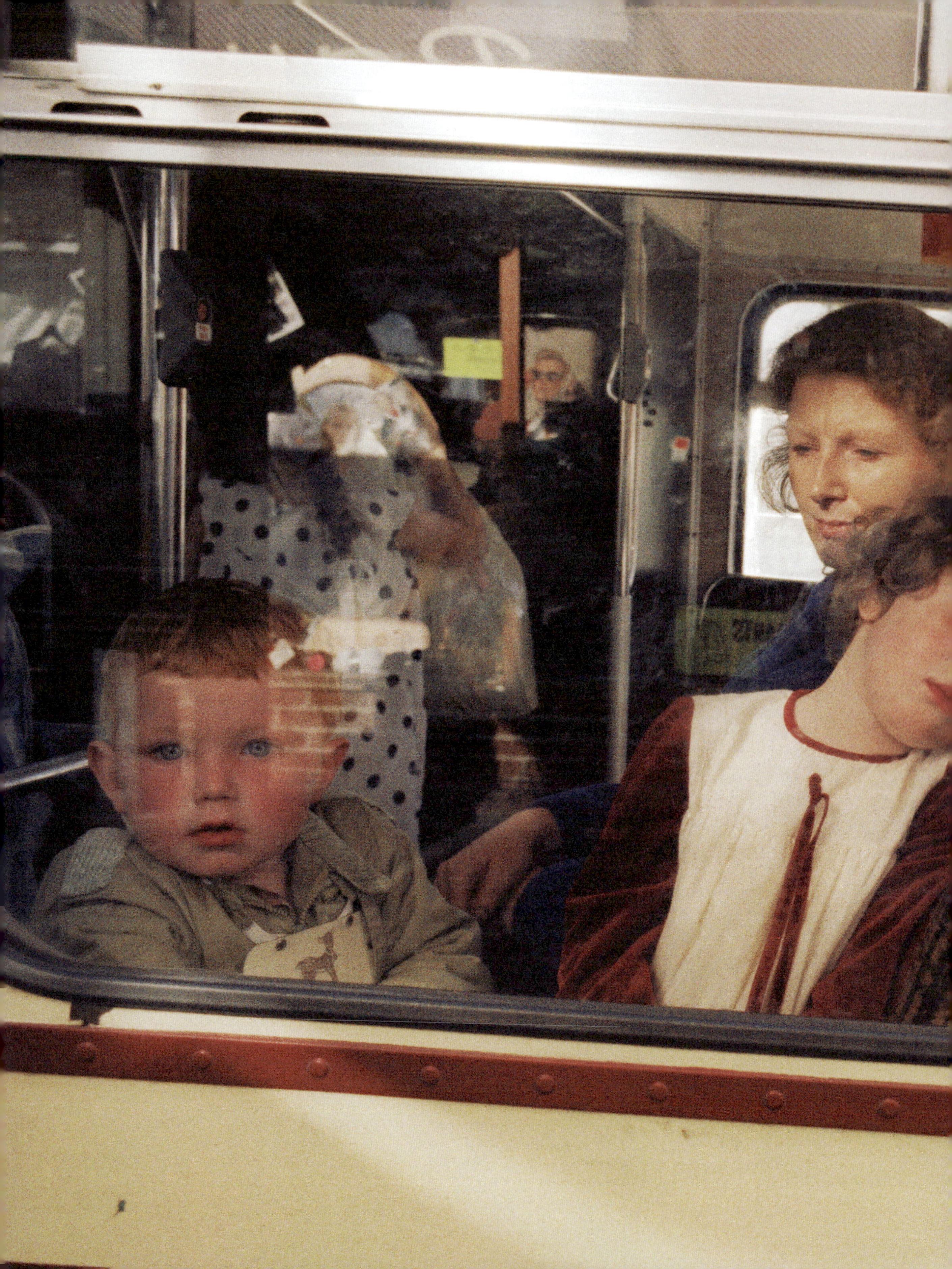

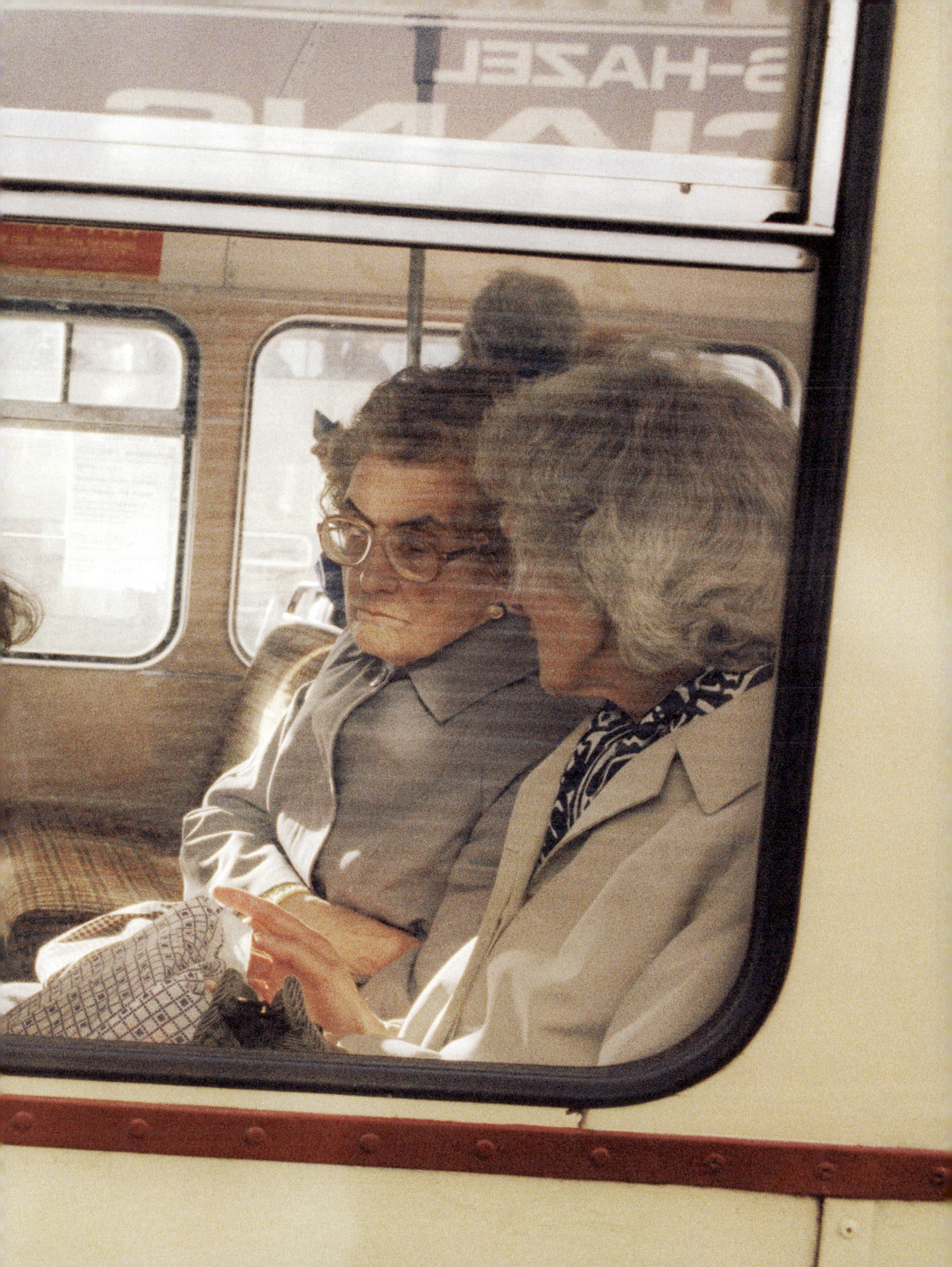
S-HAZEL
CLAIR

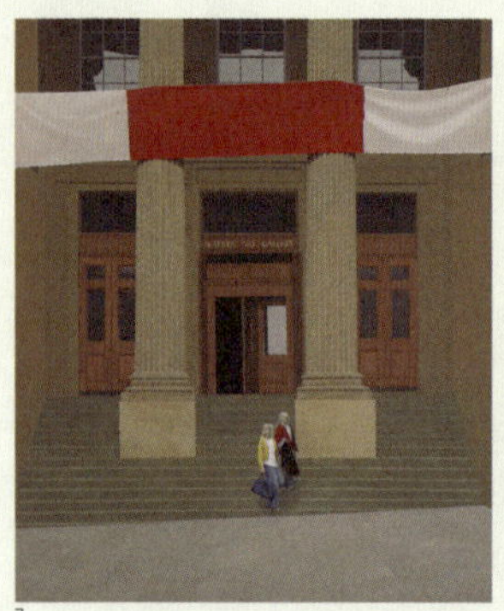
1

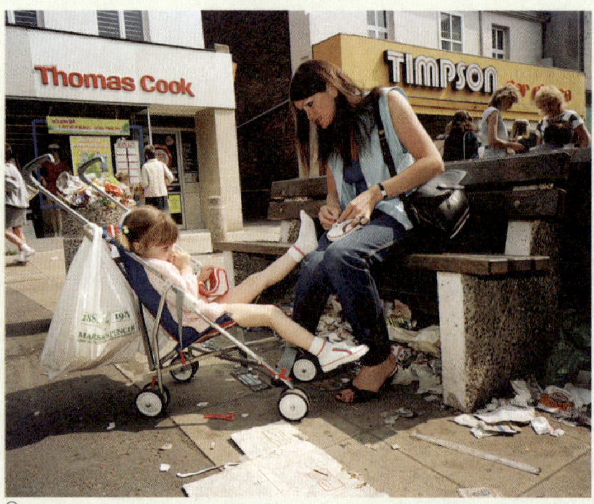
2

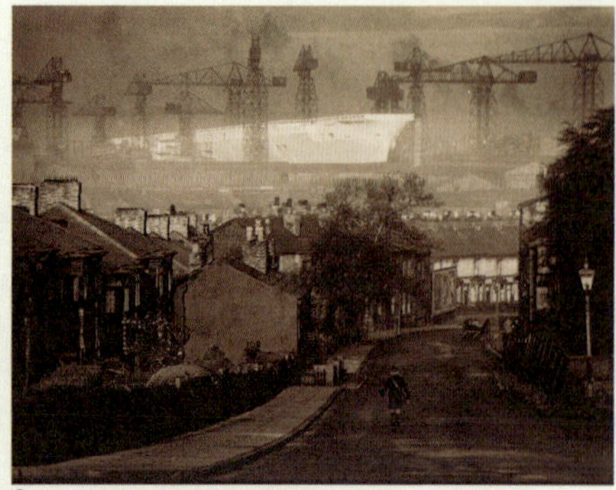
3

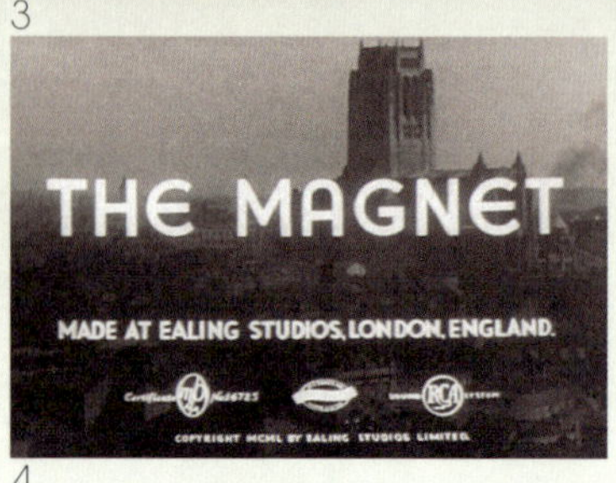

4

Contents

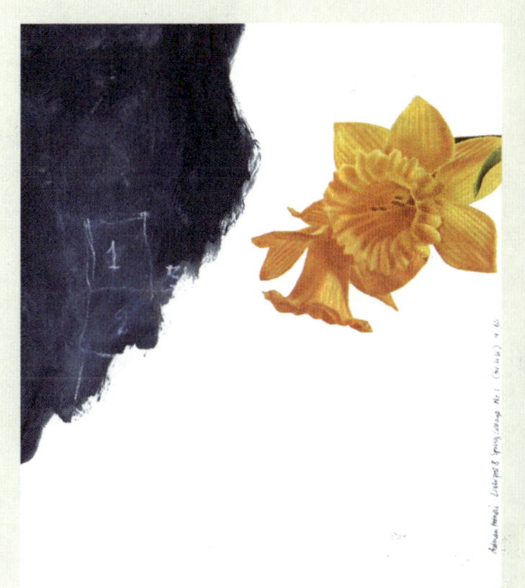

5

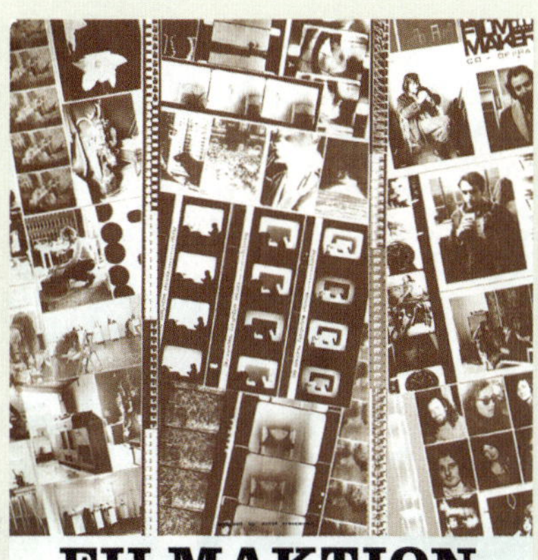

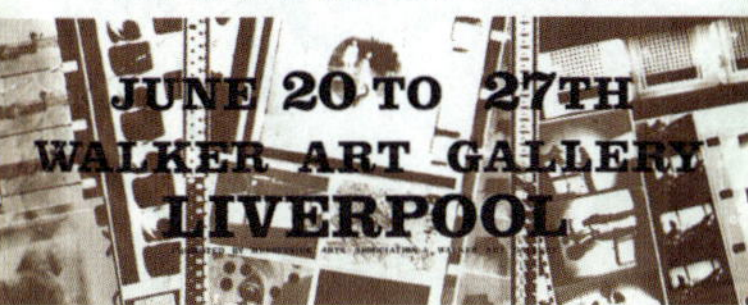

8

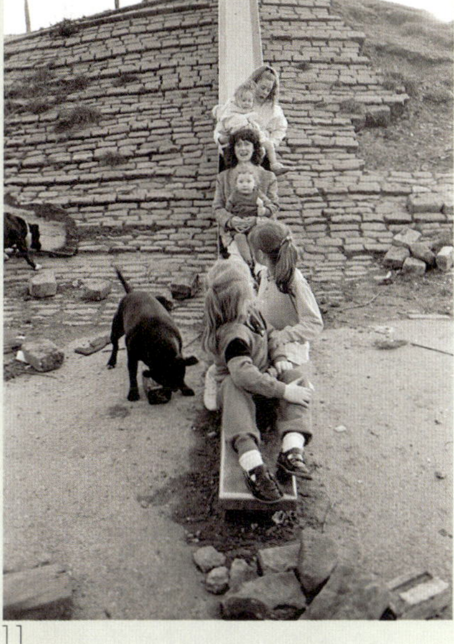

11

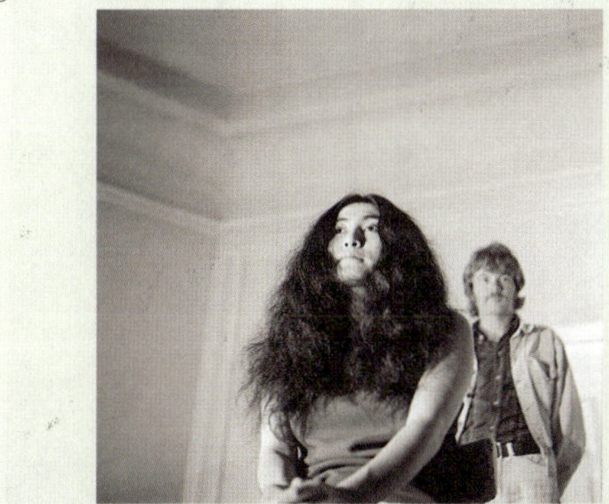

6

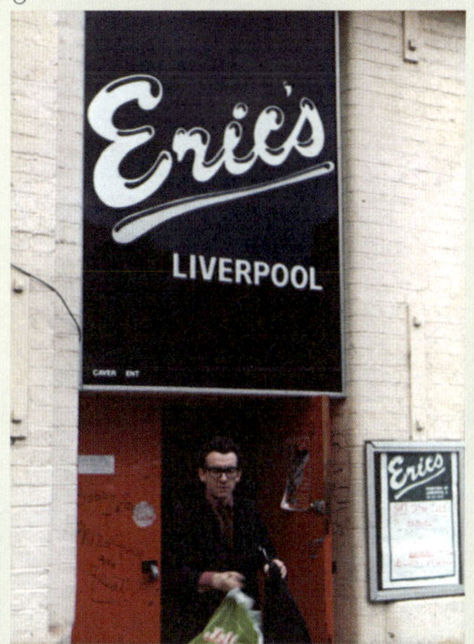

9

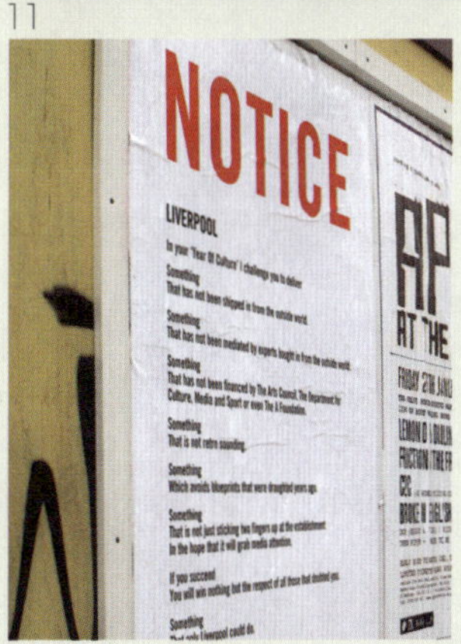

12

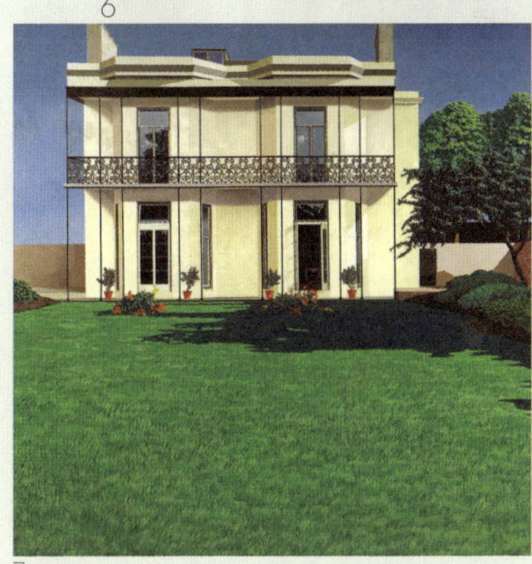

7

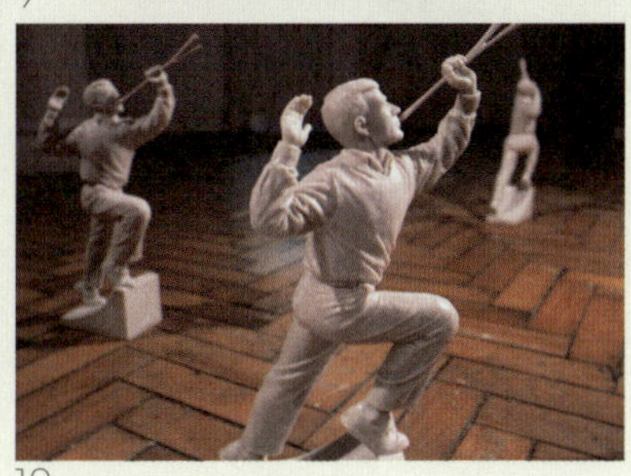

10

previous
Tom Wood
Stanley Road, Bootle 1989
C-type print
60.9 x 91.4 cm
Collection of the artist

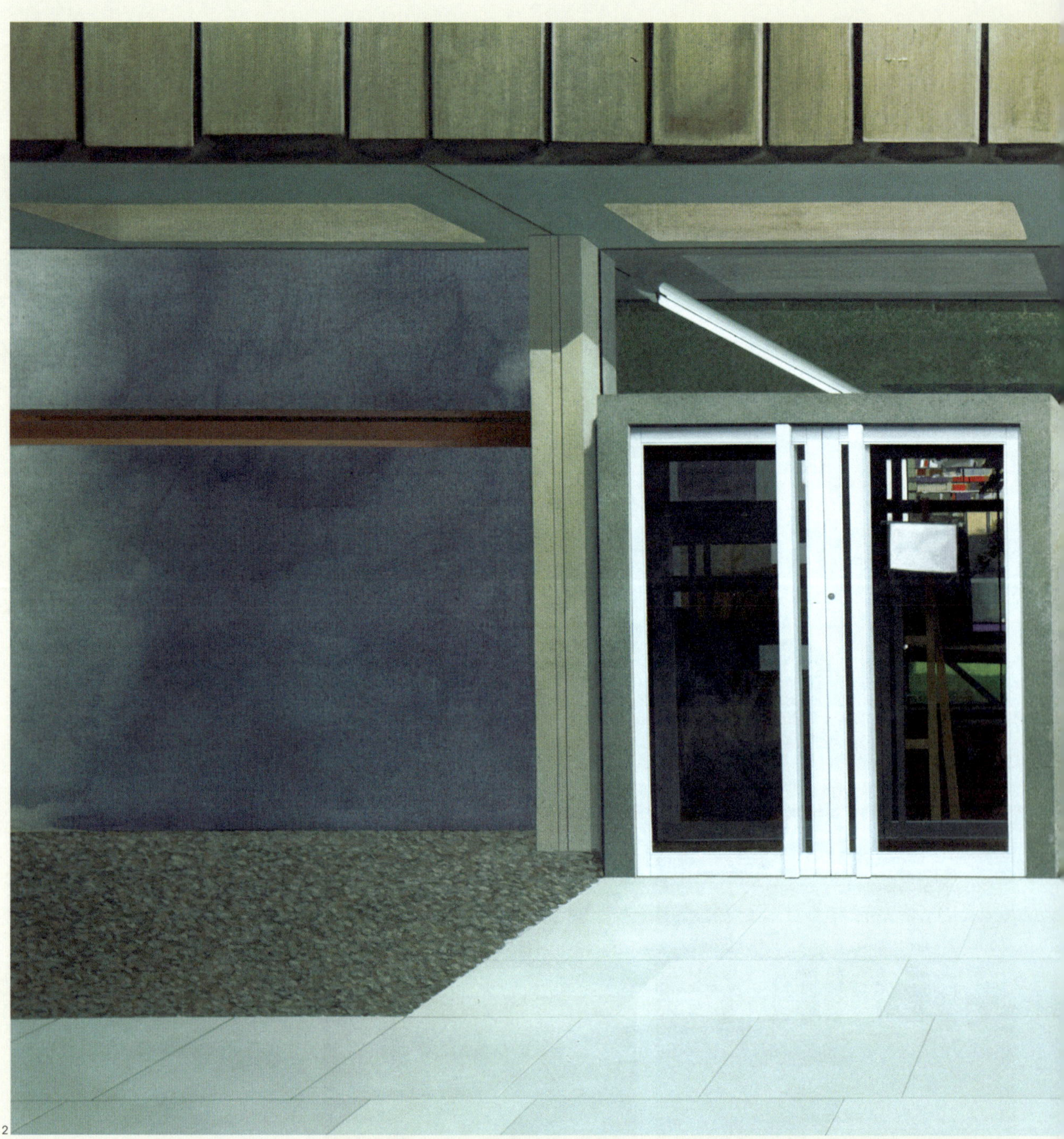

2

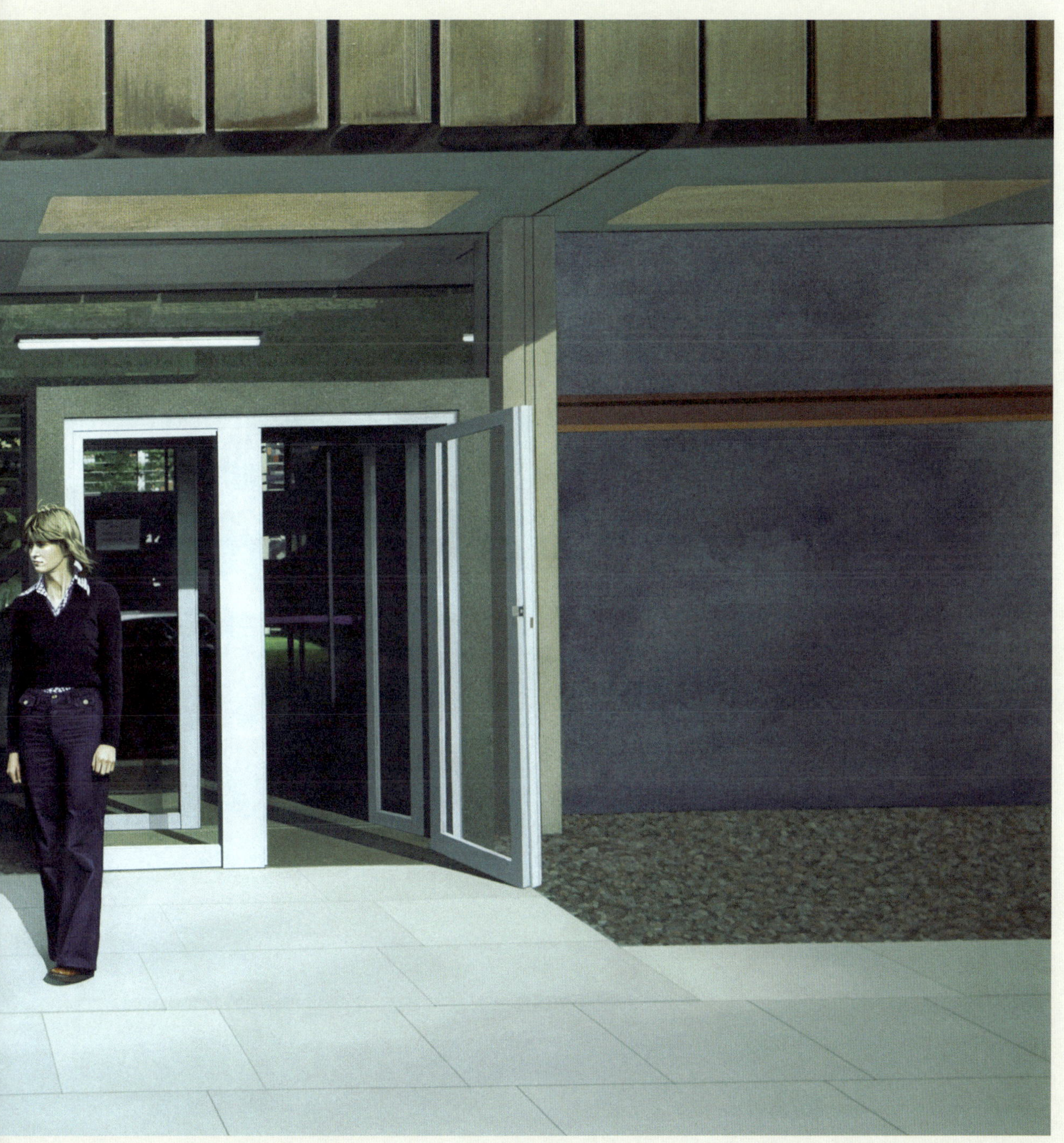

2
Maurice Cockrill
Entrance 1975
Acrylic on canvas
Diptych, each: 152.5 x 152.5 cm
University of Liverpool Art
Gallery and Collections

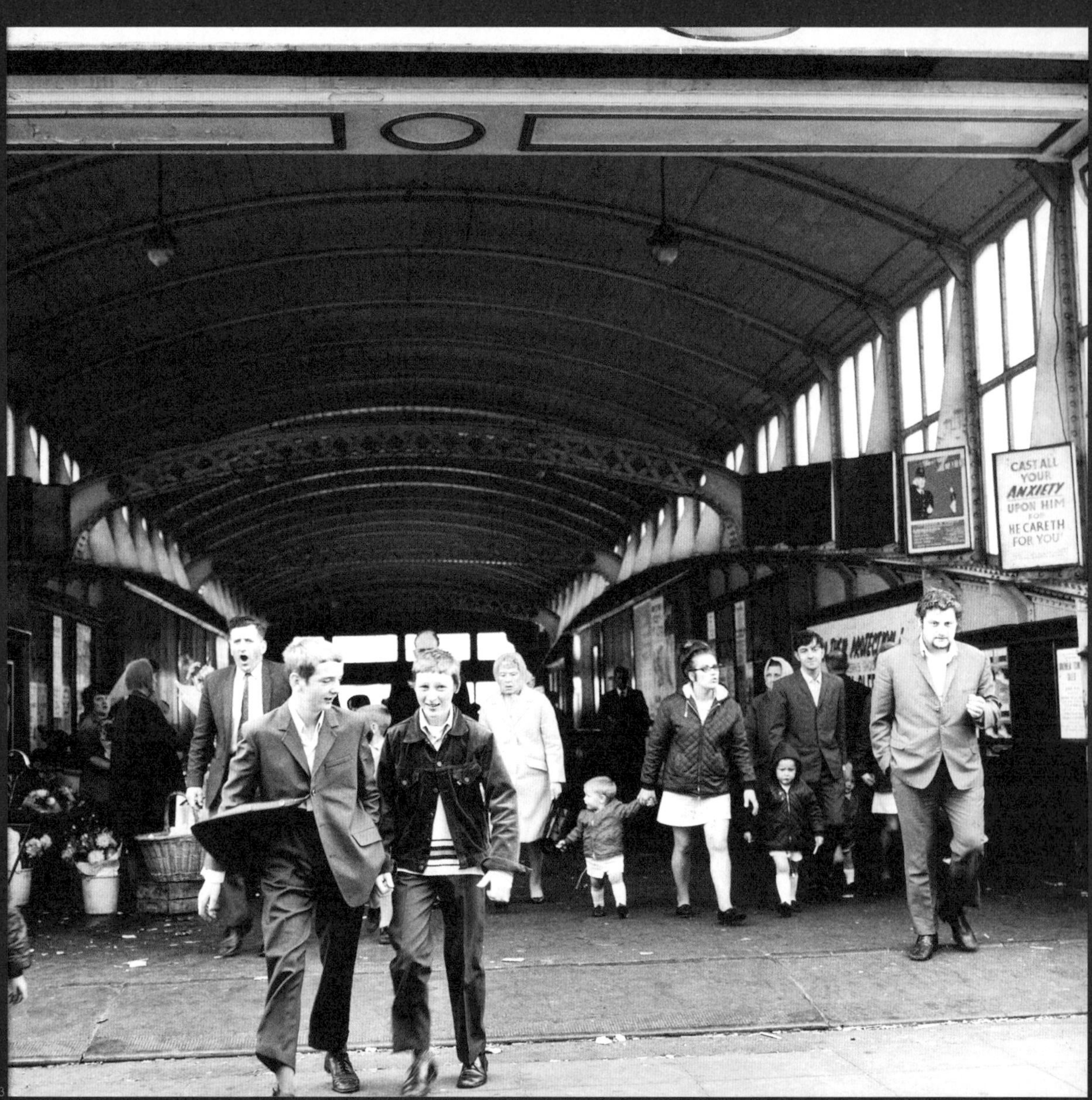

3
Candida Höfer
Liverpool X 1968
Silver gelatin print
21.1 x 20.5 cm
Photographische
Sammlung/SK Stiftung
Kultur, Cologne

Foreword
Christoph Grunenberg
& Robert Knifton

Liverpool is a place of myths – as many originating in the depth of time as generated by its inventive people and imposed from the outside. The title of this book, documenting the exhibition of the same name at Tate Liverpool, has its origins in the famous declaration by the poet Allen Ginsberg following his visit to the city in 1965, proclaiming 'Liverpool is at the present moment the centre of the consciousness of the human universe.' As with so many legends handed down over time, Ginsberg's programmatic statement was misremembered, elevating Liverpool to 'Centre of the Creative Universe.' We decided to retain this inspired mis-recollection, perfectly capturing the premise of the show but also Liverpool's, at times, hyperbolic world view.

The idea for *Centre of the Creative Universe* first occurred to me when Catherine Kinley, a former Tate Curator, mentioned a photograph of the decaying Albert Dock by Bernd and Hilla Becher from the 1960s which was presented at an exhibition about five years ago. Gradually, I came across more and more examples of British and international artists who had stayed in or passed through Liverpool and created works in the city or in response to it. What emerged was an alternative historical account of art in Liverpool, a record of the city observed from the outside. This was, however, not the usual contemptuous imposition of stereotypes dealt with by the city, in particular over the last decades. Rather, it presented a sympathetic portrait of the city by artists fascinated by an at times mythical and yet all too real place and its people.

Centre of the Creative Universe thus appropriately reflects Liverpool's status as seaport – a place of constant movement, change and exchange, playing host to a diverse collection of itinerant travellers, traders, emigrants and immigrants, passing through, temporarily stuck or settling permanently in the city. Though we have attempted to remain loyal to our original curatorial premise, the borders between local and global are necessarily fluid in an age of all-embracing transience. Photographer Stewart Bale, for example, arrived in the city from Australia, becoming one of the most intrepid chroniclers of change in Liverpool. Bale and Irish-born Edward Chambré-Hardman were also outsiders in other respects – professional photographers ambiguously positioned between art and commerce and only fairly recently accepted for the high quality of their work and contribution to shaping an enduring image of Liverpool. Martin Parr and Tom Wood made Merseyside their home for extended periods before leaving for Bristol and North Wales respectively. Most of the artists in the exhibition, on the other hand, experienced the city as short-term visitors, attracted by the myth of Merseybeat, The Beatles and Mersey Sound, the city's unique brand of poetry, as well as its perennial outsider status and notorious tendency towards nonconformity. As a guiding principle, we excluded artists and works previously presented at Tate Liverpool or the Liverpool Biennial as the establishment of these two organisations signalled an explosion of creative activity, transcending the scope of this exhibition and book. Instead we have concentrated primarily on an historical perspective and on those artists who have continued to find their way to Liverpool outside the 'official' channels.

While the primary focus of this exhibition and book is an external view of Liverpool, this is necessarily also an account of the city as an unlikely centre of avant-garde activity. As such it highlights the places, venues and personalities who have shaped Liverpool's creative scene since the 1950s. Without the College of Art, the entrepreneurial spirit of prominent figures such as poet and artist Adrian Henri or the pioneering work of Bill and Wendy Harpe at the city's first 'alternative' art centre, the Blackie, Liverpool would not have received the inspiration provided through the visits of nationally and internationally renowned figures that have included Bernd and Hilla Becher, the Boyle Family, Robert Creeley, Allen Ginsberg, John Latham and Yoko Ono. *Centre of the Creative Universe* is therefore also an account of a thriving local bohemian scene tied into a network of productive relationships and inspirational interfaces. Such centres of creativity connect the city globally, not unlike the network of shipping lines and trade links that existed before the decline of Liverpool's port and the arrival of jet travel.

If *Centre of the Creative Universe* as an exhibition acts as an alternative psychogeographic map of Liverpool, this book functions as a kind of avant-garde guidebook.

Its chapters re-animate a succession of creative moments in a number of artistic spheres, reintroduce some unjustly forgotten personalities and works, examine how the city has been imagined, and discover some of the ideological and sociological bases for that imagination. On the way we stop off at any number of intriguing spaces in the city. These spaces, where real, are reproduced on an indexical map at the back of this book, so that the adventurous visitor can interact with the final and largest work of art in the exhibition – Liverpool itself.

The organisation of *Centre of the Creative Universe* has been a journey into a mostly uncharted territory and a rediscovery of many forgotten histories. Therefore our foremost thanks have to go to the artists who have assisted us in making this exhibition possible. We are grateful to their essential contributions which were the starting point and foundation of this project. Many institutions, galleries, private collectors and artists contributed by making important works of art and documents available for the presentation at Tate Liverpool. We like to thank in particular Jake Miller, The Approach, London; Keith Arnatt and David Hurn, Chepstow; John Baum, Anglesea; Jerry Goldman, The Beatles Story, Liverpool; Bernd and Hilla Becher and Chris Durham from the artists' studio; Honor Beddard and Diana Eccles, The British Council; Sarah Wilde, British Film Institute, London; Caroline Arno and Antony Griffiths, The British Museum, London; Vanley and Carey Burke, Birmingham; Annelise Hone and Kathleen Soriano, Compton Verney Trust; Lara Blanchy, Galerie Chantal Crousel, Paris; Sheridon Davies, Sheffield; Jeremy Deller and Paul Ryan, London; Rineke Dijkstra, Amsterdam; Uwe Husslein, Dokumentationszentrum für Popkultur, Cologne; John Entwistle, Cumbria; Kathryn Dempsey, FACT, Liverpool; Anna Fox, Hampshire; Bill Harry, Merseybeat, Liverpool; Neville Gabie, Stroud; Candida Höfer, Cologne; Susanne Eder and Ulf Krüger, K&K, Hamburg; David Govier, Liverpool Central Library; Janet Martin, Liverpool John Moores University; Jacqueline Holt, LUX, London; Anne Gleave, Merseyside Maritime Museum; Ann Bukantas, Jessica Feather, Alex Kidson, Julian Treuherz and Godfrey Burke, Walker Art Gallery and National Museums Liverpool; Celia van Mullem, London; Emily Burningham and Sarah E Woodcock, The National Trust, North West Regional Office, Cumbria; Martin Parr and Conor Kilroe from the artist's studio; Gwyn Ritchards, Chester; Johanna Blask and Dr Felix Meyer, Paul Sacher Foundation, Basel; Dr Susanne Lange and Rajka Knipper, SK Stiftung Kultur, Cologne; Bob and Roberta Smith, London; Alec Soth, Minnesota; Matthew Clough and Moira Lindsay, Art and Heritage Collections, The University of Liverpool; Dr Maureen Watry, The University of Liverpool; Yvonna Elphick, Whitford Fine Art, London; Stephen Willats and Victoria Miro Gallery, London; and Tom Wood, Caerwys.

We were also fortunate enough to draw on many first hand accounts and are grateful to the many figures from Liverpool's tumultuous history who shared their expertise and memories. We would like to mention in particular Liz Royles, Atkinson Art Gallery, Southport; Bryan Biggs, Bluecoat Arts Centre, Liverpool; Dave Clapham; Maurice Cockrill; Chris Evans; Gordon Fazakerley; Leo Fitzmaurice; Alan Dunn and Laura Sillars, FACT, Liverpool; Duncan Hamilton; Bill Harpe; Wendy Harpe; Colin Fallows, Liverpool John Moores University; Julia Hallam, University of Liverpool; Marco Livingstone; Edward Lucie-Smith; Catherine Marcangeli; James MacRitchie; Ros McAlister; Edward Morris; Dr Jon Murden, National Museums Liverpool; Patrick Henry, Open Eye Gallery, Liverpool; William Raban; Peter Shield; Dorte Kirkeby Andersen at Silkeborg Kunstmuseum, Denmark; Georgina, Mungo and Roger Smith; Imogen Stidworthy; Ken Testi; Neville Weston; David Morris, Whitworth Art Gallery, Manchester; Colin Simpson, Williamson Art Gallery, Birkenhead; and all the other artists and people who made the period come alive for us.

At Tate Liverpool, our foremost thanks go to Darren Pih, Assistant Curator, who not only managed the many strands of this ambitious investigation into Liverpool's history and provided the logistic backbone with his usual efficiency but also actively shaped the exhibition through his extensive research into and knowledge of the period. Robert Knifton's research for and work on *Centre of the Creative Universe* was supported by an AHRC grant and we are grateful for this critical support as well as the supervision of Steven Gartside of Manchester Metropolitan University. The extensive programme of activities accompanying this exhibition has been shaped by Jean Tormey while the interpretative context was devised and realised by Maria Percival. Excellent registrarial support was as always provided by Wendy Lothian while Ken Simons, Barry Bentley, Roger Sinek expertly realised the installation of the exhibition. We are most grateful for the collaboration with Liverpool University Press on this publication and the excellent support provided by Robin Bloxsidge in particular. We would also like to thank Lisa Rostron of Lawn Creative, Liverpool for her sympathetic design and the efficient management of this project.

This exhibition and book is Tate Liverpool's central contribution to the city's celebration of its 800th anniversary. The exhibition has received generous support from Liverpool Culture Company and we are grateful for their help in making this show and journey into a little known chapter of Liverpool's history possible. The Granada Foundation and P H Holt Foundation have supported all public events and educational activities that accompany the exhibition.

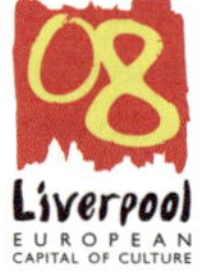

The exhibition *Centre of the Creative Universe* at Tate Liverpool was supported by the Liverpool Culture Company as part of the city's preparations for European Capital of Culture 2008

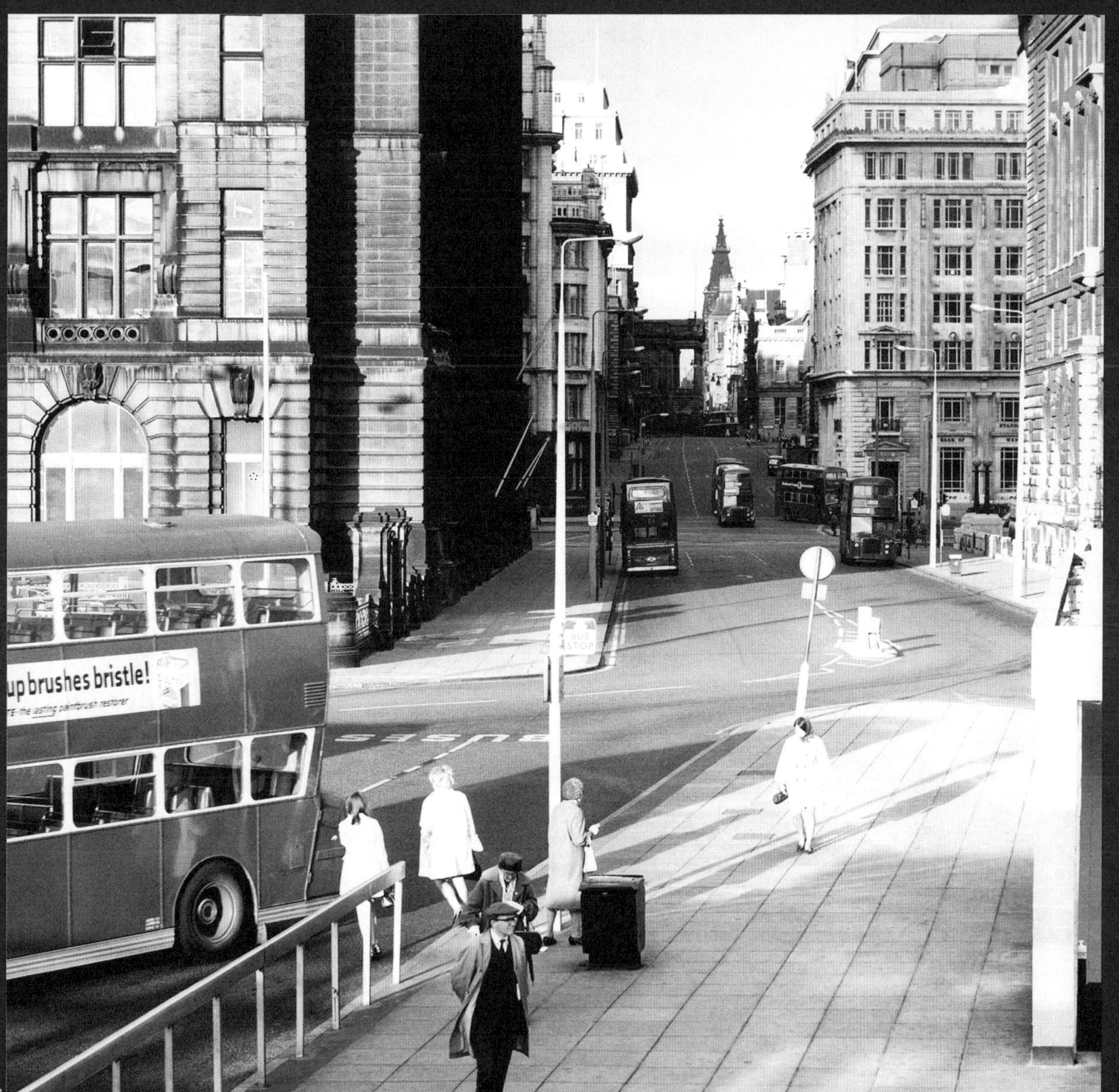
up brushes bristle!
the lasting paintbrush restorer
BUS STOP

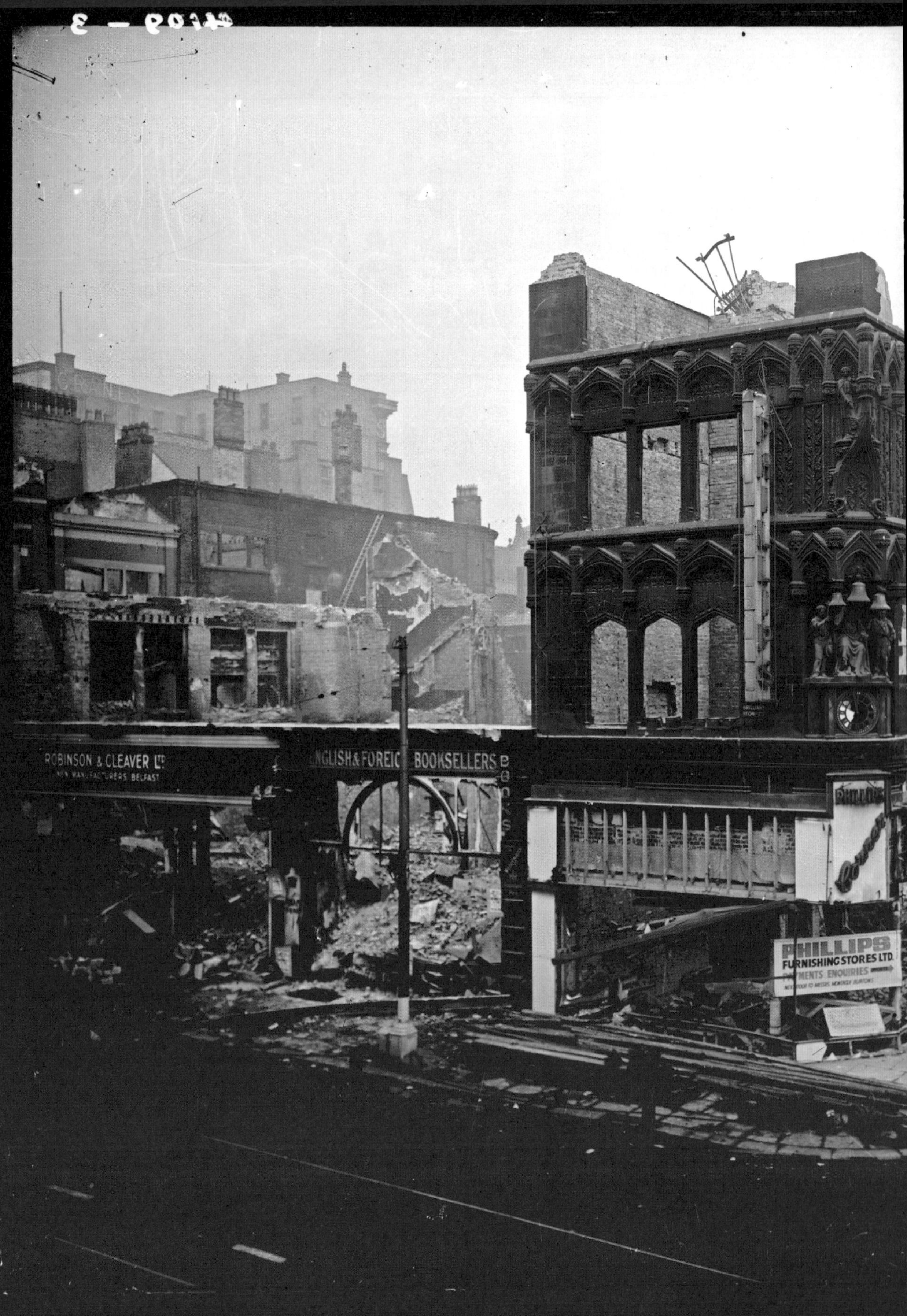
ROBINSON & CLEAVER LTD
LINEN MANUFACTURERS BELFAST
ENGLISH & FOREIGN BOOKSELLERS
PHILLIPS
PHILLIPS
FURNISHING STORES LTD.

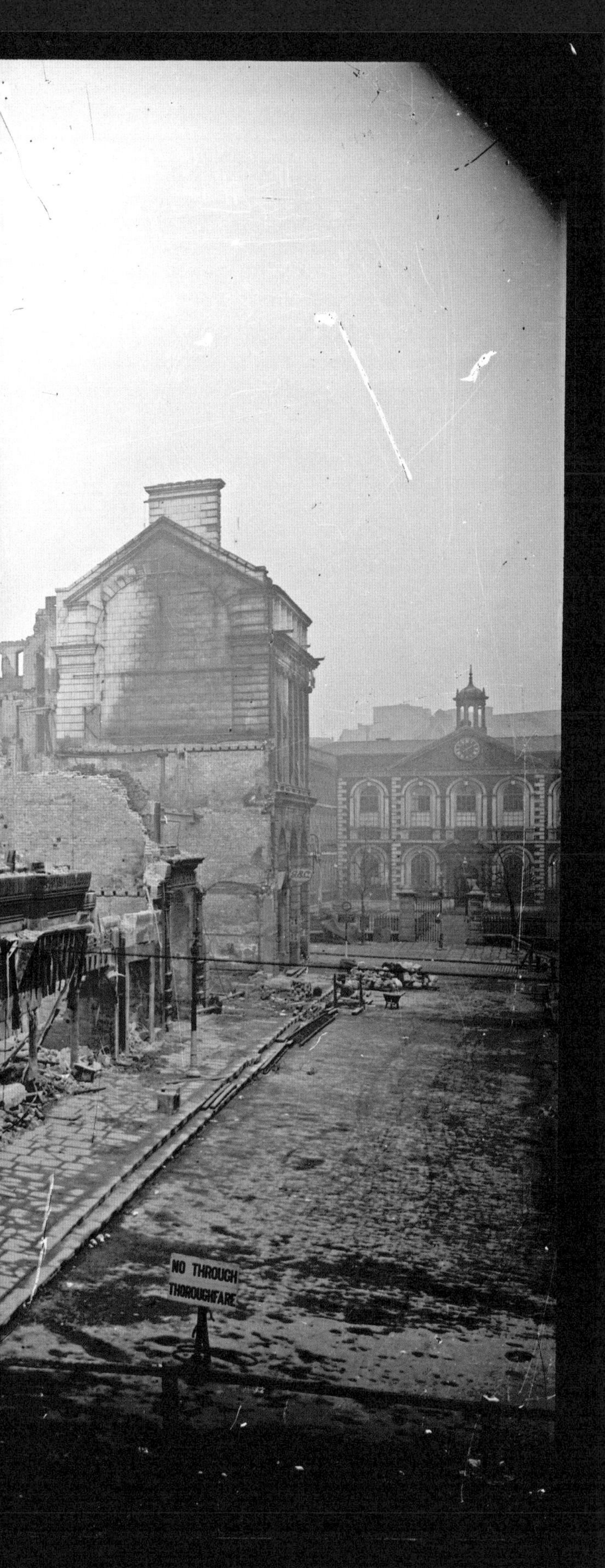

5
Stewart Bale
*Bomb Damage,
Church Street* 1941
Black and white photograph
40.7 x 50.8 cm
Courtesy of National
Museums Liverpool,
Merseyside Maritime
Museum

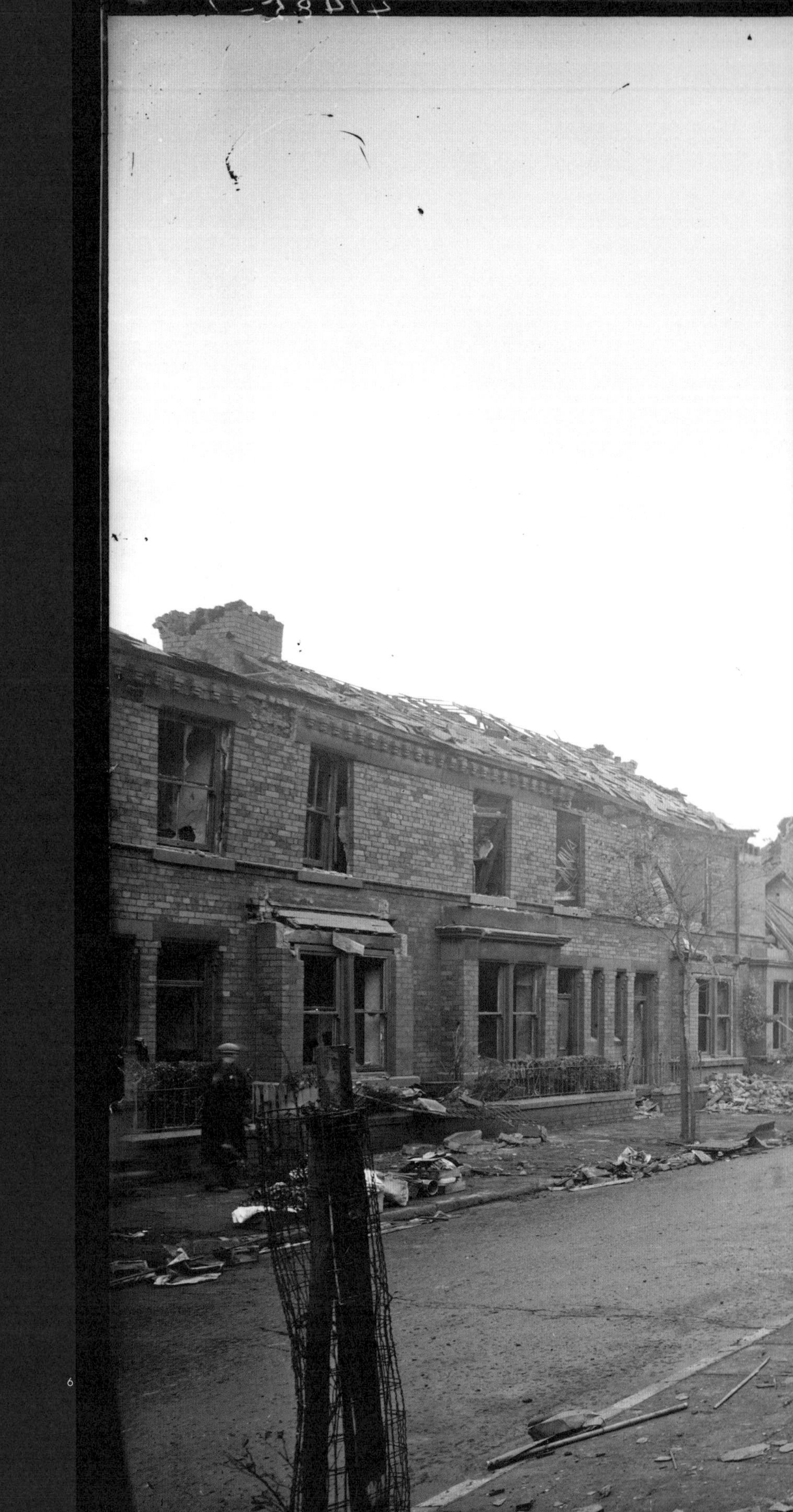

6
Stewart Bale
Bomb Damage, Bootle 1941
Black and white photograph
40.7 x 50.8 cm
Courtesy of National
Museums Liverpool,
Merseyside Maritime
Museum

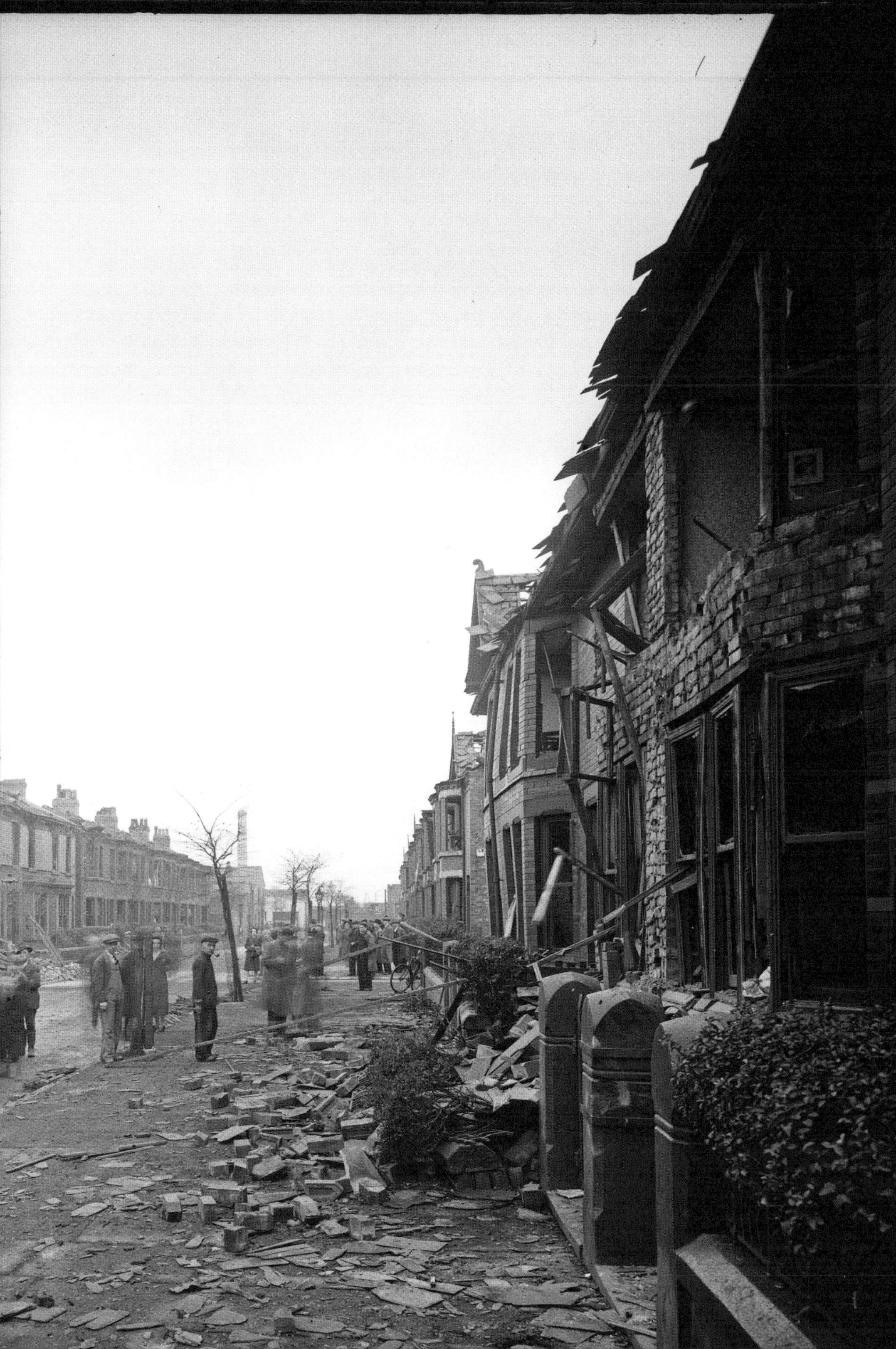

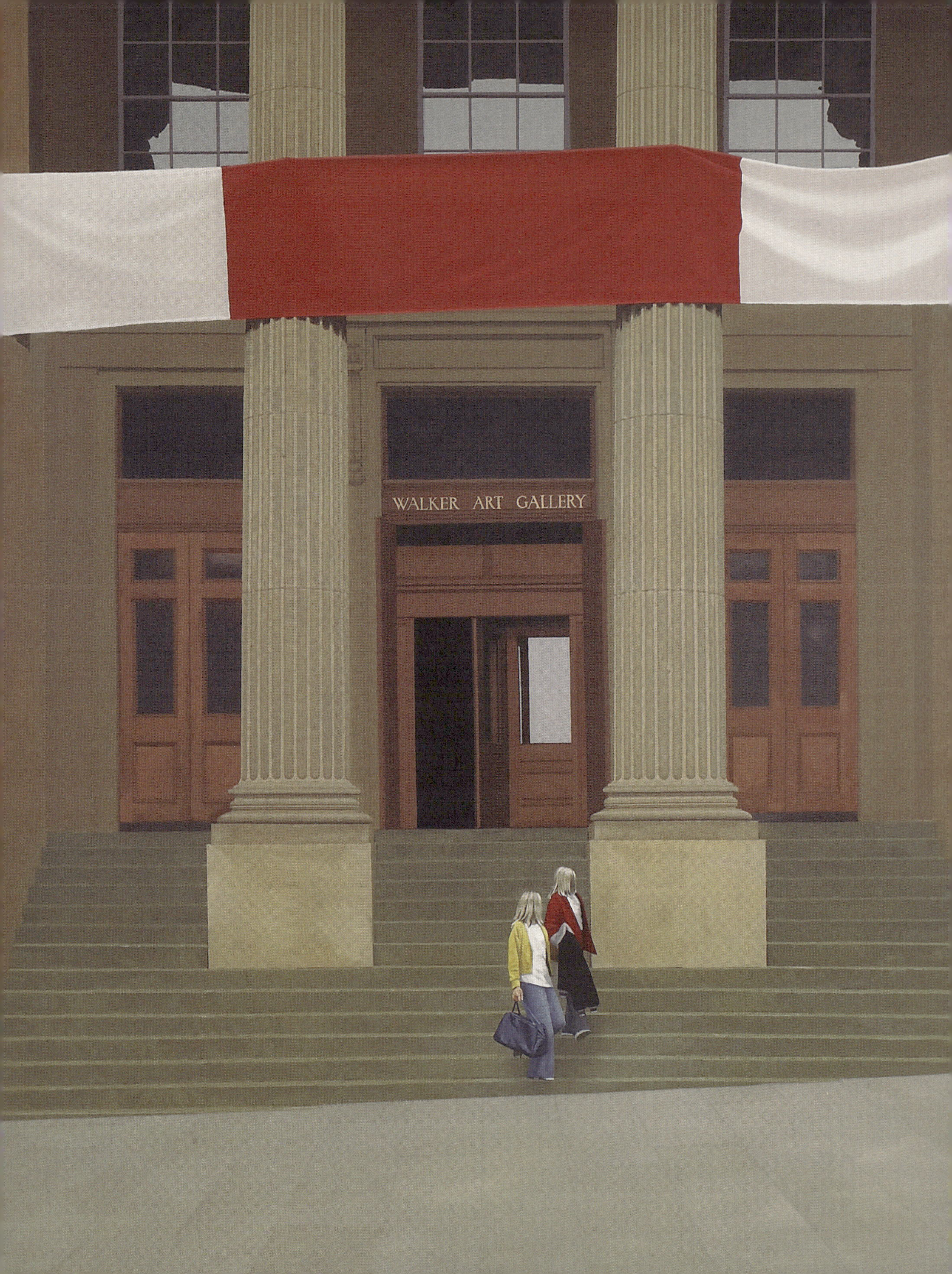
WALKER ART GALLERY

THE CRATER OF THE VOLCANO: LIVERPOOL AND THE AVANT-GARDE

Christoph Grunenberg
& Robert Knifton

The Crater of the Volcano: Liverpool and the Avant-Garde

Christoph Grunenberg
& Robert Knifton

In July 1846, when Prince Albert visited Liverpool to open the dock bearing his name, the city was at its peak. He remarked, 'I have heard of the greatness of Liverpool but the reality far surpasses the expectation'. Liverpool already had a great imaginative cachet at this time, and its name travelled far.

It was because of its seaport status that Liverpool was regarded at the time as 'the New York of Europe'.[1] From the docks ships carried trade all over the globe and as a result Liverpool became one of the most cosmopolitan cities in England. The shift in economic forces since this high watermark has been well documented: for example, Richard J. Williams portrays post-war Liverpool as an 'anxious city'[2] – its population halving in just four decades, with unemployment high and buildings decaying. It has been argued that the long and sad decline of Liverpool reminds the British of the waning and loss of the Empire.[3] The Empire's sad legacy is probably more visible in Liverpool than in any other British city, the downturn of the city's fortunes intrinsically linked with the decline of the country's position as a world player. The so-called 'Three Graces', majestically towering over the city's waterfront, speak of far more prosperous and significant times – the Edwardian years and 'Merseypride's' most pronounced period. European Union Objective One Funding followed as Liverpool was officially recognised as amongst the poorest regions in Europe, a direct result of the collapse of the city's main trade of shipping and associated industries. This loss, which sometimes was also experienced as liberation, permeates many of the works of art, plays, novels and films set in Liverpool, but was perhaps most pointedly documented in Ken Loach's 1997 documentary *The Flickering Flame*.

Yet Liverpool still looks out, and the world returns its gaze. George Melly, a prime spokesman for the city who grew up in its glory years, states the case when he comments, 'the 'Pool feels itself closer to Dublin, New York, even Buenos Aires, than it does to London…It's very aware of its own myth and eager to project it.'[4] Liverpool to this day remains a world city in mythic terms, its capacity to provoke inspired imaginations undiminished. This is the city Carl Gustav Jung cast as 'the pool of life' and of course, inescapably, the home city of the world's biggest pop group. Liverpool is, as any local would tell you, 'the centre of the creative universe'.[5]

A City on the Edge

And yet in so many ways Liverpool is on the outside, on the edge – geographically as well as culturally. Situated on the North West coast of England, just North of Wales and directly facing Ireland, Liverpool in some ways is at the end of the line. While well connected by motorway, rail, air and boat links, there is only the Irish Sea once one has reached the city. However, the cultural, political and social isolation of the city has opened a much wider gulf that no high speed rail link or direct motorway access can bridge. In the 1980s, Liverpool became a symbol for everything that was wrong with Britain after World War II: the decline of traditional industries and manufacturing; low productivity; political radicalisation and class antagonism; poor public services; and persistent social deprivation. The shift from trading and manufacturing to a service industry affected not just Liverpool but the 'North' as a whole, the term emerging not only as a description for a geographical area but as blanket synonym for some ill-defined, dark post-industrial hinterland. More than any other city, Liverpool symbolically exemplified this decline to the extent that in 1982, the *Daily Mirror* could recommend: 'They should build a fence around [Liverpool] and charge admission. For sadly, it has become a "showcase" of everything that has gone wrong in Britain's major cities.'[6] A wall of persistent cultural stereotypes was raised around Liverpool, turning it into a virtual no go area for politicians, investors and the media, dramatically reflecting its changing

1   *Illustrated London News*, 15 May 1886, quoted in Munck, Ronaldo, *Reinventing the City?*, Liverpool: Liverpool University Press, 2003, p. 39.
2   Williams, Richard J., *The Anxious City: English Urbanism in the Late Twentieth Century*, London: Routledge, 2004, p. 107.
3   Biggs, Lewis, 'Ducking and Weaving' in *Liverpool Biennial: The International 2002*. Liverpool: Liverpool Biennial, 2002, pp. 29-32.
4   Melly, George, *Revolt Into Style: The Pop Arts in Britain*, London: Allen Lane, 1970, p. 212.
5   Carl Gustav Jung's legendary statement is recounted in Paul Jones and Stuart Wilks-Heeg's essay in this volume.
6   Quoted in Lane, Tony, *Liverpool: Gateway of Empire*. London: Lawrence & Wishart, 1987, p. 13. (The second edition of Lane's book was published as *Liverpool: City of the Sea*, Liverpool: Liverpool University Press, 1997.)

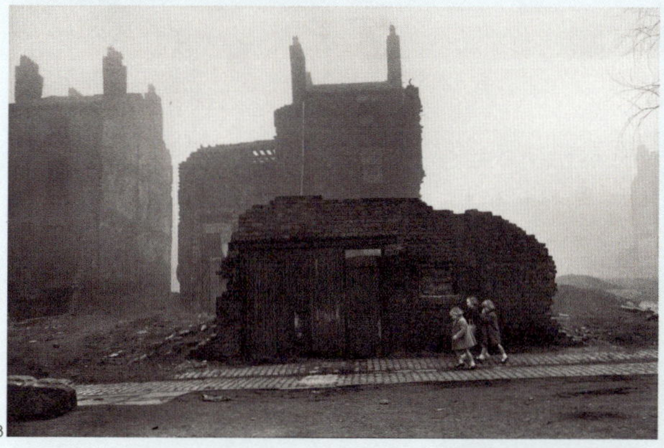

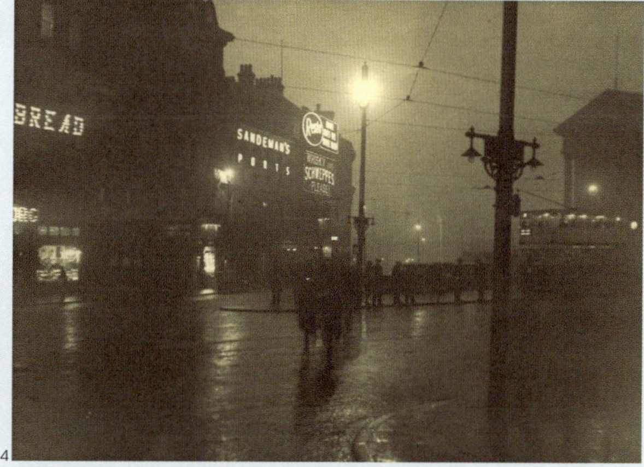

previous
Maurice Cockrill
The Walker Art Gallery
1974-5
Oil on canvas
126.8 x 101.3 cm
National Museums Liverpool,
Walker Art Gallery

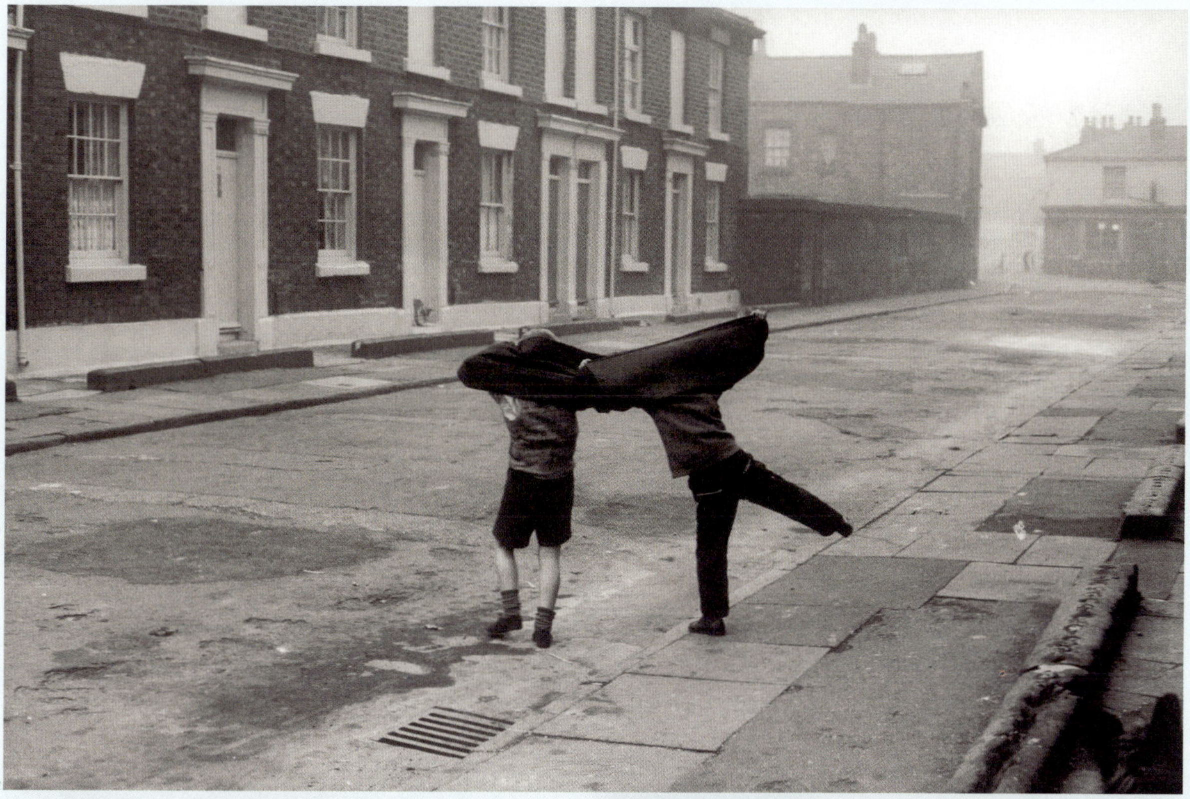

2/3
Henri Cartier-Bresson
Liverpool 1962
Black and white photograph
30.5 x 40.7 cm
National Museums Liverpool,
Walker Art Gallery

4
**Edward
Chambré-Hardman**
Lime Street at Night
c. 1950s
Black and white photograph
11.8 x 16.2 cm
The National Trust,
Edward Chambré-Hardman
Collection

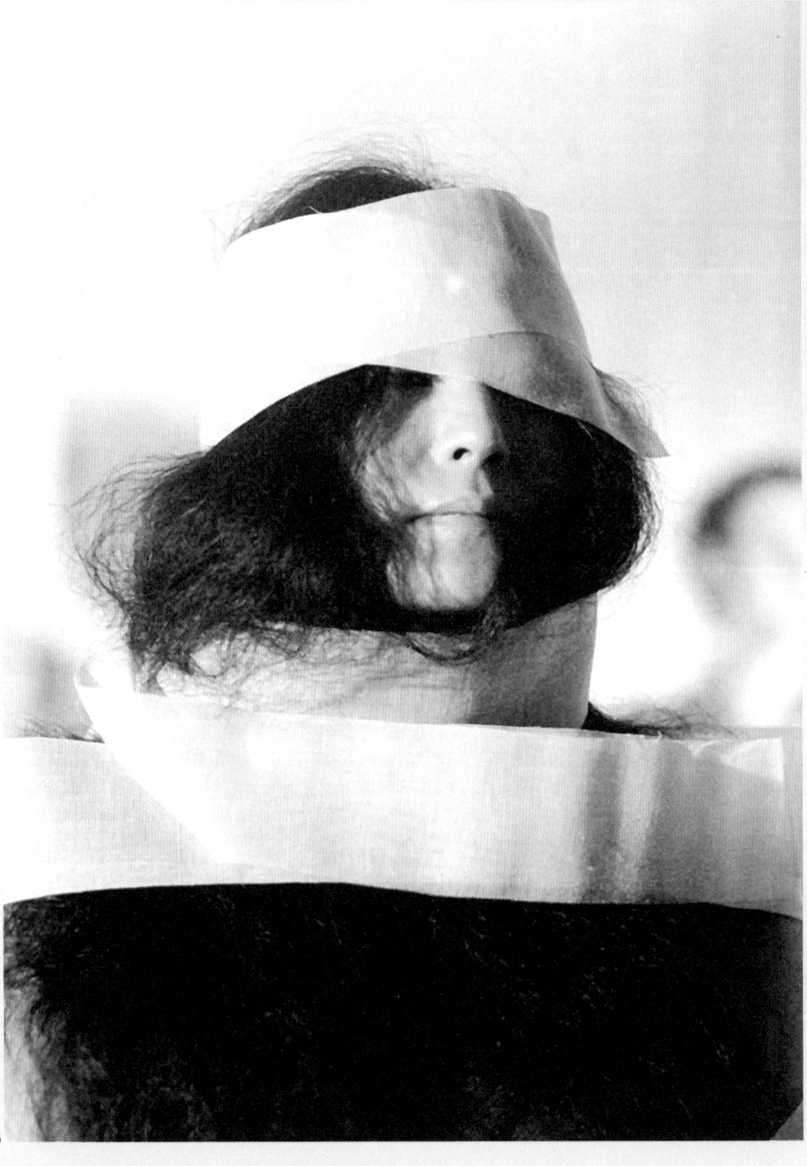

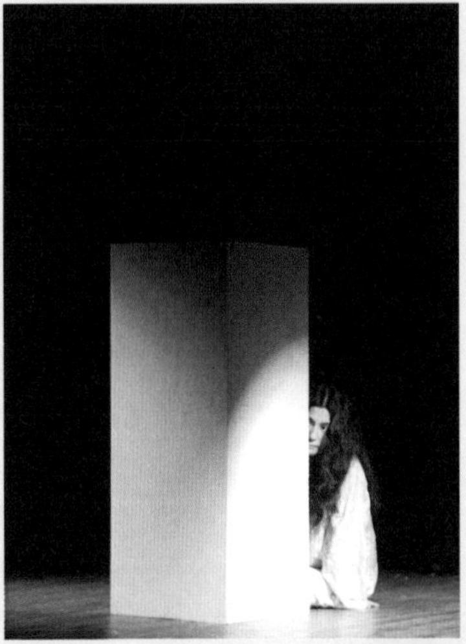

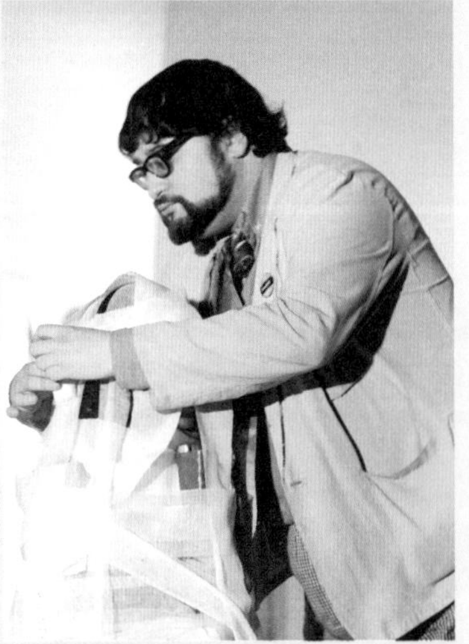

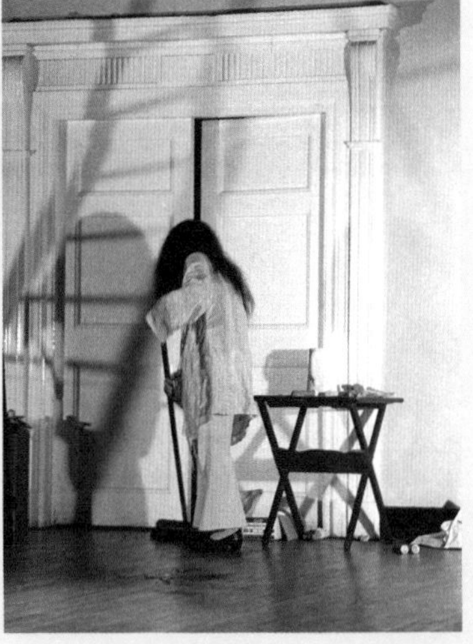

5

Sheridon Davies
Yoko Ono Bandaged
Yoko Ono Peeping
Adrian Henri Bandaging Yoko Ono
Yoko Ono Sweeping 1967
Black and white photographs
Courtesy of Sheridon Davies

fortunes and the painful transition from a wealthy port city and proud cultural centre in the 19th and early 20th century to a byword for urban decline and dereliction in the 1970s, 80s and 90s.

The isolation of Liverpool that culminated in the 1980s has its origins in the industrial revolution of the 18th century as a gap opened between the working-class North and the more 'cultured' South that continues to shape perceptions until today. The 'new relations of production and commercial exchange' brought about by the industrial revolution, as Rob Shields has analysed, established an 'uneven geography' between the North and South. This uneven geography with 'its perceptions of social anomalies, the threat of class rebellion, the debasement of living conditions, the political challenge of the rising middle classes', was reflected in the language to describe the North. It is a language that 'constituted a spatial discourse which privileged the centre – London – and sought to re-establish the North not only an economic but also a cultural periphery around this core.'[7] The Northern dialect and in particular 'Scouse', the vernacular of Liverpudlians named after a dish of Scandinavian origin and identifying both the city's idiom and its inhabitants, continues to be the object of much ridicule. It is perceived to expose the speaker immediately not only as socially inferior but also as uncultured, however rich or educated he might otherwise be. This distinction goes back to at least the 18th century and thus predates the birth of 'Scouse', as a statement by John Walker in his *Critical Pronouncing Dictionary* of 1791 illustrates: 'The grand difference between metropolis and the provinces is that the people of education in London are free from all the vices of the vulgar; but the best educated people in the provinces, if constantly resident there, are sure to be tinctured with the dialect of the country in which they live.'[8]

Despite high-level political intervention and a continuous stream of public subsidies and urban renewal programmes, the disparities between the regions continue as deep-seated structural problems are ignored. A recent report 'suggests [that] the division between north and south has become so wide that the nation is split into two separate countries: To the south is the metropolis of Greater London, to the north and west is the "archipelago of the provinces" – city islands that appear to be slowly sinking demographically, socially and economically.'[9] The inequality pervades all areas from economic productivity, employment, political participation to health and access to culture.[10] Recent trends, however, show a reversal of the century-old brain-drain to the South and, for the first time in 30 years, more people are leaving the Capital in search of a better quality of life and cheaper living than are moving there. Newcastle and Manchester have been declared as creative hotspots outdoing London while Liverpool is favourably compared to Milan.[11]

Northernness has been embraced as an identity and fosters a certain creative attitude. This creativity is under the surface, hidden behind stoicism and perhaps not visible to the uninitiated, as Henri Cartier-Bresson's rather dour first impression upon visiting Liverpool in 1962 demonstrates. He commented, 'Writing about the same people of the North at work amounts to the same as writing about them at play. Their looks are not so different neither are their clothes. There is no exuberance on their faces nor gestures. Their vacationing seems just an occupation as any other.'[12] Undoubtedly Liverpool in the early 1960s was an austere place, still recovering from the devastation of war and yet to experience the explosion of the Merseybeat phenomenon. Cartier-Bresson's iconic images stand in a long tradition that has its origins in the activities of documentary film and photography of the 1930s and Mass Observation in Britain in particular and which, with variations, continues to shape conventions until today. This 'school of miserable realism' paints an uncompromising picture of hardship, industrial decline and urban deprivation while emphatically focusing on the individual fate and almost heroic resistance in the face of persistent adversity.[13] Cartier-Bresson's views on the holidaying working class cannot help but call to mind, for example, Martin Parr's famous series of working-class Scouse daytrippers at New Brighton, *The Last Resort* 1983-6 or Tom Wood's night revellers at play in the same location. But as Parr's title for this memorable series highlights, this was already a vanishing world at the time it was being captured by these photographers.

In recent years, beginning with the DIY aesthetic of punk, Northernness has become a badge of honour for many. Katie Milestone claims there has been an 'aestheticisation of

7 Shields, Rob, *Places on the Margin: Alternative Geographies of Modernity*. London and New York: Routledge, 1991, p. 214.

8 Quoted in Belchem, John, *Merseypride: Essays in Liverpool Exceptionalism*. Liverpool: Liverpool University Press, 2000, p. 48.

9 Editorial, 'North/south divide: Seismic Shifts', *The Guardian*, Thursday, 1 July 2004, p. 27; See also Brown, Paul, 'Poverty and crime make it tough up north – but more birds are singing', *The Guardian*, 11 July 2003, p. 9; Wintour, Patrick, 'North-south divide is widening, warns report', *The Guardian*, 13 December, 2002, p. 13; Hetherington, Peter, 'The gridlocked north', *The Guardian*, 13 December 2002, p. 21; Liddle, Rod, 'Britain's great divide: London versus the rest', *The Guardian*, G2, 12 April 2002, p. 7; Hetherington, Peter, 'North-south gap likely to widen, warn researchers', *The Guardian*, 12 April 2002, p. 10; Hetherington, Peter, 'While England becomes ever more divided, Europe's provincial prosperity forges ahead', *The Guardian*, 1 March 2001, p. 15.

10 Life expectancy, for example, of a male in the South of England is over 11 years higher at 80.1 years than in Glasgow with just 69.1 years. Scotland and the North West of England also have the highest rates of premature deaths. Carvel, John, 'North-south life expectancy gap grows wider', *The Guardian*, 16 October 2004, p. 6. See also Carter, Helen, 'Third of children in north-west live in poverty', *The Guardian*, 2 March 2005, p. 11.

11 Carvel, John, 'Heading north as London loses grip on migration trend', *The Guardian*, 16 December 2005, p. 10; Firth, Maxine, 'Judged creatively, the best place to be is Manchester', *The Independent*, 26 May 2003, p. 5; Adams, Tim, 'A Tale of two cities', *The Observer*, 22 May 2005, Review section pp. 1-2; Adams, Tim, 'May the North be with you', *The Observer*, 28 July 2002, Review section, pp. 1-2. See also Curtis, Polly, 'Why it's no longer grim up north', *The Guardian*, 24 May 2005, p. 11; Hetherington, Peter, 'North scorns study of gulf with south', *The Guardian*, 1 July 2004, p. 8.

12 Cartier-Bresson, Henri, 'Notes on the North', 1962. The Walker Archive, National Museums Liverpool.

13 See Peter Davidson, *The Idea of the North*, London: Reaktion Books, 2005 for an exploration of the mythology of the North in Britain and beyond.

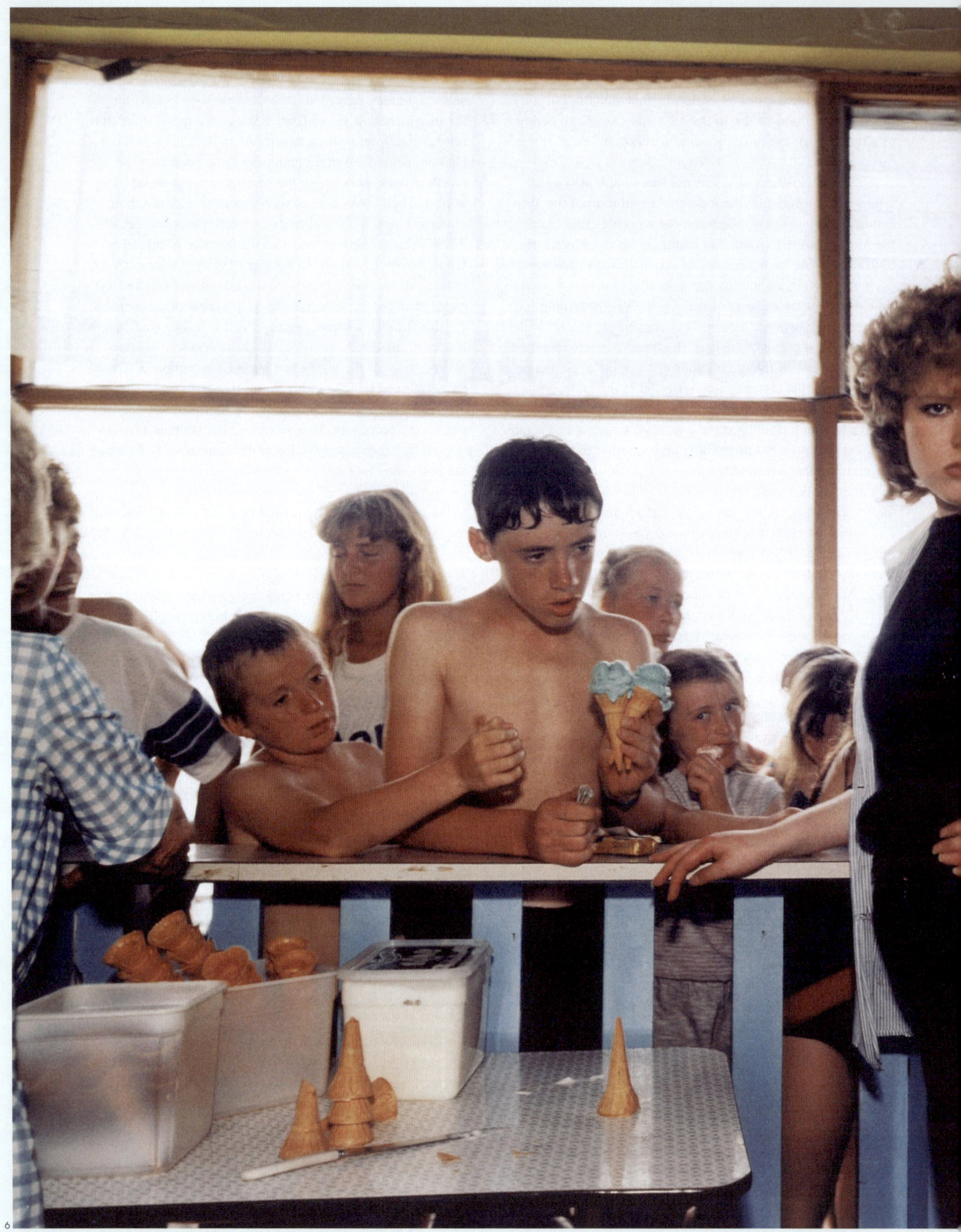

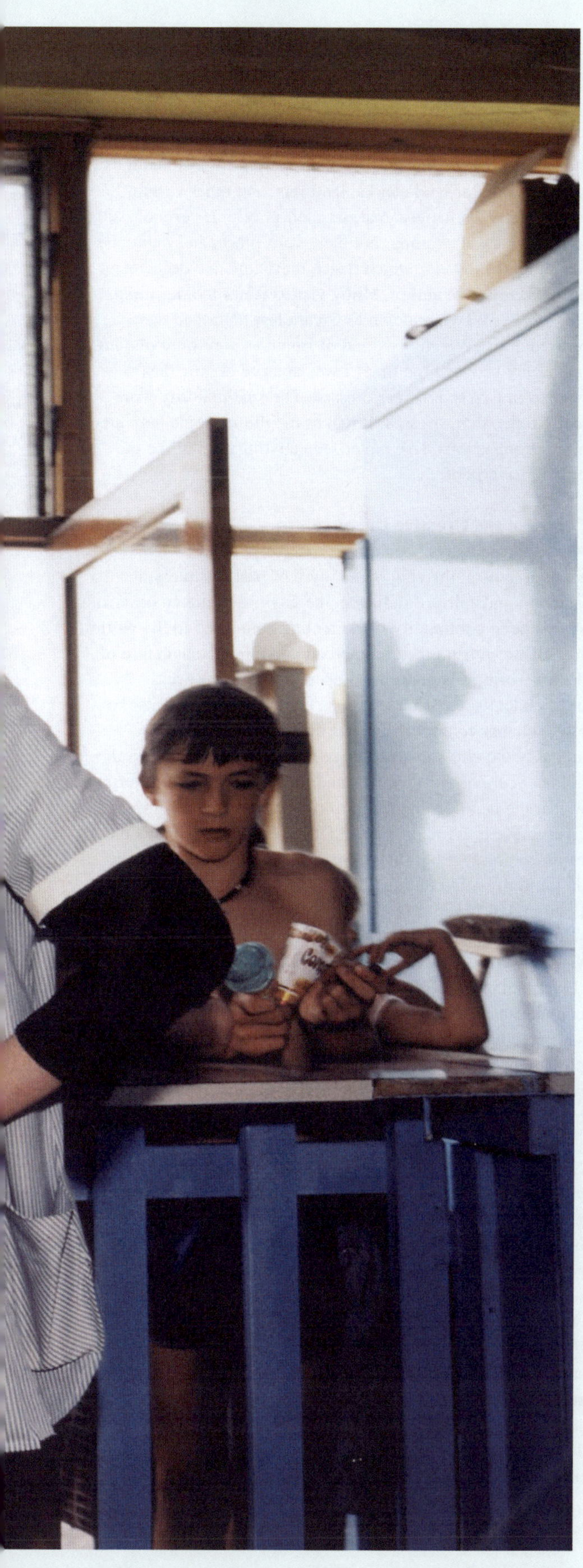

6
Martin Parr
The Last Resort 1983-6
C-type print
104 x 132 cm
Tate. Presented by the artist
and Rocket Gallery 2002

northernness', as the label is appropriated, re-packaged, commodified and sold as style: outsiders as rebels – the 'Livercool' brand.[14] For proof, see the cachet of being an outsider claimed by the Eric's punk crowd in Jaki Florek's essay, where groups such as Echo and the Bunnymen epitomised the spirit, or alternatively look at the immense success of the Liverpool superclub Cream through the 1990s and its take on music labelled 'scouse house'.

Trade and trans-Atlantic traffic have left Liverpool with a population more Celtic than Anglo-Saxon, with an accent much altered from the surrounding Lancashire towns. The Irish connection to the city in particular has had a massive bearing on its culture, with Liverpool being for many years the cheapest crossing to England from Dublin. However the Welsh and Scottish influences are discernible if not quite as huge. For example, painter John Baum recalls that the Blue Funnel Line based in Liverpool was known for many years as the Welsh Navy as so many in its service came from the principality. Artists in the exhibition have links with all three nations, from Irish-born artists like Sam Walsh, Edward Chambré-Hardman and Tom Wood, those who grew up in Wales like John Baum and Adrian Henri, and in this catalogue we have the view of Bill Drummond, a Scottish figure who had a significant bearing on Liverpool in the late 1970s and early 80s, whilst the 'fifth Beatle' Stuart Sutcliffe was born in Scotland, settling in Liverpool due to his father being a shipworker. The city also has a significant Chinese community, with one of the longest established Chinatowns in Europe, as well as one of the oldest black populations in the UK. This large non-English influence has over the years contributed to Liverpool's edginess, but also makes it such a welcoming place to other migrants and outsiders. American grunge queen and latterly actress Courtney Love is one more example of a creative soul drawn to the Liverpool scene – she spent some of her formative years living in digs not dissimilar to those John Lennon and Stuart Sutcliffe shared a generation earlier.

Liverpool's economic basis in shipping and trade historically gave it a casual working model far removed from the enforced hours and shifts of Manchester's mills, for example. As John Belchem has noted, this pattern of hours had a bearing on the cultural make-up of the city. He contends, 'Viewed from the workers' perspective casualism was not a curse, but a culture to be defended.'[15] Liverpool, much like the River Mersey it sits atop, has always ebbed and flowed to its own distinct cultural rhythm. This culture, grown in storytelling, singing, pubs and clubs, has a strong anti-authoritarian transgressive tendency.

Liverpool has also perennially been known as a good night out. Gordon Fazakerley, who was a student at the art college in the 1950s reminisces on dances played by the Merseysippi Jazz Band – who would perform until either the audience collapsed from exhaustion, or the band would from drunkenness.[16] From the days when Herman Melville came to stay in the city in the late 19th century, commenting, 'of all the seaports in the world, Liverpool, perhaps, most abounds in all the variety of land-sharks, land-rats, and other vermin, which make the hapless mariner their prey',[17] Liverpool had a reputation as an exciting, but dangerous place, and today the reputation of the city which dance musician, and descendant of the *Moby Dick* author, Moby visited is not too dissimilar. He recalls, 'We went down to Cream last night and were refused entry. Which was kind of ironic as they were playing one of my songs at the time! I was amazed at how the women in Liverpool were dressed. The vast majority wore really tight, short dresses. It makes me think people here are more promiscuous. I've never seen anything quite like the girls in Liverpool.'[18]

Centre of the Creative Universe
Artists have always been drawn to Liverpool's exceptionalism, thriving on its myth of past greatness, its isolation and spirit of defiance, the city providing an oasis and sympathetic community while feeling connected to the world. At a distance from the commercial and intellectual centre of the art world, it is possible to operate more freely and independently, to be adventurous and take risks, but also to effect change to a much greater degree. The 1960s were arguably the city's most creative period, surpassing even the golden years of the Victorian and Edwardian era, as Liverpool was at the heart of a global pop cultural revolution. As George Melly wrote in 1970: 'This great explosion was the result of pressure building up over a period, and there is no doubt in my mind that the crater of the volcano was not London, but Liverpool.'[19] The city achieved such a prominent status in the popular imagination that Allen Ginsberg, who visited Liverpool in 1965, could emphatically declare: 'Liverpool is at the present moment the centre of the consciousness of the human universe.'[20] This misremembered statement has been adapted as the title and guiding motto for the present investigation of art and creativity in Liverpool, perfectly reflecting the hyperbolic world view of the Liverpudlians even before the city had reached its creative pinnacle.

The cross-cultural renaissance which developed in Liverpool in the early 1960s was part of a wider tendency that gave Northern musicians, writers, dramatists and filmmakers a national platform to explore Northern identities in often harsh realistic films and socially engaged novels focusing on provincial working class lives. Through the appropriation and re-working of peripheral identities such as 'Northern' and 'Liverpudlian', originally intended by those at the 'centre' as derogatory markers of difference and irrelevance, artists mapped new symbolic territories on to the city, giving those rejected liminal spaces new symbolic value. In particular in the 1960s, concentrated but strong communities and networks formed in Liverpool that often crossed the boundaries of artistic styles, genres and media. Eccentric personalities with a flair for self-promotion and displaying a typically anarchic spirit of entrepreneurialism staged exhibitions, events, plays and performances in both official and underground venues, providing an extraordinarily rich cultural landscape at the forefront of artistic developments. It produced and attracted creative characters, as for example Adrian Henri, who themselves were talented musicians, poets, writers and painters while also functioning as catalysts for avant-garde activities that brought national and international figures such as the Boyle Family, John Latham, Allen Ginsberg and Yoko Ono to Liverpool. It is this strong indigenous culture, resistant to interference from London, that has more than any other aspect seen Liverpool cast as peripheral, since it posed a threat to the stratified hierarchies centred on the capital. The tension present in this dynamic is what lends Liverpool its mythic, symbolic significance. As Peter Stallybrass and Allon White perceptively argue, 'what is socially peripheral is so frequently symbolically central.'[21] So it proves with Liverpool: the very things that place it outside the centres of power and mark it as different are the features that have made it so significant to creativity and artists over the years. The art in this exhibition attempts to highlight the contradictory nature of the symbolic hierarchies and the conflicting desires within the social imagination of space. Liverpool is central because it is on the edge: it is the world's outsider.

Topophilia: An Artists' City

Artists have seized Liverpool's outsider status and melded it with their own. Like Liverpool-born sculptor Tony Cragg's wall relief *Britain Seen From the North* 1981, the perceived view is turned on its head. James Donald has remarked on artists' reclamation of the city through a process of topophilia, writing 'In the recesses and margins of urban space, people invest places with meaning, memory and desire.'[22] From the 1950s onwards, the city benefited from 'the ready-made existence of a bohemian quarter, Liverpool 8, providing cheap housing in the grand Georgian terraces close to the city centre as well as pubs and other places of convergence.[23] Gordon Fazakerley is a good example of an artist from this era melding with the outsider status of the city. His local name literally inscribes him in its fabric, whilst his story is a hidden history that links one of the most significant art movements of the last century, Situationism, back to Liverpool. Fazakerley recalls the Liverpool of his youth as a place of contrasts; a dangerous city of 'shibbins' – illegal drinking dens – and pimps loitering on street corners. It was also austere: most pubs closed at 10pm in a hangover from wartime hours. Places like Ye Cracke and the Kardomah Café were the few lively places for the artistic crowd of Liverpool 8. Leaving Liverpool in the late 1950s for London, Fazakerley fell in with people at the ICA, where in 1959 Herbert Read and Lawrence Alloway staged a small exhibition of his art in the Institute's library, even securing the young artist leave from

the military in order to install the show. It was at the ICA that Fazakerley first encountered the Situationists. He emigrated to Sweden, helping Jørgen Nash to establish the Bauhaus Situationist at Drakabygget. The group represented a break from the French Situationists led by Guy Debord, as the 'Drakabygget Declaration' upon which Fazakerley was a co-signatory indicates. In his painting-poems Gordon Fazakerley carries a Liverpool outsider spirit – the outlook of a port that expands horizons but also lends opportunity to escape. He is an artist who got away, until now at least: 50 years after he left Liverpool, through *Centre of the Creative Universe* Fazakerley is part of Liverpool once more.

Liverpool's wealth of warehouse space and cheap living quarters has meant it offers the creative individual a host of such recesses to invest in, as evidenced in the use of the city's space by organisations like A Foundation, Static, Jump Ship Rat and the Royal Standard. Thus, artists lead Liverpool's reclamation, giving it new purpose and meaning, inventing their own city that is constantly in flux. Emma Anderson comments on the '…shifting, sorting, filtering process through which the experiences of metropolitan life are made into art…'[24] as artists draw upon the particular situations of their location in forging new works. Tom Wood's Liverpool, captured from the windows of buses, has just such movement. As he travels the city, his images are inflected with the desires and hopes of his fellow travellers, resting just beneath the surface.

'A city is not just a place on the map,' Ronaldo Munck contends, 'it is a site of power, difference and contestation.'[25] It is often precisely these features of power, difference and contestation that artists have focused on when making art in Liverpool, as we can view for example in Melik Ohanian's *White Wall Travelling* 1997, which re-imagines Liverpool's docks as a psychogeographical space of power and resistance. The slow cinematic journey through the deserted docklands – empty of dockers but also of any other activity – dramatically illustrates the costs of post-industrial decline as traditional industries die and whole city quarters

14 Milestone, Katie, 'Regional Variations: Northernness and New Urban Economies of Hedonism' in O'Connor, Justin, and Wynne, Derek (ed.), *From the Margins to the Centre: Cultural Production and Consumption in the Post-Industrial City*, Aldershot: Arena, 1996, p. 93. See also 'Livercool', *Tatler*, March 2003, pp. 158-181; Rose, Aiden, 'Liverpool Cool', *The Times Magazine*, 9 October 2004, pp. 46-52.

15 Belchem, John (ed.), *Popular Politics, Riot and Labour: Essays in Liverpool History 1790-1940*, Liverpool: Liverpool University Press, 1992, p. 6.

16 Conversation with the artist, August 2006.

17 Quoted in Lane, *Liverpool: Gateway of Empire*, p. 32.

18 Quoted in Du Noyer, Paul, *Liverpool: Wondrous Place – Music From Cavern to Cream*, London: Virgin, 2002, p. 1.

19 Melly, *Revolt Into Style*, p. 212.

20 Melly, *Revolt Into Style*, p. 214.

21 Stallybrass, Peter, and White, Allon, *The Politics and Poetics of Transgression*, Ithaca, NY: Cornell University Press, 1986, p. 5.

22 Donald, James, 'The City, The Cinema: Modern Spaces' in Jenks, Chris. (ed.), *Visual Culture*, London: Routledge, 1995, p. 78.

23 Melly, *Revolt Into Style*, p. 213

24 Anderson, Emma, 'Inventing the City' in Anderson, Emma (ed.), *Out of Place: Memory, Imagination and the City*, Salford: Lowry Press, 2000, p. 3.

25 Munck, *Reinventing the City?*, pp. 6-7.

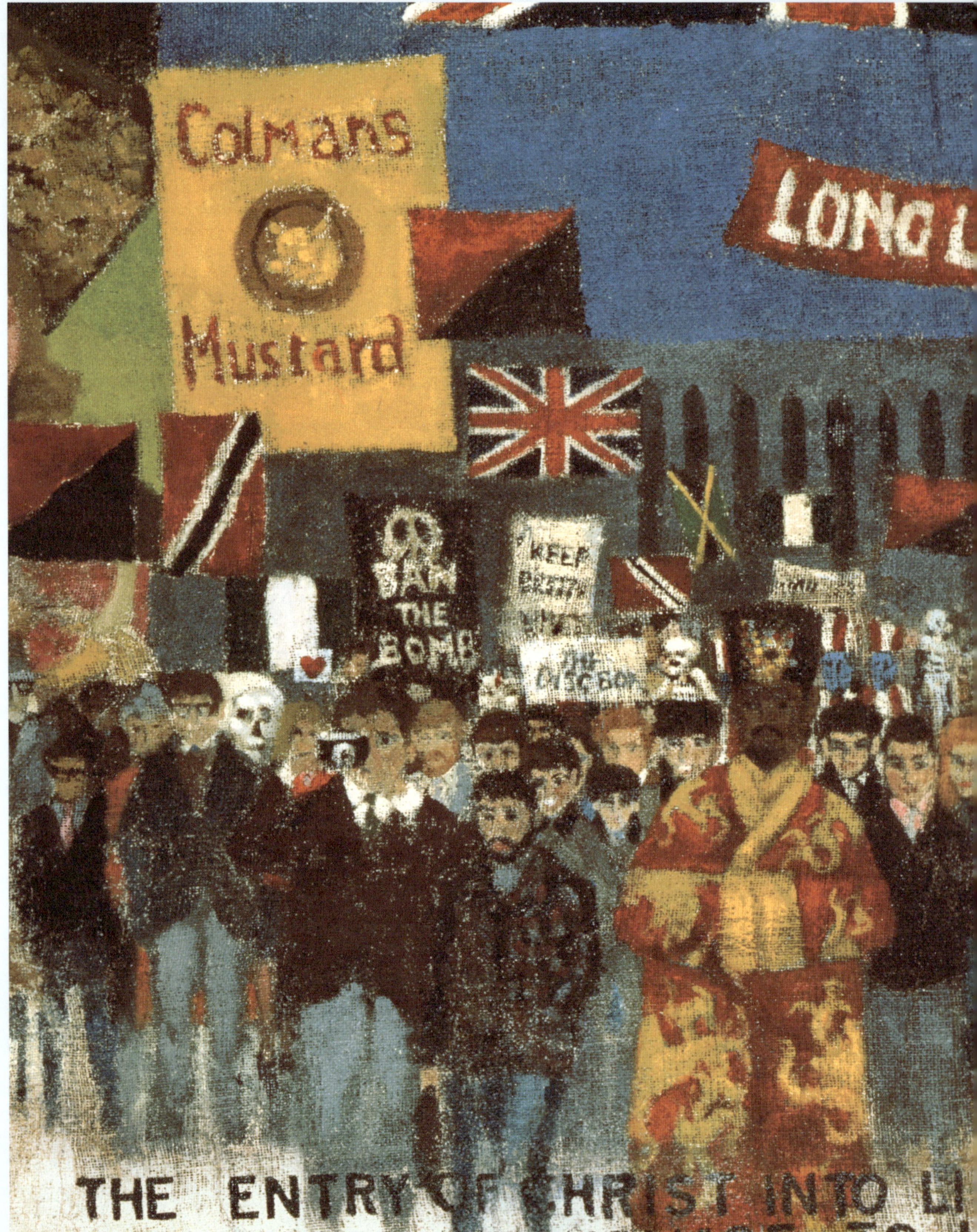

Colmans
Mustard
LONG L
BAN
THE
BOMB
KEEP
BRITH
THE GREEN
THE ENTRY OF CHRIST INTO L
HOMAGE TO J

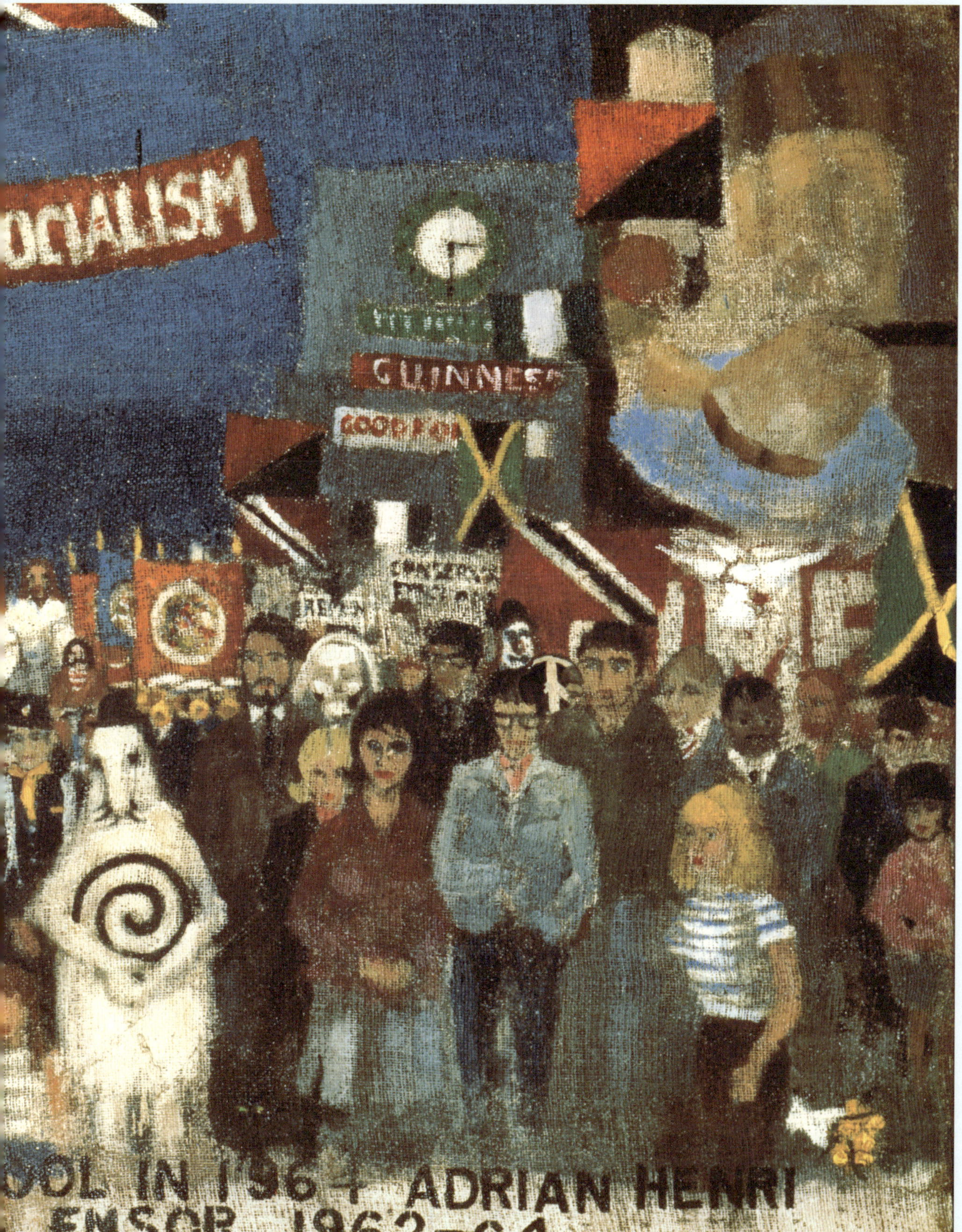

OCIALISM

GUINNESS

GOOD FOR

OOL IN 196- ADRIAN HENRI
ENSOR 1962-64

are left deserted. However, from contestation and difference also sprouts creativity as art works such as Ohanian's or Allan Sekula's account of the 1995-98 dockers' strike, produced for the inaugural Liverpool Biennial in 1999, eloquently show.

If the city has an influence upon the artist, the converse is equally true as artists receive power through picturing the city. Urban theorist Nestor Garcia Canclini proposes, 'Cities are also configured through images. These may be the plans that invent and order the city. But also, the sense of urban life is imagined… The city becomes dense as it is loaded with heterogeneous fantasies.'[26] This dense city of fantasies is that imagined by the artist, whose creative practice covers it and thus alters our perception of the urban environment, shaping the city and changing it permanently. Those fantasies may be the artists' own personal visions, such as when Adrian Henri makes Hope Street a festival of skeletons in his vision of *The Day of the Dead, Hope Street* 1998. They may also be collected memories that at a once-remove become a fantastical vision of a city's past such as in Jason Rhoades' literal translation of Jung's infamous statement into a liver-shaped and liver-coloured pool complete with stylised 'trees' on occasion of the 2002 Liverpool Biennial. It is the artist who facilitates and drives these fantasies, and *Centre of the Creative Universe* aims to view Liverpool as just such a dense city of heterogeneous fantasies.

Liverpool Avant-Gardes

The artists who first cover new urban territory are the avant-garde. Put avant-garde and Liverpool into a search engine and you'll get a hair salon. In some ways this is appropriate: just ask Jayne Casey about avant-garde haircuts in Liverpool… However, at the fringe of the city the avant-garde's influences pervade and Liverpool emerges as an unlikely centre of avant-garde activity. Adrian Henri brought in the happening from Allan Kaprow and the New York scene, Yoko Ono attracted hundreds to an event at the Bluecoat, Filmaktion formed at a Walker Art Gallery show: all these events place Liverpool on the frontline of culture and connect the city's artistic milieu to a range of art movements through Pop Art, Situationism, Conceptualism and Photorealism to name a few. Liverpool in some ways seemed like the place artists came to try out new ideas: maybe not always because they were accepted by the local audience, but because it was a challenging place to host such events, and a reaction of some sort was almost guaranteed.

Yet equally Liverpool seems to foster its own sense of the avant-garde: a democratic grass-roots culture that negotiates art, everyday life, mass culture and politics and ties artworks to the city. Ken Campbell's Science Fiction Theatre of Liverpool and Peter O'Halligan's Liverpool School of Language, Music, Dream and Pun displayed such a spirit, as do Rineke Dijkstra and Jeremy Deller's work when they engage with the club culture of Liverpool's youth. The

Bridewell, artists' studios in an old police station up the hill from Lime Street, tapped into this vernacular avant-garde, hosting art happenings such as, for example, a beach party with mounds of sand imported, thus answering the Situationist call to arms from the May 1968 Paris Student Riots, 'Sous les pavés, la plage' – 'underneath the street, the beach.' In Liverpool, the avant-garde means a close connection to the spirit of the streets, and perhaps it remains a truer vanguard for it, as Andreas Huyssen contends, 'The avant-garde…only makes sense if it remains dialectically related to that for which it serves as the vanguard.'[27]

Chronotopicity: A City Soaked in Memories

One way artists have reflected Liverpool's street spirit is by displaying the city's capacity to absorb myth and stories within its very fabric. Sites become charged with memories, added to with significance from the past. For example, sample the mythic qualities of Gambier Terrace – home to so many artists, poets and musicians over the years, including John Lennon. All this loaded memory is simultaneously acknowledged and deconstructed in Bob and Roberta Smith's text and performance work, challenging and destroying a powerful myth in order to make space for one's own imaginative activity.

The myths embedded in city-space act as chronotopes. Paul Smethurst defines the chronotope as 'a time-space in which the conscious mind frames and organises the real, but it can also be the time-space where it disorganises and re-presents the real.'[28] The chronotope examines how time and space, real and mythic become fused and through this act of synthesis produce a collective meaning that art can utilise, and helps to create. This dialogue between fiction and truth, real and imagined space seems especially pertinent in myth-making Liverpool. See Bill Drummond's anthropomorphicised account of the city in this catalogue for a fascinating example of this tendency. Further, as Mikhail Bakhtin notes, 'a locality is the trace of an event, a trace of what had shaped it. Such is the logic of all local myths and legends that attempt, through history to make sense out of space.'[29] Therefore the meaning of a site such as Gambier Terrace inevitably only makes sense to us with reference to what happened there, who stayed there, who moved on. Equally, it is impossible to not think of 1960s bohemian events and happenings when in the cellar of the Everyman Theatre since they are so imbued in its atmosphere. The same kind of trace is present in artworks that address such localities; thus John Baum's painting of Roger McGough's home near Princes Park, Windermere House,

26 Quoted in Munck, *Reinventing the City?*, p.15.
27 Huyssen, Andreas, *After the Great Divide: Modernism, Mass Culture, Postmodernism*, London: Macmillan Press, 1988, p. 4.
28 Smethurst, Paul, *The Postmodern Chronotope: Reading Space and Time in Contemporary Fiction*, Amsterdam: Rodopi, 2000, p. 5.
29 Bakhtin, Mikhail, *The Dialogic Imagination*, Austin: University of Texas Press, 1981, p. 189.

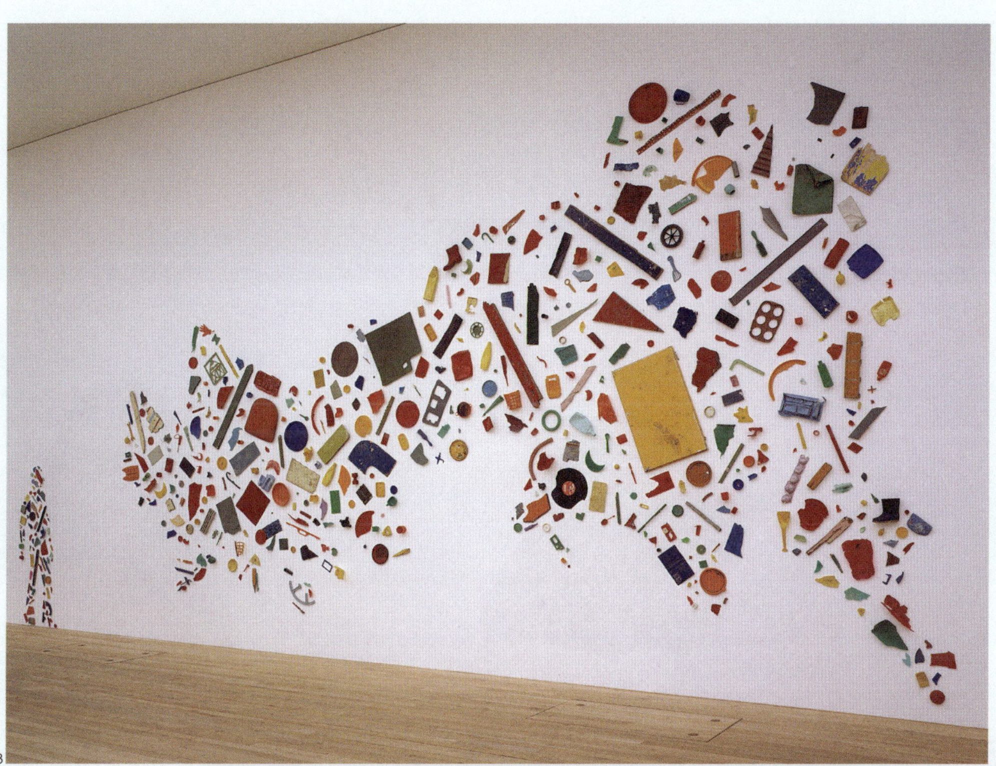

8

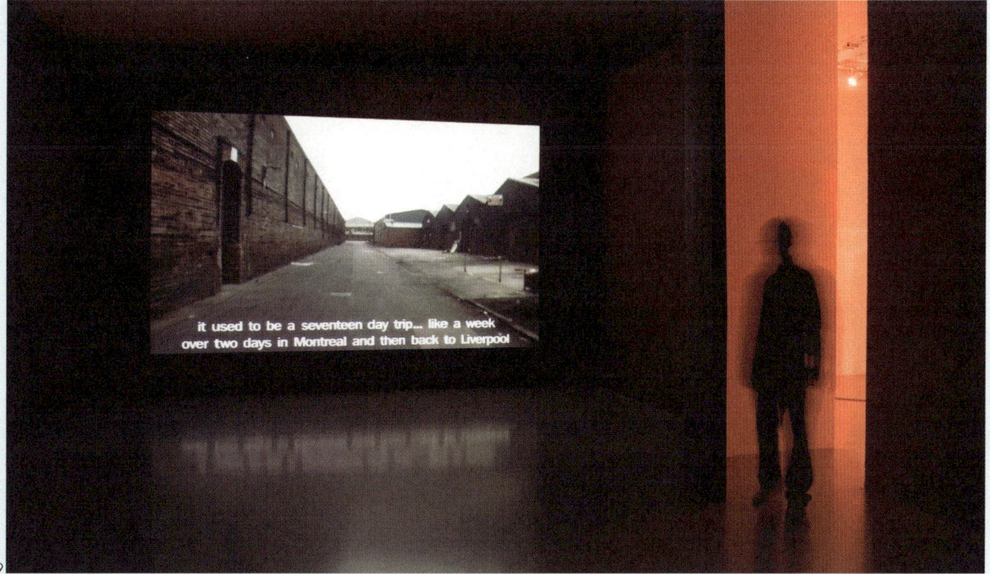

9

7
Adrian Henri
The Entry of Christ into
Liverpool in 1964
(Homage to James Ensor)
1962-4
172 x 242 cm
Oil on hessian
Private Collection, Basel

8
Tony Cragg
Britain Seen from
the North 1981
Plastic and mixed media
440 x 800 x 10 cm
Tate

9
Melik Ohanian
White Wall Travelling 1997
Film, colour, sound
38 minutes
Courtesy FRAC Rhone
Alpes / Crousel

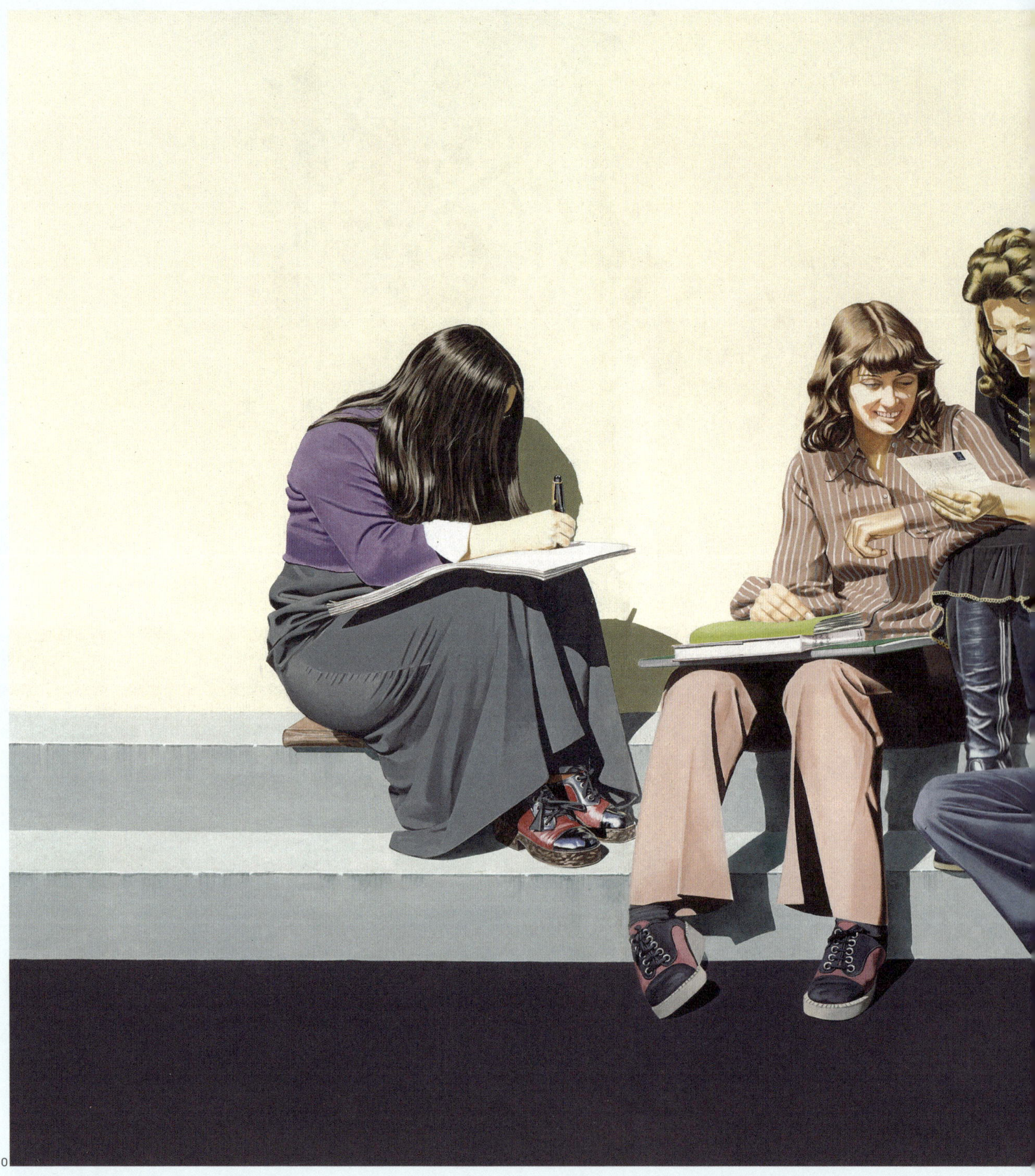

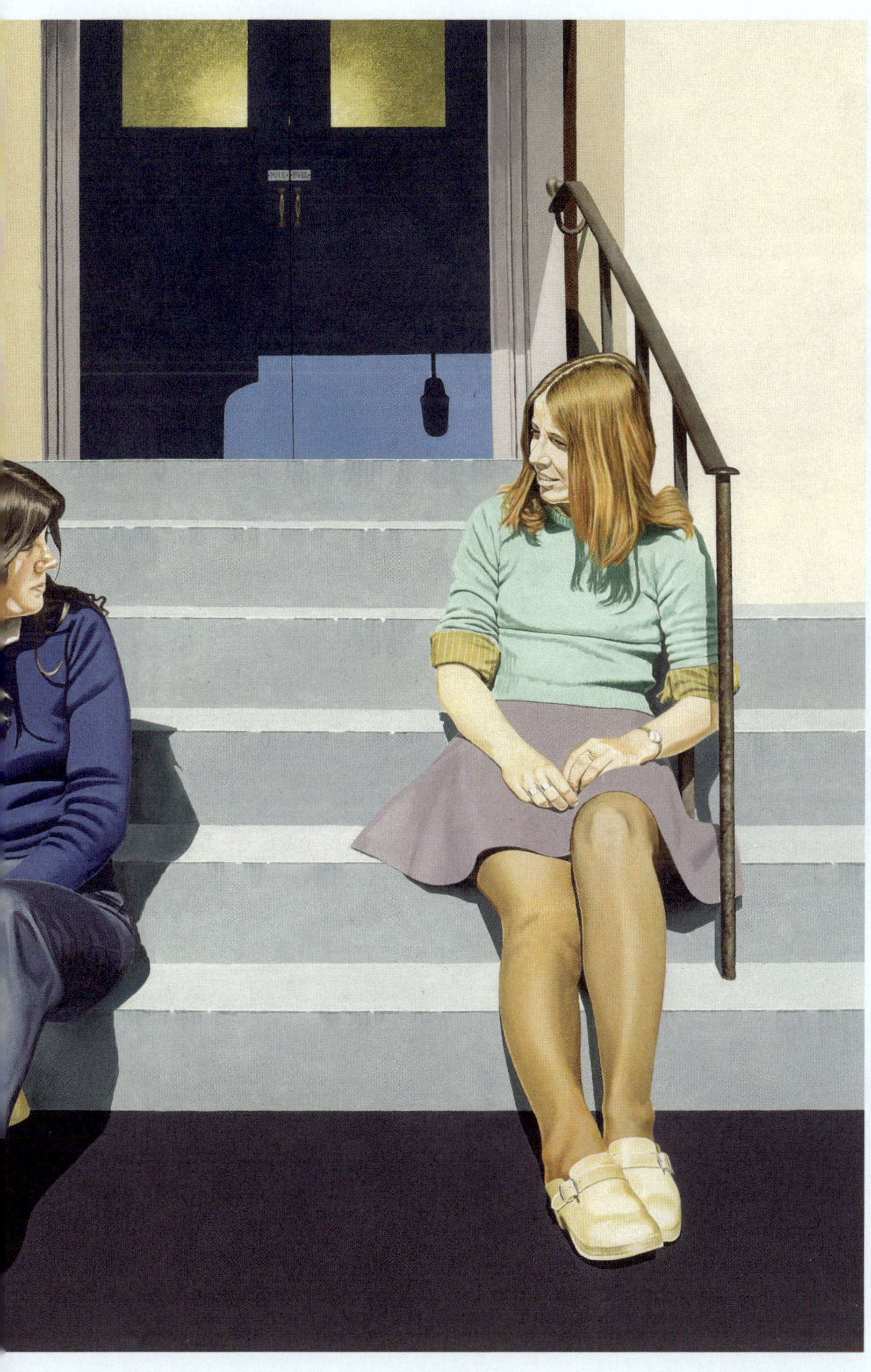

10
John Baum
Five Girls 1973
Acrylic on canvas
171.5 x 289.6 cm
Collection of the artist

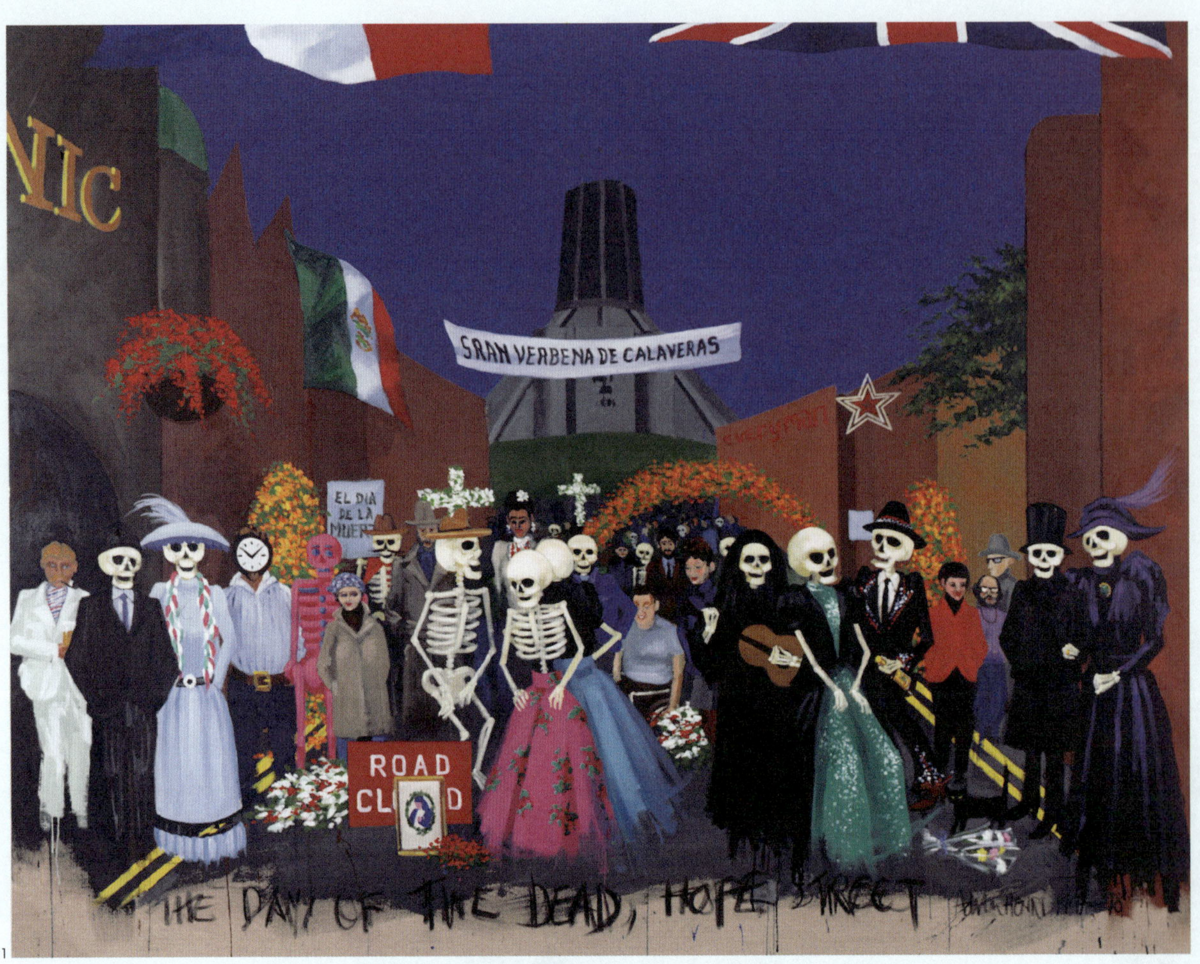

11
Adrian Henri
*The Day of the Dead,
Hope Street* 1998
Acrylic on canvas
193 x 243 cm
Collection of
Catherine Marcangeli

serves chronotopically as a trace of events that occurred there: poetry readings, happenings, parties. Similarly, Edward Chambré-Hardman's photograph of a snowy Mount Street captures the excitement of L8 at that time – the image could almost be a Bob Dylan LP cover such is its feeling of 'beatness'. In *Invisible Cities*, Italo Calvino writes about how memories infuse the fabric of a city, writing poetically, 'As this wave from memories flows in, the city soaks it up like a sponge and expands.'[30] Liverpool is similarly soaked in memories, frequently looking back and examining its illustrious past with melancholic retrospection. At the same time, these memories and associations penetrate the less picturesque corners of the city, for example Tom Wood and Vanley Burke sensitively observing the population in the pursuit of the their daily routines. In showing artworks that re-present myriad chronotopes of Liverpool, *Centre of the Creative Universe* hopes to offer a perceptive archeological reconstruction of the city's forgotten creative history.

Psychogeographies: The City as a Work of Art

The geography of Liverpool's streets host a mass of associations and affective ties; you can see this in names that link to past politicians and figures of influence such as Canning and Huskisson – memories and power have been superimposed on to the city's identity. Street names might also contain a secret history, pointing to the origins of the city's prominence in the 18th and 19th century, such as musically mythical and seemingly innocent Penny Lane concealing a hidden reference to a Liverpool slave trader. In Vanley Burke's images of Toxteth c. 1980, history is literally inscribed into the fabric of the city with graffiti, posters, signage and advertising demarcating a territorial battleground on which social, racial and political conflicts are played out. Visiting *Centre of the Creative Universe* should be like a walk through these streets of Liverpool, albeit a Liverpool refracted and kaleidoscopically altered in avant-garde ways that re-reads their meaning. It is also a journey through time, chronicling the rapid change of the post-war years as well as Liverpool's extended periods of painful immobility, defining memories and shaping history. The artists in the exhibition have in effect mapped the spaces of the city through external imagination in such a way that their representation synecdochically stands for the city, and conversely the city itself becomes a work of art, the central exhibit. Thus it is like how Henri Lefebvre envisioned the city as a vast and ungraspable text, forever being re-edited by the people who inhabit it: 'the city is an oeuvre, closer to a work of art than to a simple material product.'[31] The city becomes a work of art insofar as it is a representation of some emotional and political motive. Like the Adrian Henri painting *Entry of Christ into Liverpool* 1962-4, it defines the community as a specific group, and interprets their connections with the external world.

A psychogeographical view of Liverpool builds in the Situationist sense of a kind of living, breathing map of the city that foregrounds symbolic and affective ties. Debord defined psychogeography as: 'the study of the specific effects of the geographical environment, consciously organised or not, on the emotions and behaviours of individuals.'[32] Thus, the emotional experience of the streets is foregrounded. We hope that the exhibition visitor may be able to 'drift' through the city from within the gallery, in the manner Guy Debord called the 'dérive' – 'a technique of transient passage through varied ambiances.'[33] As a place of exchange, movement and transience, this experience of the urban space as a fluid and symbolically loaded environment is internalised in Liverpool's architecture and urban fabric. It is, however, also present on a more mundane level as photographs of tunnels, streets and, above all, ocean liners and ferries, buses and vans, evoke a highly mobile and outwardly modern experience and project the image of a city on the move (or on the flight from itself?) Frequently, it is an emotive experience that is foregrounded as the highly recognisable monuments and landmarks of Liverpool are rendered secondary in the urban experience by the mundane activities of ordinary people effectively captured by the photography of Vanley Burke, Edward Chambré-Hardman, Candida Höfer, Astrid Kirchherr and Max Scheler, Martin Parr and Tom Wood. Similarly, Jeremy Deller's and Paul Ryan's search for traces of Brian Epstein in contemporary Liverpool reconstructs an obliterated and secret history of the forgotten creative force behind The Beatles but also, more poignantly, of the tragic fate of a central figure marginalised by his religion, sexual orientation and own artistic ambitions. Through performing creativity we recognise the city and urban identity develops; the city becomes, in Andreas Huyssen's typology, 'a montage of many historical forms and spaces.'[34] In burying people to their necks on a Liverpool beach, for example, Keith Arnatt literally embedded creativity into the city's fabric, adding to the psychogeography of place. Similarly, the Boyle Family's work at Herculaneum Dock maps this space in a symbolic way: randomly selected, a space is recreated perfectly, the Boyles making us aware of the significance of everyday, overlooked, banal spaces and places, literally impregnated with traces of the city's imperial past. In the exhibition, artworks take the place of buildings and sites as an imagined Liverpool, from the monumental to the ephemeral.

30 Calvino, Italo, *Invisible Cities*, London: Secker & Warburg, 1974, p. 10.
31 Lefebvre, Henri, *Writings on Cities*, Oxford: Blackwell, 1996, p. 101.
32 Quoted in Coverley, Merlin, *Psychogeography*, Harpenden, Hertfordshire: Pocket Essentials, 2006, pp. 88-89.
33 Andreotti, Libero, and Costa, Xavier, (eds.), *Theory of the Dérive, and other Situationist Writings on the City*, Barcelona: ACTAR, 1996, p. 22.
34 Huyssen, Andreas, *Present Pasts: Urban Palimpsests and the Politics of Memory*, Stanford: Stanford University Press, 2003, p. 71.

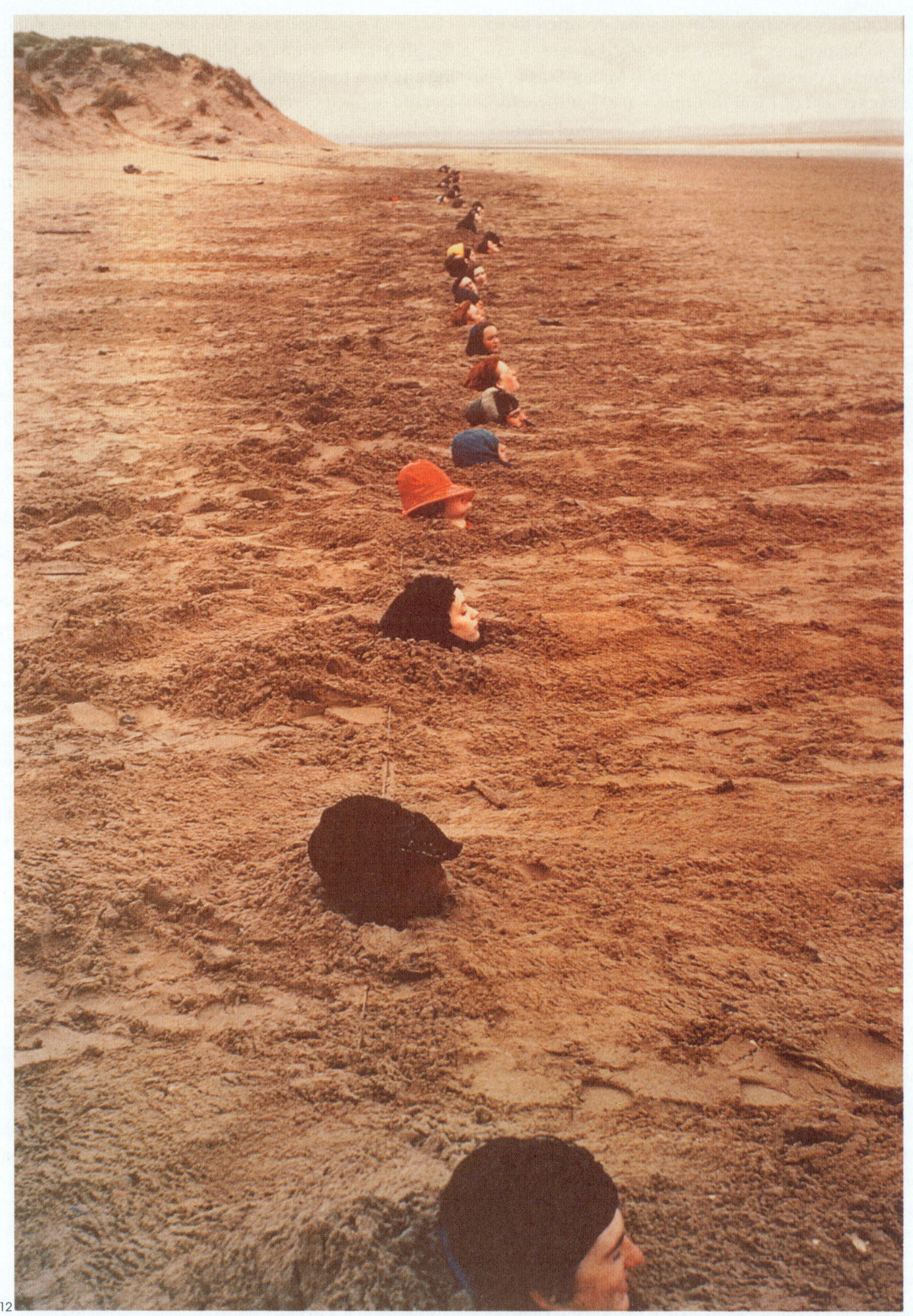

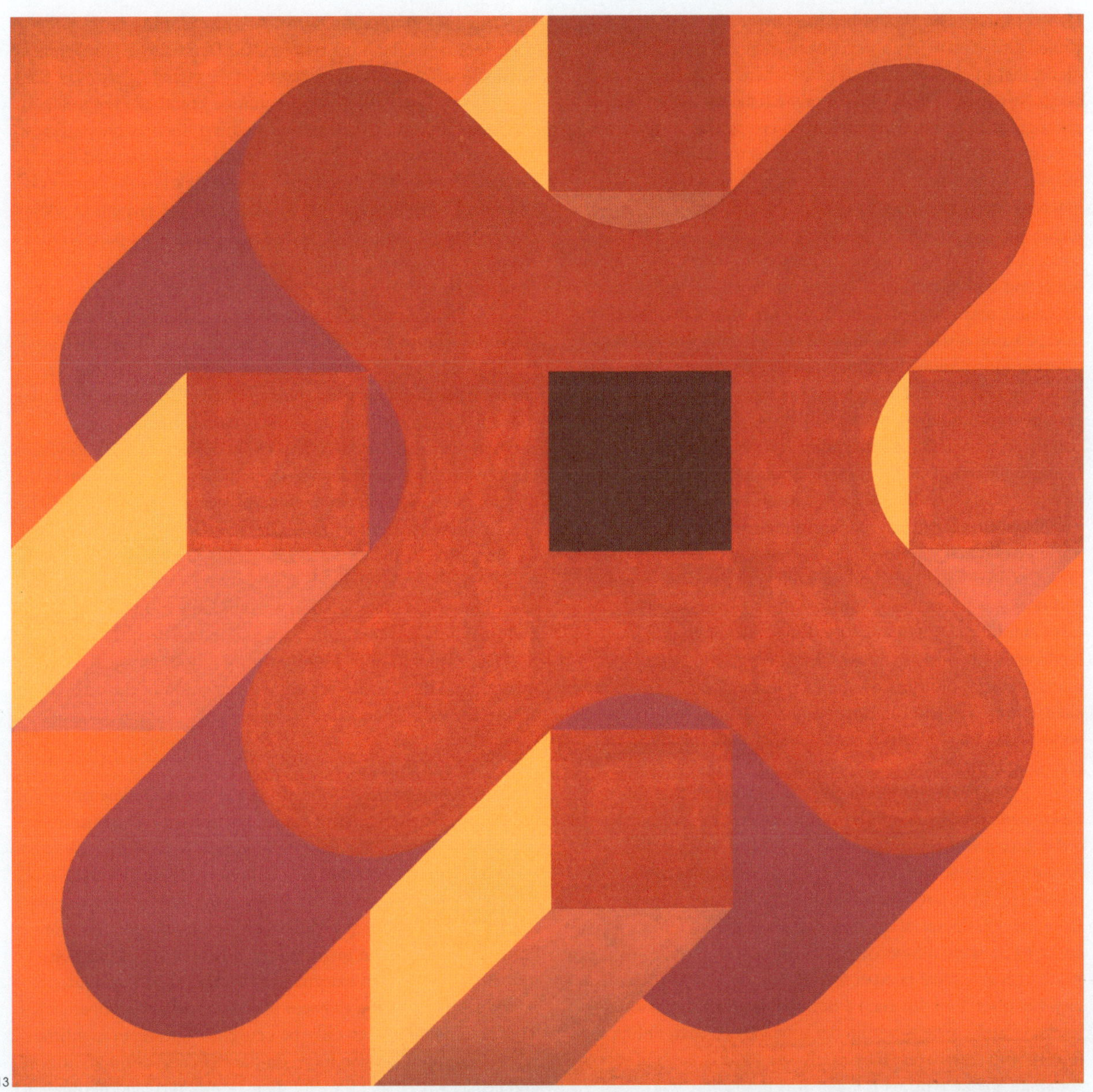

13

12
Keith Arnatt
Liverpool Beach Burial
1968
Colour photograph
50.8 x 40.6 cm
The British Council

13
John Edkins
Sing c. 1965
Acrylic on canvas
185 x 188 cm
Courtesy of Mungo Smith

Heterotopia: 'The World in One City'
If the exhibition offers a psychogeographical mapping of a place, that place is itself both everywhere and nowhere at once. Nowhere in that, like the non-existent warehouse clubs photographed by one Biennial artist-visitor duo to Liverpool, it exists purely in artistic imagination as a non-place or utopia.[35] Everywhere since if the city is 'loaded with heterogeneous fantasies' as Canclini suggests this perhaps makes the city the site of heterotopia. Michel Foucault's concept of heterotopia identified places in which all other sites are found within culture and are simultaneously represented, contested, and inverted. Heterotopia are places that possess a microcosmic quality of mirroring the wider world and thus offering incongruous combinations of experience in close proximity. As Kevin Hetherington remarks, 'It is the juxtaposition of things not usually found together and the confusion that such representations create that marks out heterotopia and gives them their significance.'[36] Liverpool as a port city offers countless heterotopic sites of marginal, liminal, shifting spaces – docks, tunnels, places of exchange, museums. When we view the photography of Stewart Bale we are presented with a plethora of such sites through shipping and docks to the delivery vans of fifties Liverpool. The city's lost centrality as gateway of the Empire leads to poignant confrontations of remnants of global economic might with manifestations of urban decline, neglect and poverty – bomb sites, empty lots and run-down housing estates that in many ways present a more pronounced reality than the stage set of past grandeur.

Kevin Hetherington goes on to suggest that this heterotopic quality is only visible from an external perspective – the juxtapositions and confusions present often being invisible to those caught up in the system themselves. He writes, 'It is how such a relationship is seen from outside, from the standpoint of another perspective, that allows a space to be seen as heterotopic.'[37] Linking to the idea of a psychogeographical perspective of the city, the resident of a city has often built up such a defined network of personal journeys and contacts within the urban space that, unlike the tourist with fresh eyes, they rarely see what is beyond this. Jonathan Raban typifies it thus: 'It is the visitor who goes everywhere; to the resident, a river or a railway track, even if it is bridged every few hundred yards, may be as absolute a boundary as a snakepit or an ocean.'[38] The focus of *Centre of the Creative Universe* is on such external viewpoints that seek out the heterotopic Liverpool: both people who were just passing through or who, in some way, had an outsider status.

A City of Transition
Thankfully, there is no shortage of such figures as Liverpool has always had a transitional, ephemeral element to its character. Transition can be a personal journey such as the immigration Stewart Bale experienced from Australia to Liverpool, or emigration, as Situationist Gordon Fazakerley undertook when he left Liverpool for Denmark; a development within an individual's art as we see in the changing styles of Sam Walsh from Pop Art to his own unique brand of Photorealism; the uncertain status of a creative medium, such as photography between commercial enterprise and art as experienced by Edward Chambré-Hardman or Stewart Bale; or the transition of an artistic movement within society as the growth of social documentary traditions in photography that were particularly strong in Liverpool through figures such as Vanley Burke, Martin Parr and Tom Wood.

Transition is also viewed when Liverpool became the stage for an important moment in art practice. The city was the choice of venue for Mark Boyle and Joan Hills' *Son et Lumière for Bodily Fluids and Functions* in January 1967, the scene for some of Candida Höfer's earliest images as a photographer, and the city's Walker Art Gallery, as Lucy Reynolds explores in this catalogue, was the unlikely yet crucial site in the development of expanded cinema pioneers Filmaktion in 1973.

Finally, *Centre of the Creative Universe* reflects upon the transition of the city itself. As Hans-Ulrich Obrist has observed, '…artists explore the forgotten zones of the city, reanimating the urban void in a formidable bid for freedom and freshness amidst the density and intensity of urban life.'[39] Such an exploration of forgotten zones, both physical and mental, and through it viewing the transition of the city, is an aim of the exhibition and this book.

A City of the Future?
Centre of the Creative Universe is a revisionist view of Liverpool. By not walking the most familiar avenues and streets, and instead heading for inconspicuous alleyways, we seek a vision of Liverpool that is not constricted by nostalgia, traditionalism, and yesterday's successes, but moves past this and proves instead that the city has a much broader and longer cultural heritage. The international artists in the exhibition, global travellers with external perspectives of Liverpool, provide the city with a richness of memories that is unparalleled. This heterogeneity can only be cause for optimism in a time when Liverpool is once more on the rise, attracting visitors and artists who make the city their (temporary and permanent) home, fascinated by its history and continuing energy. Liverpool has all the ingredients to once again become a creative centre: it can look back on a central and varied role in history; it possesses a world-class architectural heritage located in a spectacular setting; and it is home to a rich cultural landscape of art galleries, museums, orchestras and theatres of national and international importance. In some ways, Liverpool always remained a creative city even as it went through its most challenging periods. In particular musicians continued to emerge from Liverpool (such as Frankie Goes to Hollywood, KLF, Echo and the Bunnymen, to name but the most successful) as did writers such as Willy Russell and Alan Bleasdale who

continued to disseminate the city's myths and stories across the country, making them part of the national collective memory. It was a city that refused to die and continued to fight for its survival.

In the last years, we have been able to again observe pockets of creativity emerging both officially and clandestinely, feeding off the nostalgia for a mythical Liverpool long gone, on the city's more bleak realities of the present as well as chronicling accelerating change with the promise of a resurgent city. Since the establishment of Tate Liverpool in 1988, the city's arts infrastructure has grown exponentially, the arrival of the Liverpool Biennial and the opening of FACT meaning that the city now provides one the best and most diverse offers in the visual arts in the UK and internationally. The Biennial has meant that artists from around the world now engage regularly with the city and its history. However, it is impossible to engineer a successful creative scene. As Paul Jones and Stuart Wilks-Heeg argue in their essay in this volume, 'creative environments' develop at the margins and spontaneously, without and often in defiance of regulation, benefiting most from cheap rents but also a conducive cultural and social environment. It is possible, however, to provide the right conditions under which creativity can be nurtured and grow. The city needs to protect and provide those spaces where alternative and underground activity can take place, both within the city centre as well as within the neighbourhoods, maintaining and developing grown local identities. Liverpool needs to exploit its multicultural history and remain open towards the inward flow of the next wave of immigrants who for so long have shaped the city. It will have to exploit the benefits of its peripheral status while becoming part of a wider city region and a national and international creative network. We hope that this history of creativity in Liverpool might serve as a model and inspiration for future artistic activity that will continue to emerge from the city.

35 Nina Fischer and Maroan El Sani's series *Phantom Clubs Liverpool/Berlin* for the 1999 Liverpool Biennial.
36 Hetherington, Kevin, *The Badlands of Modernity: Heterotopia and Social Ordering*, London: Routledge, 1997, p. 42.
37 Hetherington, *The Badlands of Modernity*, p. 43.
38 Raban, Jonathan, *Soft City*, London: Harvill Press, 1998, p. 163.
39 *Cities on the Move: Urban Chaos and Global Change – East Asian Art, Architecture and Film Now*, London: Hayward Gallery Publishing, 1999, p. 13.

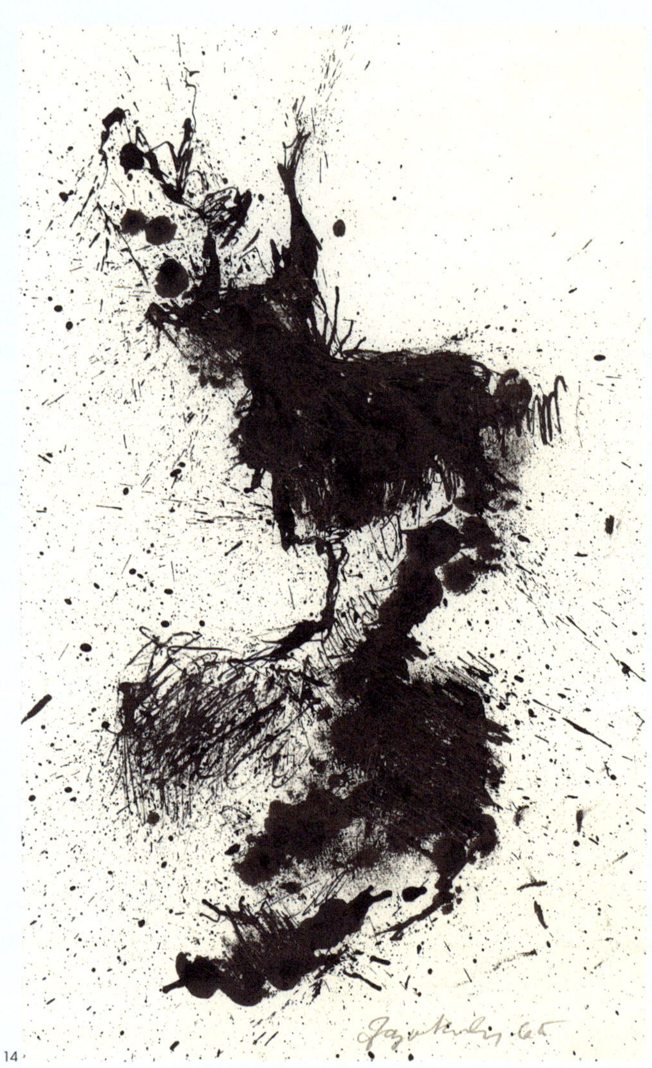

14

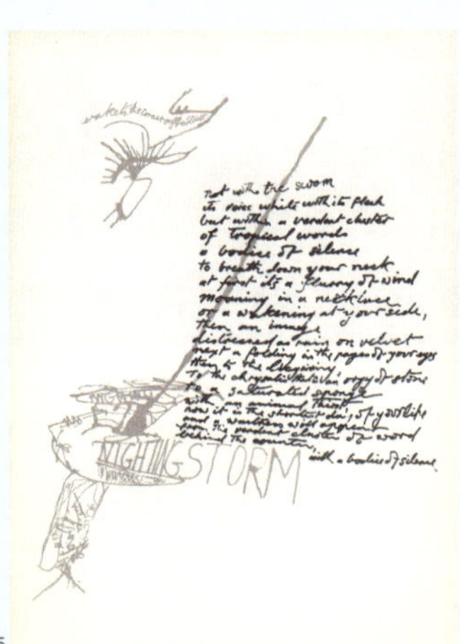

15

16

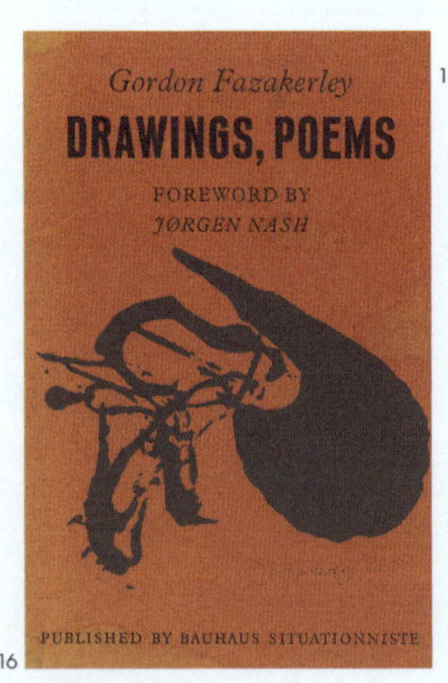
Gordon Fazakerley
DRAWINGS, POEMS
FOREWORD BY
JØRGEN NASH
PUBLISHED BY BAUHAUS SITUATIONNISTE

17

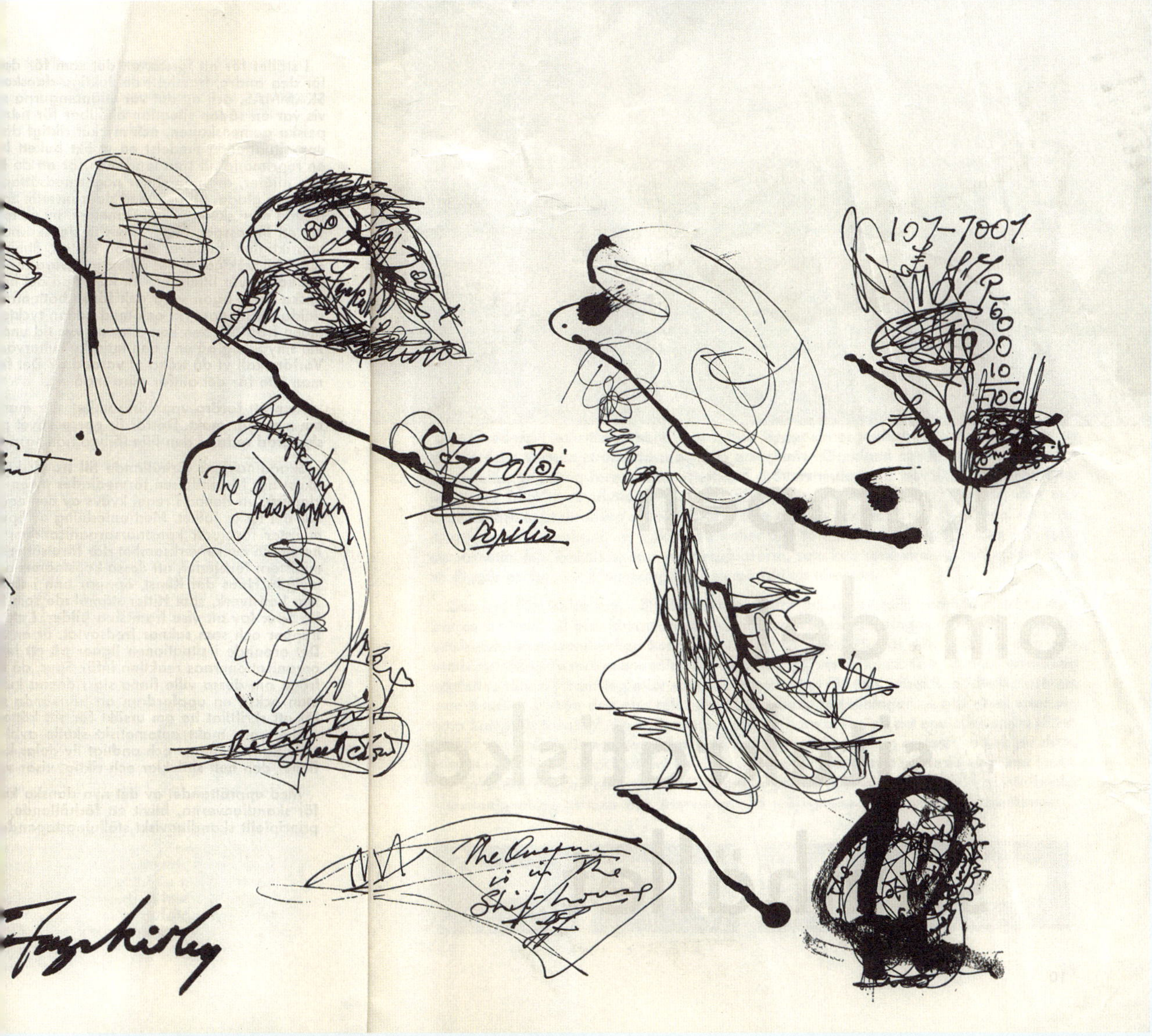

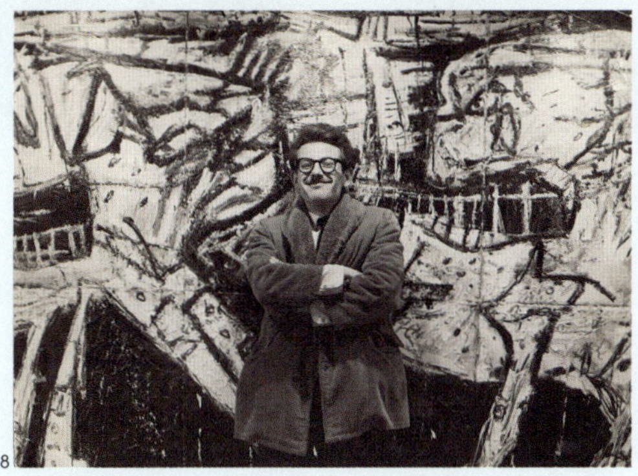

14
Gordon Fazakerley
Untitled 1965
Ink on paper
25.1 x 14.8 cm

15
Gordon Fazakerley
Nightingstorm
From Galerie
Gammel Strand
exhibition catalogue,
Copenhagen, 1962

16
Gordon Fazakerley
Drawings, Poems
Copenhagen: Bauhaus
Situationniste, May 1962

17
Gordon Fazakerley
Drakabygget, No. 2-3, 1962

18
Gordon Fazakerley
standing in front of
painting at *History of
Drakabygget* exhibition,
Charlottenburg 1982
Courtesy of the artist

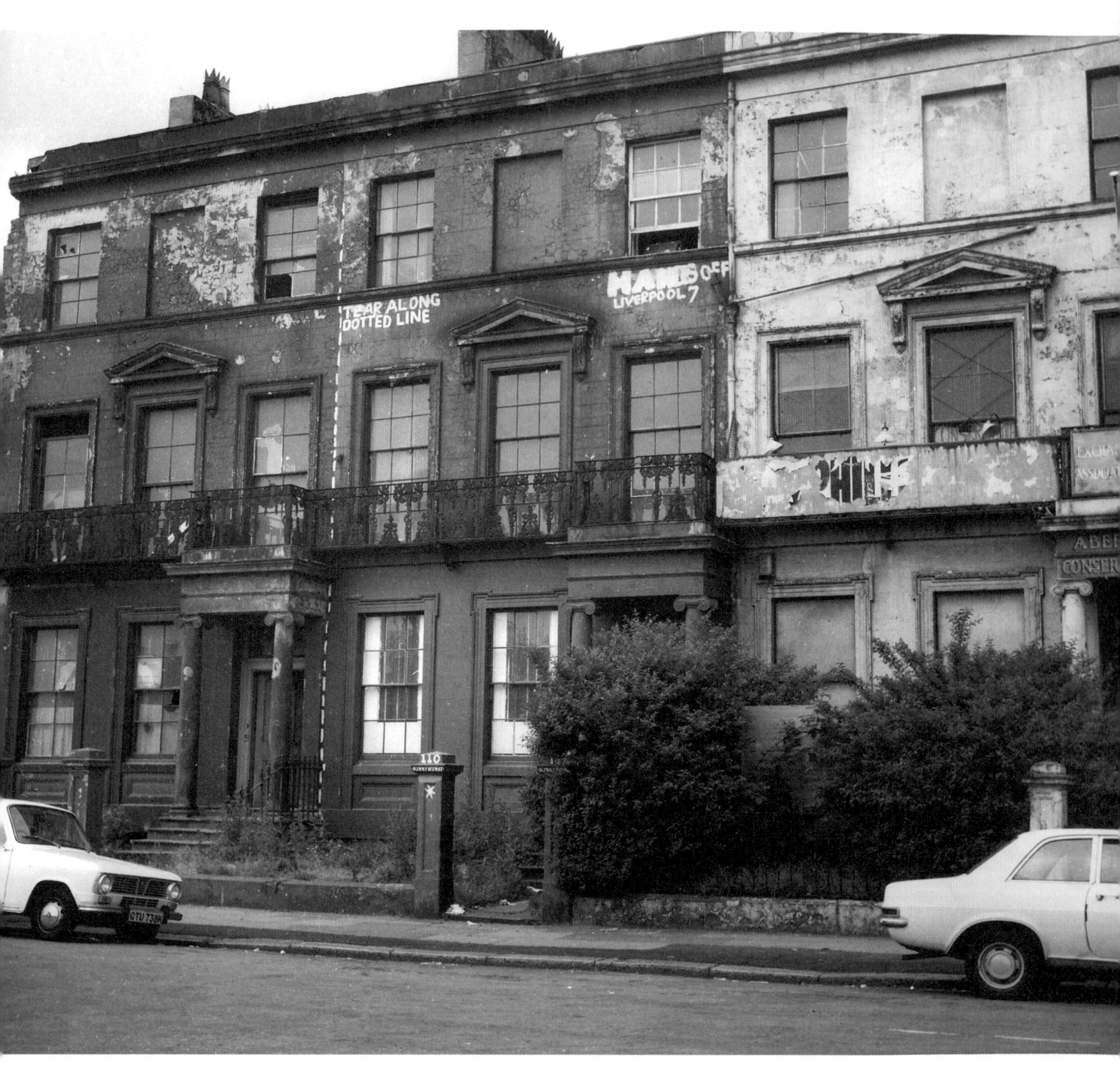

TEAR ALONG
DOTTED LINE
HANDS OFF
LIVERPOOL 7
110

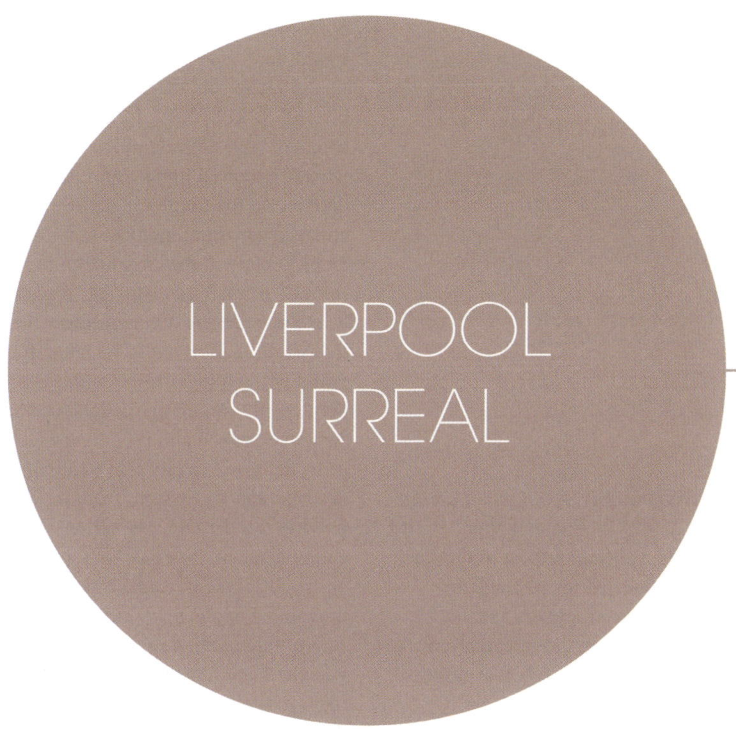

Paul Morley

Liverpool Surreal
Paul Morley

1.

Someone asked me about Liverpool. Liverpool is not part of England in the way that New York is not part of America. It is more Welsh, more Irish, a shifty, shifting outpost of defiance and determination reluctantly connected to the English mainland, more an island set in a sea of dreams and nightmares that's forever taking shape in the imagination, more a mysterious place jutting out into time between the practical, stabilising pull of history and the sweeping, shuffling force of myth.

It's where it says it is on the map, just up there, and along there, down under what's above, above what's below, and rivers and roads and railway lines draw it towards England, and a little bit further out, and you can easily find ways in and out without losing track of time or leaving behind English weather, English telly or English moods. Liverpool, though, fancies that it can just keep going, leave the green, mean and limiting England far behind. It can climb mountains, crack open new territory, even conquer space, the implacable water keeps it connected to the rest of the world, all of history, and grinding, stunning reality doesn't wreck its role as a kind of gutsy cosmic link between the tough everyday and the frail, seething fantastic.

Liverpool has always forced itself forward through the grimy thick and thin of rise and fall, success and failure, hope and hopelessness, despite what was said about it, however hostile the assault on its emphatic, bitter-sweet

rhyme and reason. Liverpool is always on guard. They know that the English look up and over with suspicion and doubt, stumped by the language, needled by the snappy, mongrel confidence, outmanoeuvred by the fast logic-shredding wit. The city is also always wary at what might appear over the horizon, from the endless heavy sea, at what unknown force, for good or evil, might wash up on their vulnerable, open shore. The city has had more money than some, and been poorer than most, it's seen better days, it's always on the up, it believes in itself, it's all on its own. It's been associated with grotesque episodes in history, it's had ideas that have contributed to the immense civilised progress of the whole world. Its hands are dirty, but its mind is open.

You can hear it in the way Liverpool talks. You can hear all its grievous, glorious past in a single sentence spoken about nothing much in particular. Local history, and its well reported impact on the planet, fizzes one way or another on the tongue of a Liverpudlian. You can hear the enterprise and belligerence, the flippancy and the rage, the ambition and the stubbornness, the influx of this, the passing through of that, the constant rumour of the exotic. You can hear the guilt, the defensiveness, the aggression, the pride, the determination not to be taken for a ride, not be taken for granted, the hunger to be in the know, first in line, on the hoof, ready for anything, dead on the money. In a single sentence spoken about nothing much in particular you can hear that this is a city that's fought off all manner of danger, derision and repression, from inside and outside, and has lived to tell the tale, and tell it with a kind of spectacular, cunning relish. You can hear arrogance and music, love and anger, a turbulent, tragic city folded into speech, centuries of movement and achievement propelling words that urge the future to happen, now, again, now and again, friendly, violent vowels that connect friends and family and streets and memories and strangers with everything that's happened, that's come and gone, that's lived and died, across 800 years. It's the sound of a people who have been loved and hated, ignored and exiled, the sound of an inspired, persecuted collection of voices, religions, myths, schools and traditions that have fused together in one place where, against all odds, they found refuge, and home, and a future.

Liverpool has always been about the future, seeing it first, digging it up out of nowhere, grasping its potential, exploiting the results. The future that is now being glossily layered over the city is a cosmetic one, a commercially contrived one, an illusion that does not necessarily represent the essential foreignness of the city, the rampant alien vigour. The glass windows, chain stores, coffee shops, waterfront apartments, architectural flourishes, tourist trails, heritage points seem all imported from the bland, paved and lacklustre England that has ignored the city for so long. The modernisation seems processed and gift wrapped and liable to rub away the urgent, chaotic but ultimately grand and

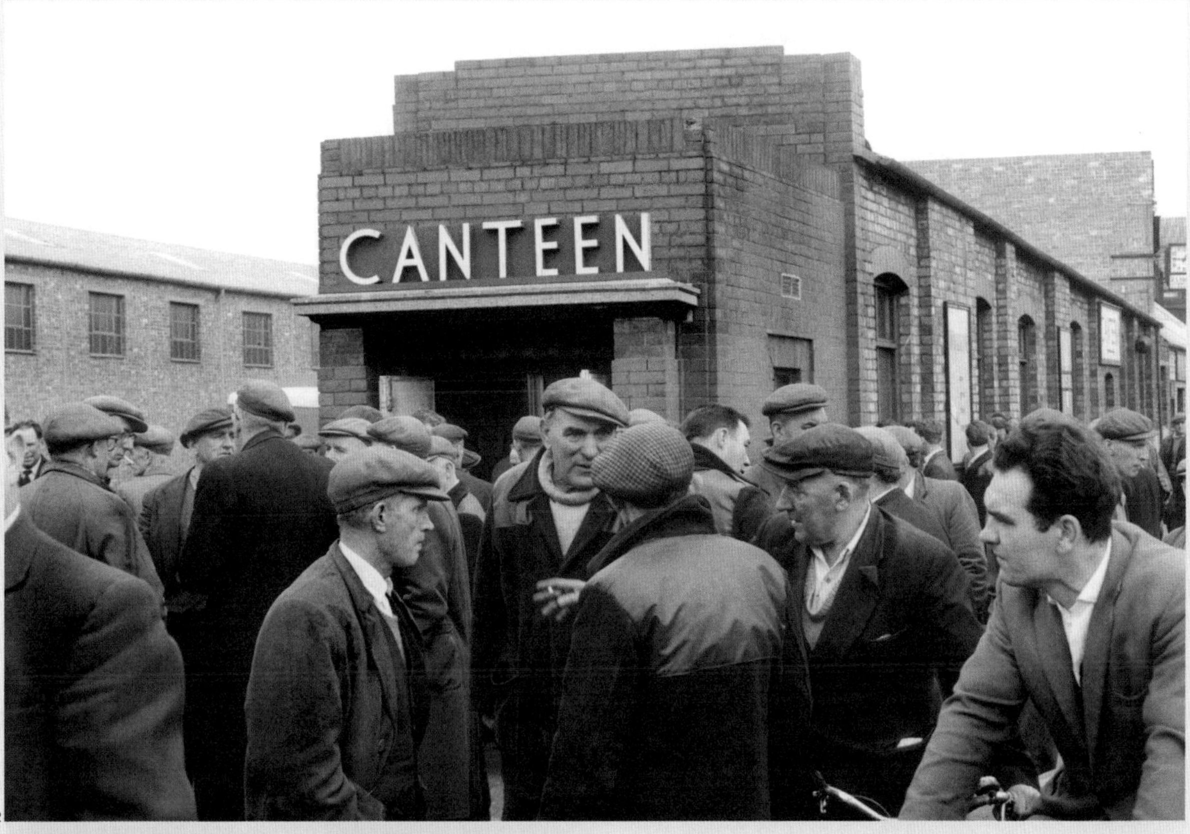

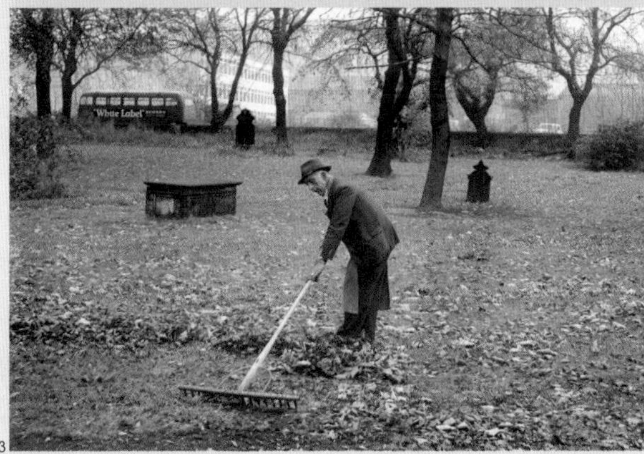

previous
Edward Chambré-Hardman
Georgian Façade, 'Hands Off L7' c. 1970s
Black and white photograph
18.8 x 22.6 cm
The National Trust,
Edward Chambré-Hardman Collection

2
Henri Cartier-Bresson
Liverpool 1962
Black and white photograph
30.5 x 40.7 cm
National Museums Liverpool,
Walker Art Gallery

3
Henri Cartier-Bresson
Liverpool 1962
Black and white photograph
30.5 x 40.7 cm
National Museums Liverpool,
Walker Art Gallery

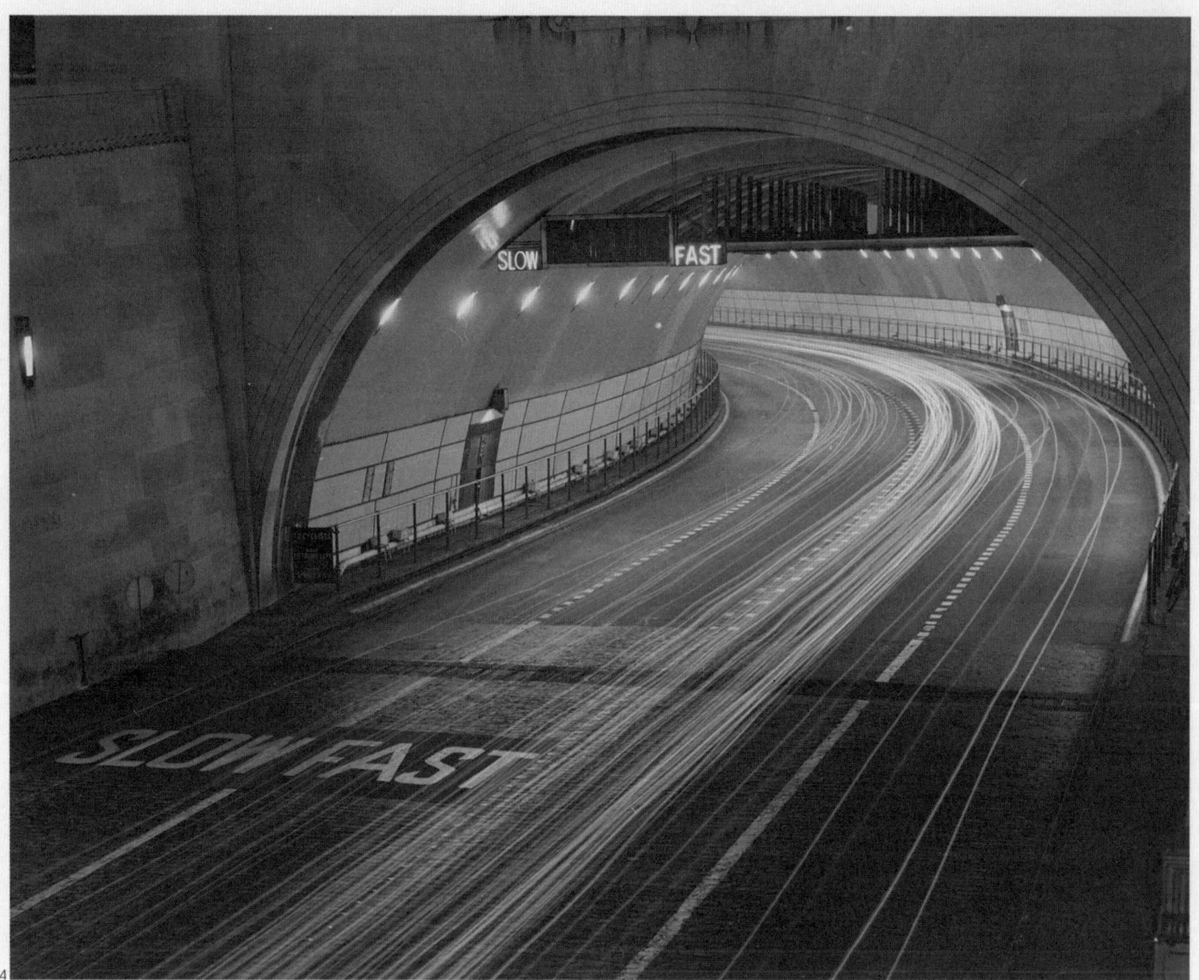

4
Edward
Chambré-Hardman
Mersey Tunnel Interior
undated
Black and white photograph
23.9 x 29.5 cm
The National Trust,
Edward Chambré-
Hardman Collection

unifying elements that have made Liverpool so different, so aggressively outside, a place that helped make England, and Britain, and Europe, a better, stranger, lovelier and more hopeful place than it might otherwise have been. The refurbishment seems not to have come from the city's people, from its thriving, maddening history, its fundamental commitment to invention and innovation, but to have been merely dropped in place, as ordered by glib, dreamless business, as designed by faceless committee.

This alluring, cheerless invasion of the artificially manufactured now is maybe just the latest threat to a city that in the end has become what it is because of its ability to somehow survive any direct or indirect attempts to undermine its natural resilience. The regeneration is not representing, except superficially, the radical, pioneering nature of the city, the way it changed with the times sometimes by being the place those changes happened first. The rebuilding and cleaning up is all second hand, and selective, and borrowed from other regions and other redevelopments, but Liverpool's battling, roguish history suggests that its radicalism will not be destroyed. The city, uniquely capable of somehow acting collectively, to represent an inner will, a common appetite, will find other ways to maintain the aura of otherness and togetherness that is the heart of its scandalous, edgy specialness.

Someone who asked me about Liverpool was asking me to obtain a soundbite for a radio show, and so was looking for something perhaps a little bit more concise, so they said. The hopeful look in their eye hinted that they would like me to have another go at what I thought about Liverpool, its history, people, art, pop music, museums, shops, its past, present, future, its frontier ability to encourage and embrace change, the quick, slick 21st-century transformation it's undergoing at the moment, the changing nature of its reputation over the years, the influence it's had on the way pop culture has colonised large parts of the modern world, its outsider status, its sentimental tendencies, its wild enthusiasm, its contrary cockiness, how the Cavern became Eric's became Cream, how The Beatles became Frankie Goes To Hollywood became Liverpool FC, did The Beatles make the city or turn it into a theme park version of itself, the change between Ringo's springy, uplifting Atlantic Lancashire accent and the shrill in-bred post-Brookie chancer accent, the annoyance people felt about the city and its self-pity at the end of the 20th century, its stylish come-back as a sort of city with very fashionable eccentric celebrity status, its endless ability to absorb disparate influences, its awkward position as a kind of promiscuous, cosmopolitan, avant-garde city tucked inside a inherently conservative, suspicious nation... I wondered if everything I had to say, the first things that leapt into my mind, could be compressed into a single sentence, a tidy thought, snipped to broadcasting size for comfortable consumption.

2.

Liverpool Surreal. Liverpool, never quite what it was. Liverpool, the home of Liverpool. Liverpool, welcoming the world. Liverpool, cutting edge. Liverpool, lost. Liverpool, as spontaneous as life itself. Liverpool, born. Liverpool, going to sea. Liverpool, set in its ways, at the end of the line, at the beginning of time, with its back to the land, its feet in the water, its head in the clouds, its heart on its sleeve, hearts in its mouth. Liverpool, the first city to rock in Britain. Liverpool, boring people to tears. Liverpool, singing for its supper. Liverpool, eagles become seagulls. Liverpool, working. Liverpool, dreaming. Liverpool, corrupt. Liverpool, uncompromising. Liverpool, playfulness turned into art, and philosophy, and business. Liverpool, a relatively small provincial city plus hinterland with associated metaphysical space as defined by dramatic moments in history, emotional occasions and general restlessness. Liverpool, the rest of the world rubbing off. Liverpool, occupation hard knocks. Liverpool, the riots of 1981. Liverpool, spirit, spirited, spiritual. Liverpool, Victorian overcrowding, malnutrition, filth and disease. Liverpool, Charles Dickens first public reading in the town at the Philharmonic Hall, 1858. Liverpool, the Irish impulse to perform, the Welsh need to sing, the sailors shanties, the movement of the mighty river, the roar of the sea, the rhythm of the wind, the beat of the factory. Liverpool, the slope by the creek. Liverpool, on the threshold of the invisible. Liverpool, pulling itself up by its own bootlaces.

Liverpool, nothing lasts forever. Liverpool, Penny Lane, moldy moldy man, a cellar full of noise, more popular than Jesus, blah blah blarney, Bill Drummond, fascination with 23, with K, with time, with novelty hits, with obscure genius pop talent. Liverpool, the centre of making it up as you go along. Liverpool, fuck right off. Liverpool, it really is a fantastic game. Liverpool, the centre of somewhere, if not everything, where something happens, most of the time, leading to something else, only in Liverpool. Liverpool, made up. Liverpool, you couldn't make it up. Liverpool, that's why mums go to Iceland. Liverpool, still nil nil. Liverpool, the Quarrymen. Liverpool, Deaf School. Liverpool, the Zutons. Liverpool, Jesus Christ. Liverpool, ban the bomb. Liverpool, the Gateway to the Empire, leaving, for America, Canada, Australia, New Zealand. Liverpool, arriving, from China, from Africa, from the Indies, from places without names, Jews, Africans, Asians, the Irish. Liverpool, offering hope to millions passing through on their way to America. Liverpool, the world in a city. Liverpool, outside. Liverpool, motivated by progressives, inspired by the classical and renaissance past, constructing public buildings that would not look out of place in Venice, Florence or Athens. Liverpool, the most heavily blitzed city outside of London. Liverpool, the trail of wrecked houses. Liverpool, small patches of wasted wasteland in the shape of President de Gaulle. Liverpool, beat. Liverpool, speaking in tongues.

Liverpool, the great unwashed. Liverpool, people passing through, sticking around, passing it on, keeping it to themselves, sharing it out. Liverpool, 1207, a tiny watery eye blinking bravely in the dense dark cold. Liverpool, lle'rpwll, Lerpwl, Lyrpul, Leverpul, Laverpul, Lyfrpwll, Leverpole, Liverpul, Lytherpwll, Lieverpull. Liverpool, Knotty Ash. Liverpool, the Summer of Love. Liverpool, no scented breeze. Liverpool, the full bodied whine of self pity. Liverpool, population 1931, 855,688. Liverpool, Herman Melville, 1839, 'In the evening, especially when the sailors are gathered in great numbers, these streets present a most singular spectacle, the entire population of the vicinity being seemingly turned into them. Hand organs and fiddles, plied by strolling musicians, mix with the songs of the seamen, the babble of women and children and the wining of beggars. From the various boarding houses, proceed the noise of revelry.'[1] Liverpool, 1565, population 700. Liverpool, step inside love. Liverpool, the O'Leannins. Liverpool, Mel Chisholm, Craig Charles, Paul O'Grady. Liverpool, Scotland Road, Scottie by the docks, the first port of call for desperate emigrants fleeing the ravages of the Great Potato Famine in the 1840s. Liverpool, 'This commercial intercourse of the inhabitants, induces a general harmony and sociability, unclouded by those ceremonies and distinctions that are met with in more polished life; hence the freedom and animation which the town has always been observed to possess.'[2] Liverpool, 1800, 40 per cent of the world's trade passing through the city. Liverpool, post-war sailors bringing American 45 rpm soul, jazz, rock 'n' roll, country and western records into the city. Liverpool, the decision by the Colonial Office to place over 300 semi-skilled West Indian volunteers in the city to help with the war effort. Liverpool, Probe Records, the best psychedelic section in the country. Liverpool, 1957, the first rock 'n' roll record from the city, Johnny Guitar and Paul Murphy's She's Got It. Liverpool, town. Liverpool, ringleaders. Liverpool, Jacaranda Coffee Bar. Liverpool, in 1958, Ronald Wycherley aged 18 of Garston becomes Billy Fury, John Lennon asks for his autograph. Liverpool, the Cavern. Liverpool, her majesty's poor decayed town. Liverpool, Hitler's brother, Yoko Ono and Malcom Lowry. Liverpool, the muddy pool. Liverpool, a good place to wash your hair.

Liverpool, a goal to the good. Liverpool, Liverpuddle. Liverpool, Liverpolitan. Liverpool, resisting. Liverpool, dissenting. Liverpool, booming. Liverpool, the names of pop groups that demand perfection, setting out to make an impression on the whole world, which they can glimpse from their bedrooms, from the waterfront, from the inside of bars and clubs. Liverpool, a cosy anarchy of pilfering, gossip, giddiness and love. Liverpool, championing the demotic in language, and in everything. Liverpool, in the 17th century, built on the River Mersey, newly built in brick and stone, handsome paved streets, fashionable and well dressed people, a large fine town, London in miniature. Liverpool, Underdog.

Liverpool, you can put your finger on it. Liverpool, a cathedral to spare. Liverpool, Derek Hatton, David Shepherd and Stan Boardman. Liverpool, moving things around from place to place, around the world, across the universe. Liverpool, stew, hotpot, hash, scouse. Liverpool, Hairy Records, the divine smell of vinyl. Liverpool, the nervous skin of sensation just this side of darkness. Liverpool, rising through the mist. Liverpool, Simon Rattle, Ladytron, The Farm. Liverpool, Muhammad Khahil, a seaport spun from the blood of slaves, in the pool of life a macabre parade, slave city in a society built on a truth that's cruel, once upon a time you were the nation's jewel. Liverpool, a dark lightless white netted over with grey. Liverpool, the enchantment sours. Liverpool, little boxes, little boxes. Liverpool, the immaterial sphere of our furious and outreaching emotions. Liverpool, a collapse of the capitalist system. Liverpool, earthy mysticism. Liverpool, cabs that smell like people have stopped wiping themselves. Liverpool, a goddess in disguise. Liverpool, Ken Dodd, Jimmy Tarbuck and Arthur Askey. Liverpool, passion. Liverpool, moving. Liverpool, moving cotton, sugar, slaves, invoices, music, ideas here, there and everywhere else. Liverpool, import, export. Liverpool, a bit raw. Liverpool, rich, richer, richest. Liverpool, slum, slummier, slummest. Liverpool, shady. Liverpool, good old fashioned, genuinly likeable, salt of the thing, with this and that thrown in for good measure. Liverpool, the problem with demoralised cities. Liverpool, one hundred and ninety thousand cousins. Liverpool, people fleeing social reforms and economic declines. Liverpool, what about us? Liverpool, John Lennon born to the sound of Hitler's bombs. Liverpool, a post-war anglicised Siberia, out of sight, out of mind, unloved, unwanted. Liverpool, Hamburg. Liverpool, The Searchers, Orchestral Manouevres in the Dark, The La's. Liverpool, gossip. Liverpool, history. Liverpool, The Kop. Liverpool, drug addict, shoplifter and burglar. Liverpool, oh you are a mucky kid, dirty as a dustbin lid. Liverpool, the founder of America was the maker of Liverpool. Liverpool, John Lennon's urban harmonica introduction to Love Me Do. Liverpool, Carl Gustar Jung, 1961, 'I had a dream. I found myself in a dirty, sooty city. It was night and winter; and dark and raining. I was in Liverpool. In the centre was a round pool; in the middle of it a small island. On it stood a single tree; a magnolia in a shower of reddish blossoms. It was as though the tree stood in the sunlight, and was, at the same time, the source of light. Everything was extremely unpleasant; black and opaque – just as I felt then. But I had a vision of unearthly beauty... and that's why I was able to live at all. Liverpool is the pool of life.'[3] Liverpool, 1961, population, 610,114. Liverpool, 1961, Gerry and the Pacemakers' version

1   Melville, Herman, *Redburn: His First Voyage*, New York, Harper, 1849, Chapter 39.
2   Moss, W, *The Liverpool Guide*, Liverpool, 1796 (facsimile reprint, Liverpool: City of Liverpool Public Relations Office, 1974).
3   Jung, Carl Gustav, *Memories, Dreams, Reflections*, London: Collins, 1961, pp. 189-90.

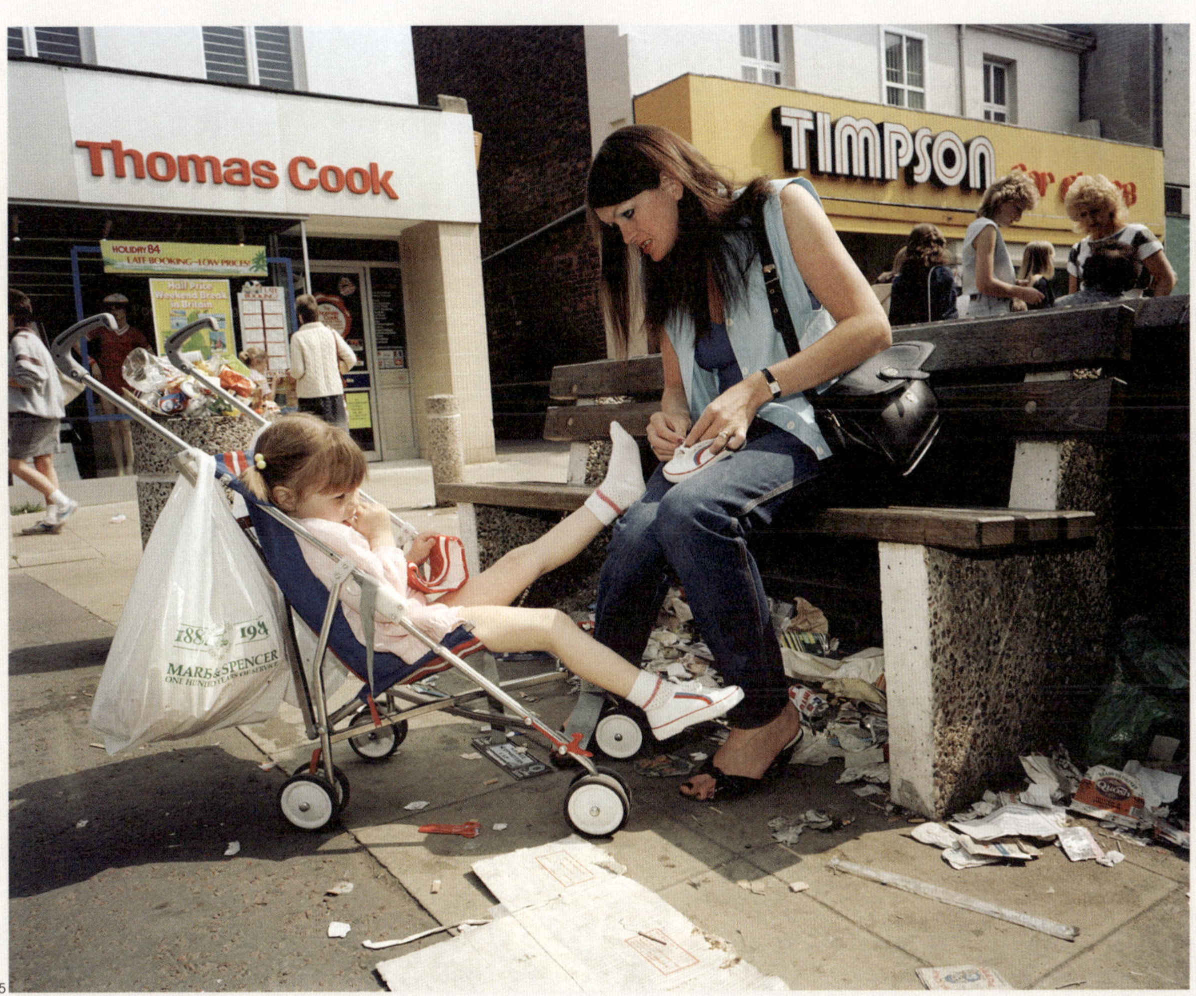

5
Martin Parr
England, Liverpool 1983-6
Inkjet print
61 x 76 cm
Martin Parr Magnum Photos/
Rocket Gallery, London

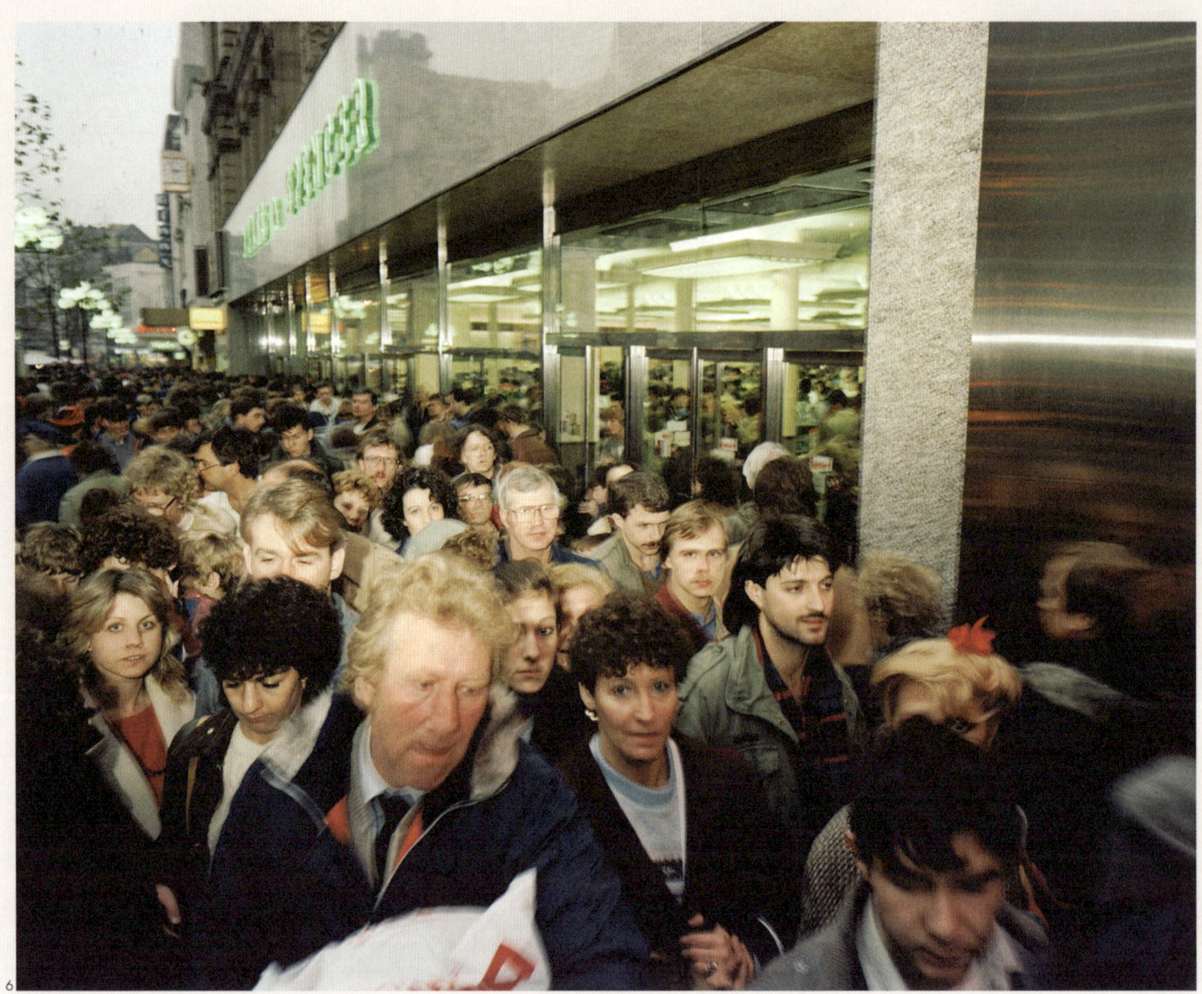

6

Martin Parr
England, Liverpool 1983-6
Inkjet print
61 x 76 cm
Martin Parr Magnum Photos/
Rocket Gallery, London

of Ray Charles' What'd I Say. Liverpool, January 25th 1961: It was a damp and foggy night as I nervously approached Hambleton Hall, a miserable little dance hall on the outskirts of Liverpool. I was tense because a gang of 'Teddy Boys' were following me to the same little dive. They were putting the boot into cars, lamp-posts and the occasional cat. We were all going to see a new group called The Beatles, who had just returned from Hamburg. Liverpool, November 1961, Brian Epstein meets the Beatles. Liverpool, 1961, poets Adrian Henri, Brian Patten and Roger McGough meet almost to the day that Andy Warhol directs his first film, Ornette Coleman releases Free Jazz, and Joseph Beuys is made professor of sculpture at the Academy in Düsseldorf. Liverpool, Bill Shankly's Liverpool FC are promoted from the second to the first division at the end of the 1961/62 season. Liverpool, 1962, happening, pre-scene, public event as work of art, Adrian Henri, mixed media event, Merseyside Arts Festival, find a flower, hold it up to the light. Liverpool, 1962, Bruce Channel was on tour with The Beatles, supported by local bands The Four Jays and The Statesmen, Channel describes Liverpool as a bleak lonely place, with bible black buildings, light shafts and a memorable seawall. Liverpool, Allen Ginsberg walking down Mathew Street, like a bloody saint, holier than Ringo or John. Liverpool, if I gave marks out of ten for towns then Liverpool would get 13, said Lux Interior of the Cramps, some time between 1852 and 1988. Liverpool, John Peel, Harold Wilson and Tom Baker. Liverpool, Brian Patten recalls 'I started writing because I was quite isolated. My family didn't talk to each other, it was one of those nightmare families. My father had left. I grew up in a quite violent and strange house and I just felt very isolated, so I started writing to try and articulate my own feelings really you know. I wasn't thinking about whether it was poetry or not, I was just trying to articulate what was going on inside me. I had one teacher at school, a guy called Mr Sutcliffe, who was really ace and he was inspirational to me. That was at a school called Sefton Park Secondary Modern; I think there is a little Norwegian supermarket there now.'[4] Liverpool, and Alan Bleasdale answers a question about why so many writers comes from Liverpool, 'I think it's the influence of the Irish, the Welsh, and the Dock economy, and the fact that nobody had proper jobs up to about a hundred years ago. My mother's family is from the Dingle and my Dad's family is from Scotland Road – that's where they were born and brought up …a lot of my mother's family especially were dockers, and when I was a kid, you'd go down to the Dingle and you'd hear stories of these six thousand men in a pen, with 300 jobs, of a 6 o'clock on a Monday morning. And the 5700 men, who went back up the hill – and they'd go into the pub...and play cards, and they'd have the crack. And that was generally, in Liverpool, that there wasn't constant labour – like, say with the industrial revolution, like Manchester or Birmingham and so there was an awful lot more time for people to talk.

To create stories, and to… I think Liverpool is very much a verbal city, and surely it comes from the, y'know, the Welsh and the Irish, and it comes from the fact that not many people had jobs a long time ago.'[5] Liverpool, John Betjeman, 1970, 'Liverpool Cathedral is one of the great buildings of the world. Suddenly one realises that the greatest art of architecture, that compels reverence, but also lifts one up, and turns one into a king, is the art of enclosing space.'[6] Liverpool, outdoor toilets. Liverpool, unconquerable charm. Liverpool, from side streets and back yards, from all directions, come more and more children, suddenly grown up. Liverpool, a fountain of things. Liverpool, sights of local interest. Liverpool, nowhere to look for amusement and mercy but towards one another. Liverpool, behind the Pier Head there are numerous narrow streets that fall down to the river; Water Street, Chapel Street, Dale Street and James Street. Liverpool, the Merseysippi Jazz Band sharing the stage with Louis Armstrong at the Liverpool Stadium in 1956. Liverpool, it's just a rumour that is spread about town. Liverpool, a dreary flat spread of streets. Liverpool, the foul disorder of bad dreams. Liverpool, daydream, trance, faith and passion all exist on the borders of waking thought. Liverpool, the patchwork landscape around the Cathedral yields a supernatural dell. Liverpool, Phil Redmond, Jimmy McGovern and Anthony Shaffer. Liverpool, several buildings have a distinctive American quality. Oriel Chambers (1864) is the most revolutionary and a frank expression of function and technology; it anticipated by 20 years the commercial buildings of Chicago and New York. The white Tower Buildings (1908) is an early example of steel frame construction. India Buildings (1924-31) is typical of North American architecture of the 1920s; it includes a central barrel vaulted arcade, another American feature. Barclays Bank (1927-32) is similarly monumental and American. The Adelphi Hotel was a grand building for trans-atlantic travellers; it exterior and interior reflected the great wealth in the city. Liverpool, I'm Bloody Sure You're On Dope. Liverpool, the true beginning place. Liverpool, somebody speaks and you fall into a dream.

Liverpool, the Reverend William Bagshaw Stevens said in 1797, 'throughout this large-built town every brick is cemented to its fellow brick by the blood and sweat of Negroes.'[7] Liverpool, artistic troublemakers. Liverpool, serious fools. Liverpool, Stan Kelly-Bootle, achieves the first post-graduate degree in computer science in 1954 and also writes the lyrics to I Wish I Was Back In Liverpool in 1964. Liverpool, shortly before the recording of *Skellington*, Julian Cope recounts Bill Drummond's belief that a line of psychic

---

4 Guy, Darren, 'Liverpool's Poetic Hero' (interview with Brian Patten), *Nerve*, 5, Spring 2005.
5 Ford, Adam, 'An Interview with Alan Bleasdale,' *Nerve*, 3, Spring 2004.
6 Quoted very widely, the exact reference to this remark of Betjeman's seems to be lost, but is said to have been made on a BBC broadcast in 1970.
7 In his *Journal* for 20 August 1797. See Galbraith, Georgina, *The Journal of the Rev. William Bagshaw Stevens*, Oxford: Clarendon Press, 1965, p. 436.

power connected the North Pole to the South Pole, travelling via Reykjavik, through a statue of Carl Gustar Jung that stands in Liverpool city centre (not far from The Cavern and Eric's, both significant local music venues) and on through Cheops in Egypt to New Zealand. As such, Drummond arranged to have The Teardrop Explodes play in New Zealand at exactly the same time as Echo and the Bunnymen, another of Drummond's managerial charges, played in Reykjavik. Drummond would then be standing at the statue in Liverpool as both bands played, hoping to achieve some kind of transcendent experience. Seemingly, and perhaps not surprisingly, nothing happened, but Cope does recount how he was surprised to discover some years later, that Donato Cinicolo, the photographer for Cope's second solo album *Fried* (1984), was responsible for driving the granite for the statue from Italy to Liverpool in the early seventies. Liverpool, decline. Liverpool, docks, obsolete. Liverpool, run down council estates. Liverpool, Woolton Parish Church Garden Fete, 1957. Liverpool, Anglican Cathedral, built using sandstone dug up in Woolton. Liverpool, John Lennon, 1971, 'Yes, well, the first thing we did was to proclaim our Liverpoolness to the world, and say "It's all right to come from Liverpool and talk like this". Before, anybody from Liverpool who made it, like Ted Ray, Tommy Handley, Arthur Askey, had to lose their accent to get on the BBC. They were only comedians but that's what came out of Liverpool before us. We refused to play that game. After The Beatles came on the scene everyone started putting on a Liverpudlian accent.'[8] Liverpool, voices. Liverpool, Al Hibbler. Liverpool, Carl Perkins. Liverpool, Ray Charles. Liverpool, the Mersey meets the Mississippi. Liverpool, the Dissenters. Liverpool, the Mersey Sound. Liverpool, Z Cars. Liverpool, Pete Best. Liverpool, Robert Mitchum. Liverpool, Stuart Sutcliffe. Liverpool, yeah yeah yeah. Liverpool, George Martin. Liverpool, MBE. Liverpool, Ravi Shankar. Liverpool, Vietnam. Liverpool, the Maharishi, transcendental meditation. Liverpool, Ringo takes several tins of baked beans with him when the Beatles go to India to study with the Maharishi. Liverpool, long haired rough spoken poets wandering into O'Connor's and screaming their poems above the bar noise. Liverpool, Abbey Road. Liverpool, the home of The Beatles. Liverpool, The Beatles, the ultimate confidence trick. Liverpool, Pete Wylie, the Wah! man, 'Everything in Liverpool was "from the home of The Beatles" so we made a deliberate effort to ignore it...we didn't want to re-create anything that had gone before.'[9] The Four Just Men in 1964 sounding just like The Coral in 1998. Liverpool, Thatcher, working out a way to cut off the rail line to Liverpool, to cut off the life supply to Liverpool, to wipe out Liverpool. Liverpool, fighting Thatcher, outliving Thatcher. Liverpool, a dry eye rubbed raw shrinking into itself. Liverpool, windows and curtains in the same position for fifty years. Liverpool, chasing rainbows. Liverpool, the train from outside the city

holding its breath before it noses into Lime Street and sinks into the earth. Liverpool, the air lashed and staggering with suction winds. Liverpool, nothing to breathe but burnt rubber and diesel fumes. Liverpool, despised. Liverpool, Brookside, lesbian kisses, bodies under the patio, the rape of Sheila Grant, calm down. Liverpool, drunk. Liverpool, repartee. Liverpool, mass redundancy, failed strikes, depopulation, gangs, guns, drugs, poverty, social exclusion. Liverpool, making a dent in national self-awareness. Liverpool, the brand names, the fads, the bastardised vistas. Liverpool, a succession of poses. Liverpool, imagine. Liverpool, frozen memories gleam amid the blackness of loss. Liverpool, hope springs eternal. Liverpool, Faith Brown, Margi Clarke and Kerry Katona. Liverpool, November 1976, Julian Cope surfaces at a Liverpool college, meets Ian McCulloch, Pete Burns, Pete Wylie etc. and forms a succession of half groups. Liverpool, an epic whodunit. Liverpool, a certain slippery ease. Liverpool, make me whole again. Liverpool, The Merseys, Lightning Seeds, Clinic. Liverpool, Hillsborough. Liverpool, The Sun. Liverpool, let's not end it this way. Liverpool, Boris Johnson. Liverpool, Harry Enfield, stupid stereotypes, calm down. Liverpool, Alexei Sayle, born in Anfield, August 7, 1952, humour was not a priority in working class 1950s Liverpool dominated by Stalinist communism and political activism, 'I think that my idea of the world is that it's random and cruel but quite sort of comical really.'[10] Liverpool, live and let die. Liverpool, making to live. Liverpool, the Real Thing. Liverpool, hate. Liverpool, well there's something else to life. Liverpool, Dunlop, Tate and Lyle, Kraft, leaving. Liverpool, scum. Liverpool, smackhead. Liverpool, scallies. Liverpool, vagabonds and thieves and scoundrels on the make always lying. Liverpool, how do we soldier on? Liverpool, 5th May 1977, The Clash play at Eric's. Liverpool, you to me are everything. Liverpool, a triumph of drift and whim. Liverpool, late into the night. Liverpool, buildings and stars laid flat for storage. Liverpool, the steady accretion of plain lived moments. Liverpool, destruction of, by bombs, town planners, politicians, indifference, 'when desolation spreads her empire here.' Liverpool, love. Liverpool, the Turquoise Swimming Pools, winds blow, the rains pour, the seas flow, the old men grow tired of sailing: The winds blow, the rains pour, the seas flow, the old ships ghosts, drifting away.

Liverpool, Surprise Surprise. Liverpool, Bill Drummond, watch the K Foundation burn a million quid. Liverpool, a moment of utter clarity. Liverpool, among people who would be lost without the cross. Liverpool, entertaining all sorts of conditions with a view to self-preservation.

8   See Ali, Tariq and Blackburn, Robin, 'Power to the People' (interview with John Lennon and Yoko Ono), *Red Mole*, January 1971.
9   See http://www.petewylie.com for views and reviews.
10 See 'Alexei Sayle: The World is Random, Arbitrary and Cruel', *The Independent*, 8 February 2005.

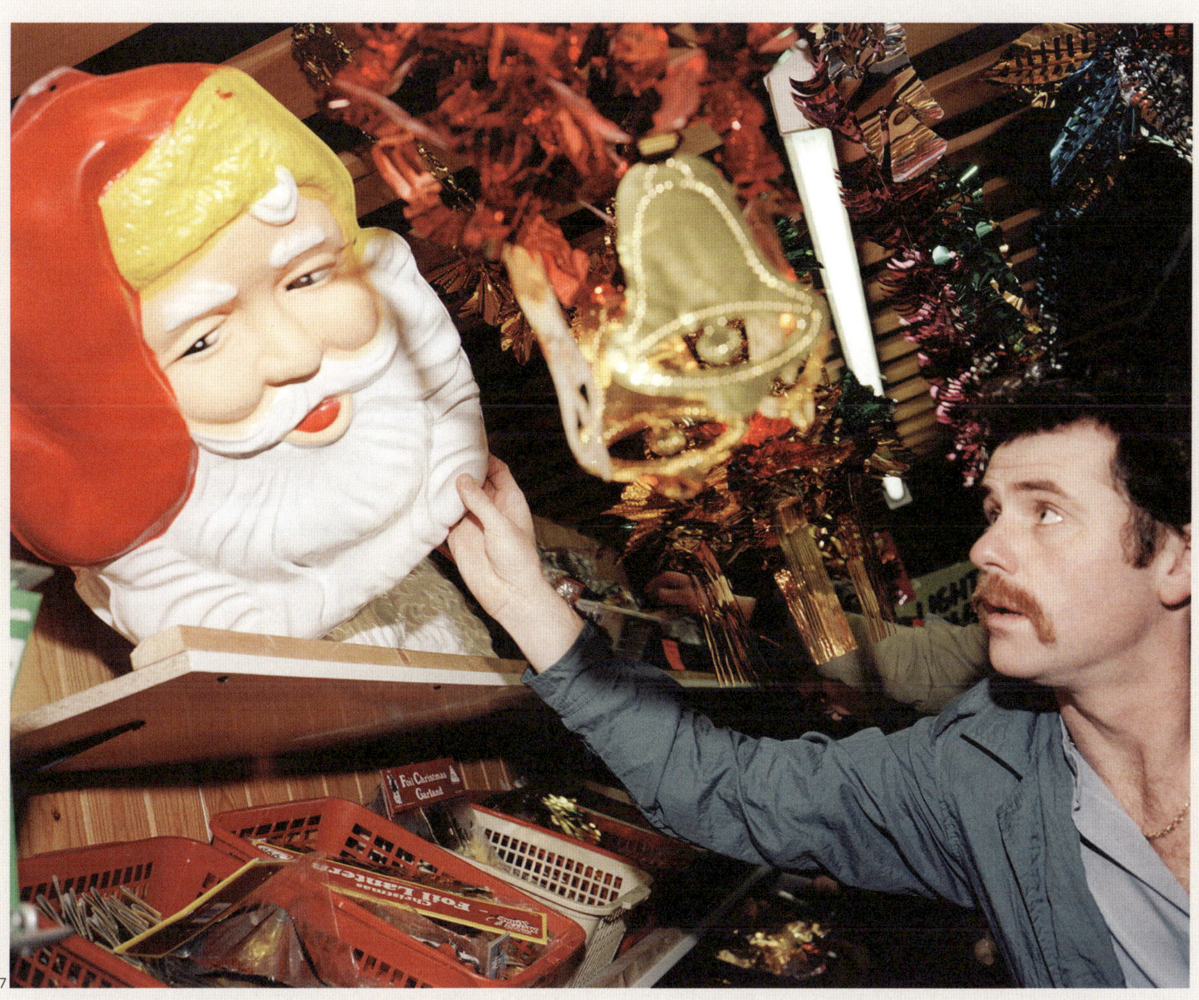

7
Martin Parr
England, Liverpool 1983-6
Inkjet print
61 x 76 cm
Martin Parr Magnum Photos/
Rocket Gallery, London

Liverpool, dogged dedication. Liverpool, industrial anxiety. Liverpool, Cream, the most famous nightclub in the world, commodification of pleasure, pop culture gets branded, hedonism gets streamlined, the wildness of repetition, the groove of expenditure, the dream of dance, the needle and the spiral, the beat and the bar, the social commitment to leisure, the movement of movement, the movement of money, the money in movement, the design of lifestyle, the escape from tomorrow, the missing link between The Cavern and Big Brother. Liverpool, Carla Lane, Lynda LaPlante and Bel Mooney. Liverpool, sound. Liverpool, Jayne Casey, bald singer in Big In Japan, brainy singer in Pink Military Stands Alone and Pink Industry, speaking in 1993, 'Well, in 1978, we were the Eric's band and everyone hated us because we were dead cocky and dead mouthy. If you walked into Eric's, there was a little platform, and that was our table. Obviously like all our mates we'd come from gay clubs. Before Eric's opened, gay clubs were the only ones that would let us in, because of the way we looked. We'd kind of been into dance music in gay clubs, so we brought that with us, and it was a very bitchy scene. People like Ian McCulloch and Julian Cope were quite young in terms, they're only the same age as Holly and Paul (Rutherford), but we'd been very isolated from our working class background, whereas they'd come straight from it; we were probably a little bit more sophisticated in the way we were looking at life. We were all cynical, we'd been around more, we'd all left home at 14 and kind of got into the same books and the same records. We'd already been well into Warhol and Lou Reed, and we'd sort of got into the New York alternative subculture, and modelled our little scene on that, really. So it separated us a bit from the others, also because all the boys in our gang were gay. So they all really hated us and they formed an anti-Big in Japan society. They got a petition together, and when they had 2,000 names on it we had to split up. Then they got t-shirts with my face printed on them, so they'd all walk around in t-shirts with my face on them, getting everyone to sign these petitions, which we all signed because we were into it you know. "He's got my face on his chest, he fuckin' hates me, I love it!" (laughs) So it was very antagonistic. They were into things like Jack Kerouac, quite dry things. We were just into "camping out" and having a laugh. It was two separate scenes, and then they started to play instruments and wanted to be in bands, which is why they hated us so much to begin with, because we were doing it and they were sort of just coming up. You know I have said that when I saw the first Echo and the Bunnymen gig at Eric's, when they just had a drum machine, it was the best thing I'd ever seen. You know I did think they were brilliant. In later years we became friends, but it was very antagonistic in the beginning. All through the 80's, Ian and Julian would slag me in the music papers at every opportunity, because that's what they felt they had to do. It was the most competitive I've ever seen in the Liverpool music scene at that time, and it was quite odd because I was the only girl really there at that time, there weren't that many girls around doing things at that point.'[11] Liverpool, the stupidly hip Eric's club. Liverpool, work shy. Liverpool, loss of civic vision. Liverpool, Bill Drummond, fuck the millennium. The Yachts, The Flock of Seagulls, Shack. Liverpool, above us only sky. Liverpool, Wayne Rooney, Brian Labone, Chris Lawler. Liverpool, 2001, population 439,471. Liverpool, Albert Dock, at the edge of the water, from old world to new world, from new world to this world, eat, drink and spend. Liverpool, and the years flare up and are gone quicker than a minute. Liverpool, 6.48 pm, 6 July 1957, Paul McCartney introduced to John Lennon by Ivan Vaughan at a parish church fete in Liverpool, Paul realised John had been drinking, 'he was a little afternoon-boozy, leaning over my shoulder, pissed.'[12] Liverpool, were the Beatles the punchline to a whole history of emotion, or were they just Bill Drummond's genial straight men, setting up the circumstances, working the room, making the introductions? Liverpool, John Lennon as Mickey Mouse, John F Kennedy, Ghandi and Chaplin. Liverpool, imagine the Pete Wylie International Airport, above us only Wah! Liverpool, trendy renovated docks. Liverpool, city centre regeneration. Liverpool, supposed city centre regeneration. Liverpool, artinliverpool.com Liverpool, the glazed buildings and top class design are meant to evoke a combination of 18th century splendour and 21st-century vision. Liverpool, 143 new shops, 360 apartments, executive office space and new bars and restaurants. Liverpool, battered by Thatcher, botoxed by Blair. Liverpool, Bill Drummond, making soup for local people. Liverpool, it's been a hard days night. Liverpool, we hope you enjoyed the show. Liverpool, thank u very much. Liverpool, your sky all hung with jewels. Liverpool, people they rush everywhere, each with their own secret care. Liverpool, diving for dear life when we could be diving for pearls. Liverpool, until you realise, it's just a story. Liverpool, relax, don't do it. Liverpool, an interview in *Nerve* with Alan Bleasdale, where he says, 'I have occasionally a serious ear infection, and so I go down to the Royal Hospital, say, three times a week – Monday, Wednesday, Friday – get up first thing in the morning to get my ears sorted, and I have to go through Kensington – which is where I used to live, in the seventies with my wife and children – and in Kensington – you'd find this in a lot of other places around Liverpool – it has declined. As much as there are the bright lights and luxury apartments, and the wine bars, in the centre of Liverpool, there is also a decline, in places like Bootle, Old Swan and Kensington and areas outside of the city. What I'm trying to say is, I would hope that – in the year 2008 – if I'm still going to the bloody hospital, that Kensington will look a damn sight better than it does now because its…by culture you'd still mean poets, and artists, and musicians, and actors, and singers, these are cultural – it should be for the cultural benefit of everyone in this city. And culture includes your culture – how you live. And it will have failed if there's still areas in Liverpool that have just have got worse. And I know when I went to Glasgow after the city of culture you could see the amazing effect it had on so many parts of the city, I think of it as a great success. I think the people who are organising this have to be aware it's for all the people of Liverpool.'[13] Liverpool, George Melly, the British saint/pope/uncle/tout/ fount/jester/pear/dean/queen of Surrealism, born in the city on the 17th August 1926, wrote in his book *Revolt Into Style*, 'Dedication to pleasure is Pop's intention: pleasure in the present for young people, before they are independent, and have to assume adult responsibilities.'[14] Liverpool, the mouth of the Mersey. Liverpool, the mouth.

3.

Someone asked me about Liverpool. Liverpool has a great mouth, I said, and I dare you to put your head inside it.

11 See http://www.appelstein.com/cif/jaynecasey.html for a previously unpublished 1993 interview with Jayne Casey by Lin Sangster. The interview was originally made for *Caught in Flux #2*.
12 For the story of McCartney's introduction to John Lennon by Ivan Vaughan, see: http://www.beatlesource.com/savage/1950s/57.07.06%20fete/57.07.06fete.html
13 Ford, 'An Interview with Alan Bleasdale, *Nerve*, 3, Spring 2004.
14 Melly, George, *Revolt into Style,* London: Allen Lane, 1970.

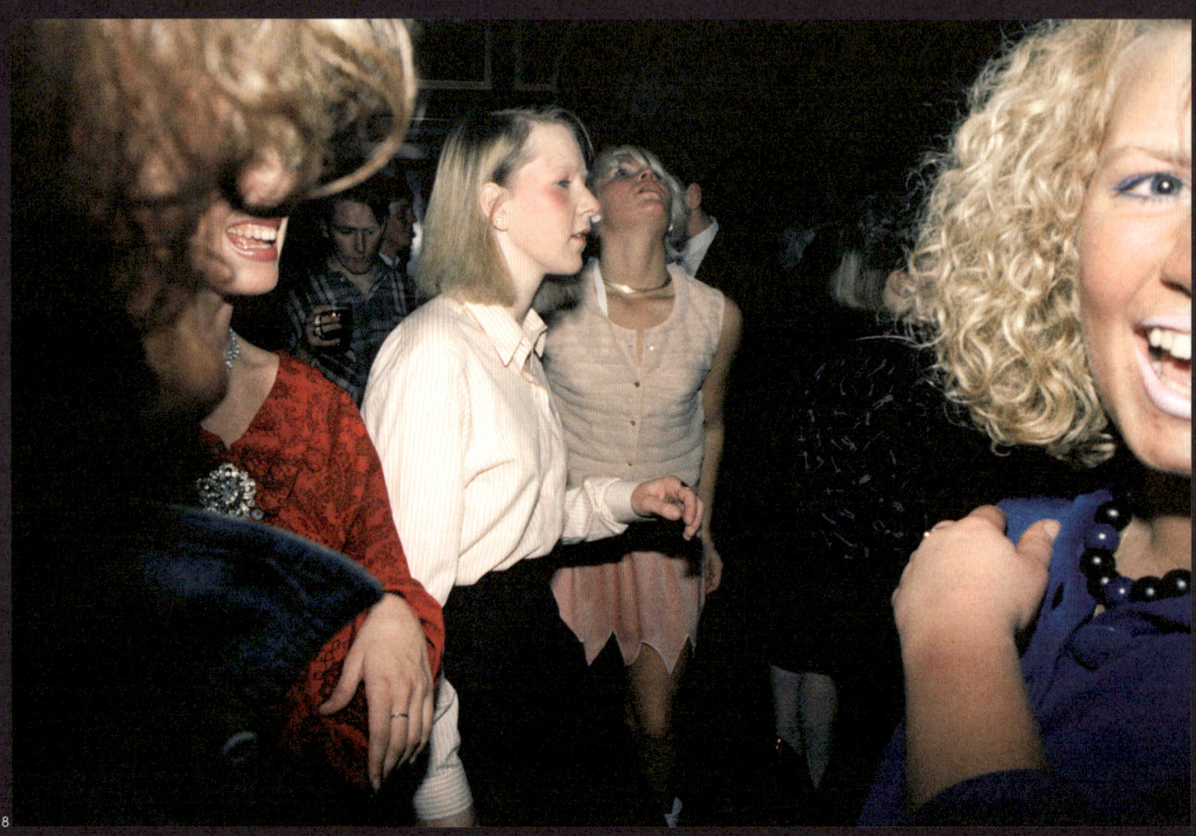

8

Tom Wood
*Untitled (Hair and
Mouth)* 1982-6
C-type print
57.5 x 77.5 cm
The Approach, London

9

Tom Wood
*Untitled (Pink
Lipstick)* 1982-6
C-type print
57.5 x 77.5 cm
The Approach, London

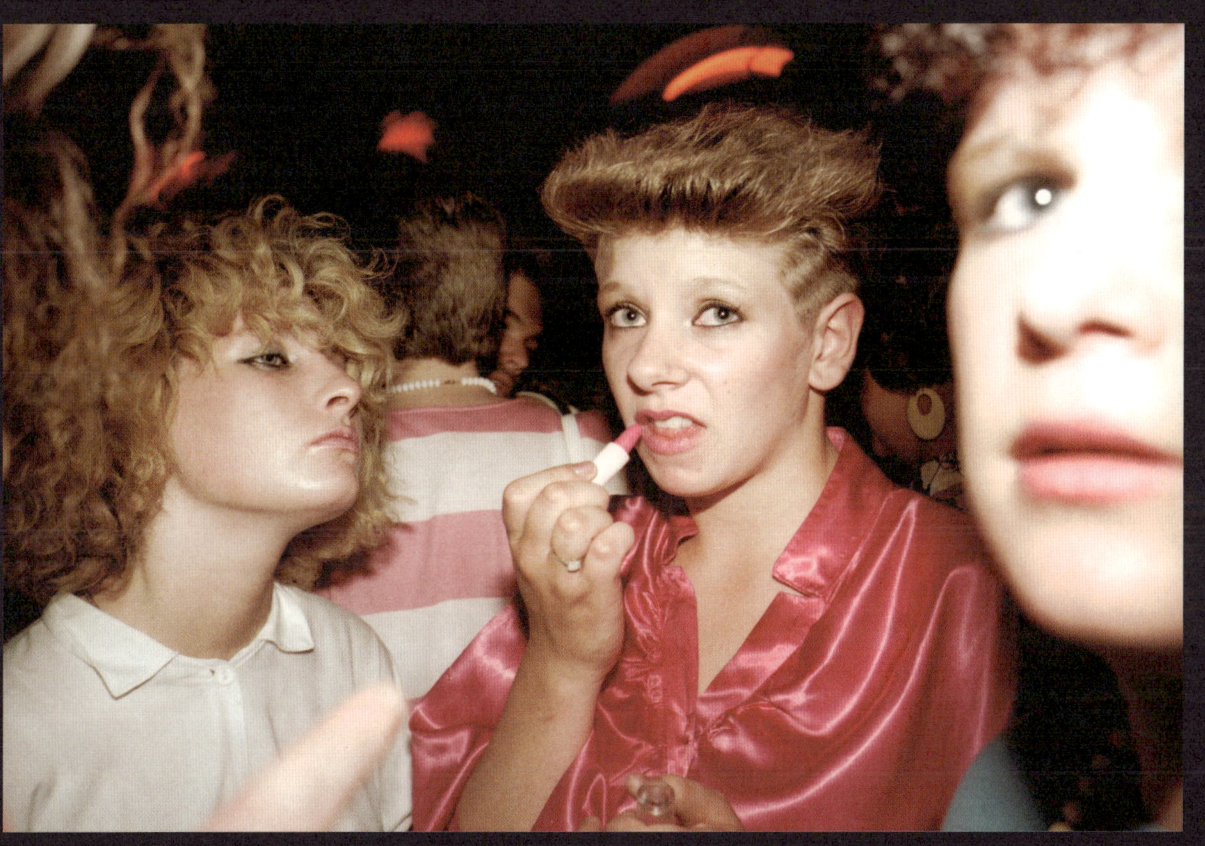

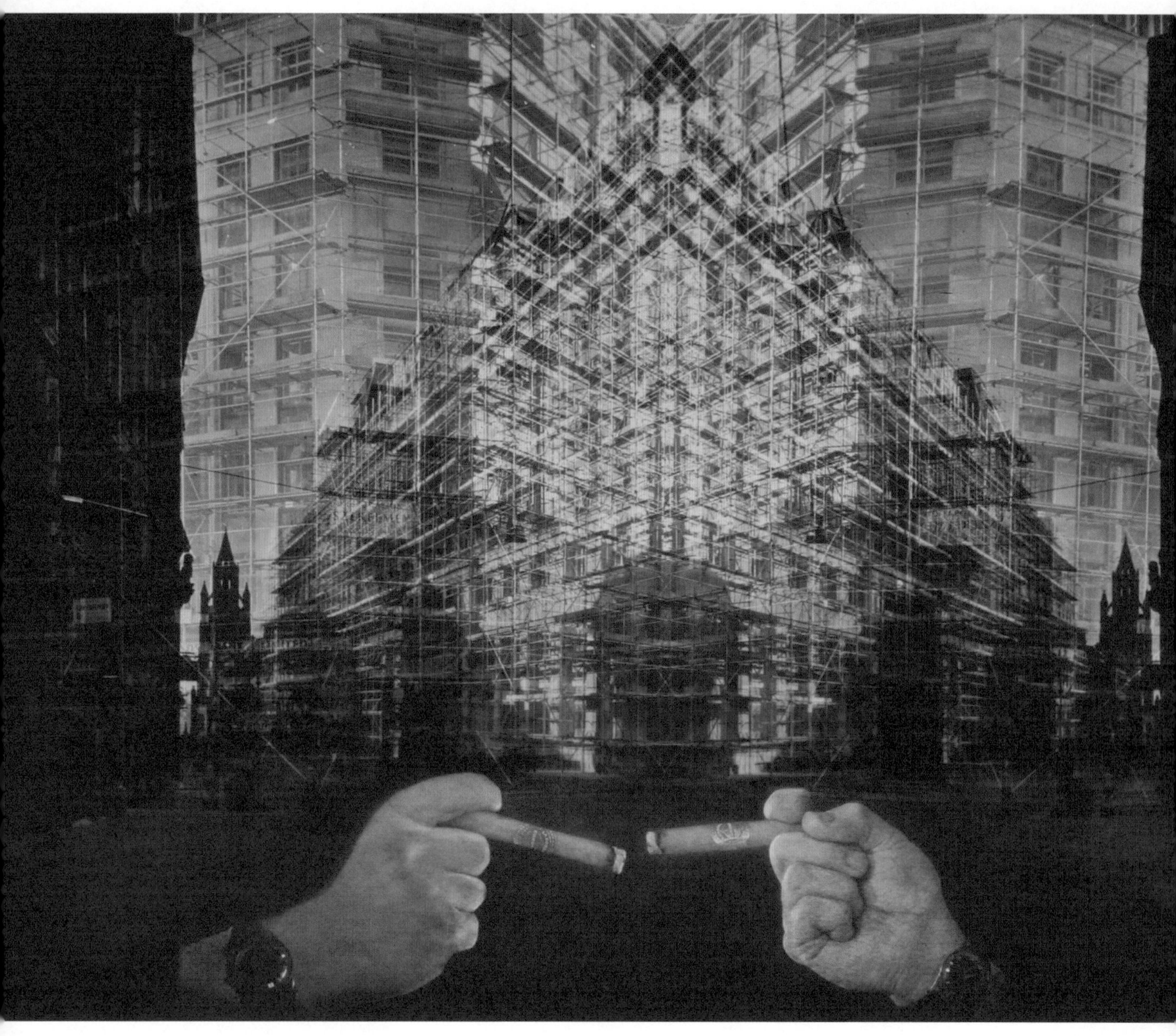

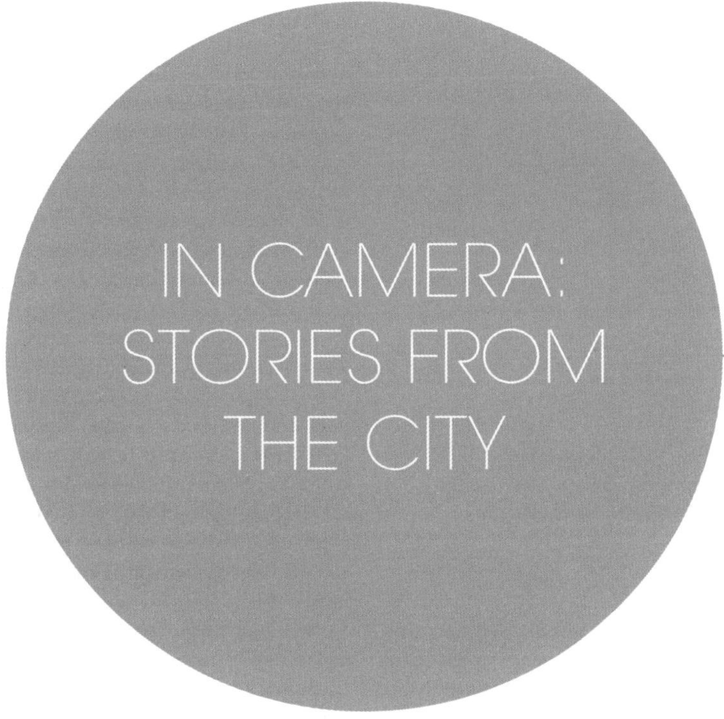

Russell Roberts

In Camera:
Stories from the City
Russell Roberts

'Cities like dreams, are made of desires and fears,
even if the thread of their discourse is secret, their rules
are absurd, their perspectives deceitful and everything
conceals something else.'
Italo Calvino, *Invisible Cities*, 1974[1]

Photography in the contexts of both art and the everyday – or as an art of the everyday, has continuously opened up the visual complexity of the city to new interpretations. Subsequently and in their various guises, photographs have generated a kaleidoscope of 'actual' and 'imaginary' urban spaces. In the multifaceted and contradictory world of images, there is perhaps something in the combination of forms of photography that brings us close to Calvino's evocation of cities as both real and illusory.

Such pictures might be aligned with studio portraiture; survey and record photography; social reform and documentary; itinerant photographers, amateur snapshots and family albums; postcards; advertising; press and editorial photography; illustrated magazines and so on. These are all photographic elements in the visual strata of the city that co-exist at any one time within a patchwork of different times and spaces. As such, they constitute a dispersed archive which reflects how photographs have shaped, as well as been moulded by urban experience.

In sympathy with the ideas behind *Centre of the Creative Universe*, this essay outlines certain images that have taken their cues from the city of Liverpool, worked with and against it, found inspiration in its buildings and people, its histories

and contemporary rhythms. It combines different photographic encounters drawn from various genres, institutions and historical periods. The selection includes images with little or no relationship with art as well as those with an established cultural profile, but such a combination relates to how different pictorial languages have defined and mythologised Liverpool; a creative and varied dialogue between photography and environment in the construction of 'place'.

The photographic elements in the *Centre of the Creative Universe* constitute a curious mix of cultural politics and visual poetics. The mix speaks of the different stylistic and conceptual approaches that have utilised the mediums expressive and functional roles and, on occasion, have been fused to create hybrid forms. One of the recurring motifs has been 'the street' and there have been several projects of significance that have examined – not always within the zone of documentary humanism – the lives of Liverpool's inhabitants. Take Martin Parr's *The Last Resort* (1983-6), a vivid account of working class leisure in the run-down resort of New Brighton during the Thatcher years, in contrast with Ken Grant's intimate record of Merseyside communities in *The Close Season* (1987-2002), or Tom Wood's travelogue through the city on its public buses in *All Zones Off Peak* (1998); we see a social landscape of differences that is tender, fragmented, stoic yet vulnerable.

The political landscapes of Liverpool have been poignantly conveyed through certain kinds of photography that, deliberately or by default, represent something deeper within the historical moment. Images that have inscribed or revealed elements of their time can be found in Bert Hardy's photo-essay on racism in Liverpool for *Picture Post* (1949) and the Exit Photography Group's study of inner city problems in the 1970s, scenes in stark contrast with the earlier imagery of Stewart Bale and Edward Chambré-Hardman during the pre- and post-war periods. This commercial work celebrated Liverpool's industrial heritage and its economic place within a global network of maritime export, traits that received conceptual attention in the work of Bernd and Hilla Becher in the 1960s, and a more rigorous analysis in the critical realism of Allan Sekula's *Freeway to China – Version II for Liverpool* in the 1990s. Considered alongside Candida Höfer's grey street scenes in the late 1960s and Peter Marlow's depiction in the 1980s of industrial entropy and social hardship, Liverpool is an enduring place. However, in more recent accounts of its urban culture, the portraits of Rineke Dijkstra and Alec Soth suggest that there is a sense of the city encompassing something more dynamic, mutable and enigmatic. In all, such contrasts in picture-making strategies reveals how the city has been cast again and again in a different light. Themes of reconstruction and invention, ruins and renewal, are ever present.

The trajectory of this essay shifts to connect post-war uses of photography to a wider network of ideas and imagery

---

1   Calvino, Italo, *Invisible Cities*, London: Secker and Warburg, 1974, p. 44.

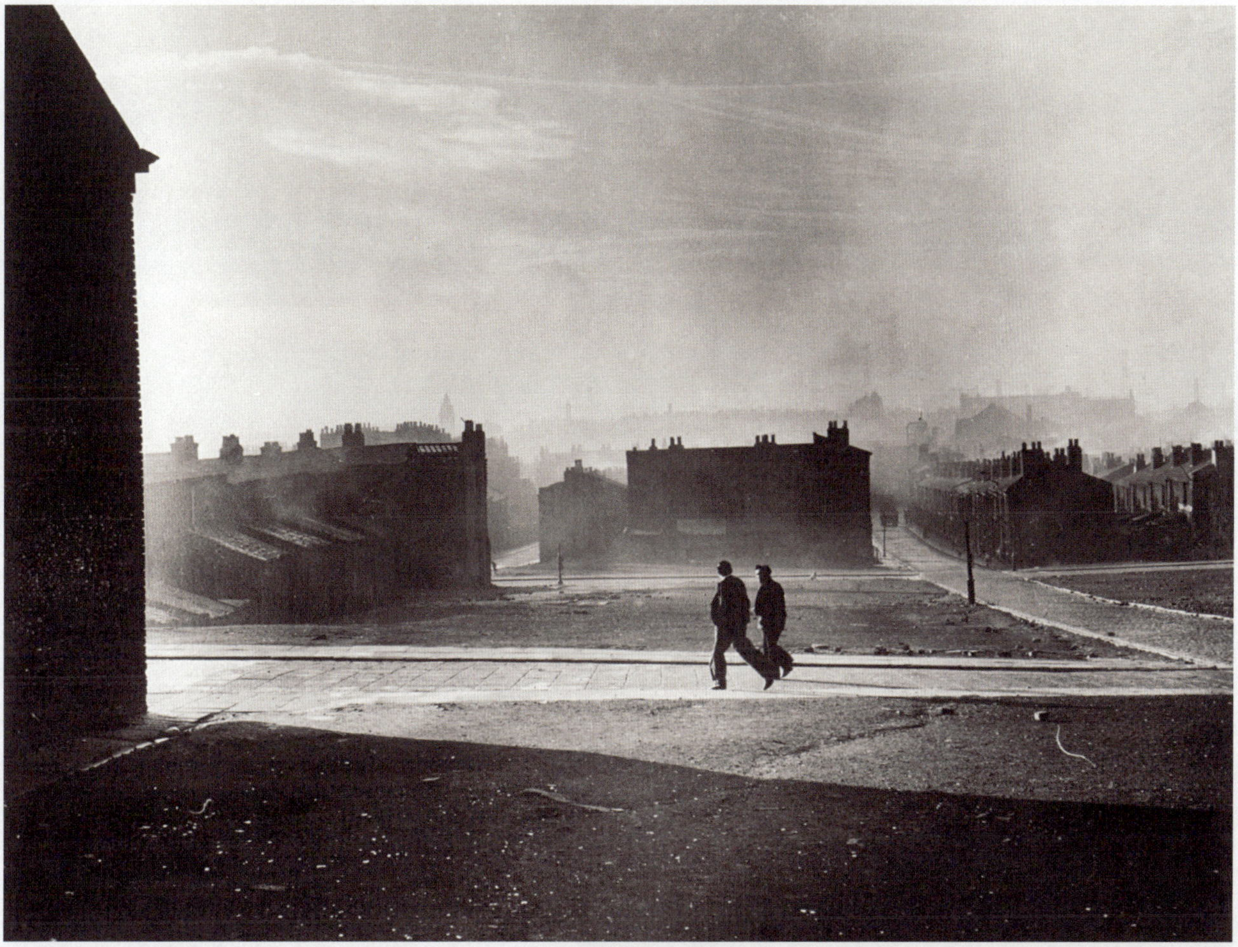

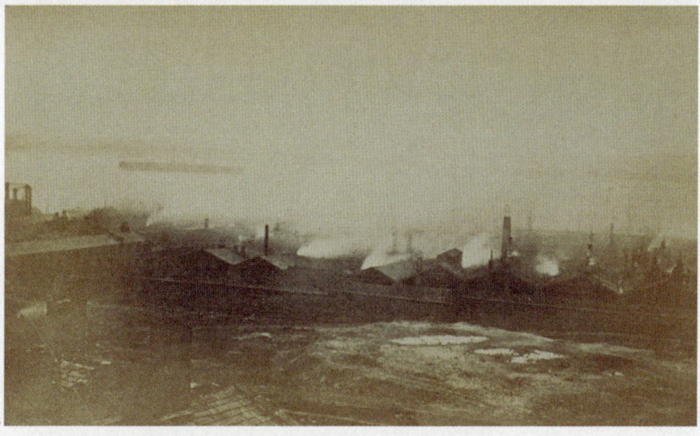

4

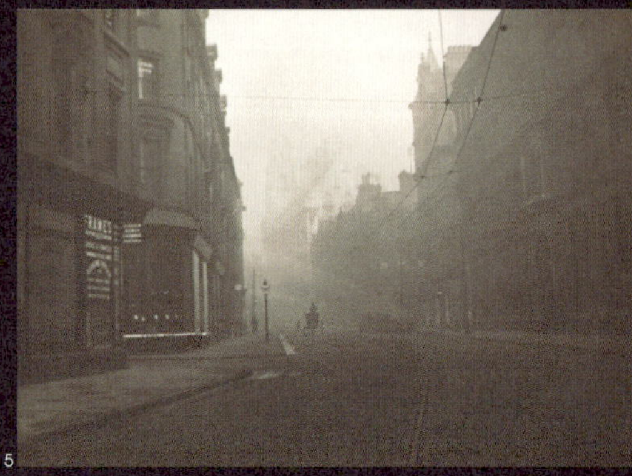

5

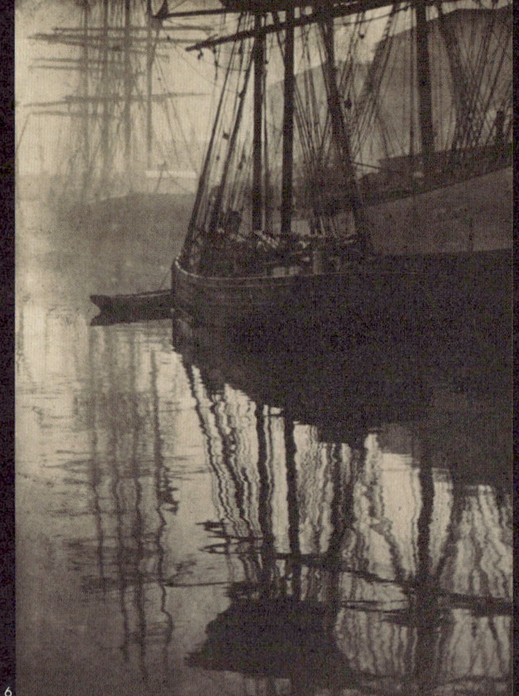

6

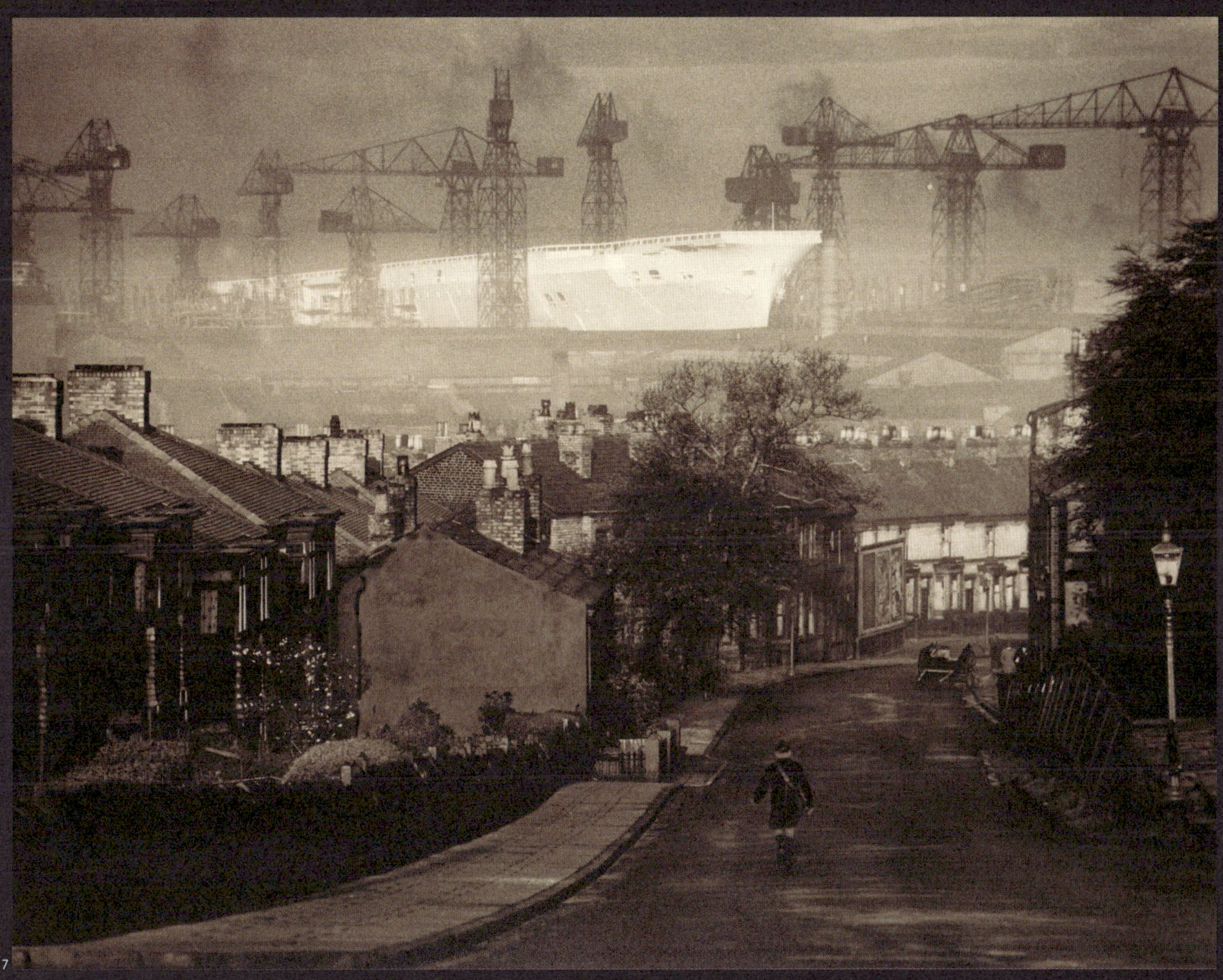

7

4
John Dudley Johnston
Liverpool – An Impression
1906
Gum-bichromate print
Courtesy of Royal
Photographic
Society/National Media
Museum/Science and
Society Picture Library

5
John Dudley Johnston
Liverpool 1906
Silver gelatin print
Courtesy of Royal
Photographic
Society/National Media
Museum/Science and
Society Picture Library

6
Alvin Langdon Coburn
The Spiders Web 1906
Albumen print
Courtesy of Royal
Photographic
Society/National Media
Museum/Science and
Society Picture Library

7
**Edward
Chambré-Hardman**
*Where Great Ships
Are Built* c. 1958
Silver gelatin print
Courtesy of Royal
Photographic
Society/National Media
Museum/Science and
Society Picture Library

as artists' themes cut across time, genres and photographic currencies. There is, in one sense, good reason for doing this as photography moves through the fabric of the city to create a dialogue between the historic and the contemporary. Many of these images reflect tensions between opposites: between desire and constraint, order and chaos, the urban and the rustic, wealth and poverty. Photography has set down multiple pathways through the metropolis, sometimes it could be argued the image is at the centre of things, other times it exists at the borders or the interstices between places. On other occasions it conflates these locations. Yet it is worth attempting a playful overview to reveal the creative 'centres' and the 'margins' where photography operates that have contributed to a sense of Liverpool's social and cultural identity.

It is no coincidence that photography turned toward the mapping and representation of urban life in its first decades. Firstly out of necessity to understand the characteristics and potential of the medium, and secondly to participate in new forms of social behaviour. The photograph and the expansion of the modern city are inextricably tied, initially creating new temporal and spatial experiences that in partnership constitute one of the more powerful and defining statements of Modernity.

Following the announcement of the invention of photography in the popular and scientific press in 1839, it was with a sense of the familiar and otherworldliness that photography arrived in Liverpool later that year.[2] The photograph was a radically new type of object, a new way of seeing the world with its graphic, matter of fact rendering of things, but with a sense of almost magical, alchemical properties.[3] For example, aside from the literal description or naming of photography that included reference to the sovereignty of invention or to its perceived inherent characteristics, a host of other terms were used to convey a sense of wonder: 'fairy pictures', 'natural magic', a 'black art', 'words of light' and 'nature's marvels'. Like many cities, photography too had its ethereal and diabolical dimensions.

In October 1839, the *Liverpool Courier* contained an advert for a 'Daguerreotype Exhibition' in Castle Street consisting of a single view of Paris.[4] In the following year the Liverpool-based scientific instrument maker and photographic pioneer John Benjamin Dancer (1812-87)[5], produced the first photomicrograph of a flea which he exhibited in the city at a Mechanics Institute meeting in 1840. Precisely how he manufactured his microscopic marvels was never disclosed, since he never published on the subject but it is known that in experimental trials he used the eyes of recently killed oxen as photographic lenses. While Dancer was exploring scientific and novelty applications of photography,[6] in 1841 the opening of a Daguerreotype portrait studio took place in Mount Gardens (one of only four in the UK) that foretold of the 'industrial madness' of photography through studio portraiture.

The movement between the macro view of the city, to an encounter with the faces of its (wealthy) inhabitants and the micro study of its invisible dimensions, typified many uses of photography in the 19th century as the 'near' and 'far' were subject to new taxonomic systems. In short, the city in many ways came to be defined, quantified and organised through the photographic document throughout the 19th century.

The formation of the Liverpool Amateur Photographic Society in 1853, for example, provided a rarefied network for the gentleman-amateur fortunate to pursue photography as an applied science and an independent art. Here experiments with photographic processes were shared but also the technical secrets of certain photographers withheld. Comparisons were made with photographs produced in other European countries and some discussion of the French and English 'atmospheres' took place in terms of which helped produce the finer picture. One member, a Mr. G. R. Berry of Apothecaries Hall, stated 'that in practice he found the Liverpool fog a great annoyance to him'.[7] Given the temperamental nature of taking photographs in the city – the chaos of streets, and smoke and industrial pollution affecting the quality of light, opinions were divided as to when the best time was to take pictures – but between 10am and 2pm seemed to cover most suggestions.

Opportunities for exhibition also gave photography a greater profile and currency in the city. In a later issue of the journal in 1855, it was announced that 'The stirring photographic feature of the day, as regards Liverpool, is the exhibition of Mr. Fenton's productions from the seat of war… It is an example of the true use of photography as a record of facts.'[8] Fenton's commission to photograph in the Crimea resulted in images that were comparatively gentile and evinced the horrors of conflict. Such photographs acted as a form of propaganda, hence the importance of them being seen in important metropolitan centres through England. Another influential exhibition coincided with the advent of the Society's journal in 1854; its members turned their cameras on the celestial sky producing collodion-based photographs of the moon to coincide with the meeting in Liverpool of the British Association for the Advancement Science.[9] These images were projected via a magic lantern onto a screen around sixty feet in diameter – a playful and spectacular precedent to

2   See the correspondence of Derek Wood from the 1990s discussing the arrival and of the Daguerreotype process in England
http://www.midleykent.fsnet.co.uk/Letters/LETTERS4.HTM

3   For further discussion of the impact of photography in Britain during the 1840s, see Batchen, Geoffrey, Roberts, Russell, Schaaf, Larry, Ware, Mike et al, *Huella de Luz: El Art los Experimentos de William Henry Fox Talbot*, Madrid: Aldeasa & Museo Nacional Centro de Arte Reina Sofia, 2001 (bi-lingual Spanish and English).

4   See Shelley Rice, *Parisian Views*, Cambridge, MA: MIT Press, 1997.

5   Articles on Dancer's photographic experiments in Liverpool are scarce. See Hallett, Michael, *John Benjamin Dancer, 1812-1867: Selected Documents* (printed privately), UK: 1979, and Prescott, Gertrude Mae, 'Public and Private Vision: The Photography of John Benjamin Dancer', in Oliphant, David, and Zigal, Thomas (eds.), *Perspectives on Photography*, Austin: Harry Ransom Research Center at The University of Texas, 1982.

6   See Benjamin, Marina, 'Sliding scales: microphotography and the Victorian obsession', in Spufford, Francis, and Uglow, Jenny, (eds.), *Cultural Babbage: Technology, Time and Invention*, London: Faber 1996, pp. 99-122.

7   'Liverpool Photographic Society', *Journal of the Photographic Society*, No. 5, May 21, 1853, p. 67.

8   *Liverpool Photographic Journal*, Liverpool: Henry Greenwood, Vol. II, No. 23, November 10, 1855, unpaginated.

9   'Photography' (From *Cosmos*, 21st *October*, 1854), *Liverpool Photographic Journal*, Liverpool: Henry Greenwood, Vol. I, 1854, p. 146.

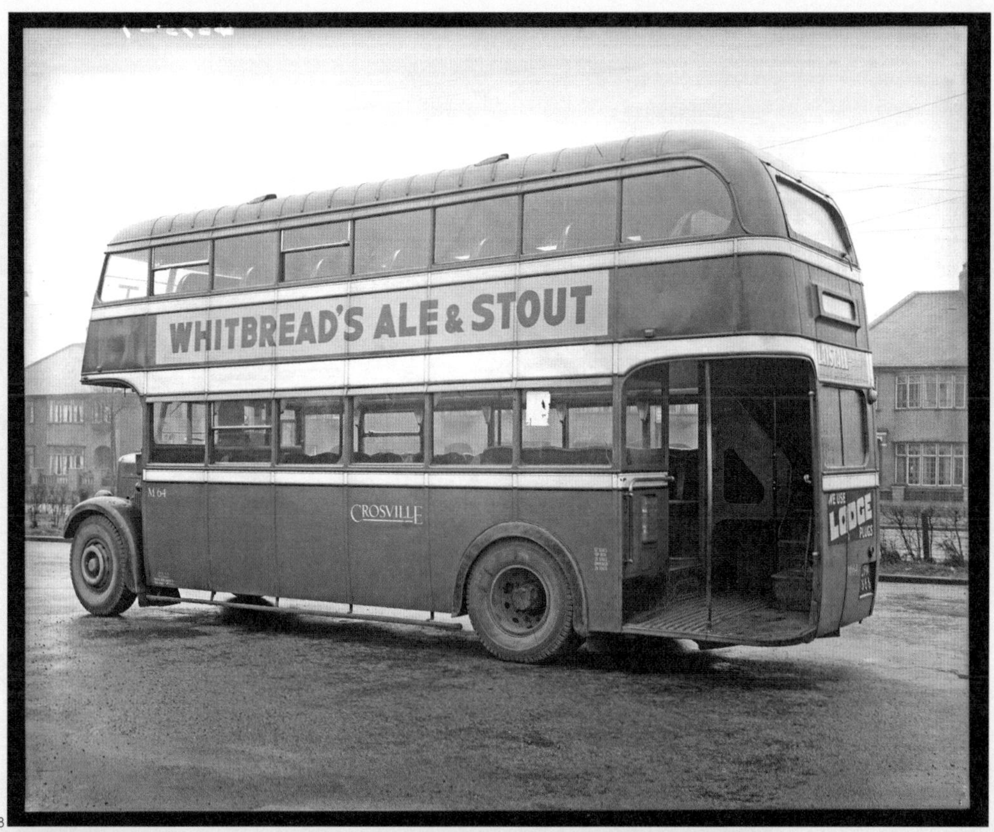

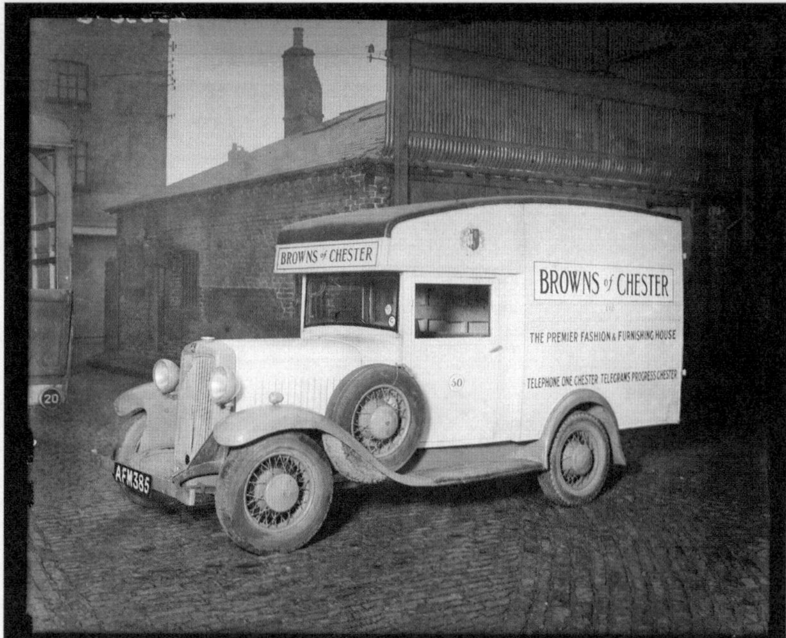

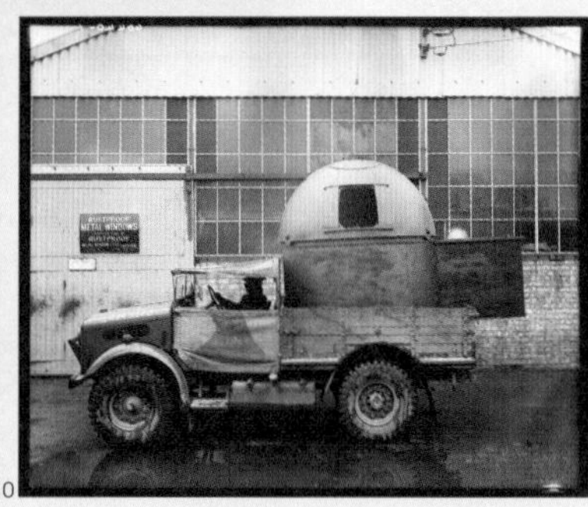

8/9/10
Stewart Bale
*Crosville Double Decker Bus
at Edge Lane Depot* 1946

*A Chester Engineering
Company Van* 1945

*Chester Works of Rustproof
Metal Windows* 1940

Black and white photographs
Each: 40.7 x 50.8 cm
Courtesy of National
Museums Liverpool,
Merseyside Maritime
Museum

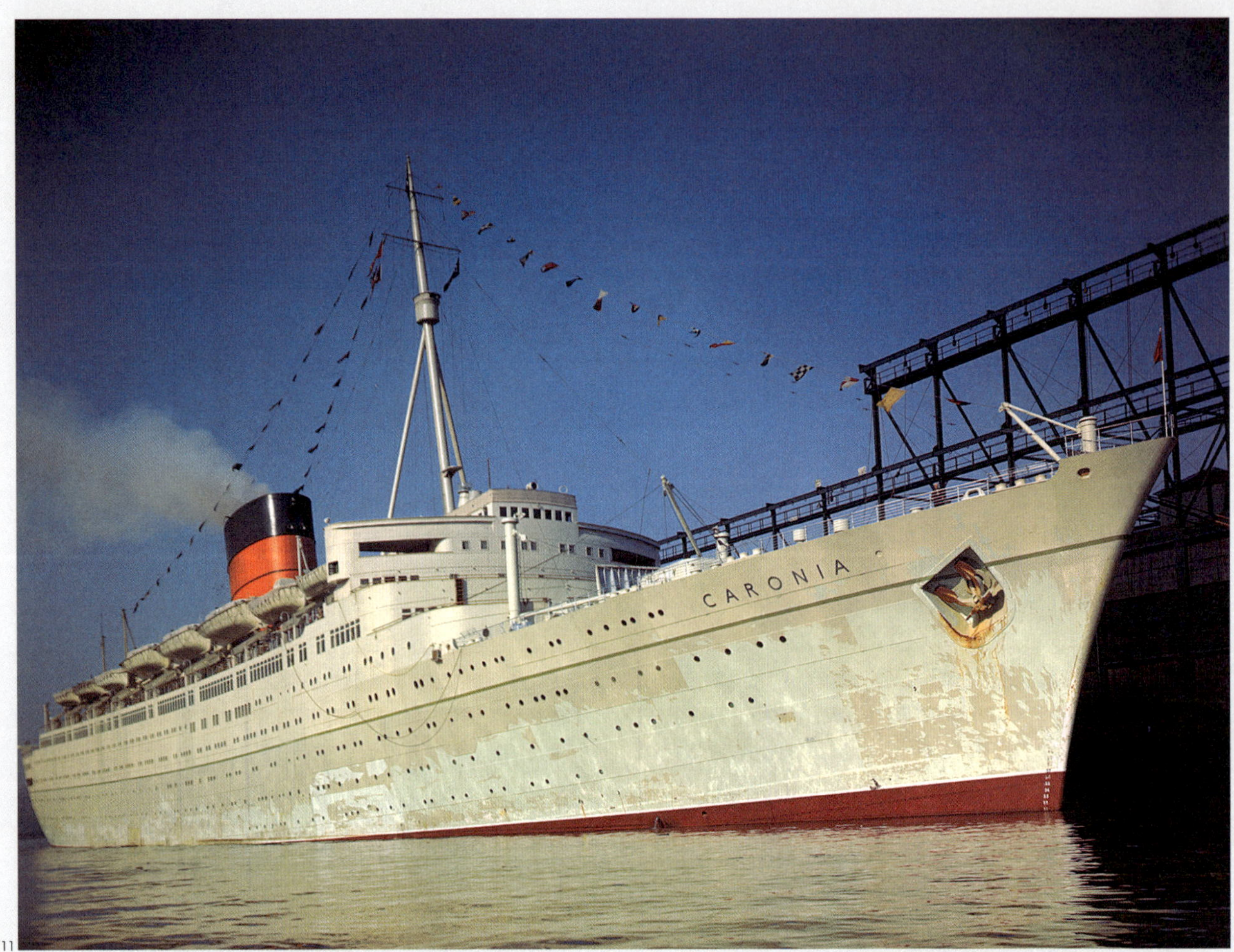

11

11/12/13/14
Stewart Bale
Caronia
Caronia
Caronia
Ivernia

Colour photographs
Each: 40.7 x 50.8 cm
The University of
Liverpool Special
Collections and Archives

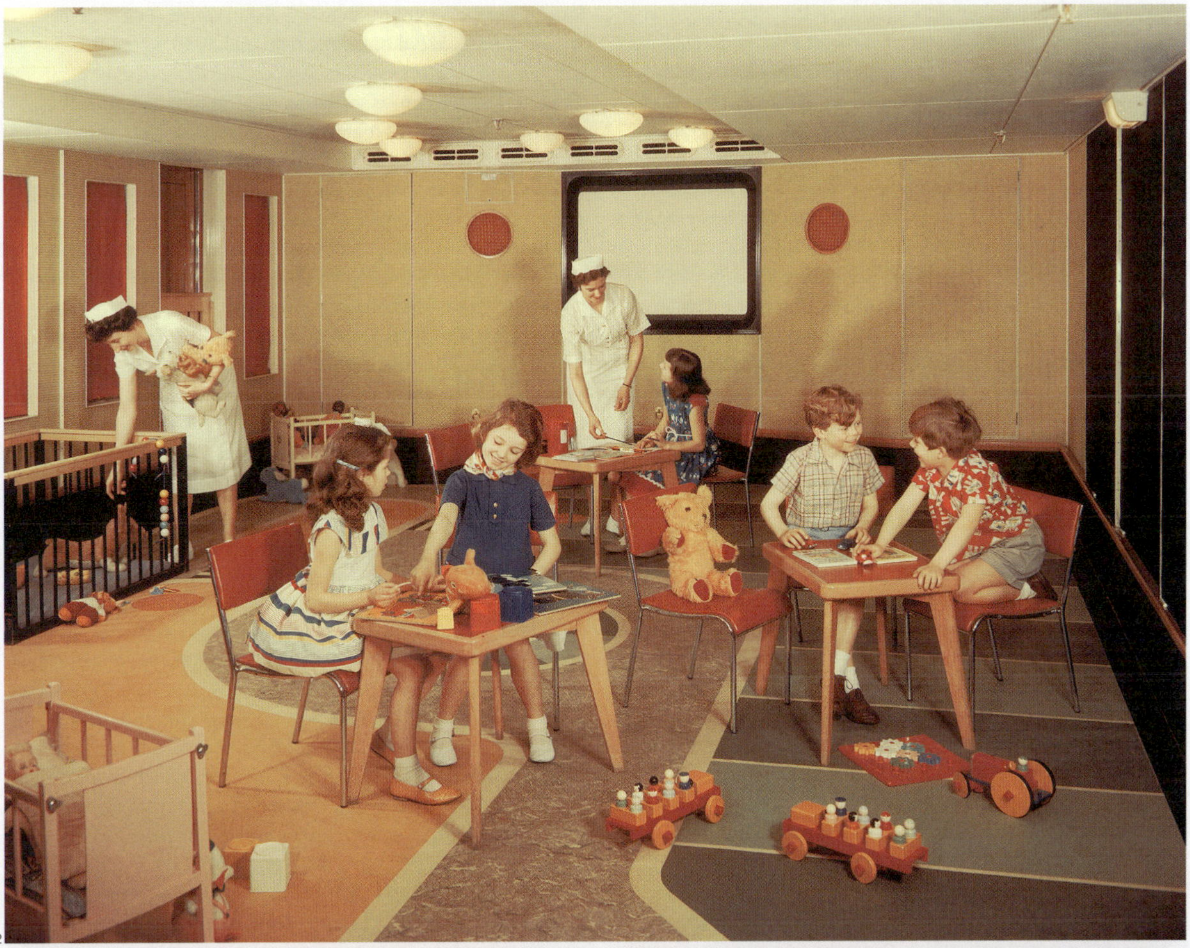

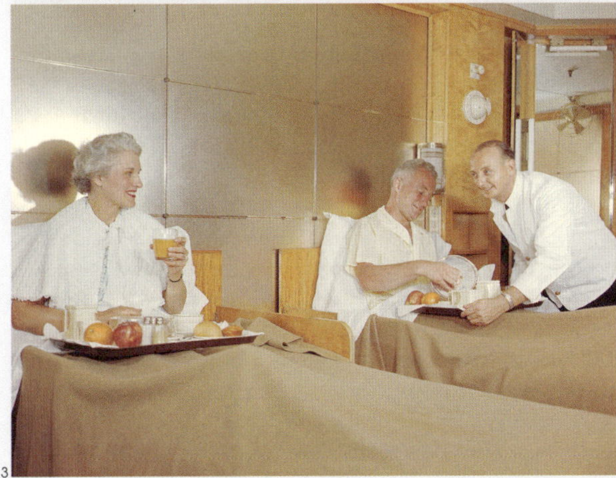

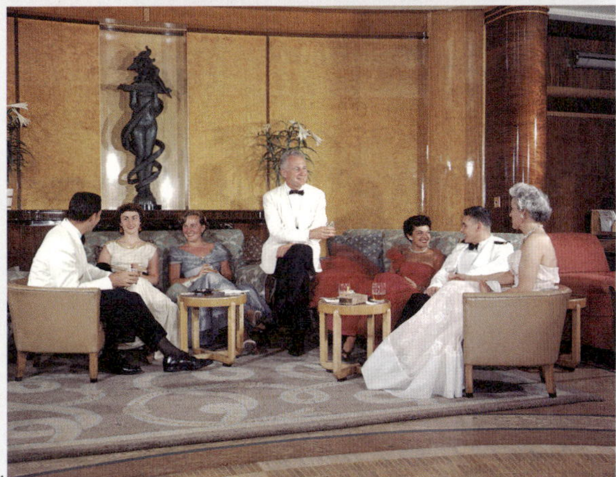

the notion of a city being at the 'centre of the creative universe'.

By the mid 19th century Liverpool was reinforcing its position as a vibrant centre for manufacturing and maritime industries, emerging as one of England's most vital Victorian cities. Expanded travel networks, tourism and photography developed in parallel. One writer in the photographic journal noted how the study of ethnographic types could be easily undertaken in the context of the city's docks. This however was more actively pursued in the expanding market for photographs of distant places that fed colonial and ruling class fantasies. For example, a founding member of the Liverpool Amateur Photographic Society, Francis Frith, embarked on a series of journeys to North Africa and the Middle East. Frith established the photographic studio Frith and Hayward in Liverpool during 1853. Following the sale of his other business interests he concentrated on photography in Egypt, Palestine and Syria. The lavish albumen prints of ruins and ethnic types were often sold as albums, as desirable commodities – hence the traffic in photographs as commercial products with their exotic subjects represented as exotic spectacle.

Photography also mapped industrial developments to some extent within the city that were linked with colonial expansion, with images such as those of the ironworks on Merseyside in Patrick Barry's *Dockyard Economy and Naval Power*. Published and illustrated with photographs in 1863[10], Barry looked to expose some of the management flaws in maritime industries ranging from administrative and procedural inefficiencies to outright corruption. However, given the technical limits of photography at this time the interior world of the factory is reduced to distant views or staged tableaux. The veiled rooftops of the Merseyside works with their plumes of white smoke, that appear as ethereal forms as a result of the long exposure, convey an industrial atmosphere that resonates with later literary and visual art accounts of the industrial North such as those of George Orwell and Mass Observation in the 1930s. In this respect it is difficult to disassociate the pictorial ambitions of the Liverpool gentleman amateur photographer of the 1850s in search of atmospheric effects from the circumstances that created them. One can find in more contemporary commentaries such as Allan Sekula's project *Freeway to China – Version II for Liverpool* (1998-9), how questions concerning the rights of dock workers and disenfranchised labour through globalisation still require active debate and intervention to make clear the true social impact of a certain economic models.

The historian Raphael Samuel in his book *Theatres of Memory* (1994) used the term 'dreamscape' to describe a longing to find the past in a particular kind of photography, a particular kind of 'view' that symbolically restores that which is missing in the present. A quality that Samuel draws out is one of focus as a quality that defines 'atmosphere': 'blurring the hard lines of detail in some more generalised aura of pastness'.[11] The question of focus in photography was central to some of the debates around its status as 'Art' at the

turn of the 19th century that saw a derivative pictorialism give way to a hard edged modernism around 1910 where the contours and surfaces of the city became increasingly clear.

The erasure or softening of temporal and spatial specificity in early photographs of the Secessionists groups (The Photo-Secession in New York and The Linked Ring Brotherhood in London), were in response to a particular place yet often rendered indistinguishable by the actual photographic treatment. The gum-bichromate process, an emulsion applied by hand whose textures were receptive to further manipulation, imparted a sense of craftsmanship in the finished object. Using this process in 1906, John Dudley Johnston took a photograph that was subsequently titled in its finished form as *Liverpool, an Impression*. The final picture is an urban palimpsest. The initial image being a conventional gelatin print of what looks to be a street early in the morning: we see shop signs, tram lines and electricity cables, a horse drawn carriage and a lone pedestrian; there is an overwhelming sense of the non-event to this picture. The reworking of this image as a gum-bichromate print veils this city in fog. It is also cropped from the landscape format to portrait, accentuating the scale of the city. The softening effect of the print process and the retouching of evidence of modern urban life – the tram lines and cables for example, transform the greyness and drudgery of the modern city to a hazy, mysterious, continental space. The dialectics between past and present in mourning urban change is in keeping with Secessionist visions of England as a lost arcadia. The effect here though is not a return to a lost ideal or idyll, but the creation of a purely imaginary space.

In contrast, the American Alvin Langdon Coburn made several photographs of Liverpool and other cities in the industrial North around the same time that Johnston was making his diffuse and painterly prints. Coburn too used alternative processes but his subjects and their optical treatment was driven by a fascination with the inherent characteristics of the medium and camera vision. Coburn travelled extensively and mixed with the artistic and literary elite. He was elected a member of the Photo-Secession in 1902, and joined the Linked Ring Brotherhood a year later. In 1906 the playwright George Bernard Shaw described Coburn as someone who '…is free of that clumsy tool – the human hand… He drives at the poetic… without any impoverishment or artification'.[12] In essence, Coburn had taken the conventions of Pictorialism and set them to work in order to explore the contemporary dimensions of the city, to find beauty in its form and geometry. This is evident in his photograph *The Spider's Web, Liverpool* (1906), a seemingly reflexive gesture on the effects of photography, hinting at an expressionistic and symbolic language towards abstraction. Another similar rendering of urban structure and form is the picture *The Rudder, Liverpool* reproduced as a photogravure in Alfred Stieglitz's lavish publication *Camera Work* in 1908. These studies of the city were part of a projected series of books entitled *The Adventures of Cities* to include not only Liverpool but London, Edinburgh, Birmingham, Paris, Boston, New York and Pittsburgh.

Such pictures by Coburn helped forge an overtly modernist language of his later abstract photography such as those images associated with Vorticism and Wyndham Lewis's publication *BLAST*. Described as the 'enfant prodige of modern photography', Coburn's innovative approach to picture-making mark him as someone who had taken vital elements of the industrial city as the basis of an avant-garde way of seeing metropolitan life.

The growth of illustrated magazines and press pictures in the 1920s and 30s heralded the growth of a greater visual and political awareness of social differences in Britain. Magazines such as *Weekly Illustrated*, *Picture Post* and *Lilliput*, along with newspapers such as the *Daily Herald*, had either a committed socialist agenda or liberal left politics. The magazine culture that had grown in the 1930s and benefited from the influence of many émigré publishers, artists and photographers, shaped a sense of social realism in Britain in the wake of political upheaval in Continental Europe.

A glimpse into the *Daily Herald's* picture library files from the 1930s and 1940s shows Liverpool as a city experiencing uncertainty. However, the *Herald* had begun to move away from its hard-line socialist position to create a newspaper that looked to juggle conflicting agendas of being financially stable with capitalist enterprise inevitably influencing editorial policy.[13] Photographs came from a variety of sources including syndicating picture agencies, as well as from staff photographers, combining a variety of photographic approaches without necessarily any political interests.

Although a selective vision, these images are indexes of micro and macro politics that relate to Liverpool, of different states of being in the city; topical stories ranging from support for Oswald Mosley's 'Blackshirts', slum dwelling, transatlantic liners and the Blitz. Each picture speaks differently of modernity. The presence of the liner blocking out the sky at the end of the terraced streets is a reminder of communal ties and a thriving industry in the city, but also an overpowering sign of mobility, luxury and glamour that is better expressed in terms of Stewart Bale's series of colour photographs. As a reportage or newspaper image it is rooted in the labour politics of the region, anchored by its monochrome. In contrast, the picture of the slum interior, though seemingly constructed, is an image of incapacity, of a permanent, miserable state of things with no means of transcendence. An unnamed man stares at the stained walls in a sparse, dishevelled room in non-regulated housing, his gaze taking in the scene where a few personal possessions are to be found. A single framed picture of a landscape fixed to the wall that exaggerates the austerity of the room and offers a romantic alternative. In its totality, it is an image of little hope.

Press photography operated within pictorial and stylistic conventions that needed to connect quickly with the reader, usually at an emotional level of empathy or sense of horror and moral outrage. The realism of the press and illustrated magazines extended to most kinds of stories which ensured both high circulation and ready identification with the editorial perspective. An interesting case in point being the photographs of Bert Hardy who was given an assignment to illustrate a feature on racism in Liverpool and published in *Picture Post*, July 1949. This magazine sold many copies and occupied a prominent place in the nation's social and political conscience. Despite its prominence, *Picture Post* looked to enlighten but did not radically overturn preconceptions rooted in stereotypes of ethnic groups, class or geographical regions.

The story 'Is there a British Colour Bar?' contained thirteen photographs by Hardy with a text by Robert Kee. Hardy recorded the overcrowding of families in tenements, unemployed seaman, workers, students, social segregation, mixed marriages, Liverpool school-children, noting how society suspends questions of 'colour' in sport, education and entertainment. According to Kee, at that time Liverpool's immigrant community from within the Commonwealth numbered around 8000 with Afro-Carribean and Asian backgrounds. The story was commissioned to provide greater understanding of the living conditions, as well as appreciating the hopes and desires of immigrants during Colonial Month – a campaign to stimulate popular interest in the life and people of the Colonies.

Hardy's revealing and compassionate pictures provided some insight into the tensions, yet he also chose to record positive scenes of interaction between different ethnic groups. In Kee's words on the question of integration he wrote that for this '…to take place there must be some revolution inside every individual mind – coloured and white – where prejudices based on bitterness, ignorance or patronage have been established'.[14] Indeed the editor closed the story with an image of Liverpool schoolchildren at play, an image that Kee returned to some years later reinforcing his belief in Hardy's photographs as embodying an '…ideal to be worked for rather than a "danger" to be feared'.[15]

In 1956 another *Picture Post* photographer – Thurston Hopkins – visited Liverpool where he made a series of pictures revealing the continued presence of slum dwelling in the city. When published, this story enraged city officials and *Picture Post's* owner Edward Hulton was lobbied to withdraw what was seen as a searing indictment of the city. In contrast, one senses a more opened-ended agenda in Henri Cartier-Bresson's Liverpool street scenes. They combine a familiar sense of the urban everyday. Cartier-Bresson's well known dictum of the 'the decisive moment' is less forceful here. There is an extended sense of time to some of these pictures, a rhythm to the curious temporality of the street that he lingers over. They are

10 Barry, Patrick B., *Dockyard Economy and Naval Power*, London: Sampson, Low, Son and Co., 1863.

11 Samuel, Raphael, *Theatres of Memory*, London & New York: Verso, 1994, p. 359.

12 Shaw, George Bernard, *Catalogue of the Exhibition of the Work of Alvin Langdon Coburn*, The Liverpool Amateur Photographic Society, 1906, unpaginated.

13 See Richards, Huw, *The Bloody Circus – The Daily Herald and the Left*, London and Chicago: Pluto Press, 1997, for a more detailed account of the *Herald's* ideological development.

14 Cited in Hopkinson Tom, (ed.), *Picture Post 1938-50*, London: Penguin Books, 1970, pp. 254-60. Hardy and Kee's article is reproduced in full with additional 'Hindsight' reflections on the story by Kee. See also Hall, Stuart, 'The Social Eye of Picture Post,' working papers in *Cultural Studies*, no. 2, 1972.

15 Hopkinson, *Picture Post*, p. 254.

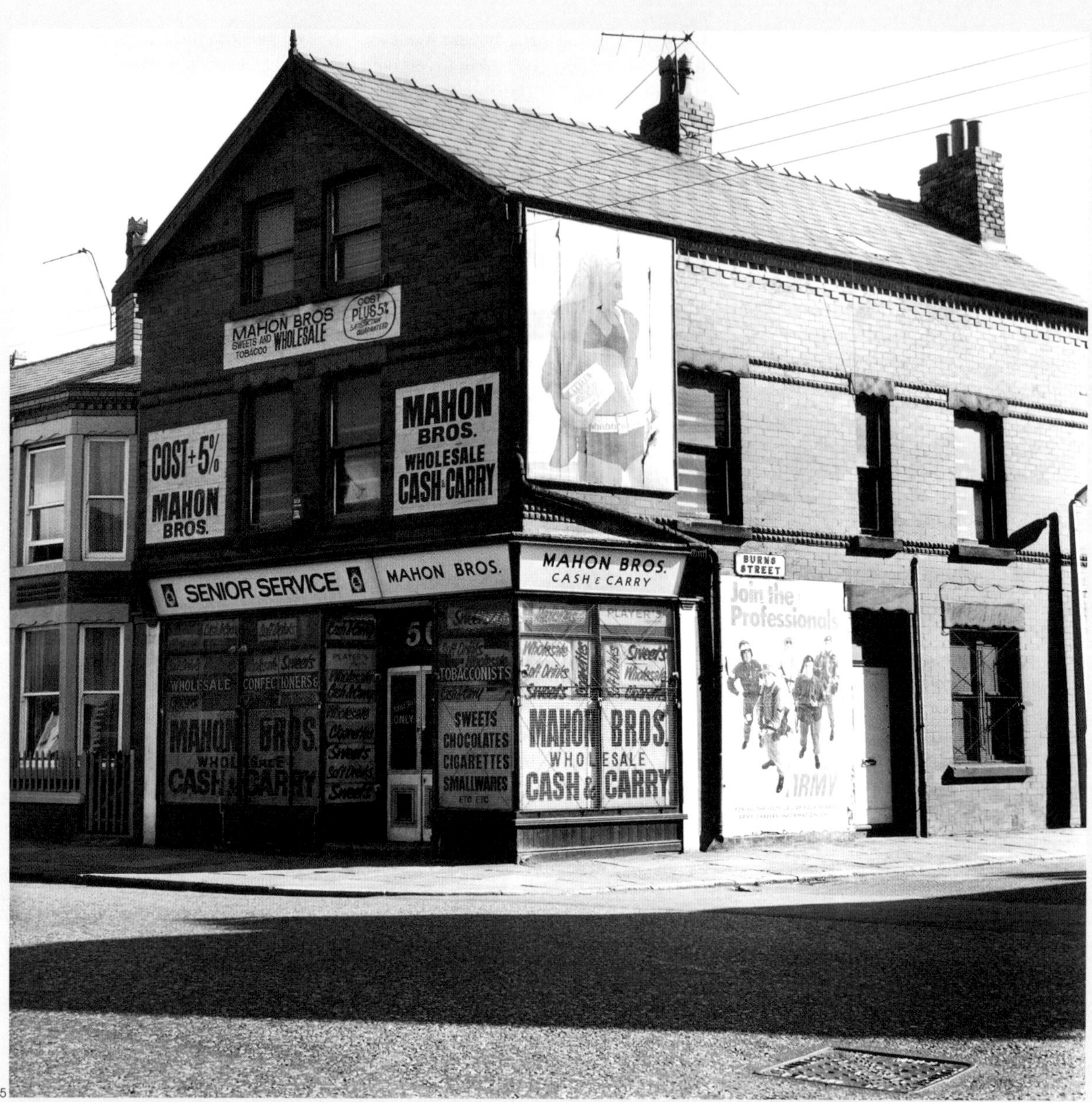

15

Candida Höfer
Liverpool IX 1968
Silver gelatin print
21.1 x 21 cm
Collection of the artist
Courtesy the artist and SK
Stiftung Kultur, Cologne

contemplative and strangely factual; taken as if to provide anthropological evidence of daily routines and leisure – a woman takes her child in a pram for a walk, children playing in the street, leaves being swept up, a rugby league match, an estranged moment between a policeman and a pedestrian, the exterior of a canteen, and the façade of the Walker Art Gallery; a world of typical activity on the one hand, and contrasts that speak of class and the civic order of things on the other. Though late in his photographic career, Cartier-Bresson's Liverpool pictures evoke that sense of wandering associated with the 'destination-less walks of discovery' of Parisian Surrealists: 'Alone, the Surrealist wanders the streets without destination but with a premeditated alertness for the unexpected detail that will release a marvellous and compelling reality just beneath the banal surface....'[16]

In the 1970s, photographers from both the Shelter project (Nick Hedges) and the Exit Photography Group continued to explore the urban underbelly and the scale of deprivation within Britain's inner-cities. Exit in particular embarked on a more discursive form of sociological journalism and documentary practice.[17] In terms of the social politics, this in many ways marked a return to the issues raised by photographers such as Hardy and Hopkins some decades previously. However, Exit were distinguished by their methods of social documentation that reinforced the political importance of the project.

A book of Exit's work published in 1982 entitled *Survival Programmes: In Britain's Inner Cities*[18], looked to expose the processes behind social conditions which were considered as mere 'symptoms'. As well as photographing their subjects along with domestic interiors and streets, hundreds of hours of taped interviews were made, excerpts of which accompanied the images. The photographs were structured not according to place but to themes such as 'Growth', 'Promise', 'Welfare' and 'Reaction'. Liverpool figures in the study alongside cities such as Birmingham, Leeds, Newcastle, Glasgow and London. The photograph taken on Christmas Day at the Petrus Community Hostel in Everton, is possibly one of the more self-conscious pictures in the book yet it conveys both through the limited presence of festive decoration and luminous presence of the Queen, the true disparity. The symptom and the process here are made quite apparent.

During the 1980s, Vanley Burke extended his photographic narrative that had focused on those generations of families following post-war migration in Handsworth, Birmingham, to explore something of the 'black' experience in Toxteth, Liverpool. Though his pictures connect geo-politically and to some extent culturally with Hardy's reportage, the emphasis has shifted in terms degrees of empathy and the picturing strategy. For Burke, there is a concern to show black British identities in a subsequent generation on its own terms, quietly confident, distinctive. Stuart Hall has written on the way that Burke's pictures utilise the qualities of the monochrome process to emphasise the richness and diversity of different ways of being 'black'.[19] His pictures are culturally incisive, relaying narratives based on working knowledge of the tensions as well the dialogues between 'inside' and 'outside' perspectives. The matter of fact titling for his Liverpool series – *Man Working*, *Young Girl* and *Young Boys with Gun* – is direct. Driven by a desire to reclaim and establish the cultural presence for African Caribbean communities, Burke's pictures are testimony to a committed documentary project from within the realms of migratory experience that reveals a range of identities and their important place in the realms of urban sub-cultures and contested sense of British identity. As Burke has stated: 'The photographs are very much a part of a documentation process which we as black people need to go through, and it is not an attempt to show the black community to the wider community, this is where we are, it is more importantly a record!'

The inclusion of prints in this exhibition from the city's commercial photographers acknowledges how this type of imagery can operate within a creative register that has its own aesthetics, but also a visual language and conceptual framework that has a wider cultural relevance and resonance. The recent salvaging of the pioneering colour work by John Hinde is a good example as part of the ongoing fascination with quotidian and vernacular photography in the both the art world and new interest in photography at the margins.[20] However, what is potentially at stake in such instances where photography and the everyday is reclaimed as art is the erosion of genre specificity.

At a functional level, advertising images constitute a valuable alternative within the concept of the *Centre of the Creative Universe*, and to some degree a populist encounter as to how the metropolis should appear in the eyes of its administrators and businesses that connects with its citizens and consumers. In the case of Liverpool, there are two distinguished commercial photographers whose images constitute rich archives charting the major historical moments in the life of the city such as shipbuilding and traumas of World War, as well as promoting Liverpool's industries and architecture. Stewart Bale Limited were founded around 1910 and continued to operate in Liverpool up until to the 1980s. During this time they established themselves as the leading commercial photographers within the city (and for some time London) specialising in advertising, industrial and architectural photography. The name of the firm derives from its founder's surname, Herbert Stewart Bale, a printer who migrated to England from Australia in the early 1900s and established an advertising agency, initially in Seacombe in 1899 and later in

16 Peter Galassi, *Henri Cartier-Bresson: The Early Work*, New York: Museum of Modern Art, 1987.
17 Exit Photography Group members were Nicholas Battye, Chris Steele-Perkins and Paul Trevor. See Exit Photography Group, *Survival Programmes: In Britain's Inner Cities*, Milton Keynes: Open University Press, 1982, to appreciate the quality of the photography and the innovative documentary approach to inner city problems.
18 Exit Photography Group, *Survival Programmes*.
19 See Hall, Stuart, 'Vanley Burke and the "Desire for Blackness"' in Sealy, Mark, (ed.), *Vanley Burke: A Retrospective*, London: Lawrence and Wishart, 1993, p. 12.
20 Hinde, John, and Parr, Martin, *Our True Intent Is All For Your Delight: The John Hinde Butlin's Photographs*, London, Chris Boot, 2002.

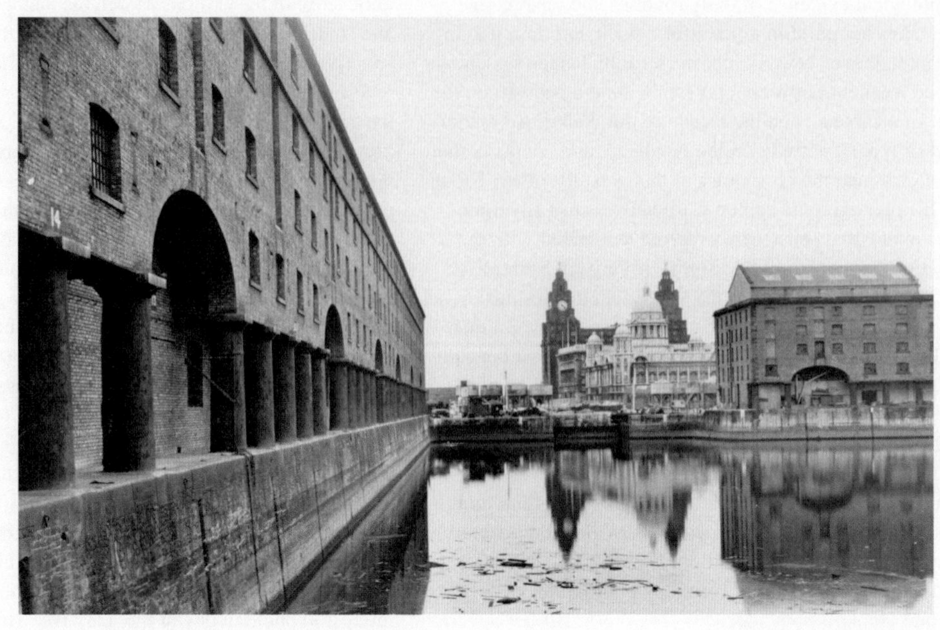

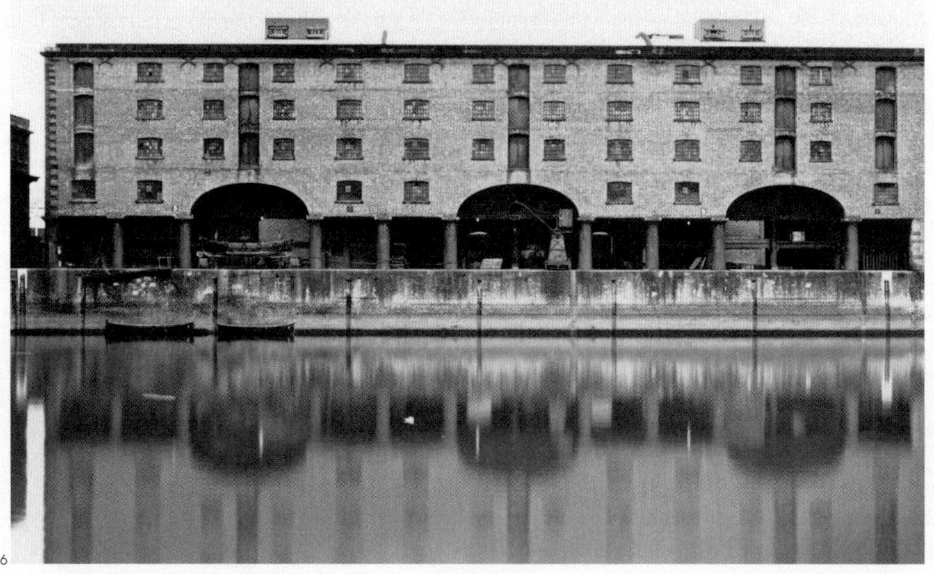

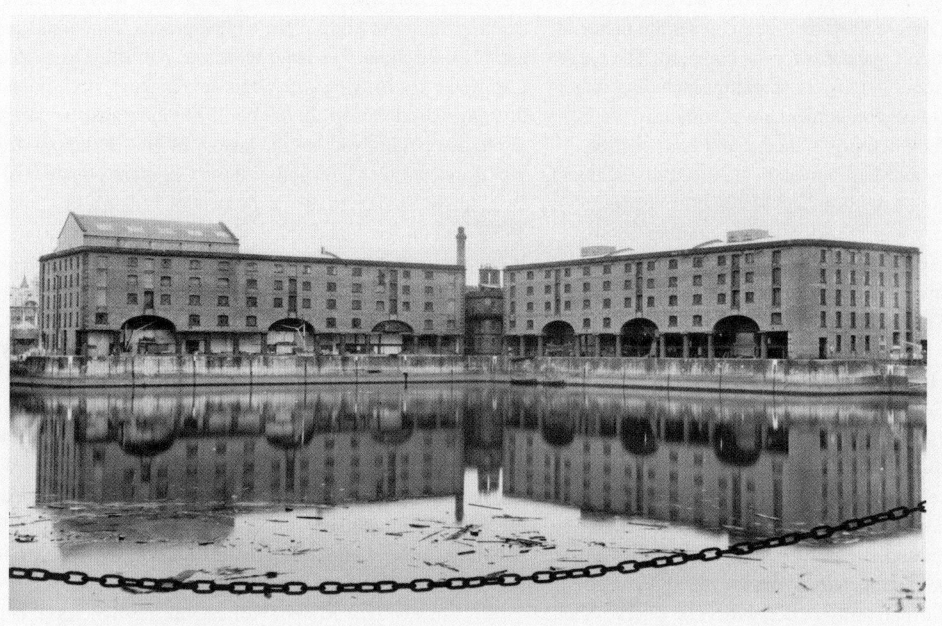

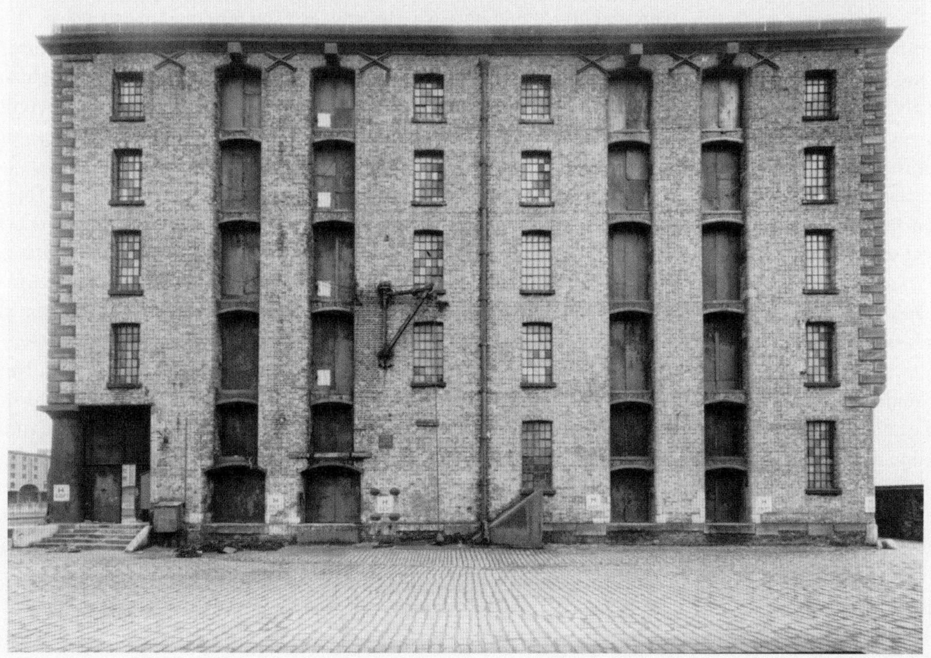

16
Bernd and Hilla Becher
*Prince Albert Dock,
Liverpool* 1966
Four photographic prints
Each: 30 x 40 cm
Collection of the artists

Liverpool.[21] Bale's enterprise grew out of the absence of high standard advertising photography, a role they were to fulfil themselves through Edward Stewart Bale, who set the pictorial and technical photographic standards for the company. The range of subject areas are great but those in shipping (including major shipping and shipbuilding companies) are particularly well represented, so too dock activity; industry and construction (including the Queensway Mersey tunnel); architecture (including construction of Liverpool's Anglican and Metropolitan cathedrals); transport, social history and World War II (including bomb damage). There is a sense of kitsch to Bale's colour work in the post-war optimism that centred on the rising consumer culture and leisure. The benign gaze and atmosphere to these pictures belongs to a kind of imagery later refracted through the anti-consumerist lens of British Pop Art such as the work of the Independent Group and Richard's Hamilton's seminal montage *Just What Is It that Makes Today's Homes So Different, So Appealing?* (1956).

In 1931, Bale's took a photograph of F.W. Woolworths window display on London Road for *Household Week*. An array of tools for carpenters and engineers set out carefully as a consumerist spectacle that appears to mirror the abundance of the harvest festival with an array of screwdrivers, pliers, saws, spanners and so forth: an instance where the size of the photograph does not do justice to the detail of the display.

Many advertising photographers in the 1930s and 40s were often affiliated with camera clubs and societies, pursuing commercial day jobs and personal art projects along different trajectories. Occasionally these would overlap, sometimes colliding incongruously. One such photographer was Edward Chambré-Hardman. Born in Ireland, he travelled to Liverpool where he made his permanent home. He first established a studio in Bold Street in 1923 and later moved to a more elaborate and long-term set up of both home and work premises at 59 Rodney Street. Establishing the photographic studio was not easy, and as an insurance Chambré-Hardman sold and repaired wireless apparatuses as a means of subsidising the studio in its early years. The studio closed in 1965 but the building remained Chambré-Hardman's home and is now a museum of his photographic career.[22]

Chambré-Hardman specialised in portraiture, though it was his landscape photography that earned him regard and respect amongst the photographic community. He received several awards from the London Salon of Photography for example, and exhibited regularly. In his photographs of Liverpool there is a graphic record of changing face of the city over more than sixty years. These images show the overhead railway and the trams, the docks, civic buildings and the changing landmarks. Some of these photographs are taken from above – the top of the Cunard Building was a favourite spot for this and from the 1940s onwards allowed him to show how Liverpool was starting to decay around him – the bomb damage at the docks and derelict housing.

The abiding sense of entropy associated with the collapse of the British economy in the 1980s is evoked with startling clarity in Martin Parr's photographs from both Liverpool and New Brighton. The latter work was published in 1986 as *The Last Resort*, portraying with a macabre pathos a once popular and thriving seaside resort. In the book, the journalist Ian Walker wrote compellingly about the history of New Brighton, from its 1830s inception as a response to the Georgian grandeur of Brighton in Sussex, to the excitement of Wilkie's fun fair of the 1930s and the gradual demise of the fairground and promenades. It includes commentary from those who lived in or visited New Brighton over the years and Walker mixes beautifully first person testimony with his own thoughts. It is a fascinating introduction to the pictures that follow and in Walker's closing words we find something of the aching melancholy that Parr's pictures perversely evoke through a kind of trash aesthetic that is uncompromising and uncomfortable: 'It was the last Sunday in August, the last Sunday of the Season. I went back into Wilkie's Covered Fairground for one last look at the thrilling modern electric galloping horses. Once an angel had fallen from the spinning carousel and hit someone on the head. People had been shocked to see a bleeding angel on the fairground floor.'[23]

In *The Last Resort*, Parr establishes a pictorial language that he would later turn on the English middle-class in *The Cost of Living* (1989); the trademark harsh flash, the garish colour and invasive camerawork. The resulting images render situations as a kind of perceptual (and social) shock, there is something visceral in the lighting of Parr's pictures from New Brighton – the dripping ice-cream cone, the sheen on human skin, overflowing bins and rubbish in proximity to the bodies of young children – this is a tactile and physical incision through the camera into a world where people are making the most of things. These pictures are about resilience but jar with the sense of spectacle and voyeurism, a deliberate and ambiguous strategy that gives the work its political tension. Above all, there is a sense of a place once associated with escapism becoming a poignant allegory to British working class culture during the Thatcher years.

At the same time Parr was photographing in New Brighton (1983-86), he was also exploring the transformation of urban space in Liverpool where the theme of 'the ruin' was also part of the pervading narrative. This is something that he shared with other photographers of the period. In the monochrome work of Peter Marlow for example there is a real sense to the decline of Liverpool's once prominent place in the international

21 National Museums Liverpool acquired the Stewart Bale Ltd. photographic archive in 1986, at which point it had already received national recognition as a collection of outstanding quality. The collection primarily consists of black and white negatives (principally 12"x10" gelatin silver glass plate negatives and 12"x10" cellulose acetate film sheet negatives), black and white gelatin silver prints and original documentation. There is a small proportion of colour material. There are approximately 200,000 negatives and 2,000 prints. There is also a body of original records from the firm dating back to 1913 and continuing, principally, to 1970.
22 To view the catalogue of the Hardman collection, visit Liverpool Record Office's website at http://archive.liverpool.gov.uk/
23 Parr, Martin, *The Last Resort – Photographs of New Brighton*, Wallasey: Promenade Press, 1986.

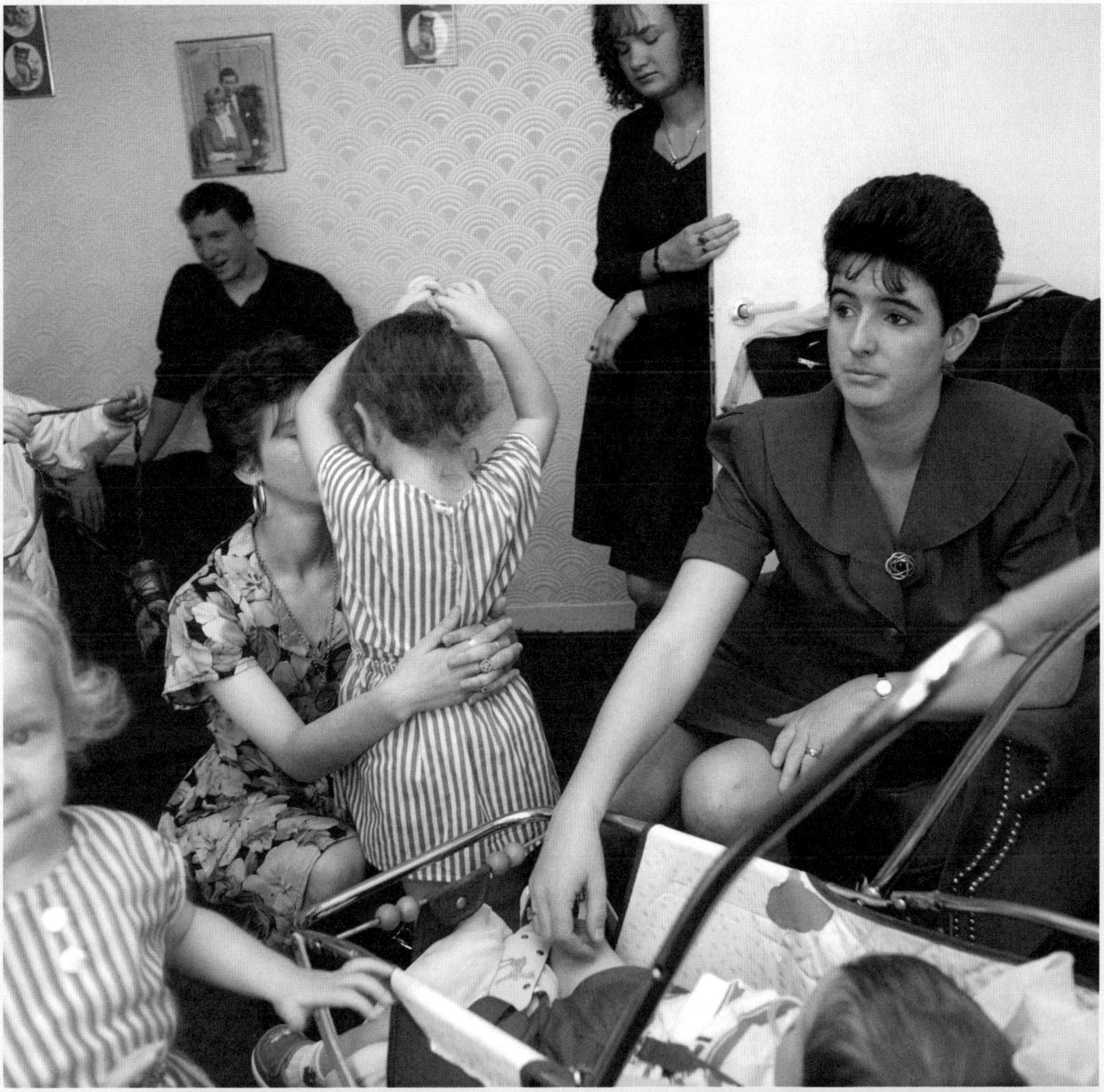

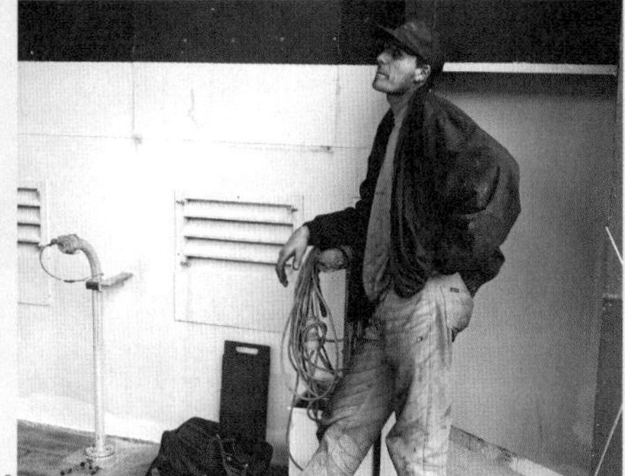

17
Ken Grant
Christening,
Norris Green 1989
Black and white photograph
45.7 x 45.7 cm
Courtesy of Ken Grant

18
Ken Grant
Keith in the
Dry Dock 1994
Black and white photograph
50.8 x 60.9 cm
Courtesy of Ken Grant

19
Vanley Burke
Crumbling Stone
Union Jack c. 1980
Silver bromide print
60.9 x 41.4 cm
Courtesy of Vanley Burke

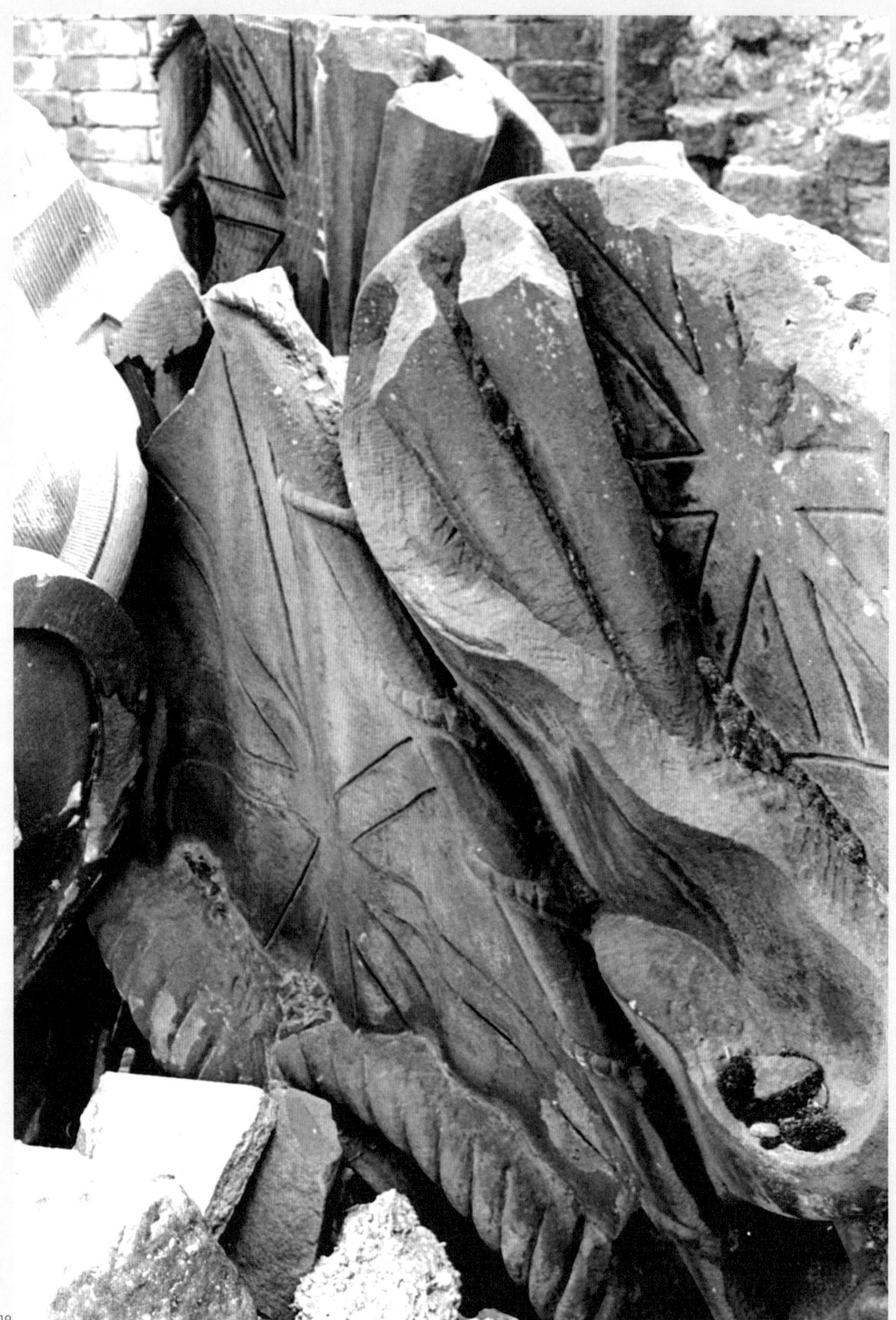

commerce of the British Empire. Marlow concentrates on the fabric of the city – its gradual decay and imminent demolition. In *Liverpool: Looking out to Sea*, there are images that speak directly about the alienation to the 'new' landscape – the run-down children's park with the skeletal, iron frame of a 17th century trade ship becomes a memento-mori in a wasteland that poignantly symbolises the loss of industry and high unemployment. In contrast with the literal and symbolic depiction of decay, Marlow conveys a greater sense of mourning in his portrayal of those who work the rubbish dumps such as the Moss Tip in Bidston.

If Marlow's urban poetry evokes some of the classical associations of the documentary form, we can find alternatives in the work of contemporaries that combine elements of conceptual art, photo-journalism and street photography with an autobiographical dimension that maps the lives of Liverpool's inhabitants in more intimate ways. Such projects are often the result of long-term involvement with a place. In Tom Wood's 'bus project' around Liverpool and New Brighton (1976-96) and Ken Grant's commemorative account of his Merseyside home begun in the mid-1980s, we are drawn into the interior worlds of both individuals and communities.

Tom Wood has been photographing in the city for many years. Like an itinerant photographer, he travels through the streets revealing stories and telling moments from everyday life. Using public transport as well as roaming the city on foot, Wood has created a unique social map of Liverpool. Metropolitan life can indeed be boring and these pictures speak of the monotony of shopping, journeys to and from work, queues and ubiquitous graffiti. As a familiar component himself within the urban landscape, Wood became known locally as the 'photie-man'. In *All Zones Off-Peak* and *Bus Odyssey*, the world unfolds in familiar and occasionally strange terms. From his seat on the bus, the experience of time appears to be slow, plodding, thick. However the usual ebb and flow of people from bus to street is punctuated by unexpected viewpoints or micro-dramas created out of ordinary behaviour and incidental details: a book held open by an anonymous passenger creeps into the frame or the condensation that veils and filters the external world, window reflections that fuse inside and outside, to the fleeting expressions of pedestrians and co-passengers.

Wood sensitively shows us the crowd while inviting speculation as to the value of the individuals within it. We see parts of the city centre as well as the periphery – the estate, the local high streets, car parks, shop fronts, flats and housing schemes. Wood's pictures from buses, like those of his other projects, are concerned with a particular class experience, whether it is on the top floor of a double-decker bus or in the smoky atmosphere of an 1980s disco as in *Looking for Love* (1982-85). Such pictures suggest an informal or snapshot aesthetic that brings with it a feeling of rawness and proximity to the flow of everyday life. This feeling of authenticity is, however, carefully crafted. On the one hand it plays with modernist

aesthetics – montage, superimposition, the photographic frame and so on, while possessing a quasi-conceptual feel to the project. Yet, there is a strong sense of locality and the work remains resolute for its adherence to a diffident vernacular. As a social history it is rich, opening out onto an overwhelming sense of the transience of life, whether it is in the routine of work and domesticity, or in the highs and lows of teenage dating.

In Ken Grant's pictures, we find sympathy with Wood's travelogue but enter into more intimate territory in terms of group dynamics that revolve around family, friends and community ties. Begun in the mid-80s, Grant looked to draw out the ways that a certain community had dealt with economic decline, emphasising the loss of labour skills in post-industrial Liverpool. If Wood's reference points are Walker Evans and Robert Frank, then Grant's Liverpool project is in the mould of Chauncey Hare's *The American Interior* (1978). Like Hare, Grant reveals the sense of desolation of working people but takes us further into its demotic richness and character. Prominent within this is domestic space but also the pub, work and football, spaces underpinned previously by the strong bonds of labour that revolved around Liverpool shipyards.

Though hard-edged in terms of the surrounding social conditions, the subject of Grant's black and white images are portrayed in gentler terms that shows the degree of intimacy that exists with vital relationships that develop around several generations. In a selection of this work published recently as *The Close Season* (2002) that celebrates community values, the narrative structure that moves between portraiture, landscape, the home and to the shores of the River Mersey, we find a fitting memorial to a period of hardship in Liverpool's history, and a strong sense of kinship and quiet optimism that confronts adversity. Such photography resonates even more in terms of its historic value if seen in relation to the work of other photographers and artists projects in the city such as Dave Sinclair's documentary of striking Liverpool dockers in the 1980s or as previously mentioned, Sekula's *Freeway to China – Version II for Liverpool* (1998-99) that linked the effects of globalisation between communities of dock-workers in Los Angeles with those based in Liverpool.

The buildings of Liverpool figure strongly in the industrial photography of Bale and Chambré-Hardman, as testimony to periods in the city's commercial growth and decline, as well as acknowledging its architectural heritage. Perhaps one of the more distinctive statements about this heritage can be found in the photographs of Bernd and Hilla Becher. From their earliest publication entitled *Anonyme Skulpturen: Eine Typologie technischer Bauten (Anonymous Sculpture: A Typology of Technical Buildings,*1970) the Bechers' work has functioned within the realms of contemporary art practice. Using picturing motifs derived from anthropological and record photography, the Bechers have isolated primarily industrial buildings – head on and in profile, with an air of ambivalence that celebrates the factoid characteristics of photography. Continuity in terms of distance, the size of prints, the quality of daylight, are adhered to closely.

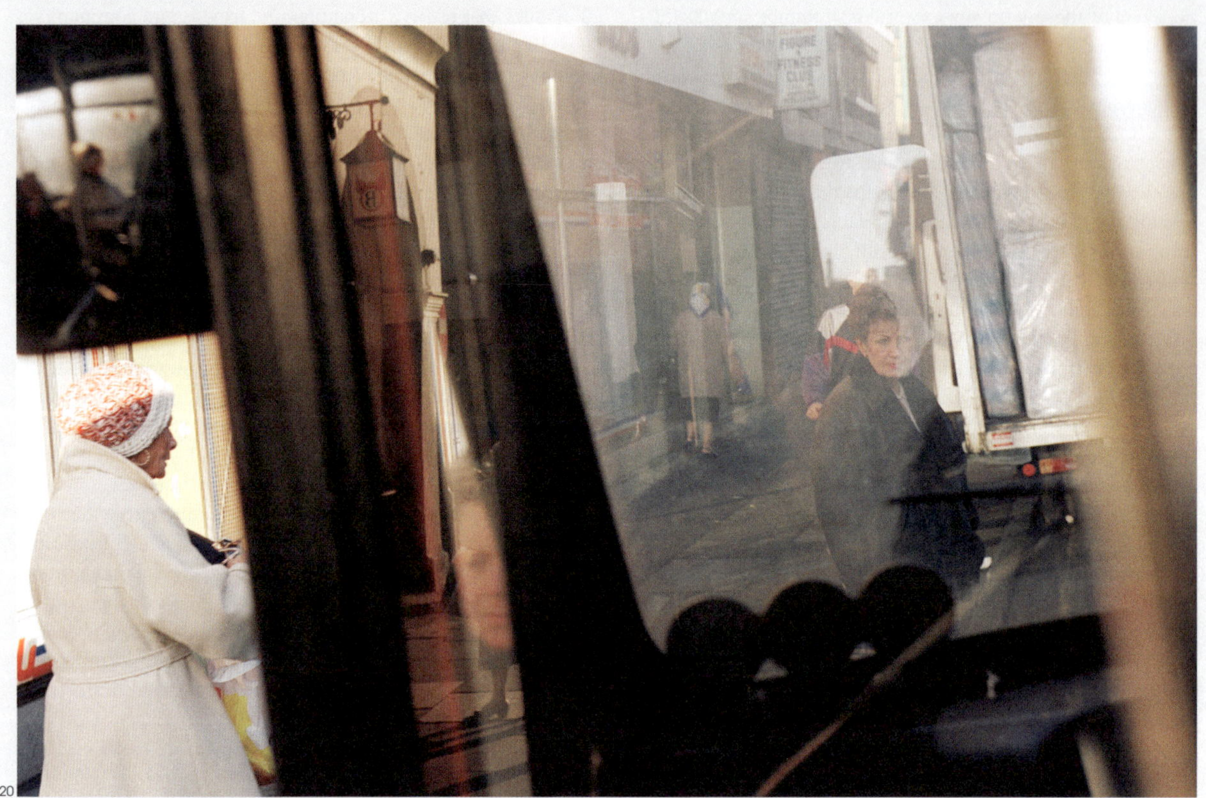

20
Tom Wood
London Road,
City Centre 1990
C-type print
60.9 x 91.4 cm
Collection of the artist

21
Tom Wood
London Road,
City Centre 1993
C-type print
60.9 x 91.4 cm
Collection of the artist

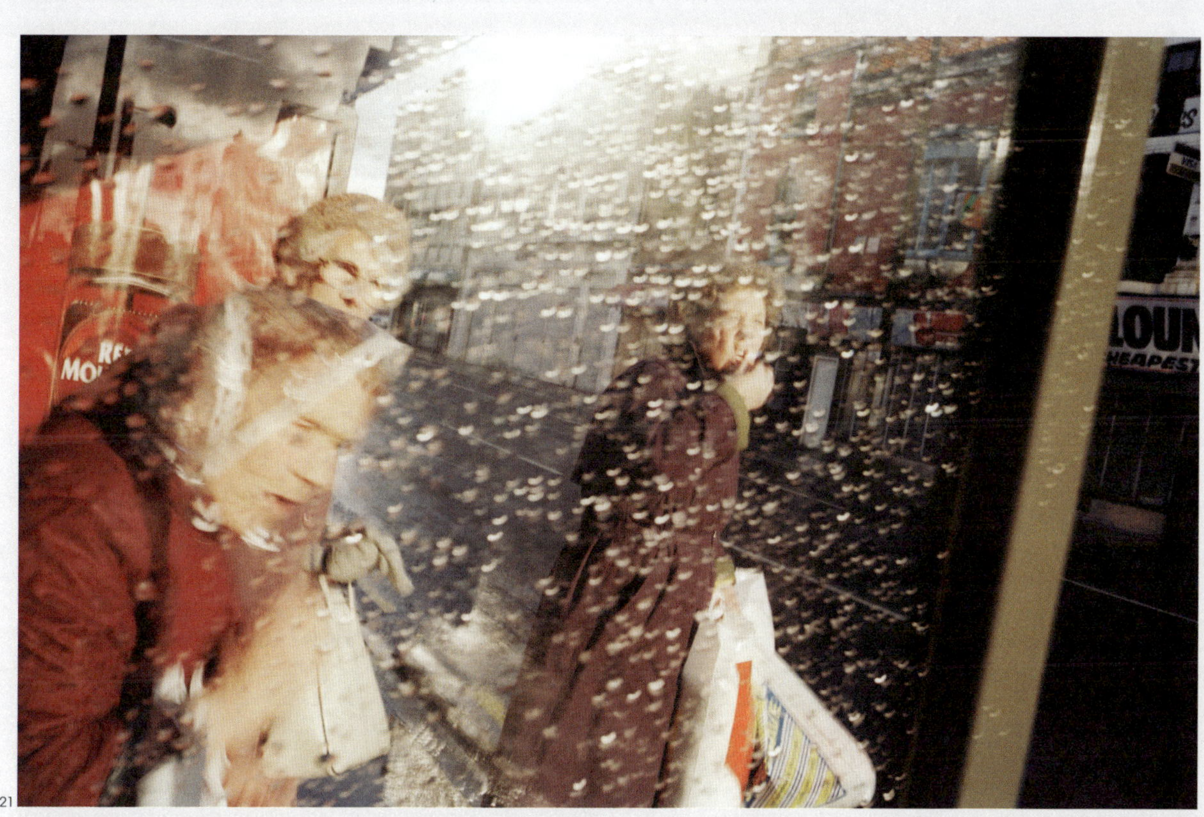
RE
MO
LOUN
CHEAPEST

The trajectory of the Bechers' vision can be traced from the beginnings of *Neue Sachlichkeit*, a pictorial tradition emerging in the Rhineland that included August Sander, Albert Renger-Patzsch and Werner Mantz in the 1920s. The adaptation of this approach in the Bechers' creation of industrial typologies required tighter parameters to emphasise similarity and difference. However, this limited expressive use of photography suggests an ascetic edge to these pictures where human presence is totally absent beyond the occasional poster or piece of graffiti. In 1966 the Bechers spent time in Liverpool and the surrounding area photographing water towers in Newton-le-Willows and in Liverpool city, pit winding mechanisms in Bold Colliery in St Helens and Lea Green Colliery in Prescot. One of their subjects from 1966 combined four photographs depicting various views of Albert Dock, the future home of Tate Liverpool. A subject that now has an ironic edge to it looking back through the words of the sculptor Carl Andre, who noted that the Bechers '…prefer to be close to the site of production rather than to the salons of consumption'.[24]

Highly influential as teachers in the Düsseldorf Art Academy, the Bechers have shaped a future generation of artists most notable among them are Candida Höfer, Thomas Ruff and Thomas Struth. It is a coincidence that Höfer also worked in Liverpool during the 1960s, adopting a more fluid approach to exploring the streets, its shop signs and cafés. Like her later and better-known work, Höfer's Liverpool pictures anticipate the depiction of public or semi-public spaces – libraries, universities, museums. The street, however, is arguably the more democratic space where different classes and politics intermingle. There is no clear narrative of the street here, more a contemplation of surface details. A cinematic or performative element does mark these medium format pictures however, with the urban background laid bare, expectant, against which the everyday unfolds. What is drawn out through Höfer's photographs is partly the visual culture of the street and an impersonal portrayal of those who inhabit a space that, in this instance, has its own equilibrium that is neither contentious nor harmonious.

More recently, photographic portraiture has been at the centre of contemporary art and Liverpool has provided artists with distinct opportunities within which to explore the genre. Arguably, the most successful approaches have been those that create an intimate distance between photographer and subject that opens out onto a psychological landscape, imbuing the subject with an intensity and presence such as that found in the portraits of Alec Soth. Soth's portraits made in various locations within the city are the result of a particular kind of negotiated space for taking the picture. His subjects look slightly stilted, knowing, but ultimately posing for themselves projecting an image of what they believe themselves to be.

In a similar vein, Rineke Dijkstra's video and still portraits made in an improvised studio space within Liverpool's Buzz Club (1995), tap into the interior world of young people caught up in the hysteria of club culture. Temporarily isolated from the crowd and music, and 'performing' for the camera, her subjects oscillate between a patina of introspection and projected sense of their social and cultural identity. Dijkstra's subjects are always photographed in isolation and always physically or mentally exposed to the gaze of the camera. The subjects appear vulnerable and on occasion we can feel their discomfort but this can suddenly change in ways that totally shatter any sense of a nervous, controlled self-image. The Buzz Club portraits (still and moving) are a gateway into a world of individual and group dynamics, partly voyeuristic and part catalyst in exploring the surface and depths of the public image and the private self.

Over the years, many institutions in Liverpool have proactively supported photography in its various forms. Many extended their interest in the medium as it became part of mainstream contemporary art, others were more attentive to a range of photographic work that was part of a committed social practice. Some of this is historically specific of course and one can find a rich seam of photography exhibited in galleries such as Open Eye which first occupied the Grapes Hotel Public Bar on the corner of Whitechapel and Hood Street in September 1977. Operating as a media workshop in the first instance, the Open Eye exhibition space did not come into play until the following year. Its programme was a mix of touring exhibitions and self-generated shows that included the likes of William Klein, Mari Mahr, Tony Ray-Jones, Tom Wood, Martin Parr and Tina Modotti.[25] Open Eye continues to play a significant role in promoting photography in the city.

Liverpool's historical and contemporary photographic cultures are fascinating and extensive. There are important bodies of work such as those by Charles Frederick Inston, Keith Arnatt, John Davies, Clement Cooper, Philip Jones Griffiths, Max Scheler and Astrid Kirchherr, Eric de Mare, Don McCullin, Michelle Sank and many more that reveal the way that photography is used and consumed as both art and document. Through these images we get close to a city that has through the means of photography demonstrated its influence on the artistic imagination in line with Ginsberg's words, yet we can also find in dialogue with photography of another kind, sensibilities that mark an understanding of 'place' that is rendered visually more complex but is all the more richer for it.

'The city…does not tell its past, but contains it like the lines of a hand, written in the corners of streets, the gratings of windows, the banisters of the steps, the antennae of the lightning rods, the poles of the flags, every segment marked in turn with scratches, indentations…'.
Italo Calvino, *Invisible Cities*, 1974[26]

24 See 'A Conversation with Carl Andre', in Lange, Susanne, (ed.), *Bernd und Hilla Becher Festschrift – Erasmuspreis 2002*, Schirmer/Mosel: Munich, 2002, p. 56.
25 See http://www.openeye.org.uk for details of Open Eye's history, exhibition listing, archive and contemporary programme.
26 Calvino, *Invisible Cities*, p. 11.

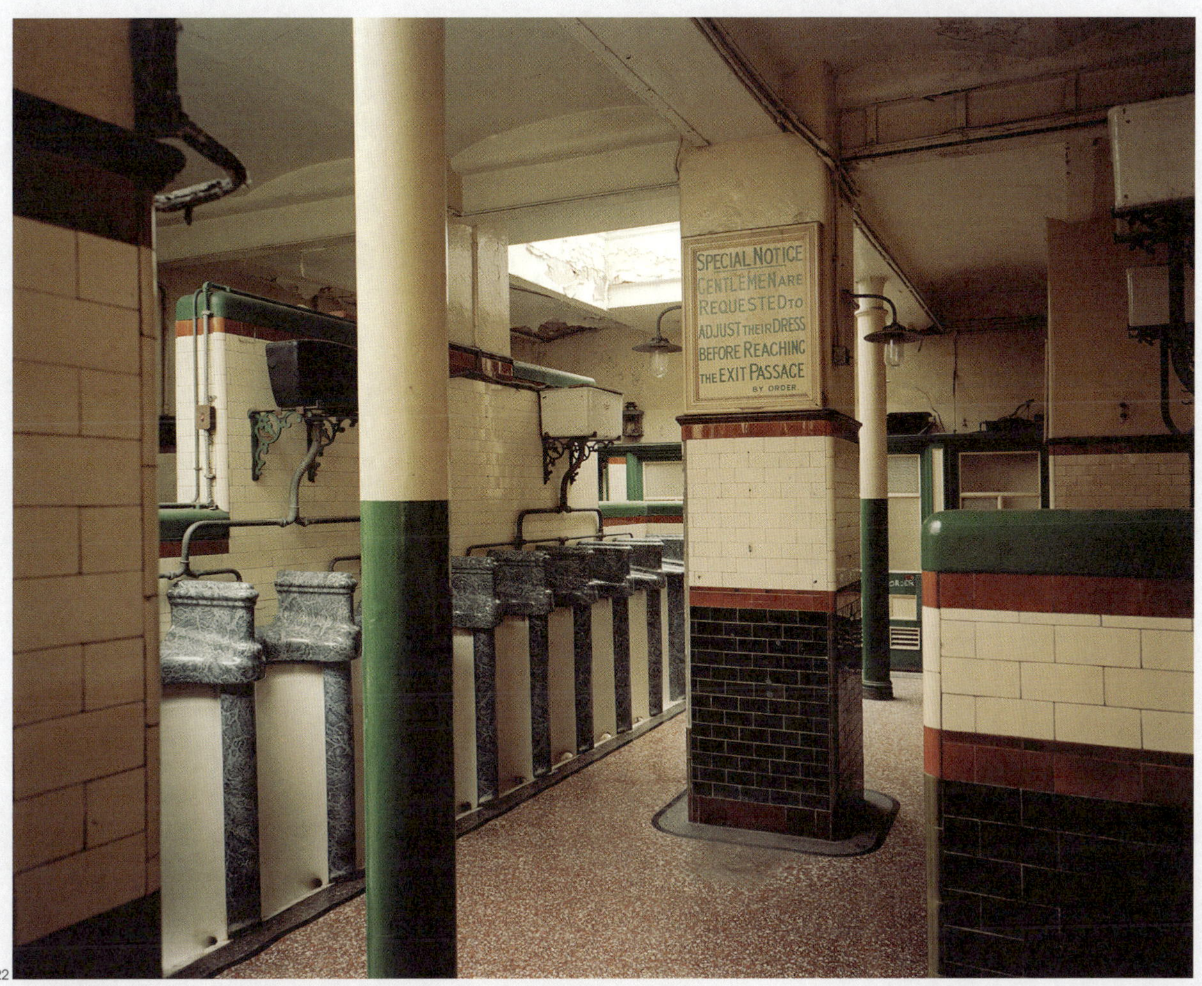

22

22
Martin Parr
England, Liverpool 1983-6
Inkjet print
61 x 76 cm
Martin Parr Magnum
Photos/Rocket Gallery,
London

23
Alec Soth
Danielle, Liverpool,
United Kingdom 2004
C-type print
94.5 x 78.7 cm
Courtesy of the artist
and Gagosian Gallery

24
Alec Soth
Michael, Liverpool,
United Kingdom 2004
C-type print
94.5 x 78.7 cm
Courtesy of the artist
and Gagosian Gallery

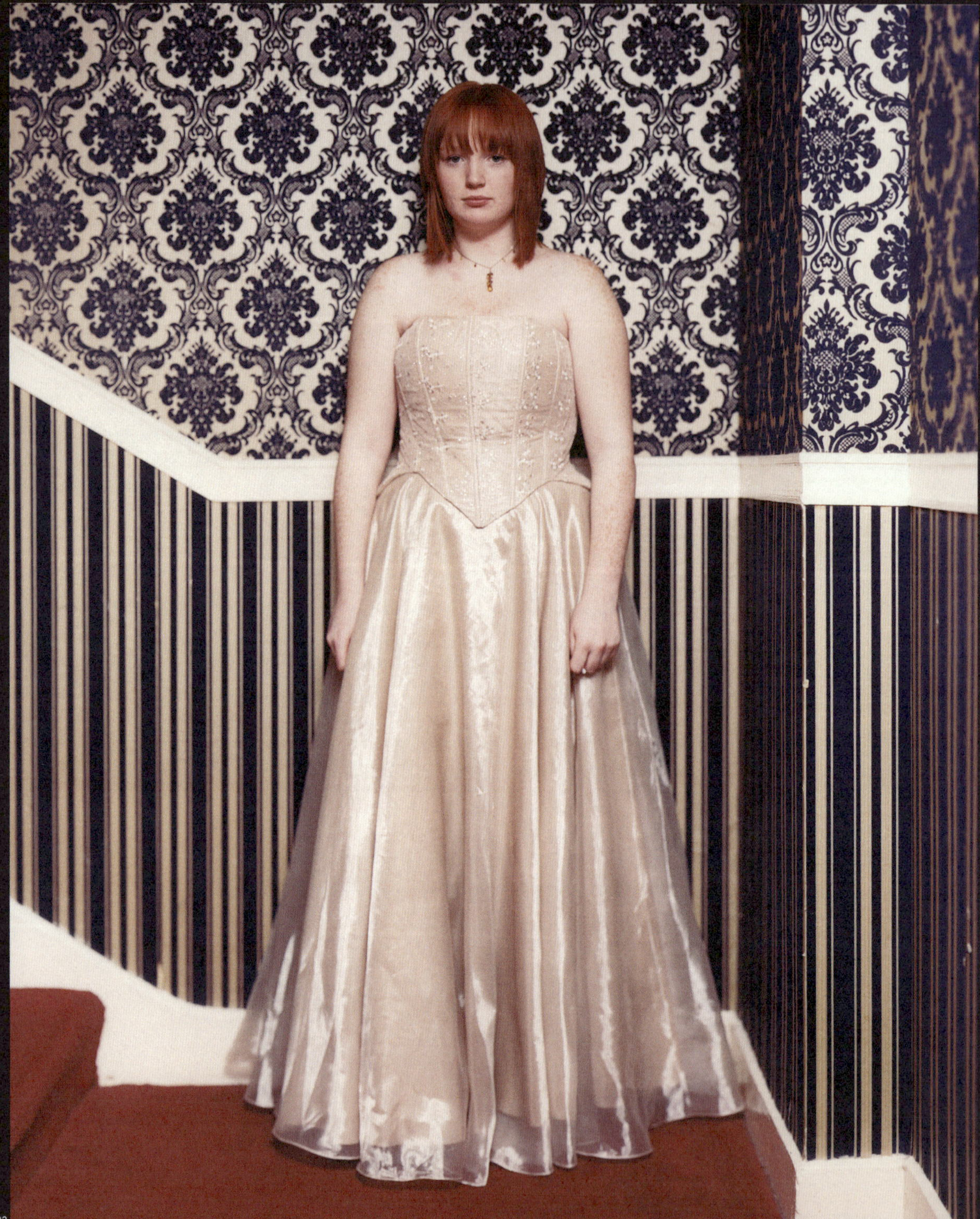

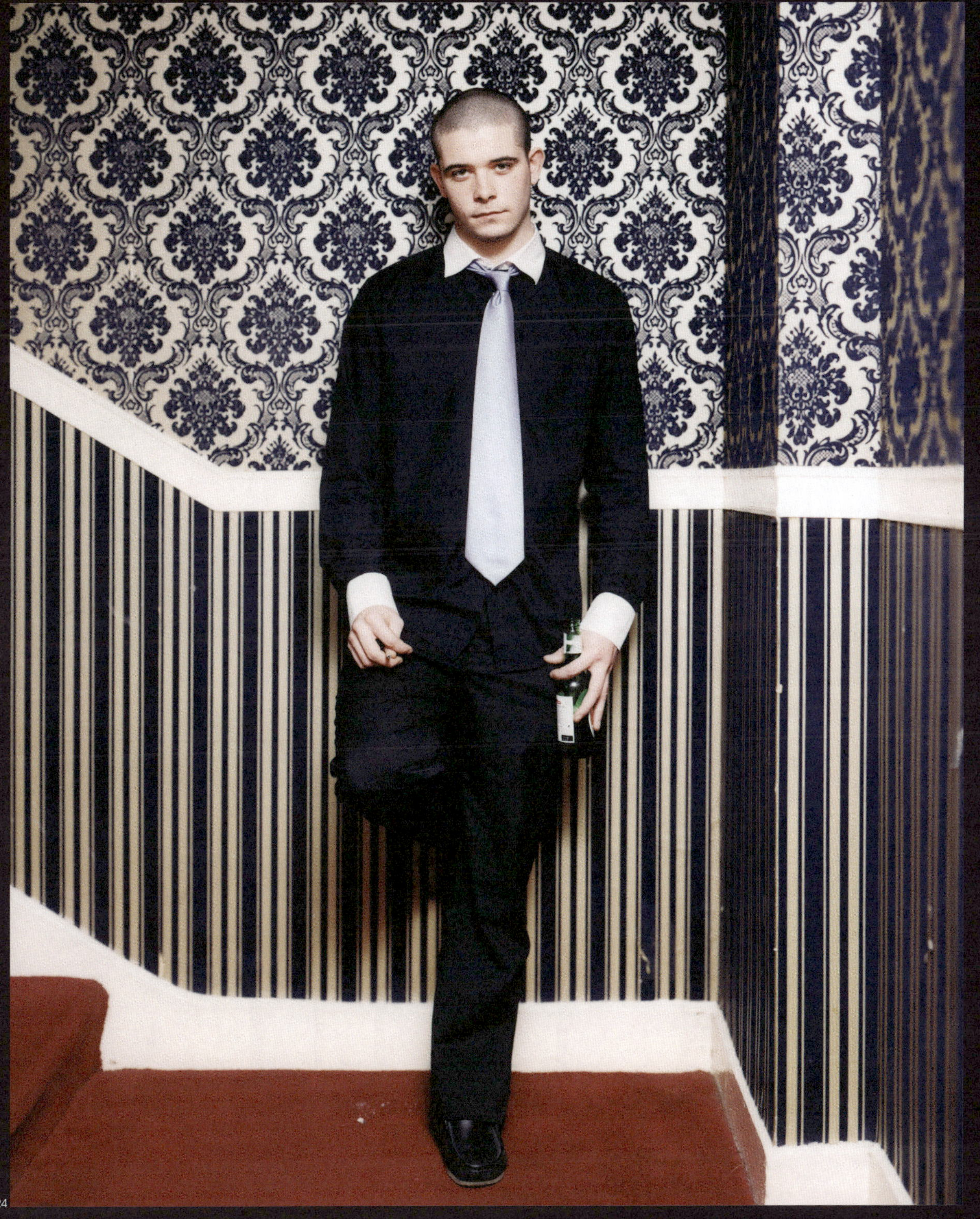

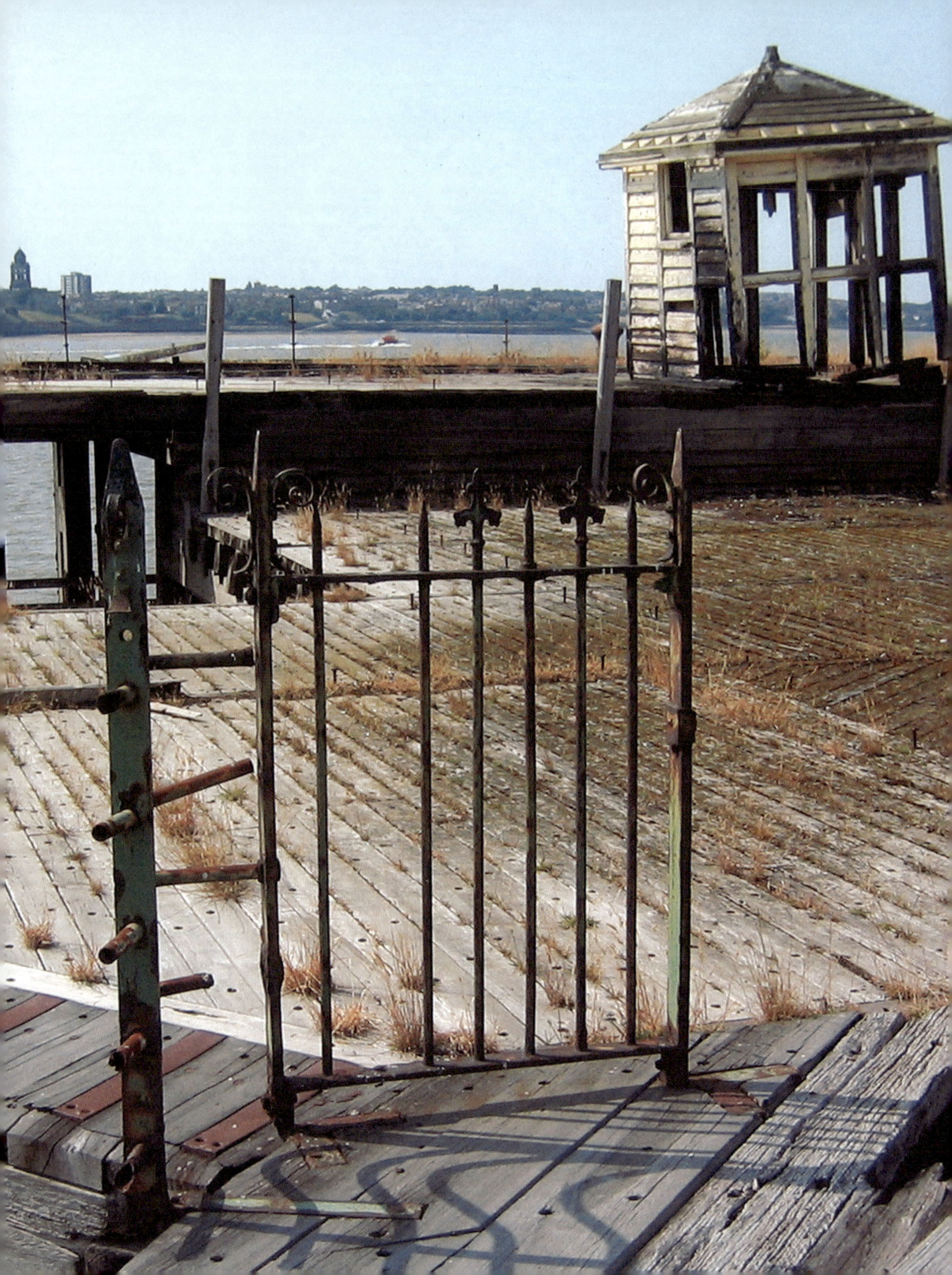

THE ARCHIVE CITY: READING LIVERPOOL'S URBAN LANDSCAPE THROUGH FILM

Les Roberts
& Richard Koeck

The Archive City:
Reading Liverpool's Urban
Landscape Through Film
Les Roberts & Richard Koeck

At a site earmarked for redevelopment on Lime Street, a virtual panorama of Liverpool's famous waterfront rises from a busy stretch of pavement leading to and from the railway station. For the urban *flâneur*, the iconography of this symbolic cityscape (enlisted to promote Lime Street's status as 'Gateway to a World-Class City') is momentarily woven into the otherwise prosaic fabric of everyday urban space. The panorama's transitory location inhibits any lingering or reflection. Yet, pause for a moment and lend the image a more incisive gaze, and what immediately becomes apparent is the striking particularity of the viewer's perspective. It is an image of the city, photographed at dusk, in which nearly all of its most prominent landmarks – the Three Graces, both cathedrals, St Nicholas' Church, St John's Beacon (all 'theatrically' illuminated) – are clustered together in perfect configuration. Geographically such a view is only possible from a singular vantage point on or across the river, yet at the same time it represents an image of the city in which maximum legibility – i.e. the ability to 'read' the cityscape as 'Liverpool' – has been invested. This economy of legibility (branding the city for global consumption) constructs a vision that is at once totalising and particular: a virtual city whose centre is everywhere and nowhere.

The idea of cityscape legibility, first proposed by Kevin Lynch in his book *The Image of the City*,[1] is one of which filmmakers with a keen eye for location and landmark have long been aware. The rich symbiosis between the

virtuality and materiality of the cinematic city has proved increasingly fertile ground for groups such as artists, architects, geographers and historians, as well as for those marketing city destinations to potential tourists (a case in point being the hugely successful US advertising campaign in 2005: 'You've seen the films, now visit the set…'). Never has 'reading' the city been so thoroughly informed by the language and geography of cinema. Yet in our everyday travels through the symbolic and material landscapes of urban living, there is also, as the cultural theorist Ben Highmore has observed, a fundamental *illegibility* that confronts us[2]: a city composed of multiple or fragmentary readings; of contradictory rhythms, temporalities and structures of feeling; a city that defies, to use Lynch's term, instant 'imageability'[3] – a city, in short, *in need of legibility*.

In the case of Liverpool – a city whose proud cinematic heritage boasts footage shot by early film pioneers such as the Lumière Brothers and Mitchell and Kenyon – the project of 'mapping' the city in film becomes, in the first instance, an exercise in rendering legible historical fragments of the urban landscape; extracting, if you will, these virtual gazes from the obscurity of the archive, and then reconstituting them in their social, historical, and geographical contexts. Reading Liverpool as an archive-city – a cinematic repository of iconic, forgotten, or half-remembered glimpses – demands not only a process of rendering present the spaces and moments of the city's past, but also, and more crucially, of plotting their absence, palimpsestically, within the multi-layered textures of the city's present. This offers a more radical potential for imaging the city; one which disrupts the corporate legibility of a consumer-led vision of the city, allowing instead for an altogether more oblique engagement with its urban form and spaces of memory: city projections defined less by the stasis of nostalgia, or the flux of simulacra, than the rhythms and syncopations of *absence*.

For a post-industrial city whose transitional hub and axis of orientation is and has been its historic waterfront, the spectral presence of absence has remained a powerful constituent in the shaping of Liverpool's affective and emotional geographies. From the disjunctive layering of the city's architecture to its embodied routes of memory and migration, the interrogative presence of a spatial or temporal *other* has proved a persistent theme in the city's cultural rendering. Nowhere is this more evident than in post-war representations of the city in film.

Consider, for example, Terence Davies' elegiac journeys into childhood remembrance. In the opening moments of *Distant Voices, Still Lives* (1988), the director's autobiographical study of working-class family life in post-war

---

1   Lynch, Kevin, *The Image of the City*, Cambridge, MA: MIT Press, 1960.
2   Highmore, Ben, *Cityscapes: Cultural Readings in the Material and Symbolic City*, Basingstoke: Palgrave Macmillan, 2005.
3   Lynch, *The Image of the City*.

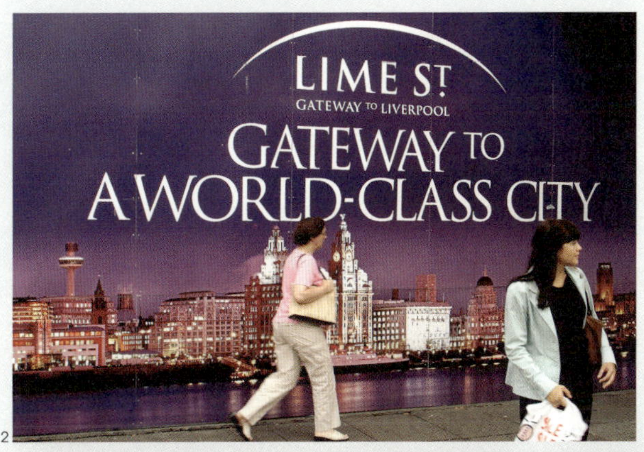

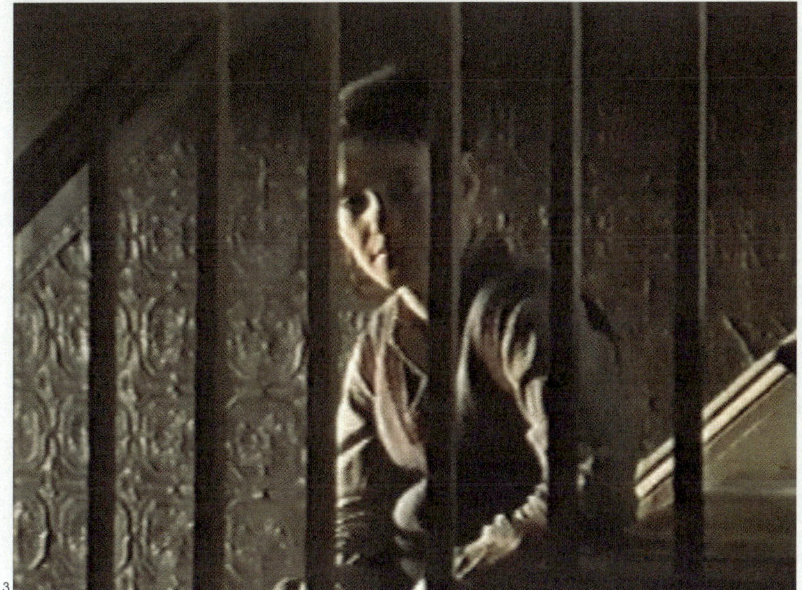

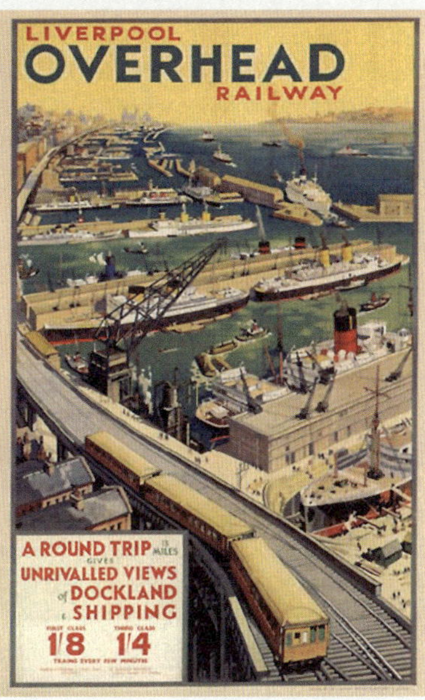

previous
Forgotten Landing Stage
Princes Dock 2006

2
'Gateway to a
World-Class City',
Lime Street Station 2006

3
Terence Davies
The Long Day Closes 1992

4
Liverpool Overhead Railway
Advertisement 1950s

Liverpool, a mother calls up to her children from the foot of the stairs. The camera remains fixed on the empty staircase as she exits the frame. When the children descend we hear the sound of their footsteps, yet the staircase remains empty. It is an image-space that offers no visual presence; a memory caught in the act of remembrance itself, temporally detached from all but the present.

Insofar as they throw past and present into reflective dialogue, Davies's intimate landscapes of memory chart an absence that is as much spatial as temporal in origin. Liverpool is presented as a place of returns – a city one comes back to to confront the trauma of its associated memories (in this case those of a violent and abusive father), but also to dwell once again in its more tender and epiphanic moments. In *The Long Day Closes* (1992), Davies's follow up to *Distant Voices,* remembrance drifts amongst oneiric landscapes of childhood reverie: subtly shifting patterns of light on a carpet; the transcendent sociality of cinema and song; the textures, rhythms and 'countless alveoli' of intimate space.[4] The wider social geography of the city rarely intrudes on the beautifully composed *mise-en-scène* of these films. The action centres almost exclusively on the domestic home and localised places of leisure such as the cinema or pub. Like the films' narrative, the urban landscape that is evoked is one comprised of ellipses, both spatial and temporal. In the same way that, as Marc Augé has noted,[5] the oblivion of memory – i.e. that which is forgotten – shapes the form and substance of particular remembrances, it is the historical and geographical lacunae in Davies's films that inform the director's singularly personal and subjective rendering of the city's presence. His is an image of the city in which the architecture of everyday domestic life, such as a staircase can be as iconic and as redolent of time and place as any public building or notable landmark.

In films where Liverpool's urban landscape commands broader legibility – that is, where recognisable landmarks and locations are incorporated into the filmic narrative – the tropes of absence and return become more self-consciously woven into narratives of the city itself. These cinematic landscapes establish sites of focused gathering in or around which particular identities and histories of the city – as a place of mobility and transition – are assembled. Films such as *Waterfront* (Michael Anderson, 1950), *The Magnet* (Charles Frend, 1950), *Violent Playground* (Basil Dearden, 1958), *Beyond This Place* (Jack Cardiff, 1959), *The Little Ones* (Jim O'Connolly, 1965), *Ferry Cross the Mersey* (Jeremy Summers, 1965), or, more recently, *Letter to Brezhnev* (Chris Bernard, 1985), *Shirley Valentine* (Lewis Gilbert, 1989), *Blonde Fist*, (Frank Clarke, 1991) and *Across the Universe* (Julie Taymor, 2006), all, to a greater or lesser degree, present an image of the city as a place of arrival and departure: a gateway to or from Elsewhere. It is not altogether surprising therefore that it is Liverpool's iconic waterfront that functions as its most prominent trope of transition in the city's imagining.

The iconographic nature of this landscape can be traced to early postcard images of the city and grew from an emergent 'tourist gaze'[6] that quickly oriented itself around the river and docks. The Liverpool Overhead Railway, which, until its demolition in 1957, ran all the way along the dockside, played a crucial role in instilling what Wolfgang Schivelbusch describes as a 'panoramic perception' of the city and its waterfront.[7] It is surely then no accident that the first moving images of Liverpool, filmed by the Lumière Brothers in 1897, were shot from the Overhead Railway (then just four years old) looking out over the busy docks. This panoramic view of the waterfront, captured in the nascent years of film, can be paralleled with that experienced by the dockworkers and travellers riding the newly-constructed railway. Together, these 'mobile, virtual gazes'[8] informed an image of the city in which the dynamism and prosperity associated with the waterfront had become emblematic of the progressive rhythms of modernity itself. As Guiliana Bruno notes, 'moving panoramas were instrumental in developing films that eschewed static, theatrical views in favour of architectural motions… [the panorama] incorporated site-seeing journeys and the spatio-visual desire for circulation that had become fully embedded in modernity'.[9] In 1897 Liverpool truly was a 'cinematic city'.

The birds-eye-view or panoramic shot from a high-angle position has since become a familiar cinematic convention to quickly situate the viewer at a distinct geographic location in which the action takes place. We all have seen films which open by showing a single or series of *vertical landmarks*, such as the Eiffel Tower, Big Ben or the skyline of New York. Cinema has played an influential role in transforming these architectural landmarks into iconographic symbols that describe, or render legible, the characteristics and collective memories of the cities they represent. Liverpool has a number of architectural landmarks of international stature which have been portrayed in film: two outstanding cathedrals, a number of neo-classical marvels such as John Wood's Town Hall and Harvey Lonsdale Elmes' St. George's Hall, as well as, of course, its world famous waterfront ensemble – the Three Graces. However, there are also a number of filmic examples in which these traditional landmarks are marginalised or even absent. In contrast to most other filmic cities, filmmakers have exploited Liverpool's *horizontal landmark* – the waterfront docks – an urban-architectural feature which, as we have noted, has drawn the attention of filmmakers since the very earliest days of the moving image.

In *Waterfront*, Michael Anderson's 1950 melodrama of working-class life on the docks, the waterfront functions as a narrative expressive space – a horizontal landscape that is not only unique to Liverpool, but also suggestive of a set of urban-industrial values associated with it. The film starts (and ends) with an impressive pan over the docks and the railway, shot from an omnipotent high-angle position. Instead of seeing familiar waterfront landmarks, such as the Liver Building, we are introduced to a vast maritime-industrial landscape in which steamships enter and leave the docks, factories exhaust their fumes, and the Overhead Railway rattles along its elevated tracks. The content of the picture and the movement of the camera itself render Liverpool as a dynamic, ever-changing site, a representation which belies the film's overwhelming sense of stasis and entrapment, which we will return to below.

Made in the same year, the title sequence of the Ealing comedy *The Magnet* reveals an equally impressive opening and as such is yet another example that uses the dockland as landmark site. Interestingly, the pan (right to left) starts with an image of the Anglican Cathedral which then dissolves into a longer shot over Princes Dock. While the portrayal of the cathedral on its own, from this distance and point of view, would perhaps be ambiguous in terms of its location, the shot of the docks situates the viewer unmistakably and instantly in Liverpool. Although these images of the dockland do not consist of singular landmark buildings, they nevertheless contain a number of legible urban-architectural elements, such as *paths* (Overhead Railway), *nodes* (the tunnel exit), *edges* (the waterfront and river Mersey). These urban features are not only in themselves important constituents to the city's perceptibility, but also, when composed into a single shot (such as that of an all-embracing pan), they are instantly recognisable urban attributes of Liverpool's waterfront.

Looking back over a century or more of Liverpool on film, the industrial legacy of the docks has, from the very outset, shaped a compelling cinematic landscape of mobility and transition in which the fortunes and vicissitudes of the city and its inhabitants have remained inextricably tied to those of the waterfront. While the Lumière film captures an early and resplendent 'moment of presence', in films such as *Waterfront* (set in the period of economic depression between the wars), the idea of *mobility* takes on altogether different connotations. As with its 1980s counterpart, *Letter to Brezhnev* (set in the Thatcher years of high unemployment and industrial decline) tropes of movement and transition are expressive of an inherent contradiction: one born of *immobility* and stasis. The desire to 'move on' or escape draws attention to the constraints, boundaries and limitations of the here and now. Transition in this sense reflects more a condition of liminality: of lives suspended or caught 'in-between' moments of presence. The dialectic between mobility and stasis, departure and entrapment is in part reflected in the gendering of the dock's (post)industrial landscape, and becomes particularly evident in the way in which female and male citizens are portrayed inhabiting contrasting patterns of mobility. *Waterfront* and *Letter to Brezhnev* (as well as more recent films such as *Dockers* (Bill Anderson, 1999) provide a good illustration of this. The plot of *Waterfront* begins somewhere in the 1920s. Nora and her family live in a poor housing estate near Liverpool's waterfront. The aforementioned panoramic shot is accompanied by Nora's voiceover which reveals the extent to which she sees herself rooted to this site: 'That's what you might call inevitable, I suppose; because I was born and brought up in this part of Liverpool; right on the waterfront; almost among the docks.' Nora's sense of stasis and entrapment is explored in the opening minutes of the film. One morning, while being on the grounds of her school, she is visited by her father. Talking to her through the railings of an iron fence, he explains to Nora that he has signed on a ship about to leave Liverpool. This is of course a traumatic moment for Nora, as she realises that she and her mother are about to lose the family's only source of income. What makes this scene so memorable is the way in which it is cinematographically portrayed. Cutting back and forwards between the two sides of the fence, this architectural feature becomes more than a simple dividing line between opinions. Nora is neither able to keep her father from leaving, nor is she able to follow him, which, visually paired with vertical iron bars, leaves the implicit impression of being imprisoned by, and entrapped on, Liverpool's waterfront.

True to its title, *Waterfront* not only starts, but also ends with shots along the shore of the river Mersey. Once again, and after a jump in time of perhaps twenty years, Nora is being left behind in the port of Liverpool when her husband, who, after years of unemployment, finally finds work on a commercial liner. As she bids farewell to her husband, who is seen crossing the empty space between her and the ship, it seems as if Nora has resigned herself to her fate. *Waterfront* portrays the period between the two world wars as a time of socio-economic uncertainty for the inhabitants of Liverpool. Seen in this context, Ben's departure can be interpreted in terms of a regained economic stability for Nora and her family as well as a promise of a better future. Interestingly, similar visual motifs are evident in *Letter to Brezhnev*. Kirkby girl Elaine falls in love with Russian seaman Peter, who, after a brief romance must return to his home country. The pivotal farewell-scene takes place at a landing stage of one of the docks. Once again, as in *Waterfront*, the fence is part of the composition of the image, which in this mid-1980s production is perhaps an oversimplified visual reminder of the iron curtain that divided East and West. Importantly, it is again the waterfront which becomes the symbolic ground on which male protagonists *have to leave*, while female protagonists are *unable to leave* Liverpool. As Peter crosses the empty space towards his Russian ship, he is visually consumed by the enormous difference in scale between him and the ships, until vanishing almost completely.

4   See Bachelard, Gaston, *The Poetics of Space*, Boston, MA: Beacon Press, 1994, p. 8.
5   Augé, Marc, *Oblivion*, Minneapolis, MN: University of Minnesota Press, 2004.
6   Urry, John, *The Tourist Gaze*, London: Sage, 1990.
7   Schivelbusch, Wolfgang, *The Railway Journey: The Industrialisation of Time and Space in the 19th-Century*, Leamington Spa: Berg, 1986, p. 63.
8   Friedberg, Anne, *Window Shopping: Cinema and the Postmodern*, Berkeley and Los Angeles: University of California Press, 1994, p. 2.
9   Bruno, Giuliana, *Atlas of Emotion: Journeys in Art, Architecture and Film*, New York: Verso, 2002, p. 19-20.

THE MAGNET
MADE AT EALING STUDIOS, LONDON, ENGLAND.
Certificate No.16725
RCA SOUND SYSTEM
COPYRIGHT MCML BY EALING STUDIOS LIMITED.
MEREDIT
GLADY
WYLI
THO
JULIE
as th

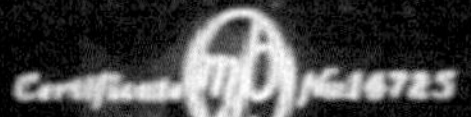

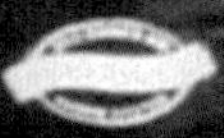

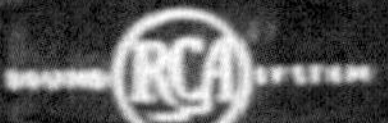

5

5
Charles Frend
The Magnet 1950

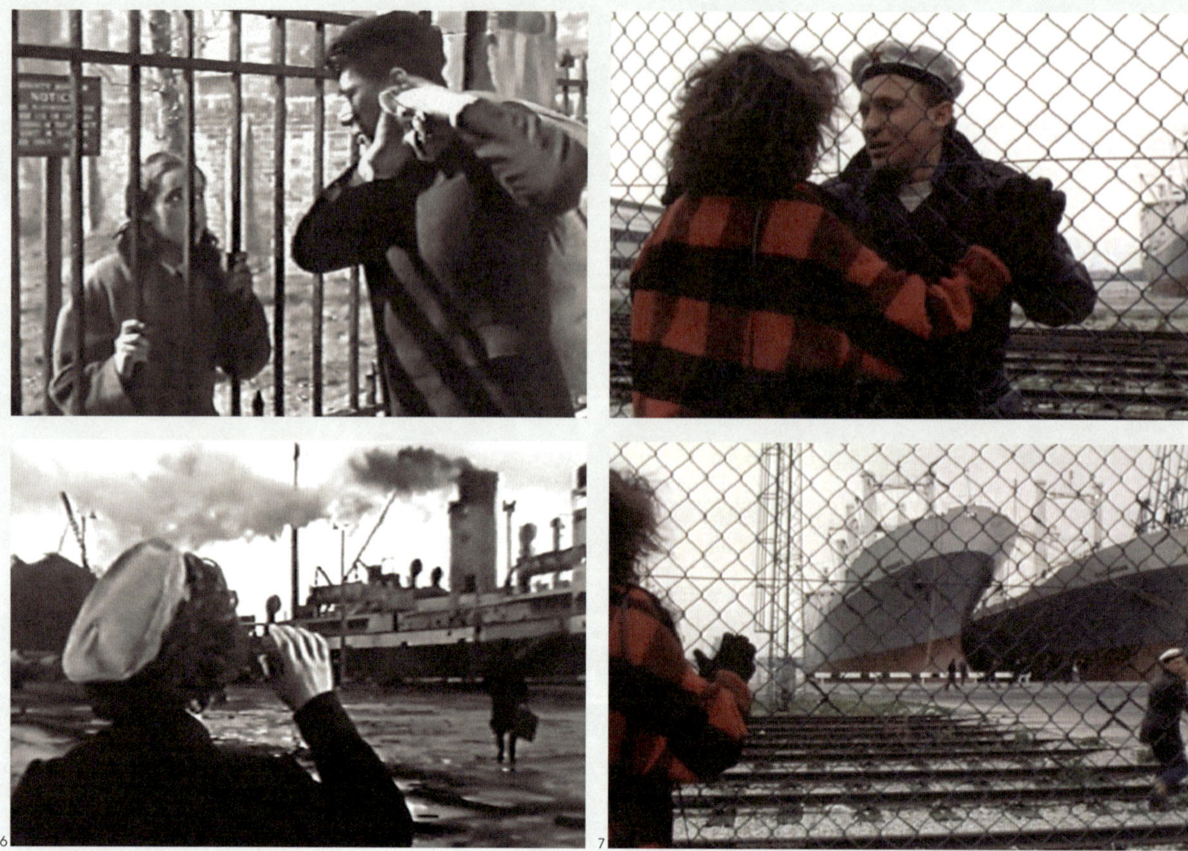

6
Michael Anderson
Waterfront 1950

7
Chris Bernard
Letter to Brezhnev 1985

Of course, the coda to *Letter to Brezhnev*, in which Elaine, despite all the odds stacked against her, flies out to Moscow to be reunited with Peter, sets the two films apart, both dramatically and historically. The reclaimed mobility of the 1980s protagonist (albeit one that has her chasing after her man) highlights, by comparison, the constraints and relative lack of agency in movement experienced by women a generation or two earlier. Women whose matriarchal domain, as films such as *Waterfront* and *The Long Day Closes* powerfully attest, was the spatial (and existential) interiority of a domestic environment in which men were conspicuously absent.

Moreover, insofar as Elaine's story can be read as a symbolic narrative of the city itself, it is an ending in which Liverpool is depicted as once again entering a state of transition. The destination to which she is travelling is Elsewhere: another time, another place, *another city* yet to be realised.

In an essay exploring the iconography of Liverpool's urban landscape in film, in particular its waterfront, it would perhaps be remiss to omit mention of *Ferry Cross the Mersey* (Jeremy Summers, 1965), a film little seen since its release in 1965, but one which in many ways encapsulates a can-do spirit and optimism that stand in marked contrast to the prevailing themes of absence and stasis. Produced by Brian Epstein, the film has few pretensions to be anything other than a vehicle for its stars, the Merseybeat group, Gerry and the Pacemakers, after whose famous song the film is titled. In this respect it is a film that bears close family resemblance to *A Hard Day's Night* (Richard Lester, 1964) and *Help!* (Richard Lester, 1965), both of which starred The Beatles (playing themselves). While in these latter films the city itself does not feature in any significant way, in *Ferry Cross the Mersey* Liverpool is cast in a central role, portraying a vibrant, creative and dynamic city that had begun to define itself in relation to an emerging pop and consumer culture, oriented in particular around its music and fashion scenes. The city portrayed in the film is one that had begun to exert a centripetal force, attracting people to its waterfront and spaces of culture. Such a reading of the film is literally translated onto the screen when Gerry Marsden and his bandmates make a symbolic passage across the river, Liverpool's waterfront landmarks framed prominently in the background.

The trope of the ferry crossing also has the effect of drawing on a wider cultural geography of the city, one that acknowledges the spatial and symbolic importance of key locations 'cross the Mersey, such as Birkenhead or New Brighton. Viewed thus, 'this land's the place I love…', from the song, may be interpreted as a tribute to an idea of place that has the Mersey *at its centre* rather than at its edge. In addition, as with the corporate image of the waterfront discussed earlier, the ferry journey enables the city to be visually objectified and apprehended *from a distance*. Again, in marked contrast to the other examples, in *Ferry Cross the Mersey* the waterfront is depicted as ostensibly a place of arrival: a gateway *to* rather than *from* the symbolic city. This more positive connotation is further enhanced by the way both men and women are portrayed in terms of their mobility.

By the 1960s, Liverpool is no longer seen as a city of mass transportation (the Overhead Railway, for example, is conspicuously absent) but one that is increasingly being explored by individual motorists. The city is filled with scooters and automobiles; modern means of transport that signal an active engagement with the physical fabric and boundaries of the city. If compared with previous representations of the city's youth culture in film, most memorably that of *Violent Playground*, made in 1958, it becomes clear as to the extent to which *Ferry Cross the Mersey* was conceived in part as a reaction against the restricted mobilities and lack of opportunity attached to the city's spaces a decade before. In *Violent Playground*, situated in the entropic spaces of a city housing scheme (the actual location was Gerard Gardens), youth alienation gives way to violence and arson, representing an altogether different engagement with the physical fabric of a city in which individual agency manifests itself in destructive rather than creative forms of expression.

The self-conscious portrayal of Liverpool in *Ferry Cross the Mersey* is thus one that is hallmarked by redemption from the past, and as such is indicative of a city in a state of transition. Forty years on, as Liverpool once more finds itself in the midst of change and transition, this search for presence represents a structure of feeling that carries a particularly contemporary resonance. The city's 800 year anniversary in 2007, and its status as European Capital of Culture 2008, have sparked the unfolding of massive urban architectural developments currently under way. In this light, the virtual panorama discussed at the beginning of this essay is already today an obsolete representation of the city and will itself need revaluation in the near future. In transforming the symbolic and material landscapes of Liverpool, the projection of an image of the city thus reflects the need to sustain a legible visual identity that somehow transcends the flux of rapid economic and cultural change. Paradoxically, such a durable vision is more likely to lie in the *illegibility* and *absence* of a cinematic city that is recognised to be in a state of constant modification and transition – a visual identity that therefore needs to be sought not so much in the *permanent* but the *ephemeral*.

In its century-long transition from 'gateway to Empire' to 'gateway to a world-class city', Liverpool's historical accretions of urban and cinematic space have continued to play host to its diverse, and at times conflicting, rhythms and mobilities. By reading and celebrating Liverpool as an *archive city*, not only can we (re)glimpse the image-spaces of the city's near and distant past, but also, and more importantly, we can (re)incorporate these absent spaces and moments within the real and imagined landscapes of the city's present and future projections.

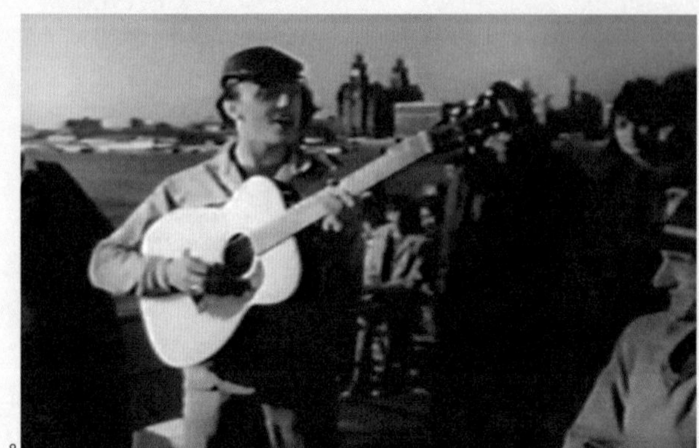 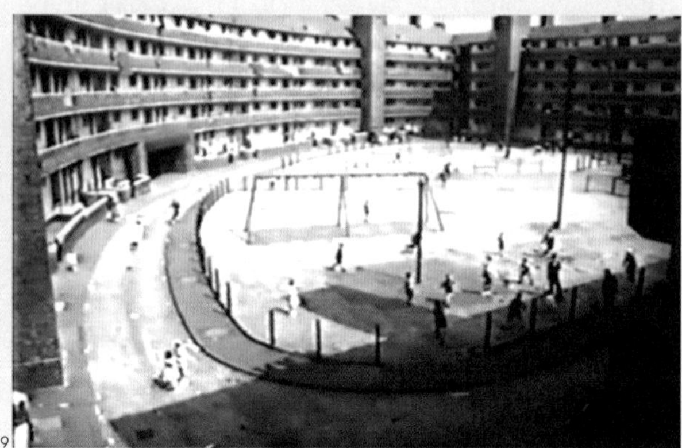

8
Jeremy Summers
Ferry Cross The Mersey
1965

9
Basil Dearden
Violent Playground 1958

10
Liverpool
City in transition 2006

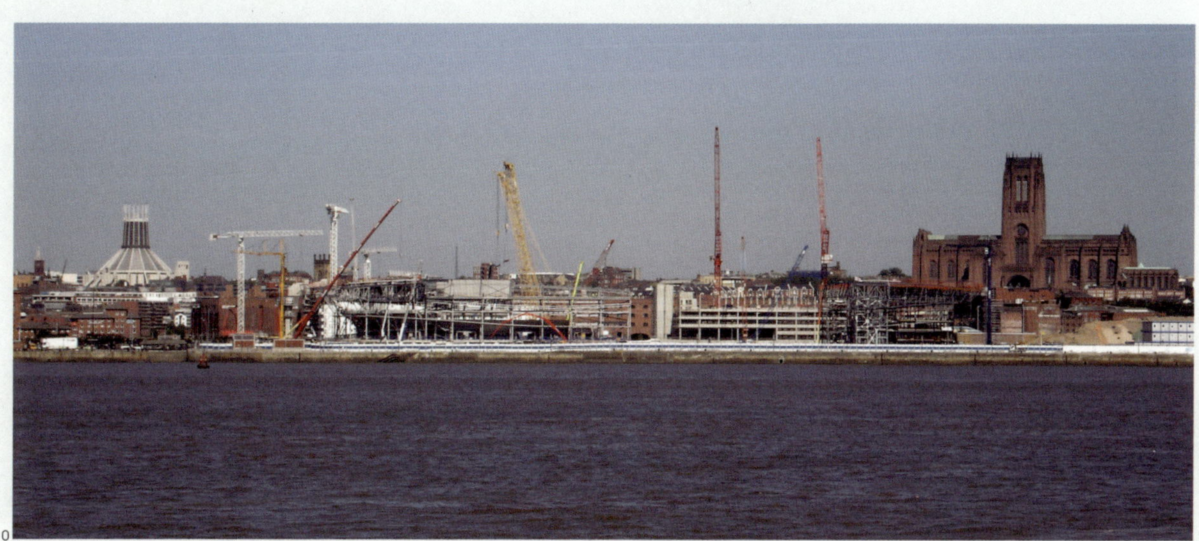

10

Filmography
Across the Universe (Julie Taymor, USA, 2006)
A Hard Day's Night (Richard Lester, UK, 1964)
Beyond This Place (Jack Cardiff, UK, 1959)
Blonde Fist (Frank Clarke, UK, 1991)
Distant Voices, Still Lives (Terence Davies, UK, 1988)
Dockers (Bill Anderson, UK, 1999)
Ferry Cross the Mersey (Jeremy Summers, UK, 1965)
Help! (Richard Lester, UK, 1965)
Letter to Brezhnev (Chris Bernard, UK, 1985)
Shirley Valentine (Lewis Gilbert, UK, USA, 1989)
The Little Ones (Jim O'Connolly, UK, 1965)
The Long Day Closes (Terence Davies, UK, 1992)
The Magnet (Charles Frend, UK, 1950)
Violent Playground (Basil Dearden, UK, 1958)
Waterfront (Michael Anderson, UK, 1950)

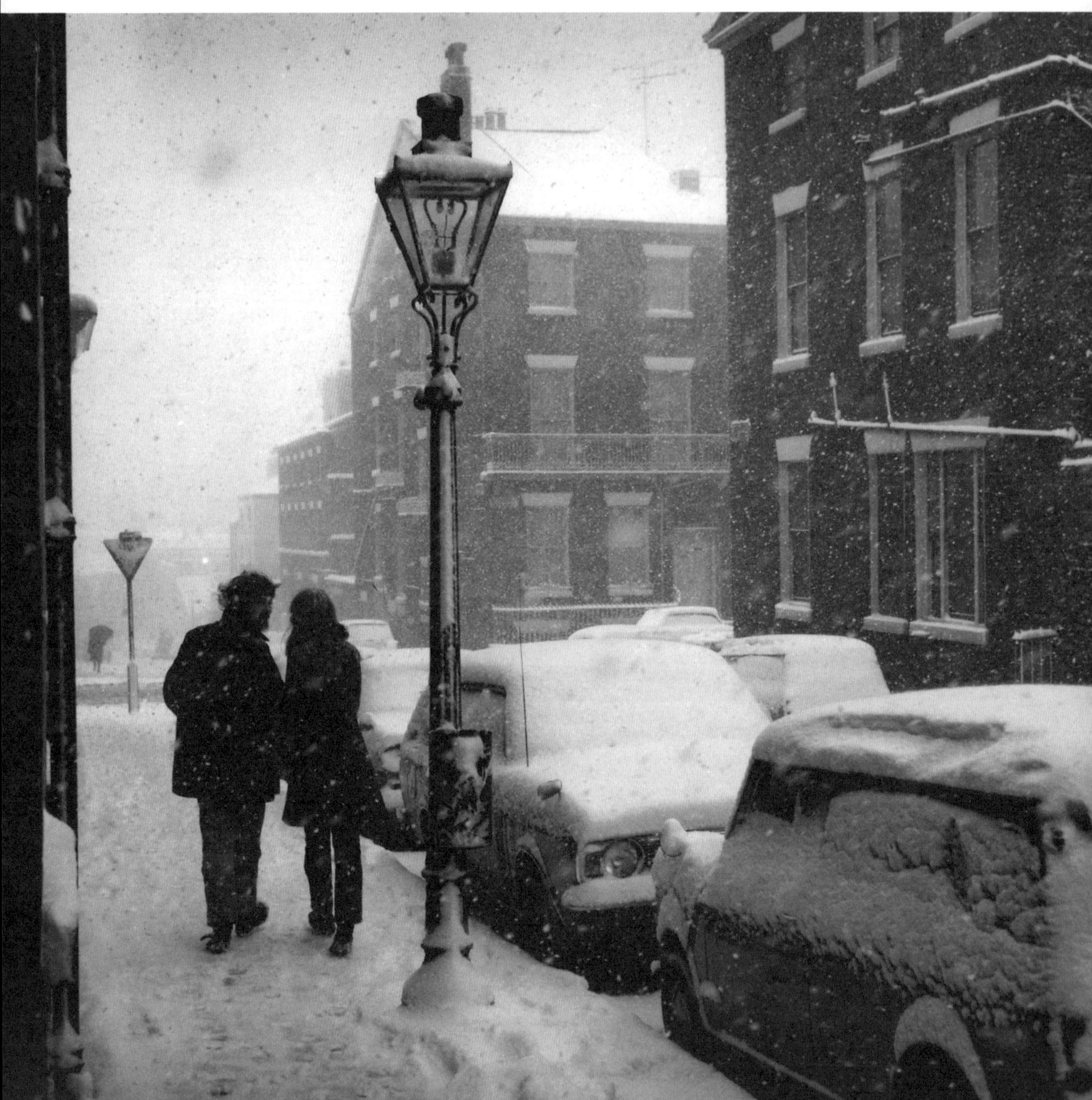

RAISING THE CONSCIOUSNESS? RE-VISITING ALLEN GINSBERG'S LIVERPOOL TRIP IN 1965

Simon Warner

Raising the Consciousness? Re-visiting Allen Ginsberg's Liverpool Trip in 1965

Simon Warner

In the very heart of the Swinging Sixties, a decade whose influence has continued to vibrate luminously through the last years of one millennium and into the first years of the next, a high profile poet and campaigning activist of Jewish-Russian-American background came to Liverpool, a place where the ley lines seemed to hum most loudly and warmly in the late spring/early summer of 1965. At the end of that May, Allen Ginsberg, Beat-politico-Buddhist-performer-poet, extended his ongoing and impromptu world tour – Cuba, Russia, Eastern Europe and on to the United Kingdom – to take in a Northern English city that had, only quite recently, unleashed on the world nothing short of a musical sensation. Yet the visitor had more to praise than just an all-conquering quartet who had left such an indelible impression across the Atlantic and beyond – but more of that later.

The Beatles, following their arrival in the New York in February 1964, had sparked little less than a cultural revolution. Until then, British pop had been a virtual irrelevance to the United States, the most powerful and lucrative marketplace of all. But the group's spear-heading of the British Invasion would, in the next few years, leave a searing brand on the American carcass. The Fab Four seized the keys to the rock'n'roll citadel and opened gates that would eventually admit home-grown artists from Herman's Hermits to the Rolling Stones, the Dave Clark Five to the Who, the Animals to the Kinks, Led Zeppelin and Van Morrison, Fleetwood Mac, David Bowie and Elton John, the Punks and the New Romantics.

So, The Beatles were one convincingly powerful reason for such outside interest in their home city at the mid-point of a momentous decade. But what would prompt Allen Ginsberg, the voluble guru of the Cold War silence and the garrulous precursor of the hippie generation, to not only spend nearly a week in Liverpool but also coin an iconoclastic phrase that would both delight – and maybe even haunt – the city for the next four decades. For Ginsberg concluded during that amiable and frenetic stay – in box-rooms and bars, in bookshops and basements – that Liverpool was 'at the present moment the centre of the consciousness of the human universe'. Although Edward Lucie-Smith, whose 1967 volume *The Liverpool Scene* would become a broadside for the city's new vibrancy, was later reported to be the recipient of that comment[1], it seems much more likely that he said it, during his stay, to fellow writer Adrian Henri, one of a community of poets who would be another appealing lure for Ginsberg to spend some time by the banks of the Mersey.

In this article I aim to contemplate that 1965 visit from a number of positions, attempting to historically re-describe the Ginsberg stay from personal and reported accounts, drawing on interviews, histories and biographies. I want to try and establish what Ginsberg made of Liverpool and attempt a reading of what the Liverpool Poets and the wider community made of this exotic guest. And, perhaps crucially, I would like to try, through more recent responses by critics and commentators, to make sense of the poet's widely remembered and oft-quoted remark, one that continues to resonate through the recent Merseyside milieu and offers succour and encouragement to the city's art-makers, its enduring bohemian quarter, even its officially sanctioned arts sector.

But first: who was Allen Ginsberg and why did he count? From the late 1940s through the early 1950s, Ginsberg was a central figure in a dynamic sub-cultural grouping, self-dubbed the Beat Generation – beaten down but also beatific, aspiring to saintliness – which had forged literary, artistic and musical cells in Greenwich Village, in North Beach, San Francisco and Venice Beach, Los Angeles. Yet it would take Ginsberg's live debut, in 1955, of his long poem 'Howl', and the subsequent acclaim then furore raised by obscenity charges eventually dismissed, to propel the Beats into a national then international phenomenon, before long 'familiar to hundreds and thousands of readers around the globe in the months and years to follow'.[2] Before that decade had ended, further members of this creative clan – novelists Jack Kerouac and William Burroughs, poets Michael McClure, Lawrence Ferlinghetti, Gregory Corso, and others would see their writings appear in

---

1 Lucie-Smith, Edward (ed.), *The Liverpool Scene*, London: Donald Carroll, 1967. See Schumacher, Michael, *Dharma Lion: A Biography of Allen Ginsberg*, New York: St Martin's Press, 1992, p. 446.
2 Warner, Simon, 'Sifting the Shifting Sands: "Howl" and the American Landscape in the 1950s', in Warner, Simon (ed.), *Howl for Now: A Celebration of Allen Ginsberg's Epic Protest Poem*, Pontefract: Route, 2005, p. 29.

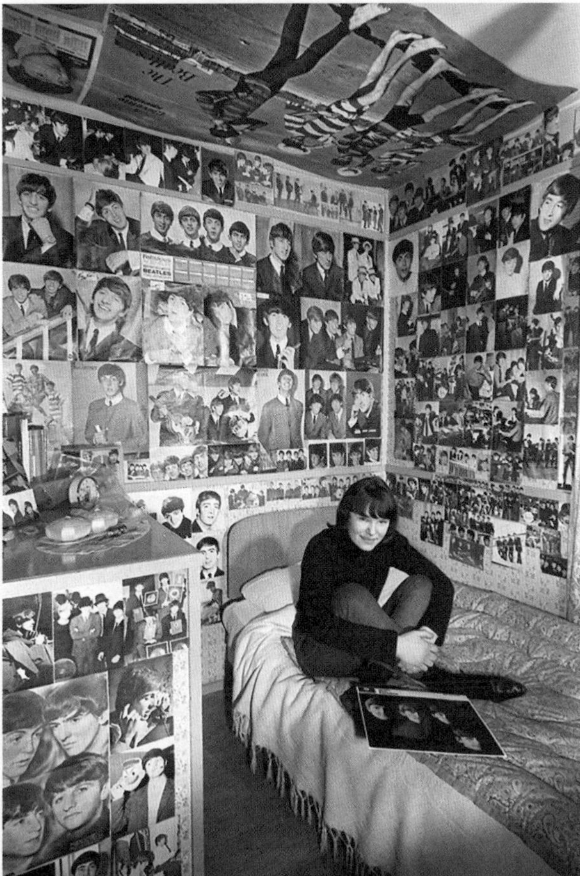

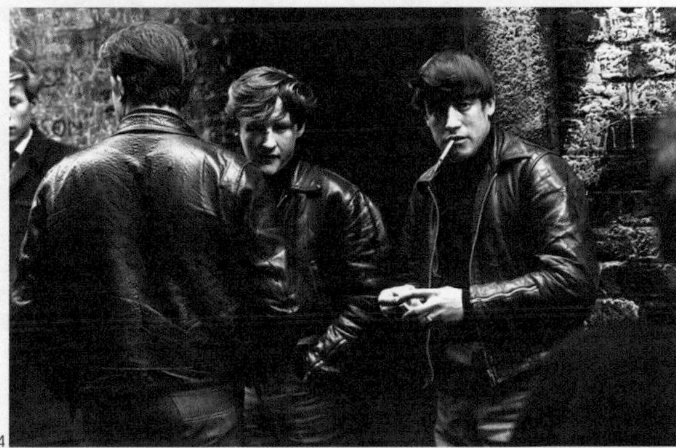

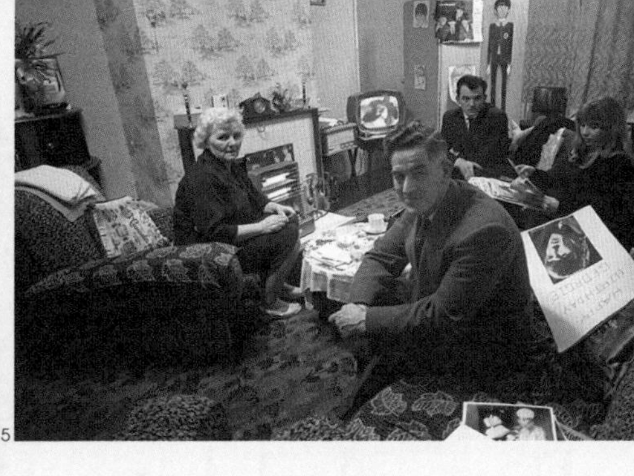

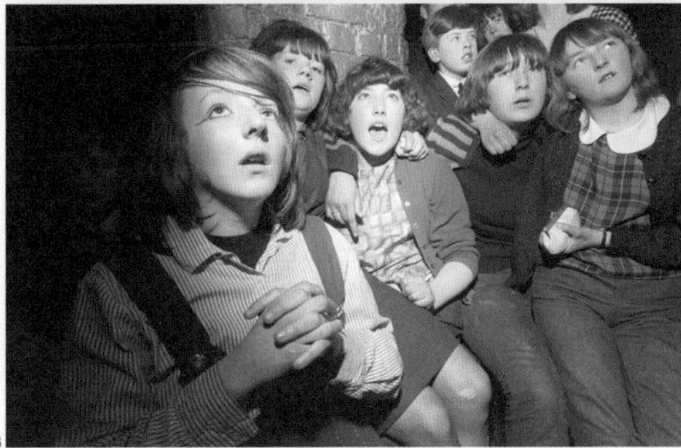

2
Max Scheler
Beatles Fan 1964
Silver gelatin print
50 x 60 cm
Courtesy Max Scheler/
K&K

3
Max Scheler
*Girls at The Cavern,
Praying* 1964
Silver gelatin print
50 x 60 cm
Courtesy Max Scheler/
K&K

4
Max Scheler
*Boys with Leather
Jackets* 1964
Silver gelatin print
50 x 60 cm
Courtesy Max Scheler/
K&K

5
Max Scheler
At the Harrison's 1964
Silver gelatin print
50 x 60 cm
Courtesy Max Scheler/
K&K

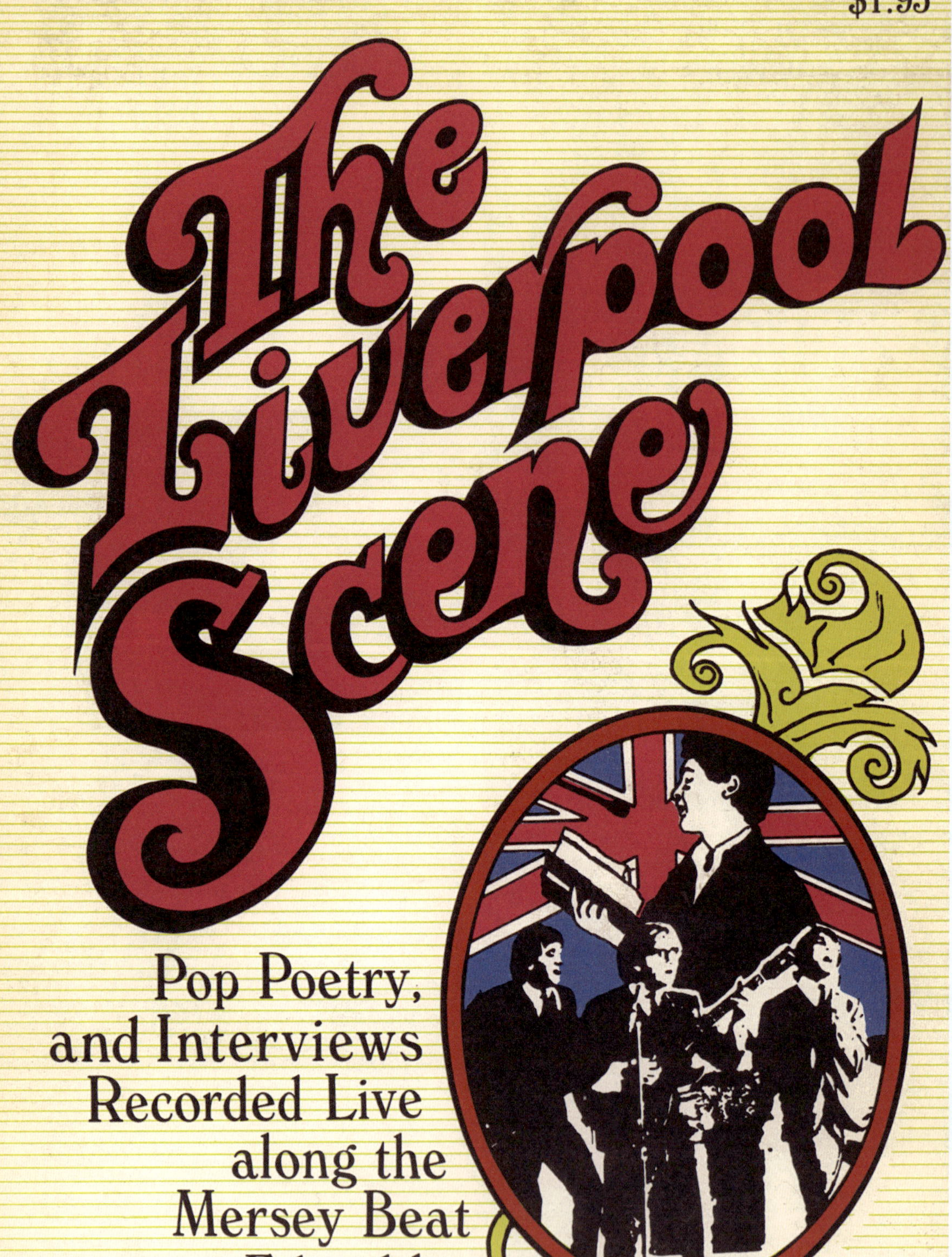
$1.95
The Liverpool Scene
Pop Poetry,
and Interviews
Recorded Live
along the
Mersey Beat
Edited by
Edward Lucie-Smith
A Paperback Original

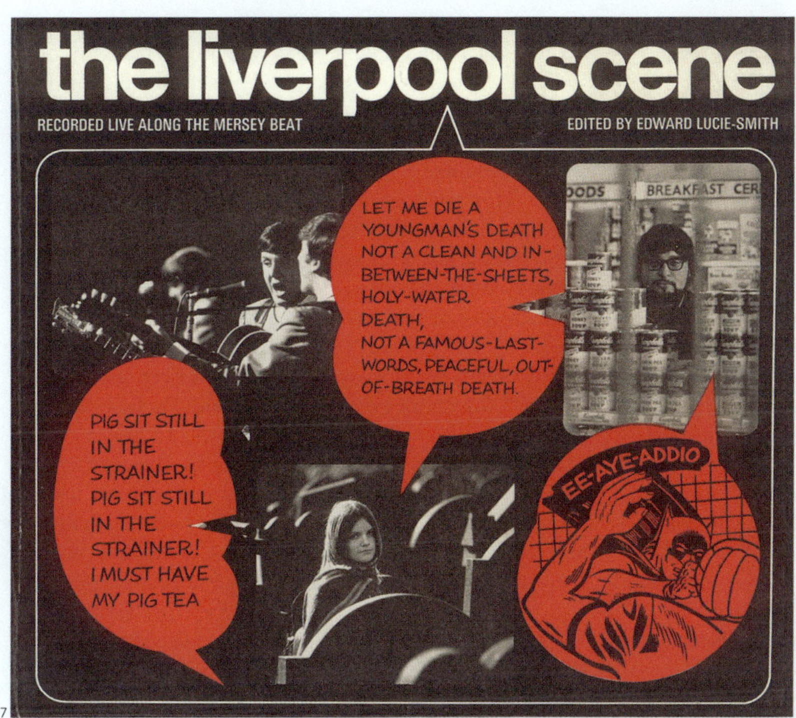

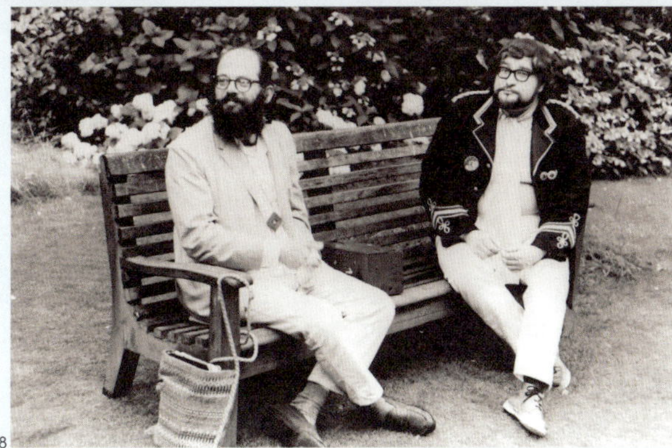

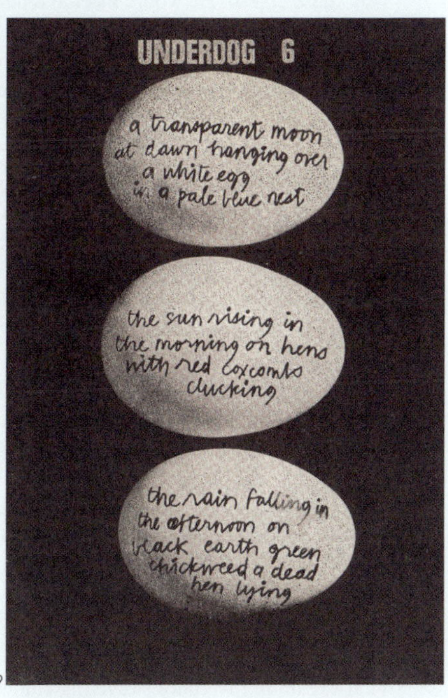

6
Edward Lucie-Smith, ed.
The Liverpool Scene
(Garden City, New York:
Doubleday & Co., 1968)

7
Edward Lucie-Smith, ed.
The Liverpool Scene
(London: Donald Carroll,
1967)

8
*Adrian Henri and
Allen Ginsberg, Holland
Park, London*, 1969
Collection of
Catherine Marcangeli

9
Brian Patten, ed.
Underdog, No. 6, 1965

10
Adrian Henri
Tonight at Noon
(London: Rapp & Whiting,
1968)

print as the Beat phalanx, for a period, surrounded the literary establishment.

By the early 1960s, the US, and by implication the wider world, was entering a period of tremorous drama. As the American Civil Rights movement battled for racial equality, the tensions between political blocs in the West and East intensified. First a 1962 diplomatic crisis saw Soviet attempts to site missiles on Cuba leaving President John F. Kennedy's finger hovering over the nuclear button. Then Kennedy's killing in Dallas in 1963 prefaced a new war in South East Asia that would set the capitalism of America against the Communist aspirations of North Vietnam the following year.

Against this extraordinary backdrop, Ginsberg became a dynamic link between the Beats of the fifties and the emerging hippies of the sixties. By 1964 Ginsberg, whose prescient messages of freedom and individualism, an anti-war manifesto underpinned by Eastern spirituality, chimed roundly with the *Zeitgeist*. He would meet and befriend Bob Dylan, then John Lennon and Paul McCartney – he was 'welcomed into their near regal circles'[3] – and an informal alliance of folk singer, rock group and Beat poet would take shape. In time, Ginsberg would perform and record with them all.[4]

In the weeks before Ginsberg came to Liverpool he had been briefly based in middle Europe, famously spending time in Czechoslovakia still, at this point, a satellite and puppet state of the Soviet regime. Here he was ritually crowned King of May by the students of Prague. But the authorities were less impressed, disturbed by Ginsberg's infectious notions of self-determination not to say his unconventional sexual mores, and he was expelled from the country.[5]

Ginsberg headed for London, in time to catch two nights of performance by Dylan at the Albert Hall on 9 May, meeting The Beatles in the singer's hotel suite after the first show.[6] Shortly afterwards the poet left London for a re-charging English odyssey, determined to celebrate his thirty-ninth birthday in the company again, he hoped, of The Beatles, back in the capital, on 3 June. His trip around the Midlands and North carried him to Lime Street Station at the start of the last week of May[7] where a figure representing another vital stream in Liverpool's reviving cultural life – poetry – would greet him. Brian Patten was the youngest member of a trio of poets who would later be gathered in *The Mersey Sound*, that much celebrated volume, published in 1967, in the Penguin Modern Poets series.[8]

On the day of Ginsberg's arrival in the city 'it was so cold that [Patten] lent him a multi-coloured jumper his grandmother had knitted him long before the coming of flowerpower' Bowen reports.[9] According to the same account, Patten had no room for the visitor to stay but he said in a 2006 interview that the visitor did reside in his flat for the first days of the trip. 'He stayed with me at 32 Canning Street in Toxteth, Liverpool 8, in an attic room I shared with a student called Tim Dawson. Allen would sit in the box room with a skylight, sing his Buddhist chants and say his Buddhist mantras. He was a bit of a showman. Tim and I were great fans but we were more fans of 'Howl' than all his chanting and bell-tinkling!'[10]

How had the Ginsberg visit to Liverpool come about? Patten explains the background: 'The American poet Robert, Bob, Creeley, had been up to Liverpool to do some readings. He enjoyed Liverpool and mentioned to Allen that the city had a great buzz. Bob had been published in the poetry magazine I was running, *Underdog*. In fact, we had published both Ginsberg and Creeley. Bob came to the city some months before; it may have been late 1964. He did two appearances – one at Sampson & Barlow's in a London Road cellar where I used to do readings and at the University. At the University, Creeley had maybe four or five people there; University people weren't interested – they were into the Movement poets. But at the other reading at Sampson & Barlow's, the place was buzzing and full of people'.[11]

Certainly Creeley's crowded reception augured well for Ginsberg's subsequent visit: there *was* an audience for US poets and poetry which remained, in Britain at least, at the *avant-garde* fringe. But Ginsberg's time in Liverpool appears to have been more of a social whirl than a performing occasion. He seems to have desired a taste of the sights and the sounds rather than a platform for himself and his poetry. He did, however, perform once during his six day stay, at 'Parry's Bookshop [...] next to the Philharmonic Hotel.'[12] But Patten recalls differently: 'Allen did a small reading in a bookshop called Wilson's at the bottom of Hardman Street, it was a kind of family run bookshop. It was a very crowded reading in a very small space with about 50 people packed in. It was not really well publicised but Allen was quite happy to do a little reading'.[13]

3 Warner (ed.), *Howl for Now*, p. 48.
4 Examples of these collaborations include: Ginsberg's recording sessions with Dylan in 1968, 1971 and 1981, compilation *Holy Soul Jelly Roll: Poems and Songs 1949-1993*; an informal musical gathering with John Lennon at the ex-Beatle's birthday party of 1971 and on-stage with Lennon in New York in 1972 (see Schumacher, *Dharma Lion*, pp. 556-57, 569); and Ginsberg's own collection *The Ballad of the Skeletons* (1996) which would involve contributions by Paul McCartney, on record and on stage.
5 Miles, Barry, *Ginsberg: A Biography*, London: Viking, 1990, pp. 362-68.
6 See Schumacher, *Dharma Lion*, pp. 445-46.
7 See Schumacher, Michael (ed.), Allen Ginsberg, Louis Ginsberg, *Family Business: Selected Letters Between a Father and a Son*, New York: Bloomsbury, 2001, p. 236. The precise days Allen Ginsberg spent in Liverpool are a matter of certain conjecture. But the poet did write to his father Louis on 1 June 1965 saying: 'I spent the last week in Liverpool where The Beatles come from', which helps to place the date of the trip with some accuracy.
8 Henri, Adrian, McGough, Roger and Patten, Brian, *The Mersey Sound* (Penguin Modern Poets 10), Harmondsworth: Penguin, 1982 (first published 1967).
9 Bowen, Phil, *A Gallery To Play To: The Story of the Mersey Poets*, Exeter: Stride Publications, 1999, p. 62.
10 Personal communication, 6 July 2006.
11 Personal communication, 6 July 2006.
12 Bowen, *A Gallery To Play To*, p. 63.
13 Personal communication, 6 July 2006.

tonight at
noon
ADRIAN HENRI

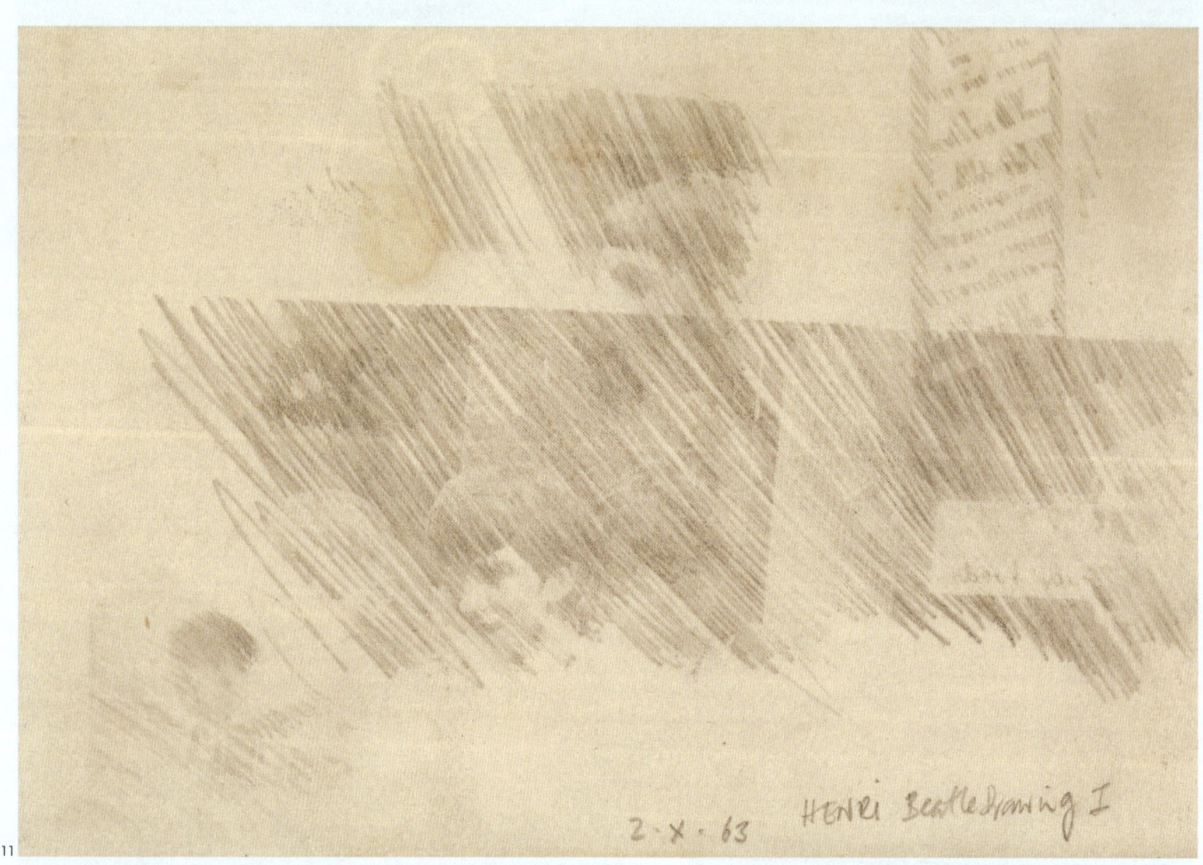

11

Adrian Henri
The Beatles Drawings 1963
Two from a set of three
drawings on paper
Each: 12.7 x 17.8 cm
The British Museum, London

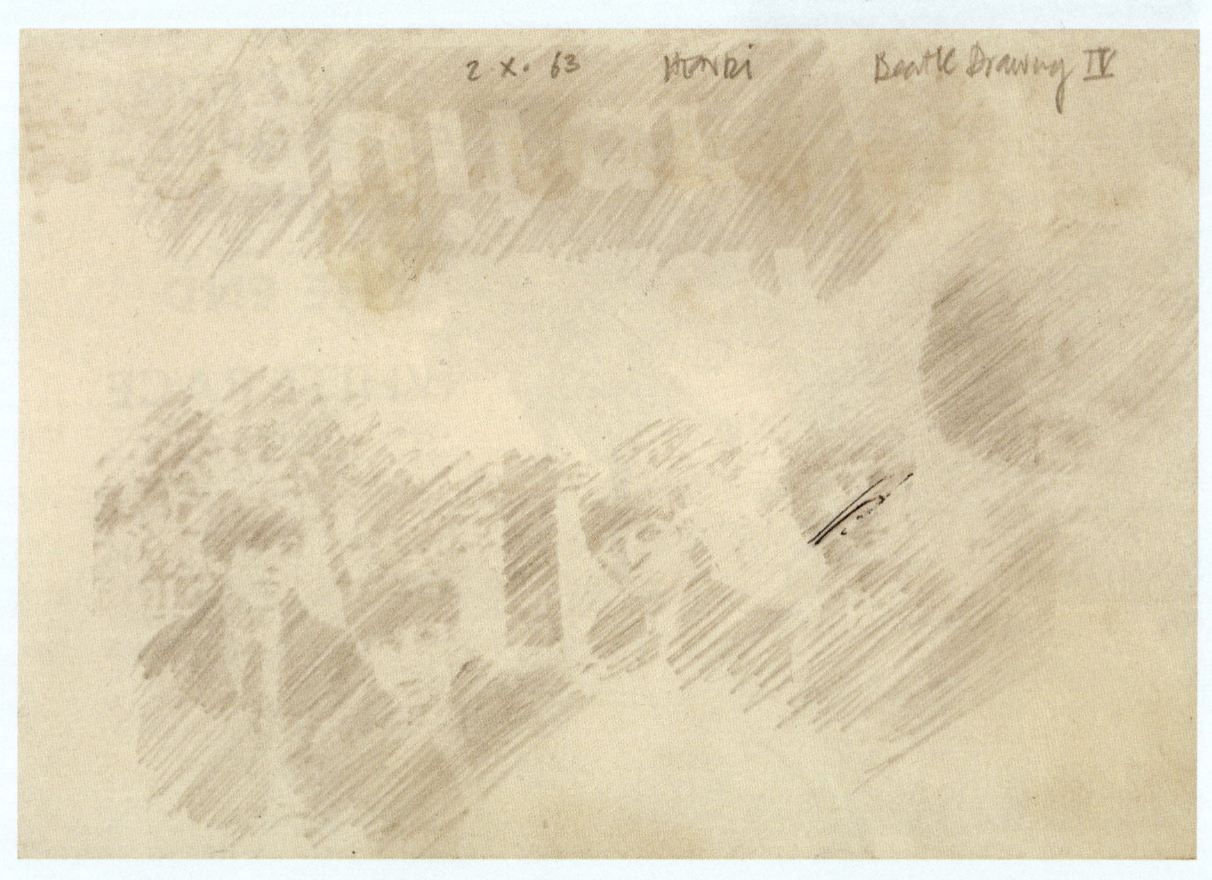

2. X. 63   Honri   Beatle Drawing IV

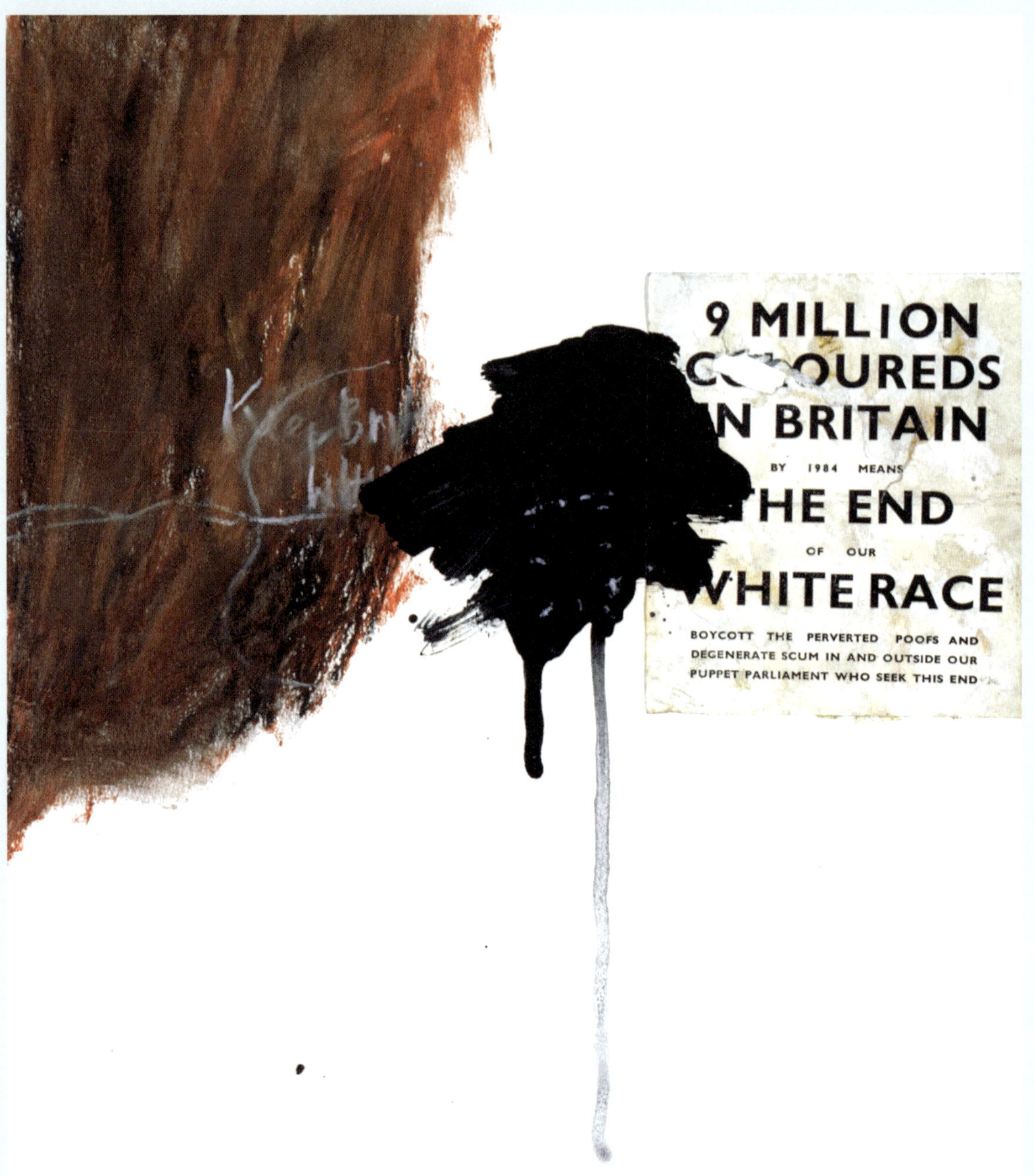

12

12
Adrian Henri
*Liverpool 8 Spring
Collage No 5 (for
P.G.W. and F.B.)* 1965
31.8 x 25.4 cm
Mixed media on board

Adrian Henri claimed that there had been some tension caused by the presence of the London-based Beat and jazz poet Michael Horovitz who 'totally monopolised proceedings'.[14] Horovitz responds to this accusation: 'Adrian clearly resented that I… should be there at all in his home turf and presumably somewhere he felt he might be more central, though "monopolising" was no part of my intention – for all that it may have looked like that to him and perhaps, via Adrian, to Allen'.[15] Horovitz's part in establishing links between the American Beats – like Ginsberg, Ferlinghetti, Corso, Burroughs, Creeley and others – and the UK throughout the early 1960s, via his publication *New Departures* and live readings, had been vital. Horovitz stresses that both he and fellow London poet Pete Brown had been engaged 'to provide substantial support performances' at Ginsberg's Liverpool reading. He feels that audience members would have been as familiar with his and Brown's work as with Ginsberg's.[16] But, despite these hints of discontent, Henri later enthused that the bookshop appearance 'had been one of the best poetry readings I've ever been to, certainly the best I've ever heard Allen do. It was a late spring evening, sunlight coming through the window, and he stayed cross-legged and just read and it was totally intimate and beautiful and it just flowed out, not even preaching, just talking to you, but talking like some sort of prophet'.[17]

Patten recalls a less meditative encounter, a more psychedelic one, during Ginsberg's Liverpool sojourn. 'I spent some time with Allen on acid,' he reveals. 'We both took a tab and spent hours and hours in the Walker Art Gallery walking around. We saw it in a new light, in fact many different lights'. What did he feel Ginsberg made of his time in the city? 'He loved the excitement of the city, full of boy bands, sweaty, tiny stages. It was paradise. He was drawn to the energy of Liverpool – there was youthful buzz in the clubs, we were hearing lots of music, lots of groups. We went drinking in the Phil and Ye Cracke,' the Philharmonic and Ye Cracke, both famous city hostelries. The visitor wrote to his lover Peter Orlovsky: 'I spent all week in Liverpool home of The Beatles and heard all the new rock bands and gave a little reading and had a ball with longhair boys – it's like San Francisco except the weather is greyer – lovely city, *mad* music, electronic hits your guts centres [*sic*]'.[18] But Patten, in his reveries with Ginsberg, recalls a human and humane figure rather than a poetic superstar. 'He was a genuinely accessible, nice man, friendly. Lots of people who were not interested in poetry found him quite fascinating, too'.[19]

After initially staying at Patten's tiny premises, Ginsberg transferred to the slightly more roomy surroundings of Henri's home at 64 Canning Street. 'It was more comfortable there,' comments Patten.[20] Ginsberg's new host was slightly anxious at what to expect. Bowen reveals that fellow Beats Ginsberg and Gregory Corso had previously stayed at the home of the celebrated Liverpudlian critic, writer and jazz

singer George Melly who had been 'appalled' when 'they behaved very badly'.[21] But Henri need not have feared. 'He duly arrived and was charming… the morning after we'd been to the Cavern… there was Allen washing the dishes and singing one of those Buddhist chants to himself. It really was an amazing revelation'.[22]

While Ginsberg was in Liverpool he was also taken to the city's Art College by poet-painter Henri, who taught there and would, some years on, win a major prize in the prestigious John Moores exhibition in 1972. They later visited a church in Everton in Albion Street and the incident prompted Henri's first poem of significance, 'Mrs Albion You've Got a Lovely Daughter', a piece that refers to William Blake, a seminal figure in the life of Ginsberg who believed he had seen the great English mystic in a vision in the late 1940s.[23] Henri later told interviewer Stephen Wade that 'Allen noticed this street called Albion Street; and of course he was entranced, because it was a Blakeian sort of sign'.[24] Ginsberg spent time in other places – drinking dens and rock haunts, most famously the Cavern, where the sexually voracious and uninhibitedly adventurous American was said to have had a liaison with a drummer he encountered.[25] 'He jammed with Trevor, drummer with Faron and the Flamingos', as the Liverpool émigré now Baltimore-based poet Christopher George says in his verse work 'Allen Ginsberg in Liverpool', a tribute on Henri's death in 2000 and published online four years later.[26] Henri said that the musicians thought Ginsberg was 'great'[27] and 'the feeling was mutual', Cook states in his book *The Beat Generation*.[28]

So, beer and verse, LSD and art, sex and music, enjoyed in the rarefied atmosphere of a Liverpool glowing in its associations with the world power who were The Beatles and a swelling poetry scene that had not only pre-dated the Merseybeat boom but, by 1965, was maturing into a movement that would soon test the thesis that the regional could not take on the metropolitan – something the Fab Four had already effectively challenged in the musical sense but one the city poets would challenge in matters literary. In many ways, as Ginsberg toured the city streets, these literary aspirations were

14 Bowen, *A Gallery To Play To*, p. 63.
15 Personal communication, 24 July 2006.
16 Personal communication, 29 July 2006.
17 Bowen, *A Gallery To Play To*, p. 6.
18 Miles, *Ginsberg*, p. 371.
19 Personal communication, 6 July 2006.
20 Personal communication, 6 July 2006.
21 Bowen, *A Gallery To Play To*, p. 62.
22 Ibid.
23 See Miles, *Ginsberg*, pp. 91-105.
24 Wade, Stephen (ed.), *Gladsongs and Gatherings: Poetry and its Social Context in Liverpool since the 1960s*, Liverpool: Liverpool University Press, 2001, p. 90.
25 Bowen, *A Gallery To Play To*, p. 63.
26 George, Christopher, 'Allen Ginsberg in Liverpool' (For Adrian Henri 1932-2000), poem at http://chrisgeorge.netpublish.net/Poems/AllenGinsberginLiverpool.htm originally published in *Electronic Acorn*, 16, September 2004
27 See Lucie-Smith, *The Liverpool Scene*, p. 17.
28 Cook, Bruce, *The Beat Generation*, New York: Charles Scribner's Sons, 1971, p. 154.

still to be made flesh – Lucie-Smith's book would be two years in the publishing, as would *The Mersey Sound* – so, in early summer 1965, this American guest, we might propose, was tasting the early juice of the harvest before it passed to the lips of the nation. What though of this iconoclastic statement, this resounding comment on the city being 'the centre of human consciousness'? Why did the great Beat bard intone a sentence of such dogmatic certainty, a summary which almost reeked of headline-seeking hyperbole? The comment has certainly been the subject of much conjecture since.

Bowen suggests in saying what he said 'Henri and others knew he was talking about The Beatles'.[29] The ubiquitous power of the group meant, for a long time and perhaps still in 2007, that the name of the city and the name of the band had become synonymous: to praise Liverpool was to praise the Fab Four. The world's gaze was so fixed on the most outrageously gifted songwriters, the most prolifically productive act of the era, that the consciousness of the people of Earth was plausibly, on that basis alone, centred on that location; to know of the group was to know what the world was listening to during that period. Jonah Raskin of Sonoma University, California, leading Ginsberg scholar who penned the 2004 'Howl' history *American Scream*, supports this analysis: 'I would say that it was The Beatles that brought the comment. And [Ginsberg] was in the habit of making grandiose and global statements and wanted to sound like a sage and an oracle, all at the same time. The Beatles did put Liverpool on the map of the world for most Americans – even hip Americans'.[30]

But there are other explanations, other interpretations. Melly in his much-praised account of the Sixties insurgence *Revolt Into Style* – a quote in itself from Thom Gunn on Elvis Presley – commented of Ginsberg's remark: 'A typical exaggeration, just the thing to set the middle-aged teeth on edge, and yet if you substitute "the young" for "the human universe" it was surprisingly accurate'.[31] Poet, critic and *Beat Scene* contributor Jim Burns admits that 'years ago I commented, probably a bit sourly, on Ginsberg's remark and was taken to task by George Dowden, his early bibliographer, who reckoned I'd taken him too seriously and the comment was only meant lightly, perhaps a little variation on Jung's statement about Liverpool being "the pool of life"'.[32] There are still more grounded, maybe cynical, takes on the Ginsberg description. Some have suggested – even Patten has hinted at it – that the visiting poet may have been liable to make such sweeping claims for other places he went to, as well. Poet Christopher George understands that Ginsberg may have made similar remarks on at least two other cities[33] – possibly about Milwaukee, maybe about Baltimore – unlikely candidates, it could be argued, in the pantheon of seminal, globe-shaping communities.

Then there are the earthier, sexual spins on Ginsberg's words, derived principally from the comments that proceed the first section of the quotation: 'They're resurrecting the human form divine there – and those beautiful youths with long, golden archangelic hair'[34], recalling St Augustine's reference to the Angles as angels when he visited England on a Christian conversion mission in the 6th century. Although we must assume the poet is making no direct allusion to The Beatles on this occasion, the long-haired fashion and implied androgyny, that was part of that new age, must have had an appeal to the sexual inclinations of the arriving Ginsberg. In *Bomb Culture*, Nuttall makes a connection in a different, broader context: 'American reporters thought that The Beatles were queer because of their hair-cuts'.[35] Maybe Ginsberg, at this point, shared the view of those members of the US media. He may have known, too, about Brian Epstein's submerged sexual preferences and the strong innuendo that he had been drawn to manage The Beatles, not because they were outstanding musically, but because he had found Lennon physically, compellingly attractive.[36] Steven Taylor, who teaches at the Beat-associated Naropa University in Boulder, Colorado, spent around 20 years as Ginsberg's guitar player up to the poet's death in 1997, hints strongly at the sexual sub-texts underpinning these matters. 'Ginsberg would have said Liverpool was the centre of consciousness or whatever because of The Beatles,' he states. 'He had a crush on them, just as he had on Dylan. Young men of obvious talent and massive fame. Al was what we call a star fucker. And he was right. Liverpool was a vortex of consciousness, on account of Lennon, for my money'.[37]

Michael Horovitz, a key catalyst of the period who would also help assemble the renowned Albert Hall poetry event a week and a half after Ginsberg's Mersey trip, brings his own first-hand insight to the poet's remark. 'It seems quite likely that Allen was asked for a quote by one or more of the bevy of media folk he attracted wherever he went, sometimes by his own design'. Horovitz adds: 'I suspect the geographical and relatively provincial aspects of parallelism between Merseyside/Lancashire (in relation to London), and the Bay Area/California – where Ginsberg hit his major-key voice and big-time stride – (in relation to New York City), seemed related to the delight he took in tracing trails and haunts of The Beatles *et al* while hanging out around Liverpool those May 1965 days and nights'. Horovitz also recalls the sexual charge the visiting American seemed to be experiencing in the city with such enormous and endearing relish. 'He had been drawn to Lennon in particular from way back, and swiftly

<hr>

29 Bowen, *A Gallery To Play To*, p. 67.
30 Personal communication, 5 July 2006.
31 Melly, George, *Revolt Into Style* Oxford: Oxford University Press, 1989 (first published 1970), p. 238.
32 Personal communication, 15 July 2006.
33 Personal communication, 6 and 7 July 2006.
34 Schumacher, *Dharma Lion*, p. 446.
35 Nuttall, Jeff, *Bomb Culture*, London: Paladin, 1970 (first published 1968), p. 229.
36 See Goldman, Albert, *The Lives of John Lennon*, London: Bantam Press, 1988, pp.139-142
37 Personal communication, 5 July 2006.

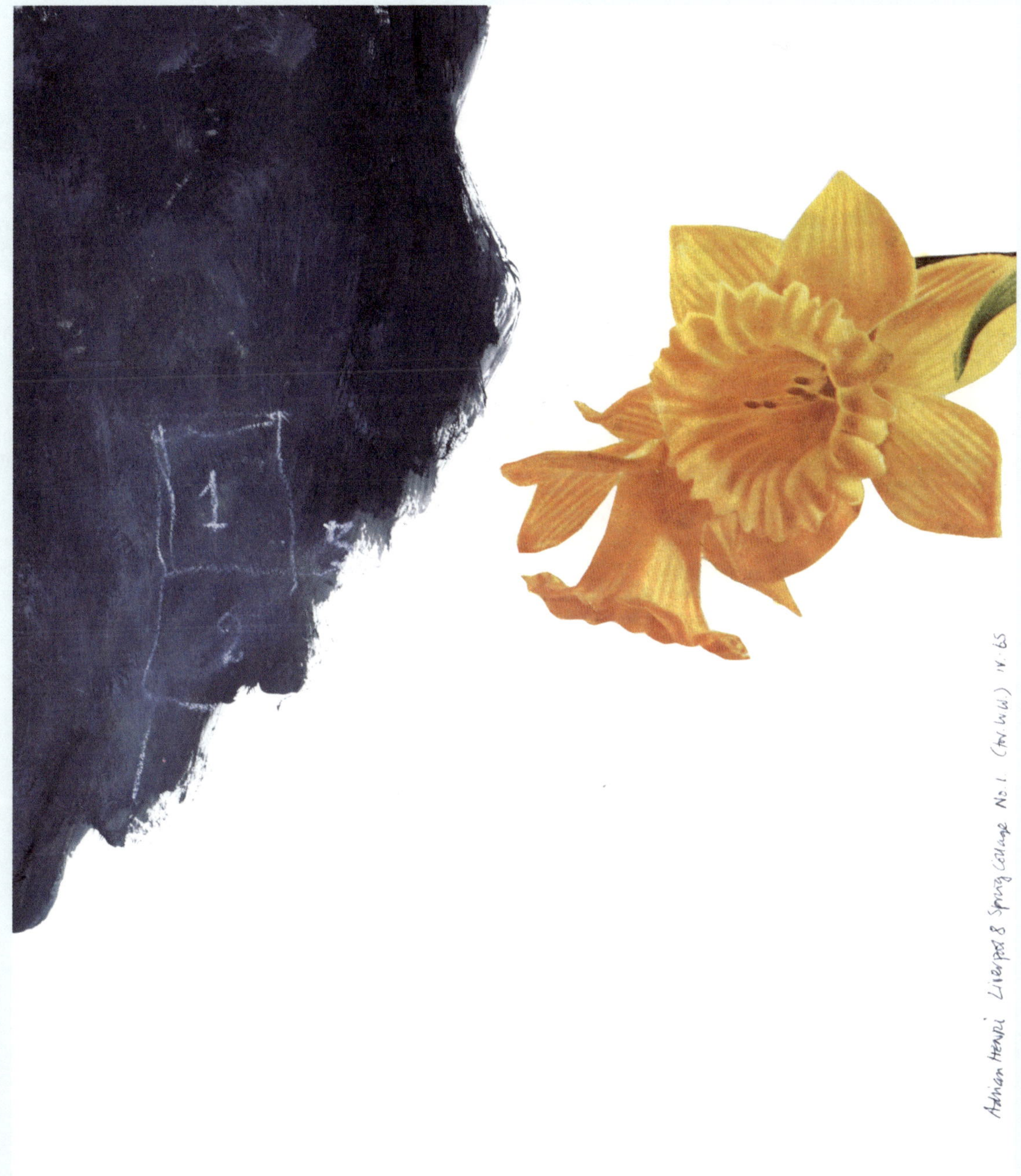

13

13
Adrian Henri
*Liverpool 8 Spring Collage
No 1 (For W.W.)* 1965
31.8 x 25.4 cm
Mixed media on board

came to fancy and adore Patten and various longhairs, musos, popsters, beatniks and dope-freaks who came his way via the Merseybeat/Liverbard wavebands, worldwide, so the city from where many of them sprang was bound to be a sort of Mecca'.[38]

Surviving Beat, Bay Area-based poet and musician David Meltzer, a friend and collaborator with Ginsberg over many years, suggests that the 'consciousness' quote may have had its roots, in part, in a volume of prose published that same year by the Black Mountain College poet Charles Olson. His *Human Universe and Other Essays* came out close to that time and Meltzer thinks that this fragment may have fed into Ginsberg's remark in an inter-textual way. Adds Meltzer: 'In 1965 Allen was still amazingly tone-deaf and rhythm-challenged but was always alert to the "new thing" – certainly The Beatles were and remain a one-of-a-kind revolution that will not be repeated. In a couple of years they advanced from a cover band to a banal song writing duo into something that changed forever pop music. I honestly don't know how "musical" Allen was. I remember playing behind him in Allendale, Michigan and realizing that, curiously, he didn't get it, he didn't swing, even though his desire was strong. Allen, McClure and Ferlinghetti were caught up in the fantasy of rock stardom. Yet Dylan told me early on that it was the poets who "had it" not the songwriters. The real movers were The Beatles who opened up the sizzle of a "scene" that the Liverpool Poets like Henri easily affiliated with'.[39]

Perhaps though, the final reflection should fall to Edward Lucie-Smith, a significant commentator and critic who was deeply influential in placing the poetry of the city in a wider context, lifting it from the parochial to a nationwide readership through his edited volume *The Liverpool Scene*. He believes that Ginsberg's comment arose on two counts: 'The rise of The Beatles, and the sense that Adrian Henri and the other Liverpool poets represented a commitment to Modernist, internationalist values missing from the British poetry being written elsewhere at that time. Philip Larkin and Kingsley Amis thought all that was rubbish and, of course, they much preferred jazz to rock. You've got to remember that Adrian was interested in popular culture, including rock, but also very much interested in the whole early Modernist culture represented not only by the Cubist Picasso, but also by Apollinaire, the Dada writers in Zurich and so on'.[40]. Ultimately, however, we might speculate that in the heady rush of rock music and popular verse immersing the city at the time, the consciousness most raised during visit to the shores of the Mersey in 1965 may well have belonged to Ginsberg himself.

38 Personal communication, 24 and 29 July, 7 August, 2006.
39 Personal communication, 9 July 2006.
40 Personal communication, 4 July 2006.

I am indebted to the letters, e-mails and conversations shared with me on this subject during July and August 2006. Thanks to Jim Burns, Royston Ellis, Christopher George, Michael Horovitz, Edward Lucie-Smith, David Meltzer, Brian Patten, Jonah Raskin, Steven Taylor and Mike Chapple (features writer, Liverpool Echo).

Discography
Ginsberg, Allen 1994 *Holy Soul Jelly Roll: Poems and Songs 1949-1943* (Rhino Wordbeat R2 71693)
Ginsberg, Allen 1996 *The Ballad of the Skeletons* (Mercury Records 697120101)

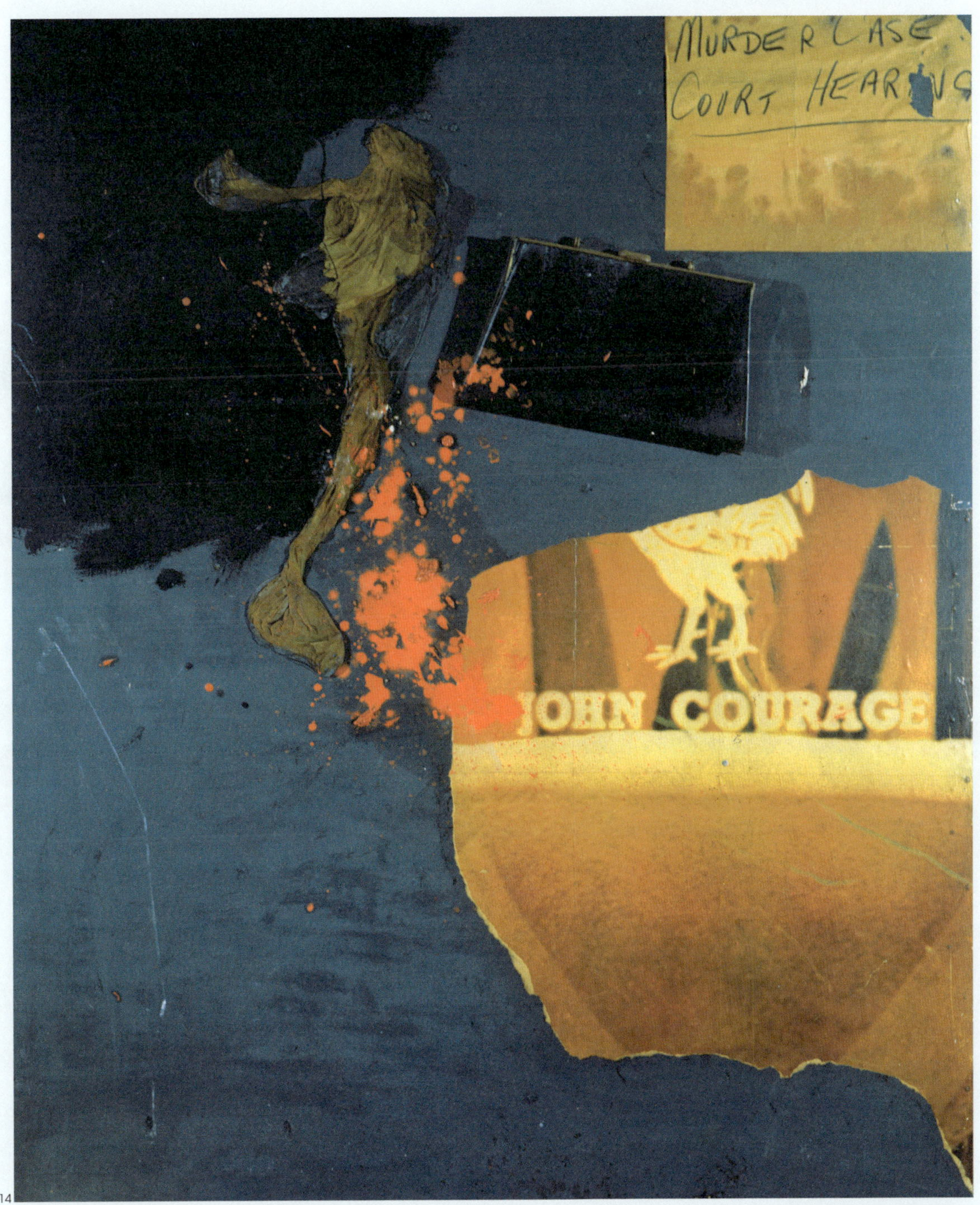

14
Adrian Henri
*Big Liverpool 8
Murder Painting* 1963
Mixed media on board
152.4 x 122 cm
Collection of
Catherine Marcangeli

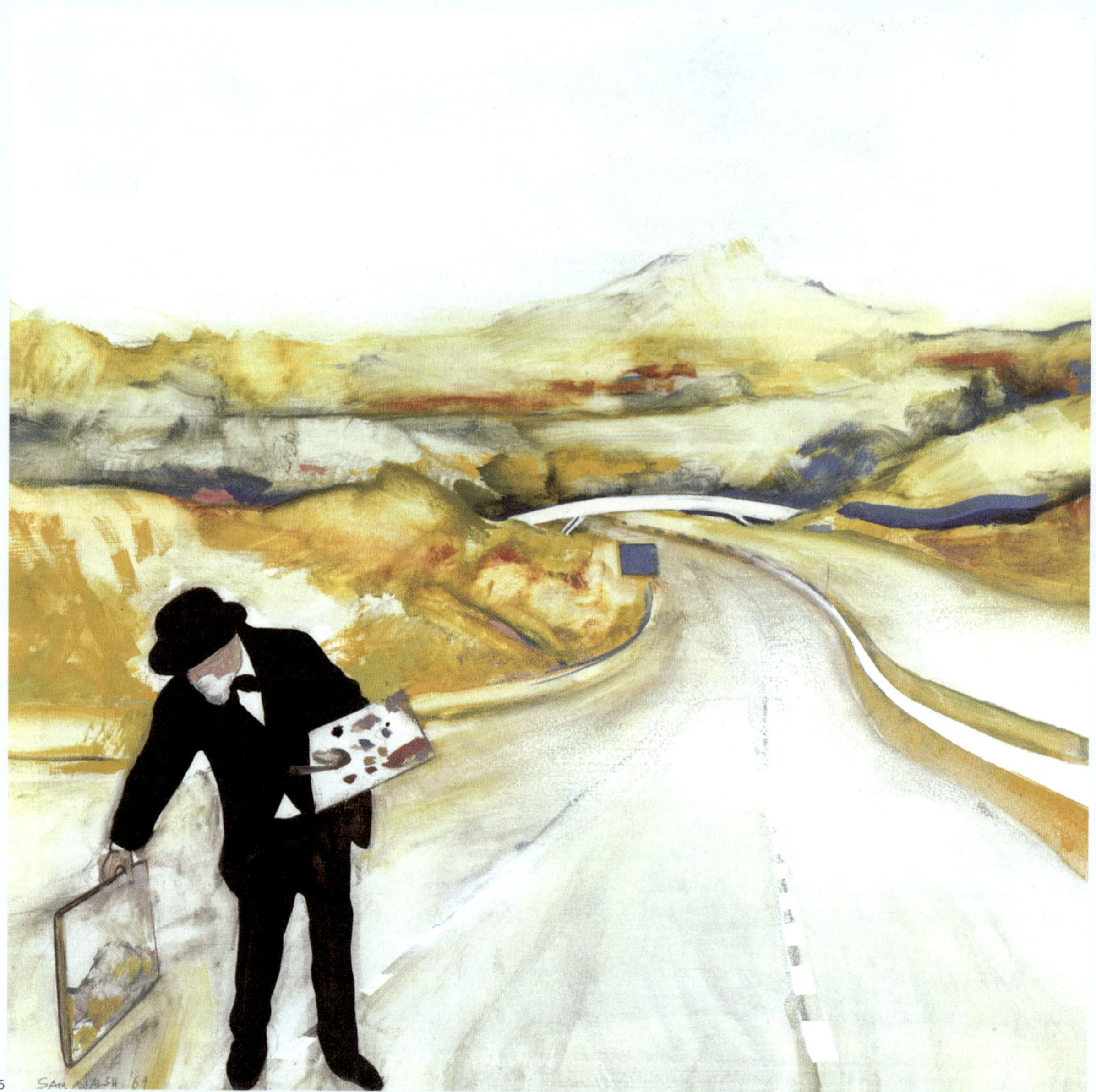

15

15
Sam Walsh
*M. Paul Cezanne
on the M6* 1969
Oil on board
61.5 x 61 cm
Collection of
Celia Van Mullem

16
Sam Walsh
*Three Figures in a
Warm Climate* 1965
Oil and plastic emulsion
on board
143 x 122 cm
National Museums Liverpool,
Walker Art Gallery

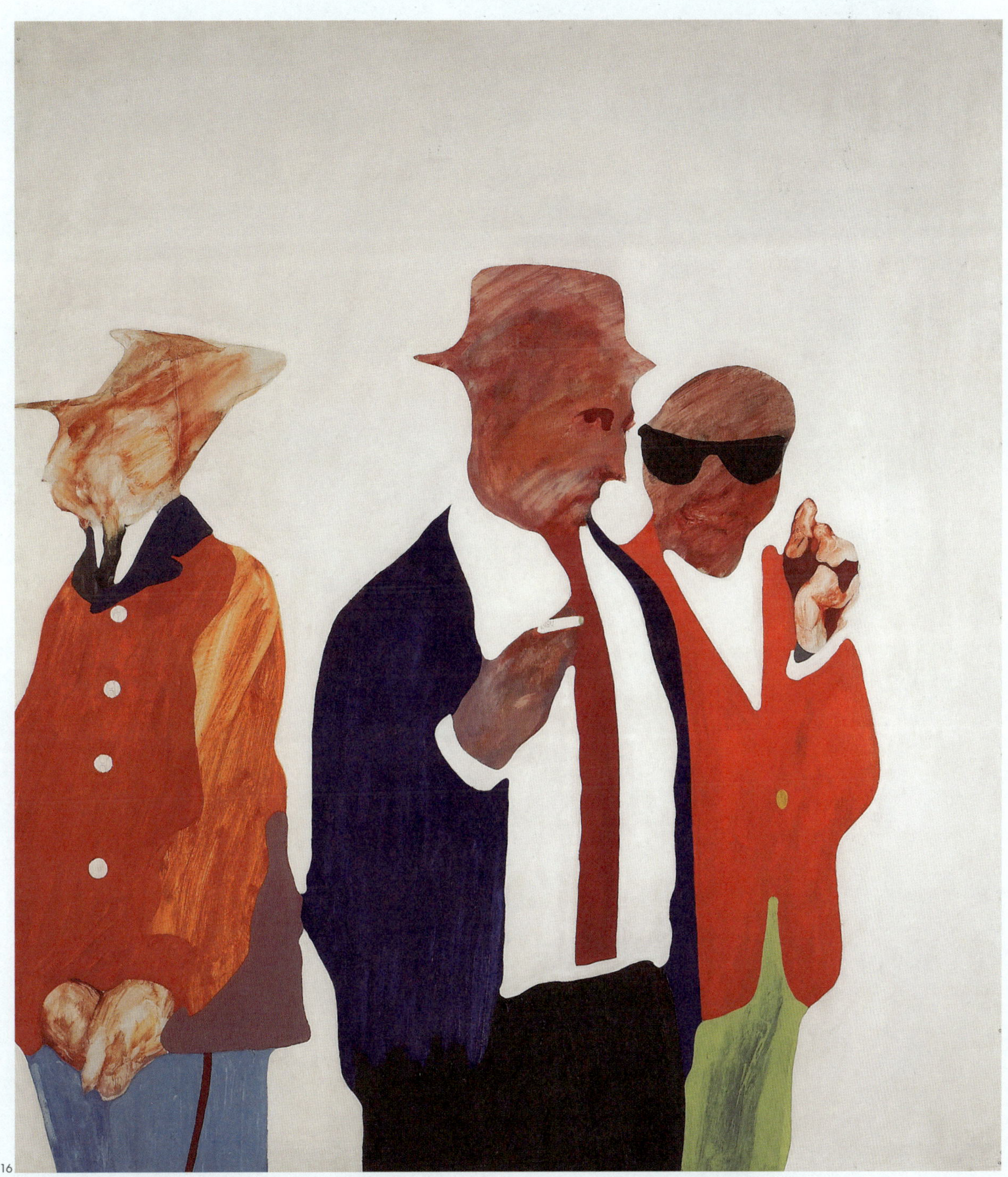

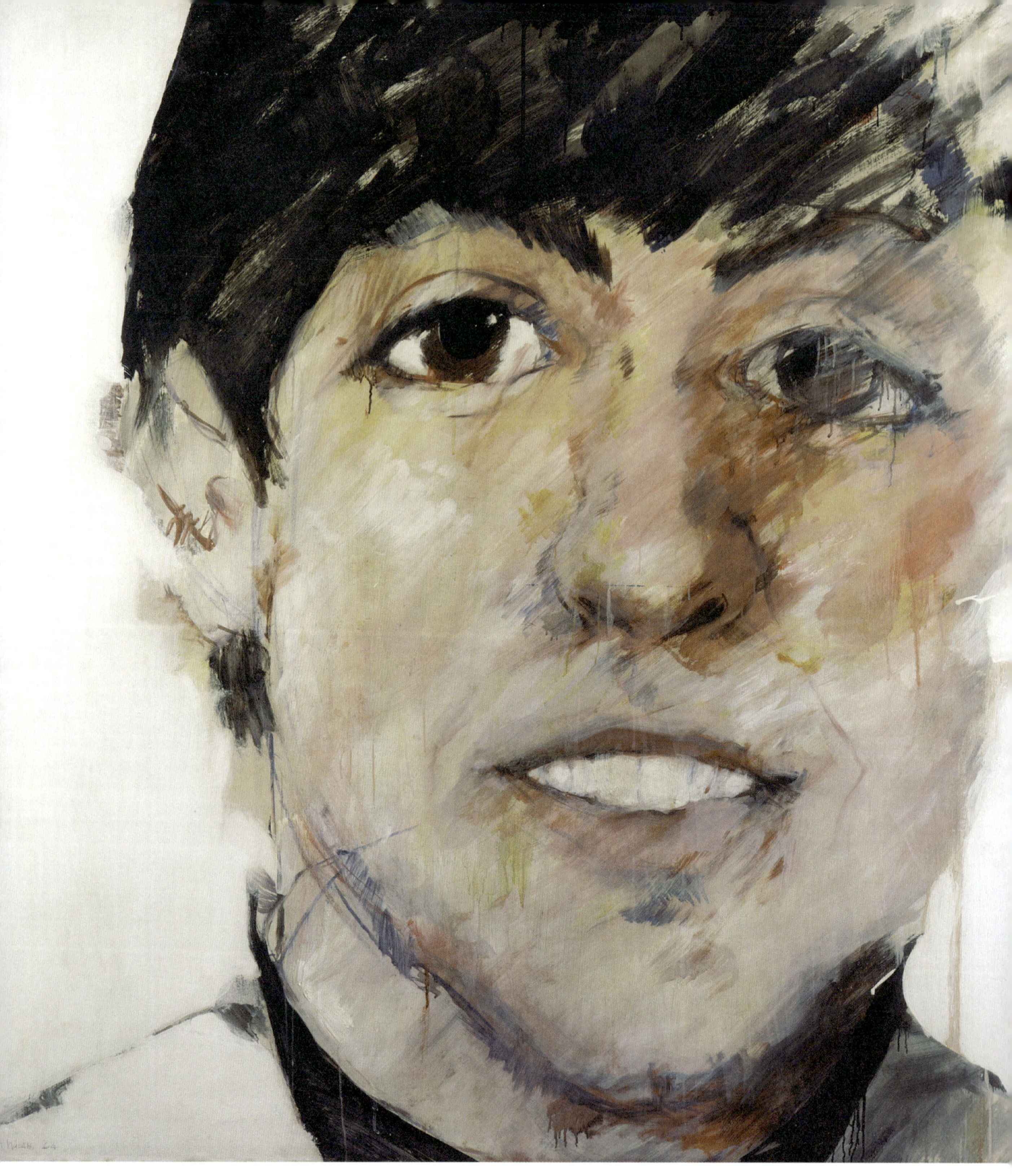

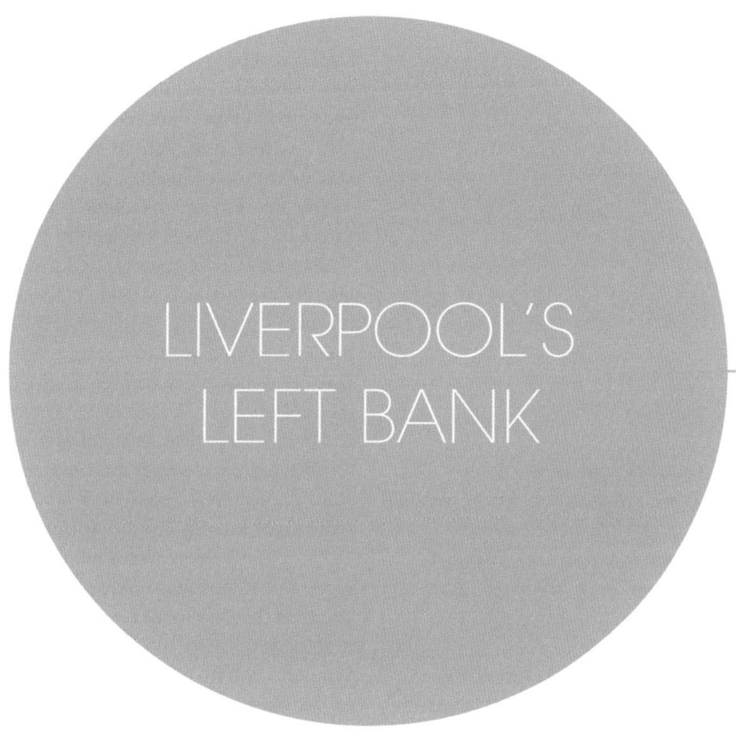

Darren Pih

Liverpool's Left Bank
Darren Pih

Liverpool 8… *A district of beautiful, fading, decaying Georgian terrace houses… Doric columns supporting peeling entablatures, dirty windows out of Vitruvius concealing families of happy Jamaicans, sullen out-of-work Irishmen, poets, queers, thieves, painters, university students, lovers…*
Adrian Henri, 'Liverpool 8', 1967[1]

In the 1960s, on a journey through Liverpool 8's Georgian streets from those nearest the city centre, where the handsome townhouses were well preserved, travelling outwards the landscape becomes increasingly scarred with un-cleared bombsites from World War II, before disappearing altogether in a sea of rubble. Against this backdrop, strung along Hope Street between the Anglican and Catholic Cathedrals, the College of Art and Sefton Park, there emerged a mythologised bohemian quarter whose reputation led to marked improvements in external perceptions of the city.[2] As Edward Lucie-Smith wrote, Liverpool and its 'mythology of the deprived, ramshackle and decrepit… had suddenly been given a place of honour in the drawing-rooms of the middle-class.'[3] In February 1967, this almost entirely self-sufficient artistic and intellectual community was the subject of a weeklong feature in the *Liverpool Daily Post* newspaper. It was described as the '…Left Bank of the North West… [here] the intelligentsia, beatnik, literati arty, tarty-arty, bohemian and dilettanti have come together to form their own inward looking society, with their own norms, uniforms, heroes, ambitions and vices.'[4]

The equating of provincial Liverpool with the symbolic centre and firmament of Parisian avant-gardism was not extravagant. Ascendant through the 1960s was the notion that wider intellectual debate could be affected by the bohemian quarter and communal intellectual activity. Just as in London's Notting Hill Gate, whose cheap rents and multiracial separation from English respectability made it a nexus of the hippy counterculture, there was a moment in the mid-1960s when a range of socioeconomic and cultural circumstances converged in Liverpool 8 to make it a fountainhead of literary and artistic endeavour. For Adrian Henri, a principal conduit of the avant-garde in post-War Liverpool, the area was bohemia akin to 'all the things I'd ever read about – Paris in the Twenties… full of artists, everybody goes to the pub, everybody knows one another…'[5]

Such observations were borne out in the *Liverpool Daily Post* feature, which described an atmosphere of fervent self-expression and vivacious social interaction. On Huskisson Street in Liverpool 8's epicentre lived Irish pop artist Sam Walsh, regarded as one of the most interesting painters in the city, declaring that he 'wouldn't live anywhere else in Liverpool… it's very stimulating.' Living nearby was Virginia Adams, pictured mini-skirted in a setting oozing mid-1960s bohemian chic, who moved to the area in order to be near her artistically inclined friends.[6] We are taken to bustling bars with 'Beards and birds everywhere, little cuties in moth-eaten fur coats ducked as pints are passed over their imitation Sassoon hairstyles… students, lecturers, musicians, actors… sculptors and artists [converge] looking for a Left Bank limelight…'[7]

The bohemian community that evolved around the Hope Street axis was unique. The *Liverpool Daily Post* declared that 'no other city in Britain has an area with such a high density of artistic and intellectual talent. Not even London, with its NW3.'[8] The following month the front page of the *Weekend Telegraph Magazine* announced a feature entitled 'The Sound of Liverpool 8.' Written by Birkenhead-born Sean Hignett and augmented by Don McCullin's photographs, it declared that the 'new Mersey Scene is ready to burst out; a scene that mixes local dialect, poetry, music, art and happenings.'[9] Hignett had earlier traded on the city's

1   Henri, Adrian, 'Liverpool 8', reproduced in Edward Lucie-Smith, *The Liverpool Scene*, London: Donald Carroll, 1967, p. 13.
2   Some sites regarded as being part of Liverpool 8 bohemia in the 1960's were outside of the L8 postal district. A number of key locations, such as Liverpool College of Art and Gambier Terrace are in L1. Streate's Coffee Bar was in L3. However, conceptually and mentally these places were central to the bohemian scene. As John Cornelius points out, 'Liverpool 8 was not so much a place as a state of mind'. See *Liverpool 8*, Liverpool: Liverpool University Press, 2001 (first published London: John Murray, 1982), preface.
3   Lucie-Smith, *The Liverpool Scene*, op. cit., pp. 5-6.
4   Neilson, Simon, 'Liverpool's Left Bank', *Liverpool Daily Post*, 6 February 1967, p. 5.
5   Cited in Bowen, Phil, *A Gallery to Play To: The Story of the Mersey Poets*, Exeter: Stride, 1999, p. 37.
6   Neilson, 'Liverpool's Left Bank', p. 5.
7   Neilson, Simon, 'Roger McGough: Poet', *Liverpool Daily Post*, Tuesday, 7 February 1967, p.10.
8   Neilson, 'Liverpool's Left Bank', p.5.
9   Hignett, Sean, 'The Sound of Liverpool 8', *Weekend Telegraph Magazine*, 31 March 1967, p. 12.

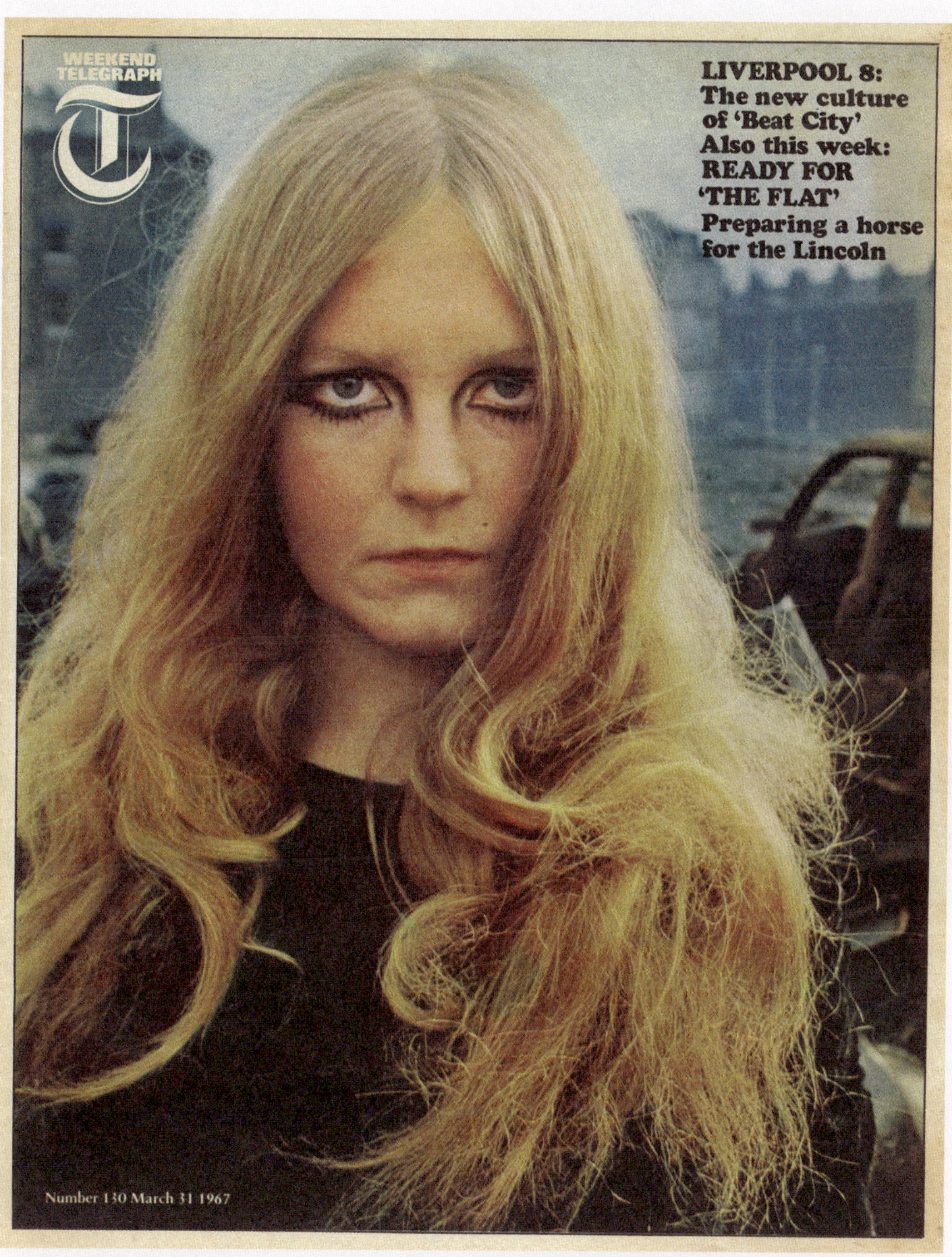

previous
Sam Walsh
Mike's Brother 1964
Oil on Masonite
162.5 x 155 cm
National Portrait Gallery,
London

2
'The Sound of L8'
Weekend Telegraph Magazine,
31 March 1967

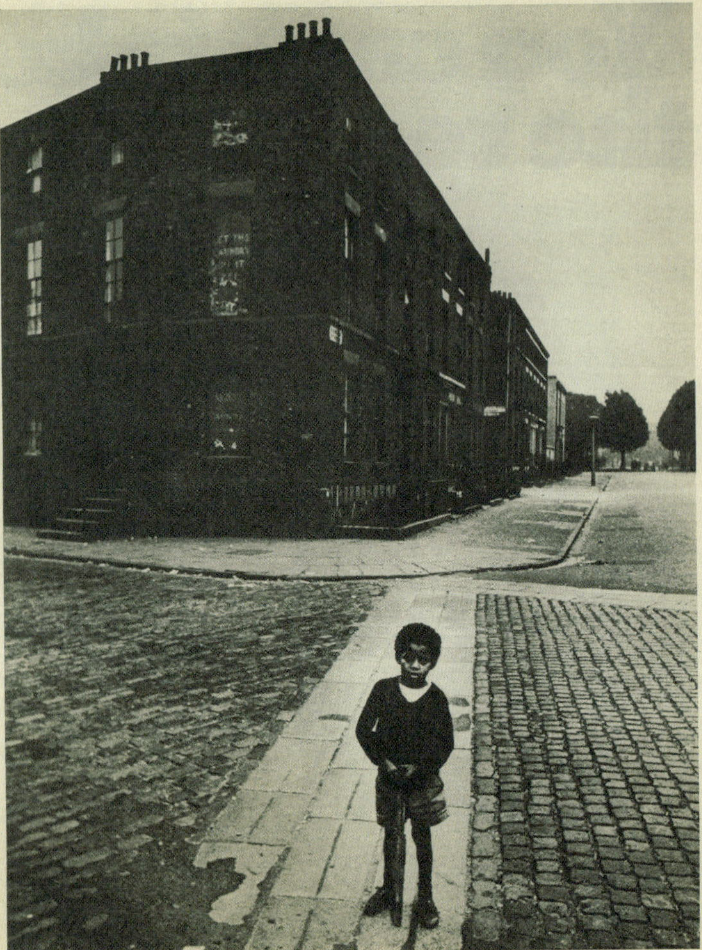

THE SOUND OF LIVERPOOL

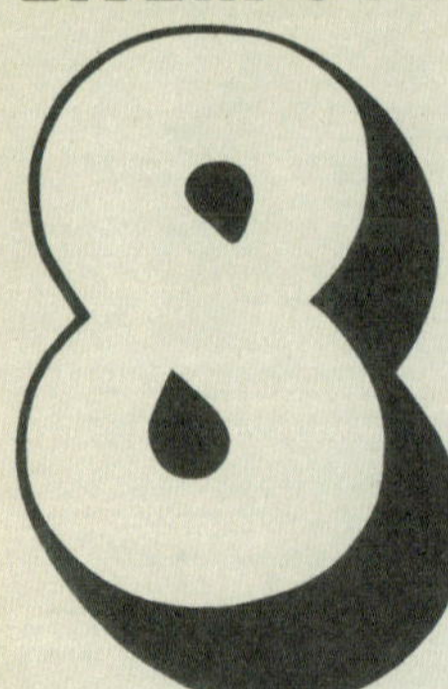

8

From a decrepit, decaying part of the Beatle City, a u
to burst out; a scene that mixes local dialect, poet
By SEAN HIGNETT.

One afternoon last summer the dolly girls in Bold Street, the smart shopping centre of Liverpool, had their eyes dragged from the minifurs in the shop windows by an extraordinary sight. Up the hill, on the steps of the blitz-blackened shell of St Luke's Church, a huge hardboard Ace of Spades was being hacked to pieces by a gang of beardies. Transparent plastic sausages, filled with multi-coloured liquids like the jars in a chemist's shop, were being pierced with darts by a litter of scruffy infants and a booming voice was declaiming across the heads of the attendant policewomen: "The daughters of Albion sleep in the dinnertime sunlight with old men looking up their skirts in St John's Gardens."

What was happening was a "happening" or, in Liverpool terminology, an "event", sponsored jointly by a local store owner and a black bearded, bespectacled, roly-poly poet, Adrian Henri. The "event" was one of several conducted in an attempt to bring an underground art into the open and bring Liverpool 8 down the hill and into the town.

Liverpool 8 postal district touches the city at the top of Bold Street. Behind St Luke's begins its grid of wide-open Georgian streets, where flaking stuccoed terrace houses stand silently in the light of gas lamps. Reasonably well preserved at the city end, where some of the houses are stone built and reminiscent of Edinburgh's New Town, the area decays rapidly after the first hundred yards and then, pock-marked by the demolition sites that have been added to the bomb sites of two decades ago, disappears altogether in a sea of rubble.

The first thing to strike one is the absence of cars, even where, in little islands, the multi-tenanted, multi-racial houses still stand. And then, as everywhere in Liverpool, the abundance of children: scrambling over the bomb sites, warming their hands round the watchman's huts on the demolition sites and playing in the wide streets themselves, where, with no threatening cars, they can kick a ball or make-believe with a battered pram or a wheelless bicycle. Stand still here and you will be asked for a penny, a sweet, have a ball thrown

[at you, be / dirty faces / be asked / biggest, bes / the Green / be covered / in birds.]

[At night / is gathered / attended b / baking pota / whole area / that cast lo / the gas lam / have, in ma / doors at all / with cardb / nations sits / slogans suc / four feet hig]

[People / musical jo / Scouse pub / actually gr / *Supplement.* / for a gen / architect / architecture / sensitive p / like Bill / festival tha / Cathedral, / 8 the only / Liverpo / and in / most fr]

[Half / Street / top of / poets a / nerve c / and goi / for Liv]

Poetic happenings

The wide-open plain of Canning Street (left)
is the main artery of Liverpool's District 8.
Half-way up the street, in a house teeming with
artists, musicians and poets, lives Adrian Henri
(right) prime propagandist for the new Mersey Scene.
Henri is a poet, "happening" organiser, painter
and lecturer at the Liverpool College of Art.
The nearest thing to a formulation of a Liverpool
attitude in painting came when in 1962 he held an
exhibition of paintings with Sam Walsh at the Hope
Hall, now the Everyman Theatre. They issued a
joint manifesto:
We would rather paint like Cannonball Adderley
than Picasso.
We would rather paint like Charley Mingus than
either.
We oppose megaton bombardments with Persil
packets, dead birds and strange apparitions with
fixed painted smiles.
We would like children to find our paintings at the
bottom of cornflakes packets.
If Frankenstein's monster didn't exist, it would be
necessary to invent him.
Henri's ambition is to have a semi-permanent
literary/beat music road show.

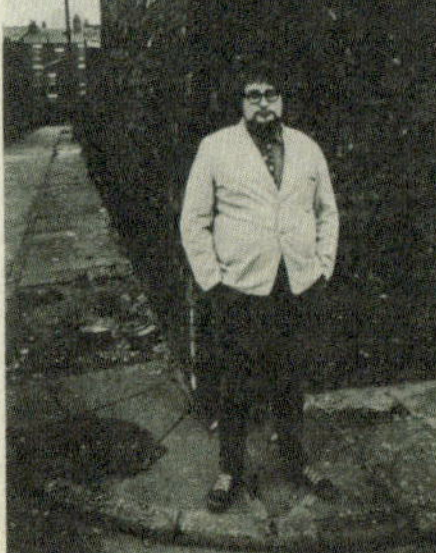

Albion's
the Mer
dangling

The dau
arriving
eating h
writing
Street
taking o
putting

The dau
see the r
Bebingt
throw at
goodnig
comb th
powder
will be t
their bo
lavende

The dau
wonderi

3
'The Sound of L8'
Weekend Telegraph Magazine,
31 March 1967

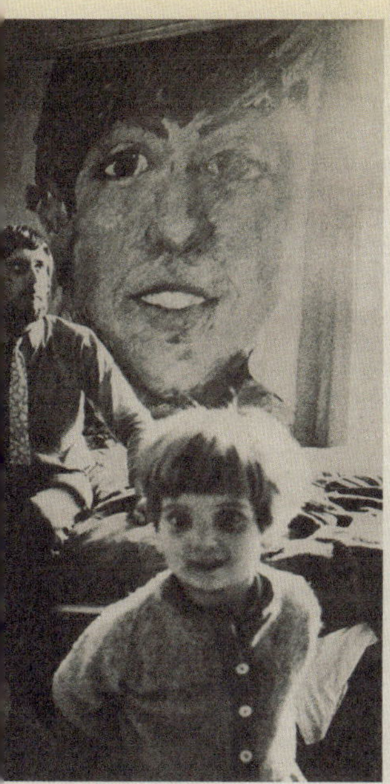

rishman, came
ears ago and
teaches at the
an attic pad in
ietly building a
lown the
ently bought
alker Art
the 5ft 6in
ontender for
ne of the
Francis Bacon,
al of

he third
n. "They're
with plastic
from us, like
t they have

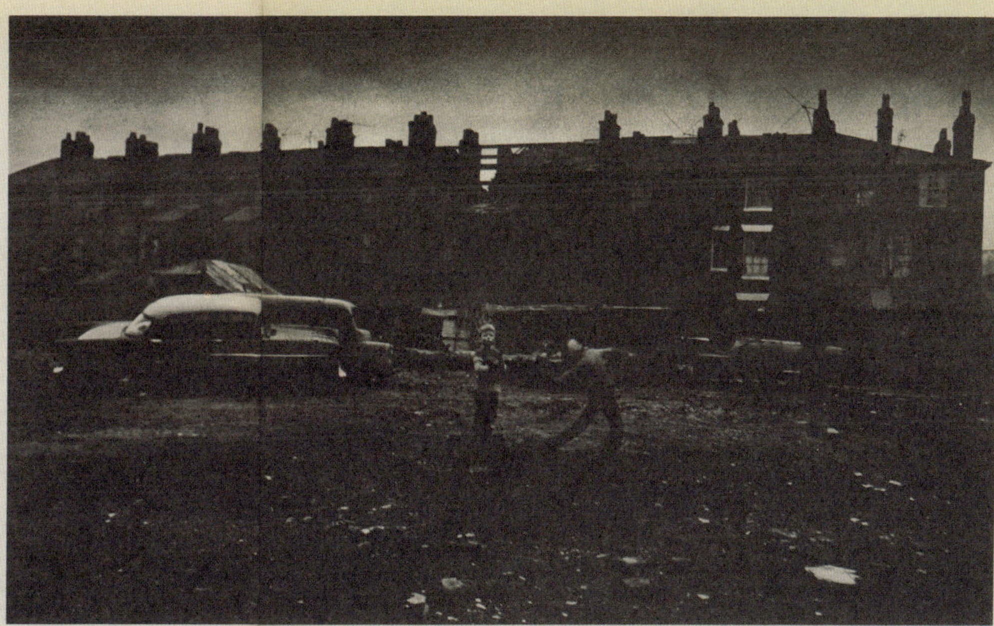

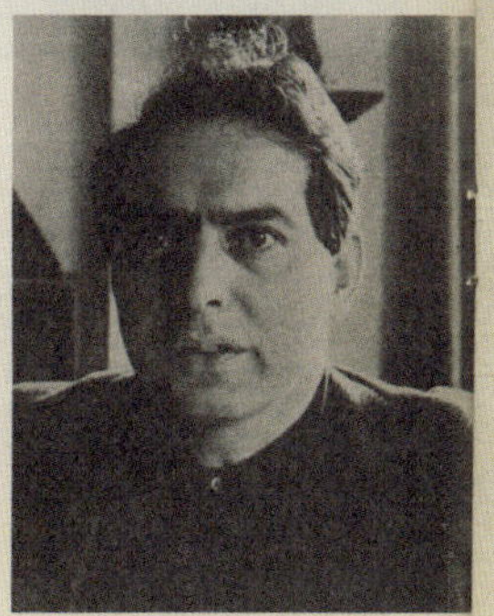

"Z-Cars" and satire

Fritz Spiegl sips sherry in the garden of his Regency house backing on to Princes Park lake, the hollyhocks and roses popping about him. The only sign of the Liverpool 8 that surrounds the house is the top of a Martian-like block of council flats that will soon fringe the park.
"We're all right now. They put a preservation order on us last week." Spiegl's whole energies are dedicated to preserving—anything and everything, from Liverpool street tunes and dialect to Napoleonic trumpet machines. And the house seems to be full of them.
He was born in Vienna in 1927 and his family came to England in 1939. They went back, but Fritz stayed. Principal flautist with the Royal Liverpool Philharmonic Orchestra for 15 years, he has a 20-year reputation for the sort of musical goonery that Hoffnung took up—this week will see his 17th "April Fool's Concert" with a do-it-yourself programme kit containing pencil, instrument and full blowing instructions.
Spiegl and his wife Bridget were responsible for taking the "Z-Cars" tune off the Liverpool streets and on to the hit parade, perversely giving it a wider circulation back on those same streets, and initiating Merseyside's invasion of the pop world. At the same time, Spiegl joined the satire league, running the newspaper mistakes column in *Private Eye* and last year producing a collection of these called *What the Papers Didn't Mean to Say*, that has run into eight editions and is still printing. His latest fry-up, *Lern Yerself Scouse*, a joky teach-yourself phrasebook of Liverpool dialect, was taken so seriously by *The Times Literary Supplement* that they ran a leader on it. Spiegl, reluctantly impressed with the gravity of his joke, is now printing "a real dictionary of Scouse" on the press he's installed in the basement.

In Canning Street—a Batmobile

It is difficult to avoid becoming involved with children in Liverpool 8. A young boy detaches himself from the football game in mid-road at the top of Canning Street, behind him an upturned car and a derelict site. His mates play on, a couple of half house-bricks marking the goal. "Eh, mister, is that a camera? Are you from the telly? Are you going to take a picture of us, too?" They spend little of their time indoors. Inside the falling-down houses, sometimes crammed a family to a room with a shared cooker on each landing, they will eat, sleep and glean enough from the telly to furnish their games with new characters, but the street is their football pitch, the derelict ground their campsite and the wrecked car their Batmobile. Even the football becomes a game of the imagination— last summer all the fights were over who was to be Eusebio. Now the Everton-Liverpool Cup Tie is being re-fought on every corner.

Photographs by DON McCULLIN

bohemian reputation in his novel *A Picture to Hang on the Wall*.[10] Though fictional, the book was populated by characters based on Liverpool artists and gives an indication of the city's position within the British popular psyche at this time. Littered with Liverpudlian slang, it follows the exploits of Keegan who swaggers down streets paved with beer to art-school parties where the city's youth mingle promiscuously. The men chat-up the 'birds' over a Beatles soundtrack. Conversation is catalysed by Bob Dylan lyrics. In a moment of fictional revelry, heightened by sexual chemistry and the grandiloquent swagger of youth, we see how Liverpool might have been regarded as 'the centre of the consciousness of the human universe.' Ginsberg's impression of the city, sparked by revelation, was doubtless ignited by the raw energy and creativity of its youth culture.

There were a number of aspects that contributed to the evolution of the Liverpool 8 scene. Predominantly working class and multi-racial, the area was home to a number of illicit drinking establishments and offered a 'sexy, disreputable atmosphere you did not encounter in ordinary Liverpool.'[11] Its reputation for non-conformity attracted young rootless artists and intellectuals seeking escape from the boredom of suburbia. Furthermore, its Georgian houses were large enough for co-habiting and provided cheap rented accommodation. Many flats became communal homes for poets, artists and musicians. Adrian Henri's flat at 64 Canning Street, described by Roger McGough as a 'cultural revelation', was where Ginsberg stayed when he visited Liverpool in 1965.[12] The cross-fertilisation of ideas within the scene was immense. Poet Brian Patten states: 'You could wander into other people's houses and get very excited about the work you saw – showing it and sharing it… people didn't live very far from each other, so there [was] a lot of interaction, between the artists and the poets.'[13]

Crucially, students and teachers lived near to the thriving Liverpool College of Art, described in John Cornelius' idiosyncratic ode to Liverpool 8 as being the 'shrine of culture… *the* place to be at that time… for Liverpudlians with leanings in the direction of art and the high life…'[14] It was headed by the charismatic Arthur Ballard whose students had included John Lennon and Stuart Sutcliffe. The importance of British art schools as the laboratory of 1960s pop culture cannot be overestimated.[15] Their relaxed entry requirements and liberal curriculum attracted creative individuals from all social backgrounds, making them 'the refuge of the bright but unacademic, the talented, the non-conformist…'[16]

The city's art scene was further galvanised by The John Moores Painting Prize, which was launched in 1957 and staged bi-annually at the Walker Art Gallery. The jury-selected exhibition quickly gained an international reputation. Liverpool-based artists were included nineteen times between 1957 and 1965. The presentation of their works alongside those by more established names such as Peter Blake and David Hockney injected a degree of vitality and competition into Liverpool's art scene. Hugh Scrutton, then Director of the Walker, was instrumental in selecting local artists. During his tenure, which lasted from 1952 to 1972, he further supported Liverpool artists by purchasing their work for the gallery's collection.

Without doubt the most important influence that contributed to the evolution of the Liverpool 8 scene was Beat culture. The city occupies an acknowledged position in the evolution of British Beat, whose sensibility reached UK shores 'through the freewheeling vernacular verse of the Liverpool poets.'[17] It was after the Beaulieu Jazz Festival of 1960 that the seeds of the Liverpool 8 scene were sown. After the festival poets Johnny Byrne and Spike Hawkins were assigned to spread the word of Beat in the North.[18] They were based in Liverpool at the time and returned there to set up regular poetry and jazz nights at Streate's Coffee Bar, 51 Mount Pleasant. Located in a candle-lit whitewashed basement, Streate's exuded a distinctly Left Bank flavour. Publicity material for the events promised: *… Exotic Atmosphere. High Adventure… Technicolor. 3-D. See the writings on the ceiling. Poetry. Folk Music… Unforgettable excitement in the heart of Liverpool.*[19]

It was at Streate's that Adrian Henri met not only Byrne and Hawkins, but also Roger McGough, to whom he was introduced by Pete Brown in December 1960. Brian Patten gave his first reading at the venue on 2 November 1961, within a week he too was in contact with Henri and McGough.[20] As such, Streate's was crucial in bringing together the figures that in 1967 were canonised as 'The Liverpool Poets'.[21] The success of the venue led to the establishment of regular poetry, jazz and folk nights at venues across Liverpool, all contributing to

10 Hignett, Sean, *A Picture to Hang on the Wall*, London: Michael Joseph, 1966.

11 Du Noyer, Paul, *Liverpool: Wondrous Place – Music from Cavern to Cream*, London: Virgin, 2004, p. 99.

12 Roger McGough describes Henri's flat as being a 'cultural revelation with its polished bare floorboards and white walls covered with his paintings. No instant coffee… but coffee beans that Adrian would polish and then grind ceremoniously, singing along to Cannonball Adderley…' In *Said and Done: The Autobiography*, London: Random House, 2005, p. 131.

13 Wade, Stephen, 'An Interview with Brian Patten', in Wade, Stephen (ed.), *Gladsongs and Gatherings: Poetry and its Social Context in Liverpool since the 1960s*, Liverpool: Liverpool University Press, 2001, p. 104.

14 Cornelius, *Liverpool 8*, p. 33.

15 The post-War economic imperative to train more scientists and engineers by widening access to higher education resulted in large increases in numbers of arts rather than the science students. Pearce Marchbank likens art schools to 'laboratories… producing musicians and designers and painters.' In Green, Jonathon, *Days in the Life: Voices from the English Underground, 1961-71*, London: Minerva, 1989, pp. 32-33.

16 See Melly, George, *Revolt into Style: The Pop Arts in Britain*, London: Penguin, 1970, p. 131. See also Sandbrook, Dominic, *Never Had It So Good: A History of Britain from Suez to The Beatles*, London: Little, Brown, 2005, pp. 402-03.

17 McDonald, Ian, *Revolution in the Head: The Beatles' Records and the Sixties*, London: Pimlico, 1995, p. 6. Also of importance are under-acknowledged figures such as the American poet Royston Ellis, the self-styled 'king of the beatniks', who briefly visited Liverpool in 1960 to read poetry at the Jacaranda Club on Slater Street, then managed by Beatles' manager Allan Williams. Ellis allegedly introduced the Beat mentality to John Lennon and Stuart Sutcliffe whilst staying at their Gambier Terrace flat, convincing Lennon to leave art school, and the band to change their name from The Silver Beetles to The Beatles to emphasise the 'Beat' influence.

18 Green, Jonathon, *All Dressed Up: The Sixties and the Counterculture*, London: Jonathan Cape, 1998, pp. 130-31.

19 Programme for 'Jazz to Poetry Concert', Crane Theatre, Liverpool, 31 January 1961, unpaginated, University of Liverpool Special Collections, Mersey Poets, Henri/I.1.5.

20 Bateman, David, 'Adrian Henri: Singer of Meat and Flowers', in Wade (ed.), *Gladsongs and Gatherings*, p. 76.

21 In 1967 an anthology of Patten, Henri, and McGough's poetry was published as *The Mersey Sound*, the tenth book in Penguin's Modern Poets Series.

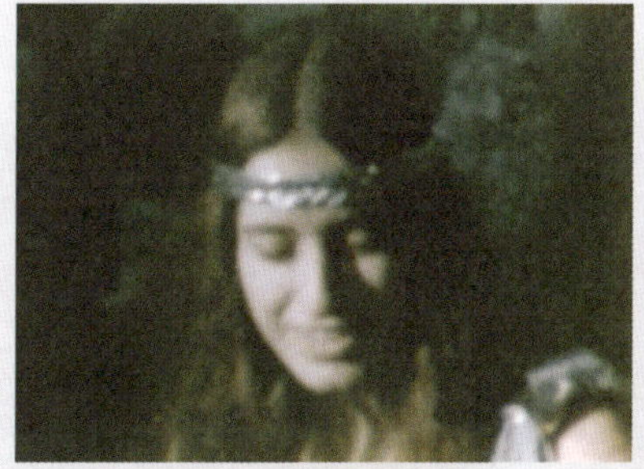
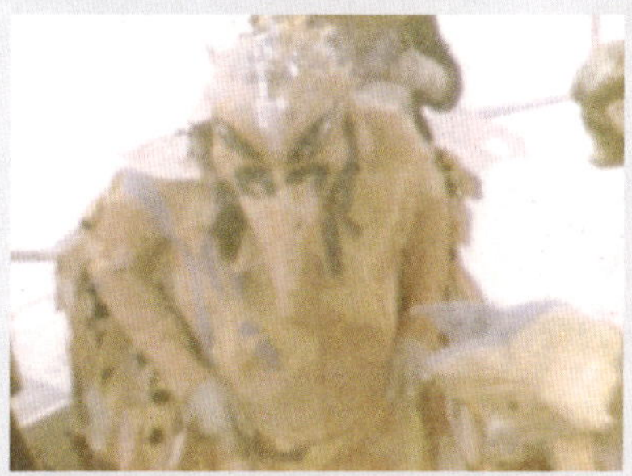
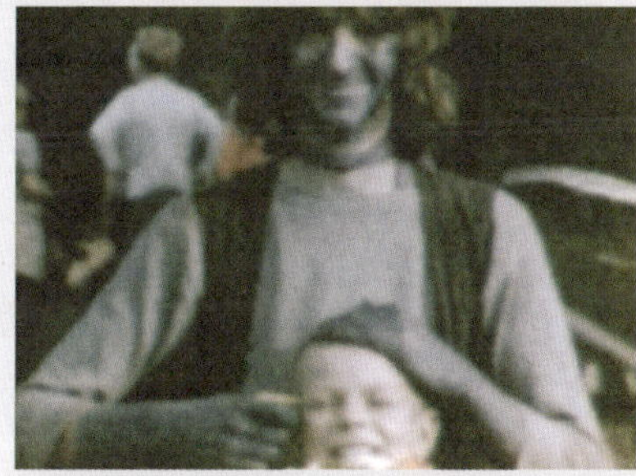
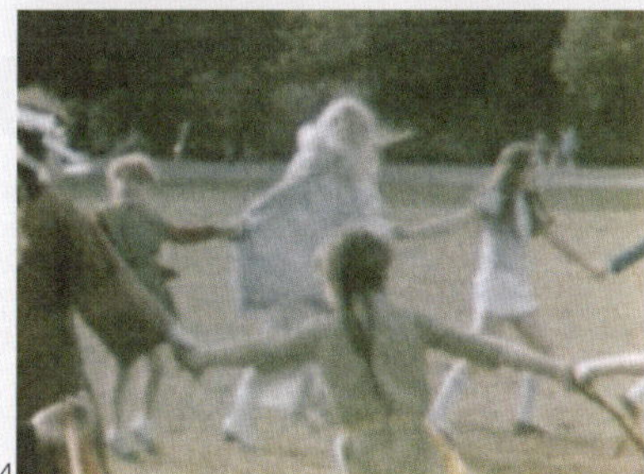

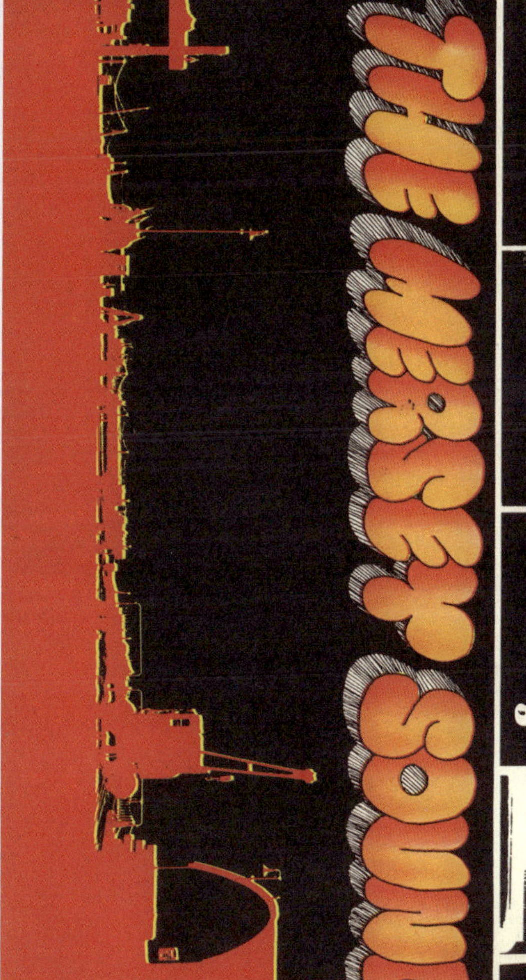

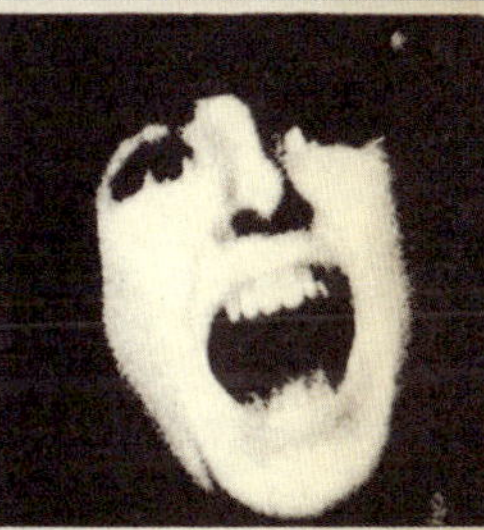
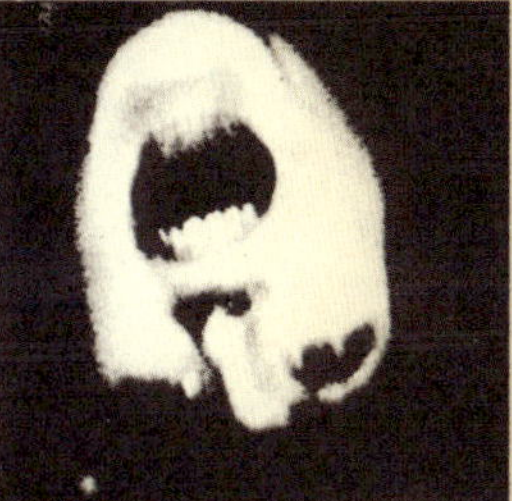
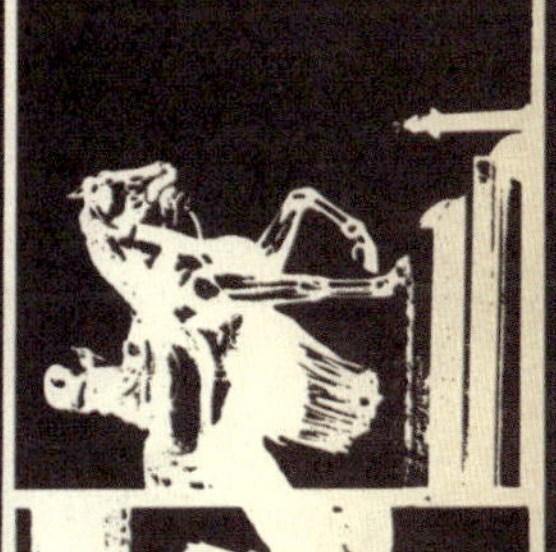
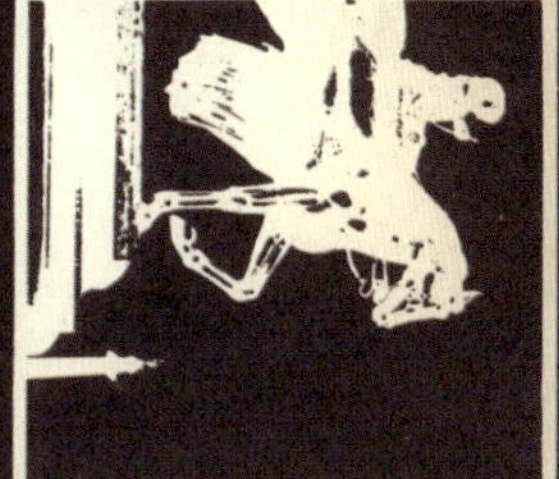

4
The Blackie – Great
Georges Community
Cultural Project
Magic in the Parks 1970
Courtesy of James
MacRitchie, Boulder,
Colorado

5
Roger McGough,
Adrian Henri,
and Brian Patten
The Mersey Sound,
Harmondsworth: Penguin
(Penguin Modern Poets 10)
1967

6

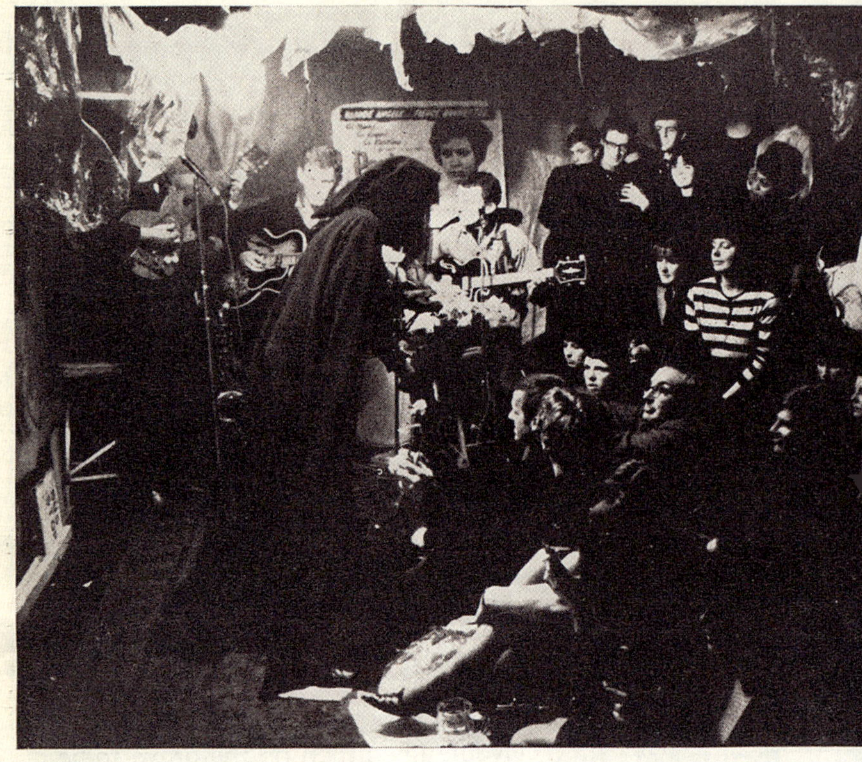

Hope Hall, Liverpool, '63.   Death Girl giving out dead flower   [see No. 8 opposite]

2: ADRIAI

" 'I want to paint' is a semi
position on the relationship o
the mass media. A sort of m
sometimes improvise on whe
experiments in communica
notes for small experiments
limited scale which are, of co
in performance. The exper
sort of mixture of painting
smells, words, etc., creating a
is carrying the technique of
clusion. I see no reason why
one medium; on the contra
part of an open continuum.
The Waste Land, a Michelar
record are all basically invol
—communication.''

16

DAFFODIL STORY
AN EXPERIMENT IN COMMUNICATION

1. Record "Along Came Jones" (The Coasters).
After 1st chorus enter Salty Sam with Sweet Sue. Struggle. Enter Jones. Face up for gunfight (end of record). Enter Gunslinger; shoots both. G. starts to read poem. Sweet Sue shoots him and takes poem; exit.

2. Enter Daffodil-Girl on decorated Daffodil bicycle. Henri/Patten 'Daffodil Variations' on tape. (2 only).

3. Re-enter girl with poem. Starts to read. Enter Gripboy. Starts to caress her, eventually end up on floor making love, she still reading the poem. At end of poem she gives it to him.

4. Enter Daffodil-Girl again on bicycle. (2nd two Variations of 'Daffodil' poems).

5. Patten reads poem. Adrian paints huge Daffodil. "Along Came Jones" for 2 minutes.

INTERVAL **DURING INTERVAL JELLY-BABIES GIVEN OUT TO GIRLS IN AUDIENCE.**

6. Record "I Want to Hold Your Hand" (The Beatles). Fade out. A. as compere announces new Teenage Idol etc. Enter Pop Idol escorted by Policeman with coat over head. Girls scream, throw Jelly-Babies. P.1. reads Wordsworth's "Daffodils".

7. Gripboy reappears. Reads 1st two lines of poem No. 2 appears. Denounces him as charlatan, plagiarist etc. Shoots him. No. 2 reads next 2 lines. Enter No. 3. Enter No. 4 etc., etc. until end of poem.

8. All lights out except one red. McGough and Patten read sad love poems to Blues accompaniment. Death Girl, hooded, black masked, gives out dead flowers to audience.

9. Lights on. Daffodil-Girl on bike gives out **live** flowers to audience. Adrian's 'Lakeland Poems' on tape, and Adrian paints huge flower.

10. "Along Came Jones"—fight as in No. 1 except with Daffodils instead of guns. All fight. Survivor reads last 2 lines.
Music—Overture to 'Ubu Roi'; at dance part all get up and dance, throw flowers etc., etc.

END OF DAFFODIL STORY A JOYOUS CELEBRATION OF FERTILITY.

NB. Gaps between the 'events' can be filled with poems, songs, dialogues etc., as required.

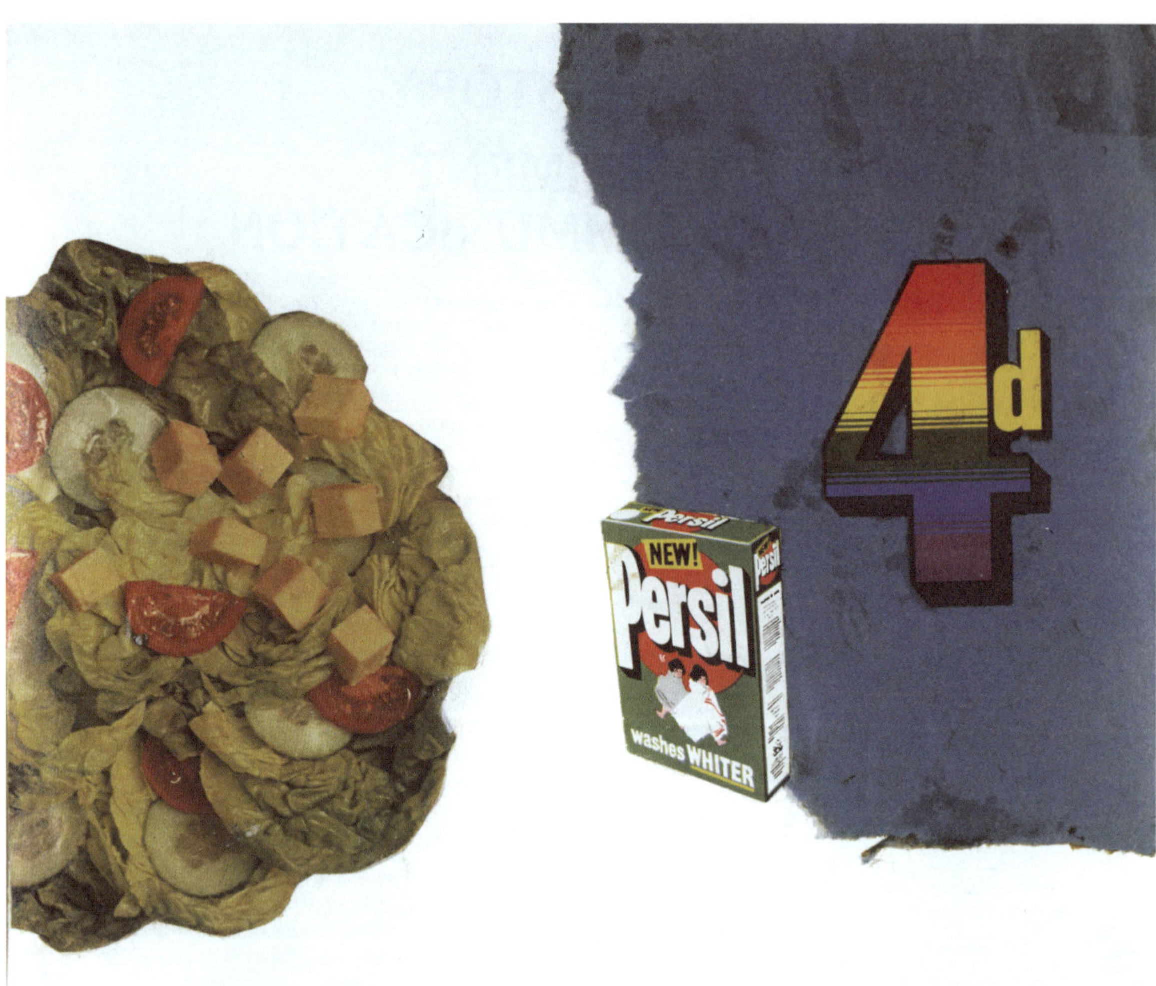

Adrian Henri   Liverpool Spring Collage No11. IV·65

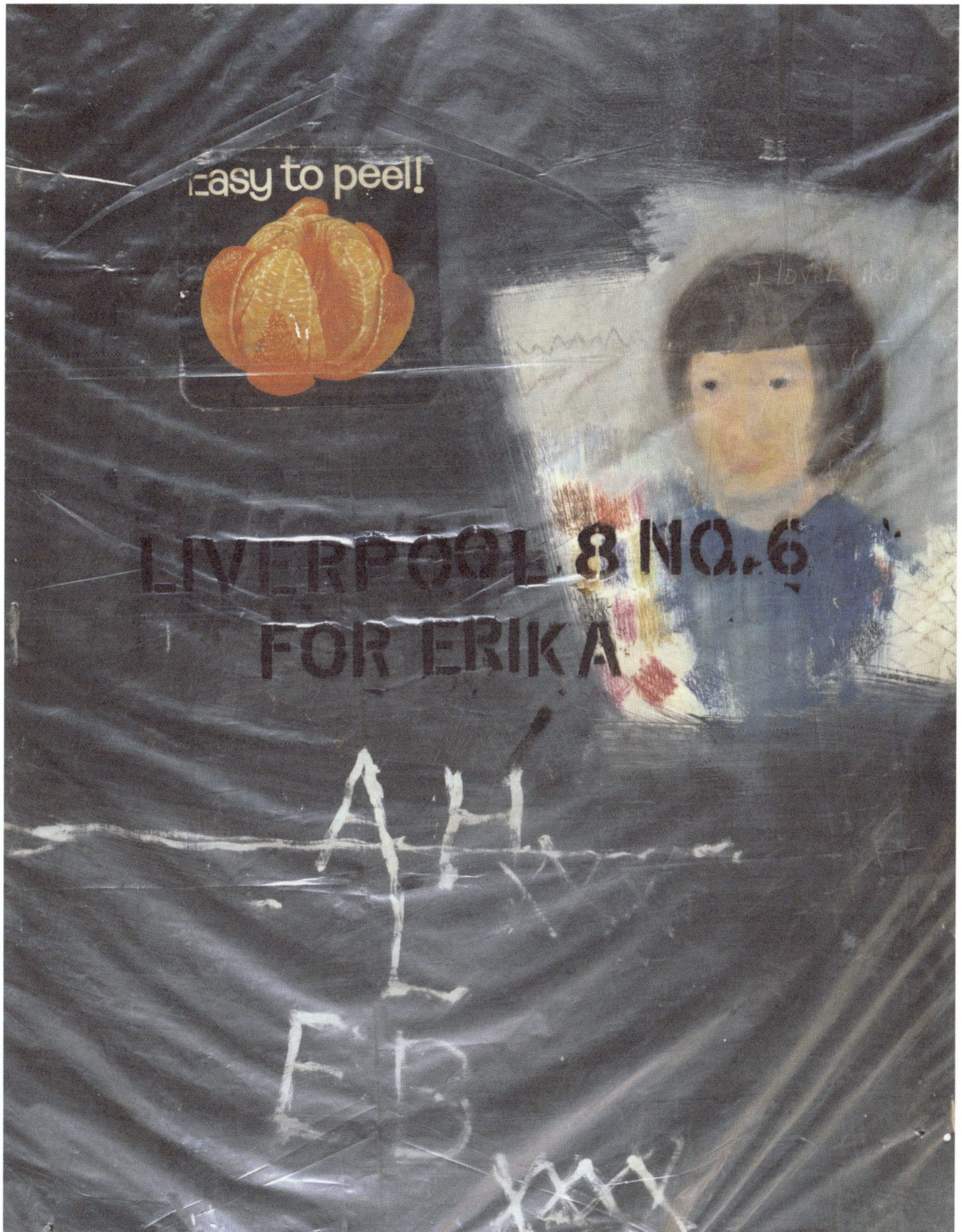

Easy to peel!
LIVERPOOL 8 NO. 6
FOR ERIKA
AH
AL
FB

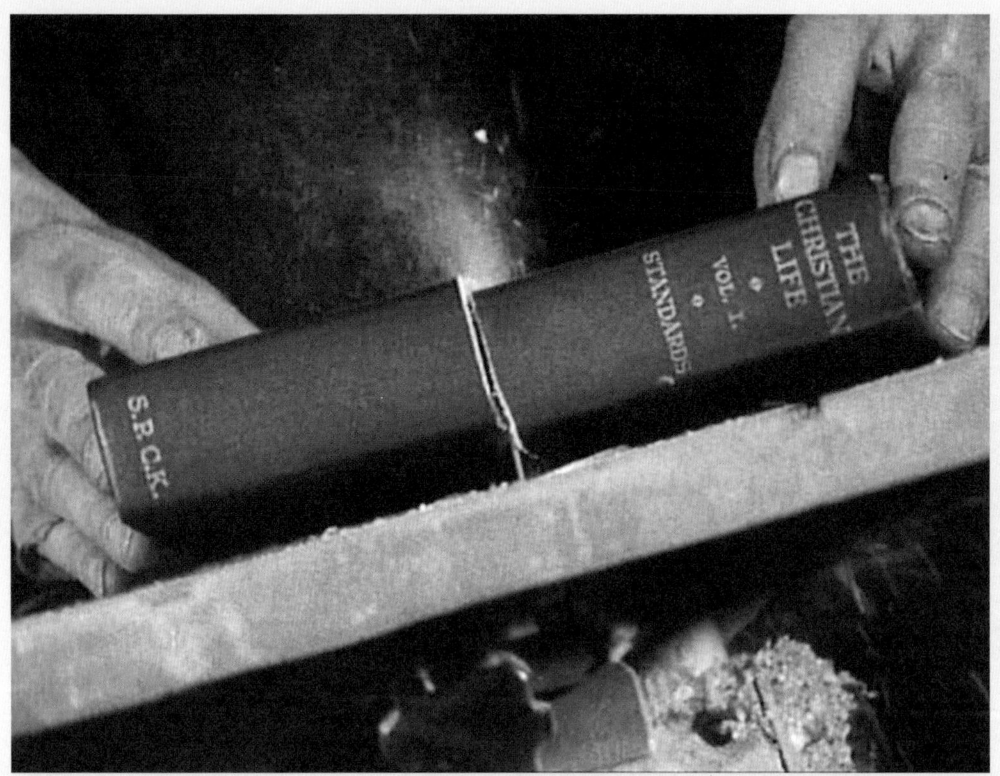

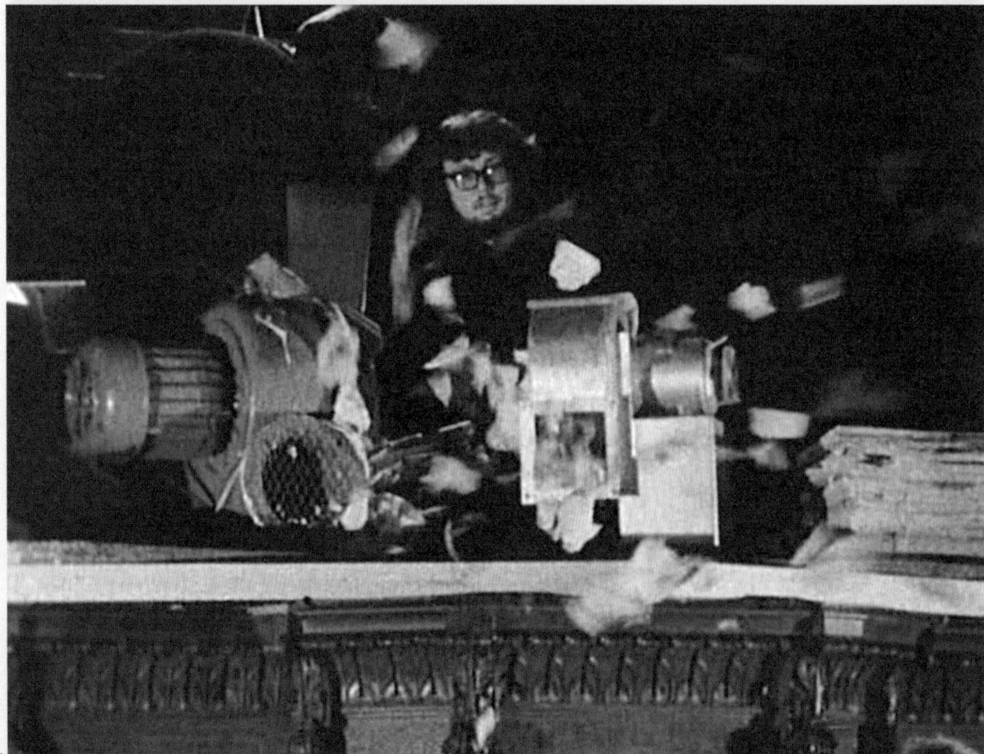

9
John Latham
Performance at
The Blackie, Liverpool
Filmed by Roger Tucker
as part of
On the Eighth Day 1969
16 mm film transferred
to DVD, black and white,
sound. Approx 30 minutes
ITV Archives

a vivacious bohemian culture. One such venue was the infamous O'Connor's Tavern on Hardman Street, described by John Cornelius as being populated by 'jostling… strangely clad figures… zonked out of their skulls on a variety of illegal substances.'[22] Its window-less interior was illuminated by a 'profane orange glow' and upstairs one could find avant-garde music and live poetry. Despite being situated next to the Liverpool Police Headquarters, this was a place of illicit pleasure and it enjoyed a distinctly exotic reputation. Along with the Philharmonic pub on Hope Street and Ye Cracke on Rice Street, O'Connor's became a main social hub of the bohemian set.

The scene's vitality mobilised the publication of a range of underground poetry magazines that tapped into wider networks of literary activity and attracted to the city Robert Creeley, the renowned Black Mountain College poet, who gave two readings in Liverpool in 1964.[23] Rather than being a part of the provincial hinterland, the city was once again a creative hub for progressive thinkers from far and wide. Democratic sentiment flowered through British culture and society during the 1960s. The levelling of social hierarchies focused attention on many provincial centres across the UK. Liverpool's influence demonstrates the fluid cultural exchange across class barriers, and between provincial and metropolitan centres at this time. Artists found it possible to 'plug out of the Liverpool student scene and… into the London student scene.'[24] Furthermore, the city's poetry scene was seen to build momentum ahead of *Wholly Communion,* the UK's largest poetry event, staged at London's Royal Albert Hall in 1965. For Ginsberg the event was made possible through the 'spontaneity of youths working together for the public incarnation of a new consciousness… thanks to the many minstrels from Mersey's shores & Manhattan's.'[25]

Despite the Liverpool poets' knowledge and appreciation of radical literary ideas fermenting in other parts of the UK and beyond, their own work adopted a uniquely indigenous slant. Indeed, for Henri this notion extended into his visual arts practice, as demonstrated in his Liverpool 8 inspired Neo-Dadaist assemblage works of the early to mid-1960s. Rather than ape the jargon of American Beat writers, common in some of their contemporary British poets' writing, it was liberating for Liverpool's poets to affirm that they came from Liverpool 8 or Birkenhead rather than pretending that they came from San Francisco.[26] As Edward Lucie-Smith points out, their poetry was 'written by people who are more interested in life than in literature.'[27] Unlike traditional English verse, it was designed to be read before a live audience and its performance was as critical as its content.[28]

In Henri's work in particular, vividly Surrealist scenes are evoked through the deployment of Liverpool's everyday iconography as subject matter. We meet Marcel Proust in the Kardomah Café eating Madeleine butties dipped in tea. This Surreal mode of address gave the work a unique accessibility to a Liverpudlian audience. As historian John Belchem points out, in the post-War period sharp phrases and idiosyncratic humour were established as Liverpool's response to its socio-economic problems, spreading '…from beyond the bonding rituals of workplace and local pub to become the defining characteristic of the scouser. Surreal word-play was highly prized…'[29] The poetry performances and events staged in Liverpool resonated with audiences with established traditions of verbal invention and live entertainment. For Henri 'the really special thing about Liverpool poetry is the audience. The front row at Streate's was practically the same as the front row at The Cavern.'[30] The popularity of these events was crucial in developing the bohemian scene that contributed to Liverpool's positioning as a symbolic site of the 1960s democratic spirit.

Against the backdrop of widespread socio-political upheaval associated with the era, a generation of international artists emerged who created art both informed and reflected by their immediate surroundings and circumstances. Seeking absolute communal liberation, for them 'the arts suddenly seemed freshly empowered… to provide a means for – indeed, to *embody* – democracy.'[31] One such figure was pioneering American artist Allan Kaprow, whose experiments with assemblage art and environments led him to organise the first Happening in New York in 1959. Happenings deployed sensory elements and everyday objects of every sort as legitimate material for creating art. Participative and anti-hierarchical in spirit, they aimed to collapse the boundaries between art and life, and performer and audience, by engaging with the particular sociological circumstances of the environment.[32] It was an active art, at once spontaneous and ludic, requiring that 'creation and realisation, artwork and appreciator, artwork and life be inseparable.'[33]

On reading of Kaprow's activities in 1962, Henri sensed the relevance of the Happening to the theatricality of everyday interaction experienced on Liverpool's streets. The writer Paul Du Noyer, for instance, likens workaday Liverpool to a play

22 Cornelius, *Liverpool 8*, pp. 33-41.
23 Creeley read at Liverpool's Gilmour Hall on 19 October 1964, as well as at Sampson & Barlow's. See Patten, Brian, 'Creeley Wuz Here', *Sphinx*, Autumn 1964, pp. 8-9.
24 Green, *Days in the Life*, pp. 46-47.
25 The event marked the moment at which the British provincial Underground went pop. It was organised by the Poets' Cooperative and staged on 11 June 1965 at London's Royal Albert Hall. It saw the British poetry scene come together with hitherto separate factions, including the 'American-orientated metropolitan flower-powered Underground…' George Melly stated that 'the event was the culmination of pressure building up over a period, and there is no doubt… that the crater of the volcano was not London, but Liverpool.' In Melly, *Revolt into Style*, p. 212. See also Allen Ginsberg's unpublished letter to the *Times Literary Supplement,* reproduced in Miles, Barry, *In the Sixties*, London: Pimlico, 2003, p. 61.
26 Cited in Bowen, *A Gallery to Play To*, pp. 47-48.
27 Lucie-Smith, *The Liverpool Scene*, p. 8.
28 Melly, *Revolt into Style*, p. 210. See also Lucie-Smith, *The Liverpool Scene*, p. 3.
29 Belchem, John, '"An accent exceedingly rare": Scouse and the inflexion of class', in *Merseypride: Essays in Liverpool Exceptionalism*, Liverpool: Liverpool University Press, 2000, p. 51.
30 Hignett, 'The Sound of Liverpool 8', p. 12.
31 Banes, Sally, *Greenwich Village 1963: Avant-Garde Performance and the Effervescent Body*, Durham, NC: Duke University Press, 1993, p. 10.
32 Bowen, *A Gallery of Play To*, p. 50.
33 Kaprow, Allan, 'The Happenings are Dead: Long Live Happenings (1966)', *Essays on the Blurring of Art and Life*, Berkeley and Los Angeles: University of California Press, 2003, p. 64.

of characters in which everybody interacts according to a script and where you 'get the impression that everybody is reacting to everybody else... Life... has a peculiar vividness... there are no spectators... everyone is obliged to take a part'.[34] Henri was inspired to organise *City,* the first of many Happening's staged throughout the decade, at Hope Hall (now the Everyman Theatre) in August 1962. Sean Hignett here describes a Happening performed in Summer 1966 on the steps of St Luke's Church on Berry Street: 'The "event" was... an attempt to bring an underground art into the open and bring Liverpool 8 down the hill and into the town [...] a huge hardboard Ace of Spades was being hacked to pieces by a gang of beardies. Transparent plastic sausages, filled with multi-coloured liquids... were being pierced with darts by a litter of scruffy infants... a booming voice was declaiming... "The children of Albion sleep in the dinnertime sunlight with old men looking up their skirts in St John's Gardens".'[35]

The theorist Marshall Berman describes 'urban montage', the celebratory embrace of urban vitality and diversity, as a key development within modernism.[36] Underpinning this is the notion that beauty and truth can be found near to the immediate surface of everyday life. It is significant that much of the most radical art of the 1960s – from Performance Art to Neo-Dada assemblage works – deployed the street either as the site of artistic production or as a metaphor for democratic and sociological intent. The street's position as a universal font of communality lent Happenings, Beat culture, and other modes of art an immediate symbolic relevance. A complex and liberating order manifest in everyday ritual and interaction exists beneath the apparent disorder of a decaying city. For Berman '...we must strive to keep [the] "old" environment alive, because it is uniquely capable to nourishing modern experiences and values...'[37]

Such privileging of communality was a founding principle of the Great Georges Community Cultural Project (The Blackie). Established on Liverpool 8's doorstep by Bill and Wendy Harpe in 1968, The Blackie integrated community involvement and avant-garde art within an organically evolving institution. Resonating with the ethos that made Happenings relevant to Liverpool's particularity, Wendy Harpe's philosophy for The Blackie was 'if you want to involve people, the activities must relate to their lives.'[38] Positioned as a site of communal creativity and play, it provided environments and activities that were sensually stimulating and physically invigorating.[39] Events such as the *Moviemovie Show,* performed by John Latham in collaboration with Eventstructure Research Group (ERG) in 1969, emphasised the visual over the verbal. This expanded arts event combined multi-disciplinary elements with Latham dressed as a judge ceremonially destroying books using an electric saw to symbolise alternative and more innate modes of communication than those possible through the written word.[40] The venue's altruistic mission led it to organise widely accessible open-air theatre events such as *Magic in the Parks,* which toured three Merseyside parks during summer 1970.

It can be seen that The Blackie harnessed the creative energy that had developed in Liverpool 8. Paradoxically, its appearance coincided with uncertainty about the future of the area, which was being threatened by urban redevelopment plans. The urgency to savour a cityscape that many feared was about to undergo radical change was palpable. John Kelly, a student at the time, declared: 'The romance and squalor of Liverpool 8 need little more description. To the transient, the immigrant, the criminal, the social misfit and the student, it has its separate attractions... If the planners move in Liverpool 8 will die.'[41]

Accompanying this was anxiety that the bohemian scene itself was stagnating. Where, many asked, were the successors to the giants of the past? *Sphinx* magazine reflected on how Liverpool had become 'rich at the feet of the Titans of Showbiz... (and) the Great God Art... its glittering long-haired fame shot around the planet several times or so and started a revolution... Now this city slumbers and dreams of bygone days.'[42] Such ruminations were indicative of the comedown associated with the end of the so-called Swinging Sixties. What was clear, however, is that the scene's heyday was over.

The Liverpool 8 scene constitutes a vital cultural legacy of the city's post-War period. For Brian Patten the area symbolises a mythologised 'idea, not a place in a complete sense... [like] The Left Bank or certain areas of San Francisco....'[43] Its influence was acknowledged in traditional avant-garde centres. The energy within Liverpool 8 was tangible, as was the impulse to maintain momentum. As Sean Hignett wrote in 1967, 'stand still and you will be asked for a penny, a sweet... be threatened by Batman, menaced by dirty faces... asked to settle a million arguments... Eight is where the new Mersey sound and scene will come from... provided it's left standing long enough.'[44]

34 Du Noyer, *Liverpool: Wondrous Place*, p. 165.
35 Hignett, 'The Sound of Liverpool 8', p. 12.
36 Berman, Marshall, *All that is Solid Melts into Air: The Experience of Modernity*, Harmondsworth: Penguin, 1988, p. 315.
37 Berman, *All that is Solid Melts into Air* pp. 317-18.
38 'Project at Great Georges', *Sphinx*, Summer 1969, p. 28.
39 The Blackie's programme in November 1969 featured 'Kinetic Theatre Workshops' for children. These combined play, environments, assault courses, films, soul and electronic music, illuminated by psychedelic lights from Nova Express, their resident light show.
40 'Project at Great Georges', p. 29.
41 'An Unpopular Move', *Sphinx*, April 1966, p. 6.
42 *Sphinx*, Lent 1970, p 36.
43 Wade (ed.), *Gladsongs and Gatherings*, p. 104.
44 Hignett, 'The Sound of Liverpool 8', pp. 12-13.

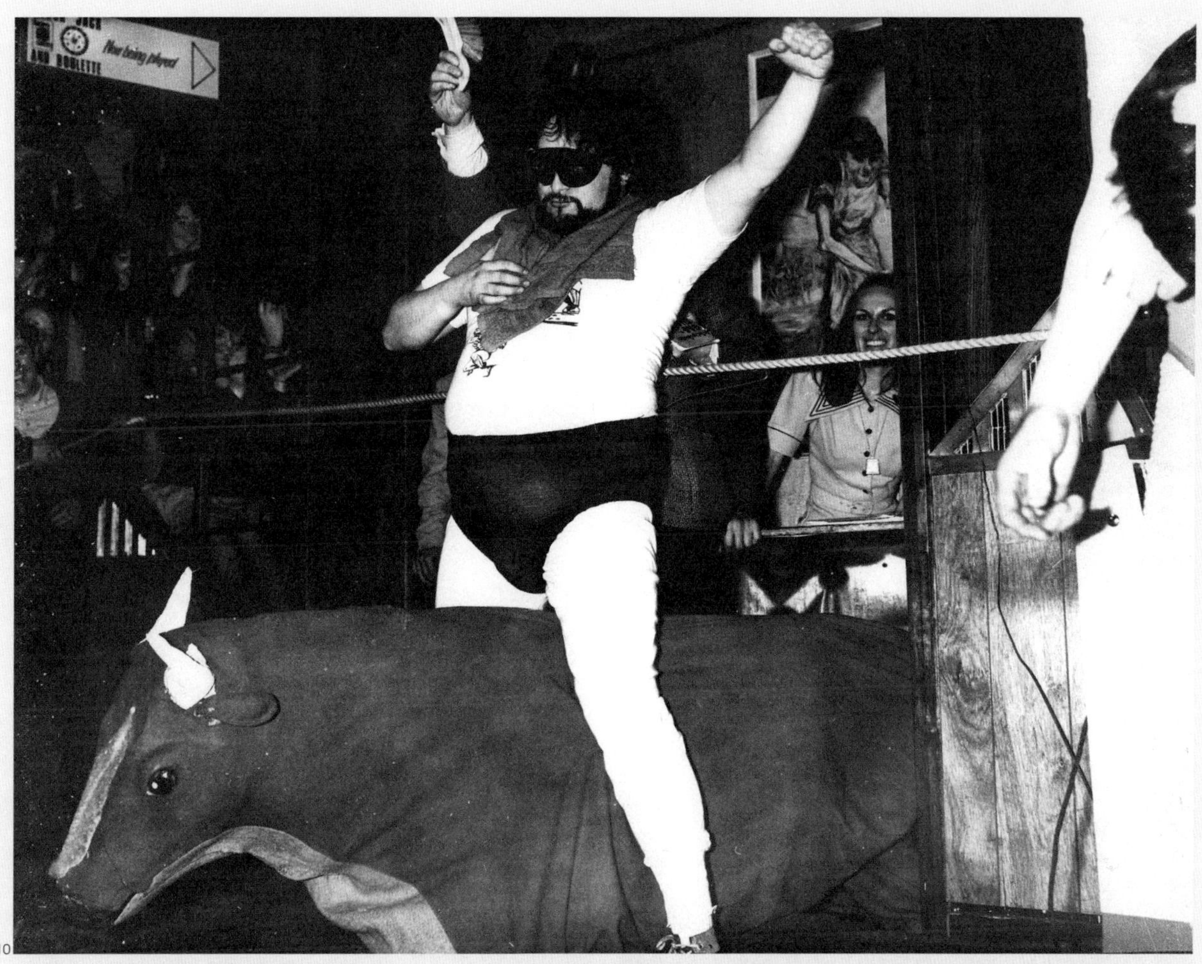

10
*Adrian Henri performing
in a Happening,
Liverpool*, c. 1965
Collection of
Catherine Marcangeli

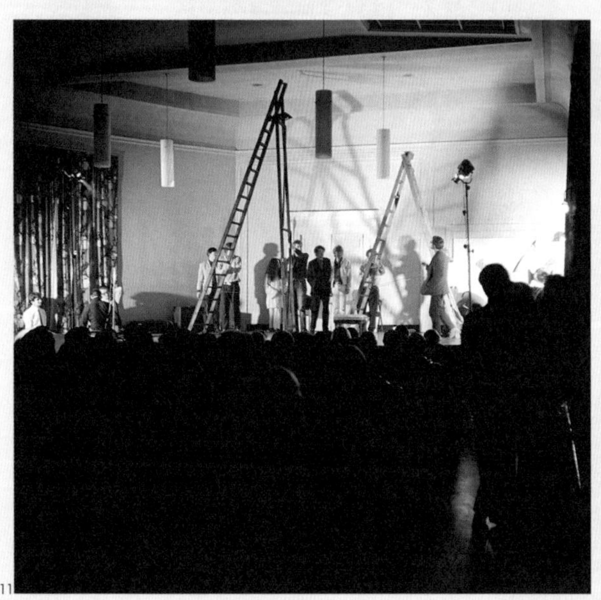 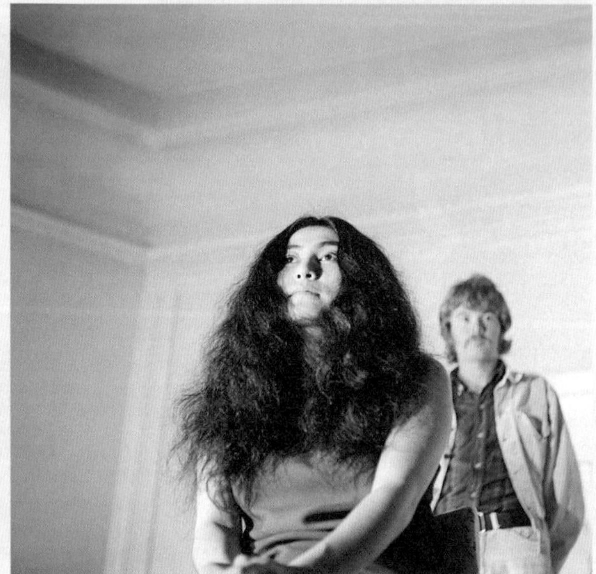

11

Gwyn Ritchards
Yoko Ono Performance
at the Bluecoat Gallery,
Liverpool 1967
Black and white photographs
Each: 40 x 40 cm
Courtesy of Gwyn Ritchards

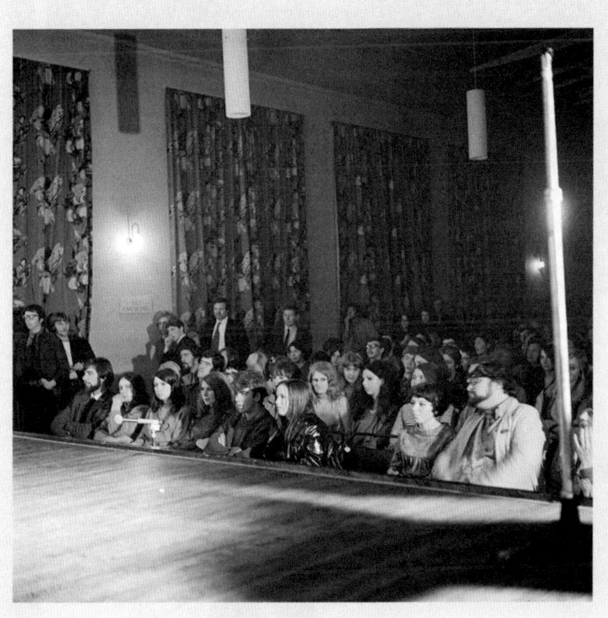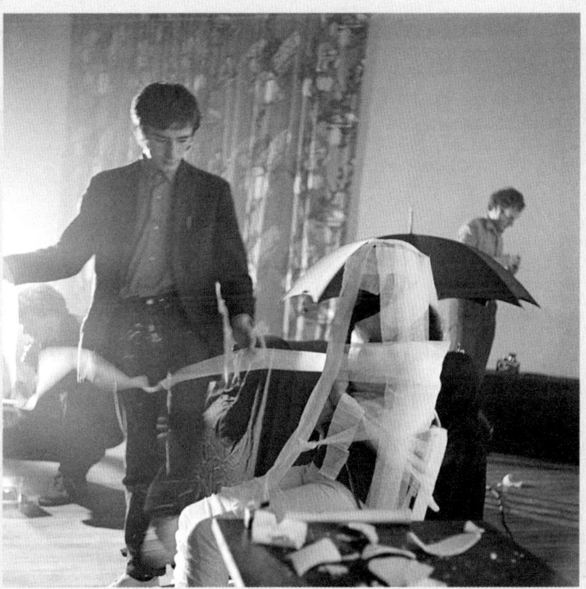

12/13/14/15
Jeremy Deller and Paul Ryan
Drawings for *A Guidebook to Brian Epstein's Liverpool* 2006
Ink and pencil in sketchbooks
Each page: 10.5 x 14.8 cm
Courtesy of the artists

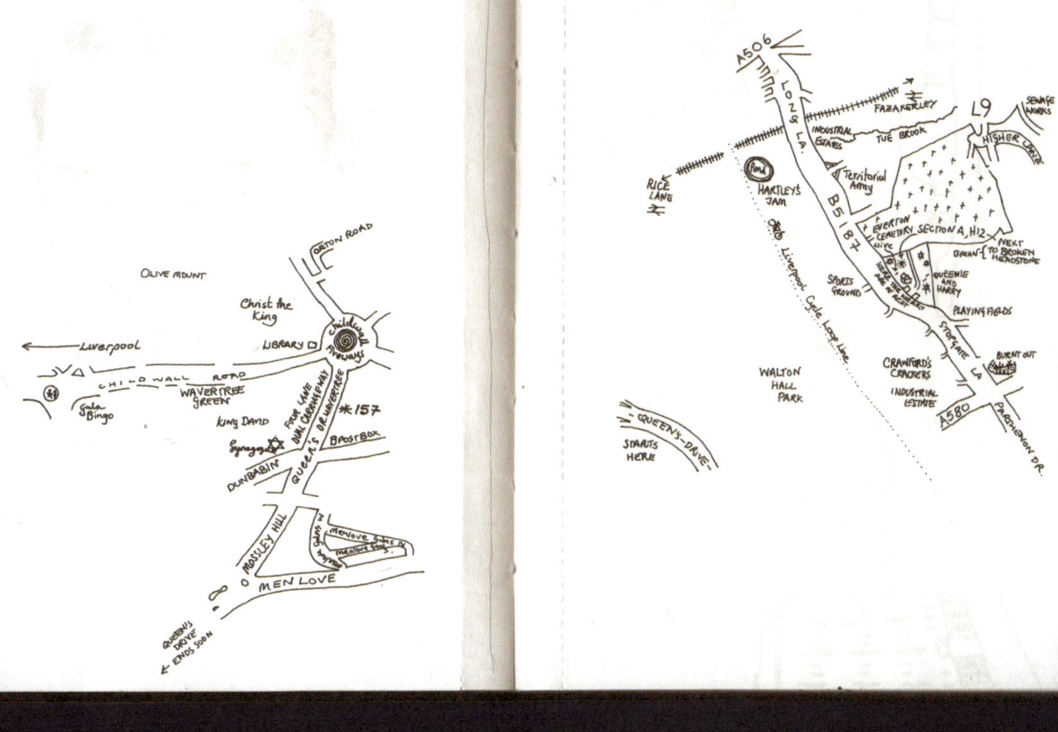

OLIVE MOUNT
ORTON ROAD
Christ the King
Childewall Fiveways
LIBRARY
Liverpool
CHILD WALL ROAD
WAVERTREE GREEN
Gala Bingo
KING DAVID
FIVE LANE
DUAL CARRIAGEWAY
DR. WAVERTREE
157
Synagogue
POST BOX
DUNBABIN
QUEEN'S DR.
MOSSLEY HILL
MEN LOVE
QUEEN'S DROVE ENDS SOON
MENLOVE GDNS N
MENLOVE GDNS E
MENLOVE GDNS S
A506
LONG LA.
FAZAKERLEY
L9
SEWAGE WORKS
RICE LANE
INDUSTRIAL ESTATES
TUE BROOK
HIGHER LANE
Pond
HARTLEYS JAM
Territorial Army
B5187
EVERTON CEMETERY SECTION A, H12
GRAVE
NEXT TO BROKEN HEADSTONE
BRIAN
OLIVE
Old Liverpool Cycle Loop Line
SPORTS GROUND
QUEENIE AND HARRY
PLAYING FIELDS
STOPGATE
WALTON HALL PARK
CRAWFORD'S CRACKERS
INDUSTRIAL ESTATE
BURNT OUT
A580
PARTHENON DR.
QUEEN'S DRIVE
STARTS HERE

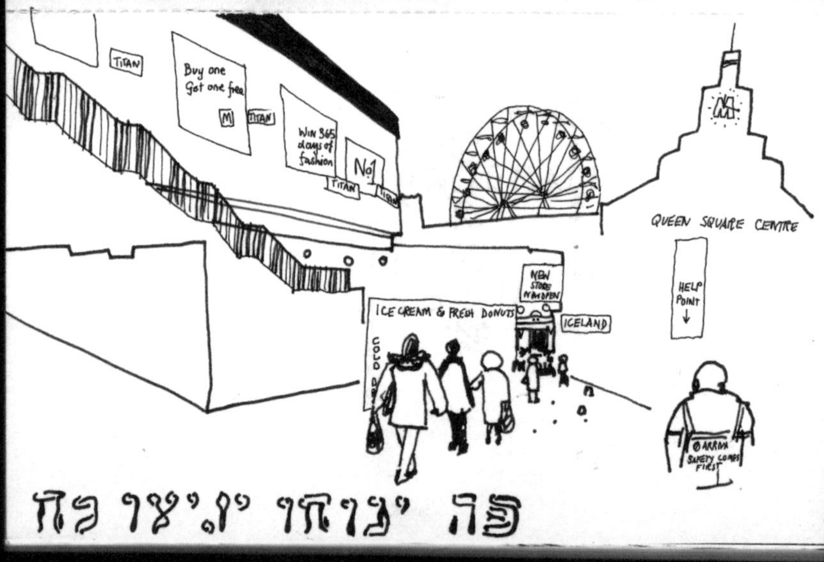

TITAN
Buy one Get one free
M TITAN
Win 365 days of fashion
No.1
TITAN
QUEEN SQUARE CENTRE
HELP POINT
NEW STORE NOW OPEN
ICE CREAM & FRESH DONUTS
ICELAND
ARRIVA SAFETY COMES FIRST
פה יגוה׳ יו׳׳ יצו׳ הפ

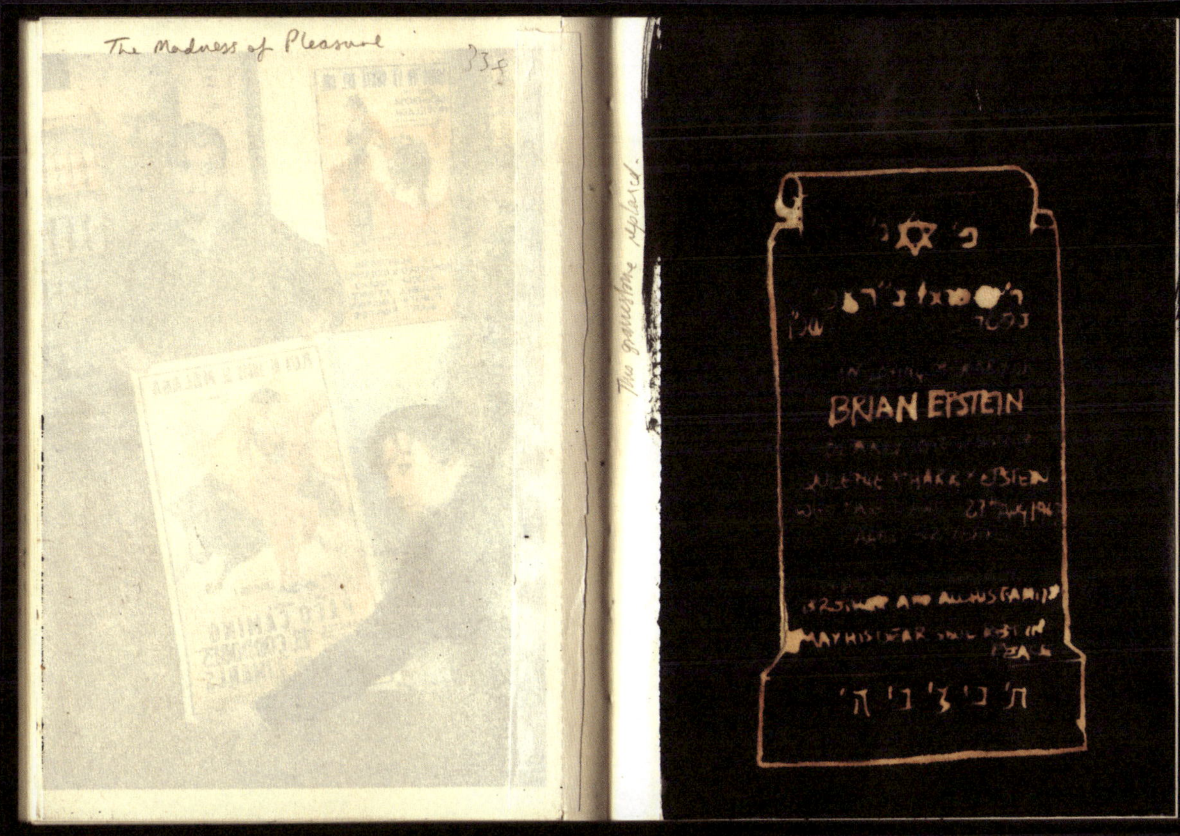
The Madness of Pleasure
33
The gravestone replaced.
BRIAN EPSTEIN

15

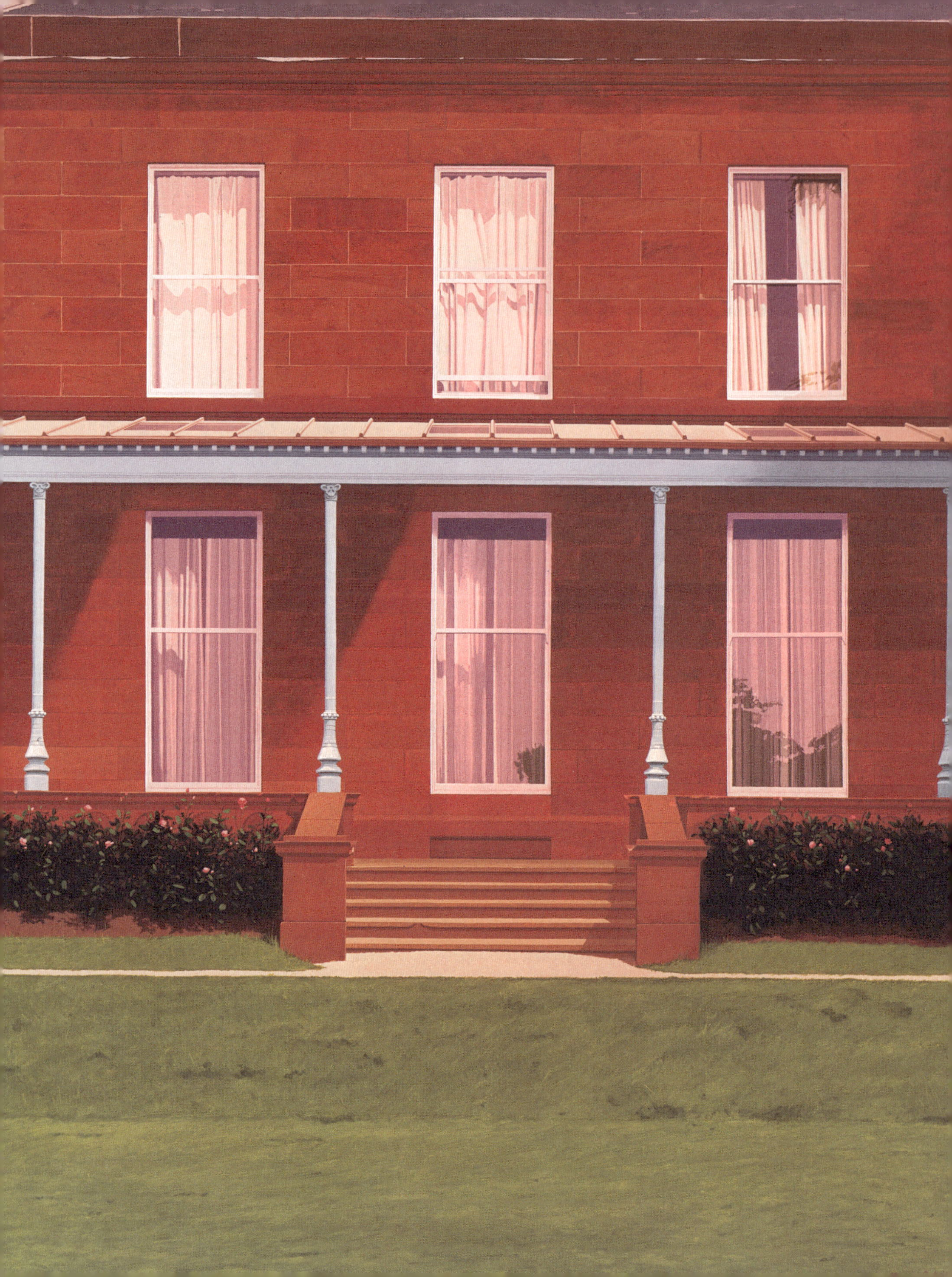

FACTS & FICTIONS: LIVERPOOL AND THE AVANT-GARDE IN THE LATE-1960S AND 70S

Sam Gathercole

Facts & Fictions:
Liverpool and the
Avant-Garde in the
late-1960s and 70s
Sam Gathercole

According to Jeff Nuttall, an anarchist who would later become Head of Fine Art at Liverpool College of Art, the Liverpool of the 1960s was a 'roaring, seedy, working-class port'.[1] It had 'the whimsicality and drunken restlessness of an Irish docker. It lack[ed] completely the "Swinging London" feeling, the Kings Road, debby, two-seater, sports model element. There [was] nothing toffee-nosed about Liverpool.' *Liverpool was a 'real' place.*

The story of Liverpool and its avant-garde art scene of the late 1960s and 70s is one of locals and visitors, and of the established and the experimental. Each passage of the story seems to tell of a different city and of different things happening there: Nuttall's Liverpool is one, but there were others. The story is inevitably fragmented and incomplete, and has to start somewhere. It does so in one version of the city and its people in the bohemian district where Liverpool 1 meets Liverpool 8 (but to one side of the avant-garde ranks that massed there).

In 1971, a 31-year-old nightclub bingo-caller, Eddie Ginley, was living in a small flat in Gambier Terrace. Unsatisfied with his lot, Ginley resolved to reinvent himself as a private detective of the hard-boiled variety by simply advertising himself as such in the local paper. Immediately plunged into a world of guns, drugs, a black South African liberation movement, and, of course, a fat man, whilst all the time maintaining the fantasy of his assumed new self, Ginley battled to distinguish fact from fiction. In 1970, an experimental community arts group, the Great Georges Project, had organised *A Cultural*

Bingo Show that made a 'happening' out of its regular bingo nights for local mothers.[2] Perhaps Eddie Ginley called the numbers; it did, after all, take place at The Blackie, a short walk down the hill from his flat.[3] Lots of things were going on, but it's difficult to recover the facts of exactly what happened, and who was involved.[4]

Around the same time, and around the corner from Gambier Terrace, the story goes that the young painter Maurice Cockrill was living in a house on Canning Street. He didn't stay there long though, preferring the peace and quiet of Windermere House, on the edge of Princes Park and just round the corner from Sefton Park, owned by the poet Roger McGough. Cockrill painted very formally organised pictures of Liverpool as a sunny and largely unpopulated place. He liked to quote Albert Camus, who had said, 'A painter's style is essentially a way of conjugating the natural with the impossible, of presenting that which is perpetually in the process of becoming, and of presenting it in an instant which is endless'.[5]

One of Cockrill's pictures, *Two Windows/Two People*, painted in 1973, is an image of a man standing behind one window and a woman standing behind another. The windows look like those of the poet's house near the park. In the windows, we see the two figures again, this time reflected on the surface of the panes: on the window in which the man stands, we see an image of the woman photographing him; and, on the other, we see the man photographing the woman. It is a very controlled work of heightened realism, that betrays little of the artist, but implies a lot about the relationship of the two figures in it that is at once intimate and remote. The artist talked about using a camera 'simply as an aid and the resultant image [being] a composite one refined from extensive photographed information'.[6] He called his work 'synthetic realism',[7] and distinguished it from contemporaneous 'photo-realist' painting in the United States with its claims of representational neutrality and

1 Nuttall, Jeff, *Bomb Culture*, London: Paladin, 1970, p. 123.
2 In 1968, the Liverpool-based couple Bill and Wendy Harpe had founded the 'Great Georges Project' at The Blackie. This, it is claimed (by The Blackie website), was the first community arts project in Britain, and revived something of the culture of live events and 'happenings' that had been a feature of Liverpool's art scene in the early 1960s. It is also claimed that Britain's first 'happenings' happened in Liverpool as part of the Merseyside Arts Festivals in 1962 and 1963 (see, for example, Henri, Adrian, *Environments and Happenings*, London: Thames & Hudson, 1974, p. 116).
3 Unfortunately, Eddie Ginley did not call the numbers at *A Cultural Bingo Show*. This is clear, because he is a character in a fiction – played by Albert Finney in Stephen Frears' 1971 film, *Gumshoe* – whereas *A Cultural Bingo Show* involved real people.
4 Among the number callers at *A Cultural Bingo Show* was the local poet and painter, Adrian Henri (who customised and politicised the conventional bingo number shorthand). Each bingo number corresponded with one allocated to a performer (such as a poet, a dancer, a musician, etc.), and when called, it prompted a short performance of around one minute. In subsequent games, two and then three numbers would be called together, this time meaning that two or three artists would perform simultaneously; not competing, but working together whilst presenting their prepared pieces. 'High' and 'low' cultural forms and reference could and would share the same stage at the same time. Bill Harpe (in conversation in August 2006) remembers a 'wonderful anarchy'.
5 Camus, Albert, quoted in Maurice Cockrill's statement in *Real Life* exhibition catalogue, Liverpool: Walker Art Gallery, 1977, p. 16.
6 Cockrill, statement in *Real Life* exhibition catalogue, p. 16.
7 Cockrill, Maurice, quoted in Peter Davies, *Liverpool Seen*, Bristol: Redcliffe Press, 1992, p. 163.

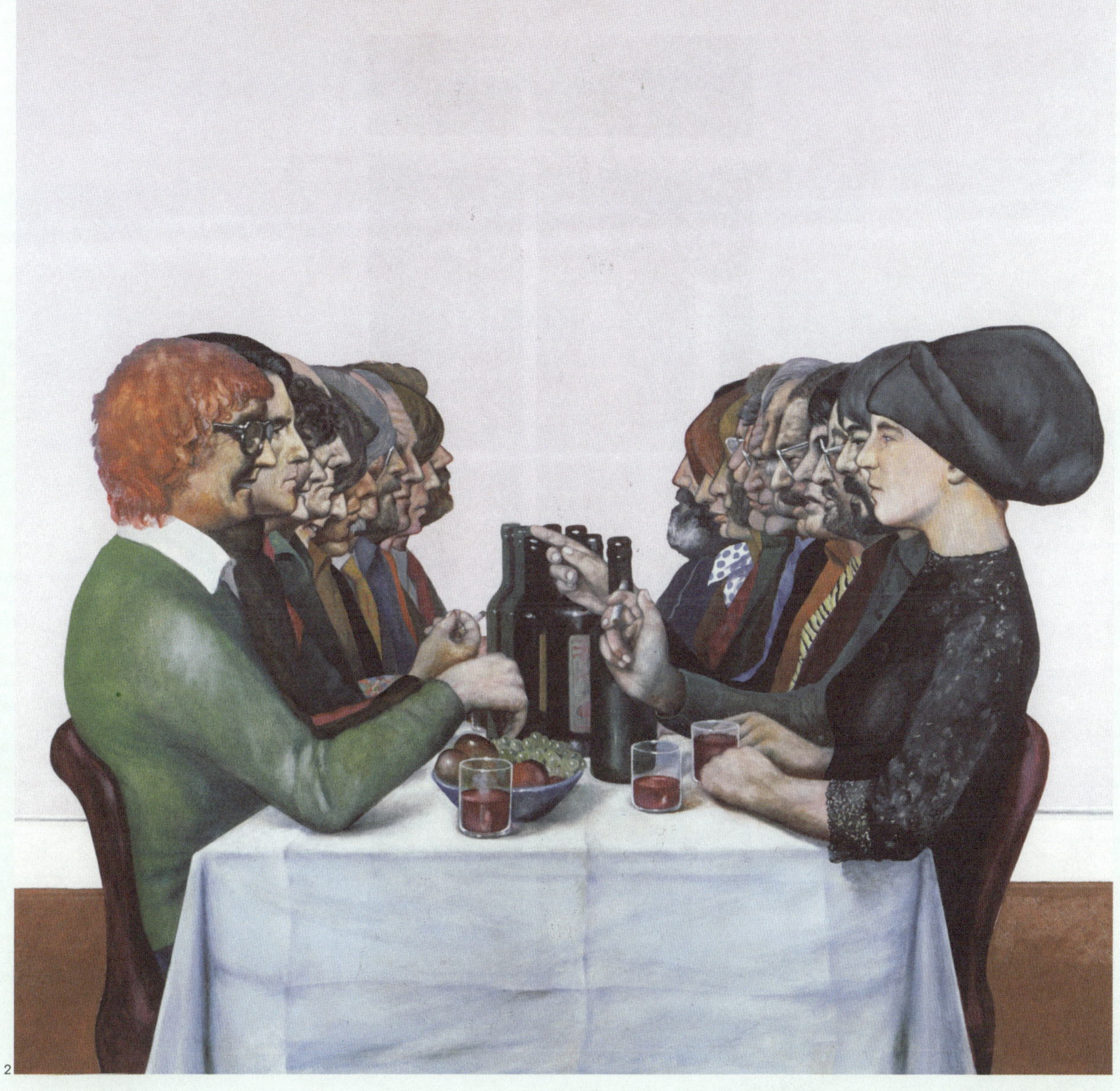

2
Sam Walsh
The Dinner Party 1980
Acrylic on canvas
152 x 152.5 cm
Collection of
John Entwistle

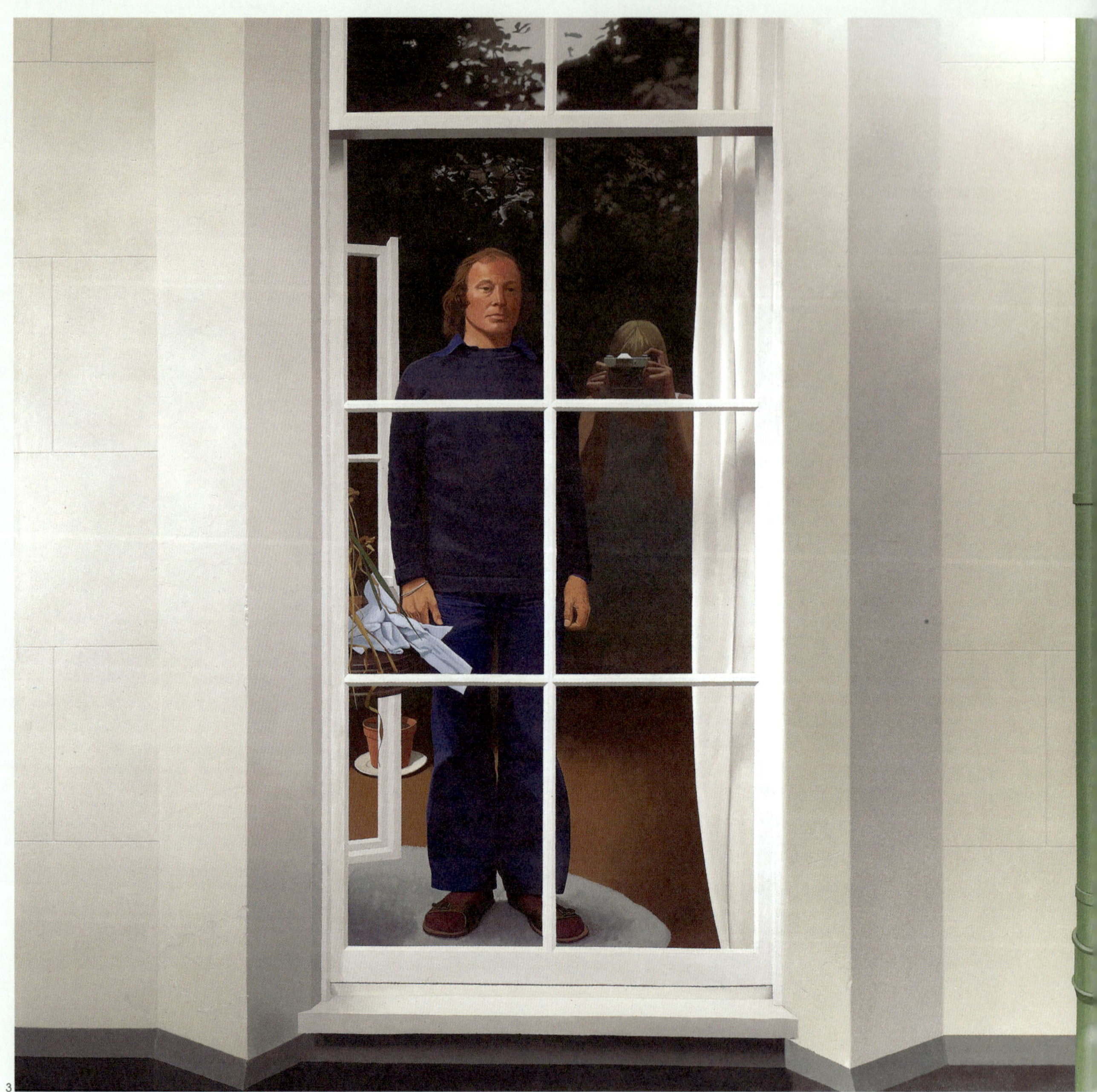

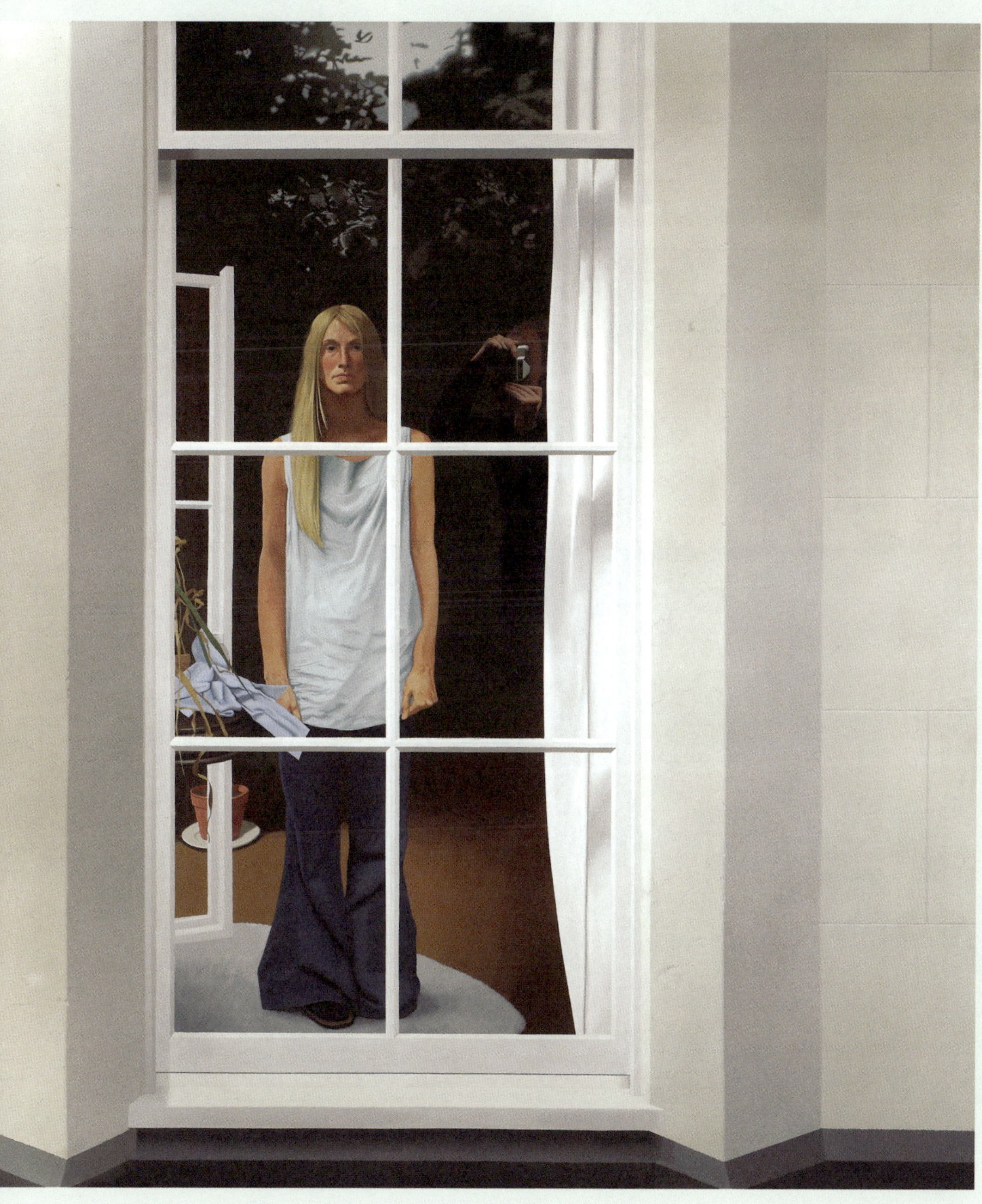

3
Maurice Cockrill
Two Windows/
Two People 1973
Acrylic on canvas
Triptych, overall:
213.3 x 428 cm
National Museums Liverpool,
Walker Art Gallery

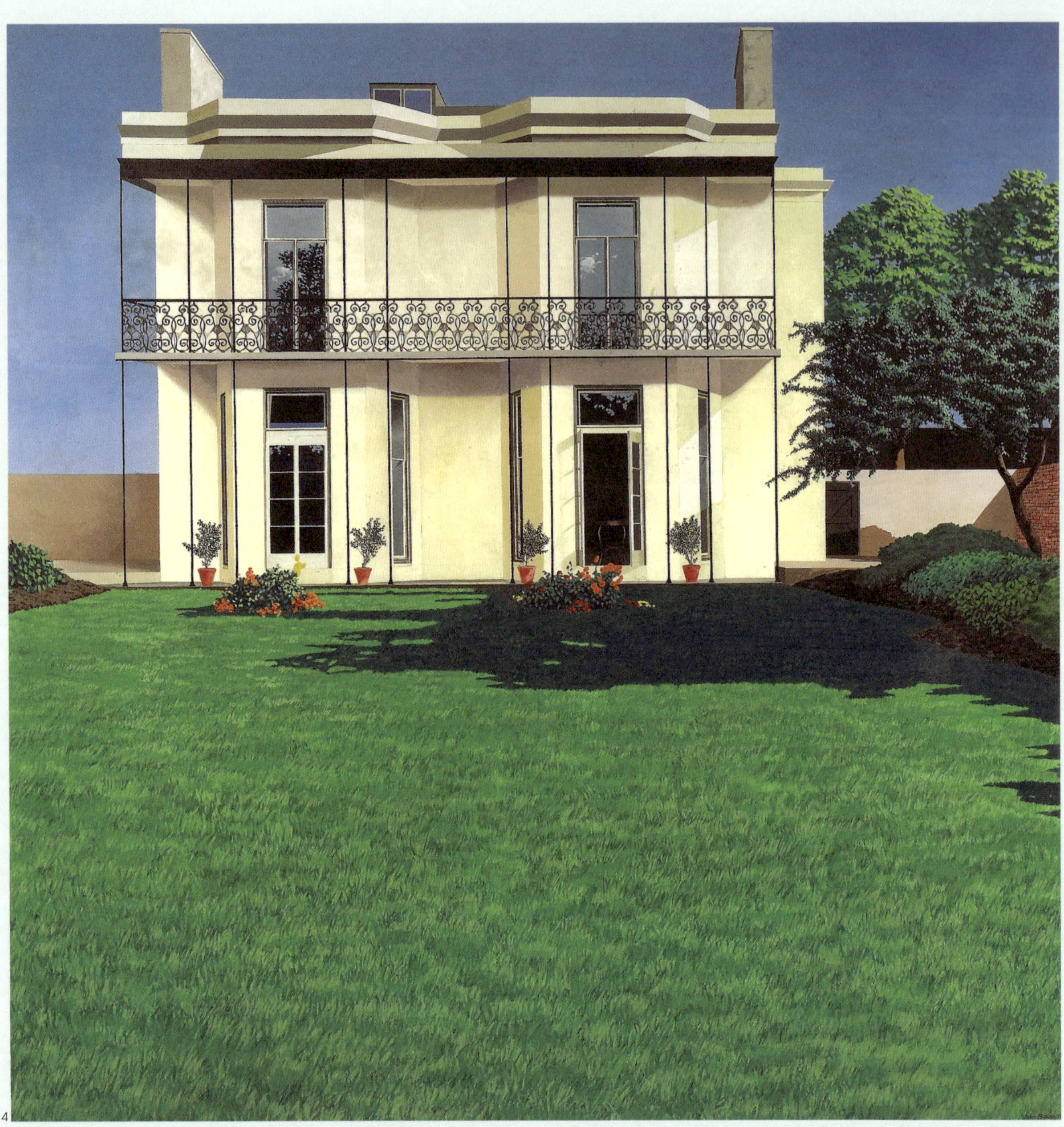

4

John Baum
Windermere House 1972
Acrylic on canvas
193 x 180 cm
National Museums Liverpool,
Walker Art Gallery

indifference to content. He preferred to cite the atmosphere conjured by artists like Edward Hopper as an influence. So, like his former neighbour, Eddie Ginley, Cockrill responded to an American 'noir' culture, albeit with a rather sunnier consequence than that encountered by the bingo-caller. *Fact and fiction are being deliberately confused.*

Another local artist, John Baum, painted Cockrill's retreat, *Windermere House*, in 1972. Baum's paintings of this time look very much like those made by Cockrill: they both used multiple photographs leading to a synthesised image; they both flooded their pictures with sunlight. Baum thought that this made 'things become questionably real because they can be seen so clearly'.[8] Both artists were in one commentator's mind when he wrote of a recognisable local style of painting that was figurative and fascinated by the immediate environment of Liverpool itself.[9] But theirs was not the working-class Liverpool that Nuttall described. In Baum's and Cockrill's Liverpool, there is an uncanny sense of the familiar: physical, objective fact (and an apparently objective treatment) is instantly transformed into a subjectively experienced reality. More than being present, their Liverpool looks like a memory or a dream. *Liverpool was a synthetic, 'super-real' place.*

Historically, the European avant-garde was suspicious of synthesised images in which an attempt is made to collect disparate facts of a subject, and summarise them in a single image.[10] The feeling was that the synthetic was susceptible to over-simplification, manipulation, and capable of deceit. More authentic was the destabilising of conventional (cultural) terms through the declaration of artifice, or through the employment of depersonalised, unmediated processes of making (sometimes mechanical and technological, sometimes automatically dictated by chance). The consequence of such means would be a changed relationship between the artist, the object, and, finally, the audience. The avant-garde believed that art had come to be too separate from the everyday, and that the idea of a detached, disinterested audience of art created a distance between the artist and the people. The avant-garde's ambition was to reintegrate art and real life, to produce a culture that was active, critically engaged and participatory, and expected the same of its audience. John Baum, for one, was little interested in this project: he said that he would rather 'retain a gap between the onlooker and the painting, just as with the stage or cinema there is a gap between the onlooker and the performance'.[11]

Back in Liverpool's city centre, attempts were being made to bridge the gap so keenly maintained by Baum. Here, there was an idea of the arts as being performed by both artists and their audience. Commencing in May 1968, the Great Georges Project sustained, for some years, the radical spirit of the events that had taken place in Paris that month. The Great Georges Project was both 'underground' and 'community' based. In 1970 it declared, 'Play is a revolutionary activity'. And, for *Towards a Common Language*, a mini-communiqué was issued:

1. Democracy cannot exist without a common language, and we don't have a common language.
2. The Great Georges Community Arts Project (The Blackie) in Liverpool is planning and building a bridge across a gap which has been well documented but rarely spanned.
3. Building and planning are proceeding simultaneously, requiring a mixture of very old and very new techniques. The project involves a collaboration of artists and vandals, toddlers and businessmen, arts lab youngsters and local mothers, students and unemployed, those interested in the arts and those interested in fighting.
4. It is estimated that traffic over the bridge will begin to release energies at present restricted or buried by divisions of class, sex, education, work, money, culture, and language.[12]

Towards these ends, the Great Georges Project staged mixed media shows, workshops, discos, the aforementioned bingo sessions, and even something recorded as 'lorry theatre'.[13]

Several visitors to Liverpool also arrived with the intention of agitating cultural conventions, particularly in relation to notions of audience and participation. 'Conceptual artist' Stephen Willats came to town in 1972 with an idea that art could have a social function as what he called a 'meta language', and that it could be used to connect communities 'separated geographically, economically and socially'.[14] He worked for a short time with Fine Art students at Liverpool College of Art and targeted communities in the city towards a collaborative 'examination of social behaviour, and the operation of socially orientated goals'.[15] Willats talked plainly about the emphasis being placed on 'the relationship the artist has to society and the development of a theoretical basis, ideological intent, goals, etc. which are both meaningful/operational within it', and functioned 'outside traditional areas of operation for art'.[16]

The work that Willats made didn't look like art in any traditional sense, but then the avant-garde were much more likely to reference sociological models, or stage a 'happening', as they were to paint a picture. When London-based artists Mark Boyle and Joan Hills first performed their *Son et Lumière for Earth, Air, Fire and Water* and *Son et Lumière for Bodily Fluids and Functions* it was at the Bluecoat Arts Centre in

8   Baum, John, statement in *Real Life* exhibition catalogue, Liverpool: Walker Art Gallery, 1977, p. 15.
9   Lucie-Smith, Edward, 'What is Reality in Modern Art?', *Real Life* exhibition catalogue, Liverpool: Walker Art Gallery, 1977, p. 12.
10 See, for example, Rodchenko, Aleksandr, 'Against the Synthetic Portrait, For the Snapshot' (1928), in Bowlt, John E. (ed.), *Russian Art of the Avant-Garde: Theory and Criticism*, London: Thames & Hudson, 1976, pp. 250-54.
11 Baum, statement in *Real Life* exhibition catalogue, p. 15.
12 Great Georges, statement published in *Magic & Strong Medicine* exhibition catalogue, Peter Moores Liverpool Project 2, Liverpool: Walker Art Gallery, 1973, pp. 50-51.
13 'Drama in Education: the annual survey, 1/1972', edited by Hodgson, John and Banham, Martin, quoted in *Magic & Strong Medicine* exhibition catalogue, p. 50.
14 Willats, Stephen, *Beyond the Plan: The Transformation of Personal Space in Housing*, Chichester: Wiley-Academy, 2001, p. 7.
15 Willats, Stephen, letter to Reg Hayden (Principal of Liverpool College of Art), dated 11 October 1972 (in Stephen Willats' personal papers).
16 Willats, letter to Reg Hayden.

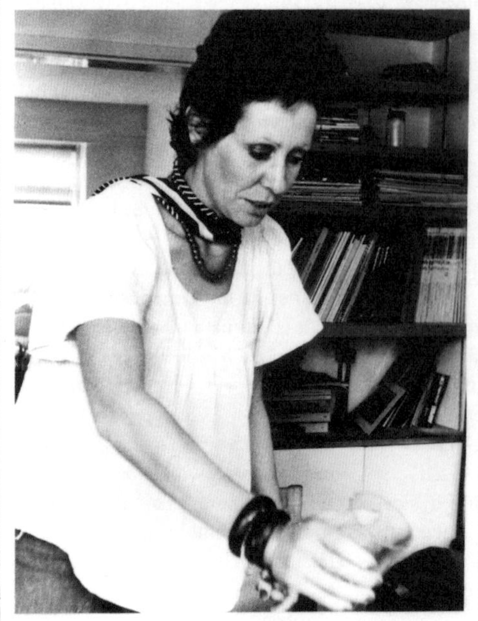

Context.

Select from the list of variables below
one that you consider is appropriate to
the context depicted above.

1)A reunion.
2)A diversion from house hold routines.
3)A break from work at the office.
4)A visit to the neighbours.
5)A reaction to bad news.
6)A settlement to a contract.
7)A party.
8)A moment before an important event.
9)A personal celebration.
10)An afternoon get together with friends.

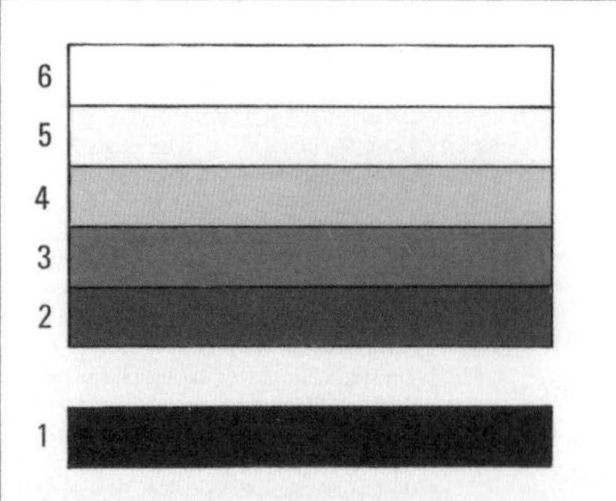

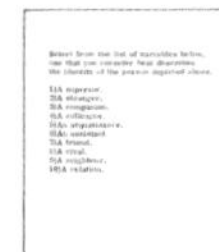

Identity.

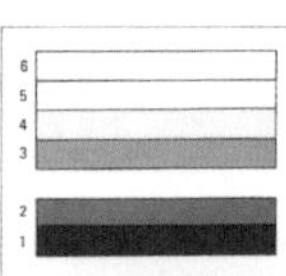

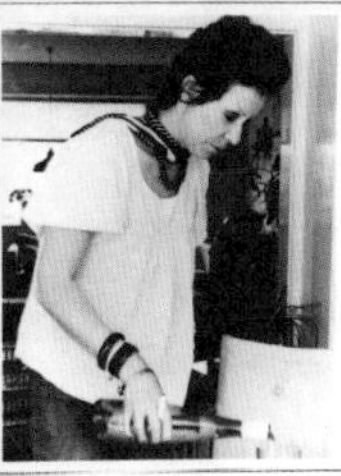

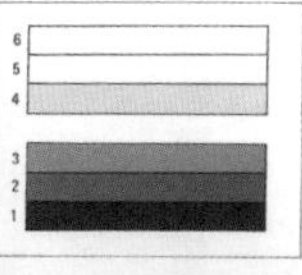

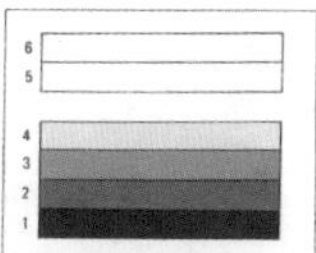

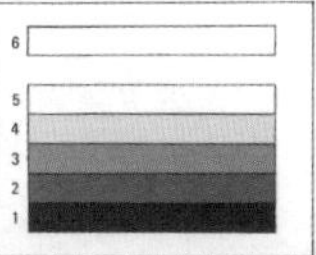

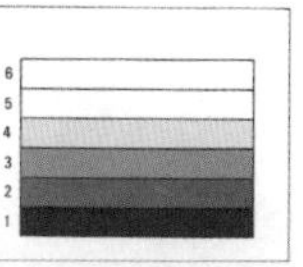

5
Stephen Willats
A Moment of Action 1974
Photography, gouche, ink,
letraset and typed
text on card
40.7 x 63.5 cm
Courtesy of Stephen Willats
and Victoria Miro Gallery

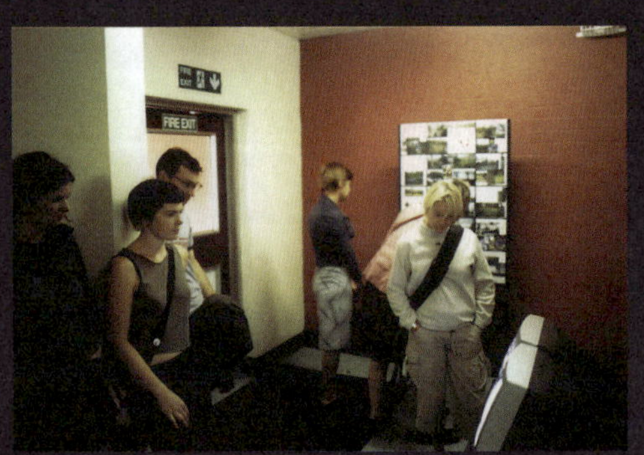

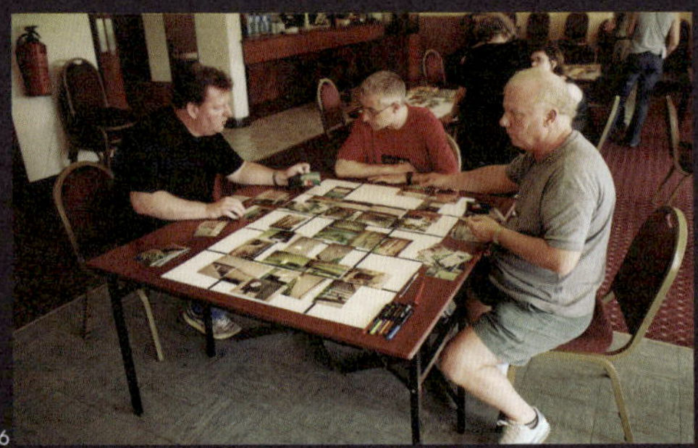

6

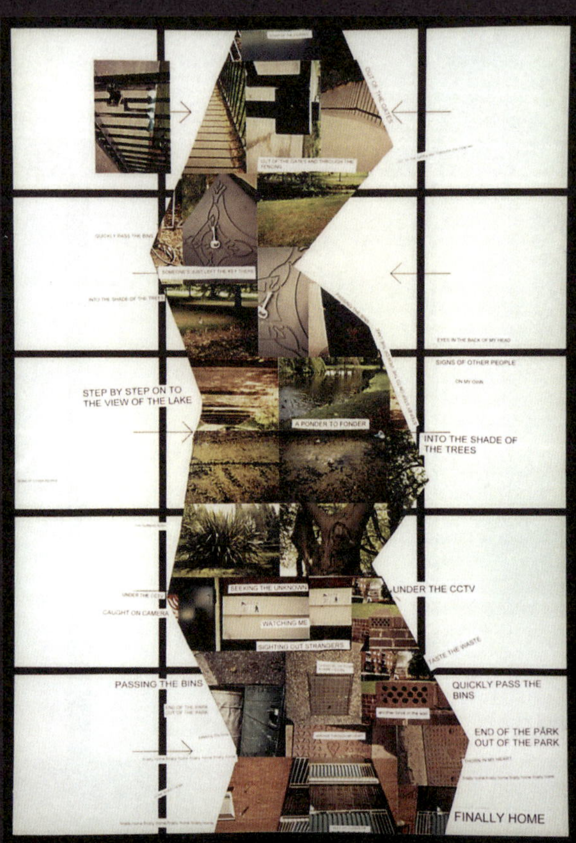
OUT OF THE GATES AND THROUGH THE FENCING
OUT OF THE GATES
QUICKLY PASS THE BINS
SOMEONE'S JUST LEFT THE KEY THERE
INTO THE SHADE OF THE TREES
EYES IN THE BACK OF MY HEAD
SIGNS OF OTHER PEOPLE
ON MY OWN
STEP BY STEP ON TO THE VIEW OF THE LAKE
A PONDER TO PONDER
INTO THE SHADE OF THE TREES
UNDER THE CCTV
SEEKING THE UNKNOWN
CAUGHT ON CAMERA
WATCHING ME
SIGHTING OUT STRANGERS
TASTE THE WASTE
PASSING THE BINS
QUICKLY PASS THE BINS
END OF THE PARK OUT OF THE PARK
END OF THE PARK OUT OF THE PARK
THORN IN MY HEART
FINALLY HOME

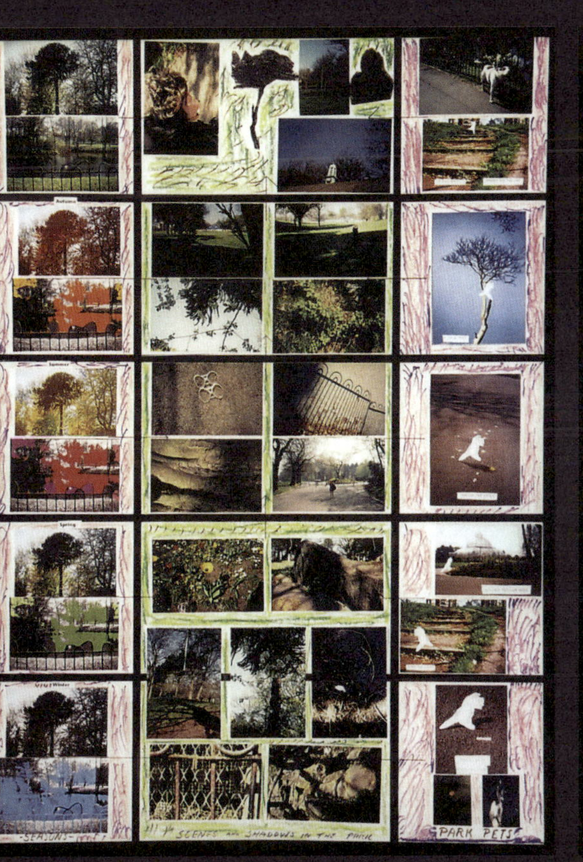
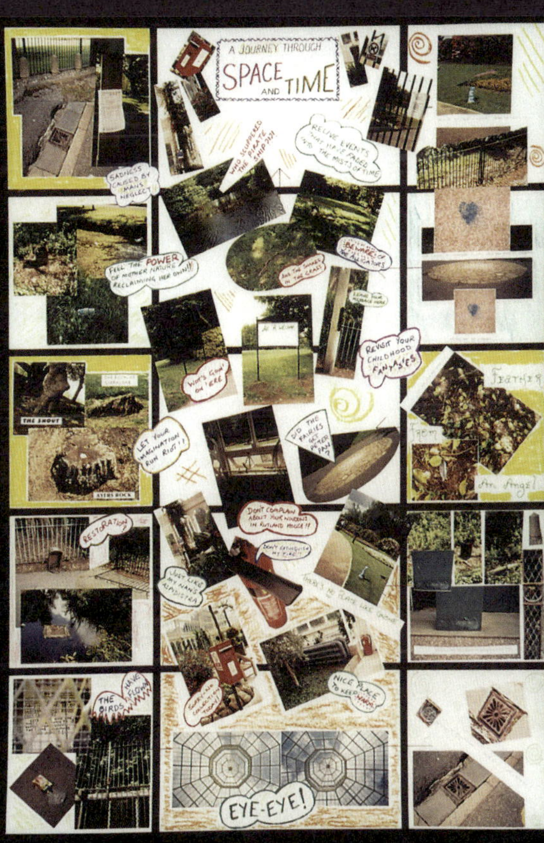
A JOURNEY THROUGH SPACE AND TIME
EYE-EYE!

Liverpool on successive nights in January 1967. A late-running train from London delayed Hills, so the first performance opened with Boyle improvising with toffee papers, that he'd collected from Liverpool's gutters, projected on to a screen. 'As you can see, this has absolutely no art value at all, like all my work', Boyle said whilst marvelling at the images produced by the sweet wrappers. He went on to add, 'I really dig this city. It's got some really beautiful stuff around'.[17]

Once Hills finally arrived at the Bluecoat, the performance proper could begin with a variety of mini chemical and physical reactions projected by means of a micro-projector, and accompanied by amplifications of the sounds made by the reactions and pre-recorded sounds of things like the eruption of volcanoes. One reviewer, writing the day after the first performance, wrote about 'some beautiful and dramatic effects', and warned Boyle that he was getting 'dangerously close to art' (whilst also looking forward to the x-rated potential of the following night 'that might restore the balance').[18] The second performance involved the projection of the artists' bodily fluids, and a soundtrack of body sounds picked up by contact microphones. Reality was amplified and enlarged by Boyle and Hills. All this was done live, and the processes used to produce the fluids were always likely to stretch the limits of taste, and be an act of endurance for both performer and audience. The story goes that the performance was well received in Liverpool,[19] whereas when *Son et Lumière* was restaged in Bristol in February 1967, the *Bristol Evening News* reported a 'sick performance' and 'an insult to civilized man'.[20]

In 1969, again at the Bluecoat, another London-based artist, John Latham, exhibited his *Review of a Dictionary*. Latham's *Review* presented single enlarged pages from a dictionary, photographically copied and silk-screened onto canvases. The pages were, however, subjected to disruptive intervention so as to only part-reveal their linguistic content and therefore undermine the idea of dictionaries as authoritative fixers of meaning and, by extension, fixers of the terms and facts of the real world. Latham regarded the 'given material' – the dictionary – as containing 'preconceptions about words' that he resolved to review 'without using words'.[21] 'Define the least', he recommended. Mark Boyle agreed: 'From the beginning', he said in 1973, 'we are taught to choose, to select, to separate good from bad, best from better; our entire upbringing and education are directed towards planting the proper snobberies, the right preferences. I believe it is important to accept everything'.[22]

In 1968, Candida Höfer, a young German photographer, spent time in Liverpool and documented the city in a series of what might be regarded, not as synthetic images, but as snapshots.[23] Her photographs are seemingly unmediated by the artist herself. She did not seek to define, interpret, or change the city in these images; rather she accepted what appeared. In Höfer's Liverpool, fashionable PVC macs and mini-skirts are to be seen alongside traditional raincoats and flat-caps,

and sharp suits and Beatles haircuts alongside workers' overalls. These are inclusive, democratic images, apparently of real people, not actors; and real spaces, not stage-sets. No one image tells all, but Höfer's series as a whole tells something of Liverpool in 1968. *Liverpool was just as it was.*

What links the work of Willats, Boyle and Hills, Latham and Höfer, is a looking again at the facts, and a starting again in negotiating a position in relation to reality. The terms of the 'given' reality (and the 'given' culture) were regarded as suspect: Willats completely re-thought what an artist was and the kind of things that an artist might produce; Boyle and Hills went back to basic elements of which the functions of the body were one; Latham threw previously accepted truths into doubt; and Höfer recorded a (photographic) trace of reality. The avant-garde was in Liverpool, looking for an unmediated reality, and, in their different ways, adopting unmediated procedures through which to find access to it.

In the 1970s, the French writer Jean Baudrillard was talking about reality and suggesting that, even in its purest form, it was already mediated. He proposed a 'possible definition of the real' as '*that for which it is possible to provide an equivalent representation*'.[24] This is straightforward enough until we – as Baudrillard suggested we should – regard reality as something that is itself a reproduction, and we are thrust into a world of the 'hyper-real'. Indeed, to look again at Höfer's photographs, is to see, quite literally, a city of signs, and the city as a stage for performance. What Baudrillard referred to as 'the crisis of representation' (traditionally, the danger of deceit associated with any synthesis, but, by now, much more complicated) was resolved only through a 'looping around' and a process of 'pure repetition': 'At the conclusion of this process of reproduction', he noted, 'the real becomes not only that which can be reproduced, but that which is always already reproduced'.[25] *Liverpool was a 'hyper-real' place.*

In the early-1970s, the businessman and philanthropist Peter Moores commenced his 'Liverpool Projects', each of

<hr>

17 Boyle, Mark, quoted in McNay, M. G., 'Son et Lumière at the Sandon Theatre, Liverpool', *The Guardian*, 11 January 1967.
18 McNay, 'Son et Lumière at the Sandon Theatre, Liverpool'.
19 See, Locher, J. L., *Mark Boyle's Journey to the Surface of the Earth*, Stuttgart: Edition Hansjörg Mayer, 1978, p. 71.
20 *Bristol Evening News* review, quoted in Boyle, Mark, *Journey to the Surface of the Earth: Mark Boyle's Atlas and Manual*, Cologne: Edition Hansjörg Mayer, 1970, unpaginated (Appendix 9).
21 Latham, John, quoted in Lippard, Lucy, *Six Years: The Dematerialization of the Art Object*, Berkeley and Los Angeles: University of California Press, 1997, p. 93.
22 Boyle, Mark, statement in *Magic and Strong Medicine* exhibition catalogue, Liverpool: Walker Art Gallery, 1973, p. 16.
23 It should be noted that, in the late-1960s, the recognition of Höfer's photographs as 'art' would have been a less than straightforward exercise. Photography itself was nothing new, of course, but it was rarely presented in an art context in the same way as, say, painting and sculpture. In Liverpool, the Merseyside Visual Communications Unit (MVCU) was set up in 1973, leading to the Open Eye Gallery opening in 1977 as among the first institution of its kind in Britain to be dedicated to lens-based media.
24 Baudrillard, Jean, 'The Hyper-realism of Simulation' (1976), in Harrison, Charles and Wood, Paul (ed.), *Art in Theory 1900-1990: An Anthology of Changing Ideas*, Oxford: Blackwell, 1992, p. 1050.
25 Baudrillard, 'The Hyper-realism of Simulation', p. 1050.

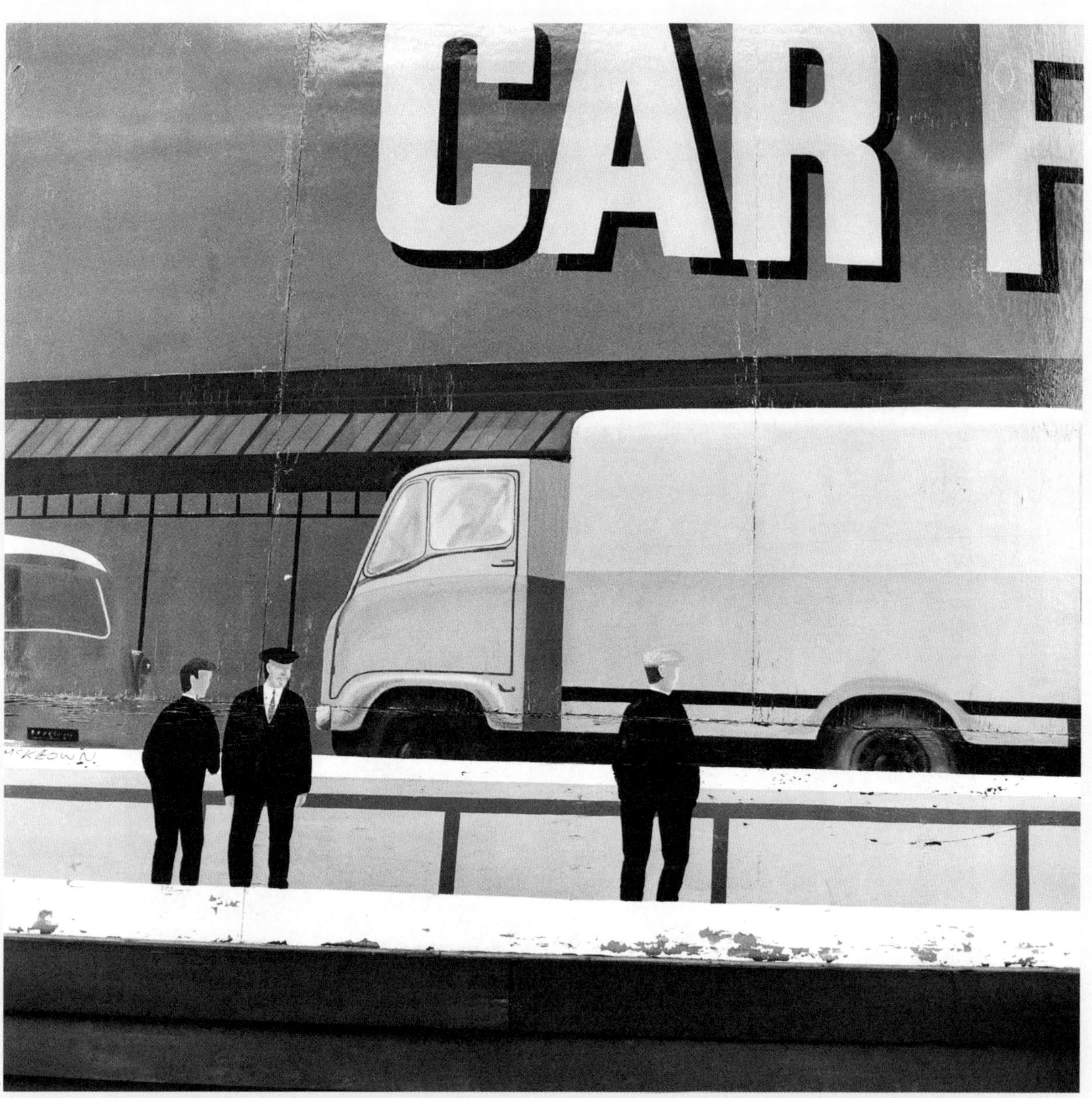

7
Candida Höfer
Liverpool IV 1968
Silver gelatin print
21 x 21 cm
Photographische
Sammlung/SK Stiftung
Kultur, Cologne

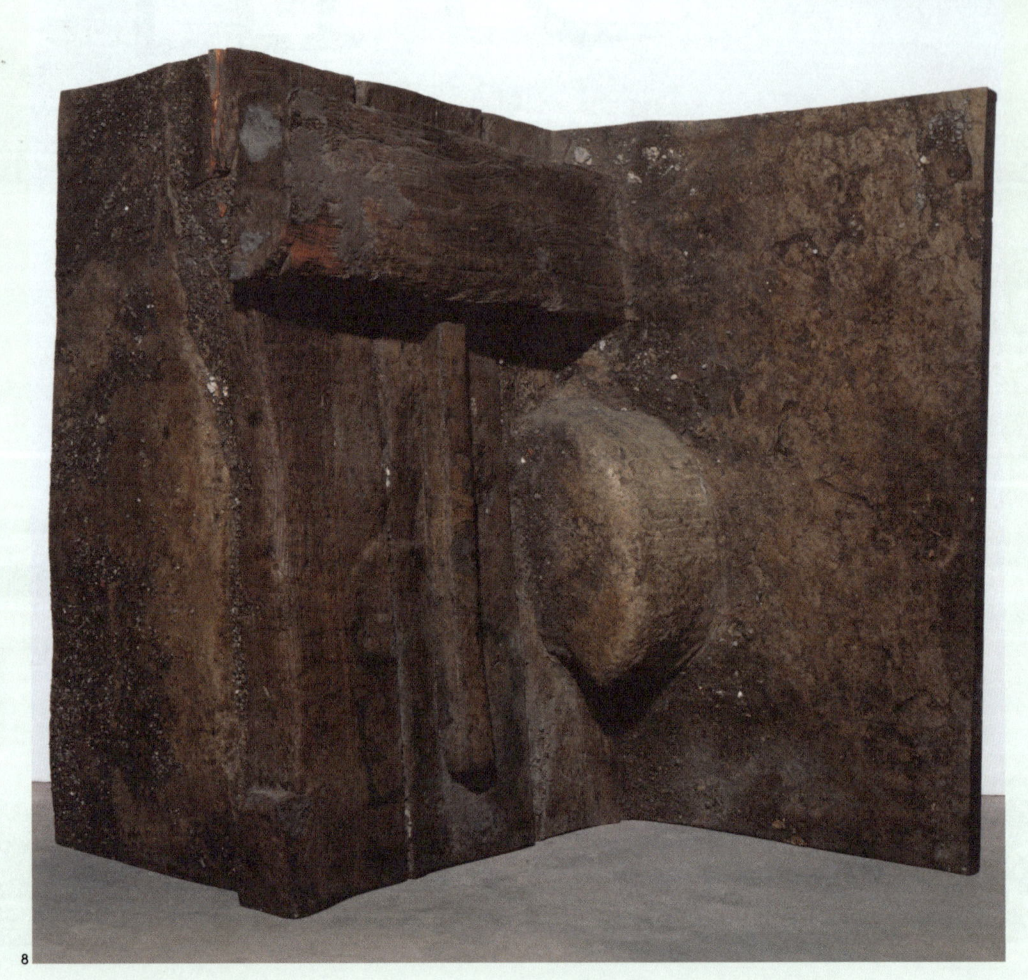

8

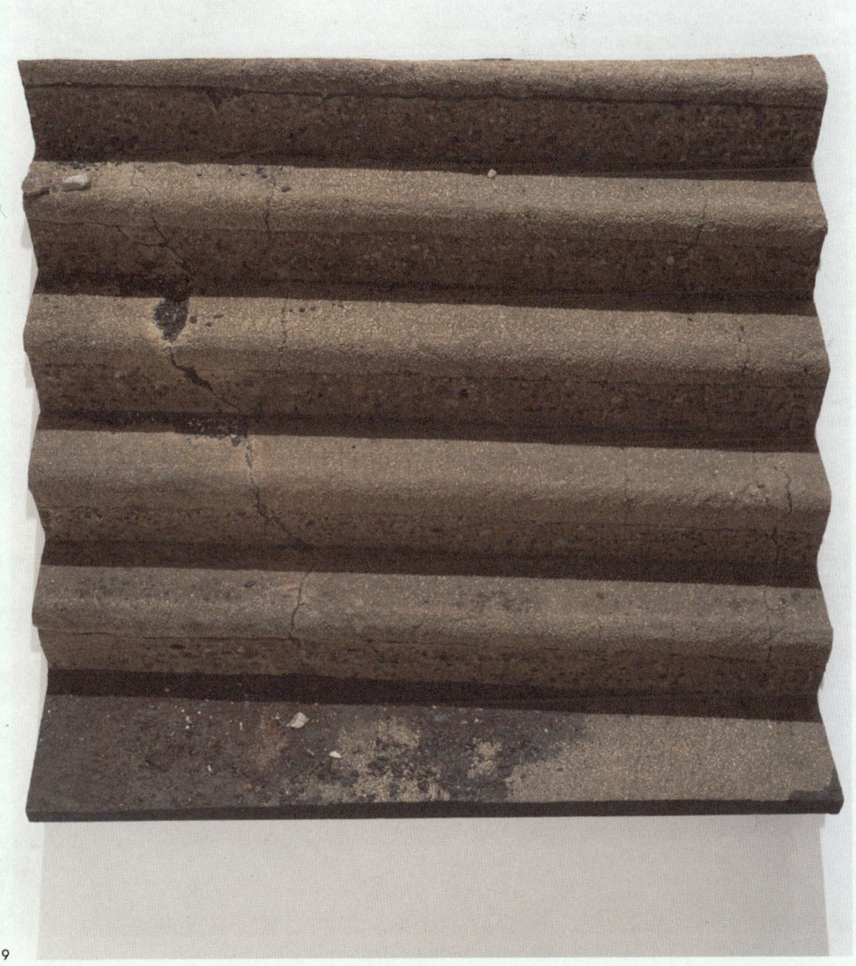

9

8
Boyle Family
*Herculaneum Dock
Series* 1976
Mixed media, resin and
fibreglass floor relief
171 x 183 x 133.5 cm
Compton Verney

9
Boyle Family
*Herculaneum Dock
Series* 1976
Mixed media, resin and
fibreglass floor relief
180 x 183 x 20 cm
Compton Verney

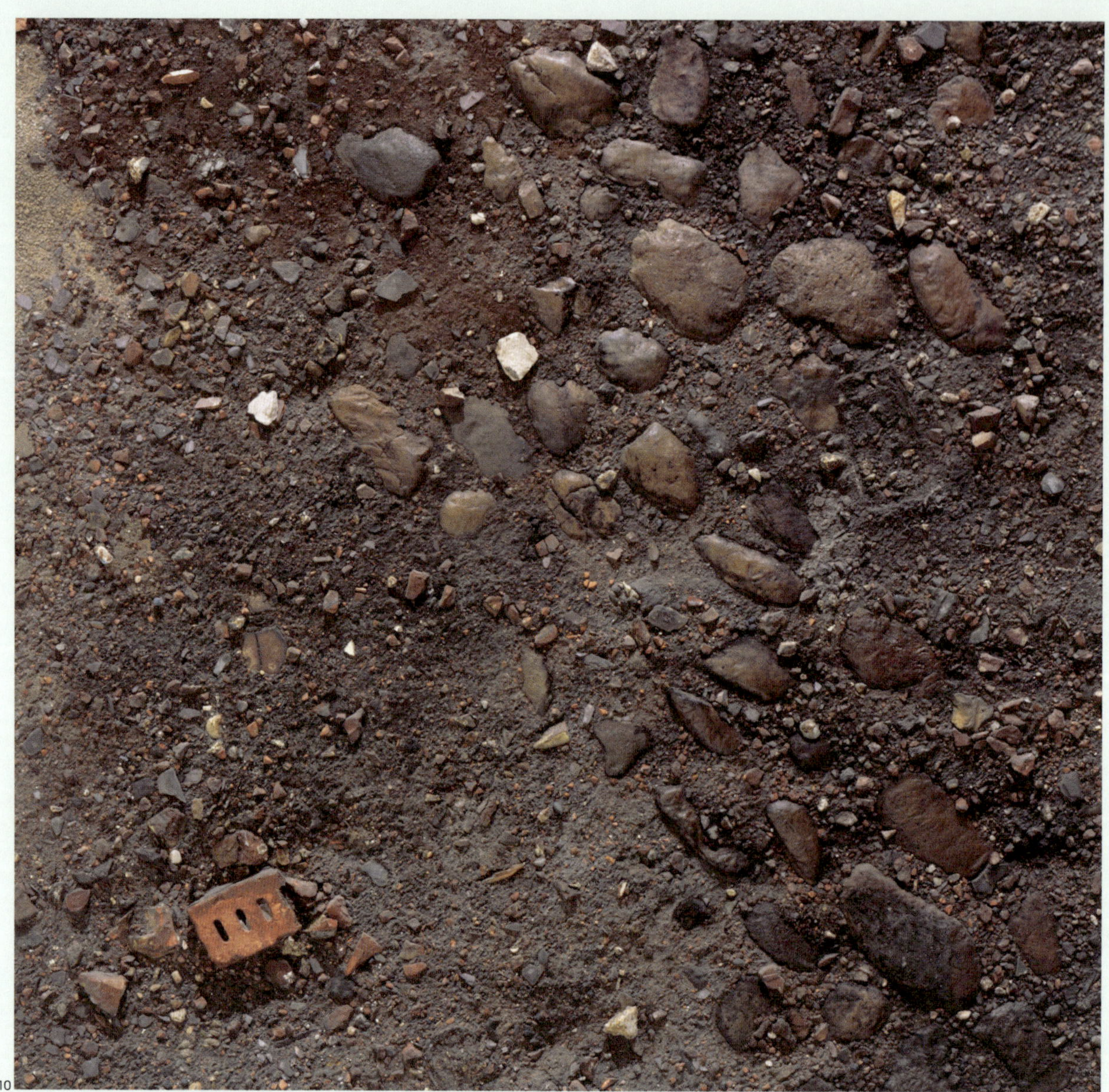

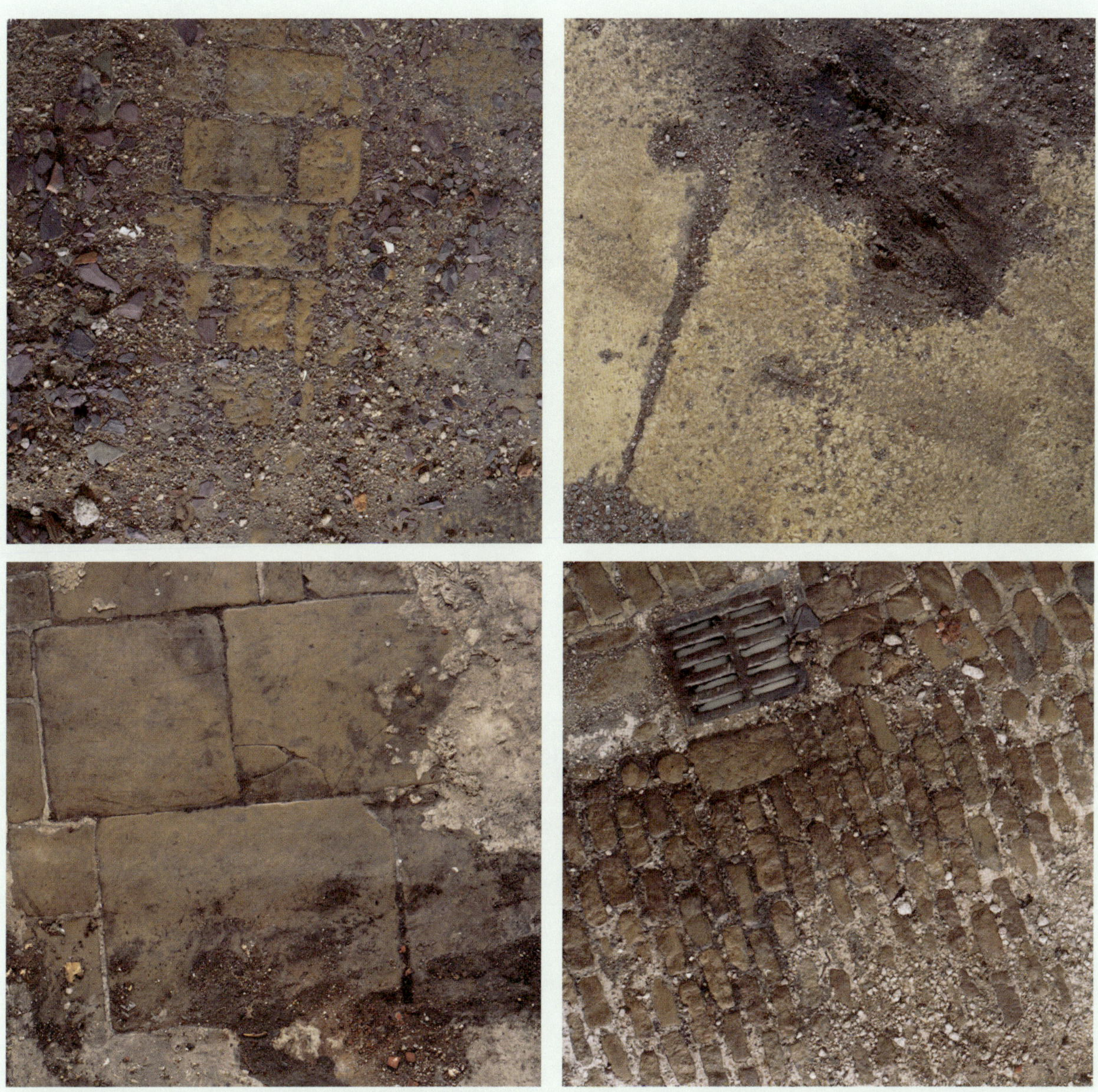

10
Boyle Family
Herculaneum Dock Series 1976
Mixed media, resin and fibreglass wall reliefs
Each approx:
183 x 183 x 8.5cm
Compton Verney

which culminated in an exhibition at the Walker Art Gallery.[26] In 1977, the 'Liverpool Project 4' occasioned an exhibition called – regardless of Baudrillard's critique – *Real Life*.[27] *Real Life* mainly featured figurative paintings by well-known artists like Michael Andrews, Frank Auerbach, William Coldstream and Lucian Freud, along with local artists including John Baum and Maurice Cockrill. Overall, the work on show indicated a belief that there was an apprehensible reality of which it was possible to fashion an accurate representation and which maintained distinctions between reality (the world) and its signs (in this case, paintings). Among the few works that disrupted this claim was a series of studies made at the Herculaneum Dock in Liverpool by the Boyle Family. Mark Boyle and Joan Hills were back in the city – as they had been on a number of occasions since the Bluecoat performances of 1967 – to record randomly chosen sites in the city's docks. The couple went to each site, and meticulously and exactly reproduced what they found there in the form of six-foot-square coloured casts.

In the *Liverpool Dock Series*, the Boyle Family left several significant choices to chance, systematised the random, and accepted its consequences. The idea of causality as an axiomatic truth was, around this time, being widely rejected by many people in Western Europe and North America. From a counter-culture attraction to Far Eastern philosophy, to the most advanced modern scientific research, chance processes excited much interest because they seemed more real than controlled actions that were limited by preconceptions and guided only by what was already known. In August 1968, a New York-based psychiatrist called Luke Rhinehart began a new life as 'Dice Man', guided only by decisions made according to chance, and wreaking havoc as a consequence.[28] During the same month, in London, the Boyle Family commenced the random selection of sites for their

World Series (Journey to the Surface of the Earth). The *World Series* sites were chosen by individuals – strangers to Boyle and Hills – who were blindfolded and invited to shoot darts at a large map of the world. The idea was for the artists to travel to each site, and produce a 'multi-sensual presentation' of it. The *Liverpool Dock Series*, made in 1976 and 1977, was an extension of the *World Series*.[29]

To create works based on such modest, incidental events as those determined by chance is to recognise something approaching what Swiss psychiatrist Carl Gustav Jung had regarded as a pattern characteristic of a given moment. 'Whatever happens in a given moment', wrote Jung, 'possesses inevitably the quality peculiar to that moment'.[30] He summed this notion up with the word 'synchronicity': synchronicity 'takes the coincidence of events in space and time as meaning something more than mere chance, namely, a peculiar interdependence of objective events among themselves as well as with the subjective (psychic) states of the observer or observers'.[31] That chance events might yield the truth of the moment is taken further by Jung: 'such an obvious truth as this reveals its meaningful nature only if it is possible to read the pattern and to verify its interpretation'. Finding profound consequence in such patterns was of little interest to Mark Boyle. He wrote about a more simple end: of looking – or attempting to look and see – 'without motive and without reminiscence'; of attempting 'to look at anything without discovering in it our mother's womb, our lovers' thighs'.[32] To find meaning in the random was, according to people like Boyle, to once again resort to what was already known. The more meaningful (or meaningless but authentic) alternative was simply to accept it as a fact on its own terms.

Jean Baudrillard may, if he had visited *Real Life*, have accused the *Liverpool Series* of being 'reality for its own sake, the fetishism of the lost object: no longer the object of representation, but the ecstasy of denial and of its own ritual extermination'.[33] He would, however, have been countered by Boyle, who said that in 'a context of everything, anything is a fair sample, or, to put it another way, nothing is a fair sample. […] To study everything we may isolate anything'.[34] Regardless, the French writer would certainly have nodded knowingly at the audience in the gallery intently studying the exact replicas of sites elsewhere in the city. The sign had indeed come to be more real than the reality it referenced.

In 1968, Jeff Nuttall wrote, 'The future is a void. In these days this seems particularly apparent. The only way to deal with void is by a game of chance, some absurd pattern of behaviour.'[35] Candida Höfer was recording, through her camera, the chance encounter in the streets of Liverpool, and John Latham was employing chance processes to disrupt the apparent order of knowledge. Mark Boyle and Joan Hills were going anywhere that darts thrown by strangers told them to. Chance was provoked by all, but, for others, the emphasis was on the absurd: in 1969 at The Blackie, a man dressed in a barrister's wig and gown was using an electric saw to cut in half a book called The Christian Life;[36] and in 1971, half-a-dozen mourners, in full, formal Victorian dress, laid wreaths on demolished sites across the city for no obvious reason.[37] In 1968, on a beach near Liverpool, a lot of people had been buried up to their necks.[38] They all faced out to sea, and stretched as far as the eye could see in a single line. The following year, the man responsible turned the shovel on himself.[39] Nine photographs document his gradual, and ultimately complete, burial. By the ninth photograph, however, the suspicion is that fact has become fiction. Maybe Eddie Ginley went on to investigate the man's disappearance. *Liverpool was an absurd place*.

26 Peter Moores wad an important figure in terms of supporting contemporary art in Liverpool at this time. His 'Liverpool Projects' included, *New Italian Art* in 1970, *Magic and Strong Medicine* in 1973, and *Body and Soul* in 1975. These exhibitions took place biennially, between the John Moores Exhibitions of painting that his father sponsored. Peter Moores used money generated from the family business, Littlewoods, in 'identifying cultural projects that deserve wider public notice and making these projects available to the public and working to involve the public in them' (Moores, Peter, *Real Life* exhibition catalogue, Liverpool: Walker Art Gallery, 1977, p. 2). Among many cultural involvements, Peter Moores sponsored the Great Georges Project in Liverpool.

27 In the accompanying catalogue, an interested local politician called John Last described the theme as being one that tackled 'aspects of the problem of what constitutes reality' (Councillor John Last, Chairman, Arts & Culture Committee, Merseyside County Council, *Real Life* exhibition catalogue, Liverpool: Walker Art Gallery, 1977, p. 1). Along with a number of texts about art and reality in the catalogue, there were advertisements for companies like 'Palitoy', who promoted their new video games (including TV tennis, football, handball, and squash) as 'just like the real thing'. A world of virtual-reality and simulation – the very 'reality' being registered by Baudrillard as now dominant – was thus being made commercially available, and entering popular, consumer culture.

28 Like Eddie Ginley, Luke Rhinehart is a fictitious character, in the novel, *The Dice Man* (1971) by author Luke Rhinehart.

29 According to Boyle, the Liverpool series explored 'various factors of random selection' (Boyle, statement in *Real Life* exhibition catalogue, p. 15). Nine works were made: in some, the random factor was simply in what had accumulated within a six-foot square; in others, the general location was selected but the particular square of ground chosen by chance; and in others still, the location was determined by chance, but the particular square selected. Several of the randomly selected locations turned out to be in water, and these were recorded with film.

30 Jung, Carl Gustav, 'Foreword' (1949), *I'Ching*, translated by Richard Wilhelm and Cary F. Barnes, London: Routledge & Kegan Paul, 1951, p. xxiii.

31 Jung, 'Foreword' (1949) p. xxiv.

32 Boyle, Mark, *Beyond Image: Boyle Family*, London: Hayward Gallery, 1987 (see www.boylefamily.co.uk).

33 Baudrillard, 'The Hyper-realism of Simulation', p. 1049.

34 Boyle, Mark, untitled statement, *Control Magazine*, No.1, 1965, unpaginated.

35 Nuttall, *Bomb Culture*, p. 67.

36 It was John Latham, inappropriately dressed and misusing the power-tool, performing part of a multi-media event organised by the Eventstructure Research Group of which he was a member.

37 This was the Great Georges Project performing *Gifts to the City: Six Memorials*.

38 This was *Liverpool Beach Burial*, the work of the artist Keith Arnatt, who taught at Liverpool College of Art from 1961 to 1964. By 1968, he was working at Manchester College of Art.

39 Arnatt, Keith, *Self Burial*, 1969. Arnatt recalled, 'the continual reference to the disappearance of the art object suggested […] the eventual disappearance of the artist himself'. Arnatt, Keith, quoted in *1965 to 1972 – when attitudes became form*, Cambridge: Kettle's Yard, 1984, p. 29.

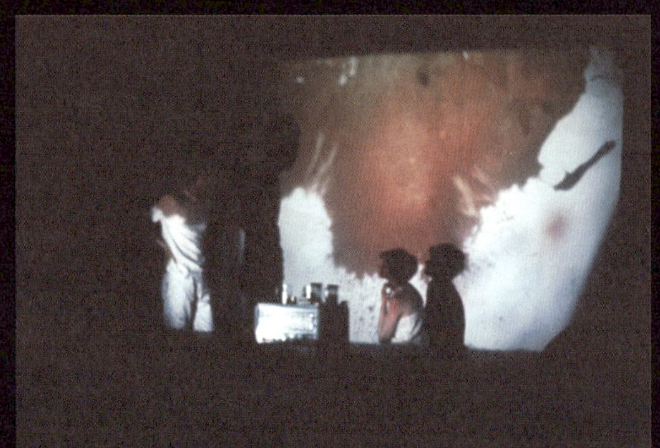

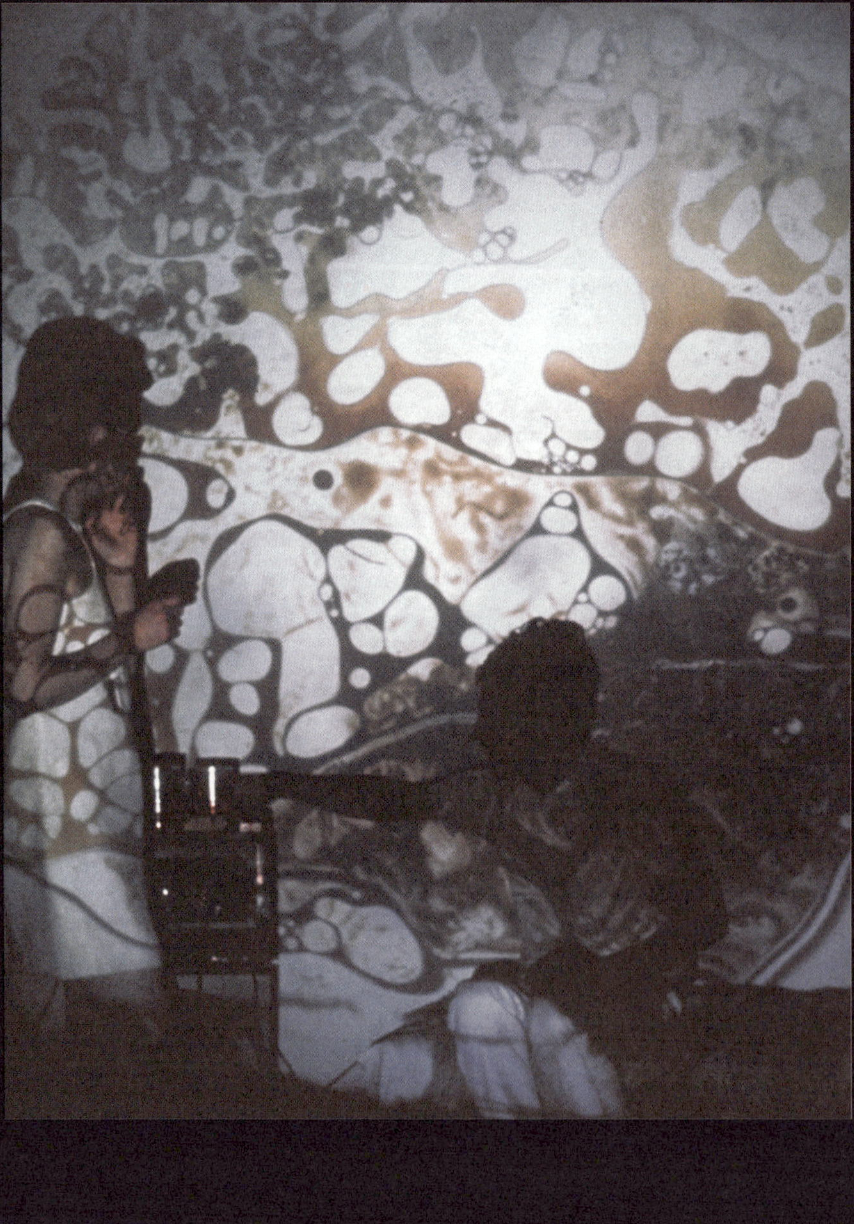

11

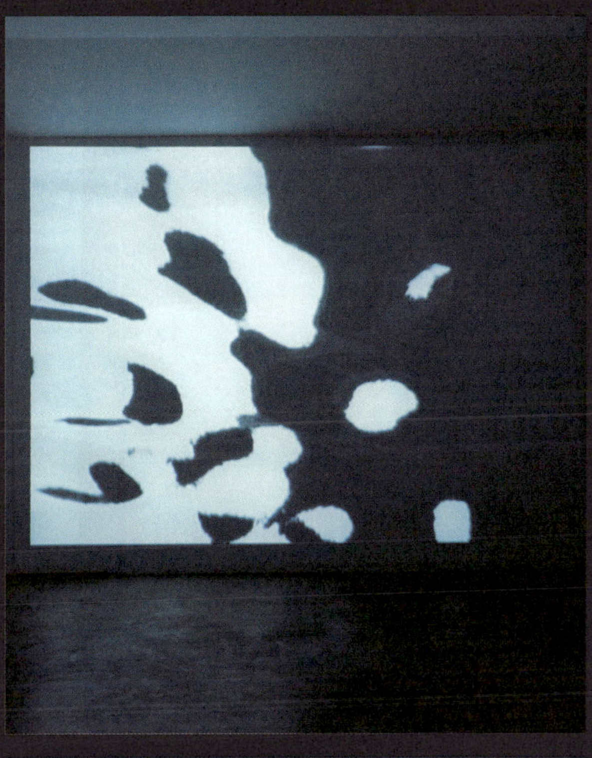

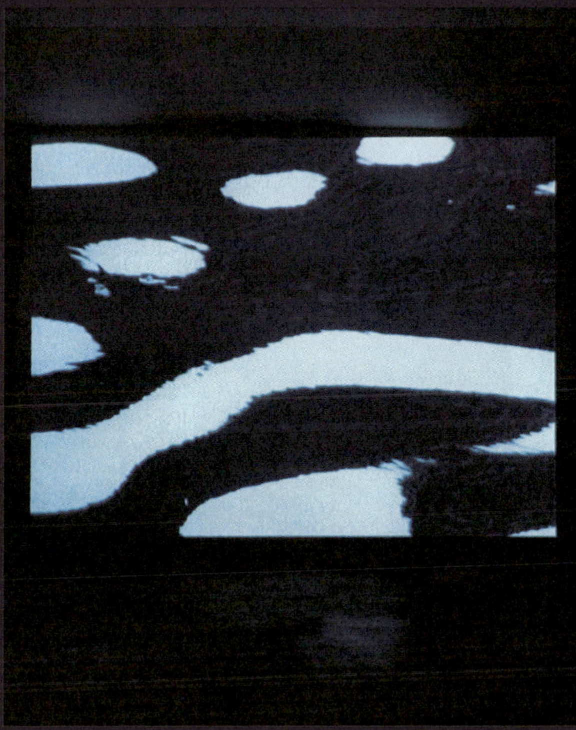

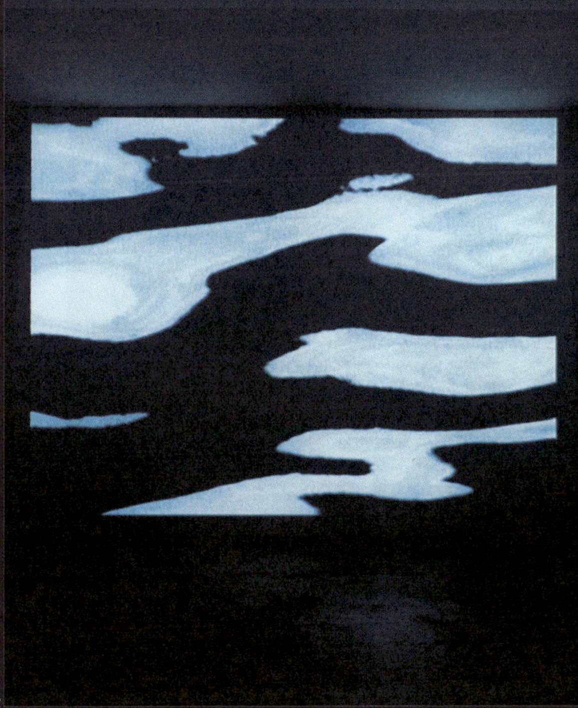

11
**Mark Boyle and
Joan Hills**
Performance of
*Son et Lumière for Bodily
Fluids and Functions*
at the Bluecoat Gallery,
Liverpool 1967

12
Boyle Family
*Herculaneum Dock
Series* 1976
Three black and white films
2 minutes 56 seconds;
3 minutes 23 seconds;
4 minutes
Compton Verney

NOBOTCH

1 2 3 4 5

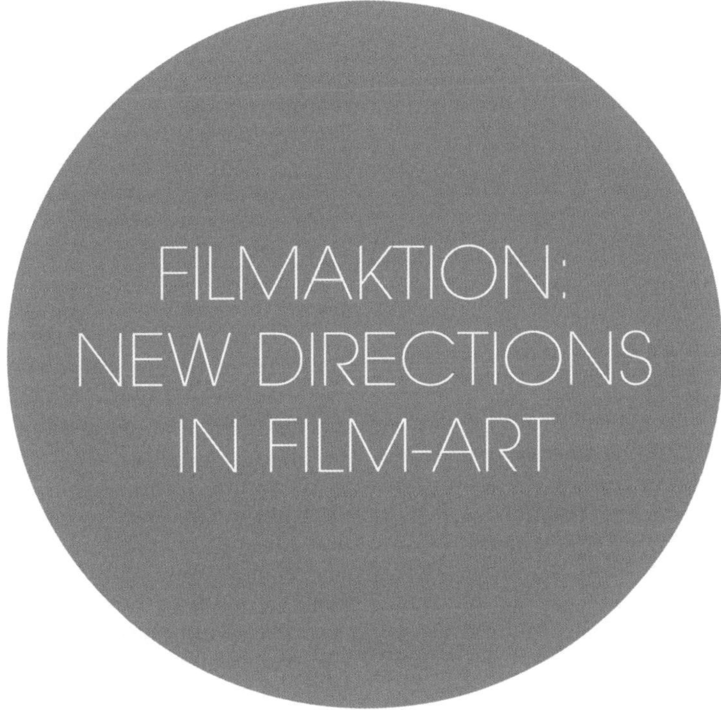

FILMAKTION: NEW DIRECTIONS IN FILM-ART

Lucy Reynolds

Filmaktion:
New Directions in Film-Art
Lucy Reynolds

In the week of 22 to 28 June 1973, a unique and unprecedented series of film screenings and events took place at the Walker Art Gallery in Liverpool under the title of 'Filmaktion'. Scant evidence remains of what happened there beyond a single timelapse film record, a scattering of previews, passing mentions in the texts of avant-garde film histories and the recollections of the filmmakers themselves. These fragments present a partial and tantalising snapshot of a significant moment in the history of British avant-garde filmmaking; not only one of the earlier instances of film crossing over into the gallery space but a portrait of a distinct approach to film form, an 'expanded cinema' which manifested itself as a diverse array of experimental multi-screen projections, film performances and installations. The group of British avant-garde filmmakers who organised and presented their work over the course of the week in Liverpool were all associated with the London Filmmakers' Co-operative (LFMC); they were filmmakers who had come to the medium predominantly from backgrounds in painting and sculpture, bringing a modernist sensibility to their filmmaking, yet one infused with the political and cultural influences of the underground counterculture from which the London Filmmakers' Co-op had emerged in the mid 1960s. Their combination of political and formalist radicalism, tempered by the loose collective working practices of a co-operative structure, resulted in the brief flowering of a uniquely coherent period of avant-garde filmmaking in

Britain. The open gallery spaces at the Walker provided ideal conditions for the experimental 'workshop' framework first developed at the Co-op, enabling the Filmaktion participants to realise ambitious multi-disciplinary film events which called into question existing notions of the cinematic viewing space and the role of the spectator.

The idea for Filmaktion was originally sparked by a letter which William Raban, then workshop organiser at the Co-op, sent out speculatively to film theatres and galleries around the country in December 1972. Intended to solicit interest for screenings of his films and those of his fellow Co-op filmmakers, Raban's letter resulted in three positive responses which led to a series of screenings the following year at the Edinburgh film festival, Camden Festival and the Filmaktion events at the Walker Art Gallery. In retrospect, Raban's letter reflects the growing confidence of the British avant-garde filmmaking community at this point in the early 1970s. He refers to the 'rich situation in this country with artists turning towards film as the medium of their expression',[1] indicating a new-found sense of identity, in which filmmakers such as himself saw themselves aligned to practices in art rather than those of the cinema. Indeed, the origins of the London Filmmakers Co-operative were more closely linked to the alternative culture of London in the latter part of the 1960s, intrinsic to a wider cultural explosion in the arts which was characterised by the music and happenings of the UFO club, and the diversity of theatre, performance and poetry readings at venues such as the Arts Lab on Drury Lane and Better Books, where it was first based. The legacy of this early period of Co-op history remained in the political, anti-establishment ideals of many of the filmmakers at Filmaktion, as did the collective sensibility and non-commercial ethos which was enshrined in the LFMC's co-operative constitution. It might also be argued that echoes of the multi-disciplinary, performance-based art forms of Better Books and the Arts Lab, with their emphasis on the live event, were later to be found in the expanded cinema experiments of events such as Filmaktion.

By 1971-72 there is evidence that the Co-op's confluence of politics and art had produced a certain conceptual approach amongst its members which engaged a critique of mainstream cinema at the level of film's actual image-making processes, rejecting the conventions of cinematic narrative and concentrating on the specific materials and processes used in filmmaking, which became the main shape and content of the film. This new materialism was not only encouraged by the process-based modernism of other art forms, but also by the printing and processing facilities available at the Co-op from the late 1960s. Access to this equipment enabled filmmakers to intervene artistically at every stage in the film process and allowed greater control over the production of the film image, even, as Michael

---

1   Extract from copy of William Raban's letter; courtesy of the artist.

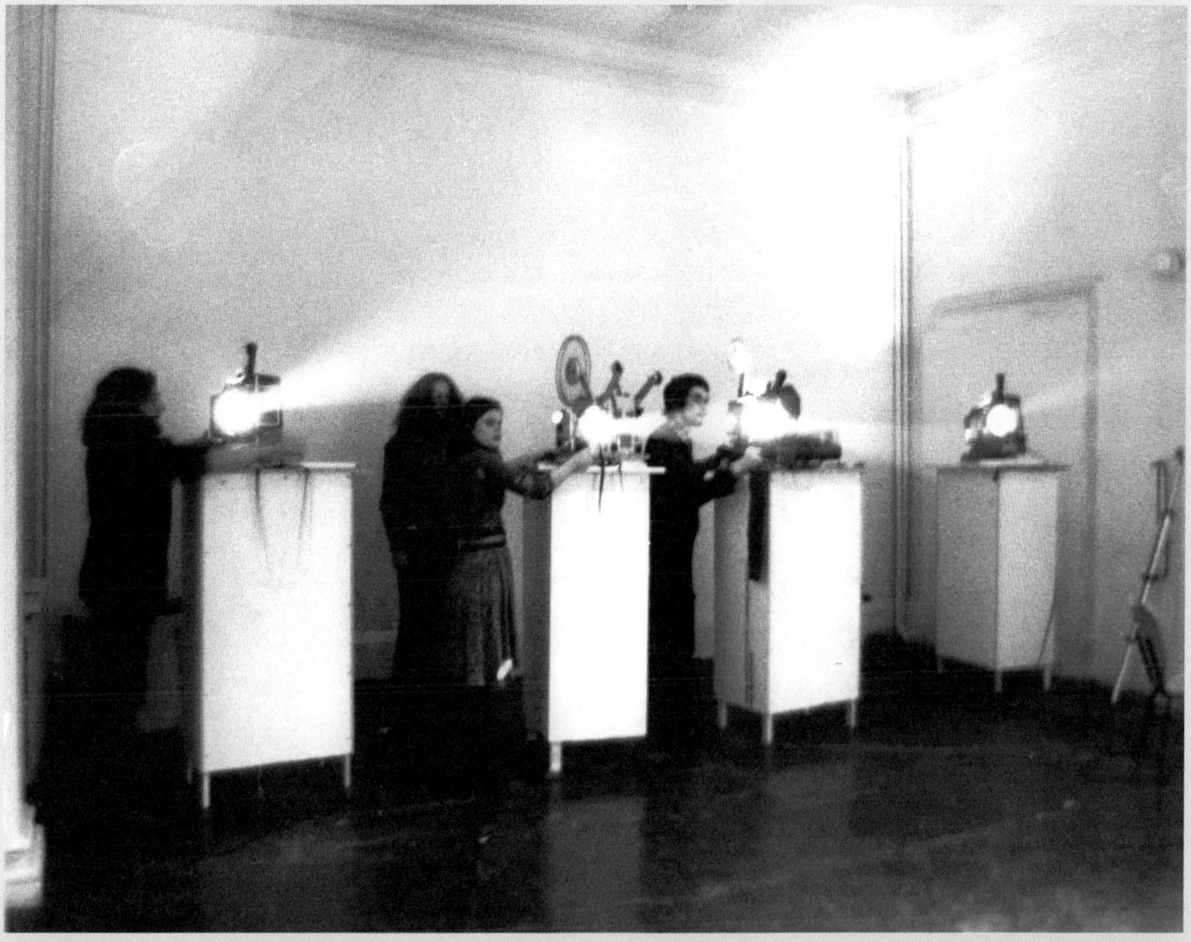

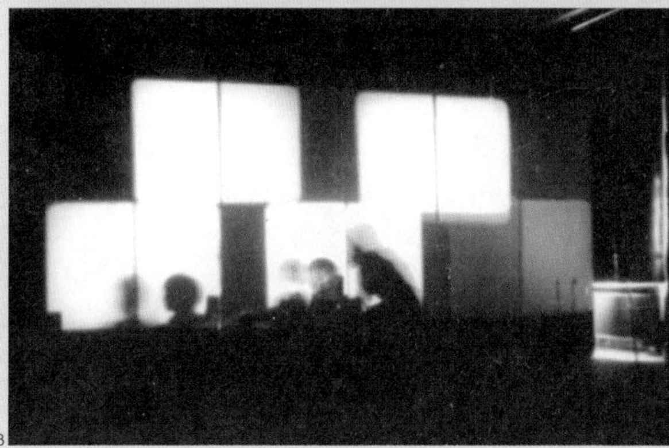

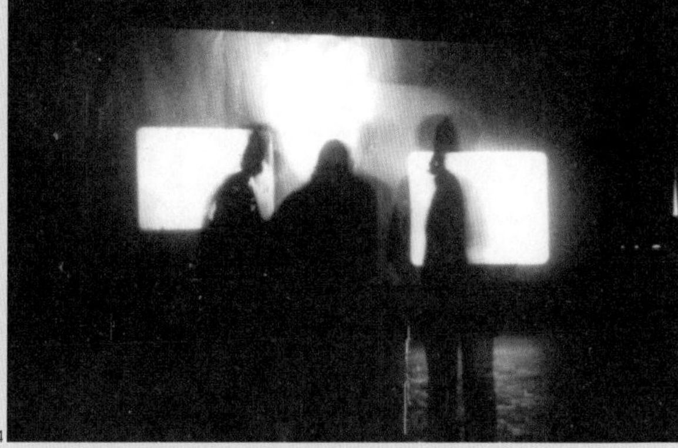

previous
Filmaktion: Mike Dunford,
Roger Hammond,
Malcolm Le Grice,
David Crosswaite and
William Raban in 1973

2
Malcolm Le Grice,
Gill Eatherley,
David Crosswaite
and William Raban
Gallery House,
London, March 1973

3/4
William Raban
Filmaktion Timelapse 1973
Film, black and white
5 minutes

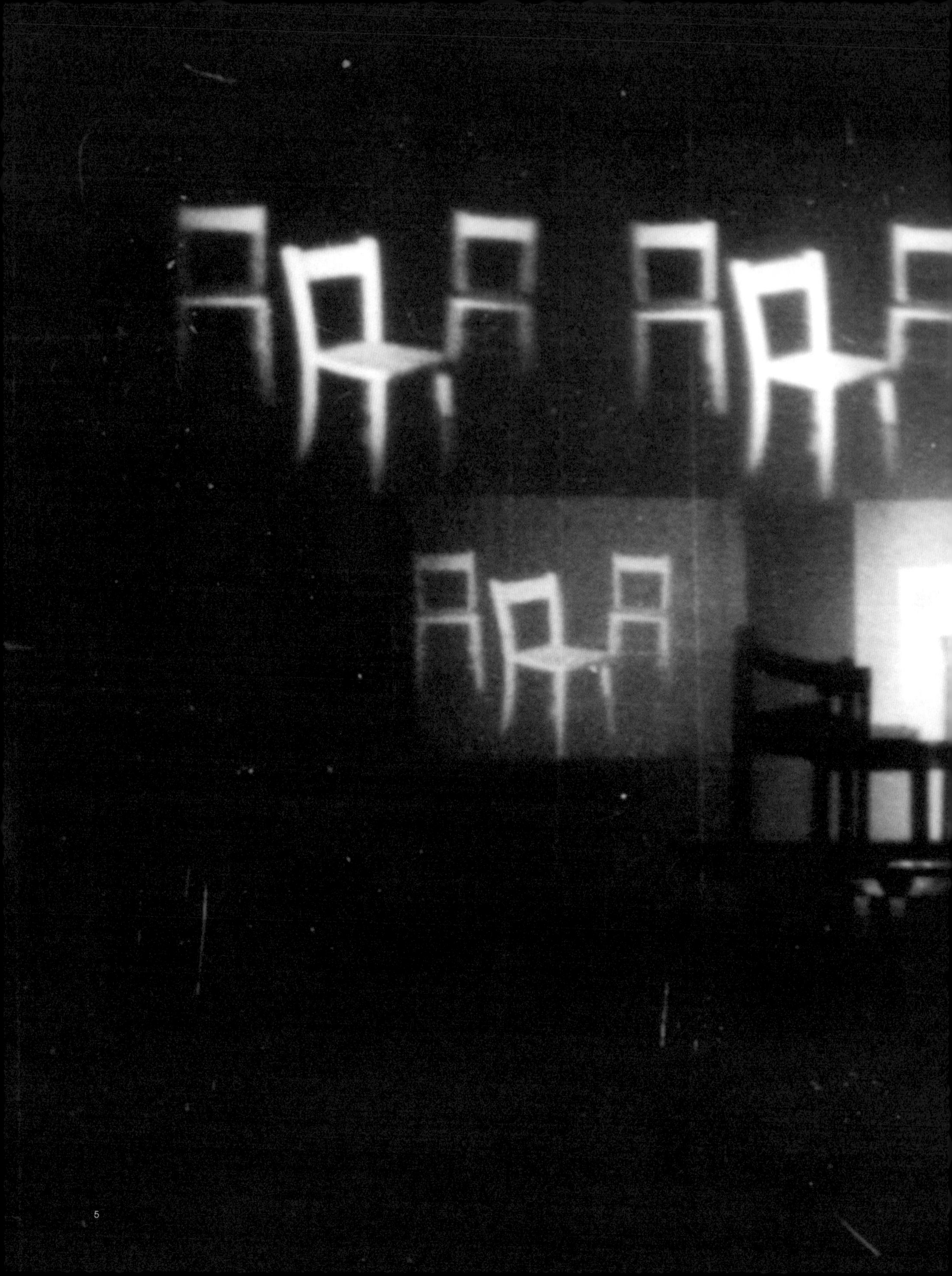

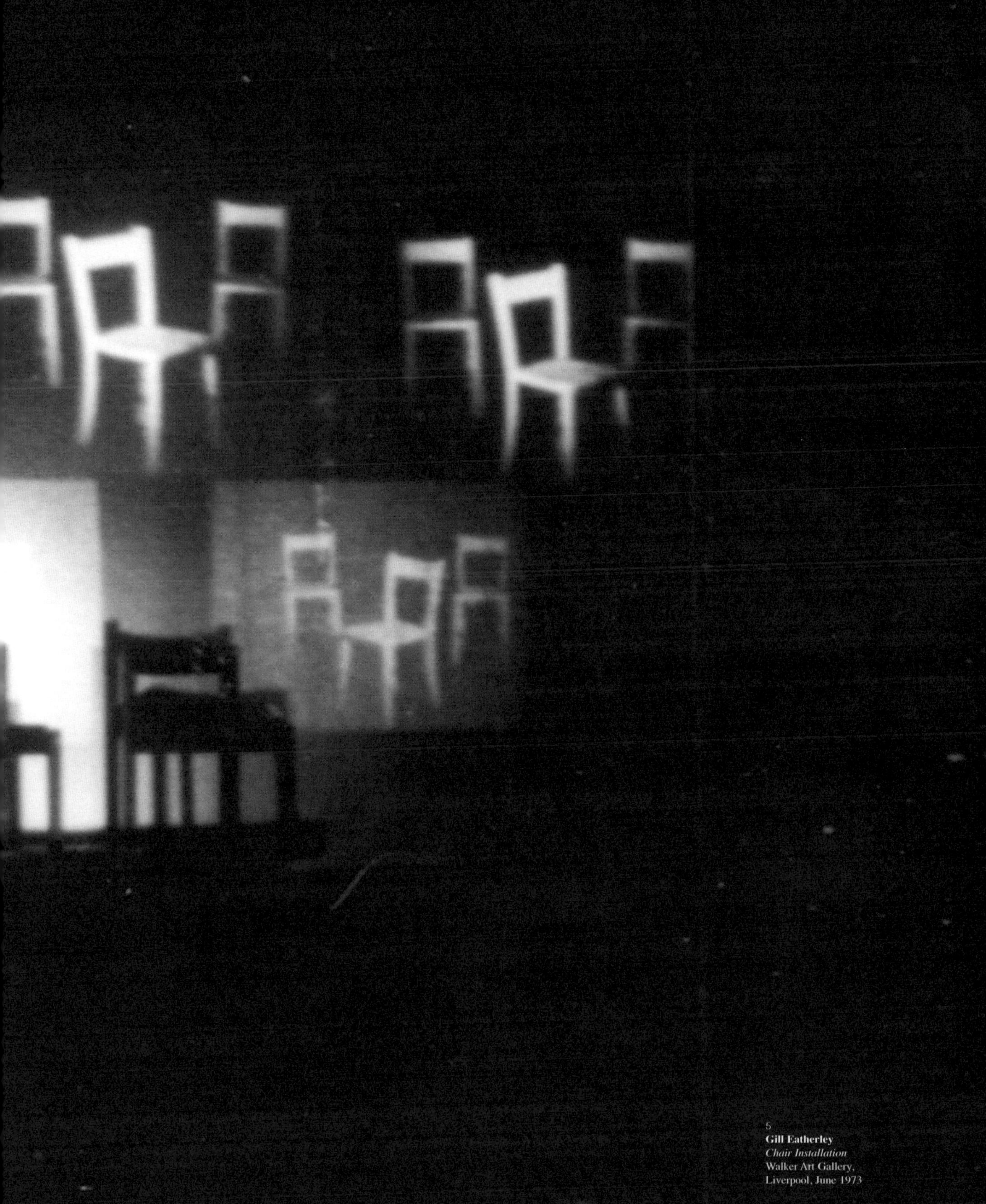

5
Gill Eatherley
Chair Installation
Walker Art Gallery,
Liverpool, June 1973

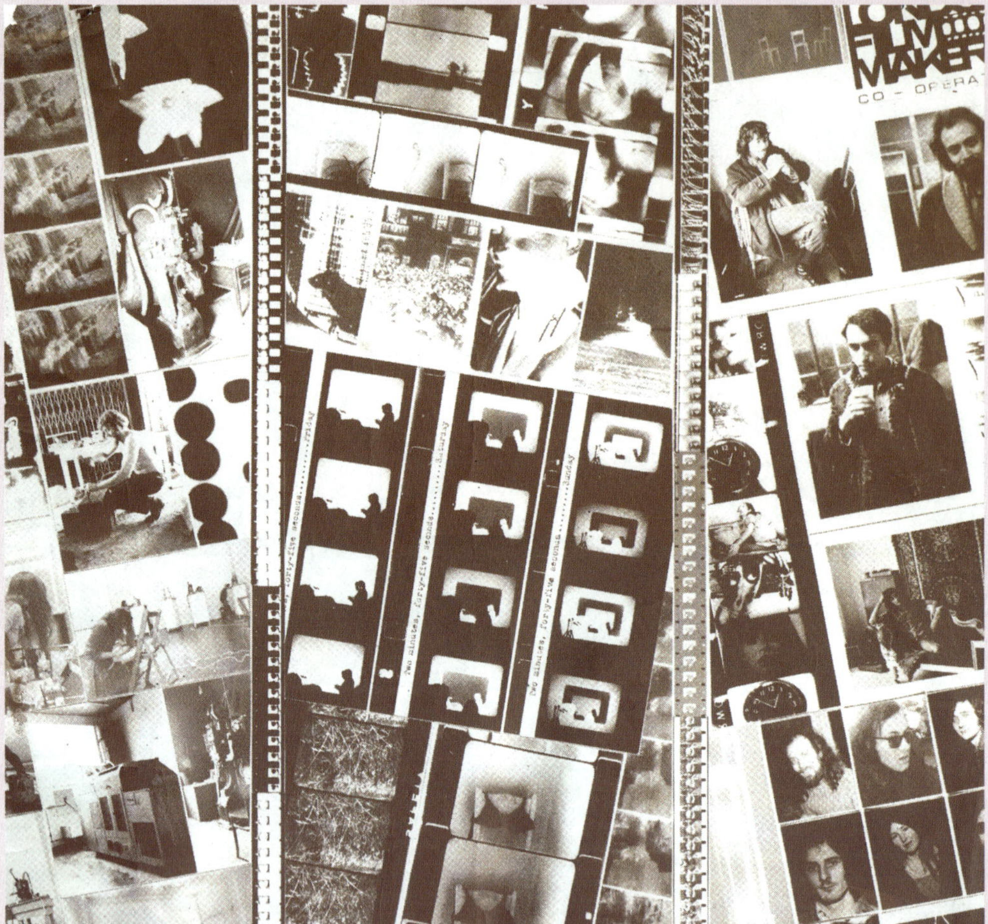

6
Filmaktion,
Walker Art Gallery,
publicity poster by
David Crosswaite, 1973

O'Pray has observed, introducing an artisanal or 'painterly aspect'[2] more associated with the singular work practice of artists rather than the mass production of a film lab. Thus by 1972 Malcolm Le Grice could talk confidently in 'Thoughts on Recent "Underground" Film' of a 'new formal tendency'[3] distinct from the previous aesthetic of American underground cinema. In the same year, in his introduction for a screening of 'English Independent Cinema' at the National Film Theatre Peter Gidal declared, 'these are the only filmmakers in England who treat film as *film* and not as mere illustration to narrative.'[4] The descriptions of the films in the NFT programme gives an indication of how far conventional notions of content had been rejected in favour of a process-based materialism; David Crosswaite, for example, was producing 'strongly textured loops, superimposed, coloured, mathematically structured', and Roger Hammond's 'hard-core structuralism takes film in the direction of pure speed.'

However, the screening facilities of venues such as the National Film Theatre were not conducive to the increasingly ambitious multi-screen works of some of the Co-operative filmmakers. Indeed in his letter to the Walker Art Gallery Raban speaks of how '[F]or some of us who are using projection as part of the creative film process the conventional cinema is redundant.' Raban's views were shared by Malcolm Le Grice, who had been working with an expanded film form for several years, and also saw the ideal conditions for his work as the 'art gallery situation' rather than the auditorium. In an 1972 article 'Real Time/Space', Le Grice argued that the commercial cinema created an illusory, 'retrospective' and manipulative image of reality that bore no relation to the actual experience of the viewer, and wrote of 'reacting strongly against the passive, subjectivity to a prestructured substitute and illusory reality which is the normal situation for the audience of the commercial film.'[5] Instead Le Grice proposed a improvisational and participatory cinema where the viewer was made aware, through a number of different formal strategies and interventions such as multi-screen film projections, performance and shadow play, of the cinema experience as a live event, or rather, 'the Real TIME/SPACE event at projection, which is the current, tangible point of access for the audience'.[6] Le Grice's article has an important prescience in relation to the later events in Liverpool. It not only pinpointed the inherent problems that he saw with the viewing experience offered by mainstream cinema, but also acted as a statement of intent for a form of expanded cinema which would later find its most complete expression at Filmaktion.[7] Many of the notions that Le Grice had outlined in his article were put into practice early in 1973 when he was joined by other Co-op filmmakers, Raban, Annabel Nicolson, Gill Eatherley and David Crosswaite, to initiate a series of film events at Gallery House. One of the few galleries in London at that time which was sympathetic to artist filmmaking,[8] the success of events at Gallery House proved

that it was possible to stage ambitious multi-screen film events by sharing skills and resources. It also established the gallery space not only as a point of presentation to an audience but also as a studio situation where new expanded works could be experimented with and developed. For Raban it was 'an unconscious precursor' to Filmaktion and many works later shown in Liverpool, such as Le Grice's multi-screen film *Matrix*, and Gill Eatherley's installation, *Chair Installation*, were first developed there.

Meanwhile, Raban's letter to the Merseyside Arts Association, forwarded to the Walker Art Gallery, had drawn an enthusiastic response from the gallery education officer Anthea Hindes, who came to London to meet Raban and other members of the Co-op. Raban recalls how the shape of Filmaktion was decided over a meal at Jimmy's, a restaurant in Greek Street, with Malcolm Le Grice in particular keen for a collective name for the events and suggesting Filmaktion with a 'k' in a nod to the expanded cinema activities of Austrian and German contemporaries such as Valie Export, Peter Weibel and Birgit and Wilhelm Hein, with whom he had close connections and many shared ideals. The 'k', could also be seen as another way of distancing Filmaktion events from those of an earlier American expanded cinema characterised by the Vortex shows of West Coast filmmakers such as Jordan Belson and the multi-screen 'moviedrome' environments of Stan Vandeerbeck.[9] As Le Grice's article had signalled, British expanded cinema, like that of the Heins, was more concerned with the temporal/spatial dynamics of the cinematic experience than creating a sensory multi-media environment or multi-screen spectacle.

Looking back to the Filmaktion events in Liverpool, one of the most illuminating visual records exists in the form of a time-lapse film by William Raban. Condensed into four minutes of screen time, it provides a glimpse of the sheer diversity of filmmaking and filmmakers who were represented at the Walker in the week of 22 to 28 June. In the film's speeding frames rooms are emptied, blacked out, figures bend over

2   O'Pray, Michael, 'The Aesthetic Impact of Film Printing Processes on British Avant-Garde Film Since 1966', *Issues in Architecture, Art and Design*, London: Polytechnic of East London, 1988, p. 116.

3   Le Grice, Malcolm 'Thoughts on Recent "Underground" Film', *Afterimage*, no 4, Autumn 1972, republished in Le Grice, Malcolm, *Experimental Film in the Digital Age*, London: BFI Publishing, 2001, p. 13.

4   Extracted from primary source, National Film Theatre programme, 1972. Source: British Film and Video Artists Study Collection.

5   Le Grice, Malcolm, 'Real Time/Space', *Art and Artists*, December 1972, p. 39.

6   Le Grice, 'Real Time/Space', p. 39.

7   Le Grice, 'Real Time/Space.' In his article Le Grice mentions some of the artists already exploring the potential of projection as a live event, giving examples of multi-screen projections from Americans such as Beverley and Tony Conrad to his own performance related work and that of English contemporaries such as Annabel Nicolson, David Dye and Tony Hill.

8   The preceding year the curators Sigi Krauss and Rosetta Brooks had mounted 'The Survey of the Avant-Garde in Britain' which attempted to bring together artists working with time-based media and performance from a range of positions, including Stuart Brisley and John Hilliard. It featured Raban, Le Grice and other Co-op members in its film programmes.

9   For a more in-depth picture of American expanded cinema see the contemporaneous book by Gene Youngblood, *Expanded Cinema*, London: Studio Vista, 1971.

projectors, chairs and audiences appear and disappear. Amongst its fleeting images it is possible to recognise films which have since become part of the canon of British experimental filmmaking, such as William Raban and Chris Welsby's double screen landscape film *River Yar* (1971) or Peter Gidal's single screen *Upside Down Feature* (1969-72). It is even possible to make out the crouching figures of children, attending one of three children's filmmaking workshops. The leaflet produced for the events, entitled *Filmaktion: New Directions in Film-Art*, shows that events at the gallery were divided between film installations which would run throughout the day and evening film shows and events. Whilst the single screen works of other Co-op artists such as Peter Gidal, John du Cane and Stuart Pound were represented, the emphasis was on the 'film installations, live action pieces, expanded events and multi-screen work'[10] first pioneered at Gallery House.

Raban stresses the 'lack of ownership of ideas' at Filmaktion. This suggests a fluid collaborative working process which may have shaped the outcome of the piece, although ownership remained with the originating artist. Thus, Filmaktion represents a rare example of a situation where a collective agenda sparked off a range of different strategies for its realisation. Le Grice also confirms that the free exchange of ideas influenced all their work, talking of a 'considerable sharing of ideas and thoughts and inter-influence.'[11] Encouraged by Filmaktion's loose, improvisational framework and supported by fellow filmmakers, evening screenings were an opportunity to experiment with ambitious multi-screen projections and performance, which were often combined with the use of shadow play to accentuate the live nature of the projection process. The work of many of the participants also displayed an effacement of any representational image, using the projector beam either as pure light, or abstract squares of filtered colour. In *Horror Film* (1971), for example, Le Grice cast his shadow across three inter-layered projected loops of coloured film to create an array of coloured shadows. Moving back from the screen towards the light source of the projector, Le Grice's looming shadow appeared to contain the coloured screens within the span of his arms.[12] In *Precarious Vision* Annabel Nicolson explored the relationship between actual presence and projection in a 'duet between projectionist and performer with light the medium'.[13] As a performer read aloud from a projected screen of text, the light source was alternatively obscured and revealed so any sense of coherence in the flow of language is lost. Nicolson's piece playfully exposed the gap between the experience of actual time, embodied in the words of the performer, and the projected time represented by the words on the screen. In Gill Eatherley's double screen performance piece *Aperture Sweep,* the presence of the artist becomes a means of exploring the interplay between the film past and the live present, as she performed the action of sweeping the screens with a broom beside a filmic shadow self who unsettlingly followed the same actions. The sounds of her sweeping motion was further accentuated and magnified by the microphone attached to the broom.

The flexible spaces of the Walker Art Gallery, which could be quickly transformed from screening space to gallery, also enabled Filmaktion participants such as David Crosswaite, Roger Hammond, Nicolson and Eatherley to create installations during the day, treating the space as a creative studio situation of works in progress. Employing film loops, shadow play and sculptural elements, their installations developed in response to the space and mobile audience, who were encouraged to engage directly with the work and the artist. Free from the time constraints of a conventional auditorium-based event, for example, Gill Eatherley's *Chair Installation* incorporated film loops with ultraviolet strobe light, four chairs and her own performative intervention to create a three dimensional installation piece. As Eatherley later recalled 'The interesting thing there for me was the idea of building up something, starting from loops and bringing it off the screen down into the actual gallery situation and working with objects and movement.'[14] Her installation created a ghostly interplay between positive and negative images of the chairs, which blurred the distinctions between what was real and what was filmed. For Eatherley the expanded dimensions of the gallery enabled her to introduce sculptural elements as well as performance into her film, whilst Annabel Nicolson's installation, also running throughout the day, was an elegantly simple response to the objects already in the room. In *Sideways Projection*, light beams were projected obliquely onto the roll of paper which functioned as the Filmaktion film screen. The light beams threw into relief the ripples and dents in the surface of the screen, transcending its primary function as a projection surface to become an object of beauty and contemplation in its own right.

The mobile audience of the art gallery space also enabled Filmaktion filmmakers to build a different relationship to the viewer. No longer distanced to the darkened immersion of the cinema auditorium the viewer was now free to become more directly involved in the processes of performance and projection occurring around them, sometimes becoming the subject of the work. Each night, William Raban filmed a seated audience for the length of a 100ft roll of film announcing the day and the date, as a camera recorded this interaction from the back of the room. Raban processed the film record of the audience and his announcement and projected it the following day, continuing every night throughout the week so that the image became the sum of those filmed previously. In the resulting film, *2'45"* (named after the length of a roll of 100ft film) the film image resembles a never-ending set of reflecting and receding mirrors, flipping between positive and negative, as a receding picture of the screening space accumulated; the screen, the heads of the audience and the filmmaker making his announcement.

2' 45", *Horror Film* or *Precarious Vision* are just a few of those works from Filmaktion for which a description survives, either provided by the filmmaker or from those of latter re-enactments. Many of the works enacted there will remain tantalising titles in the Filmaktion leaflet. What of Roger Hammond's *Audition Phonation*, for example, or Mike Dunford's *Logical Proposition*? The ephemeral nature of the work devised and performed at the Walker has meant that what actually took place there cannot be reconstructed in any detail, and relies on the memories of the filmmakers involved, those that attended and Raban's fleeting film record. This seems to be in keeping with the ethic behind the work, that the projection situation be 'an immediate reality in time and space'.[15] Beyond the clearly stated aims of its participants, the actual events at Filmaktion defy description, a confluence of elusive experimental works many of which were never repeated, in adherence to the notion of film as a live event. Furthermore, whilst the participants' rigorous systematic approach to the medium of filmmaking sought to challenge the seductive nature of mainstream cinema, there is no doubt that their events had a seduction of their own. Evoked in description, and evidenced in later reconstructions, these multi-screen projections of shifting colour, shadow play and light must have been works of great beauty, which transcended their anti-illusionist brief. It could also be argued that the use of their own bodies through performance, and sometimes even echoed in film as in Eatherley's *Aperture Sweep*, raised other profound or existential questions about identity and self-expression.

Filmaktion was one of the high points in a burst of further expanded cinema activity throughout 1973. It was followed by expanded shows at the ICA as part of the International Festival of Independent Avant-garde Cinema in September and events at the Camden and Edinburgh Festivals, in which the title Filmaktion resurfaced as a collective term for film performances by Le Grice, Nicolson, Raban, Crosswaite and Eatherley. Whilst many of the artists involved at Liverpool continued to work with an expanded practice in the years that followed, the unique combination of radical content and experimental workshop conditions offered by the situation at the Walker was an opportunity never to return. The last major event for British expanded cinema was the Festival of Expanded Cinema at the ICA in 1976. It presented a much broader picture of expanded practice than Filmaktion; embracing a wide and inter-generational selection of British artists from 60s pioneer Jeff Keen to newcomers like Tony Sinden and Ron Haselden, even a young Derek Jarman. More a survey than Filmaktion's tight work-shop situation, the 1976 festival was one of the last events of the expanded cinema model pioneered at Gallery House and Filmaktion, as younger film-makers turned to other mediums and interests.

However, Filmaktion could be said to have had other repercussions following the week of events in Liverpool.

The willingness of the Walker to host Filmaktion encouraged further galleries across the country to offer their spaces for the use of experimental multi-disciplinary events which included film, thus slowly shifting the perception that film should be restricted to the conditions of the cinema and not considered a viable art form. Indeed the plethora of events, discussions and workshops in which the Filmaktion participants sought to engage Liverpool gallery visitors also worked to dispel this perception, whilst at the same time offering a new way of experiencing cinema. Installations such as *Chair Installation* could thus be seen not only as an early instance of film entering the gallery, but as one of the earlier examples of film liberated from the prescriptive temporal frameworks of narrative cinema. Works such as these allowed the viewer to engage with the film image in their own time and opened up new readings for film as a sculptural, material form. It was important, therefore, that the experiments of Le Grice, Eatherley and others should have been made in a public space where they could be measured by audience interaction, which was such a crucial part of the Co-op project. The views of local visitors, however, is not on record. What is certain is that the intense week of events at the Walker Art Gallery produced a radical and unprecedented form of expanded cinema, one nurtured by a unique configuration of conditions. Significant beyond its historical context, the rigorous conceptual framework and experimental, collaborative working practice pioneered in that week of events in Liverpool continues to challenge our understanding and perception of the spatial and temporal nature of film, radically realigning the possibilities and potential for how the cinematic viewing space might be experienced.

10 Extract from the Filmaktion programme leaflet, Liverpool: Walker Art Gallery, 1973.
11 Zoller, Maxa, 'Interview with Malcolm Le Grice', Michalka, Matthias (ed.), *X-Screen: Film Installations and Actions in the 1960s and 1970s*, Museum Moderner Kunst Stiftung Ludwig Wien, 2002, p. 146.
12 This was accompanied by a soundtrack of the artist breathing.
13 Extracted from retrospective correspondence with the artist.
14 Gill Eatherley in conversation with Annabel Nicolson extracted from 'Annabel Nicolson at the Co-op', in *Light Years: 20 Years of the London Filmmakers' Co-operative*, London: London Filmmakers Co-operative, 1986.
15 Extracted from the Filmaktion leaflet, Liverpool: Walker Art Gallery, 1973.

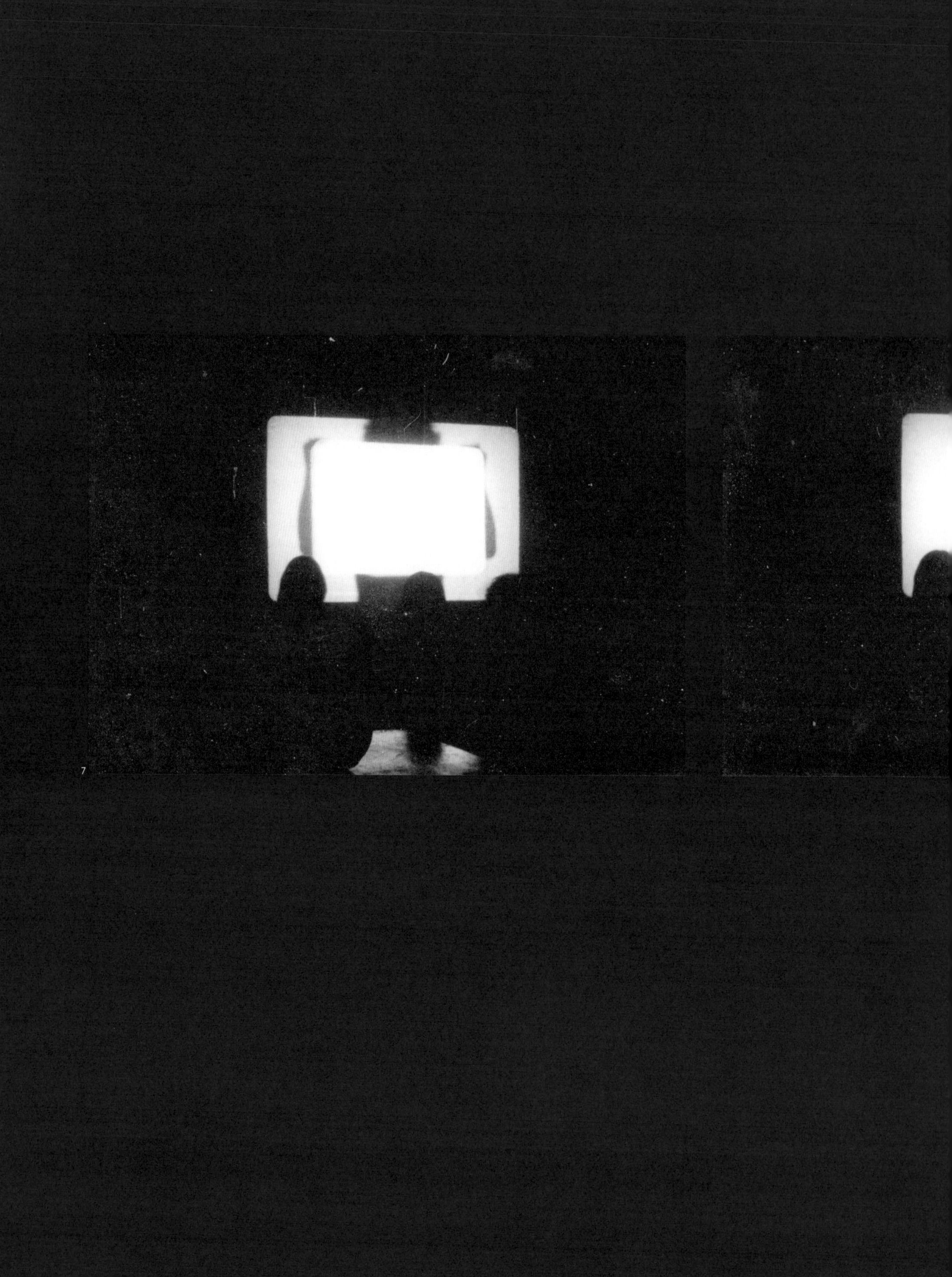

7

7
Malcolm Le Grice
Horror Film 1 1971
Film-shadow performance

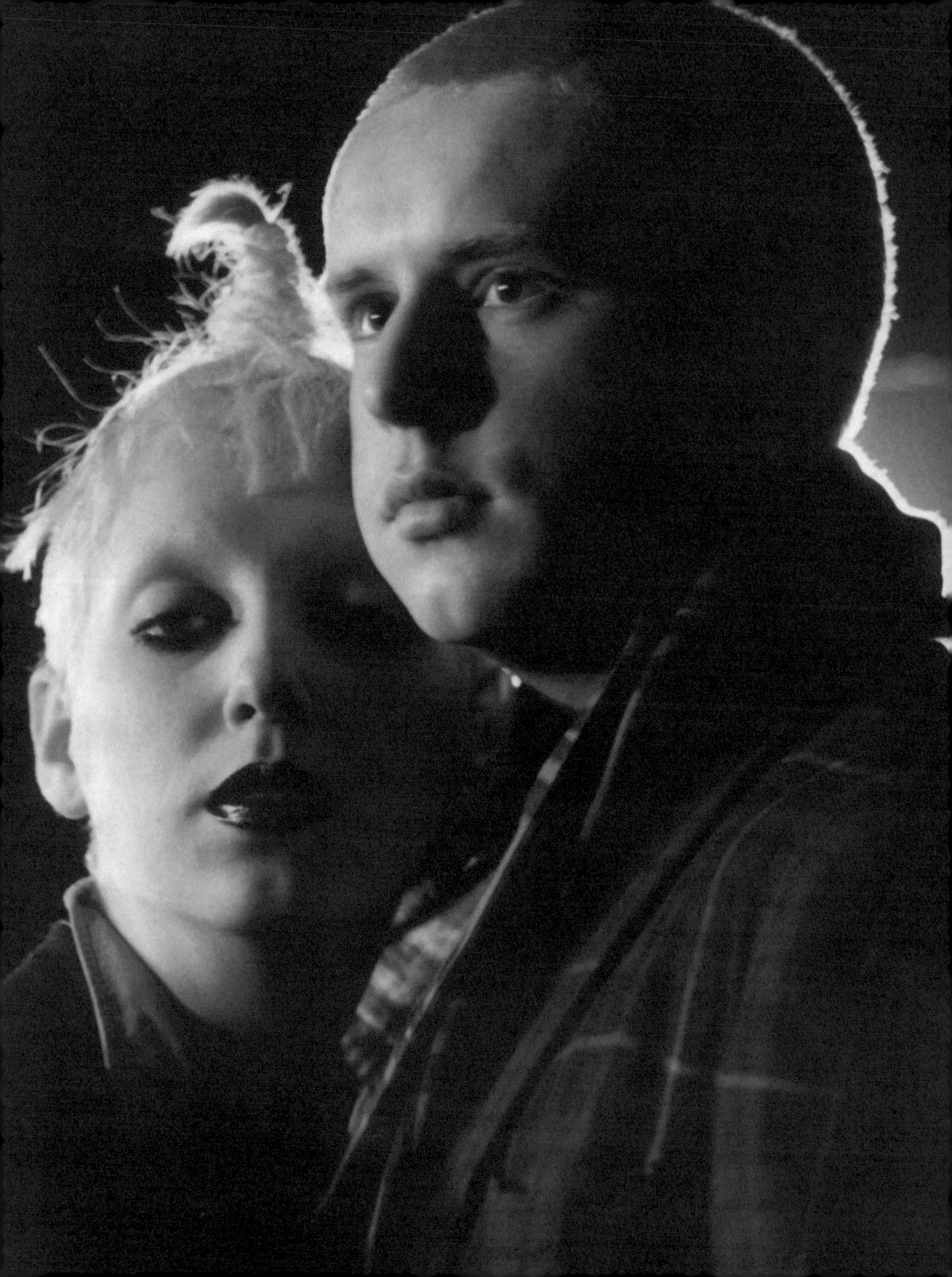

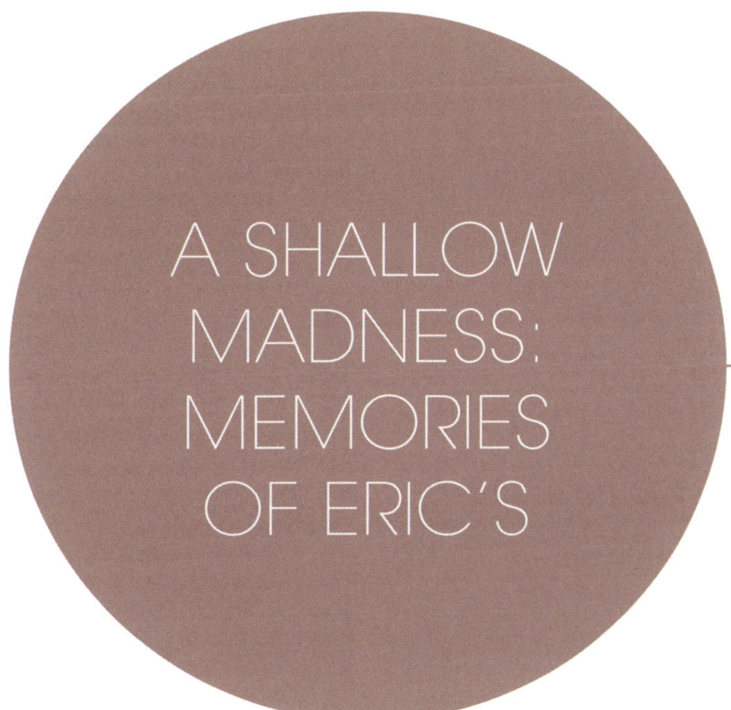

Jaki Florek

A Shallow Madness:
Memories of Eric's
Jaki Florek

Fact: Liverpool will *always* be synonymous with The Beatles and The Cavern. The Beatles phenomenon has passed from innocent folklore of the 1960s into the realms of 21st century commerce, well beyond the point of no return, and light years away from the original buzz.

In the aftermath, many of the local musicians professed to be very 'anti-Beatles' but others *actively chose to move to Liverpool*, to go to Art College or the University *because* of The Beatles' legacy, and because *Liverpool was Liverpool*. After all, Liverpool was 'the pool of life, the very centre of the life force itself' according to some dream that Swiss mind-explorer Carl Gustav Jung had and documented in his autobiography *Memories, Dreams, Reflections*.[1]

Mathew Street specifically was a centre of creative activity. The Cavern opened as a cellar jazz club in Mathew Street in January 1957, but as early as August 1957 The Quarrymen Skiffle Group played the venue, with John Lennon in the band. Around the same time, Ringo Starr also performed there, with The Eddie Clayton Skiffle Group. In January 1958 Paul McCartney made his Cavern debut, having joined John in The Quarrymen. Skiffle bands were in some ways a forerunner of the DIY Punk Revolution, with their home-made tea-chest basses and washboards and their disdain for their elders' 'proper music'. But it was the Beat Groups, and of course one group in particular, that made The Cavern globally famous. On 25 May 1960 Rory Storm and The Hurricanes (with Ringo on drums) played The Cavern's first

Beat Night session, Bob Wooler was putting on the lunchtime band and DJ sessions, and jazz was taking a back seat. In February 1961, The Beatles, back from their stint in Hamburg, made their first appearance at The Cavern.

To have a 'scene' you need the bands, the audience, a club that catches the spirit of the times, and someone who is fairly obsessive to book the bands and run the show. Had there been no 'scene', the spotlight would have been only on The Beatles. Bob Wooler was the driving force behind the Beat Scene at The Cavern and by the summer of 1962 had persuaded the owner Ray McFall to start booking big names, starting with Gene Vincent, with The Beatles on the same bill. More big named artists played there, as well as local bands King Sized Taylor, The Hideaways, Gerry and The Pacemakers, Rory Storm, The Searchers, etc. The Cavern's reputation grew massively, and Bob Wooler took on young Billy Butler to help him out.

Liverpool musician Al Peters: 'To get on at The Cavern we used to hang round The Grapes and The White Star, and buy Bob Wooler pink gins to encourage him to give us gigs! We'd do the all-night sessions; I've played for so many people there, Stevie Wonder and B.B. King, many times. We'd support The Exciters, The Drifters, Lee Dorsey…' Other notable artists who played The Cavern include Chuck Berry, Sonny Boy Williamson, Howlin' Wolf, Eric Clapton, The Rolling Stones, Status Quo, Judas Priest, Joe Cocker, The Who, The Kinks, Rod Stewart, Queen, Stevie Wonder, The Temptations, Elton John, Edwin Starr, Jimmy Page and Jimi Hendrix.

Roy Adams took The Cavern over in 1969, but in May 1973 it closed as a compulsory purchase order was placed on the club and the council demolished the warehouse above The Cavern. The Cavern was *filled in* and the waste ground above it was used as a carpark. The original Cavern Club was gone forever. Well, it was only some old club, wasn't it? 1984: Another re-built 'Cavern Club' opened on the original site. It was closed by Merseyside Police in December 1989, re-opening in July 1991. 2006: It is still a music venue, but with a heavy bias towards nostalgia and tribute bands

In 1973 Roy Adams opened a 'New Cavern Club' in Mathew Street, opposite the original site, then in 1974 it was re-launched as the Revolution Club downstairs, and Gatsby's upstairs. In October 1976, Roger Eagle and Ken Testi (who had been promoting at the Liverpool Stadium) took over Gatsby's for one night a week, and Eric's club was born. Pete Fulwell came aboard as a third partner, they bought the lease from Roy Adams, and Eric's moved downstairs into what had been The Revolution Club.

Eric's, as it turned out, was in the right place, at the right time, with the right people involved. Pure synchronicity.

---

1   Jung, Carl Gustav, *Memories, Dreams, Reflections*, London: Collins, 1961.

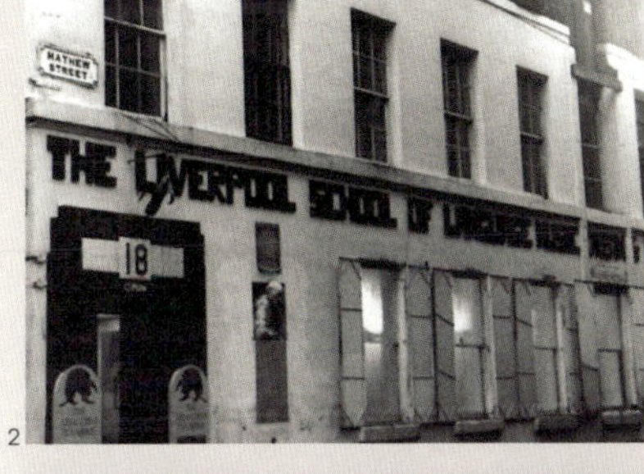

2

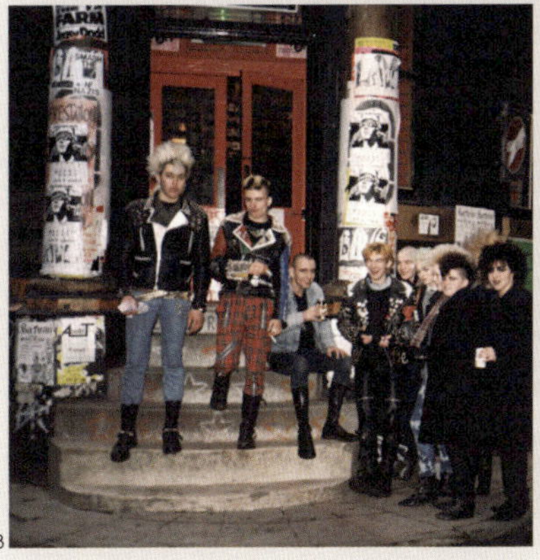

3

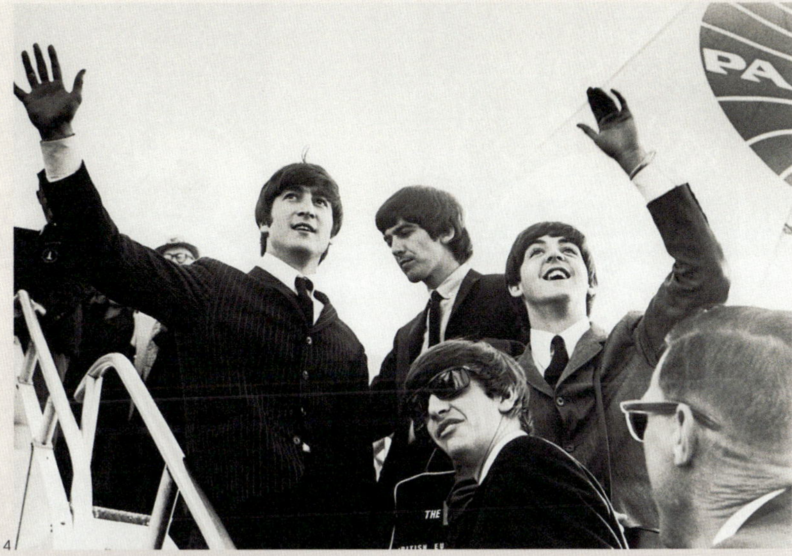

4

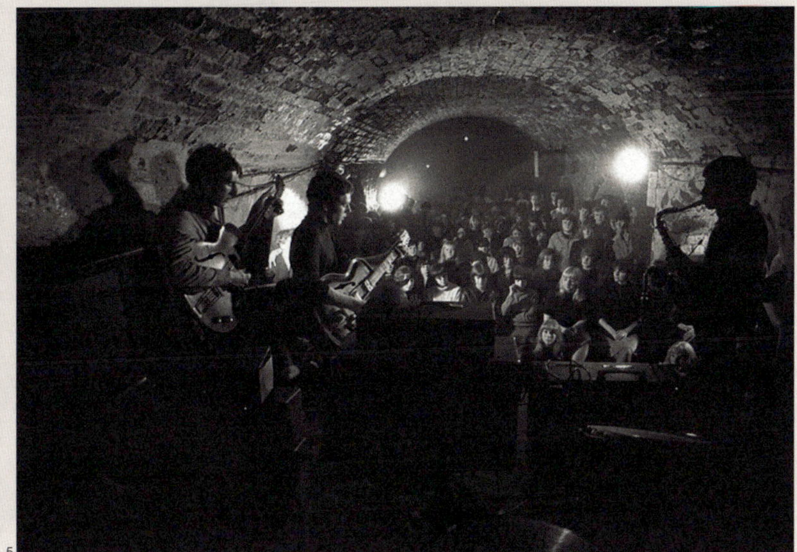

5

previous
Jayne Casey and
Holly Johnson 1977

2
The Liverpool School
of Language, Music,
Dream and Pun

3
Probe Punks

4
The Beatles Waving
from Airplane 1964
Miami, Florida, USA

5
Max Scheler
*The Roadrunners at
The Cavern* 1964
Silver gelatine print
50 x 60 cm
Courtesy Max Scheler/
K&K

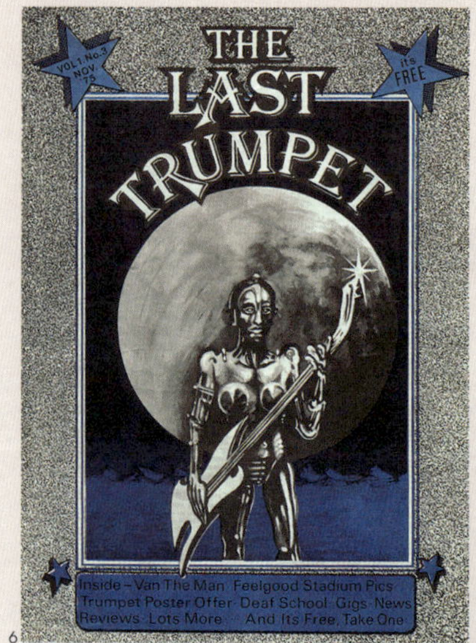

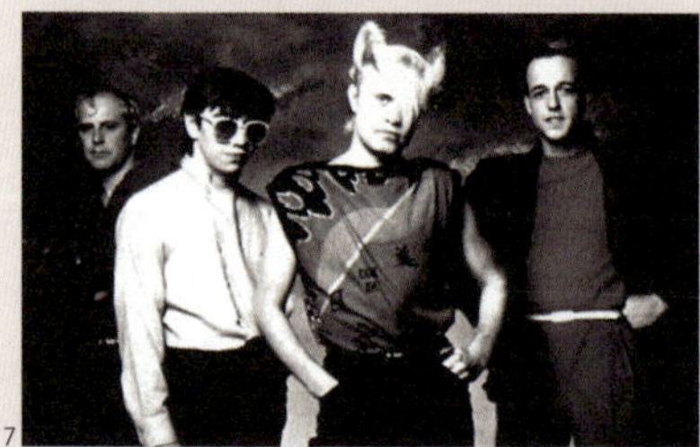

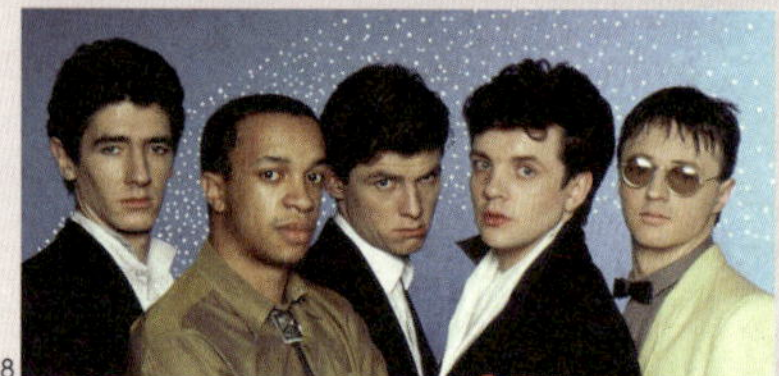

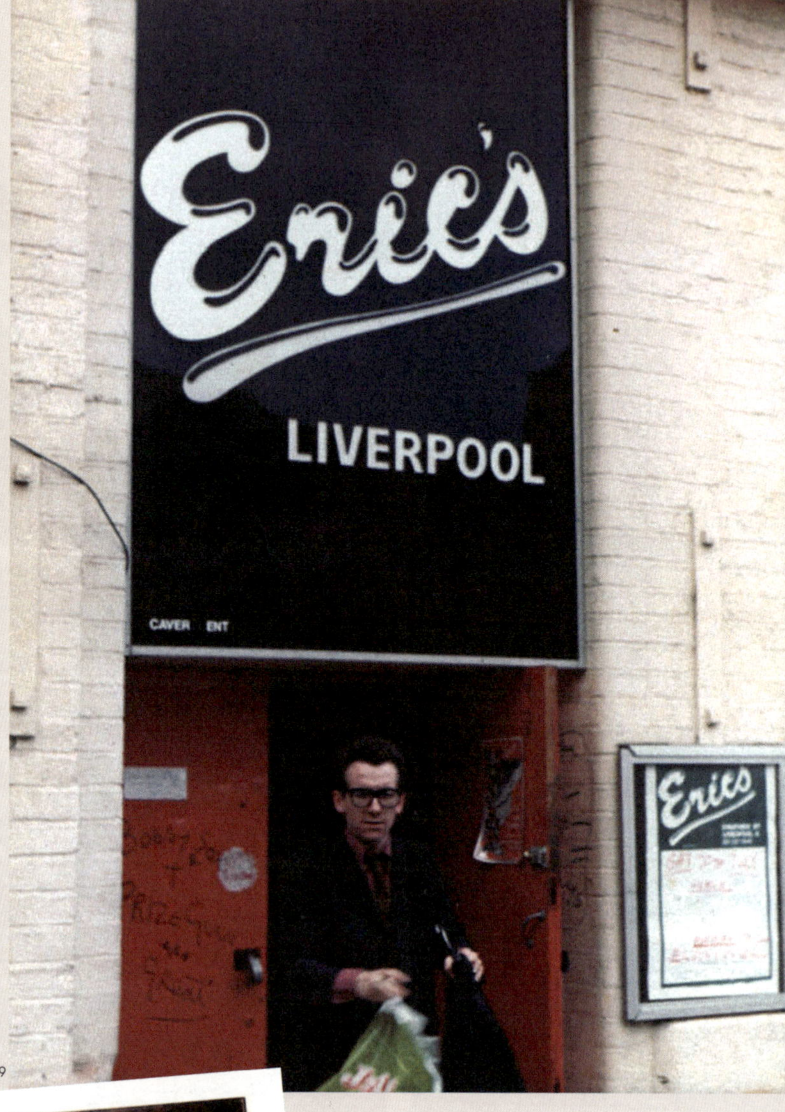

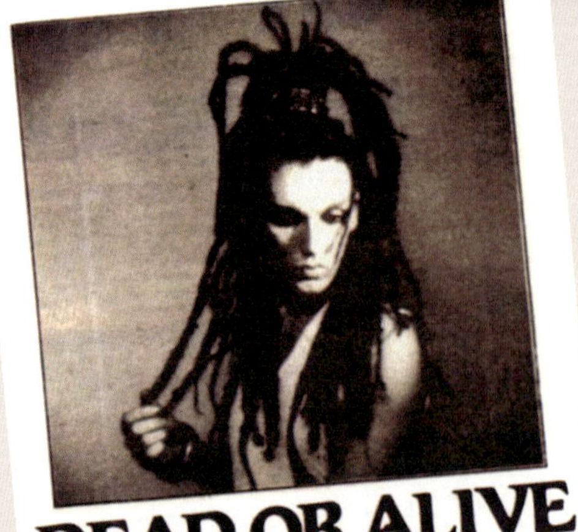

6
Roger Eagle
The Last Trumpet
Vol. 1 No. 3
November, 1975

7
A Flock of Seagulls, 1984

8
WAH! and Pete Wylie

9
Elvis Costello

10
Pete Burns
Dead or Alive, 1980

Dave Balfe: 'Eric's was the reason so much talent emerged from that generation in Liverpool.'[2]

Roger Eagle was truly a music evangelist, devoted to spreading the word of what he considered to be worthwhile music, inspiring and educating all who would be educated. A self-confessed 'Southerner by birth – but a Northerner by emotion'[3], Roger had moved up to Manchester in the 60s, famously DJ-ed at The Twisted Wheel, then in the early 70s was promoting bands at The Liverpool Stadium. He put on big name bands, kept admission prices low, and often gave local bands support slots including Albie Donnelly's Supercharge. He started a little magazine, *The Last Trumpet*, with help from Steve Hardstaff, Bryan Biggs, and others. Assisted by Doreen Allen, who also put on live music events, he moved over to Liverpool. She worked for him at The Stadium, and later at Eric's until it closed, and went on to open her own excellent live music club in Liverpool, Planet X.

Mathew Street was also where Peter O'Halligan and his cousin Sean Halligan set up a converted warehouse, The Liverpool School of Language, Music, Dream and Pun. They were devotees of Jung, and Jung's Liverpool dream was central to their thinking. Before the Eric's nights started in October, the Jung Festival was held in Mathew Street, in the summer of 1976, organised by Peter O'Halligan and a group of people. Martin Dempsey was at Liverpool College of Art, and he made the sign that went round Peter O'Halligan's building. Martin played the Jung Festival and other early gigs with Albert Dock and The Cod Fish Warriors who later on became The Yachts.

Martin Dempsey: 'I started the set by abseiling down the front of the building and onto the stage in skiing gear and skis, and all our stage gear was in suitcases; we got changed at the side of the stage.'

Bryan Biggs: 'Because Jung was Swiss, they invited the Mayor of Zurich over… he was greeted by this mad anarchic event with bands playing in the street. Charlie Alexander, or possibly Sean Halligan, jumped out of the warehouse window into a skip full of custard!'

A far cry from the Mathew Street Festival as it is today – the largest free annual music event in Europe, four days of live music spread over five stages across the city. It was estimated that 370,000 people attended the 2005 festival.

The Liverpool School of Language, Music, Dream and Pun was home for a while to Ken Campbell's Science Fiction Theatre of Liverpool, where his surreal *Illuminatus* plays were rehearsed and presented in November 1976, before moving down to The National Theatre in London.

Martin Dempsey: 'They installed a theatre space that had pumped-in smells through pipes, the audience were actually sat in a big cage of scaffolding, and my girlfriend at the time had made a soft-sculpture tablecloth; all the food, it was all knitted.'

Bill Drummond designed and built the stage sets. He had previously been at Liverpool Art College, had worked at The Everyman Theatre, and by 1977 had formed the band Big in Japan.

Chris Langham was working with Ken on the production, and he asked Albert Dock to do the music for the play. Other young musicians were involved, including Ian Broudie, later of The Lightning Seeds. Bill Drummond: 'Ken Campbell taught me to entertain *the possibility of everything*. I was 23 years old – a very good age for entertaining possibilities.'[4] Later, Bill theorised about the possibility of ley lines being present in Mathew Street, to explain why it was such a centre of creativity.

Peter O'Halligan took it to be of significance that his building was at the point where a number of streets met at the end of Mathew Street, as Jung had written about in his Liverpool dream: 'We found a broad square, dimly illuminated by street lights, into which many streets converged.'[5]

Bryan Biggs: 'It was a fantastic place. You couldn't pin it down – if they were to apply for an Arts Council grant now, would they apply for theatre, or music or what? It was one of those free spaces where all sorts of things happened.'[6]

The building housed Aunt Twacky's market stalls and O'Halligan's Parlour/The Armadillo Tearooms. Young local lads such as Pete Wylie, Julian Cope, Ian McCulloch would make a cup of tea last all afternoon, whilst they plotted to form bands, exploring the concept well in advance of the real thing. By the end of 1978 Les Pattinson really was playing bass in Echo and The Bunnymen, but first he was 'Geoff Lovestone', in his band The Geoffs where the whole imaginary line-up were called 'Geoff'. He went on to form The Love Pastels with three imaginary girls. There was also Bernie Connor and Tim O'Shea in The Cicero Gymnasts, or rather, there *wasn't*!

Thirty years on, the 2006 'Mathew Street Festival' opened with Pete Wylie singing with the Liverpool Philharmonic Orchestra.

In retrospect, this gathering together of like-minded people was an important stage in the development of the Liverpool music scene. Nowadays it would be called 'networking'; back then it was called being on the dole. Besides in The Tearooms, people met up in the café in the Open Eye (gallery, recording studio, record label) in nearby Whitechapel, and in Geoff Davies's legendary Probe Records shop at the top of Mathew Street, on the corner of Button Street. People were drawn to Probe from miles around.

2   Florek, Jaki and Whelan, Paul, 'Liverpool Eric's – all the best clubs are downstairs, everyone knows that', *Feedback*, 2007 (see www.feedback.org).
3   Roger's last interview before he died in May 1999, by Paul Welsby and Neil Henderson, appeared in Issue 2 of their fanzine *The New Breed*, reprinted in Florek and Whelan, 'Liverpool Eric's'.
4   Drummond, Bill, *45*, London: Abacus, 2001, p. 50.
5   Jung, *Memories, Dreams, Reflections*, p. 189.
6   Florek and Whelan, 'Liverpool Eric's'.

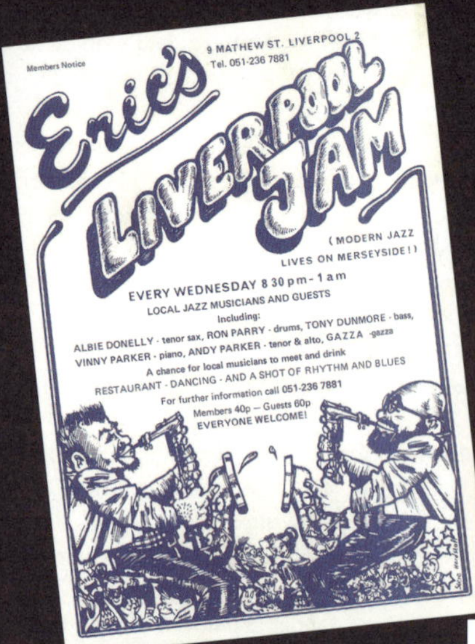

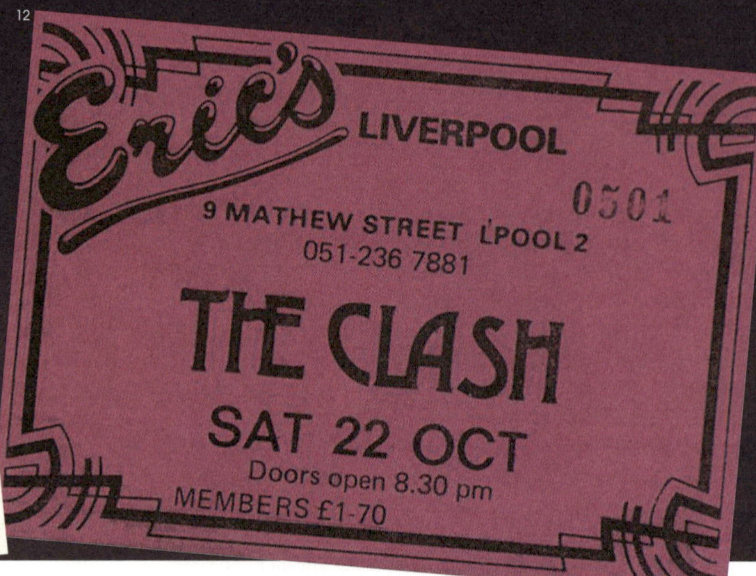

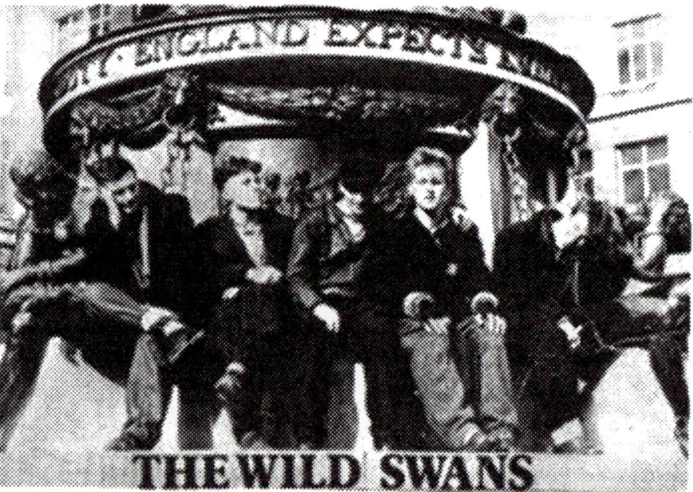

11
Poster for *Liverpool Jam*,
Eric's, Liverpool

12
Entrance Ticket for
The Clash, Eric's,
Liverpool, 22 October 1976

13
Roger Hill, *Mersey Sound*,
No. 23, 1980

14
Poster for Sex Pistols and
Albert Dock, Eric's,
Liverpool, 15 October 1976

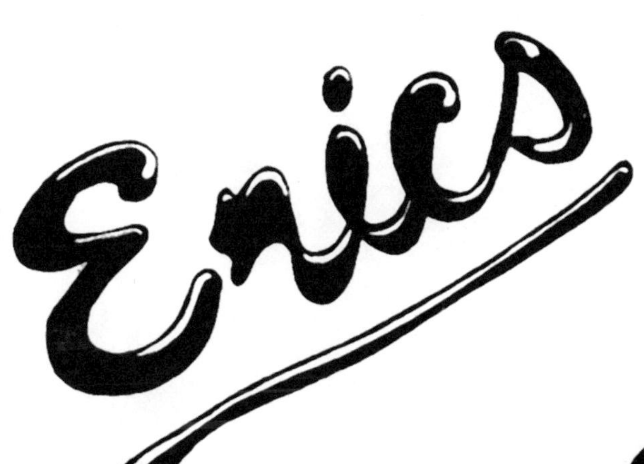

Erics

keeps on keeping on . . .

MATHEW STREET, LIVERPOOL 2
051-236 1118

FRIDAY OCT 15   8pm-2am

SEX PISTOLS

Johnny? Rotten isn't the half of it

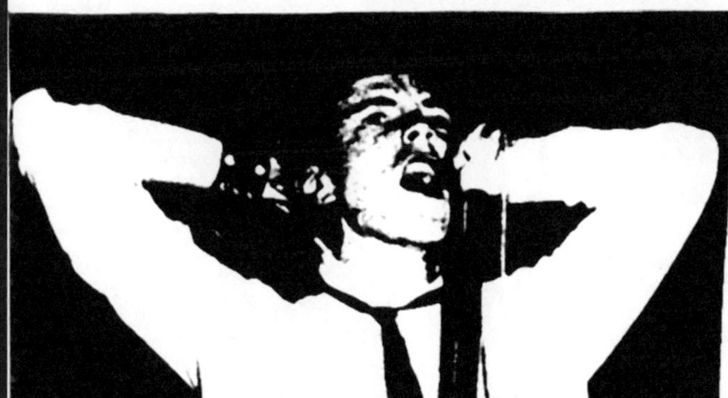

AND!!
ALBERT DOCK

MEMBERS £1·00   GUESTS £1·25

COMING SOON   THE COUNT BISHOPS
RACING CARS
ROOGALATOR
FLAMIN' GROOVIES

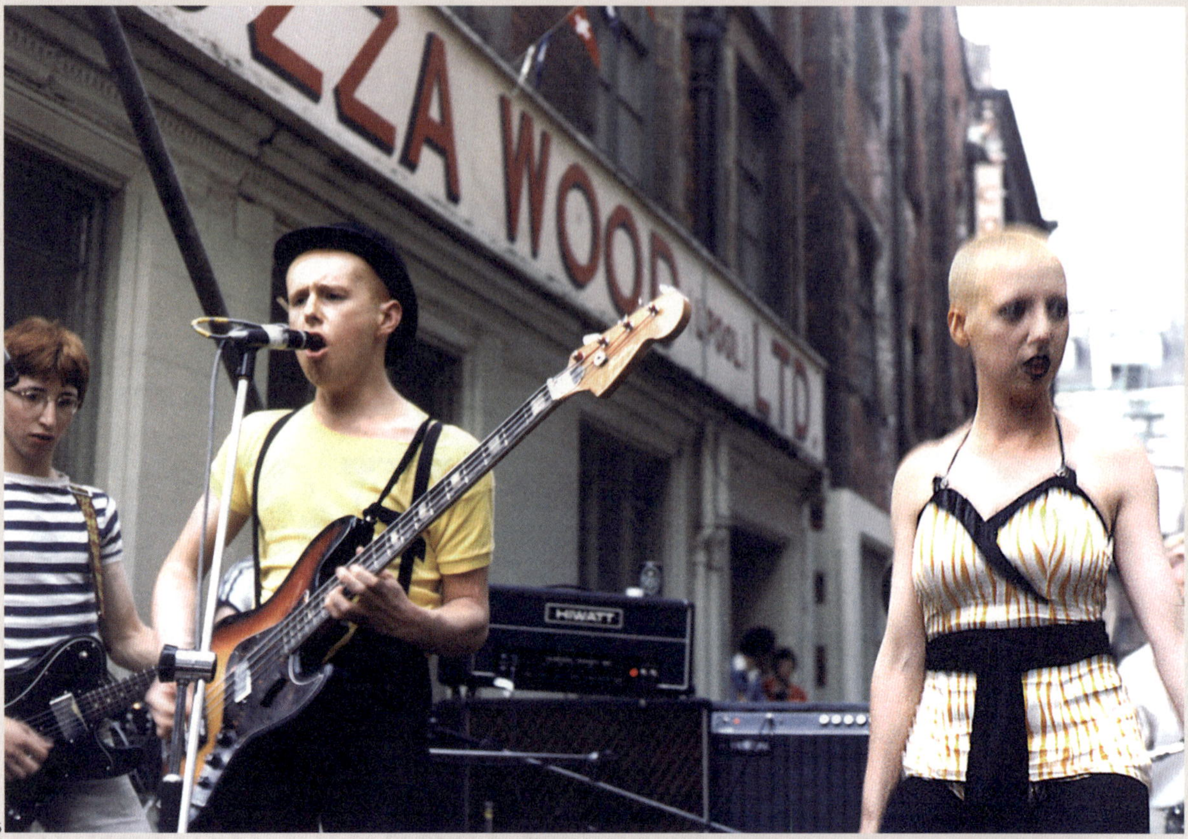

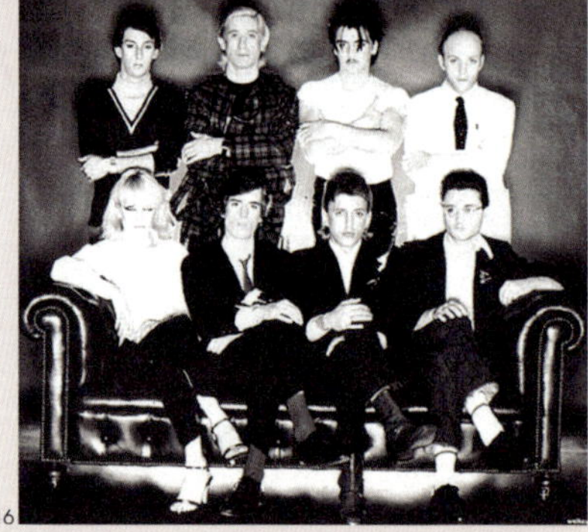

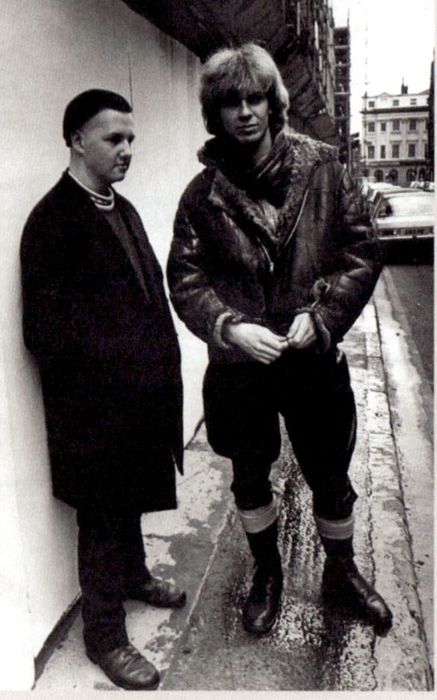

15
Big in Japan playing a
festival in Mathew Street,
1977. From left: Ian
Broudie (later Lightning
Seeds), Holly Johnson,
(later Frankie Goes
To Hollywood) and
Jayne Casey

16
Deaf School
Back cover of their 3rd
album *English Boys/
Working Girls* 1978. Album
artwork by Kevin Ward –
artist, and a founder
member of Big in Japan

17
Julian Cope c.1979 (in
jodhpurs and flying jacket)
chatting to Yorkie (later
the bass player in Space)

18
Big in Japan
*From Y to Z and Never
Again* 1978
EP cover, Zoo Records

Geoff Davies opened a record shop because there was nowhere he could listen to and buy the records he wanted. Later, when he started the Probe label, he put out records that *he felt like putting out*. This was very much the same type of attitude Roger had to Eric's – he booked artists to play Eric's *who he wanted to see*. Making money was never the driving force for either of them.

Jeff Young: 'The point about Eric's was that it was a meeting place for all the other kids like me from the suburbs who were looking for something but they hadn't known what it was up to that point. It wasn't just some club where you could go and hear The Stranglers play – The Stranglers didn't matter. What *mattered* was that it was a place where you got the secret information. It nurtured unorthodoxy, the fugitive, the left field and it was always much more "art school" than the conventional Punk movement.'[7]

Not a bad way to start a club though: The Stranglers, The Runaways, and The Sex Pistols (supported by Liverpool band The Yachts.)

Roger had intended to kick off with Liverpool's very popular and influential theatrical Art School band Deaf School, and they did in fact play the week before the official opening night. Though formed in late 1973/early 1974, well before Punk reared its defiant head, band members were enlisted more for their *attitude* than their playing ability, with names such as Enrico Cadillac, Eric Shark, Max Ripple, Bette Bright.

Life was grim in so many ways in the mid 70s – the high level of unemployment resulted in thousands of school leavers going straight on the dole. In many ways though, it was a creative time *because* of the unemployment – young people had *time* to think and question, they had *time* to form bands and hang out. They had *time* and inclination to experiment with 'found fashion'. Shortage of money made it a necessity to trawl the jumble sales and second-hand shops, and garments were added to/altered/customised. And people *could* dye their hair bright green – there were no concerns about getting the sack, cos they didn't have a job anyway!

Paul Simpson: 'If I was heavily into my look that's because I'd been an early member of Liverpool's premier Punk club Eric's. I'd been hothoused around such freak luminaries as Pete and Lynne Burns, Holly Johnson, Paul Rutherford and my particular favourite Jayne Casey of (the band) Big in Japan. These people were seriously extreme and a big influence on me. Just the way they would swan around the town centre on a Saturday afternoon like exotic birds oblivious to the catcalls and threats of violence.'[8]

There was this spirit of 'anything goes' partly as a nationwide kick against the greyness of the times, and partly sheer youthful rebellion: '*What are you rebelling against?*' '*Whadda ya got?*' Not Johnny Lydon, but Marlon Brando as 'Johnny', in the 1953 film *The Wild One*.

The mid to late seventies Liverpool Scene was more arty, quirky, and literate than the straight-ahead London-based Punk movement. The very names of the bands were a kick against conformity too: A Shallow Madness which mutated into The Teardrop Explodes, Echo and The Bunnymen, Those Naughty Lumps, Orchestral Manoeuvres in the Dark, Big in Japan, Wah! Heat, Dalek I Love You, A Flock of Seagulls…

Before Eric's opened, Roger went into Aunt Twacky's where Jayne Casey had a stall selling retro clothes. She says 'One day a big brute of a man came in and told me he had a club opening and he wanted me and my posse to come to the opening night. He handed me tickets and left. It was of course the legendary Roger Eagle. Because of the way we all looked in '76 (bald head, black lips, gay boys and all), we were constantly knocked back from clubs… So to be *invited in* by the owner was really something.'[9]

A year later, Jayne was fronting Big in Japan. She was fabulous with her short cropped bleached-white hair, or head totally shaven save for a few plaits or dreadlocks that hung over her face… and she had great *style*, typically wearing a lampshade like a big Chinese coolie hat. If Jayne was Queen of The Scene, Pete Burns was the undoubted King of Outrageous Fashion, as well as Outrageous Sarcasm.

Paul Simpson: 'Back in the late 70's, at his pre-hit peak, he was magnificent to behold. A genuine high street superstar… You just have to remember that once, just for a few years, he was the King of Liverpool. But then again, weren't we all?'[10]

The stage in Eric's was very low – which meant you could be literally inches away from The Damned, The Cramps, Joy Divison, The Clash, The Ramones, Talking Heads, Devo, Pere Ubu… if you can think of them, they played Eric's. After they played, you could chat to them at the bar. And after that, you formed your own band. Crucially, when bands formed, there was *somewhere appropriate* for them to play.

Back in the late 1970s Phil Hayes was on the dole – he saw The Clash, cut his hair, formed a band. From the early 80's until 2004, he ran The Picket in Hardman Street, a live venue which gave many a young band their first gig, plus a small recording studio. The building is to be re-developed as luxury apartments. At least it hasn't been demolished – the 2006 fate of the beautiful Quiggins building, a kind of latter day Aunt Twacky's. A hive of alternative culture has been sacrificed to make way for another soulless shopping mall.

Eric's was known as a Punk club *simply because it was 1976*. It wasn't planned that way.

Steve Hardstaff: 'Roger had a great nose for knowing what was coming up, whether he liked it or not. He wouldn't

<hr>

7 Florek and Whelan, 'Liverpool Eric's'.
8 Florek and Whelan, 'Liverpool Eric's'.
9 Florek and Whelan, 'Liverpool Eric's'.
10 Florek and Whelan, 'Liverpool Eric's'.

dismiss any music if he didn't like it, but he would dismiss it if it wasn't any good.'[11] He would pack the club out with The Clash one night, then blow the profits bringing some revered old bluesmen over from America at great expense, to play to a half empty club. There was a vast range of artists booked, from Planet Gong to Steel Pulse to Richie Havens.

Eric's regulars were also musically informed by the music that was on the Eric's Jukebox.

Mick Hucknall: 'The jukebox in Eric's just summed Roger up – you'd have "Anarchy In The UK" on next to "A Night In Tunisia" by Charlie Parker. That eclectic thing had a huge effect on my attitude towards the music I make.'[12]

There was also the eclectic mix of music Roger Eagle and Norman Killon played when DJ-ing in the club. Roger, with his love of dub reggae, Ray Charles, Bo Diddley; and Norman with his similarly eclectic music background. Norman had DJ-ed at The Sink Club in Hardman Street, which Neil English had opened in the late 1960s.

Norman Killon: 'Neil English was from the period before us and he was into jazz, traditional jazz, which was quite nice and broadened your horizons a bit – up until that time I'd never heard of Sydney Bechet, I'm now a lifelong devotee. And you'd get some blues records, Beatles and Rolling Stones, jazz, rock 'n' roll, blues, R&B… We put on

the likes of The Clayton Squares and The Hideaways, and also jazz groups, folk groups, comedy, all kinds of stuff…'[13] Norman also worked in Probe, so he had access to all the latest records and imports.

Ken Testi: 'We were a platform for popular culture. There's a lot of talk now about "cultural industries"… We premiered a considerable number of shows of different types, drama from The Everyman – we did the world's premiere of "Trafford Tanzi" which later became a film by Channel 4. We put on really top class jazz acts, and comedy. We did lots of ground-breaking stuff, developing new acts, exposing local individuals to what was possible… if you're talking about cultural industries, we had it all.'[14]

There was the Eric's record label, Pete Fulwell's Inevitable label, the Zoo label started by Balfe and Drummond in 1978 when Big in Japan ended, the 'More Or Less Monthly' magazine for Merseyside musicians which Fulwell started up, the Saturday matinees for U18s… and there were of course other pockets of creativity in Liverpool around the same time – Open Eye for instance, and Roger Hill's *Merseysound* magazine.

Eric's club was a breeding ground for creativity and a safe haven for oddballs and misfits from its first night 4 October 1976 to its *very dramatic* closure on 14 March 1980.

11 Florek and Whelan, 'Liverpool Eric's'.
12 Florek and Whelan, 'Liverpool Eric's'.
13 Florek and Whelan, 'Liverpool Eric's'.
14 Florek and Whelan, 'Liverpool Eric's'.

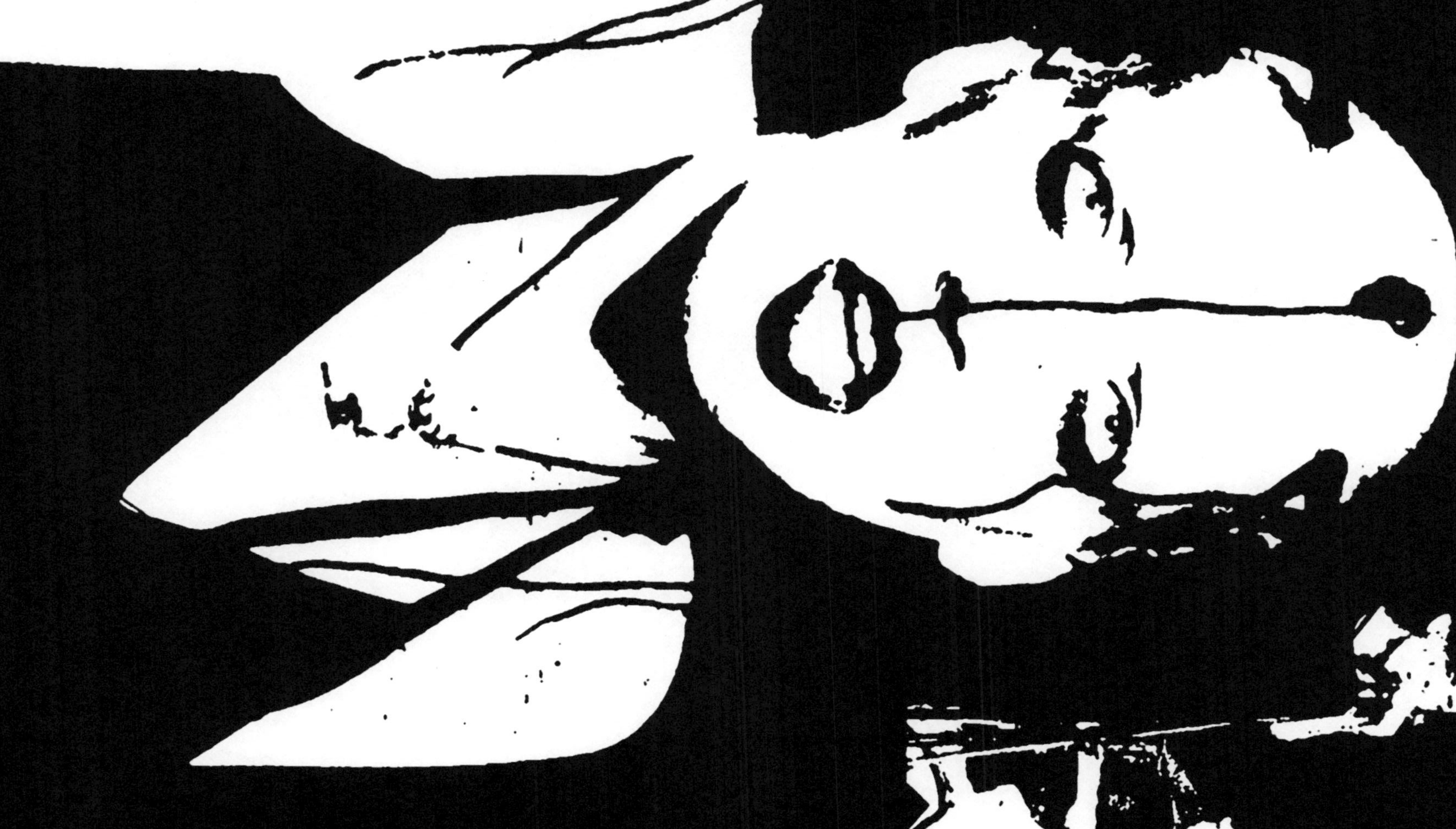
BIG IN JAPAN

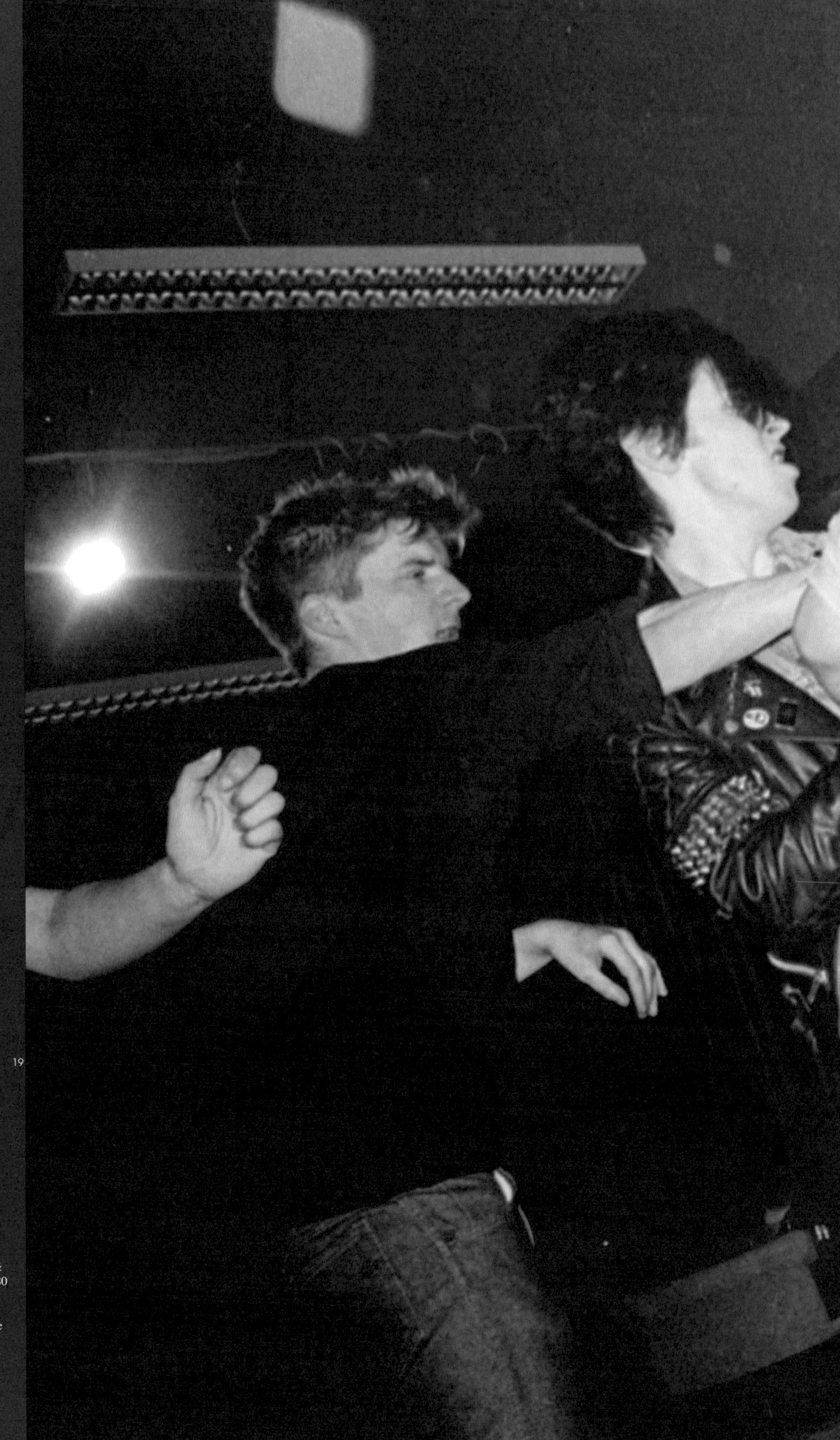

19
Vanley Burke
*'Society's Problem' Punk
Band – with Bullet Belt &
Union Jack T-Shirt* c. 1980
Silver bromide print
41.4 x 60.9 cm
Courtesy of Vanley Burke

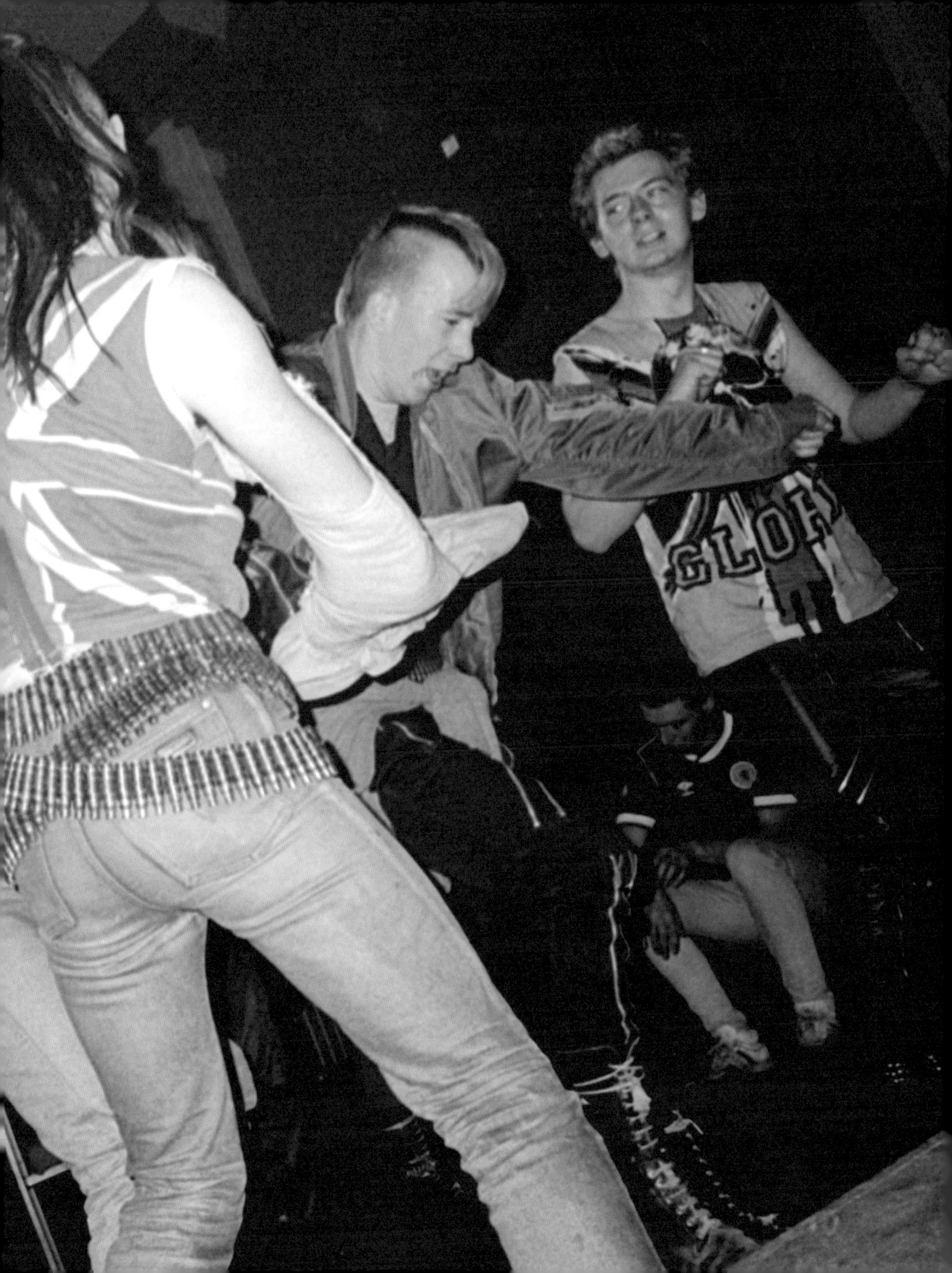
GLOR

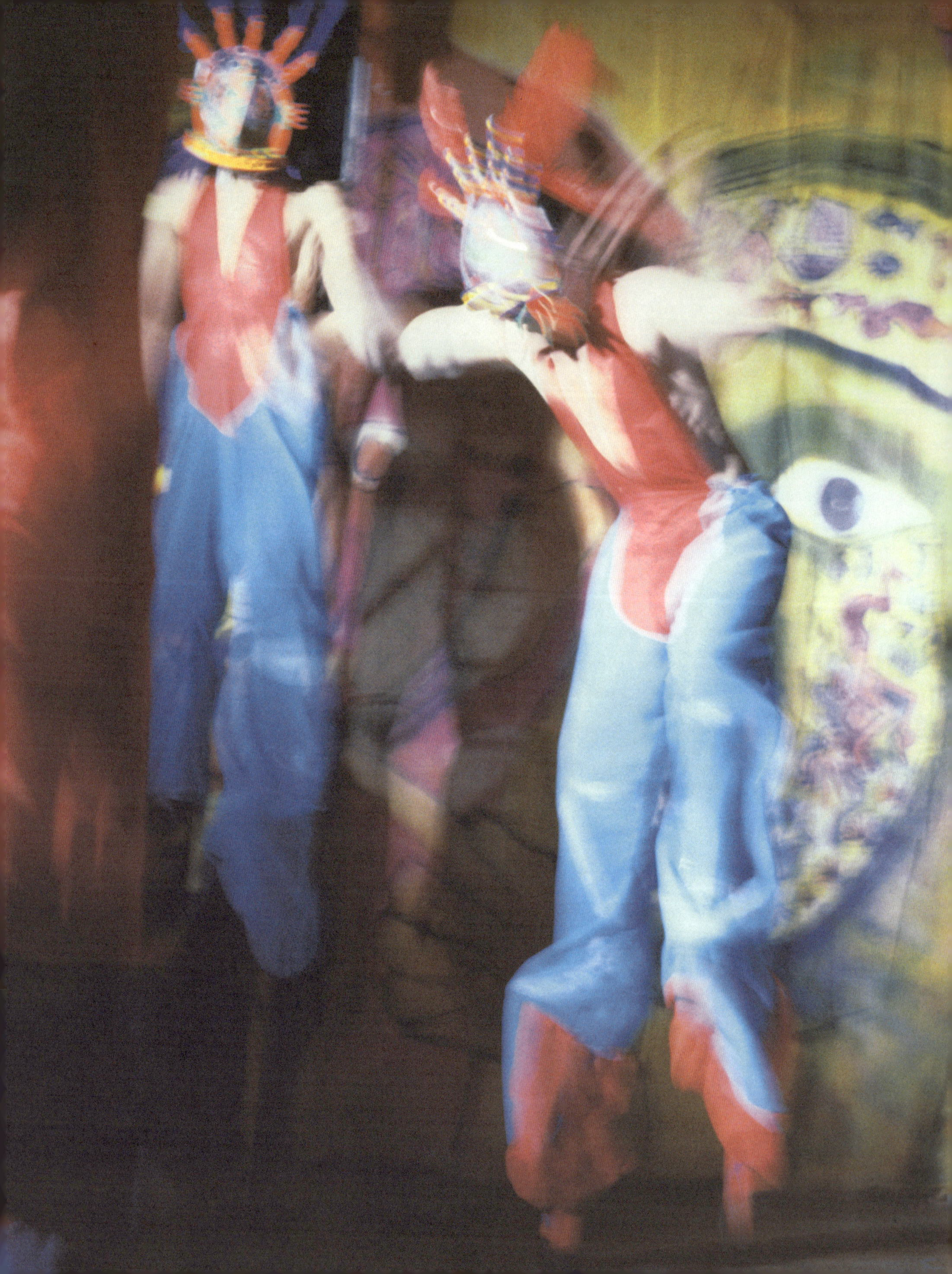

WELCOME TO THE PLEASURE DOME: ART IN LIVERPOOL 1988-1999

Bryan Biggs

Welcome to the Pleasure Dome: Art in Liverpool 1988-1999
Bryan Biggs

Between the arrival of Tate Liverpool at the end of May 1988 and the UK's first biennial of contemporary art in the city in September 1999, Liverpool witnessed a growth in the visual arts that can be seen as being born out of the first of these events, as well as paving the way for the second. Such an interpretation, however, would overlook both the arts infrastructure that already existed before Tate's decision to locate the largest museum in the country dedicated solely to modern art on the banks of the Mersey, and the plethora of arts initiatives that emerged thereafter independently of Tate.[1] Equally it would be misleading to suggest there was a groundswell of arts opinion in Liverpool demanding an international biennial, when the driving force for this was in fact an individual, James Moores, who, continuing a family tradition of arts patronage, galvanised a few key institutions in the city to get behind the idea, which he substantially funded through his A Foundation.

The post-war development of contemporary art in the city does not necessarily represent a continuum. Certainly the annual John Moores painting prize at the Walker, the presence of the Art School and a distinctive and self-sustaining community of artists can be seen as representing a legacy stretching back to Liverpool's progressive approach to art in the late 18th and 19th centuries. But it was key individuals, opportunism and the impact, later, of politically driven regeneration and arts funding agendas that were significant in this development, rather than any civic enlightenment or

overarching strategic vision of the type laid out in John Willett's seminal study *Art in a City*, published in 1967.[2] Willett's report, commissioned by the Bluecoat Society of Arts, concluded with proposals for setting the visual arts in Liverpool in a new framework, one located within a wider societal context. He called for a decentralised, 'uninhibited' art that didn't follow a London template, and he pointed to international models, for instance in the area of public art, that Liverpool should look to. Some of Willett's recommendations were taken up, certainly by Bluecoat, while others aimed largely at the local authority remained on the shelf. It was over twenty years later, during the period under discussion here, that Willett's calls for a more social art rooted in and engaging with the specifics of place, whilst at the same time having an international ambition, began to seem possible.

Both Tate Liverpool and the Biennial have substantially influenced the combination of local differentiation and global reach that has come to characterise Liverpool's art scene. There is however a history of initiatives in the city, much of it under-documented and too large to be given more than a brief overview of here, involving artists, venues and agencies – conveniently book-ended by Tate's opening and the first Biennial – that helps to give an understanding of why the visual arts developed in particular directions, creating a fertile environment in which the Biennial was able to take root.

Even before Tate arrived (indeed part of the reason why it chose Liverpool as the location for its 'Tate of the North') the city's arts scene had a national profile: the Walker's aforementioned John Moores exhibitions, its series of major shows by British Pop artists curated by Marco Livingstone, and its artist residencies, hosted in partnership with Bridewell Studios, by amongst others Anish Kapoor, Ian McKeever and Adrian Wisniewszki; Open Eye's prominent position within the developing network of photography galleries in the UK and its commissioning of new documentary image making, much of it focusing on Merseyside, by the likes of Martin Parr and Tom Wood; and Bluecoat's diverse programme, described by *Guardian* art critic Robert Clark as a 'model for provincial galleries',[3] with its mixing of the local and the global, live art and site specific practices, and nurturing of culturally diverse artists: all these contributed to the city's reputation as a thriving centre for contemporary art.

In the year before Tate Gallery Liverpool opened, Bluecoat secured sites for a billboard project by New York artist Barbara Kruger, part of a nationwide installation

1 As first the Gallery Director, then overall Director, of Bluecoat during the period under discussion, I have to declare an interest in writing about the arts scene at this time. The focus of the text is unavoidably on this organisation's activity, though not, I hope to the exclusion of other initiatives in the city.
2 Willett, John, *Art in a City*, London: Methuen for the Bluecoat Society of Arts, 1967.
3 Clark, Robert, 'New Art Merseyside', *The Guardian*, 25 April 1989.

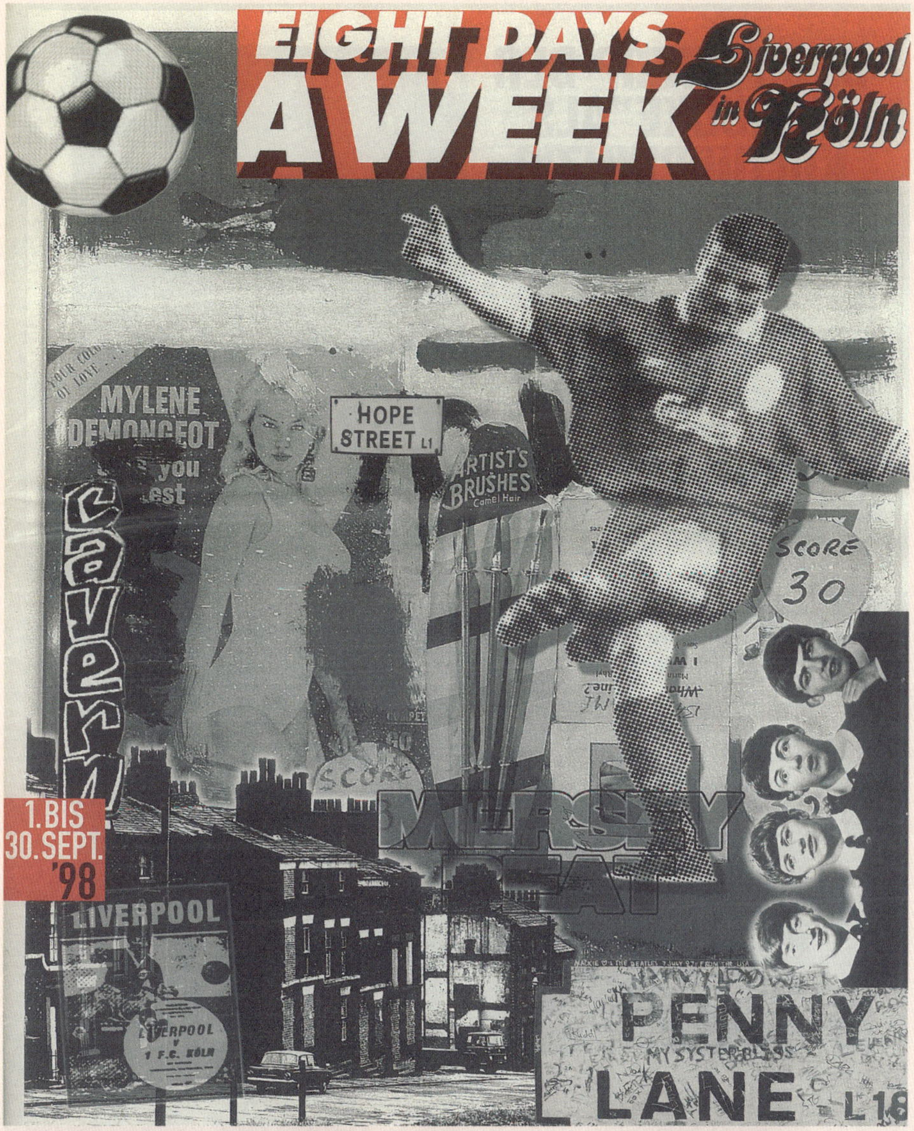

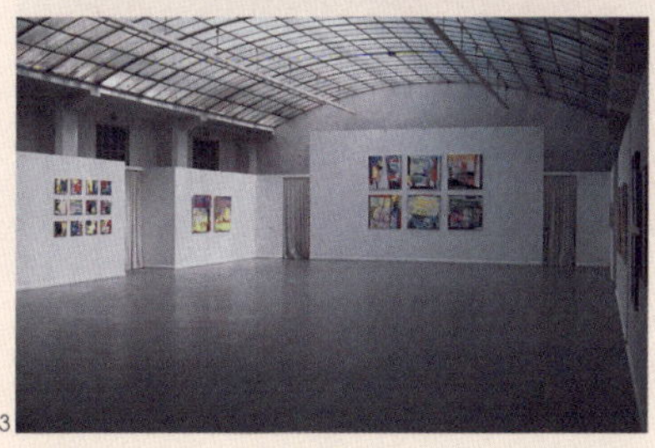

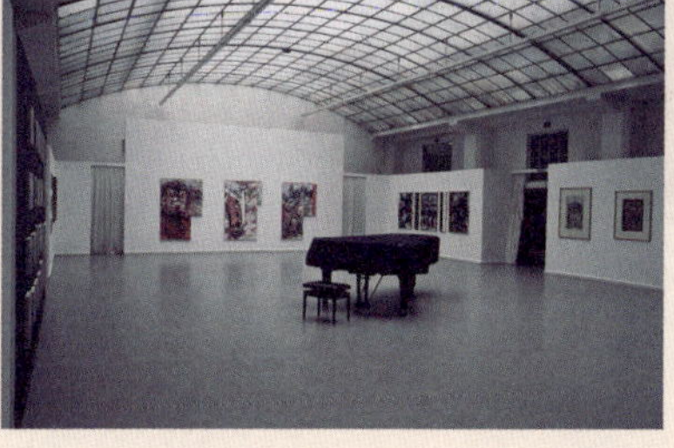

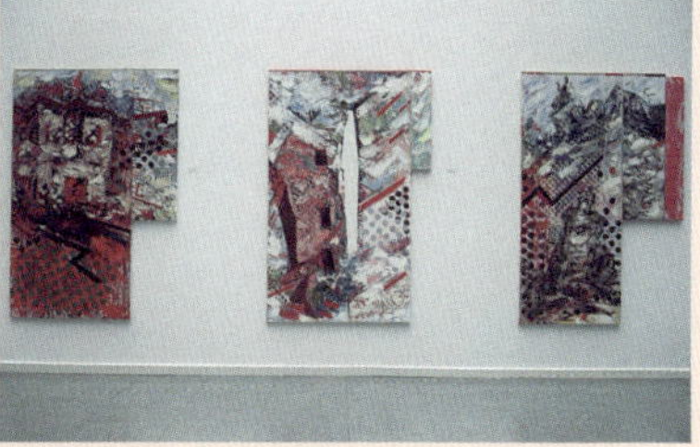

previous
Keith Khan
Soucouyan performance,
Bluecoat Arts Centre,
Liverpool, 1989

2
Newspaper catalogue for
the first *Eight Days A Week*
Liverpool/Cologne cultural
exchange, 1998

3
Installation views of
Engagement, an Eight
Days A Week exhibition at
the Lichthof, Cologne, 1998

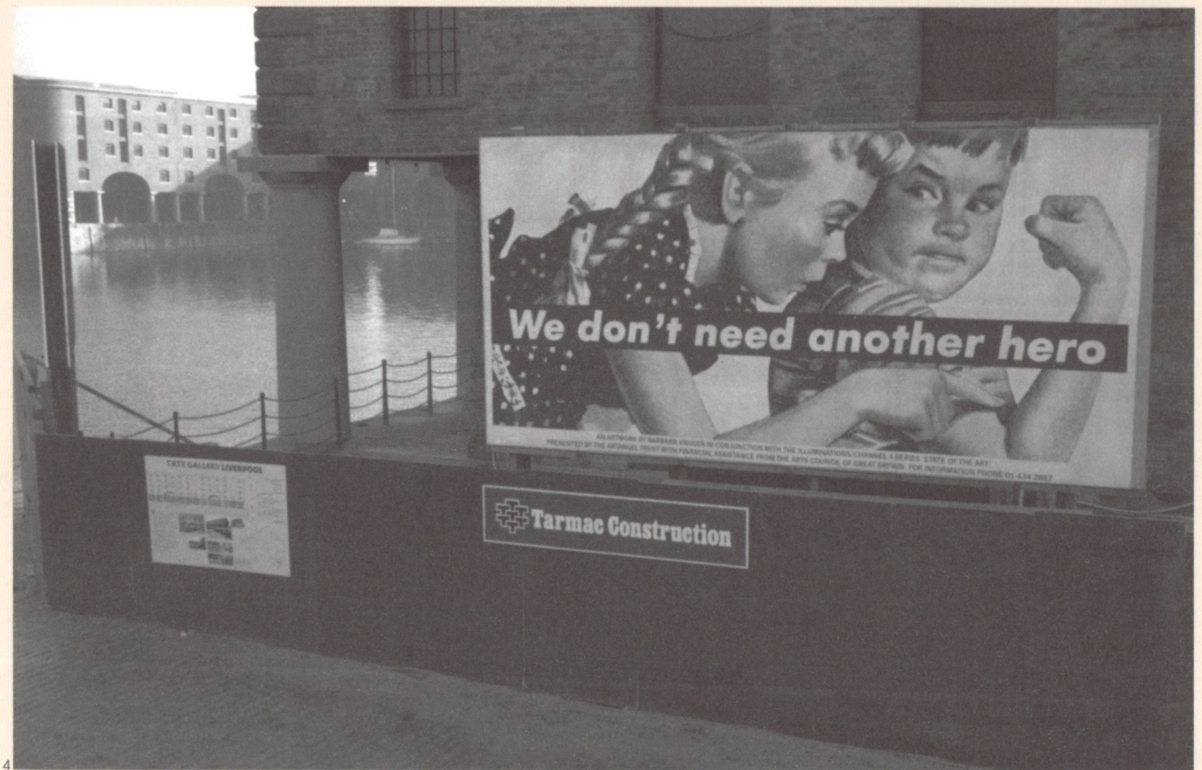

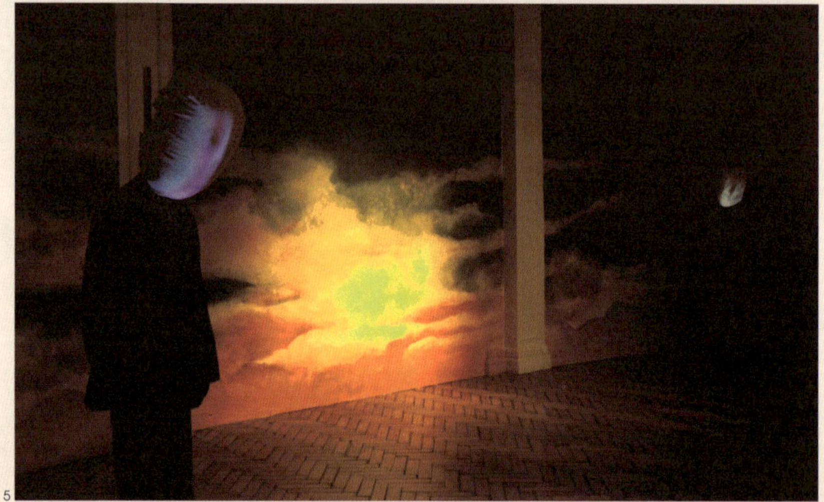

4
Barbara Kruger
We Don't Need Another Hero, Artangel billboard project, Albert Dock, Liverpool, 1987

5
Tony Oursler
Cigarettes, Flowers and Videotape exhibition, Bluecoat Gallery, Liverpool, 1993

organised by the London-based public art agency Artangel. The billboard wording in Kruger's bold trademark style read, 'We Don't Need Another Hero', across a 1950s image of an all-American boy flexing his muscles for an admiring girl. One billboard was located at the Albert Dock construction site that would soon become the Tate, a juxtaposition that took on added resonance for locals critical of what they saw as the imposition of a powerful London cultural institution (white and male, to boot.) Neither had the irony of choosing as Tate's home a former warehouse complex, symbolic of Liverpool's imperial mercantile heyday, and the gallery's past connections with Tate and Lyle sugar, been missed within debates about the continuing exclusion of Black voices from the city's cultural and public life in the wake of the media-dubbed 'Toxteth riots' of 1981. Liverpool's amnesia about its involvement in the transatlantic slave trade was to some extent addressed when National Museums and Galleries on Merseyside opened a gallery devoted to this subject in 1994, next door to Tate.

Tate's opening programme – a trio of shows: Surrealism from its collection, Rothko's Seagram Mural Project and *Starlit Waters*, a survey of British sculpture in an international context – was accompanied by a commissioned performance, *The Invention of Tradition*, by composer Gavin Bryars and artist Bruce McLean. The event was somewhat dampened by inclement weather and defeated by the sheer scale of the Albert Dock, however a more modest yet arguably more pertinent and powerful public intervention took place that week outside Bluecoat. In response to Tate's arrival, Liverpool performance groups Urban Jazz and the Goat People came together as Visual Stress to present *Urban Vimbuza Part 1: Death by Free Enterprise*, a daring multi-media performance in which Bluecoat's own slave history (the original school building, like many Liverpool institutions at that time, was founded by merchants involved in the trade) was 'exorcised' by a combination of Zambian ritual dance and drumming, priests abseiling from the building, plastic planes flying overhead, bikers revving up, live radio broadcast and cacophanous music, all achieved, as *Liverpool Echo* arts correspondent Joe Riley reported, for 'a fiftieth of the cost of *The Invention of Tradition*',[4] whilst inside the gallery British Nigerian artist Sokari Douglas Camp's kinetic sculptures contributed with rattling abandon.

Visual Stress went on to create other Vimbuza rituals, *Lemon Day* in 1990 outside St George's Hall, their take on the underwhelming *Lennon Day* pop concert the following day organised by the City Council in John's memory, and for the opening of the Transatlantic Slavery 'Against Human Dignity' Gallery at Merseyside Martime Museum. Each event, a potent combination of visual art, music and ritual, drew on the city's colonial past as embedded in the fabric of its buildings and institutions. The group's *Mobile Auto Mission* in 1992, a performance motorcade through the city centre, was part of

Trophies of Empire, a commission series responding to the Columbus quincentennial devised by artist Keith Piper and Bluecoat in collaboration with venues in two other maritime cities, Arnolfini in Bristol and Hull Time Based Arts. It was described by Gilane Tawadros as a project about 'forgetting and remembering... (as) artists re-trace the historical lines of slavery and empire in the fabric of contemporary life'.[5] As a multi-site, three-city partnership it was unique at the time for the way in which venues and artists collaborated and how they engaged with and problematised the specifics of the local in a global historical context.

The project brought together emerging Black British artists alongside others involved in 'issue based' practice.[6] One artist, Nina Edge, later moved to Liverpool, creating interactive gallery and participatory site specific works that disrupted cosy notions of multiculturalism and drew on the politics of place, such as her 1995 processional performance *Sold Down the River*, borne out of a collective and continuing sense that Merseyside had been left on the shelf, abandoned by departing industries and penalised by central government policies. A decade on from the 1981 uprisings in Liverpool 8, many of poet/photographer Leroy Cooper's sprayed bands of red, gold and green graffiti were still visible on the area's street signs, as large swathes of the inner city showed little sign of economic recovery and social exclusion increased. Another *Trophies* artist, Paul Clarkson, interrogated his own Liverpudlian identity, deconstructing official histories of the Black diaspora by celebrating overlooked local heroes like John Archer, Britain's first Black Lord Mayor (of Battersea), whose portrait by Clarkson eventually found a permanent home in Liverpool Town Hall, whilst Chila Burman returned to her home town for a solo show at the Bluecoat of her vibrant autobiographical images.

The period saw an upsurge in interdisciplinary, often grass-roots, culturally diverse art activity, as spoken word practitioners like Asian Voices Asian Lives, Muhammad Khalil and Levi Tafari brought together dance, theatre, visuals and music into a live art mix that was both celebratory and provocative. Interrogation of Liverpool's colonial past was a constant theme, but when artist Eddie Chambers was invited to create a flag for Liverpool Town Hall in October 1994, the resulting Union Jack in the colours of rasta proved too sensitive and was ordered by the Leader of the Council to be removed within hours of complaints being received. The offending flag spent the rest of the month flying off the mast of the pirate Toxteth Radio in Lodge Lane, whilst Fred

<hr>

4   Riley, Joe, 'Stroll on Fella!', review of *Death By Free Enterprise*, *Liverpool Echo*, 10 June 1988.
5   Tawadros, Gilane, 'Sweet Oblivion' in *Trophies of Empire*, Liverpool: Bluecoat Gallery, 1994, p.18.
6   Across the three cities the exhibition included sculpture, painting, video, merchandising, installation and performance from, amongst others, Juginder Lamba, Rita Keegan, Shaheen Merali, Veena Stephenson, South Atlantic Souvenirs, Donald Rodney and Sunil Gupta.

Brownell's flag for the newly reconstituted Republic of South Africa flying above the Liverpool Daily Post and Echo offices encountered no such problems. Both were part of *Signification*, a Visionfest project involving 74 flags flown across the city, designed by Liverpool and international artists, designers and architects like Will Alsop, Daniel Buren, Nigel Coates and Jamie Reid.

Visionfest was an annual visual arts celebration held every October. Growing out of a coordinated artists' studios weekend, it was launched in 1992, with the idea, in the words of its director for five years, John Brady, of putting 'artists and art everywhere – on the street, in pubs and football clubs, on billboards, in warehouses, galleries, ferries, schools and doctors' waiting rooms'.[7] Visionfest aimed at opening up the processes and practices of art, not just exhibiting it. It had an inclusive approach, both in terms of accommodating artists at different stages of their career and a wide embrace that took in architecture and design as well as fine art practices. Visionfest had an international ambition too, bringing artists from Europe and beyond to the city. Relying on modest resources and individual energy to create a concentrated visual impact on the city, it was not dissimilar from festivals of this kind elsewhere, but its distinctiveness lay in the way it used Liverpool as a site, to exploit the range and proximity of temporary spaces, coupled with foreign connections and liaison with the city's mainstream galleries and institutions (whilst remaining fiercely independent of them.) The festival demonstrated the 'critical mass' it was possible to achieve for the visual arts in Liverpool. This and the way Visionfest explored the fabric of the city, 'encouraging artists to devise work for previously unconsidered locations and to develop audiences for these strategies'[8], prepared the ground two years after the final festival in 1997 for the independent strand of the first Biennial, which was dubbed *Tracey* by its coordinator, Jonathan Swain, with characteristic irreverence for the Biennial's main international exhibition, *Trace*.

According to Adrian Henri, Visionfest testified 'to the variety and vitality of the current art scene', which was brought about by Tate's presence, despite the gallery being criticised for not having a local element. He suggested another knock-on effect of Tate was the growth of artists' studios, like Arena, and the emergence of small galleries such as the Merkmal, Acorn, Academy, Domino and Hanover.[9] Not all of these, however, survived, those with a commercial ambition finding it difficult to overcome the perennial problem for provincial galleries, not just those in Liverpool, of generating a market for contemporary art. The Liverpool Academy of Arts, resurrected in the 1960s and greatly expanded with a new venue in Pilgrim Street and a lively mixture of touring exhibitions and opportunities for local artists, had collapsed in 1981,[10] and its last director Murdoch Lothian's subsequent attempts to run a serious commercial gallery had not succeeded. Instead more flexible and sometimes temporary

venues such as 3 Month Gallery, Parking Space and Static, became an important feature in the city's gallery infrastructure, part of a nationwide trend for artist-led spaces whose prime aim was not selling work. At a time before the value of city centre real estate escalated, Liverpool seemed to have the potential to attract more of these initiatives, but even districts designated as 'creative quarters' failed to live up to expectations, the Duke Street/Bold Street (Ropewalks) area, for instance, succumbing to bar culture and the night-time economy of clubland, rather than becoming the thriving artists' scene envisaged in the rhetoric of regeneration, the presence of the enterprising Arena studios notwithstanding. To a degree Visionfest 'filled the vacuum left by the demise of the Liverpool Academy', the difference being though that artists did things themselves without recourse to a formal organisation.[11]

Visionfest's confidence grew: from hosting an international festival of pavement art in its first year, to its *Art, Lies and Documentation* theme in 1996, guest curated by Richard Hylton, who commissioned works such as Yinka Shonibare's ceramic installation at Croxteth Hall. In 1994, the year that the city bid, unsuccessfully, to host the Year of Architecture and Design in 1999 in the Arts Council's *Arts 2000* programme, the festival collaborated with the architecture and design magazine *Blueprint* on a publication, *Visions*. Its editor Deyan Sudjic highlighted how Liverpool was starting to overcome its post-industrial malaise and change 'accumulated perceptions' of the city through embracing regeneration, revealing its remarkable architecture, and articulating its urban fabric through Visionfest's artistic interventions.[12] This process anticipated the more ambitious public realm works that were to become such a prominent feature of the Biennial.

In the 1980s, Liverpool was very much 'a synonym for decay in the British media',[13] its demonisation in the post-Militant period continuing through events like the Jamie Bulger murder case, to the point where even attempts to defend itself against negative stereotyping earned the label of 'self pity city'. In contrast to this inward looking capacity, at a cultural level in the 1990s the city witnessed increasingly global perspectives. In addition to displays from its collection, Tate Liverpool staged around 80 exhibitions over this period, many curated in-house and with a strong international flavour (albeit rarely venturing beyond the known territory of Western

7 Brady, John, 'Stretching the Canvas', introduction to *p/review: Visionfest Review 1992/1993 Preview*, Visfac, 1993.
8 Brady, John, email to Bryan Biggs, 19 August 2006.
9 Henri, Adrian, 'Still Liverpool After All These Years', in *Visions*, produced for Visionfest in collaboration with *Blueprint* magazine, October 1994, p. 30.
10 This was one of a long line of institutions called Liverpool Academy, or Liverpool Academy of Arts, to fail. Yet another arose in 1989 and still exists in Liverpool's Seel Street.
11 Henri, 'Still Liverpool,' p. 30.
12 Sudjic, Deyan, 'Britain's Most Architectural City' in *Visions*, see note 7, pp. 20-25.
13 Cubitt, Sean, 'Going Native: Columbus, Liverpool, Identity and Memory', review of *Trophies of Empire* in *Third Text*, 21, Spring 1993, pp. 106-20.

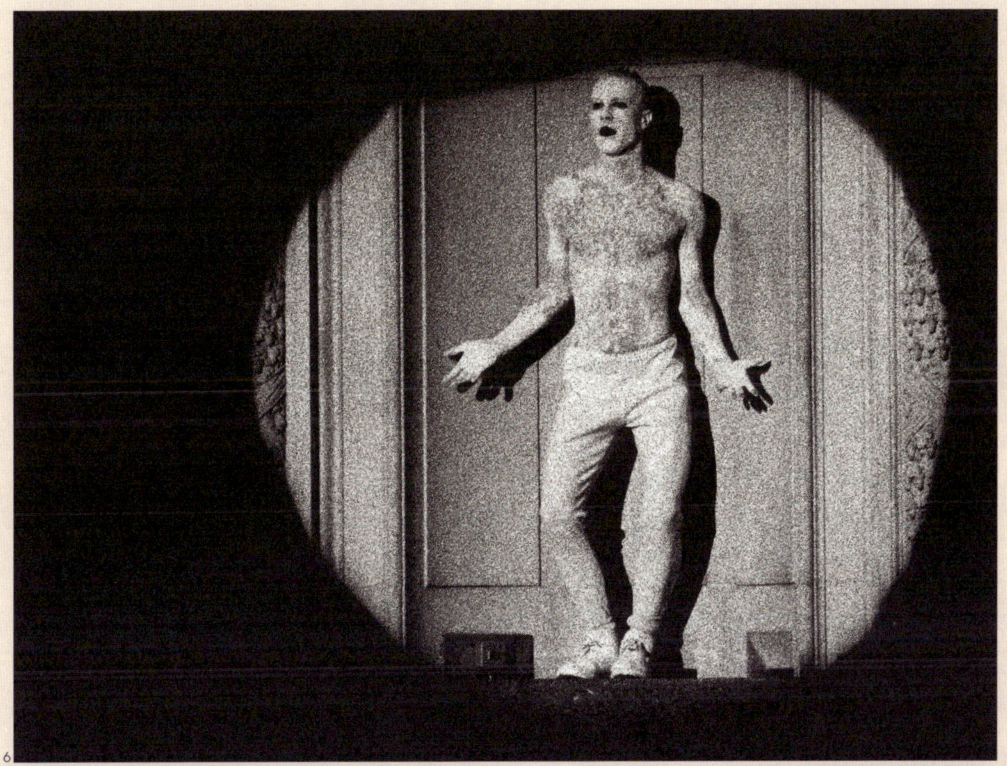

6
Robin Blackledge
(a Liverpool-based
performance artist and
recipient of the 1989/90
Bluecoat Award) during a
multi-media performance
by Leningrad's Pop
Mechanica at St. George's
Hall, Liverpool,
January, 1989

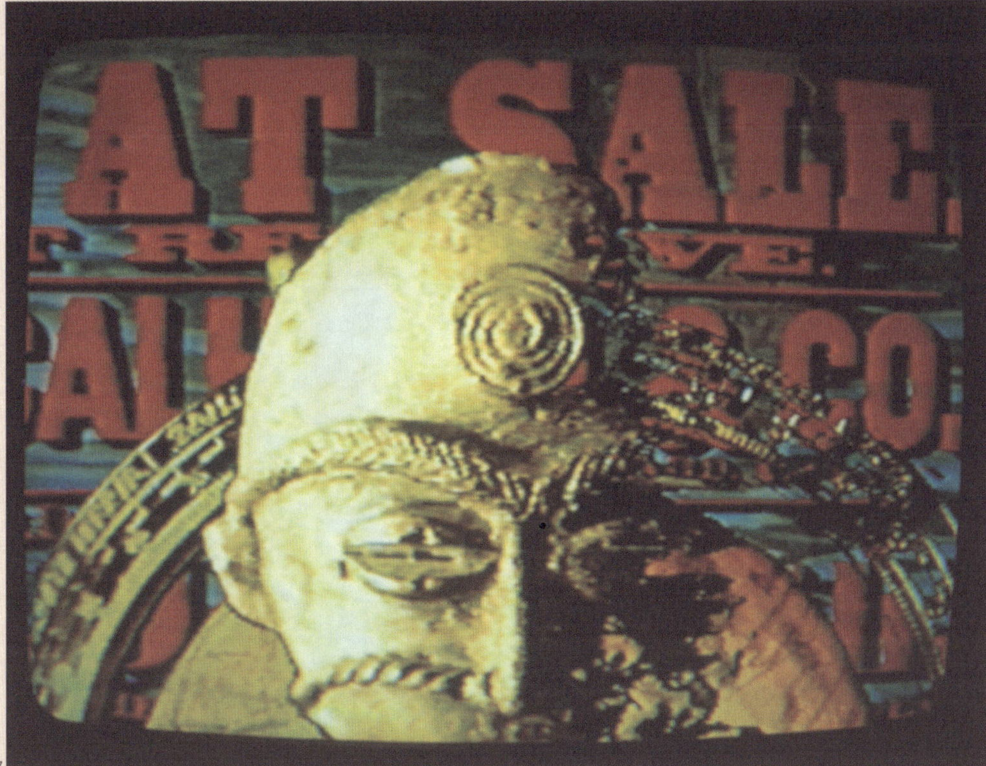

7
Keith Piper
Balance of Trade,
part of the Trophies of
Empire exhibition,
Merseyside Maritime
Museum, Liverpool, 1992

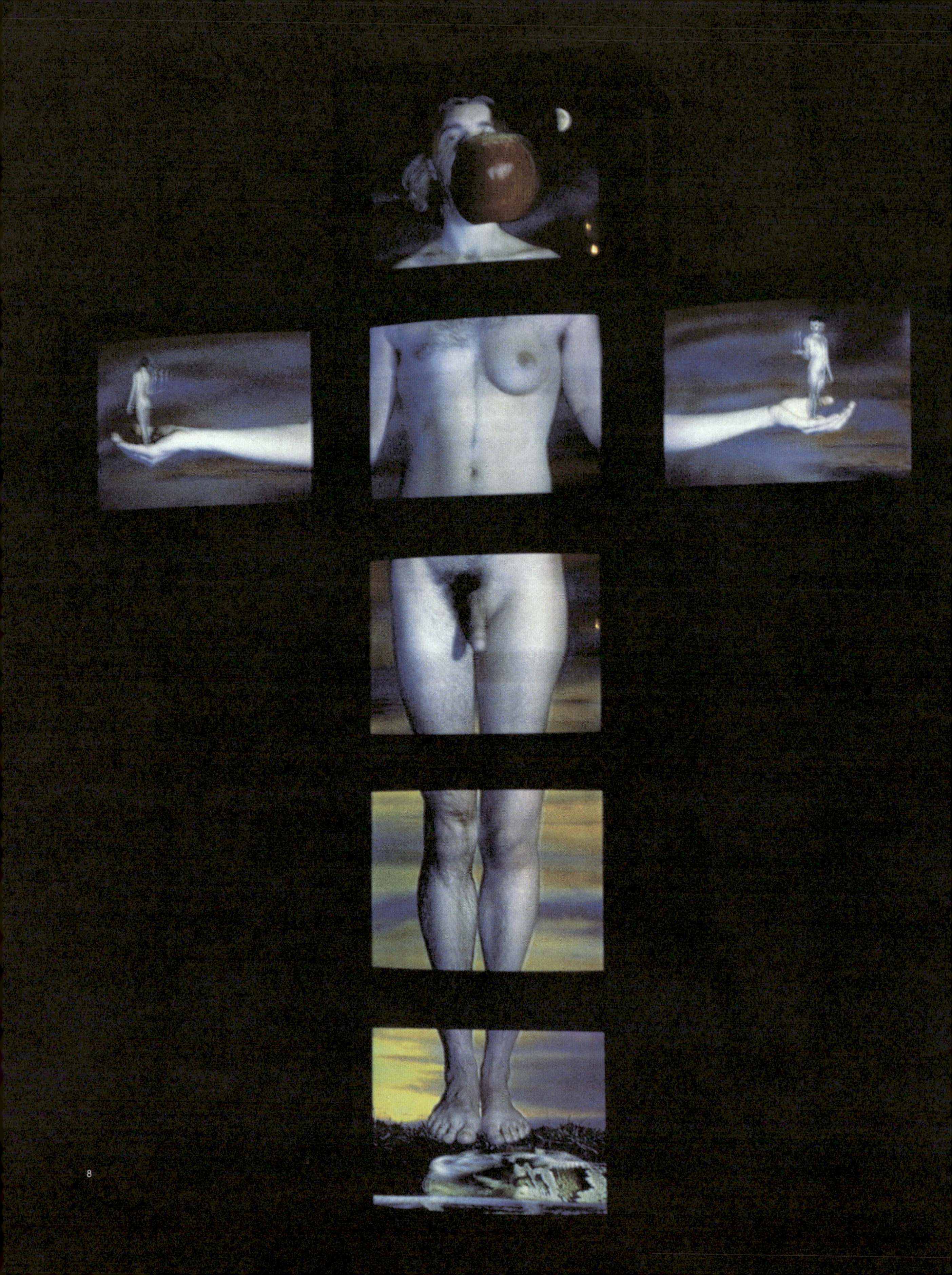

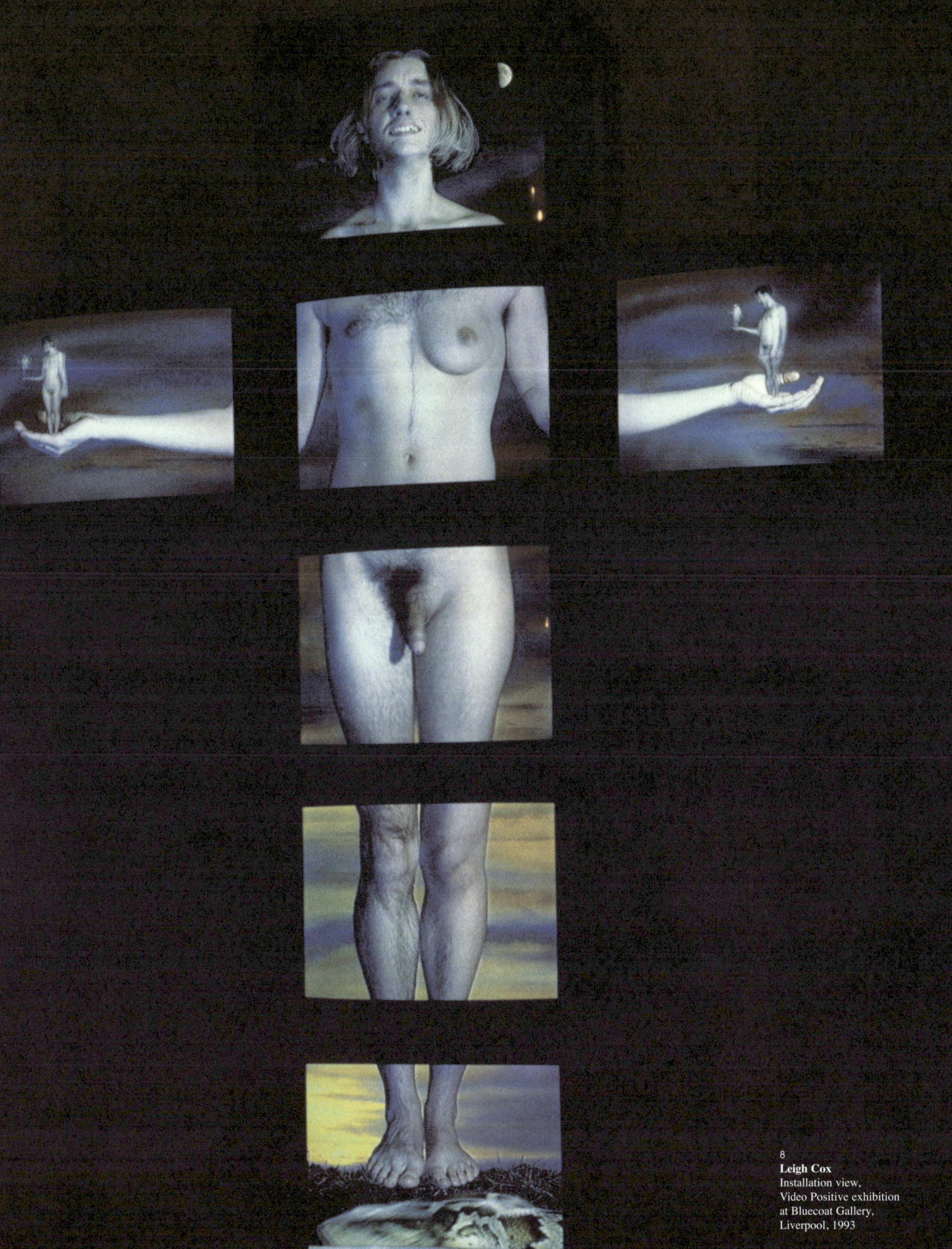

8
Leigh Cox
Installation view,
Video Positive exhibition
at Bluecoat Gallery,
Liverpool, 1993

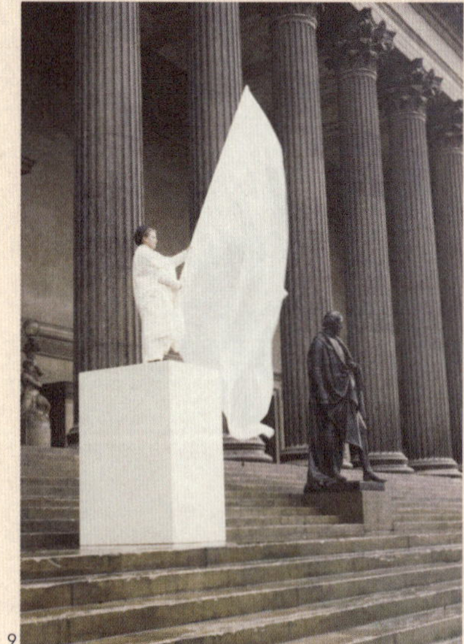

9

10

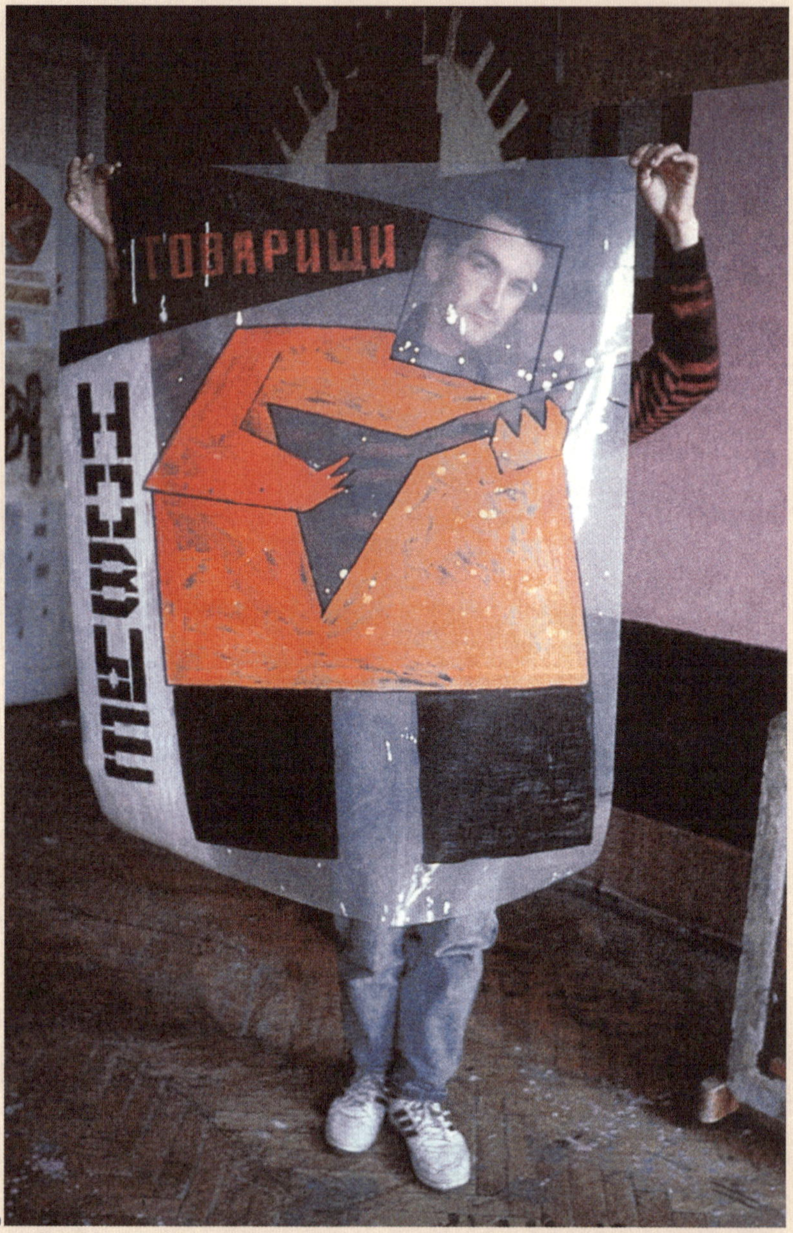

9
Peter McRae
Avenue of Hopes
Performance on St.George's
Plateau, Liverpool,
March 1989
A Bluecoat Live Art
Commission

10
*Perestroika in the
Avant-Garde*
Timur Novikov, one of the
artists in an exhibition by
the New Artists from
Leningrad staged at the
Bluecoat, January 1989

Europe and the US, notable exceptions being exhibitions of work largely unseen before in the UK from Japan, Korea and Africa).

And it was not only Tate that had an international perspective. 1989 marked the arrival of a new organisation on the scene, one whose connections to a global and UK-wide network of artists and institutions were quickly established. Set up four years earlier, Merseyside Moviola collaborated with Bluecoat, Birkenhead's Williamson Art Gallery and Tate on the first of what would be six biennial *Video Positive* festivals, positioning itself in the process as the UK's main commissioning and exhibition agency specialising in artists' film and video. From modest beginnings in a small office at Bluecoat, the operation grew through the drive and determination of director Eddie Berg, supported by regional and national Arts Council funding. It changed its name to FACT (Foundation for Art and Creative Technology) in 1997 and developed a distinctive programme through its festivals and other year-round projects, an outreach collaboration programme and the establishment of a touring and exhibition service for the sector, MITES (Moving Image Touring and Exhibition Service). Responding to the increasing number of artists working with moving image and new media, FACT was well placed to establish Liverpool, whose galleries contributed by providing exhibition space, as an international centre for this area of practice. FACT's story is told elsewhere,[14] but it is worth emphasising the role it played in exposing UK audiences to some of the most innovative video art throughout the decade. Leading US artist Tony Oursler, for instance, had his first two exhibitions in the UK in Liverpool at Bluecoat long before London recognition, and the list of names that FACT supported reads like a who's who of international video art.

Bluecoat at this time was also making international connections, with exhibitions from Australia, Pakistan, India and Senegal, and collaborations with independent curators like Olu Oguibe (*Seen Unseen*, presenting British African artists), Brian McAvera (*Parable Island*, showing art from Ireland), OVA (*Simryn Gill*) and Eddie Chambers (several group shows of Black British art), but by the end of the 1990s the idea of the 'geographic-specific' exhibition was being challenged by the increasing globalisation of the art world, whilst there was also a sense in which the identity politics that emerged in the 1980s in the UK 'had to a large degree been exhausted'.[15] With this in mind, Bluecoat developed a series of commissions, *Independent Thoughts*, through discourse with artists and galleries in the North and Midlands of England in 1997/98. Focusing on the 50th anniversary of India's independence and the partition of Pakistan, the project sought a fresh approach to the idea of independent contemporary practice in relation to a lasting historical legacy. Adopting a similar organisational framework to *Trophies of Empire*, it offered an alternative model to commissioning and touring

new work, and led to a conference and publication, *Independent Practices*, which further extended debates around artists' practice in the international sphere.[16]

This global reach was not however confined to institutions. Bypassing London, artists were already developing strong regional exchanges and collaborations with each other, and this period saw such connections extending abroad. Lin Holland and a working group of Liverpool artists set up the Cyfuniad international artists' workshop in North Wales in 1999, based on Robert Loder's Triangle model, bringing artists from Australia, Brazil, the Caribbean, Indonesia, India, Japan, Kenya and Southern and West Africa, together with regional artists to create work over a two week period, plugging Liverpool into a developing global art community beyond traditional European and US centres. The same year Godfrey Burke and Alan Dunn, two artists with wide experience of curating projects in a range of public contexts, instigated the Liverpool Billboard Project, with UK and international artists, including Fiona Banner, Willie Doherty, Felix Gonzalez-Torres, Pierre Huyghe and Erwin Wurm, creating billboards along with Liverpool artists such as Sue Leask and David Jacques. Culminating during the first Biennial, the project presented hand painted and digitally printed artworks over a seven months period, setting out to 'break into the commercial world of publicly-displayed open-all-hours imagery'.[17]

When the cultural exchange Eight Days A Week started in 1998, there were already strong connections between Liverpool and its German sister city of Cologne. Bluecoat had an ongoing exhibition exchange programme with BBK gallery there, begun over a decade earlier, bringing emerging artists from Cologne to Liverpool and enabling Liverpool artists to exhibit in one of Europe's leading centres for contemporary art. Tate Liverpool too had staged a major survey from Cologne in 1989, including amongst others Sigmar Polke, Gerhard Richter, Rosemarie Trockel and Walter Dahn, accompanied by a conference – arranged unfortunately on the day of the FA cup final between Liverpool and Everton – that examined the 'architecture of art' in both cities. The event revealed the huge differences between the two cities' arts provision, with Liverpool very much the poor relation to Cologne, with its wealth of galleries, museums, collectors and thriving artists' community. However, by focusing at a grass roots level, Eight Days A Week developed a programme of exhibitions, residencies and events that provided common

---

14 See the *Factors* series of publications, published on the opening of the FACT Centre in 2003.
15 Biggs, Bryan, Introduction to *Independence Practices*, Liverpool: Bluecoat Arts Centre, Liverpool John Moores University and Saffron Books, 2000, p. 7.
16 Exhibitions took place in Liverpool, Birmingham, Wolverhampton, Middlesbrough, Oldham, Bradford, Leeds and Nottingham. Artists included Juginder Lamba, Mohini Chandra, Rasheed Araeen, Tim Brennan, Balraj Khanna, Iftikhar Dadi, Nalini Malani, Pervaiz Khan and Permindar Kaur
17 Burke, Godfrey and Dunn, Alan, *Documentation from Liverpool Billboard Project*, Liverpool: Liverpool Billboard Project, 2000.

ground between a large number of artists from both cities. Initiated by Cologne art critic and writer Jürgen Kisters with assistance from Bluecoat, the project's first manifestation was a month-long programme of some 30 exhibitions and events in Cologne involving Liverpool artists. This was reciprocated in 2000 in Liverpool and the project grew into an ongoing artists-led dialogue driven by steering groups of artists, notably Pete Clarke in Liverpool and Georg Gartz in Cologne (who continue to collaborate by making paintings together), with several exhibitions and other exchanges staged every year. Always more than just an artists' exchange programme, Eight Days built into its remit a wider ambition to generate dialogue between the cities through projects involving football, writing, music, film, educational residencies and workshops.

Such exposure to working in an international context contributed to developing the quality and ambition of local art practice. In 1995 Tate's *Making It* exhibition, looking at how artists make art and how galleries and visitors contribute to that making, reflected the strength of the city's art scene, with exhibiting artists Janet Hodgson, Sarah Raine and Padraig Timoney all resident in the city at the time. Throughout this period Bluecoat too continued its commitment to emerging regional artists, some of whom went on to establish careers beyond the city, like Dave Campbell (Common Culture), Leo Fitzmaurice, Richard Hughes, Dave Mabb, Paul Morrison, Gary Perkins, Paul Rooney and Amrit and Rabindra Kaur Singh (Twin Studios). Artists coming to the city from outside for residencies made an impact, such as Tate Fellows Laura Godfrey Isaacs, Maud Sulter and Emma Rushton. A residency scheme for artists from 'non-European perspectives' at the Centre For Art International Research (CAIR), based at Liverpool John Moores University's School of Art and Design and developed by Jagjit Chuhan and Bashir Makhoul, included Walid Sadek from Beirut. In a publication accompanying his residency's resulting exhibition at Bluecoat in 1998, Sadek perceptively highlighted the complexities of a local art practice operating in opposition to 'globalisation's ravenous mobility', claiming that such a practice was already co-opted terrain.[18]

The same year an ambitious initiative that encompassed a large area of Northern England, proposed an alternative to Sadek's somewhat bleak analysis, aiming to 'consider the relationship of art to its public in terms which go beyond its commodification as a "nomadic" item of market exchange'.[19] *Artranspennine98* was devised by Lewis Biggs, then director of Tate Liverpool, and Robert Hopper, director of the Henry Moore Sculpture Trust, and though its geographical spread was larger, stretching from West to East coasts (the region named Transpennine by the rail network that covers it), it was in a sense a precursor to the Liverpool Biennial, in that it made as its subject a region, sought to redefine public art in relation to the specifics of place and

audience, commissioned ambitious new work, depended on collaboration with galleries, and sought to create a lasting legacy. Liverpool's site-specific participation in the project beyond gallery installations at Tate, Bluecoat and the 3 Month Gallery, included Taro Chiezo's *Superlambanana*, a 'curious fusion of animal and fruit', whose popularity has endured, as the sculpture continues to move from site to site around the city. Importantly, *artranspennine* demonstrated that it was possible to create the UK's largest visual art exhibition outside of the capital, and that in Liverpool a willing gallery infrastructure, a richness of public sites and an eager audience existed.

Participation by local people would also become a distinctive feature of the Biennial, and this element of the visual arts in Liverpool grew significantly over this period, as new models for engaging local communities were developed. From early on, Tate created a pioneering learning and inclusion programme that moved beyond traditional gallery education provision, FACT ran its collaboration programme as an integral part of its work, and Bluecoat started its outreach programme, Connect, bringing together in creative collaboration a diverse range of local people with artists from across the arts spectrum. Considerations of access, both intellectual and physical, informed these institutions' participative work. Anne Whitehurst for instance brought a disability perspective to the public realm in her Bluecoat live art commission *On the Map,* which highlighted the disabling environment of the city centre.

Since Adrian Henri's happenings in the 1960s and mixed media events at the Blackie, at Bluecoat – where Yoko Ono's performance in 1967 had sold out – and at the Liverpool Academy in the 1970s, live work had been a feature of the visual arts in Liverpool. It found a new lease of life in this period, Bluecoat taking a leading role. In addition to the live events already discussed, the organisation presented experimental performances that defied easy categorisation, both off-site and in its venue's various spaces. An artist invited from outside to work with local artists was often a feature, such as in Keith Khan's *Soucouyan* in 1989 that drew in elements from camp, carnival and bhangra, whilst, also that year, *Perestroika in the Avant-Garde* proved to be one of those audacious Liverpool events that soon passed into legend.

Pop Mechanica, or Popular Mechanics, were a group of musicians and artists from Leningrad's simmering cultural underground, led by brilliant pianist Sergey Kuryokhin. Their first album in the West had been put out by Liverpool label ARK, who subsequently worked with Bluecoat's Jayne Casey to stage Pop Mechanica's first UK performance in Liverpool and an accompanying exhibition by their compatriots, the New Artists. Welcoming *glasnost*, US President Ronald

18 Sadek, Walid, *Karaoke*, Liverpool: CAIR and Bluecoat, 1998, p.13.
19 Biggs, Lewis and Hopper, Robert, 'Introduction to *artranspennine98*', Mullins, Charlotte (ed.), *artranspennine98. Exhibition Guide*, London: Aspen Publishing, 1998, p. 5.

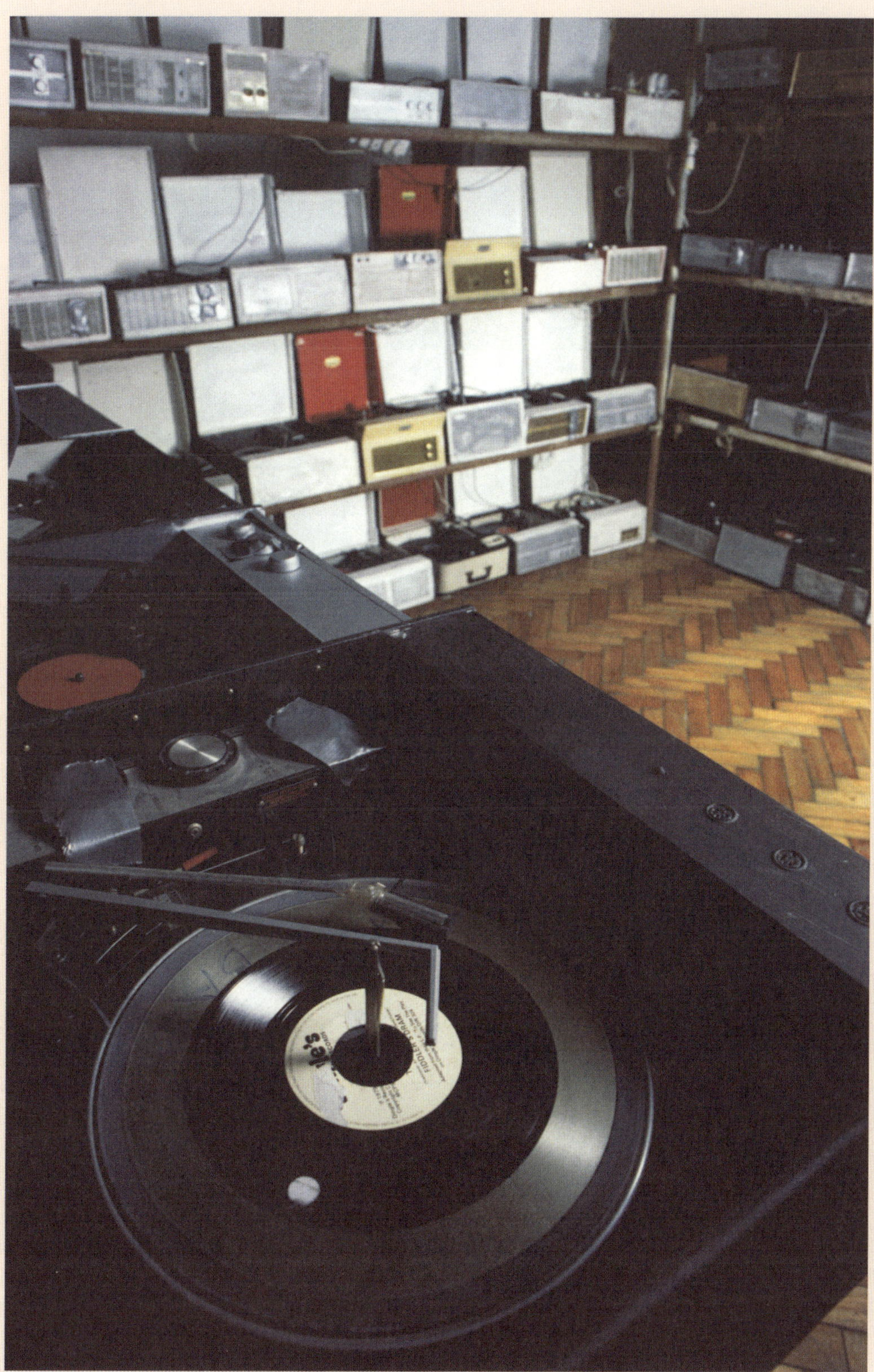

11
Philip Jeck
Off the Record installation,
Bluecoat Gallery,
Liverpool, 1996
A Live From The Vinyl
Junkyard commission

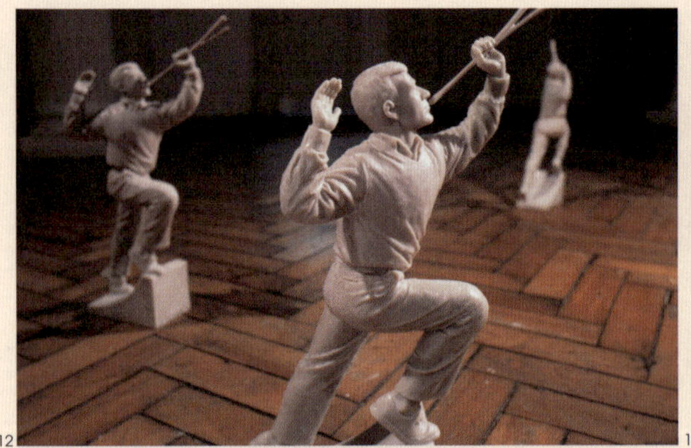

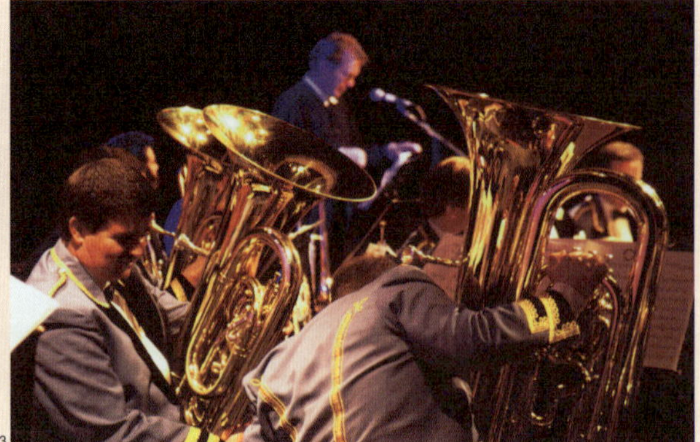

12
Walid Sadek
Karaoke exhibition,
Bluecoat Gallery,
Liverpool, 1998

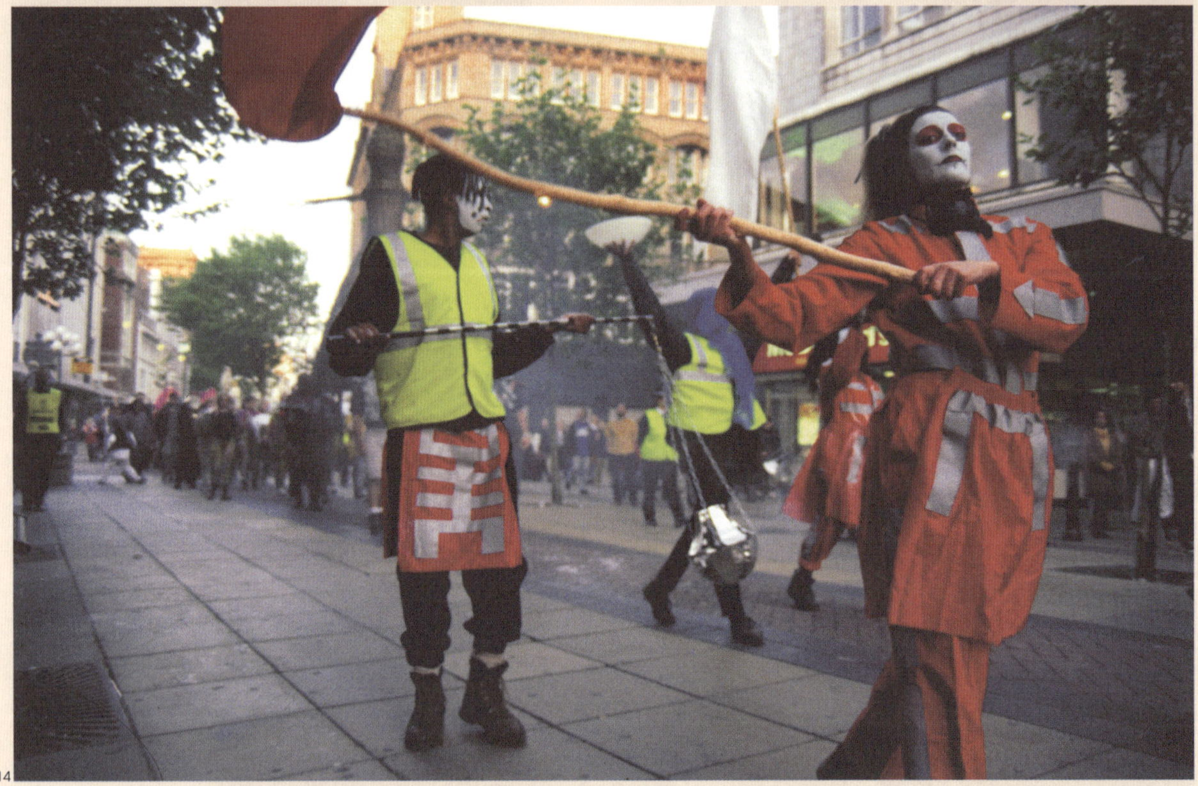

13
Jeremy Deller
Acid Brass performance
at LIPA, Liverpool, 1997
A Bluecoat Mixing It
Commission

14
Nina Edge
Sold Down The River
performance, Liverpool
city centre, 1995

Reagan had announced in 1988 that, 'Nothing would please me more than to see the day that a concert promoter, in say England, could call up Soviet performers and have them playing in Liverpool the next night. Is this just a dream?' The *Liverpool Echo* printed this quote as the headline to a supplement produced for the Pop Mechanica concert to be held at St George's Hall,[20] an event involving 150 performers. The Russians were joined by an array of Liverpool's finest: an Irish pipe band, an opera singer, fiddler, string quartet, brass ensemble, concertina orchestra, African drummers and dancers, Greek musicians, fashion models, performance artists, Kung Fu fighters, a pony, two goats and musicians from Echo and the Bunnymen and other Liverpool bands. Jamming together under Kuryokin's direction, the ensemble revived the spirit of Mayakovsky and Dada in the birthplace of The Beatles, and at the finale pelted a stunned audience with raw sausages. Audience member and cult US filmmaker John Waters allegedly said, echoing Ginsberg's hyberbole about Liverpool, 'from now the world will be divided into those who were here and those who weren't.'[21]

Art and pop music, natural bedfellows in Liverpool since the late 1950s, were a constant theme for Bluecoat over this period, from an exhibition reworking The Beatles' *Sgt Pepper* sleeve tableau 30 years after the original, to the live art commissions *Live from the Vinyl Junkyard/Mixing It* between 1996 and 1997. This series, contextualising the demise of vinyl in the digital age of the re-mix, included engaging installation, performance and turntable works by Philip Jeck and other artists from the region, alongside others who went on to develop national and international profiles: Iain Forsyth and Jane Pollard's tribute supergroup, Cornford

and Cross turning the gallery into a record fair for a day, and Jeremy Deller's *Acid Brass*, whose pumping brass band versions of acid house anthems, played by the Williams Fairey Band, achieved nationwide success following their premiere at the Liverpool Institute for Performing Arts.[22] These artists provided a new soundtrack for the 'Pleasure Dome' that Margi Clarke and Holly Johnson had welcomed us to the previous decade.[23]

This dome – representing Liverpool at its most dangerously seductive – witnessed during the decade under discussion a flowering of its visual culture as it harnessed local passion with global reach. An amalgam of the homegrown and the outsider captivated by the city's possibilities, the art scene was variously irreverent, irresistible and infuriating. Its defiantly anti-metropolitan stance produced art, much of which went unnoticed by the outside world. But the local/global dynamic and making Liverpool itself a site for creative exploration started to attract greater external interest with the arrival of the Biennial. By then, however, the city's independent visual art landscape had shifted. Although there were new artist-curator voices and spaces appearing and greater opportunities for artists to engage with communities and other public contexts, Visionfest had run out of steam, a culturally diverse dimension seemed strangely absent, and the anarchic cross-fertilisation between artists became less frequent, as, after years of relatively paltry funding, application writing fatigue took its toll amongst some of the city's most creative practitioners. The challenge for the Biennial was to provide a new catalyst that picked up and reinvigorated the various strands that had thread through and distinguished the previous decade's visual arts.

20 Ronald Reagan, from a televised discussion with students at Moscow State University, 31 May 1988, quote printed on the front cover of *Liverpool Echo*'s Bluecoat Supplement, 30 January 1989.

21 Interview with ARK's Colin Fallows, who was instrumental in bringing the event to Liverpool, August 2006.

22 The publication *Live From The Vinyl Junkyard: The Ultimate Mix*, Liverpool: Bluecoat/Liverpool Art School, 1998, documents the commissions.

23 The hedonistic promise of actor Clarke's and musician Johnson's phrase found expression in their respective film *Letter to Brezhnev* and chart-topping band Frankie Goes To Hollywood's records, including *Welcome to the Pleasure Dome*.

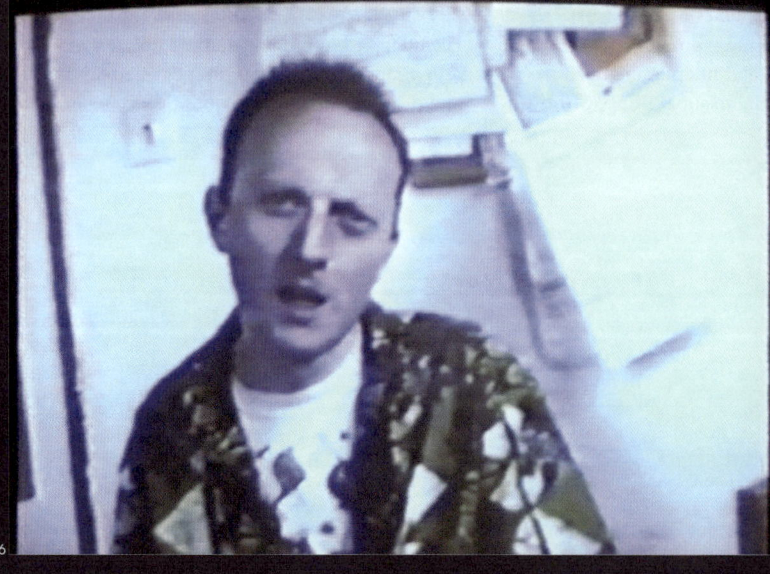

15

16

15
Bob and Roberta Smith
Lennon Text 2006
Sign-writers enamel
on found timber
229 x 115 cm
Collection of the artist

16
Bob and Roberta Smith
Humiliate 1993
Video, colour, sound
Approx 20 minutes
Collection of the artist

17
Rineke Dijkstra
*The Buzz Club, Liverpool
(UK); Mystery World,
Zaandam (NL)* 1996
Two-channel video
projection, colour, sound
26 minutes 40 seconds
Courtesy of the artist

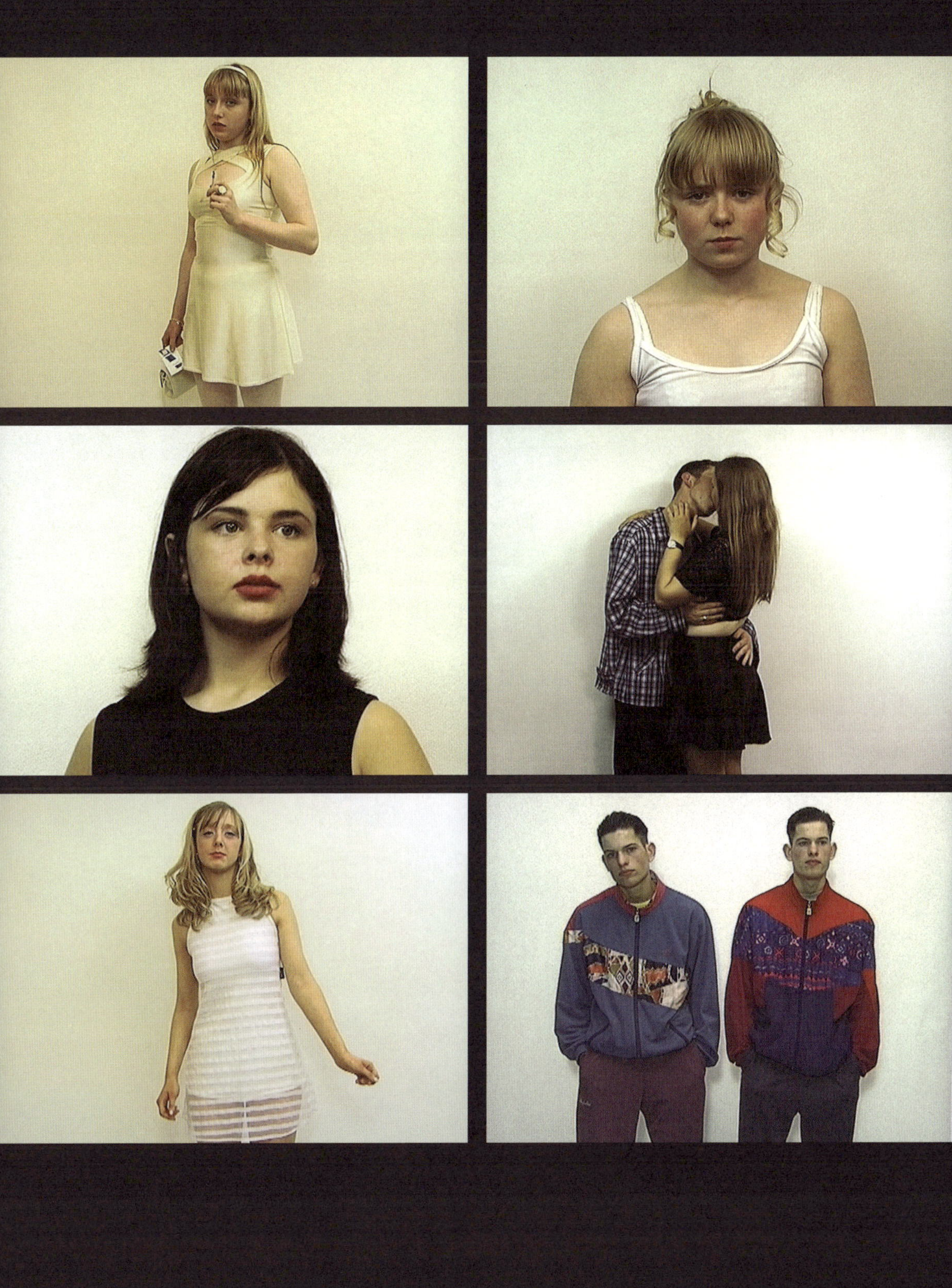

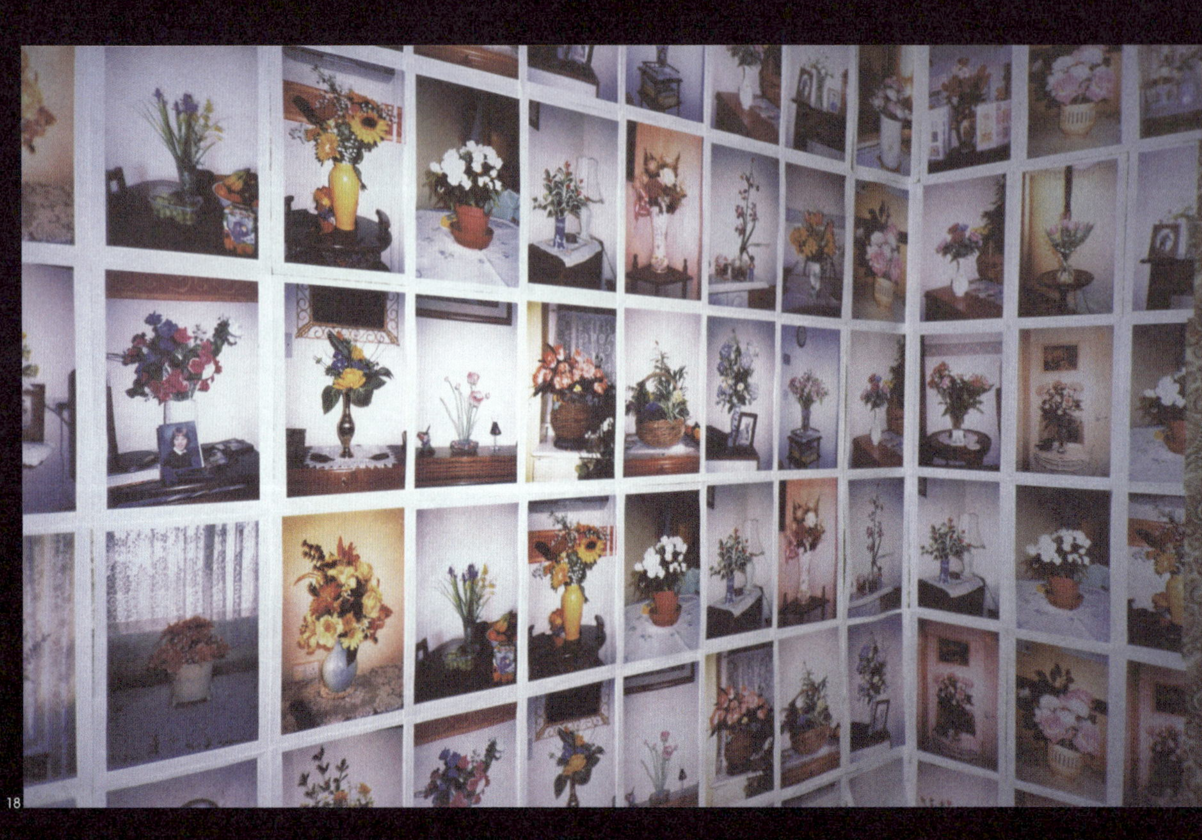

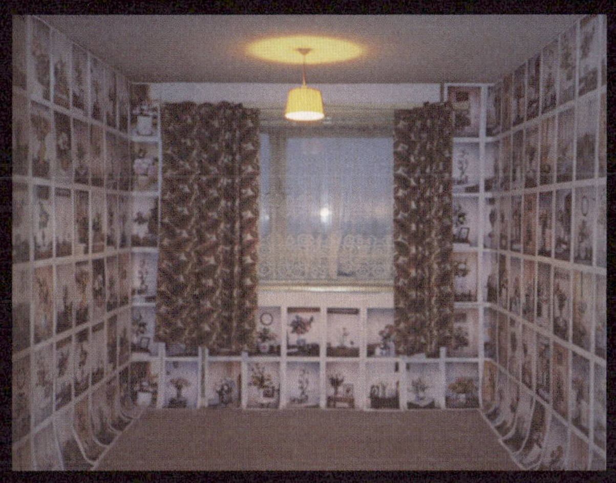

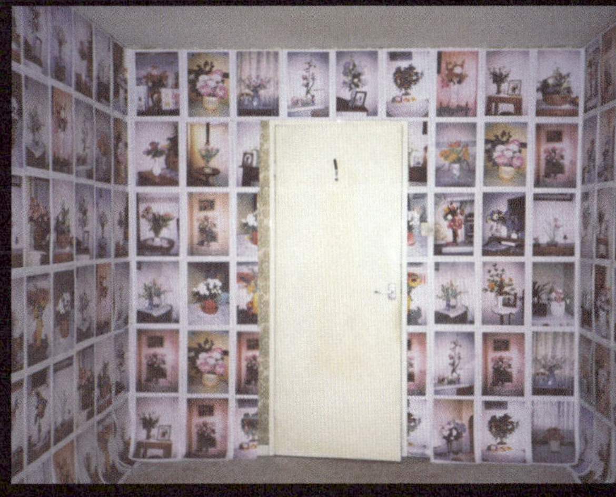

18
Anna Fox
Mum in a Million 2003
Installation views
Further Up in the Air,
Sheil Park, Liverpool

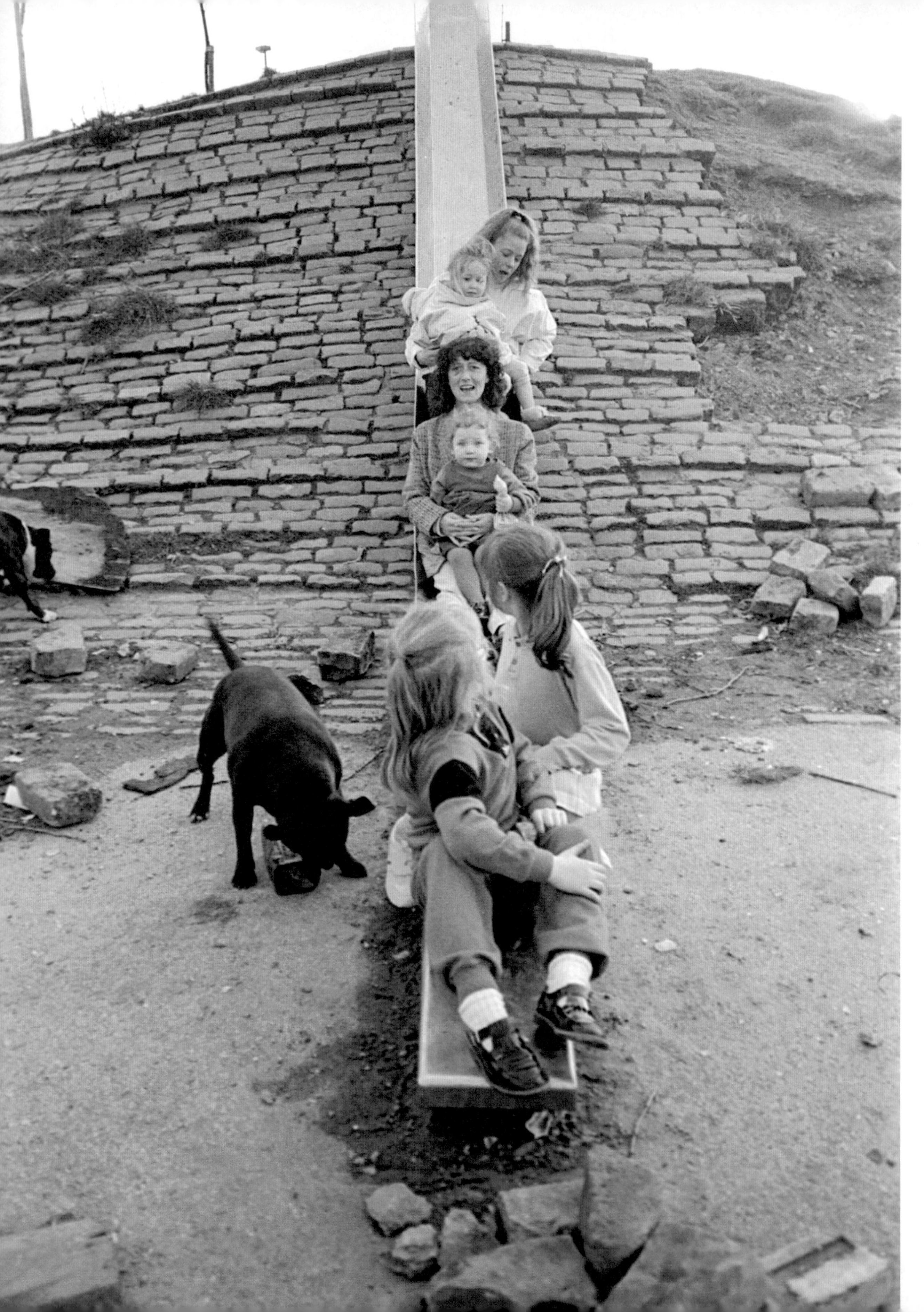

PACKAGING CULTURE, REGULATING CULTURES: THE RE-BRANDED CITY

Paul R. Jones
& Stuart Wilks-Heeg

Packaging Culture,
Regulating Cultures:
The Re-branded City
Paul R. Jones &
Stuart Wilks-Heeg

Today cities occupy an ambiguous position in media and political discussions alike. Sometimes fêted as sites of creativity and sociality and other times decried as centres of criminality and danger, contemporary commentators reflect tensions that have as long a lineage as cities themselves. While some early urban theorists celebrated the potential of the restlessness, anonymity and diversity of the social interactions that characterise modern city life, others condemned the decadence, disorder and chaos associated with the emerging urban centres. However, across this spectrum of opinion all acknowledged the fact that city life provided unrivalled potential for cultural creativity. The extent to which such potential is inherent to any urban contexts is something of a moot point, and one that is explored in various ways in *Centre of the Creative Universe: Liverpool and the Avant-Garde*. Furthermore, and with regard to Liverpool specifically, it is important to note that this exhibition takes place at a time when the city's cultural creativity is in the process of being actively (re)written as a central part of a broader project of social change aimed at reviving the city's economic fortunes.

This 'rebranding' of Liverpool is designed primarily: (a) to persuade entrepreneurs that the city is a profitable place in which to invest; and – relatedly – (b) to put the location on the 'must do' list of the profitable city break tourist market. Against the backdrop of the exhibition it is also interesting that these recent attempts to sell the city have involved certain aspects of Liverpool's history of cultural production coming

to the fore in marketing discourses, while less saleable expressions of cultural creativity have faded away to the background. This is perhaps not surprising, as 'branding' any city presents an objectified, static, and necessarily narrow vision of a much wider, messier social reality; marketing a place unavoidably reduces a hugely diverse range of lived experiences into a readily-consumable package, slogan or image. It is precisely because the process glosses over the tensions and conflicts inherent in any genuinely creative context that 'rebranding' cities is not a neutral process, and that the images and slogans used in 'selling places' are value-laden political constructions, that 'celebrate' certain spaces and people and – crucially – not others.

While Liverpool's reinvention was underway before its successful European Capital of Culture bid, the 2008 deadline has accelerated many of the processes already in progress. So, although Liverpool is far from the only city in which there has been a 'conscious and deliberate manipulation of culture'[1] to an economic end, the dramatic transformations of some of the city centre's spaces, coupled with the aggressive marketing of the city, has raised many pertinent questions about the relation between regeneration, branding and cultural creativity. Whereas the Capital of Culture bid literature suggests that the award provides the city with an opportunity for 'self-discovery', Liverpool's cultural identity is actually in the process of being actively created rather than being simply revealed. As part of the reconstruction of the city's image 'diversity' and 'alternative culture' – but not an avant-garde *per se* – have been incorporated into official marketing lines.

The European Capital of Culture 2008 bid was organised around the slogan 'The World in One City', which alludes to social and cultural diversity as self-contained values. Certainly throughout the twentieth century Liverpool's artists, actors, musicians, poets, and playwrights – not to mention those who passed through the city or had some other creative association with the place – have ensured the city's prominent representation on national and international cultural stages. As we have argued in more detail elsewhere, 'The World in One City' can equally be read as a comment on the social, cultural and economic inequalities that persist in Liverpool and globally.[2] The vague allusions to diversity and cosmopolitanism are misleadingly partial; the lived reality of Liverpool as including large degrees of inequality, racism and poverty that, while not in keeping with the re-branded image of the city, shape the lives of many people in Liverpool.

In addition, the self-evident contradiction of using 'culture' or 'creativity' as marketing lines to legitimate economically-motivated activity opens up a number of interesting questions. For example, many find their capacity for cultural

---

1   Kearns, Gerry, and Philo, Chris (eds.), *Selling Places: The City as Culture Capital, Past and Present*, Oxford: Pergamon Press, 1993, p. 3.
2   Jones, Paul R., and Wilks-Heeg, Stuart, 'Capitalising Culture: Liverpool 2008', *Local Economy*, 19 (4) 2004.

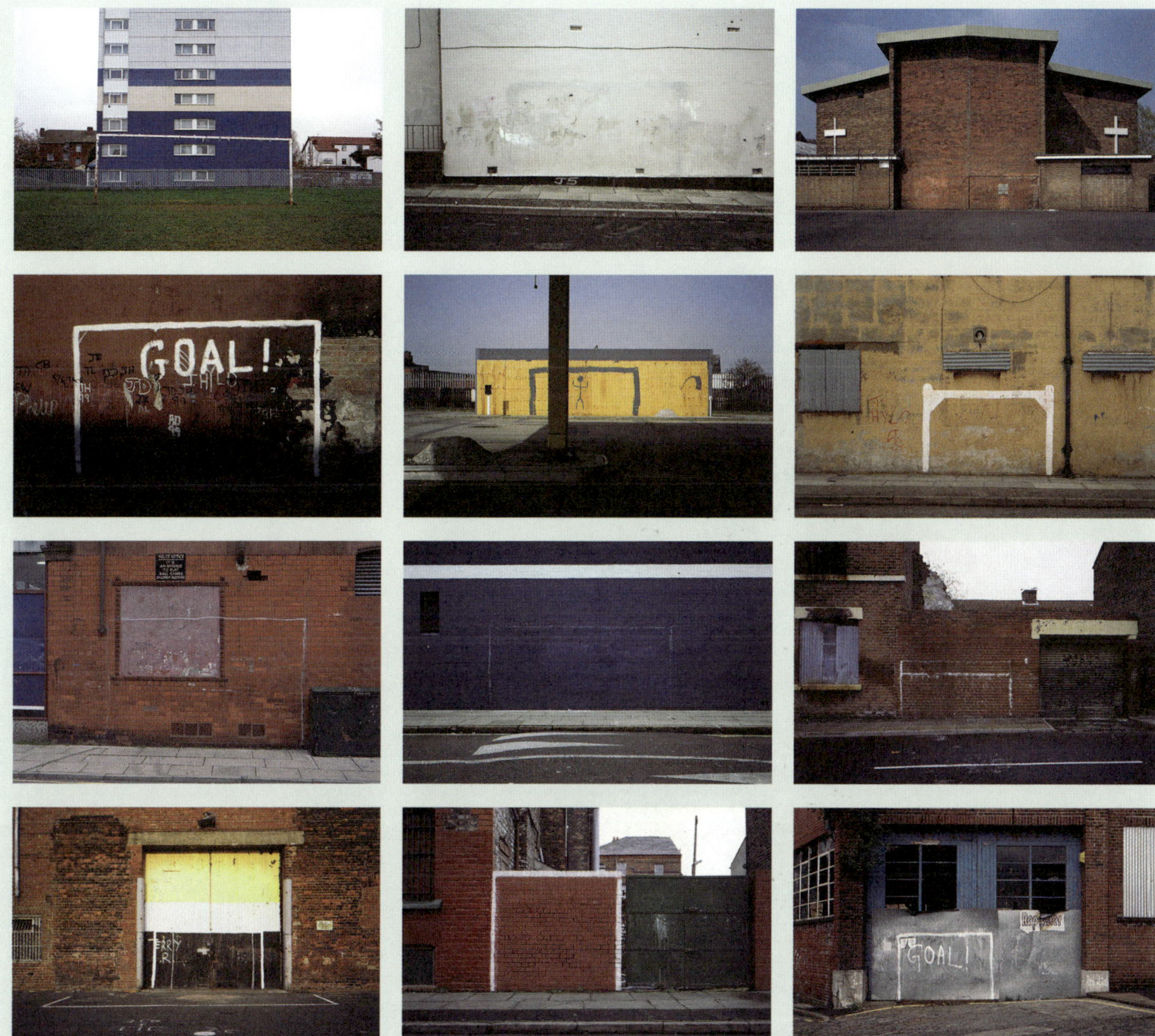

2

previous

Vanley Burke
*Dog Chewing on a
Brick* c. 1980
Silver bromide print
60.9 x 41.4 cm
Courtesy of Vanley Burke

2

Neville Gabie
*Playing Away UK –
Liverpool* 1998-2005
Lambda prints mounted
on aluminium
Each: 40 x 60 cm
Courtesy of the artist

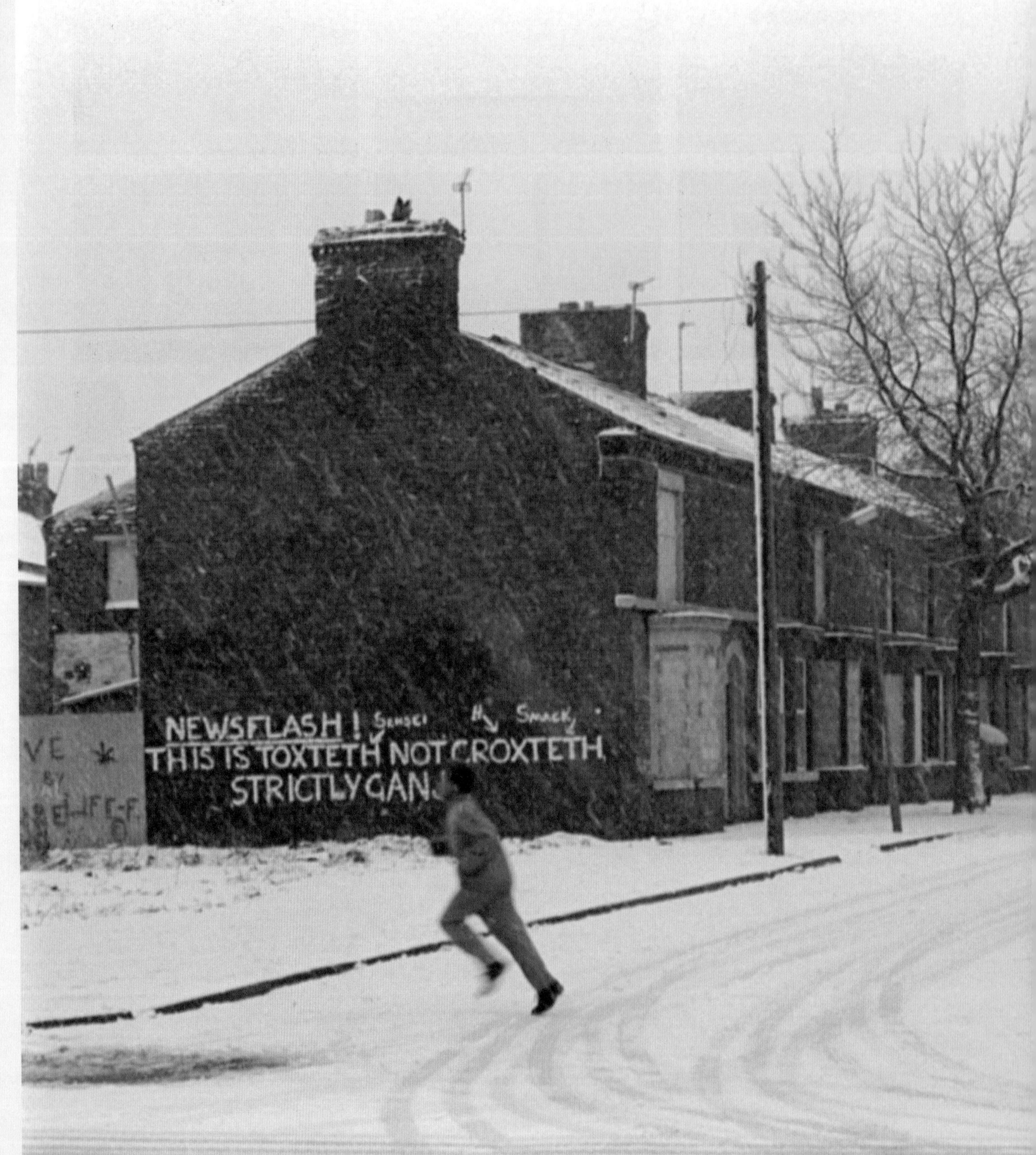

NEWSFLASH! Sensei Smack
THIS IS TOXTETH NOT CROXTETH.
STRICTLY GANJ

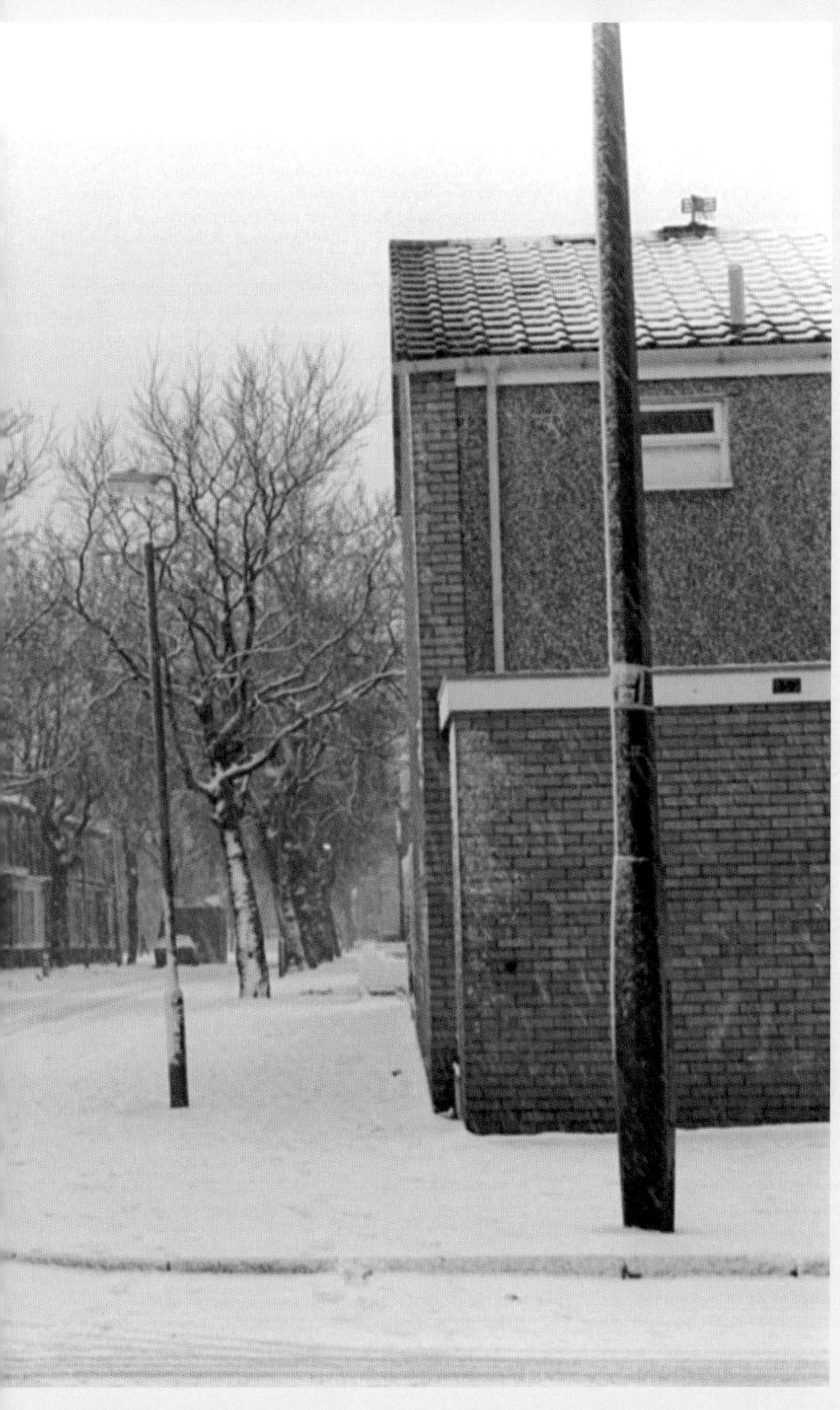

3
Vanley Burke
'Toxteth not Croxteth'
Graffiti c. 1980
Silver bromide print
41.4 x 60.9 cm
Courtesy of Vanley Burke

expression in the city highly conscribed, with the re-invigorated emphasis on consumption in the city centre narrowing the acceptable range of cultural expressions. Practical provision, like the availability of buildings for artists' studios, band rehearsal space, and other alternative cultural venues are all based on the idea of 'surplus' space. In other words, when more buildings exist than the market has use for, they can be occupied, generally on a short-term basis, for relatively low-rent and are therefore open to a range of uses. The social change associated with the regeneration of the city has aimed to fill many of its 'surplus' spaces with new buildings, new shops and new flats. As these regenerated spaces are designed exclusively for consumption, behaviour and cultures that do not fit in with such logic are excluded. In other words, attempts to encourage more shops, and in fact to refashion areas of the city centre exclusively for shopping and nothing else (as in the Met Quarter and to a great extent in the Paradise Street Development Area) are arguably the antitheses of creative urban spaces; such spaces preclude behaviour that is not shopping, and even 'loitering' in such spaces becomes seen as a problem. What's more, the consolidation of regulation to control city spaces with City Wardens, private security, additional police, gold zones, and more CCTV (see Coleman for a more detailed discussion of social control in the city[3]) alongside increasing rents and changed land use serves to limit behaviour in the city. The paradox in all this is that the 'creative' environments that policy makers seek to create are the ones that tend to develop spontaneously, or at least (in a less romantic sense) due to a lack of regulation; increased social control coupled with the extension of the market into new parts of the city are antithetical to this.

Squaring the Circle of Cultural Quarters

In keeping with the broader marketing of cities as 'brands', policy-makers have placed growing emphasis upon the development of 'cultural quarters'. This notion of designating a distinct geographical area of the city as its supposed cultural/creative hub owes much to the tradition of land-use 'zoning' in urban planning and has become a central element of 'culture-led regeneration' strategies. Yet, it also takes inspiration from authors who have suggested that significant advances in the arts and popular culture frequently emerge from city-based clusters.[4] However, in practice such clusters generally develop in an organic, 'bottom-up', even chaotic fashion often arising from the 'creative milieu' that a particular city provides during a specific period in its history. In contrast to a 'planned' environment, a creative milieu arises from the almost random ways in which creative individuals are thrown together by city life. Indeed, among the numerous common factors that might explain the emergence of cultural crucibles as diverse as Elizabethan London, inter-war Berlin and modern-day Los Angeles, 'serendipity' is one of the most powerful causal variables.[5]

While a creative milieu will often emerge in a defined district or neighbourhood of a city, it is likely to differ in a number of important ways from the more formal creative quarters established by planners. A creative milieu will not be created via slogan or logos for tourists, consumers and investors. It will neither be triggered via the creation of 'flagship' buildings for the arts and culture, nor through public-private partnerships with major property developers. All of these may follow in time but, in the first instance, what gives birth to a creative milieu is often a seemingly random combination of artists, musicians, writers, and others from across creative fields, working in conjunction with maverick entrepreneurs. A lack of regulation, often in the form of local agencies overlooking certain types of activity can be crucial; in some instances the effective 'tolerance' of illicit drugs has been a key feature in the emergence of creative milieu – witness the central role of ecstasy in Manchester's music scene of the late 1980s and early 1990s. Even more commonly, a creative milieu will involve the unapproved or even illegal occupation and use of property.

The New York art scene that grew up around artists occupying disused textile factories in the tenement blocks of Manhattan's SoHo during the 1960s and 1970s is a prime example here. Utilising the empty properties as both residential and studio spaces, artists chose to live in buildings which the planning system still officially earmarked for industrial and commercial use only. This clear transgression of the city's planning regulations was tolerated in the short term by the local authorities. Yet, the SoHo case aptly illustrates that such unplanned cultural quarters tend to be highly ephemeral, all the more so if they come to acquire public acclaim and attention. The presence of some artists in SoHo provided the impetus for the establishment of a cluster of independent art galleries and, by the mid-1980s, SoHo was firmly part of the New York tourist itinerary. At the same time, the district also became the focus for frenzied property development and a desirable location for professional middle-class residents, who actively bought into the 'loft aesthetic' that, in turn, owed its origins to the 'sweat equity' of generally impoverished artists.[6] Yet of course, with SoHo now seen by planners, property developers and tourists as a vibrant 'cultural quarter', most of the artists that had been so instrumental in establishing that reputation now found themselves priced out and displaced to other areas of the city.

The SoHo case also reminds us how, with surprising regularity, a 'cultural milieu' will come to be absorbed into a more mainstream approach to cultural quarters. This dynamic tension between artistic and cultural 'scenes' and the formal activities of public agencies and property developers frequently results in a city's creative centre constantly shifting location. Liverpool's recent experience reflects this very tendency. Over the past five decades a succession of grassroots cultural quarters have emerged, blossomed, faded and died. Among the most prominent of these were the Georgian quarter of Liverpool 8 during the 1960s, and the Mathew Street/Whitechapel area during the 1980s. More recently, during the 1990s, the Ropewalks district of the city centre was 'officially' designated by planners as Liverpool's cultural quarter. The legacy of this designation is today reflected in the presence of, among others, the FACT Centre, Arena and the Open Eye Gallery in the Ropewalks area. However, arguably more characteristic of the formal regeneration of the area has been the squeezing out of cultural activity by residential development and the proliferation of bars and restaurants. Recognition of this dynamic led to the proposal to create a so-called 'Independents District' – an ostensibly 'anti-brand' brand – in the Jamaica Street area of the city, a project which initially stalled but appears to have been reinvigorated by the preparations for 2008.

Intriguingly, visitors to Liverpool will currently find that if they follow the 'tourist' signposts in the city centre towards the 'cultural quarter', they will in fact be directed to William Brown Street. This is a useful reminder that the city's original, planned cultural quarter dates from the nineteenth century and was centred upon St George's Hall, the Walker Art Gallery and the Central Libraries.[7] Yet it is equally instructive to remind ourselves of some forgotten history of Liverpool's creative scenes – those that rarely feature in official narratives. Consideration of one such example, the Mathew Street/Whitechapel area from 1976-83 underlines that cultural creativity is frequently borne of the most surprising, if not simply bizarre circumstances. To understand its origins, we must first consider another modern-day marketing slogan: 'Liverpool, the pool of life'.

The 'Pool of Life', 1974-2006:
From Avant-Garde to 'Irish' Pub

(Liverpool) has enjoyed staggering economic regeneration over the past decade …the 'pool of life' is a now a festival city with a thriving arts and cultural scene.[8]

At weekends Liverpool's bars, clubs, theatres and international restaurants attract half a million visitors to this vibrant pool of life – all fuelling demand for new business and services.[9]

As the above quotations highlight, the description of Liverpool as 'the pool of life' has become a common phrase in the promotion of the city to tourists and investors. Moreover, the phrase also crops up in an astonishing range of other local contexts. 'The pool of life' has been adopted by the University of Liverpool's School of Biological Sciences to attract students; served as the name of a short-lived local 'listings' magazine during 2001-02; borrowed as the title of a local history/photography book by Colin Wilkinson[10]; and at the

time of writing acts as the name of a local arts project celebrating Liverpool's history in the context of its 800th anniversary in 2007. The appeal of 'the pool of life' in such promotional and celebratory contexts is self-evident; the phrase evokes the very same notions of vibrancy, creativity, diversity and cosmopolitanism implied by slogans such as 'the world in one city'.

From time to time, those making use of the term indicate that it was originally coined as a description of Liverpool by the Swiss psychiatrist Carl Gustav Jung. Perhaps, in the popular imagination, this direct association with one of the founders of psychology also implies some sort of 'scientific' basis for regarding Liverpool as 'the pool of life'. Yet, in actual fact, the phrase is taken from Jung's account of one of his own dreams, about a city that he had never visited. Recorded in his 1961 book *Memories, Dreams, Reflections*, Jung's 'revelation' about Liverpool was far removed from the city marketing discourses of today and, as such, is worth quoting at length:

I found myself in a dirty, sooty city. It was night, and winter, and dark, and raining. I was in Liverpool. With a number of Swiss – say, half a dozen – I walked through the dark streets. I had the feeling that there we were coming from the harbour, and that the real city was actually up above, on the cliffs. We climbed up there… When we reached the plateau, we found a broad square dimly lit illuminated by street lights, into which many streets converged. The various quarters of the city were arranged radially around the square. In the centre was a round pool, and in the middle of it a small island. While everything round about was obscured by rain, fog, smoke, and dimly lit darkness, the little island blazed with sunlight. On it stood a single tree, a magnolia, in a shower of reddish blossoms. It was as though the tree stood in the sunlight and was at the same time the source of light. My companions commented on the abominable weather, and obviously did not see the tree. They spoke of another Swiss who was living in Liverpool, and expressed surprise that he should have settled here. I was carried away by the beauty of the flowering tree and the sunlit island, and thought, 'I know very well why he has settled here.' Then I awoke.

3   Coleman, Roy, *Reclaiming the Streets: Surveillance, Social Control and the City*, Cullompton: Willan, 2004.

4   See, for example Landry, Charles, *The Creative City: A Toolkit for Urban Innovators*, London: Earthscan, 2000; Hall, Peter, *Cities in Civilisation: Culture, Innovation, and Urban Order*, London: Weidenfeld and Nicolson, 1998.

5   Hall, *Cities in Civilisation*.

6   Zukin, Sharon, *Loft Living: Culture and Capital in Urban Change*. New Brunswick, NJ: Rutgers University Press, 1989.

7   We are grateful to Victoria Durrer for making this connection. See also Sudbury, Patrick, and Forrester, Jim, 'Some museum developments in Liverpool, their benefits to the community' in Lorente, Pedro, (ed.), *The Role of Museums and the Arts in the Urban Regeneration of Liverpool*, Leicester: University of Leicester, 1996, pp. 71-89.

8   Virgin Trains, 'City Guide: Liverpool', at **http://www.virgintrains.co.uk/cityguides/city/liverpool/default.aspx**

9   Liverpool City Council, *Liverpool, The World in One City: Winner*, Liverpool: Liverpool City Council, 2003, p. 10.

10 Wilkinson, Colin, *Liverpool: The Pool of Life*, Liverpool: Bluecoat Press, 1993.

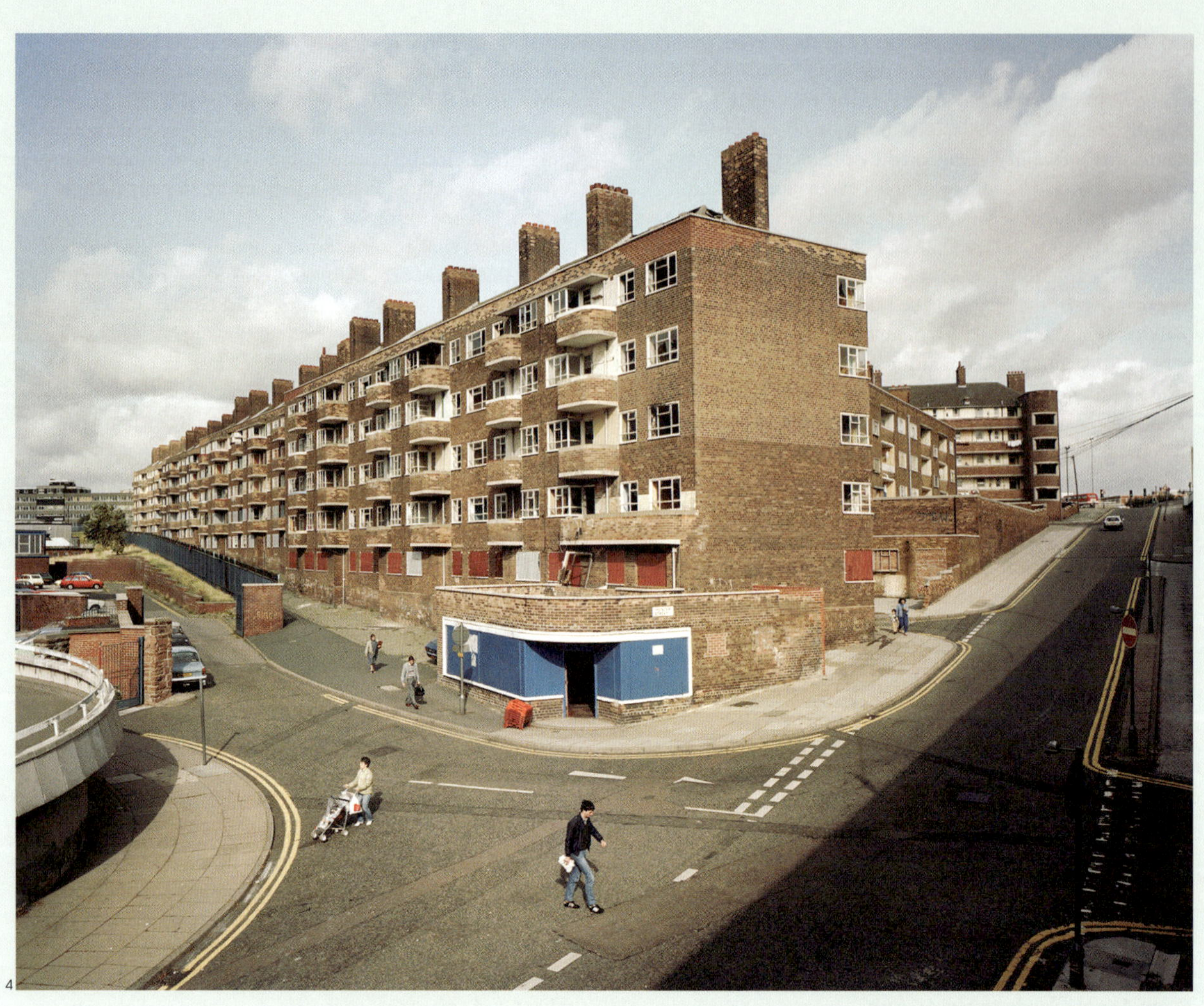

4

4/5
Martin Parr
England, Liverpool 1983-6
Inkjet prints
Each: 61 x 76 cm
Martin Parr Magnum Photos/
Rocket Gallery, London

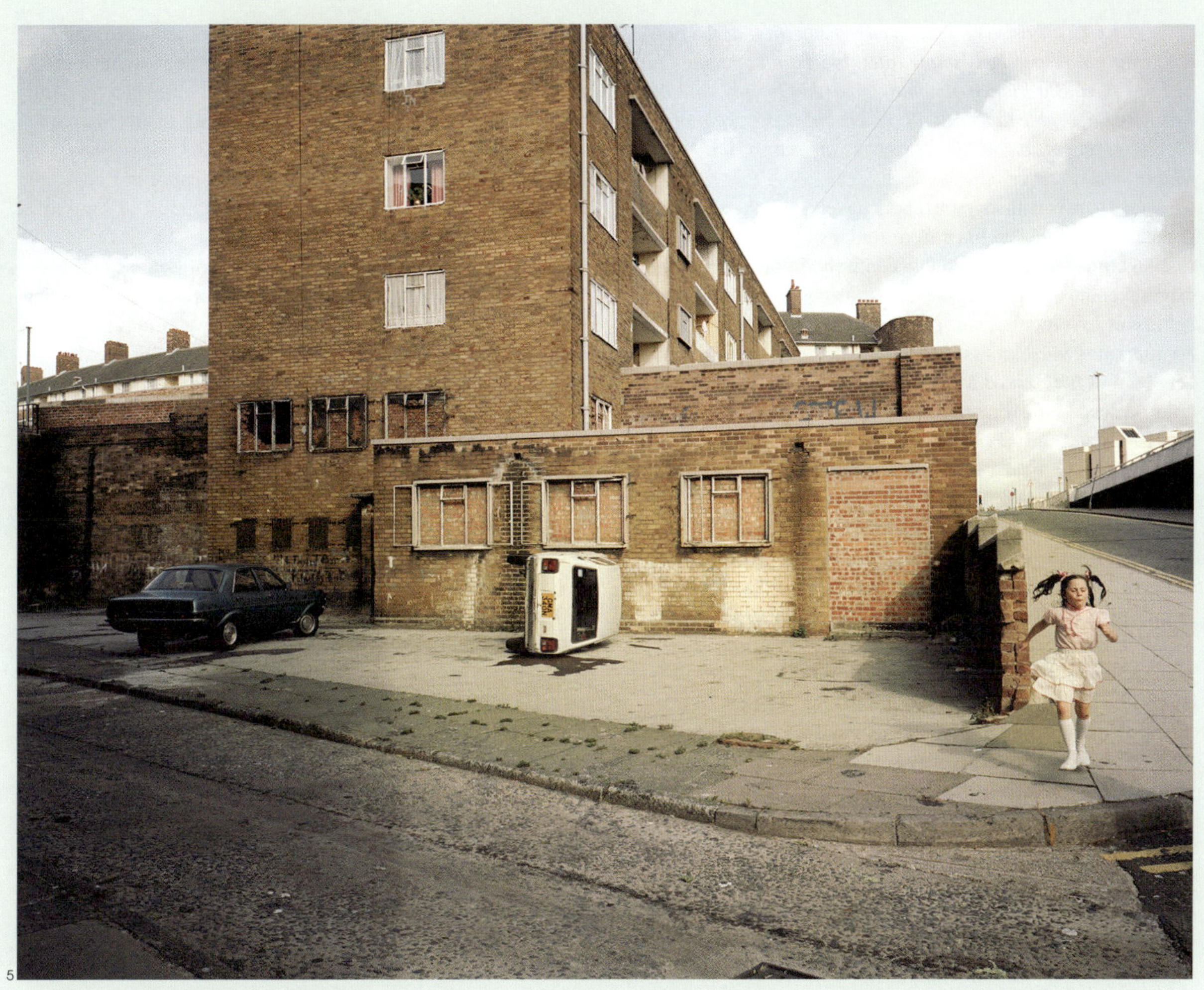

5

[…] This dream represented my situation at the time… Everything was extremely unpleasant, black and opaque – just as I felt then. But I had a vision of unearthly beauty, and that was why I was able to live at all. Liverpool is the 'pool of life'. The 'liver' according to an old view, is the seat of life – that which 'makes to live'.[11]

There is nothing particularly novel about the selective plundering of quotable lines from famous figures being used to evoke images and associations entirely divorced from their original context.[12] Yet, there is also a forgotten contemporary history of Liverpool as the 'pool of life'. For, prior to its appropriation via discourses of city marketing, Jung's vision of 'the pool of life' served as the catalyst for a vibrant alternative cultural scene in Liverpool, centred on Mathew Street in the late 1970s and early 1980s.

This particular piece of 'forgotten history' begins in 1974 when Liverpool resident, Peter O'Halligan, was told by his cousin Sean about Jung's dream. Inspired by the text, O'Halligan reasoned that it would be possible to locate the place in Liverpool that Jung was describing. With this thought firmly planted in his head, O'Halligan was also to gain apparent insight from the subconscious; having dreamt one night of a spring bubbling out of a manhole cover on Mathew Street, he set out to investigate the following day. To his amazement, he found that there was indeed a manhole cover, located exactly at a point where several streets converge – East Mathew Street, West Mathew Street, Button Street, Rainford Square and Temple Street. Convinced that this was the very spot described in Jung's dream, O'Halligan also noticed a disused warehouse for sale at this intersection. Intrigued by his discovery, he determined to research the history of the area and later read in the city library that an ancient spring under Mathew Street had been covered during the nineteenth century and diverted into the city's sewer system. Convinced that he had located Jung's 'pool of life', O'Halligan made the instant decision to buy the warehouse.

Having purchased it, O'Halligan established a flea market on the ground floor selling goods such as second hand clothes and records, health foods and hand-made crafts, and opened a café upstairs. Originally known as 'Aunt Twacky's', the building quickly became the hub of an emerging avant-garde cultural scene in Liverpool.[13] From the late 1970s, the building hosted a variety of arts exhibitions, including the *Even Moore* exhibitions, which showcased work by artists rejected by the John Moores Exhibition. A chance visit from theatre director Ken Campbell led him to select it as the location for his Science Fiction Theatre of Liverpool, which opened with a staging of *The Illuminatus!* in November 1976. Meanwhile, the café came to attract a bohemian crowd, including Bill Drummond, then a set designer at the Everyman, and many of the budding young musicians circulating in Liverpool at the time, including Julian Cope, Ian McCulloch and Pete Wylie.[14] Clearly, Aunt Twacky's was becoming more than just a flea market and café – it was the centre of a burgeoning creative scene. During a spell in prison for non-payment of rates to Liverpool City Council, O'Halligan decided to re-name the building in light of its growing centrality to alternative cultural production in the city. Following his release, he re-christened the building The Liverpool School of Language, Music, Dream and Pun and commissioned a bust of Jung to be set into the front of the building.[15]

Thereafter, The Liverpool School of Language, Music, Dream and Pun provided the impetus for a wider transformation of the Mathew Street area into an alternative cultural quarter. While the city as a whole experienced severe economic decline, job loss, escalating unemployment and severe urban decay, Mathew Street and Whitechapel blossomed, much like the magnolia tree in Jung's dream. On 1 October 1976, Roger Eagle and Pete Fulwell opened Eric's, a club devoted to Punk and new wave music just along Mathew Street. Probe Records, the city's best alternative record shop was also located close by. Aspiring popular musicians drawn together via Eric's and Probe went on to form acts such as Big in Japan, Echo and the Bunnymen, Deaf School, Elvis Costello and the Attractions, and Orchestral Manoeuvres in the Dark, the collective influence of which was arguably as great as 'Merseybeat' had been in the early 1960s. Many of the new Liverpool bands released their first recordings on a local, independent label, Zoo Records, established by Bill Drummond, with offices on Whitechapel, just across from Mathew Street.

Within this 'grassroots' cultural quarter, it was O'Halligan's School of Language, Music, Dream and Pun that acted as the classic example of the 'meeting place' that theorists suggest is so central to the formation of a creative milieu. It was within O'Halligan's school that people from diverse backgrounds and with varied cultural, artistic interests encountered one another, when they would not have done otherwise. As Bill Drummond recalls in his memoir, *45*, the School had a magnet draw and was characterised, above all else, by the spontaneity and stubborn insularity of its pupils: 'I jacked in my job building and painting stage sets at the Everyman and became a pupil of the School. Moved all my tools and workbench into the basement of the warehouse…. It soon became the creative hub of Liverpool. For the price of a mug of tea a generation of dole-queue dreamers spent their days discussing the poems they were writing, the happenings they were staging, the bands they were forming.

11 Jung, Carl Gustav, *Memories, Dreams, Reflections*, London: Collins, 1961, pp. 189-90; emphasis added.
12 The extraction of the lines 'above us only sky' from John Lennon's utopian (1971) song *Imagine*, to be used as a promotional slogan for 'Liverpool John Lennon Airport' provides another local example. Although, for cost-conscious 'budget airlines' such as Easyjet the subsequent lyric 'imagine no possessions' might also encapsulate their advice to passengers before packing their bags prior to travelling.
13 Merrifield, Jeff, *Ken Campbell and the Science Fiction Theatre of Liverpool: An Analytical History*, unpublished PhD Thesis: University of Liverpool, 2001.
14 Drummond, Bill, *45*, London: Little, Brown, 2000.
15 Merrifield, *Ken Campbell*.

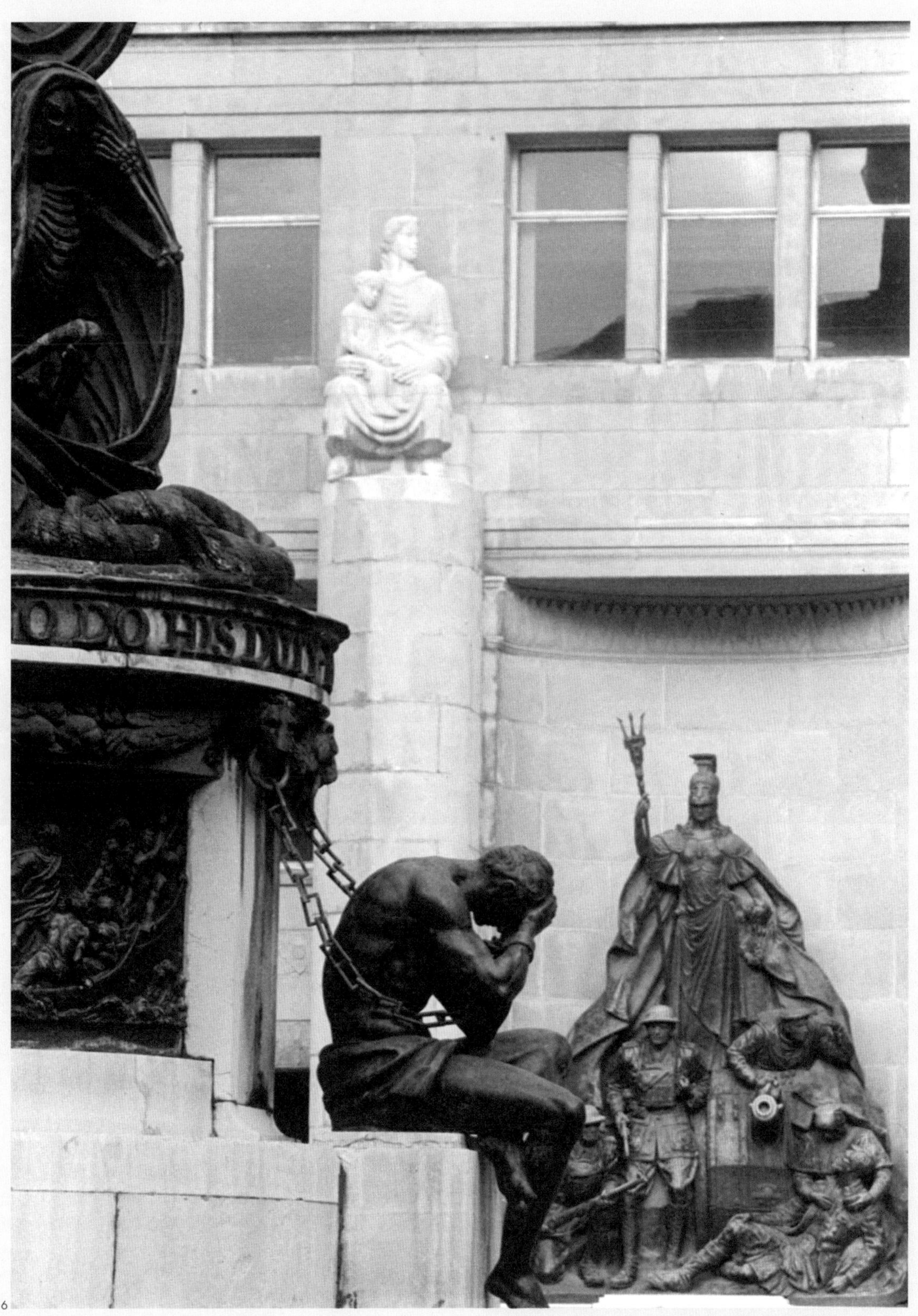

O DO HIS DUTY

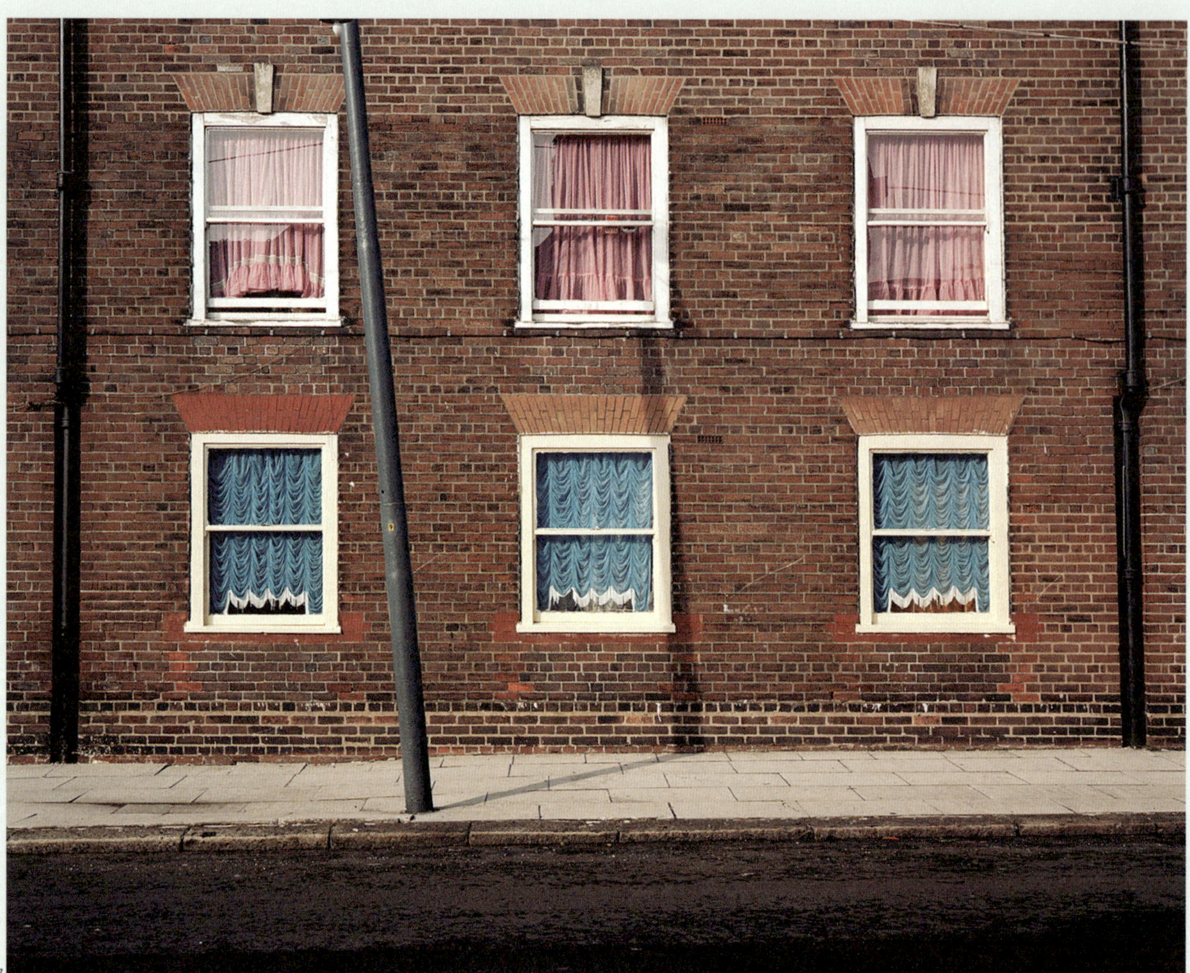

6
Vanley Burke
England Expects Every
Man to Do His Duty c. 1980
Silver bromide print
60.9 x 41.4 cm
Courtesy of Vanley Burke

7
Martin Parr
England, Liverpool 1983-6
Inkjet print
61 x 76 cm
Martin Parr Magnum Photos/
Rocket Gallery, London

The people of Liverpool were proudly insular; none of my fellow pupils at the school sipping their mugs of tea gave a shit whether anybody in London has ever heard of their existence or if any quarter of the media ever documented their creativity. All that mattered was what other people thought within the city state of Liverpool. Every day people staged impromptu performances, happenings, readings, installations, exhibitions, while Peter O'Halligan communicated his wisdom from behind the tea bar.'[16]

During the 1980s, the unique character of the Mathew Street creative quarter progressively eroded, beginning with the closure of Eric's on 14 March 1980. By 1984, the old warehouse hosting the Liverpool School of Language, Music, Dream and Pun had become a faux Irish Pub, while Bill Drummond and others had moved on. By the end of the decade, local agencies struggling to find a formula to spark the regeneration of Liverpool turned to the city's cultural heritage as a means of promoting tourism. Mathew Street was earmarked for redevelopment, becoming the centrepiece of attempts to capitalise on its earlier associations with The Beatles, by virtue of being the location of the Cavern club.[17] In the process of reinventing the area as a 'celebration' of Merseybeat, all trace of the legacy of the vibrant cultural scene of the late 1970s and early 1980s was effectively obliterated. The impact of the transformation is again captured by Bill Drummond, who recorded the following thoughts after a return visit to Mathew Street in 1997: 'I've been for a walk down through the old city, down to where the four streets meet, to the drain lid, up Mathew Street... I'd heard all about the understandable commercialisation of the area, the Cavern walks, the restaurants, the bars and all the other shite. The original pink granite cobbles in Mathew Street have been ripped up and replaced by the modern pedestrianised-walkway type of brick. A fake Cavern Club is open for business... Peter O'Hallaghan's [sic] Liverpool School of Language, Music, Dream and Pun is now a bogus Irish pub. Strangely there is still a bust of Jung on the wall, but it's different from the one that was placed there in 1977. I nod my respects to the man and hope I'm not the only remaining pupil of the school who's still dreaming dreams.'[18]

Beyond Nostalgia: The Paradoxes of City Cultures

Bill Drummond's sense of nostalgia and loss upon returning to a 'regenerated' Mathew Street would surely strike a chord with many contemporary residents of Liverpool, who are witnessing cherished buildings being demolished and entire city spaces being 'regenerated' beyond recognition. However, 'celebrating' alternative spaces and cultures risks becoming reactionary and sentimental, as it can lead us to fetishise spaces as 'creative', instead of acknowledging the talents of those who inhabit them. And, at the very least, we must recognise that nostalgic memories of Mathew Street in the late 1970's co-exist with traumatic memories of job loss, poverty and desperation among many Liverpudlians.

The processes that are constraining alternative cultural expression in Liverpool city centre have a recent precedent in the city's history. The Mathew Street case illustrates how alternative creativity – with all its deviance, drug-taking, and randomness – was ultimately driven out by officially-sanctioned (and of course more profitable) tourist and heritage industries. While it would be overly-simplistic to set up alternative vs. mainstream culture as a zero sum game, there is an important wider lesson here: in present-day Liverpool there is the paradoxical yet very real danger that contemporary 'official' celebrations and subsequent objectification of the city's cultural production constitutes a threat to the very deregulated and chaotic milieu that have been crucial to their emergence. We must also acknowledge the fact that in order to maintain the vitality that we apparently cherish, cities must support a range of activity – cultural and otherwise – some of which we may not like or even want to see. This reminds us of some of the most basic questions in urban sociology: who has the right to the city? Whose identities are recognised by those in power? How should our cities be controlled?

As the 'renaissance' of Liverpool is reliant on the symbolic reinvention and re-branding of the city there will always be a tension between the construction of a city image by organisations that are actively and self-consciously engaged in 'place marketing' and the social reality they purport to represent. At the same time, we are not suggesting that there is some kind of authentic 'Liverpool culture' that can simply be discovered and packaged. But, and as with any type of place marketing project, it is necessary to draw attention – through culture – to the contradictions that emerge with attempts to reconcile 'culture-led' regeneration strategies with instrumental economic rationales.

16 Drummond, *45*, p. 49.
17 The original Cavern had closed in 1973, although the club reopened in 1984 in a different location on Mathew Street.
18 Drummond, *45*, p. 65-66.

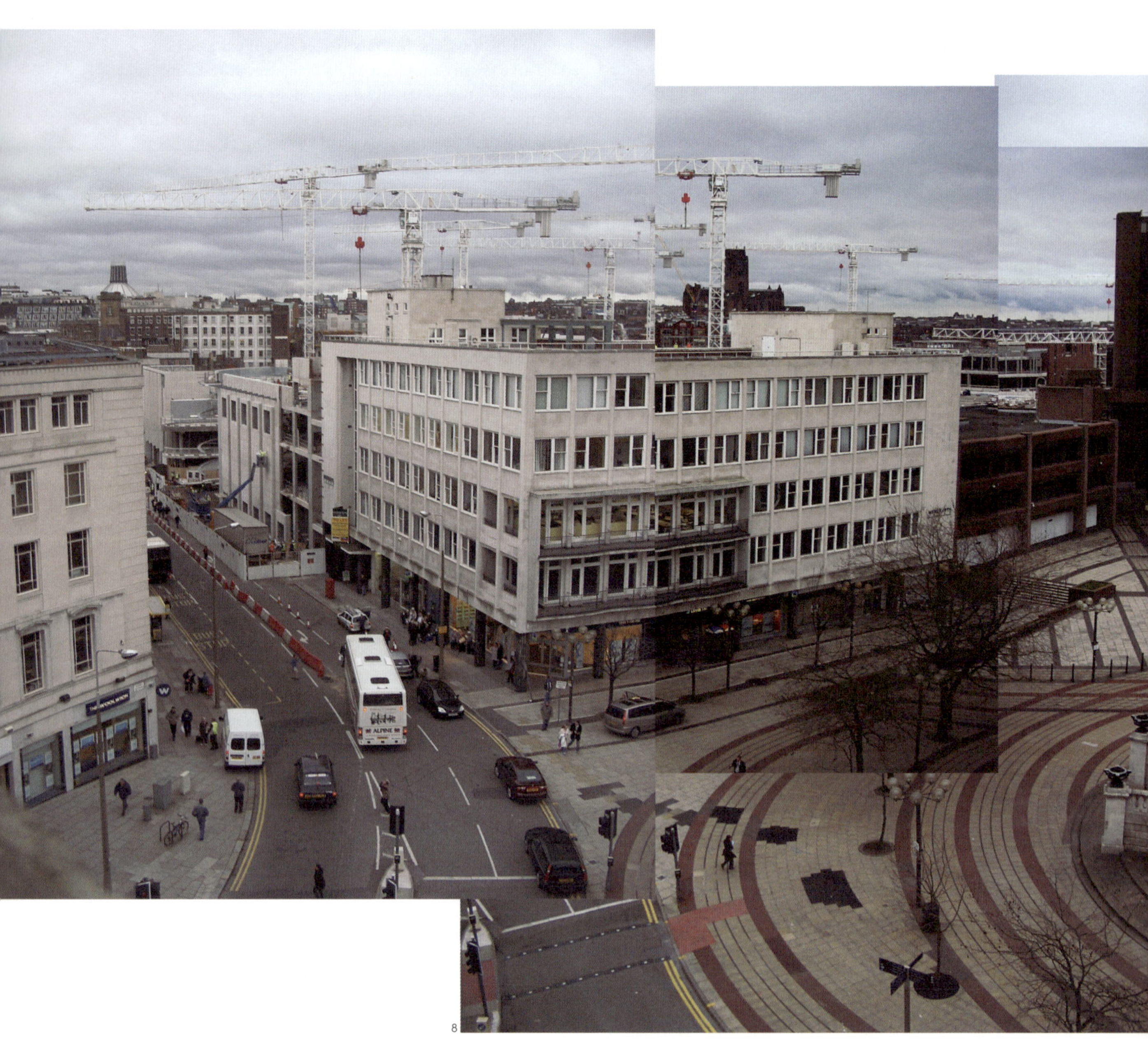

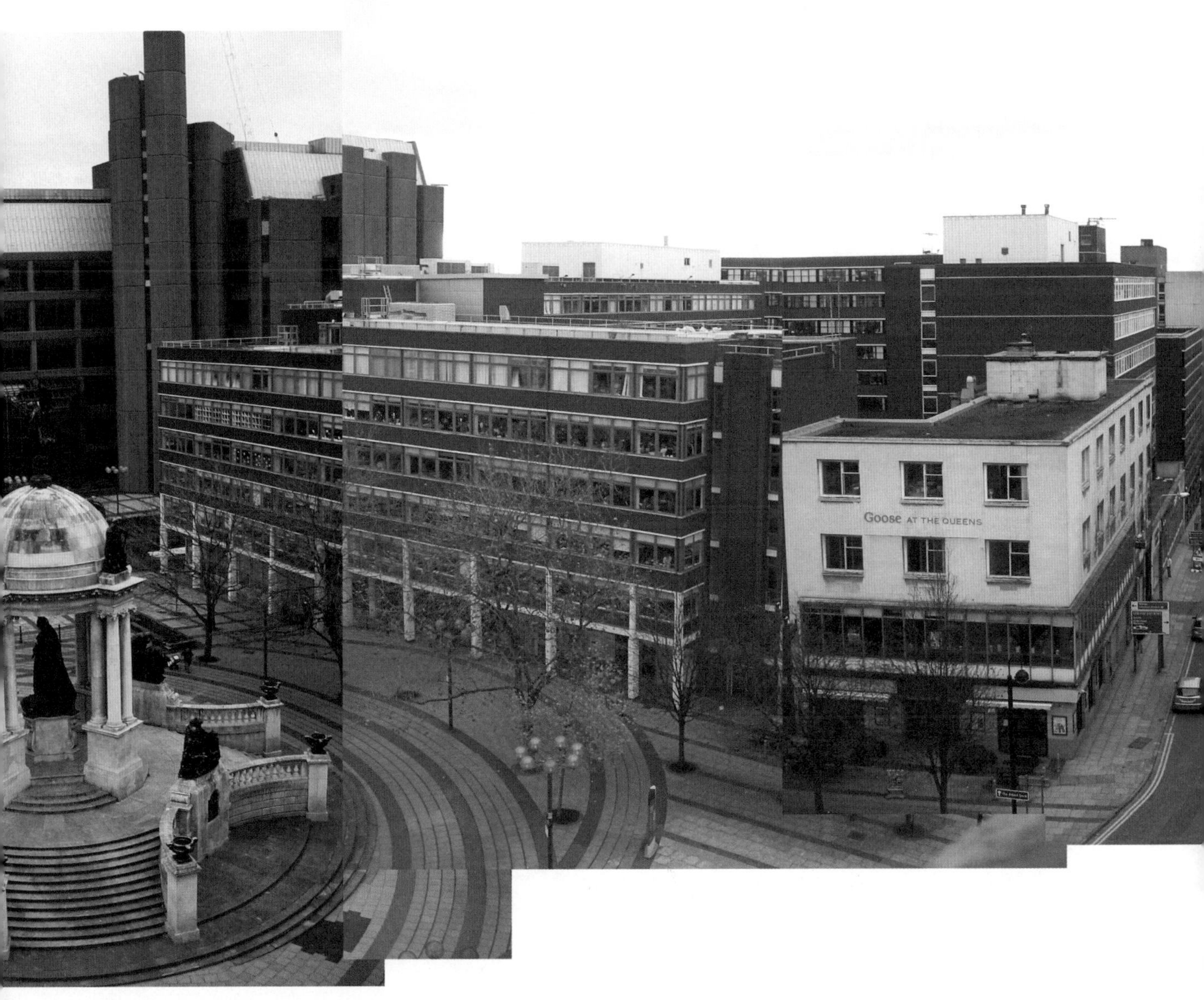

8
Paul Ryan
*Construction site near
the Victoria Monument,
Liverpool,* 2006
Colour photograph montage
Courtesy of the artist

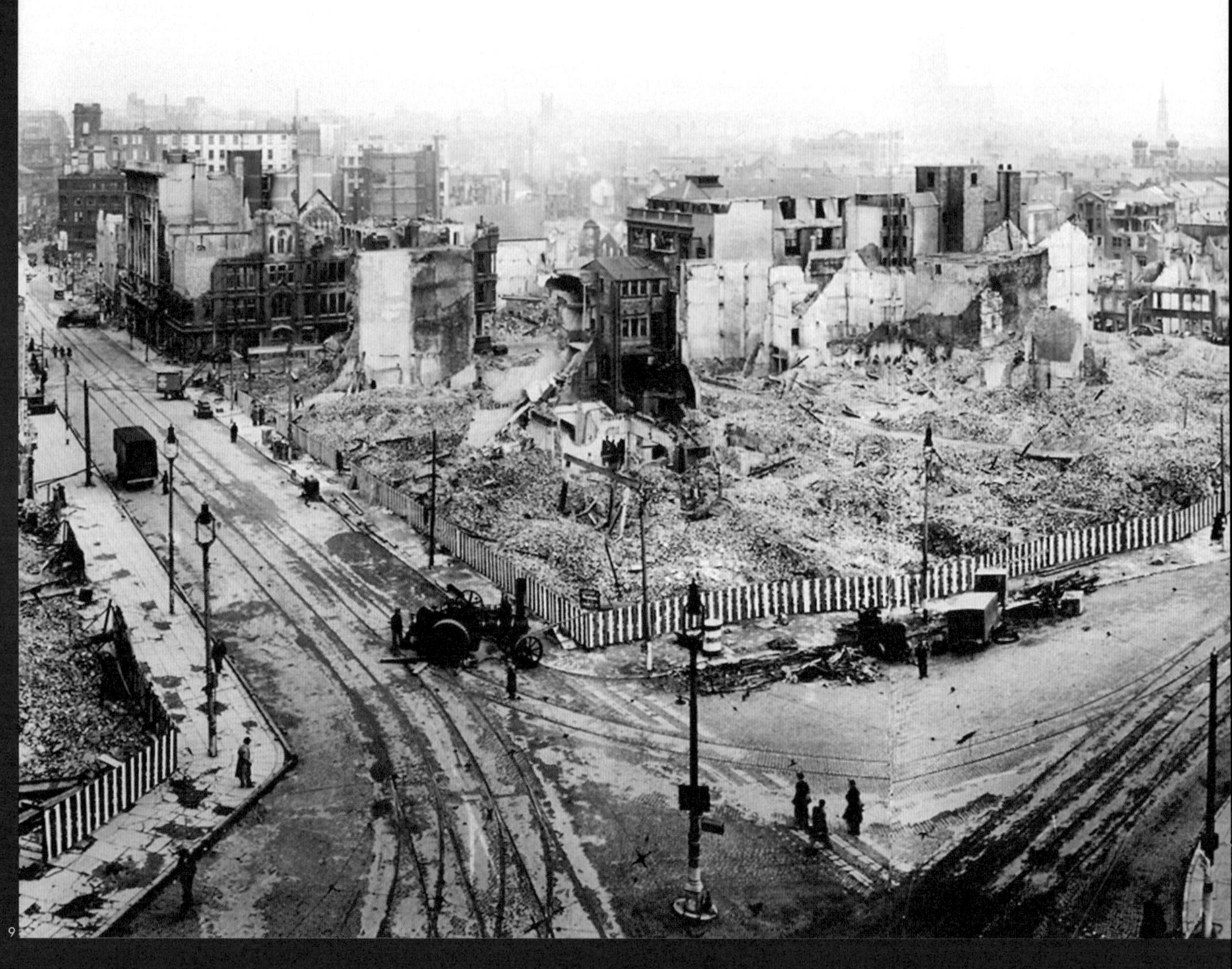

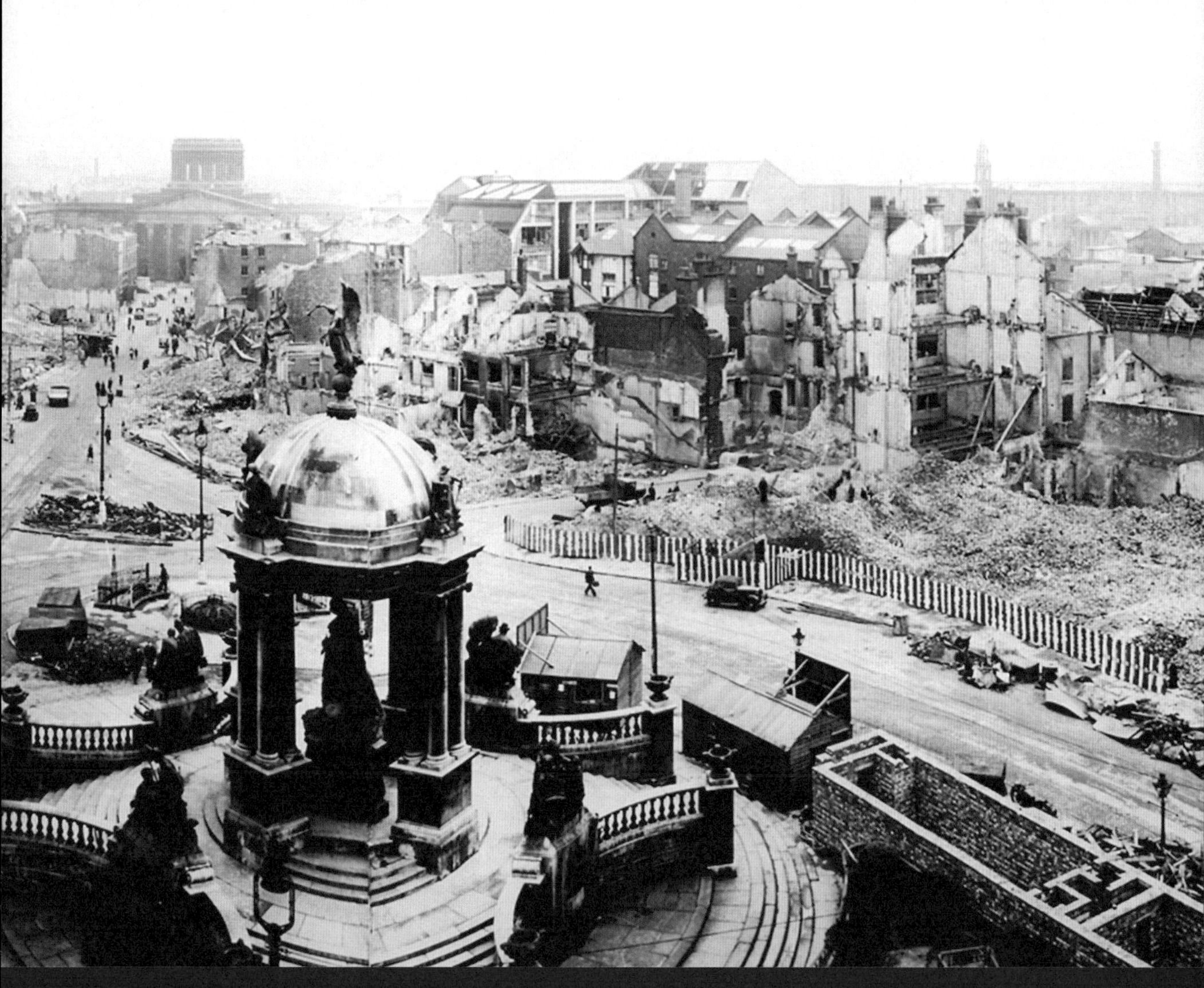

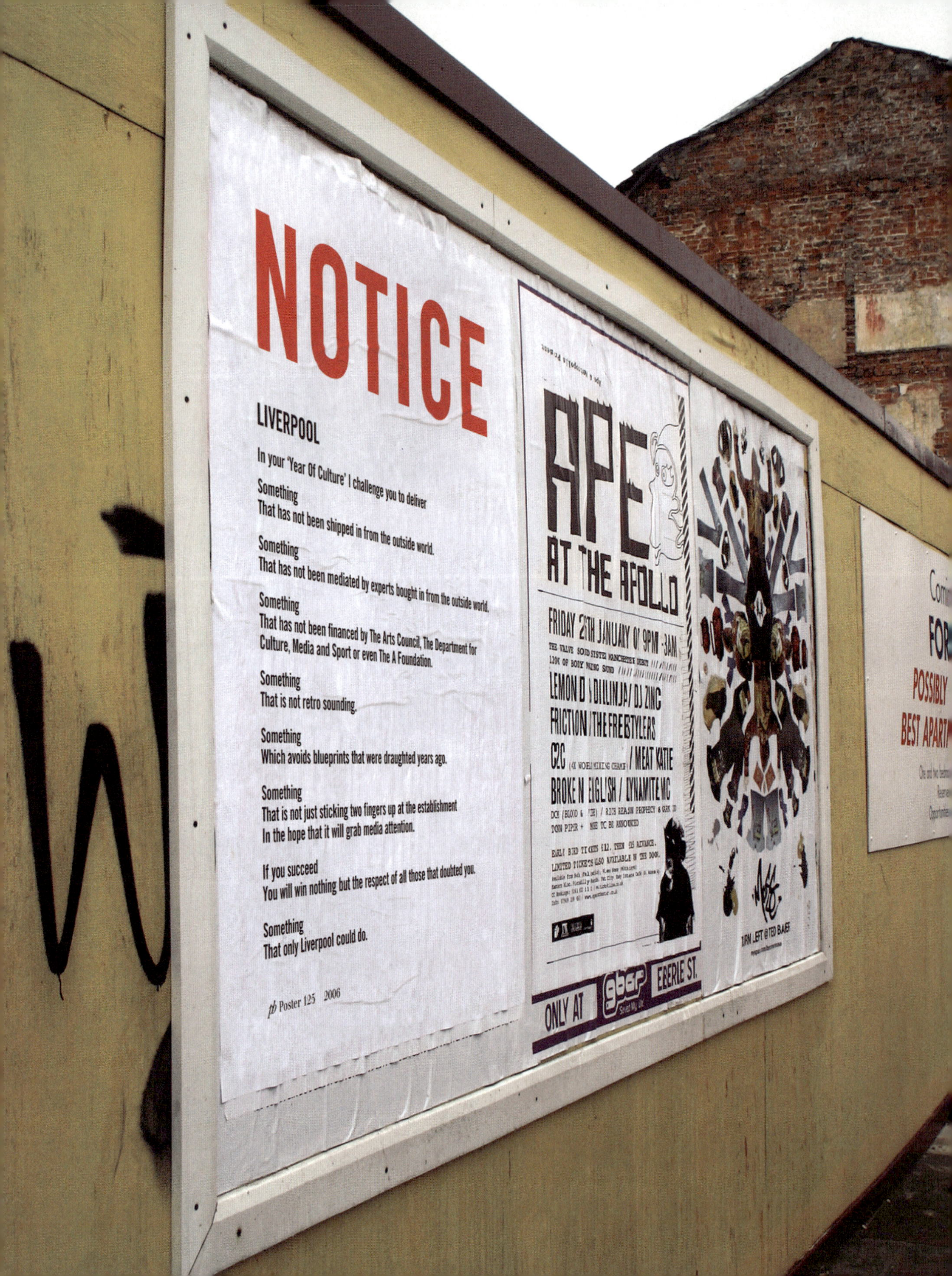
NOTICE
LIVERPOOL
In your 'Year Of Culture' I challenge you to deliver
Something
That has not been shipped in from the outside world.
Something
That has not been mediated by experts bought in from the outside world.
Something
That has not been financed by The Arts Council, The Department for Culture, Media and Sport or even The A Foundation.
Something
That is not retro sounding.
Something
Which avoids blueprints that were draughted years ago.
Something
That is not just sticking two fingers up at the establishment
In the hope that it will grab media attention.
If you succeed
You will win nothing but the respect of all those that doubted you.
Something
That only Liverpool could do.
pb Poster 125   2006
APE
AT THE APOLLO
FRIDAY 27TH JANUARY 9PM - 3AM
LEMON D / DILLINJA / DJ ZINC
FRICTION / THE FREESTYLERS
C2C / MEAT KATIE
BROKE N ENGLISH / DYNAMITE MC
ONLY AT   EBERLE ST.
Comm
FOR
POSSIBLY
BEST APART

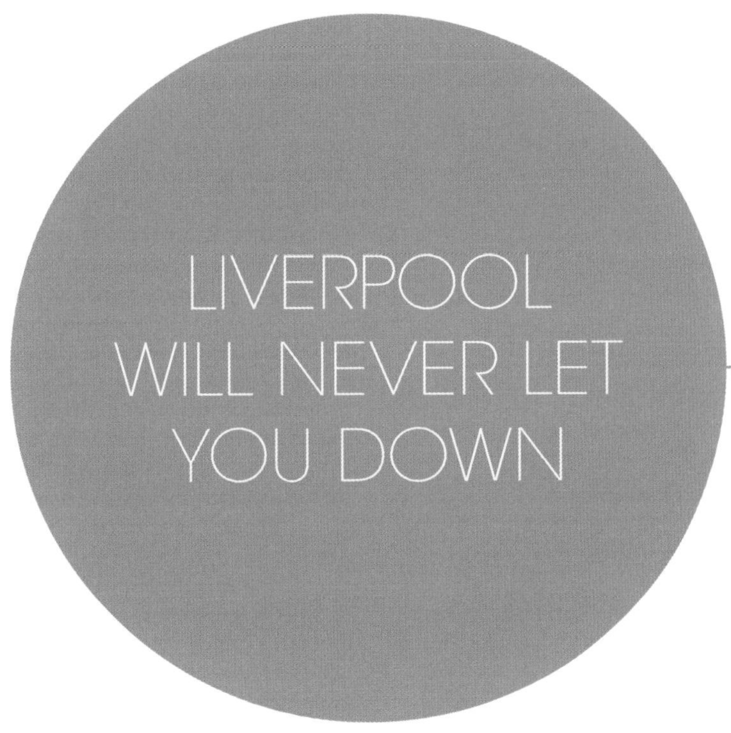

Bill Drummond

2 August 2006

'Liverpool serves no purpose whatsoever.'
100 years ago it had a purpose, but now if it were to be cut off and thrown into the Irish Sea, the rest of the country would be better off.

Maybe if England had won the World Cup, the rest of the country would have had Liverpool to thank for Steven Gerrard and Wayne Rooney, but they didn't. All that is left for Liverpool to do is look back and dream of glory years long ago.

The week before last I got an email from Christoph Grunenberg, the Director of Tate Liverpool. He was inviting me to write a text for the catalogue of an exhibition at Tate Liverpool. If you are reading this, you may already have the catalogue in your hands and the exhibition will need no explanation. If you are reading this elsewhere, I will quote from Grunenberg's email to me. 'To coincide with Liverpool's 800th birthday celebrations, Tate Liverpool is organising an exhibition entitled *Centre of the Creative Universe: Liverpool and The Avant-Garde* which will take place from 20 February – 9 September 2007. Taking its title from a celebrated statement by Beat poet Allen Ginsberg, this major exhibition will investigate how the city has influenced and inspired a wide range of artists. The focus will be on the post-1945 period, especially from the 1960s to the present day.'

I can't deny I was flattered to get this invite but there was a problem. I will quote from another bit of his email to

me then make plain the problem. 'You might be able to provide an interesting perspective on the relationship between the mainstream and underground culture, the avant-garde and everyday life of Liverpool in the 1990s.' He also suggested it needn't be a wholly new text.

There was a phone number at the end of the email. I phoned it. We spoke. I explained the problem: that I was not the right person to write about Liverpool in the 1990s as I hadn't lived in the city since 1983. But I did have a plan to write a book about the city I discovered and explored between October 1972 and December 1973; about the city I fell in love with and how it raped me; how there was nothing I could do in the confines of my studio in the Liverpool School of Art which could compete with what the city had to offer; how I would spend my days wandering around, as if in a spell, the miles and miles of its derelict docks – some of these docks that were later transformed into things like Tate Liverpool; how it almost killed me with pneumonia and pleurisy; how it threatened to lock me up for three years for a crime I had never done; how I did a runner under the cover of darkness, promising myself I would never return. But I did.

So I told Christoph Grunenberg about my plans for this book and how I would be up for writing a text for the catalogue about the city and me, that it would sort of be a summarised version of this book that I might never get around to writing and how 1972/73 is an under-reported era in the city's cultural history. That is, other than what has been written about the Everyman Theatre.

He seemed to be interested in what I was offering. And that was that. I had to get it done before the end of August.

But over the last week my mind has started racing, all of my conflicting emotions about Liverpool started to resurface. This city that filled in the original Cavern and turned it into a car park, that a couple of decades later cynically changed the name of Speke Airport to Liverpool John Lennon Airport. A city with so many chips on its shoulders which still thinks it's cool with its ridiculously arrogant swagger. A city that will always let you – and inevitably itself – down. Where Manchester can reinvent itself and march confidently on into the 21st century, Liverpool will just carry on doing dodgy deals, cutting corners and trying to do the lot on the cheap.

I first came across the Ginsberg quote some time in 1976, I was impressed – even flattered in some sort of weird way – that my adopted city was so highly thought of by one of my heroes. Even though I knew it was a load of bollocks in reality and Ginsberg probably only said it in an attempt to chat up some cute young Liverpool poet.

But still, one of the holy trinity of Kerouac, Ginsberg and Burroughs proclaiming Liverpool to be… But there lies the problem. Something about the quote that was being used in the title of this major exhibition didn't look right to me. Not quite how I remembered it. So I Googled 'Centre of the creative universe' and 'Allen Ginsberg'. Only a couple of things came up and both related directly to this proposed exhibition. So I tried once again by putting in the words 'Liverpool Centre' and 'Allen Ginsberg'. This time lots came up and there were numerous references to what Ginsberg had to say about Liverpool, none of which were even particularly close in meaning to what is being used in the title of this show. These were the variations:

Conscious centre of the human universe.
Centre of the consciousness of the human universe.
Centre of the consciousness of the universe.
Centre of human consciousness.
Centre of the consciousness for the entire human universe.

As I said, not one of these variants of whatever he actually said comes close in meaning to the line 'centre of the creative universe'. Allen Ginsberg died in 1997 so we can't check with him about what he said or meant. Now I am not going to blame any one individual for tampering with sacred quotes, I blame the whole of Liverpool. Liverpool has never been interested in the facts when it comes to weaving its own myth. It's as if the city has hired a PR executive to sell the city back to itself and the executive has decided words like consciousness won't go over well to those up the Scottie Road or down the Dingle, so why not dump the original quote and come up with a new one which will make Liverpool feel good about itself? And anyway, the dead poet's not going to be around to argue the case for what he actually said.

But it is not only those up the fabled Scottie Road and down the Dingle we have to be concerned about. It is the oft-derided chattering classes down in London. They are the ones in control of the national media, they will see through Liverpool's posturings and expose it for what it is. Liverpool may like to think of itself as the nation's loveable rogue but the nation preferred Coronation Street and EastEnders to any of the shenanigans in Brookside Close. The nation voted with their collective channel changer.

There is another angle on this deliberate misquote and for this I will go back to the email from Christoph Grunenberg: it's that bit about the relationship between the mainstream and underground culture. Ginsberg was underground. He openly celebrated his homosexuality at a time when he could get arrested for it. He walked around naked exposing his corpulent figure in public whenever he felt it his duty to do so. He wrote poetry that the American mainstream of the 1950s would have had him locked up for, if they had understood it. But as the decades roll past, the mainstream – or the literary mainstream anyway – has decided that Ginsberg is one of the greatest American poets of the 20th century.

The mainstream has always picked over the corpse of past underground cultures for the bits and tasty morsels it can use in any way it sees fit to show itself in a good light, and probably always will. There is nothing like a romance with a past underground culture. The mainstream never truly wants to know what is going on in a contemporary underground culture, one that is happening right now. Maybe that last statement is not quite true. Maybe things have so speeded up that the cultural mainstream is desperate enough for new underground cultures to pick over that it is handing out grants to anybody that it thinks might do something a bit underground in an attempt to bribe them into existence. Now there is no time for underground cultures to evolve before they are gobbled up and neutered by the mainstream.

Added to this, or maybe because of this, we now have the situation where artists (in the broad sense) are behaving in ways (making work) that they think might look a bit dangerous and threatening in an underground culture sort of way, in the hope it gets noticed by the mainstream so they can be gobbled up in exchange for a bit of fame and fortune. Maybe we are in an age where underground culture only exists in paedophile chat rooms, white supremacist websites or Islamic fundamentalist bookshops. Maybe there are no longer any battles to be fought for what we used to call the underground, just cultural career paths to be followed in Liverpool or any other city in the United Kingdom.

I came up with the title of this text 'Liverpool Will Only Let You Down' over a week ago, at a time when I really had no idea what I was going to write. Last Friday I put all my clothes in the washing machine. An hour or so later the programme was done and I was all set to hang them on the line. I opened the door of the machine to find all my clothes covered in little bits of soggy paper. My fear was that it was a twenty quid note that I had left in the pocket of my shorts.

Worse. Far worse. Stuck to the inside of the drum were the remains of the cover of my passport. Panic. I was supposed to be flying to Ireland for a few days work stuff, a week the following Monday and then on the day after getting back, flying to Greece for two weeks' family time.

Phone calls got made to various passport offices around the country. None of them had any free appointments in the next week before we fly to Ireland. There was one office left to be tried. Liverpool. Liverpool had just had a cancellation. I was given an appointment next Wednesday at 2.30. Irony of ironies. The one city that will have me is the one that I am proclaiming will always let you down.

I decided I would write the text for this catalogue on the train journey up to Liverpool for the appointment. Next Wednesday is now today. I've been writing all the way up from Euston. Before I left my flat in London this morning I printed off two texts I wrote in the past, one in July 2005 called *A Love–Hate Relationship,* the other from 1999 called *Just Ask.* The first was about how a work of art in the first Liverpool Biennial in 1999 had inspired me to go out and buy 1000 sledgehammers; the second was about how I planned to

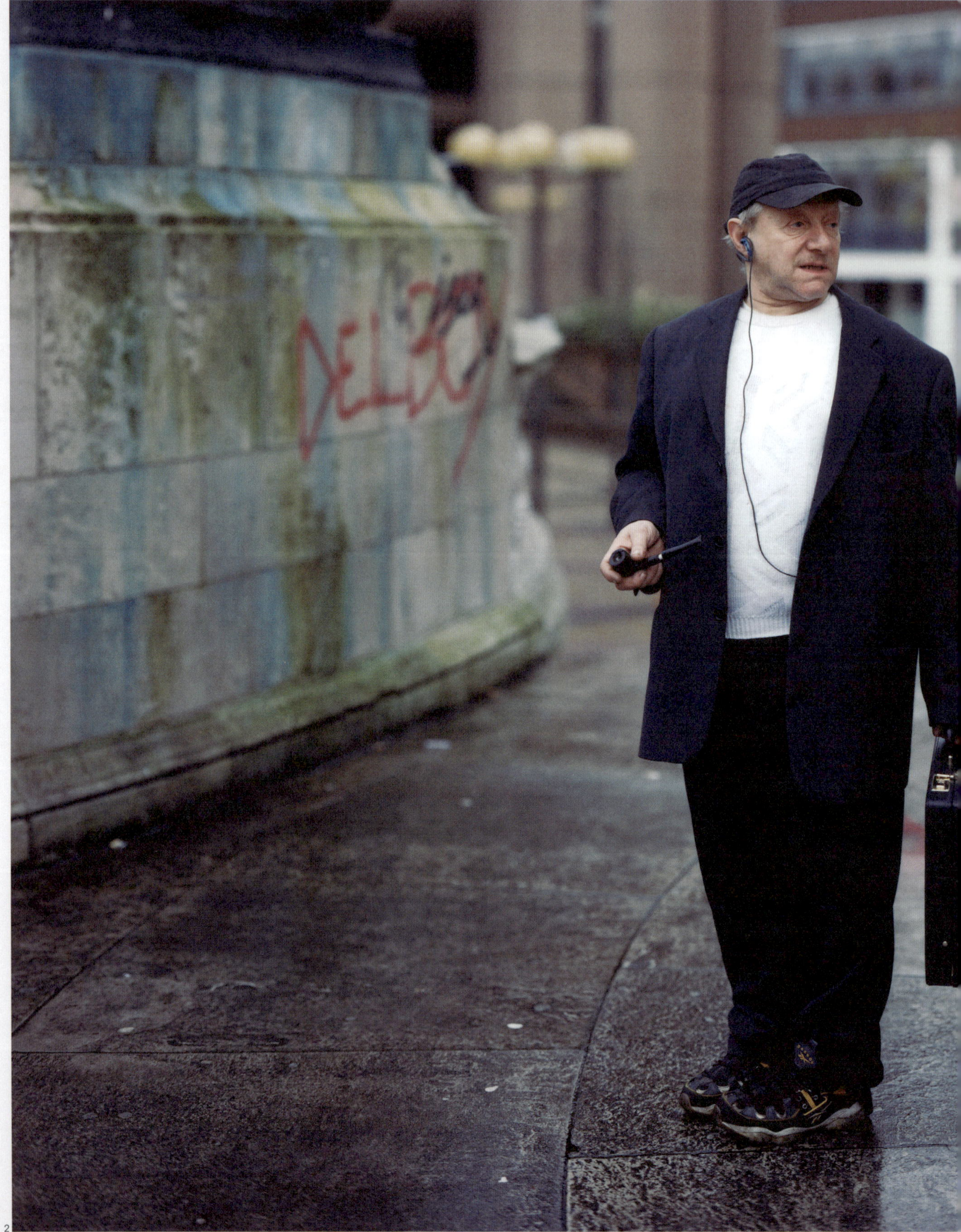
DELBOY

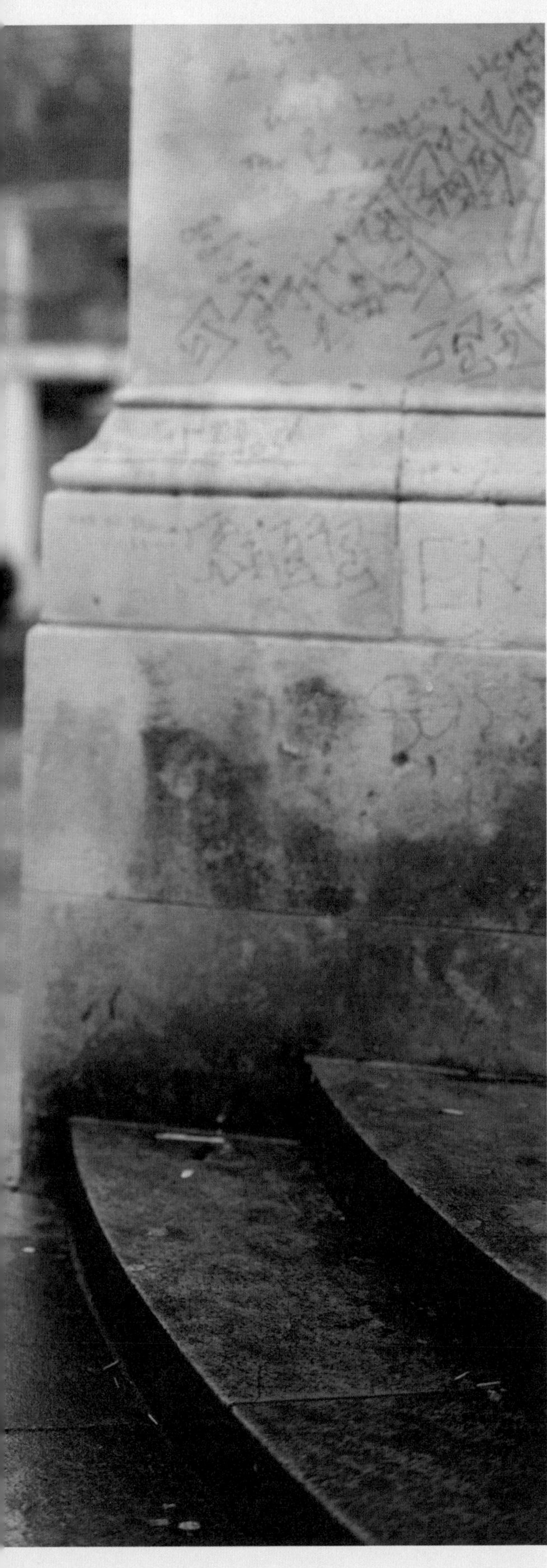

NOTICE

LIVERPOOL

In your 'Year Of Culture' I challenge you to deliver

Something
That has not been shipped in from the outside world.

Something
That has not been mediated by experts bought in from the outside world.

Something
That has not been financed by The Arts Council, The Department for
Culture, Media and Sport or even The A Foundation.

Something
That is not retro sounding.

Something
Which avoids blueprints that were drafted years ago.

Something
That is not just sticking two fingers up at the establishment
In the hope that it will grab media attention.

If you succeed
You will win nothing but the respect of all those that doubted you.

Something
That only Liverpool could do.

pb Poster 125   2006

use these 1000 sledgehammers in an exhibition of my own as part of the Liverpool Biennial in 2008. In this proposed exhibition I plan to sell off the 1000 sledgehammers at a tenner a go. The reason for me printing these two texts off and bringing them with me was because in some way they almost qualify for being about the relationship between underground culture and the mainstream in Liverpool in the 1990s.

Any time I get near Liverpool my emotions start spiralling. The only recurring dreams I have are always set in Liverpool at the time when I was managing Echo and the Bunnymen in the early 1980s. At a time when Liverpool did have an emerging underground culture, a culture that was going to willingly engage with and ultimately sell itself short to the mainstream. Those recurring dreams are all too often about me doing the selling short. Making the compromises.

I had been told that the quickest they could get me a passport was in five working days. That means things would be fucked up for going to Ireland. But somebody has told me they can sometimes fast track them through for you.

An hour after I wrote the last paragraph and I am sitting in the passport office in Old Hall Street, Liverpool, waiting for my ticket number to be called. I'm doing a deal with Liverpool: if my passport gets fast tracked through, I will change the title of this text from *Liverpool Always Lets You Down* to *Liverpool Will Never Let You Down*.

And it is now three hours since I made the deal with Liverpool. I'm lying on a bed in the Adelphi hotel writing these notes and the title of this text has been changed. My papers were all in order and I was told they could fast track my passport through in four working hours. It was then 3.00, and this means I have to go back to the passport office at 9.00 tomorrow morning to pick up my brand new and virgin passport.

I celebrated by walking down to Tate Liverpool to have a look at the Bruce Nauman exhibition. Then headed up through the city, stopping off to have a look in at the Open Eye Gallery and FACT. The weather has been wet and miserable and I was still dressed in the shorts and T-shirt that was all that has been required over the past few weeks of the summer.

Everywhere around the city centre there is building going on and the Liverpool 08 logo everywhere. I hate being cynical but that logo for Liverpool's European Capital of Culture looks tacky. As for the building that's going on, it all looks like it's being done on the cheap. It looks like, even if they get the work done for the beginning of 2008, it will be starting to fall to bits by the end of the year.

As I walked up Wood Street between the Open Eye and FACT an idea started to evolve. I think it must have been all the tatty posters advertising themed club nights that kickstarted the idea. I want to do one of the NOTICE posters that I have a habit of doing. This poster will tie in with the opening of this *Centre of the Creative Universe* exhibition.

The text on the poster, which I will work out on the train back down tomorrow, will be a challenge to Liverpool to come up with some culture for their special year that isn't being shipped in, hasn't received all sorts of funding from the A Foundation or the Arts Council, that isn't some retro sounding music following blueprints that were drafted decades ago; that isn't just about sticking two fingers up at the establishment in the hope it will get some media coverage. But in some way taps into the true soul of the city and is something that has never been seen before. It's a tall order but Liverpool deserves it and owes it to itself to do it.

This poster will be printed in the usual edition of 100 that I do. Usually those numbered 1–89 go for a tenner each, those numbered 90–99 for a 1000 quid each and number 100 for £10,000. This time I won't bother selling them. Instead I will paste 50 of them around the city. The other 50 I will fold into paper boats and launch them on the Mersey in the hope that they will drift out with the tide and sail the seven seas and in time land on distant shores and in that way the knowledge of my challenge will reach the world at large.

As for this text being used in the *Centre of the Creative Universe* catalogue, with the way that it has been turning out, I doubt it will be suitable. But if they do use it, I hope they print a copy of the proposed poster to go with it. Now that I've got this writing done I am going to go up to Chinatown to get something to eat, then off into the night to look for some underground culture far from the mainstream.

3 August 2006

On the train back down, the Cheshire plain flashing past and I'm feeling the pangs of guilt. I was in the city for less than 24 hours. I didn't even get as far as Chinatown, settling for a curry house on Renshaw Street. As for heading out into the night in search of underground culture far from the mainstream, I went back to the Adelphi instead and watched Beirut being bombed on BBC News 24.

All my shots seem cheap now. It's always so much easier to stand on the outside and point out the obvious faults than step in, get your hands dirty and try and do anything about it.

While rereading all the above I have just remembered how Astrid Proll, one of the Baader-Meinhof gang (the Red Army Faction) and possibly the most wanted women in Europe in the 1970s, was one of my fellow artists in the Liverpool Biennial 1999. We got to know each other as we both exhibited work in the same gallery space in Parr Street. She was hanging her photos that documented the death and terror the Red Army Faction meted out across Germany in the early 1970s as I made my sculpture in honour of Roger Eagle. I can't deny that I did have a bit of a crush on her. You could not get more underground than the Baader-Meinhof gang and here she was 25 years later being fêted by the art establishment.

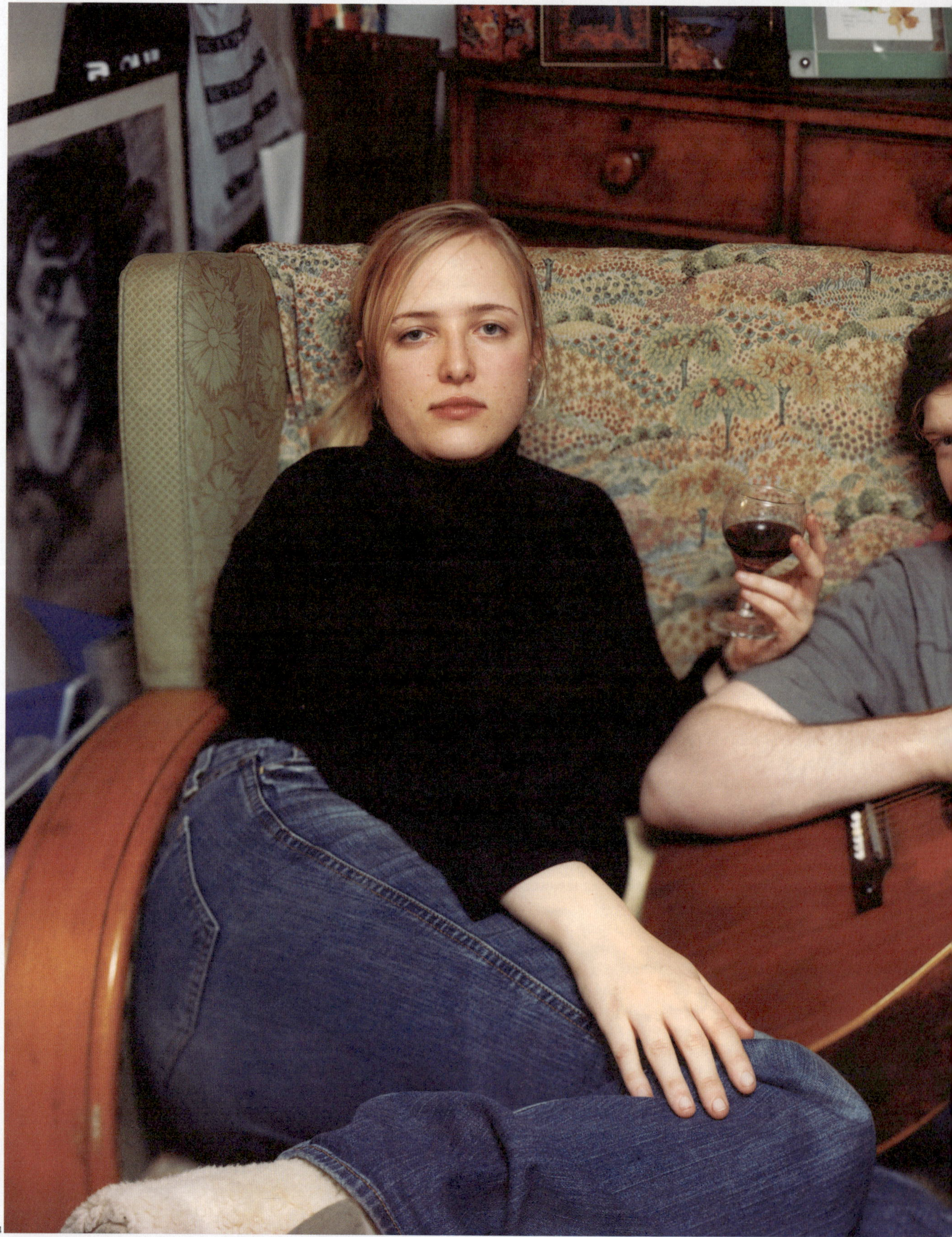

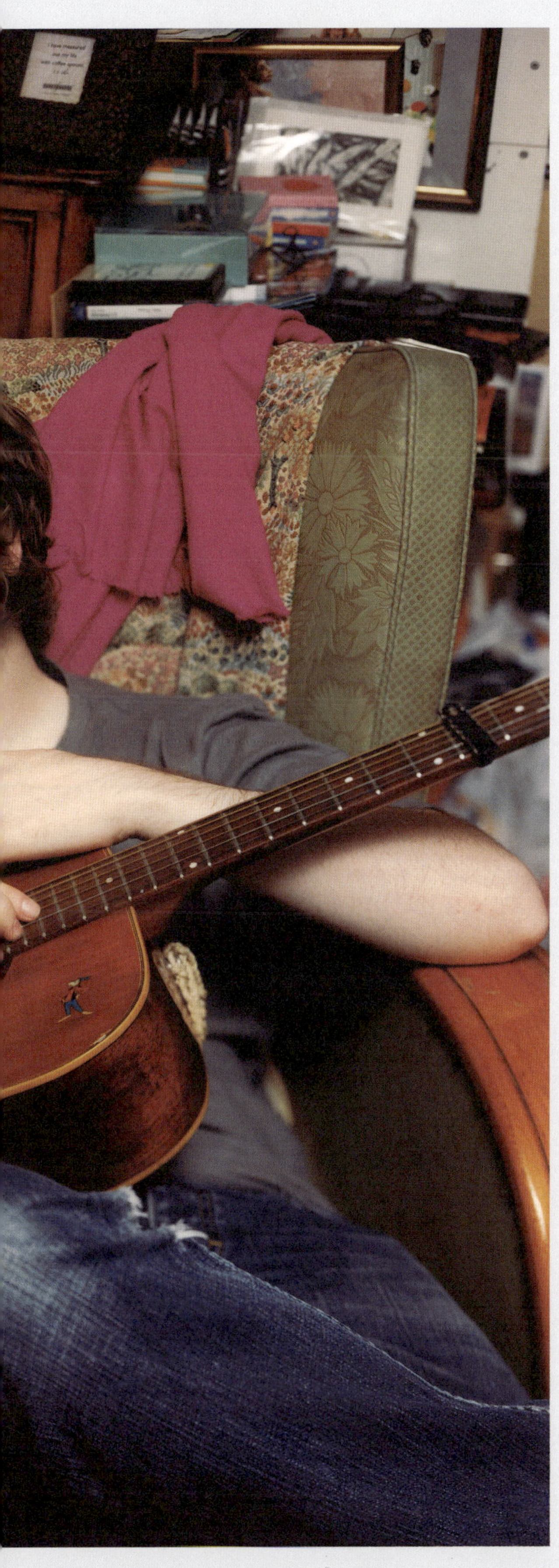

4
Alec Soth
*Laura and Steve, Liverpool,
United Kingdom* 2004
C-type print
78.7 x 94.5 cm
Courtesy the artist and
Gagosian Gallery

1
The Basement
Mount Pleasant
Bar owned by artist Yankel Feather.
Located directly opposite Streate's, it
attracted a more eclectic mix than its
more bohemian rival

2
Bridewell Studios
Prescot Street
Established in 1976 in a derelict police
station, artists such as Adrian Henri,
Maurice Cockrill, Ian McKeever and
Anish Kapoor have had studio spaces here

3
Blue Angel
108 Seel Street
Night club owned by Allan Williams

4
The Cavern
10 Mathew Street
Opened by Alan Sytner in 1957, this
venue was inspired by the 'caveau'
basement bars on the Parisian Left Bank
and became synonymous with the rise
of Merseybeat

5
Ye Cracke
13 Rice Street
Public house near to Liverpool College of
Art, often frequented by John Lennon,
Stuart Sutcliffe and Bill Harry

6
Eric's
9 Mathew Street
Live music venue established in 1976 by
Roger Eagle, Ken Testi and Pete Fulwell.
Eric's became one of the centres of punk
rock before closing in 1980

7
Frank Hessy's Music Shop
60 Stanley Street
Music shop favoured by
Merseybeat musicians

8
Jacaranda Club
21-23 Slater Street
Popular art-school hangout and live music
venue, opened by Beatles' Manager Allan
Williams in 1958

9
Kirkland's Wine Bar
35 Hardman Street
Opened in the mid-1970s by John
Hewson, this was Liverpool's first
successful wine bar

10
NEMS
12-14 Whitechapel
Electrical and record shop on Whitechapel
managed by Brian Epstein

11
O'Connor's Tavern
Hardman Street
Infamous 1960s hangout for Liverpool
artists, musicians and poets

12
Parry's Bookshop
49 Hardman Street
Venue of Allen Ginsberg's poetry reading
in 1965

13
The Philharmonic
36 Hope Street
Arts and crafts public house and cornerstone
of the Liverpool 8 bohemian scene

14
Sampson and Barlow's
London Road
Live folk music and poetry venue. Adrian
Henri gave his first reading here in 1963

15
Streate's Coffee Bar
51 Mount Pleasant
Throughout the 1960s Liverpool's leading
poets performed at this candle-lit
basement venue

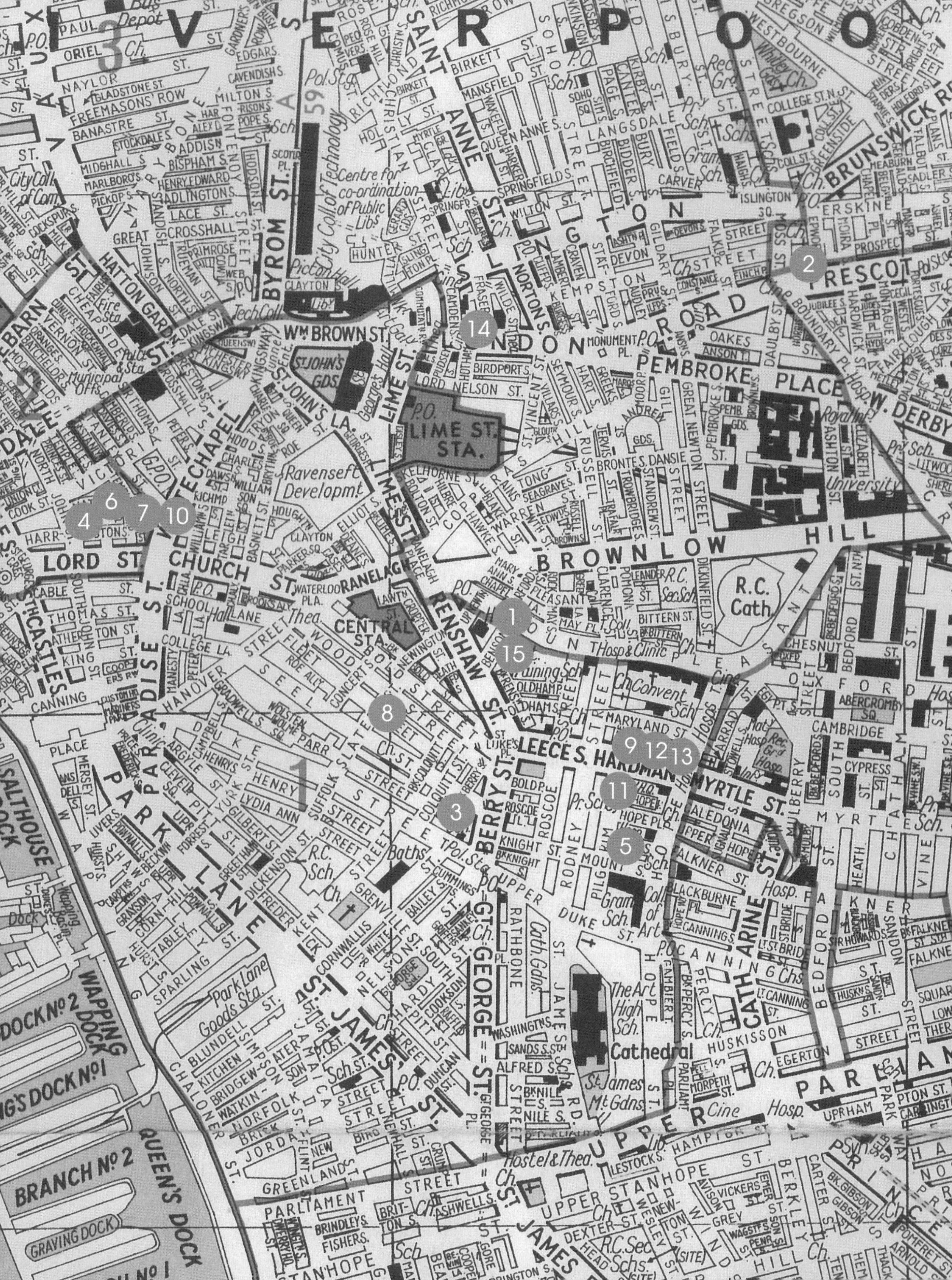

16

**The Blackie – Great Georges
Community Cultural Project
Great George Street**
Arts venue with strong community
directed programme, established by
Bill and Wendy Harpe in 1968

17

**Bluecoat Arts Centre
School Lane**
Based in the former Blue Coat School,
whose origins date back to 1708, this
venue has nurtured artistic activity
since 1906

18

Everyman Theatre (formerly Hope Hall)
13 Hope Street
Important venue for Liverpool's performers
and literati. Many of Adrian Henri's
Happenings were staged here in the 1960s

19

**FACT (Foundation for Art
and Creative Technology)
88 Wood Street**
Arts venue and cinema established in 2003
and dedicated to presenting and developing
works in new and emerging media

20

**Liverpool Biennial of
Contemporary Art Limited
The Tea Factory, 82 Wood Street**
Administrative headquarters of the UK's
only Biennial of international contemporary
visual art, based at this address from
2002 to 2007

21

**Liverpool College of Art
68 Hope Street**
Founded in 1910 – the heartbeat of the
creative Liverpool

22

**Liverpool School of Music,
Dream, Art and Pun
18 Mathew Street**
Established by Peter O'Halligan in 1976,
this was the venue for the stage adaptation
of the Robert Shea's and Robert Anton
Wilson's seminal work of conspiracy
fiction *The Illuminatus!* trilogy, the
opening production of Ken Campbell's
Science Fiction Theatre of Liverpool

23

**Open Eye Gallery
28-32 Wood Street**
Internationally renowned photography
gallery

24

**Playhouse Theatre
Williamson Square**
Built in 1866 as the Star Music Hall, the
Playhouse's programme today emphasises
creative interpretations of the great plays

25

**Sheil Park
Linosa Close, L6**
Venue for Up in the Air (2000-1) and
Further Up in the Air (2001-4), two
ambitious artists' residency programmes.
The residencies coincided with the
redevelopment of the Sheil Park site, which
included the demolition of 1960s tower
blocks and the creation of new housing

26

**Tate Liverpool
Albert Dock**
Opened in 1988 to present selections from
the national collection of international
modern art to the North of England

27

**Unity Theatre
1 Hope Place**
One of the best-loved theatres in the city,
its origins date back to the 1930s and the
establishment of the Merseyside Left Theatre

28

**Walker Art Gallery
William Brown Street**
Opened in 1877 and home to an outstanding
art collection, the Walker is the 'national
gallery of the North'

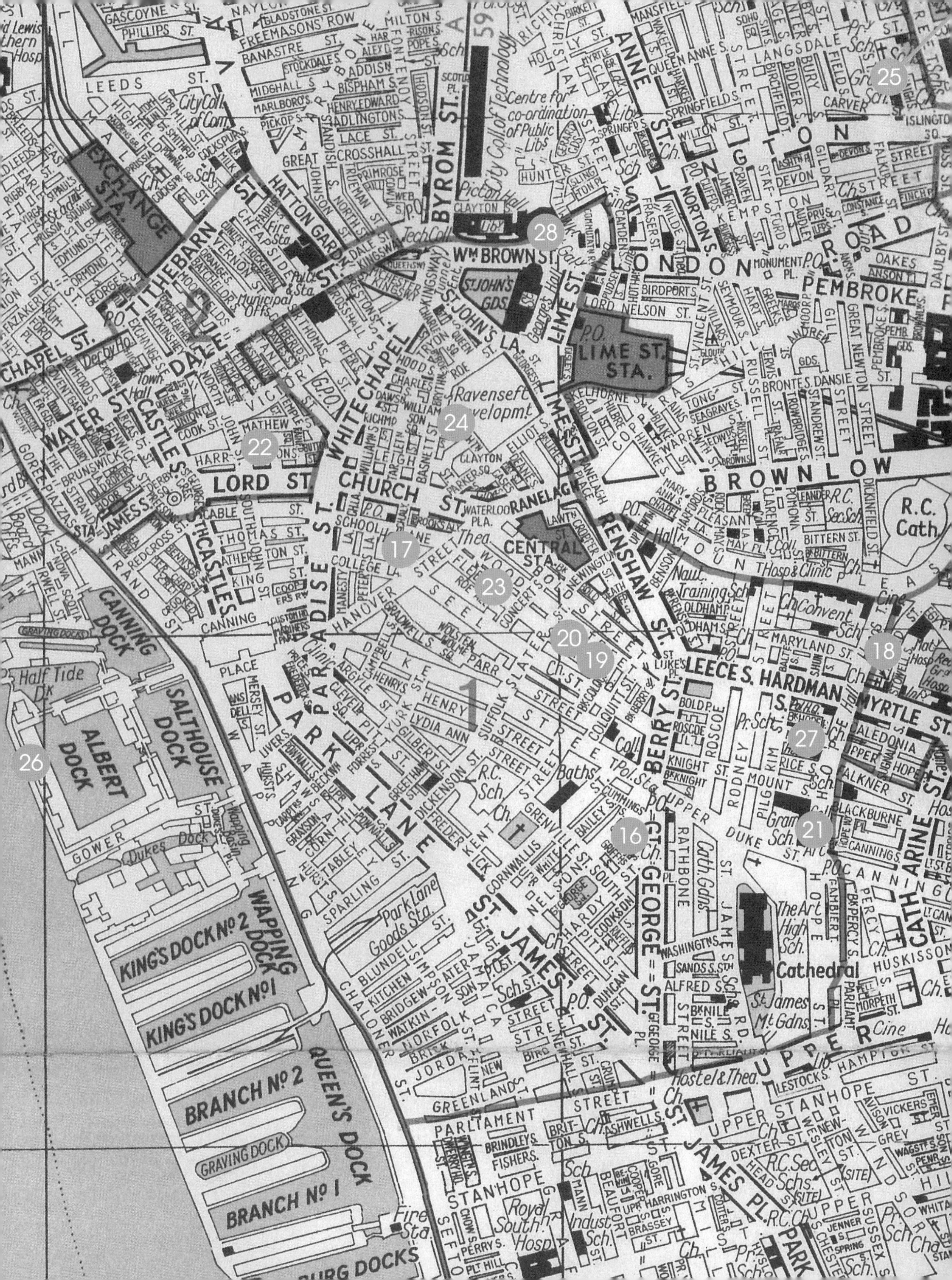

29
18 Canning Street
Brian Patten lived at this address

30
64 Canning Street
Adrian Henri lived here during the 1960's.
This communal home of poets, artists and
musicians is where Allen Ginsberg stayed
when he visited Liverpool in 1965

31
83 Canning Street
Stuart Sutcliffe lived in the basement flat
at this address when he became
an art student in Liverpool in 1957.
During his second year of study he
lives on the same street at No. 12

32
24 Falkner Square
Adrian Henri lived in the basement flat at
this address c.1953-57. Sam Walsh also
lived here, in an upstairs bedsit,
on first moving to Liverpool in 1960

33
**Flat 3, Hillary Mansions
Gambier Terrace**
Home of Stuart Sutcliffe and Rod Murray.
Sam Walsh also lived here c. 1961

34
20 Forthlin Road
Childhood home of Paul McCartney

35
6 Huskisson Street
Roger McGough lived here

36
84 Huskisson Street
Sam Walsh lived here through most of
the 1960s

37
251 Menlove Avenue
John Lennon lived at this address with
his Aunt Mimi and Uncle George

38
21 Mount Street
Adrian Henri lived here from 1969,
opposite the Art College

39
9 Percy Street
Stuart Sutcliffe moved here in the winter
of 1957-58

40
59 Rodney Street
Photographer Edward Chambré-Hardman's
home and studio

41
Windermere Terrace
Roger McGough lived at this address.

Residences

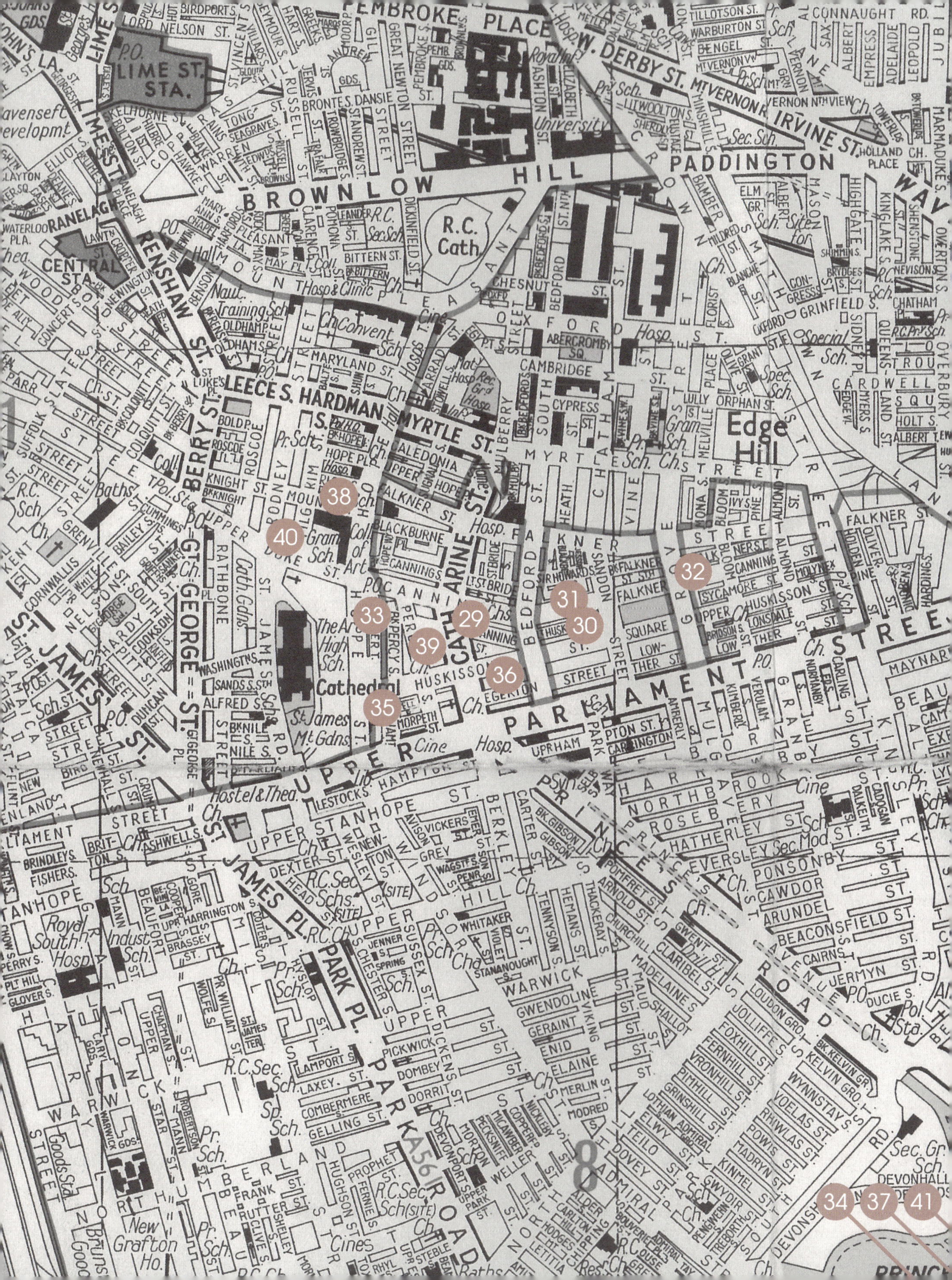

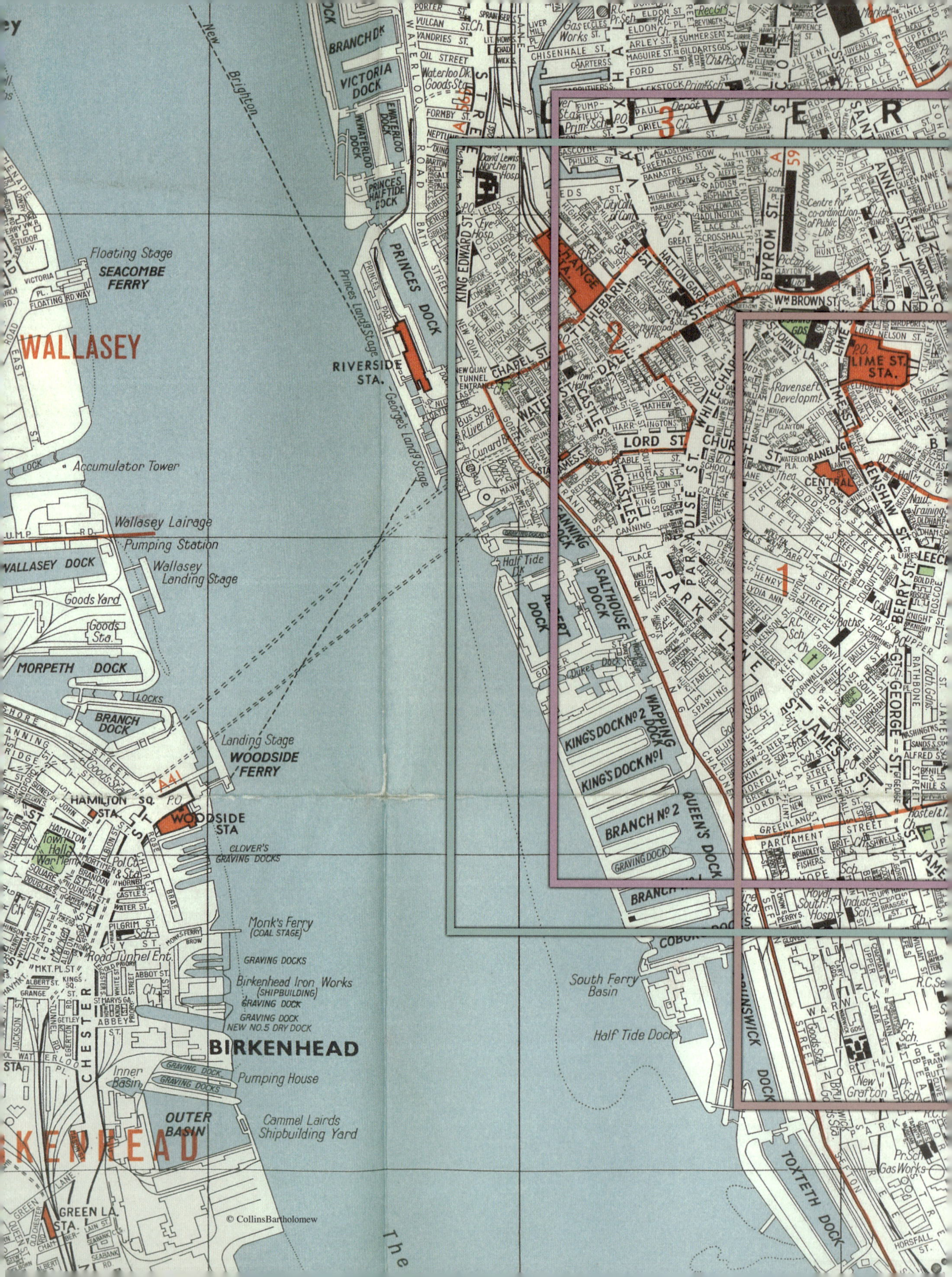

WALLASEY
Floating Stage
SEACOMBE FERRY
VICTORIA DOCK
Waterloo Dk. Goods Sta.
BRANCH DK.
OIL STREET
WATERLOO DOCK
E. WATERLOO DOCK
WHITEWATER DOCK
FORMBY DOCK
NEPTUNE ST.
PRINCES HALF TIDE DOCK
PRINCES DOCK
RIVERSIDE STA.
Princes Landing Stage
George's Landing Stage
Accumulator Tower
Wallasey Lairage
Pumping Station
Wallasey Landing Stage
WALLASEY DOCK
Goods Yard
Goods Sta.
MORPETH DOCK
BRANCH DOCK
LOCKS
Landing Stage
WOODSIDE FERRY
HAMILTON SQ. STA.
Town Hall
War Mem.
WOODSIDE STA.
CLOVER'S GRAVING DOCKS
Monk's Ferry (COAL STAGE)
GRAVING DOCKS
BIRKENHEAD
Birkenhead Iron Works (SHIPBUILDING)
GRAVING DOCK
GRAVING DOCK NEW No.5 DRY DOCK
Pumping House
Inner Basin
OUTER BASIN
Cammell Lairds Shipbuilding Yard
GREEN LA. STA.
BIRKENHEAD
CHESTER
LIVER
RIVER
Depot
King Edward St. Ch.
David Lewis Northern Hosp.
Eye Hosp.
City of Com.
EXCHANGE STA.
TITHEBARN ST.
Wm. Brown St.
BYROM ST.
JOHN'S LA.
LIME ST. STA.
Ravenseft Development
Centre for co-ordination of Public Libs
WHITECHAPEL
LORD ST.
CHURCH ST.
RANELAGH ST.
CENTRAL STA.
PARADISE ST.
PARK LANE
ST. JAMES
GREAT GEORGE ST.
WATER ST.
CASTLE ST.
CANNING DOCK
ALBERT DOCK
SALTHOUSE DOCK
Dukes Dock
WAPPING DOCK
KING'S DOCK No.2
KING'S DOCK No.1
BRANCH No.2
GRAVING DOCK
QUEEN'S DOCK
BRANCH No.1
South Ferry Basin
Half Tide Dock
COBURG DOCK
BRUNSWICK DOCK
New Grafton
Royal Southn. Hosp.
TOXTETH DOCK
HORSFALL DOCK
Gas Works
The Mersey
© CollinsBartholomew

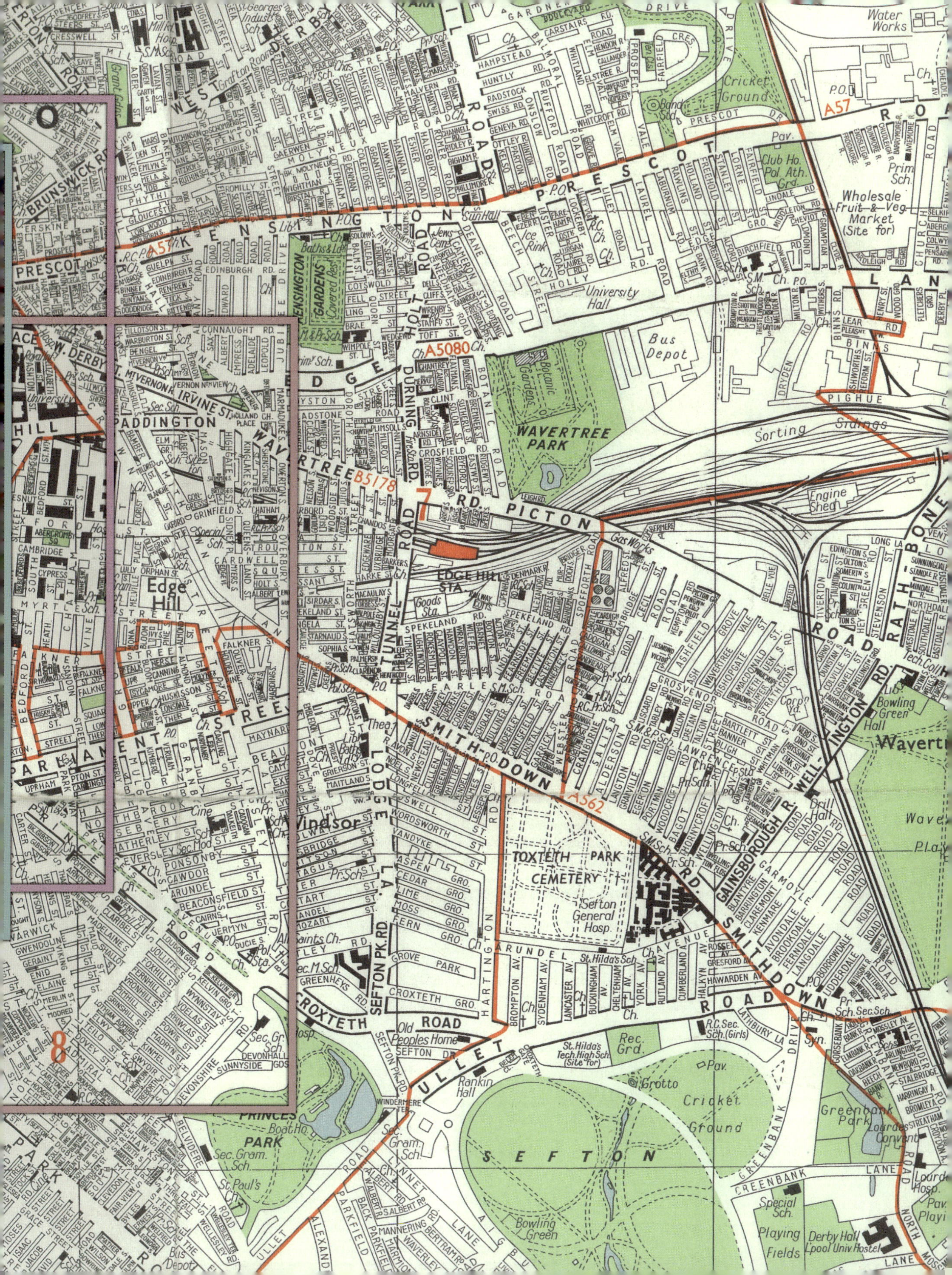

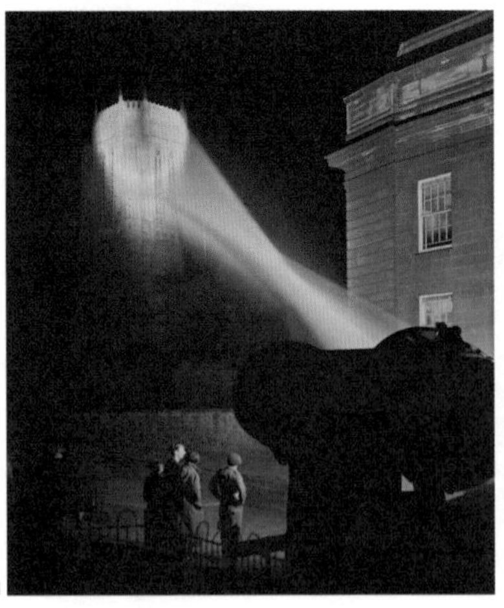

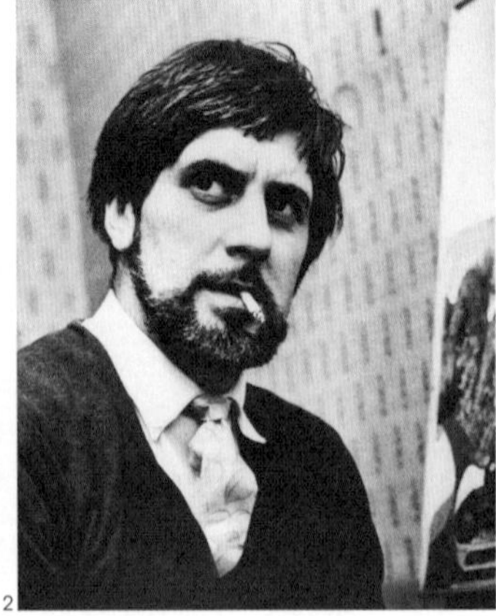

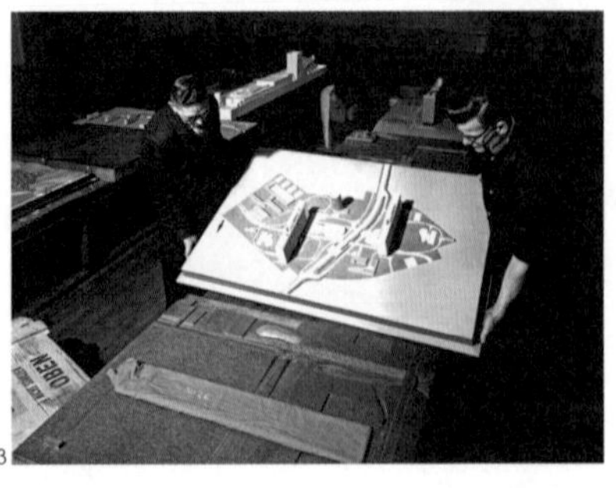

Timeline
Darren Pih
& Robert Knifton

1946-47
Liverpool FC win the first post-War League Championship

1948
Edward Chambré-Hardman photographic studio moves to 59 Rodney Street. His studio had previously been established at 51a Bold Street in 1923

1951
The Walker Art Gallery re-opens after the War. In 1952 Hugh Scrutton is appointed Director of the Walker Art Gallery. The gallery supports Liverpool artists by regularly purchasing their work for its collection until 1972

Gordon Fazakerley enrols at Liverpool College of Art. In 1962 he becomes a founding member of the Bauhaus Situationists in Drakabygget, Sweden

1954
Jacob Epstein's *Resurgent* is unveiled at Lewis's department, Lime Street. The sculpture of a naked youth with arms flung out triumphantly on a ship's prow is intended to symbolize Liverpool's rising from the flames of World War II

1956
Adrian Henri moves to Liverpool after studying art at King's College, Newcastle, where he was taught by Richard Hamilton

Stuart Sutcliffe enrols at Liverpool College of Art

1957
6 July – John Lennon and Paul McCartney meet at the annual Garden Fete, St Peter's Church, Woolton, where Lennon's skiffle group The Quarrymen were performing

John Lennon enrols at Liverpool College of Art. Liverpool-born sculptor and future Royal Academician Michael Kenny enrols in the same year

John Moores biannual painting prize and exhibition launched at the Walker Art Gallery. The first prizewinner is Jack Smith's *Creation and Crucifixion, 1955-56*

Arthur Ballard, artist and Lecturer at Liverpool College of Art, awarded a grant to study in Paris, where he exhibits the following year

Alan Sytner opens The Cavern in the basement of 10 Mathew Street. Inspired

by the 'caveau' bars on Paris's Left Bank, the venue becomes synonymous with the emergence of Merseybeat

1958
Le Corbusier exhibition at the Walker Art Gallery

1959
Lawrence Alloway and Herbert Read organise a solo Gordon Fazakerley exhibition, which is staged in the library of London's Institute of Contemporary Arts

Denis Mitchell of the BBC Northern Film Unit makes *Morning in the Streets,* a study of life in Liverpool's slums

1960
The Beatles leave for Hamburg

Irish artist Sam Walsh moves to Liverpool from London, where he had been studying at the Royal College of Art

George Mayer-Marton, former head of Liverpool College of Art, dies in Liverpool. A memorial exhibition is held at the Walker Art Gallery

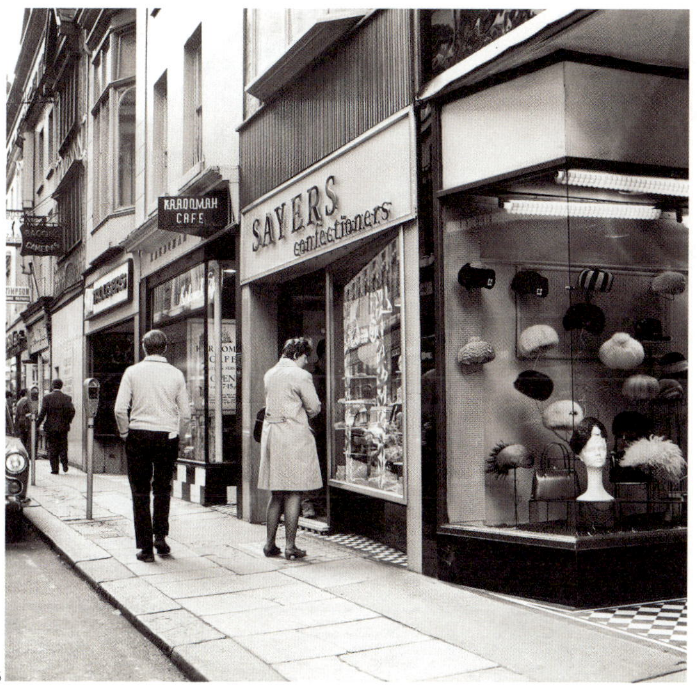

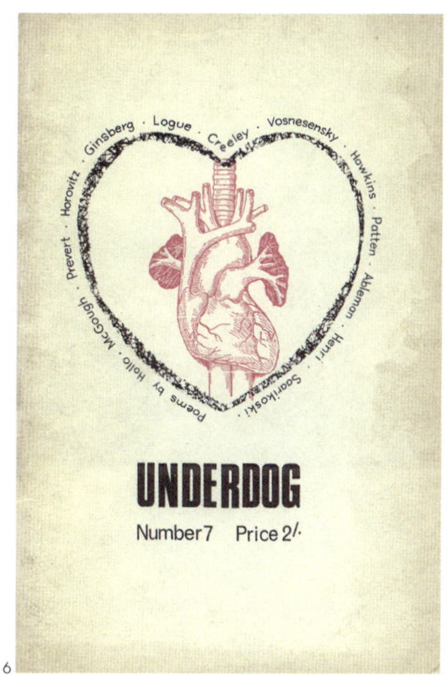

Poets Johnny Byrne and Spike Hawkins set up jazz and poetry nights at Streate's Coffee Bar, 51 Mount Pleasant. It was here that Adrian Henri meets Roger McGough. Brian Patten gives his first poetry reading at the venue the following year

1961
John Edkins and Neville Weston become Lecturers at Liverpool College of Art. Pop artist Weston had previously studied at the Slade School of Fine Art and the Courtauld Institute of Art

The Beatles second trip to Hamburg. Stuart Sutcliffe leaves the band and enrols at the city's State School of Art, where he studies under Eduardo Paolozzi

Merseybeat, a fortnightly newspaper dedicated to the Liverpool music scene, launched by Bill Harry

Bluecoat Arts Forum formed by cultural societies within Bluecoat Chambers 'to develop the building as a live arts centre'

1962
Keith Arnatt becomes a Lecturer at Liverpool College of Art

Brian Patten produces the first issue of *Underdog*, an underground poetry magazine. It ceases publication in 1966

Adrian Henri becomes aware of the activities of pioneering American Happening artist Allan Kaprow. That August, as part of the Merseyside Arts Festival, he helps organise *City*, the first Happening in England, at Hope Hall (now the Everyman Theatre). Other Happenings staged through the 1960s include *Death of a Bird in the City* (Hope Hall, 1962); *Nightblues* (Hope Hall, 1963); *Bomb* (Cavern Club, 1964); and *Black and White Show* (The Cavern, 1965)

Henri Cartier-Bresson takes photographs in Liverpool for American TV programme *TEMPO*

Adrian Henri and Sam Walsh joint exhibition at the Portal Gallery, London

Stuart Sutcliffe dies of a brain tumour

The Beatles' first UK single *Love Me Do* is released

1
Edward Chambré-Hardman
Searchlight on Anglican Cathedral 1951
Black and white photograph
37 x 29.4 cm
The National Trust, Edward Chambré-Hardman Collection

2
Sam Walsh (1934-1989)
Courtesy of National Museums Liverpool, The Walker Art Gallery

3
Technicians installing the Le Corbusier exhibition, Walker Art Gallery, 1958
Courtesy of National Museums Liverpool, The Walker Art Gallery

4
Max Scheler
Cavern Queue, Lunchtime Session 1964
Silver gelatin print
50 x 60 cm
Courtesy Max Scheler/ K&K

5
Candida Höfer
Liverpool IIA 1968
Silver gelatin print
21 x 21.3 cm
Collection of the artist

6
Underdog No. 7, 1965
Collection of Catherine Marcangeli

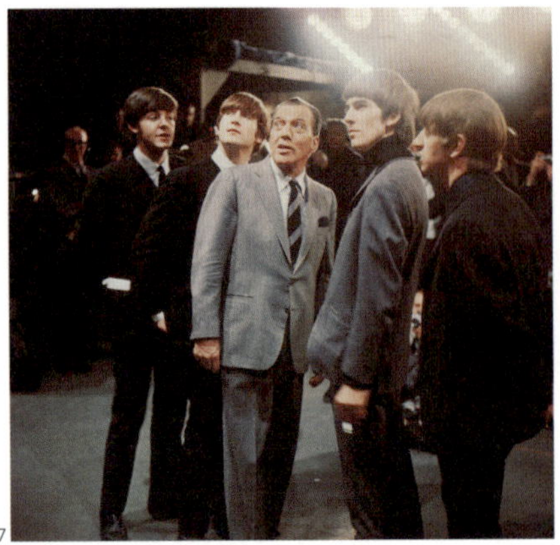

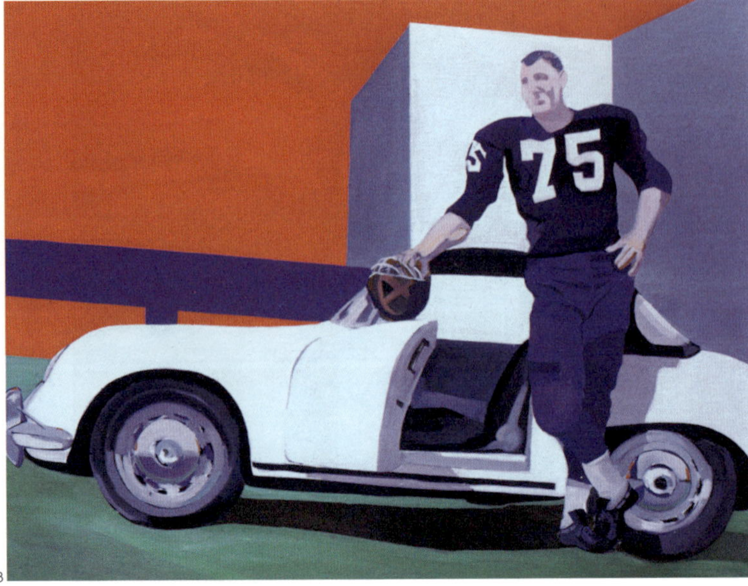

1963

Formation of WEBA Group of 'designers and consultants in colour, mural decoration, exhibition design, display and typography' by Keith Arnatt, Arthur Ballard, John Edkins, and Neville Weston. Between 1963 and 1966 they undertake several commissions for Liverpool-based architects

Theatrical satire music group The Scaffold form. Their original line-up is John Gorman, Mike McGear (a pseudonym for Mike McCartney, brother of Paul), Roger McGough, and Adrian Henri, who leaves shortly after joining the group

Sam Walsh's *Pin up 1963 – for Francis Bacon,* 1963, is included in the John Moores exhibition and purchased by the Walker Art Gallery

Pop Art exhibition at Midland Group, Nottingham, includes work by Adrian Henri, Sam Walsh, as well as by Pauline Boty, Peter Blake and David Hockney

1964

Max Scheler and Astrid Kirchherr travel to Liverpool from Hamburg for a photographic feature on Merseybeat for *Stern* magazine

Adrian Henri paints *The Entry of Christ into Liverpool (Homage to James Ensor)*, 1962-4, and in the same year becomes a Lecturer at Liverpool College of Art

Everyman Theatre is established in Hope Hall, Hope Street. It quickly builds a reputation for groundbreaking theatrical work, becoming an important venue for a number of Liverpool writers and performers

Maurice Cockrill moves to Liverpool, he becomes a Lecturer at Liverpool College of Art in 1967

The Beatles' first US tour opens the door to the 'British Invasion'. On 9 February 1964 around 73 million watch them perform on The Ed Sullivan Show

Stuart Sutcliffe retrospective at the Walker Art Gallery

Northern premiere of Beatles' film *A Hard Day's Night* at the Liverpool Odeon, around 50,000 people crowd outside the Town Hall for a glimpse of the band

Black Mountain College poet Robert Creeley gives readings at The University of Liverpool poetry society, and at Sampson & Barlow's

1965

Beat in Liverpool, photographic book of Liverpool music scene, by Juergen Seuss, Gerold Dommermuth, and Hans Maier is published in Germany

John Baum becomes Senior Lecturer on the Art Foundation course at Liverpool College of Art and holds his first exhibition in the city

Allen Ginsberg visits Liverpool in May and describes the city as 'the centre of the consciousness of the human universe.' Whilst in Liverpool he meets poets and artists, and gives a reading at Parry's Bookshop, Hardman Street

1966

German artists Bernd and Hilla Becher awarded British Council grant to photograph the industrial regions of England and South Wales. They visit Liverpool and photograph the Albert Dock

Sean Hignett's Liverpool-based novel *A Picture to Hang on the Wall* is published by Michael Joseph, London

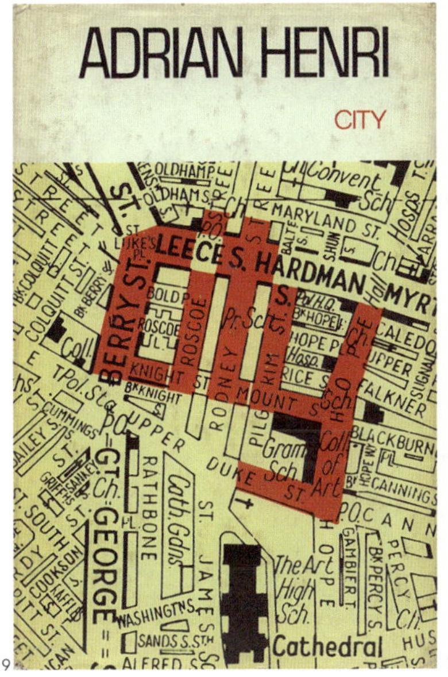

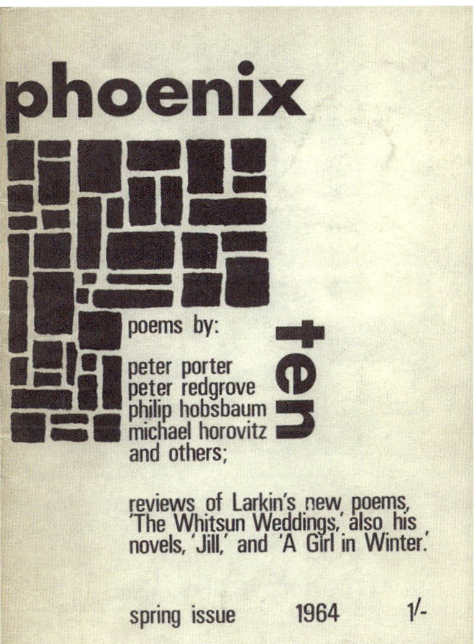

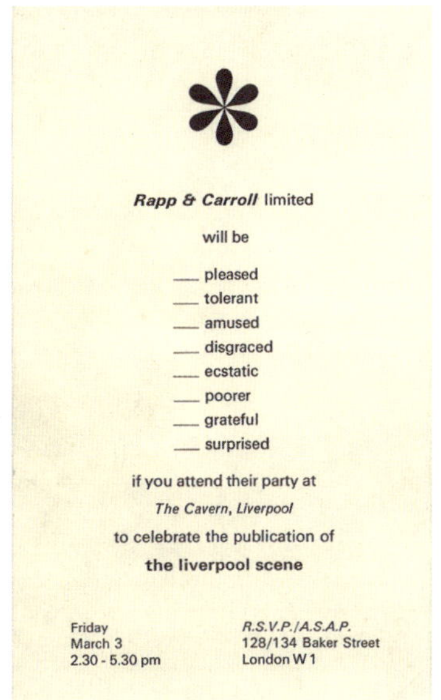

John Edkins, artist and Lecturer at Liverpool College of Art, dies at 35 of a heart attack

John Lennon meets Yoko Ono at Indica Gallery, London

1967
Penguin publishes *The Mersey Sound*, anthology of poems by Adrian Henri, Roger McGough and Brian Patten

Brian Patten's first volume of poetry *Little Johnny's Confession* is published by Allen & Unwin, London

Frinck, A Day in the Life Of and *Summer with Monica,* Roger McGough's first novella and volume of poetry is published by Michael Joseph, London

John Willett's *Art in a City* is published by Methuen & Co Ltd, London. Commissioned by the Bluecoat Society of Arts, this study of Liverpool's cultural scene proposes a blueprint for how its arts might be developed in future

Edward Lucie-Smith's *The Liverpool Scene* published by Rapp & Carroll, London. The book documents the city's poetry and live music scene

Mark Boyle and Joan Hills exhibition at the Bluecoat Society of Arts. They perform *Son et Lumière for Earth, Air, Fire and Water,* and premiere *Son et Lumière for Bodily Fluids and Functions* over the first two evenings of exhibition opening

The *Liverpool Daily Post* runs a weeklong feature about the Liverpool 8 bohemian area in February, which it describes as the 'Left Bank of the North West'

On 17 February The Beatles release double A-sided single *Strawberry Fields Forever/Penny* Lane. The LP *Sgt. Pepper's Lonely Hearts Club Band* follows in June and becomes the soundtrack to the 'Summer of Love'

On 31 March the *Weekend Telegraph Magazine* publishes Sean Hignett's feature about the Liverpool 8 scene

Art in a City: The Liverpool Look, the exhibition to accompany John Willett's book, is staged at the Institute of Contemporary Arts, London

Exhibition in honour of Liverpool-based artist John Edkins is held at the Walker Art Gallery

7
The Beatles with Ed Sullivan on the occasion of their first live American television appearance, New York, 1964

8
Neville Weston
Big Ben Davidson 1964
Oil on canvas
91.5 x 122 cm
Courtesy of the artist

9
Adrian Henri
City
(London: Rapp and Whiting, 1969)
Collection of Catherine Marcangeli

10
Phoenix, No. 10,
Spring 1964
Collection of Catherine Marcangeli

11
Invitation for the launch of *The Liverpool Scene,* Edward Lucie-Smith, ed. 1967
Collection of Catherine Marcangeli

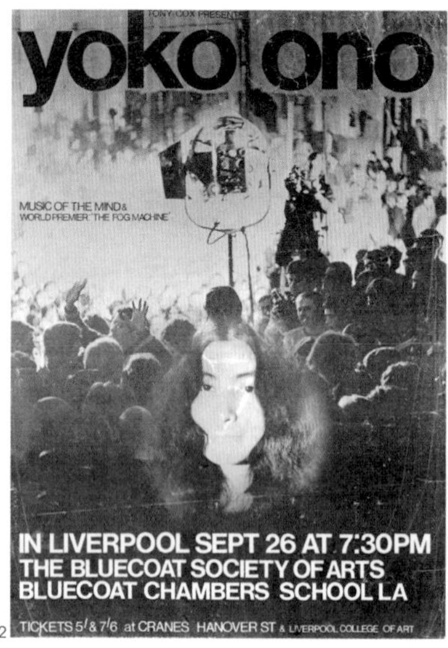

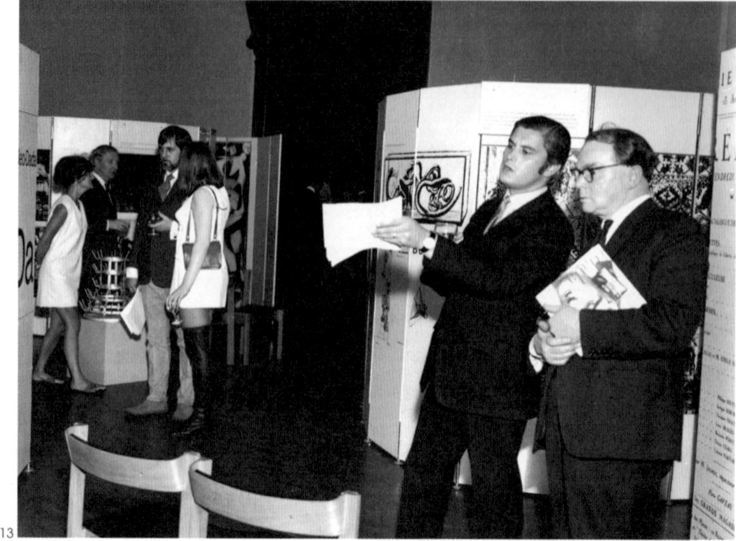

Yoko Ono performs *Concert of Music for the Mind* and premieres *The Fog Machine* at the Bluecoat Society of Arts

Poetry/Rock group *The Liverpool Scene* formed by Adrian Henri, Andy Roberts, Mike Evans, Percy Jones, Brian Dodson and Mike Hart. Their debut LP *Amazing Adventures of…* is produced by John Peel and released on RCA Records the following year. In 1969 the band tour to America and play the Isle of Wight Festival. They break-up in 1970, shortly before the release of their final LP *Heirloon*

1968
Adrian Henri's first book of poetry *Tonight at Noon* is published by Rapp & Whiting, London. Its title is taken from a Charlie Mingus LP. In the same year he has a solo exhibition at Institute of Contemporary Arts, London

German photographer Candida Höfer accompanies a friend to Liverpool who was interested in finding out more about the city's poetry scene. Whilst in Liverpool she takes her earliest exhibited photographs

Great Georges Community Cultural Project is founded by Bill and Wendy Harpe. Known as The Blackie due to the sooty exterior of the former church they inhabit, it pioneers the use of avant-garde arts practice in education and community work

Dada 1916-1966: Documents of the International Dada Movement exhibition is held at the Walker Art Gallery

1969
John Latham exhibition at the Bluecoat Gallery opens in January. The following month Latham collaborates with Eventstructure Research Group (ERG) for a performance at The Blackie

1970
George Melly's *Revolt into Style: The Pop Arts in Britain* is published by Allen Lane

1971
Probe Records opens on Clarence Street. The shop relocates to Whitechapel and later Button Street. It becomes a focal point for the local music scene with many staff members later becoming members of prominent Liverpool bands. The shop later moves to its present home on Slater Street

Timothy Stevens appointed Director of the Walker Art Gallery. Its role changes to showcase the best contemporary art in the widest sense with no discrimination in favour of local artists

The Walker Art Gallery stages *New Italian Art 1953-71,* the first in a series of Peter Moores Liverpool Project exhibitions

1972
Adrian Henri's *Painting 1,* 1972, wins Second Prize in the John Moores exhibition. In the same year he becomes president of the Liverpool Academy of Arts, a position he holds until 1981

Cult Californian rock musician Captain Beefheart visits Liverpool to perform at the Liverpool Stadium, finding time to have the first public exhibition of his abstract paintings at Bluecoat Gallery

1973
An exhibition of Liverpool Academy artists entitled *18 Special Works on Communication* is staged at the Walker Art Gallery. Paintings include John Baum's *Five Girls* 1973 and Maurice Cockrill's *Two Windows/Two People* 1972

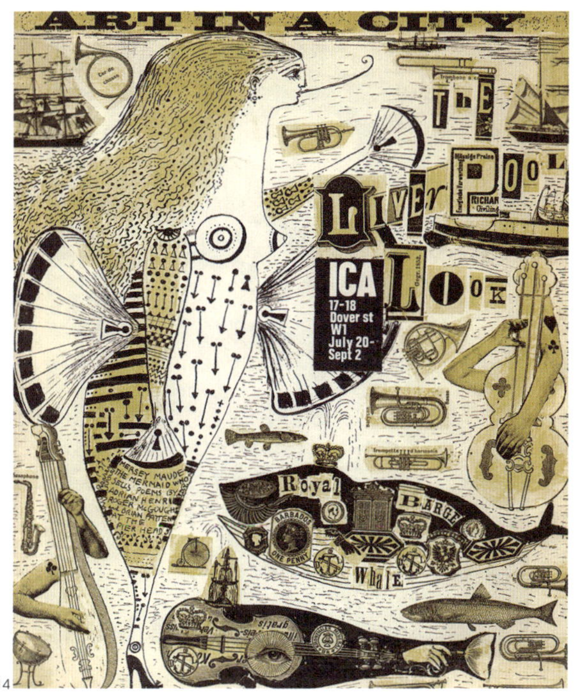

14

Filmaktion residency at Walker Art Gallery, 22 to 28 June 1973. The filmmakers involved are David Crosswaite, Mike Dunford, Gill Eatherley, Malcolm Le Grice, Annabel Nicolson and William Raban

Peter Moores Liverpool Project 2, *Magic and Strong Medicine* at Walker Art Gallery

Edward Lucie-Smith's article 'The New British Realists' is published in the *Sunday Times Magazine* of 14 October. It focuses on a number of Liverpool photorealist painters, including John Baum and Maurice Cockrill

Contemporary Art from Africa at Bluecoat Gallery, includes work by Ronald Moody, Uzo Egonu and Errol Lloyd

1974

Maurice Cockrill's *Scillonian Pumps,* 1974, wins a prize in the John Moores exhibition. In the same year he exhibits at the Bluecoat Gallery

Adrian Henri's *Environments and Happenings* is published by Thames & Hudson, London. The book offers a

historical overview of the origins of assemblage, environment, and performance art

Deaf School formed by students and staff at Liverpool College of Art. An archetypal 'art school band', they go on to win the Melody Maker best new band competition, securing a deal with Warner Brothers and releasing three albums

1975

Peter Moores Project 3, *Body and Soul* at the Walker Art Gallery. Exhibited works include Stephen Willat's *A Moment of Action*, 1974

1976

The Face of Merseyside, exhibition of works by Liverpool Academy artists, held at the Walker Art Gallery

Ken Campbell forms the Science Fiction Theatre of Liverpool to stage his play *Illuminatus!* at the Liverpool School of Language, Music, Dream and Pun, 18 Mathew Street

Roger Eagle and Pete Fulwell establish Eric's on Mathew Street. A number of eminent

12
Publicity poster for
Yoko Ono performance
26 September 1967,
Bluecoat Gallery, Liverpool

13
Dada 1916-1966:
Documents of the
International Dada
Movement
Walker Art Gallery,
15 August to 25
September 1968

14
Art in a City:
The Liverpool Look,
Exhibition leaflet,
(London, Institute of
Contemporary Arts, 1967)
Collection of
Catherine Marcangeli

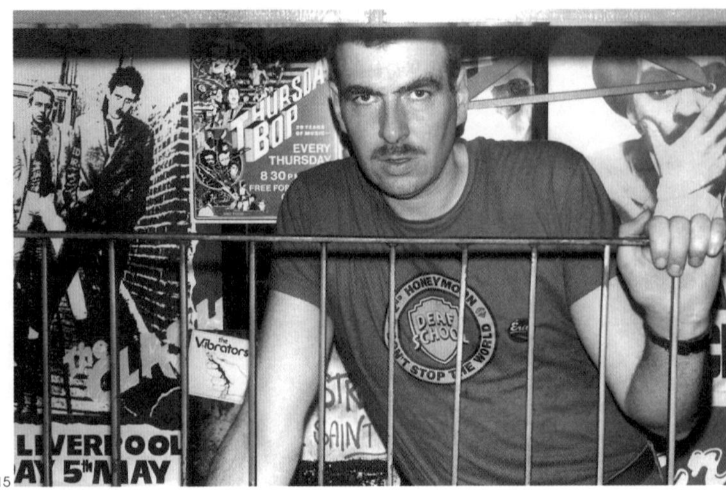

Punk and New Wave acts play at the venue, which becomes instrumental in developing the city's music scene. It closes in 1980

1977
Peter Moores Project 4, *Real Life* exhibition at the Walker Art Gallery. Works include Boyle Family's *Herculaneum Dock Series*, 1976, and four paintings by Maurice Cockrill

Open Eye Gallery opens in the former public bar of the Grapes Hotel on the corner of Whitechapel and Hood Street. The gallery moves to Bold Street in the early 1990s, before re-launching in November 1996 at its current Wood Street premises

1978
Adrian Henri becomes president of Merseyside Arts Association

Bill Drummond and David Balfe form Zoo Records, an independent Liverpool-based record label which releases records by Echo and the Bunnymen, The Teardrop Explodes and others

Photographer Tom Wood moves to Wallasey

Phil Redmond's *Grange Hill* first broadcast on BBC

1979
Seven in Two, Maurice Cockrill's public art commission is installed at Lime Street Station. He has a solo exhibition at the Bluecoat Gallery the following year

Peter Moores Project 5, *The Craft of Art* at the Walker Art Gallery

1980
John Lennon murdered in New York

Liverpool Artists' Workshop established. It initiates projects and develops a lecture programme around the idea of art in a social context. Speakers include Terry Atkinson, Pete Dunn and Griselda Pollock

1981
On 3 July racial tension and social deprivation erupts into three nights of street rioting centred in the Liverpool 8 area. The event is quickly dubbed the 'Toxteth Riots' by the media

Art and the Sea, a nationwide collaboration involving coastal venues and artists working around maritime themes is shown in Liverpool at Bluecoat Gallery and other venues

The Liverpool Academy of Arts closes

1982
Alan Bleasdale's *The Boys from the Blackstuff* is broadcast by the BBC

Phil Redmond establishes Mersey Television to produce *Brookside* broadcast for Channel 4. The series runs until 2003. In 1995 he produces *Hollyoaks,* also for Channel 4

Albert Dock acquired by Merseyside Development Corporation

Martin Parr moves to Wallasey. The following year he begins to photograph New Brighton – these works become *The Last Resort* series

1983
The film adaptation of Willy Russell's *Educating Rita*, starring Julie Walters and Michael Caine, is released

Peter Moores Project 7, *As of Now* staged at the Walker Art Gallery

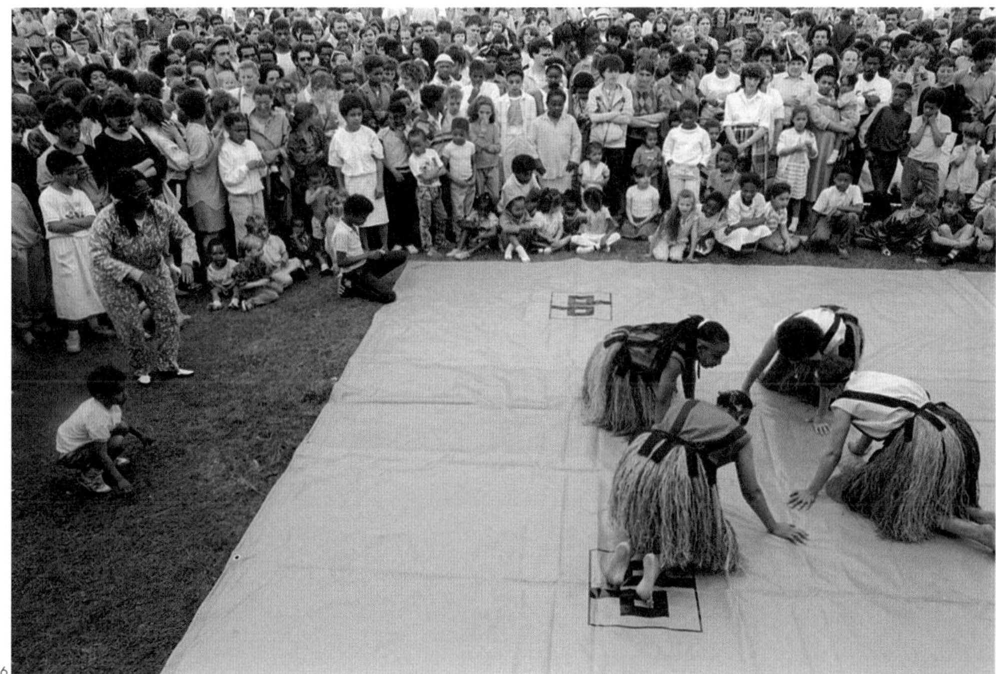

Bridget Riley commissioned to paint a mural at the Royal Liverpool Hospital

1984
The International Garden Festival takes place in Otterspool. Occupying 100 hectares, this 'five month pageant of horticultural excellence and spectacular entertainment' attracts 3.4 million visitors. The festival includes a major sculpture exhibition curated by Sue Grayson

Artists, designers and craftspeople move into a warehouse on Duke Street, converting it into studios and workshops. Gaining charitable status in 1986 as the British Art and Design Association, the group later becomes known as Arena in 1997

1985
Joint exhibition of photographs by Martin Parr and Tom Wood at the Open Eye Gallery

Black Skin, the first exhibition to reflect the emerging Black art movement in UK, is staged at the Bluecoat Gallery. It features works by Eddie Chambers, Keith Piper, Sonia Boyce and Tam Joseph

Letter to Brezhnev, Liverpool-based film, is released

1986
Phil Hayes establishes *The Picket,* a rehearsal space, recording studio, and live music venue on Hardman Street

Under the Directorship of Richard Foster, National Museums and Galleries on Merseyside (NMGM) is established following the abolition of Merseyside County Council.

In the same year it acquires the Stewart Bale photographic archive

Connections, an exhibition exploring the links between Manchester and Liverpool, is staged jointly at Open Eye and Bluecoat Galleries and Cornerhouse in Manchester. The exhibition includes work by Vanley Burke, Peter Clarke, John Davies, John Hyatt, Martin Parr and Jenny Wilson

1987
The Granby Street Festival, Liverpool 8, is photographed by Vanley Burke

Barbara Kruger *We Don't Need Another Hero* billboard appears in Liverpool and on

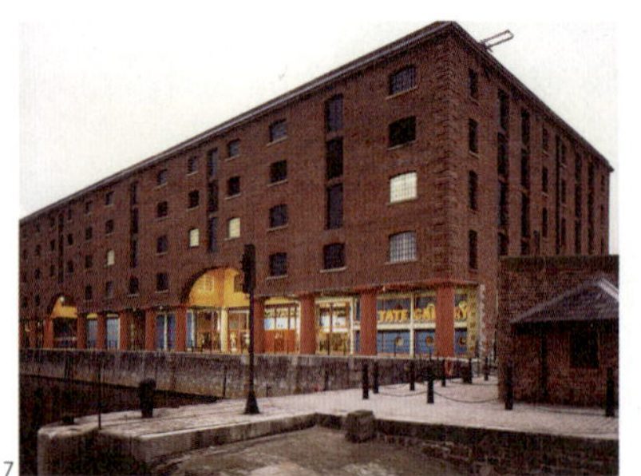

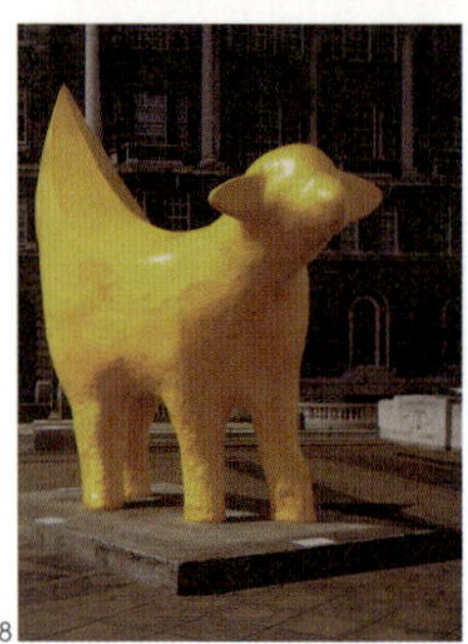

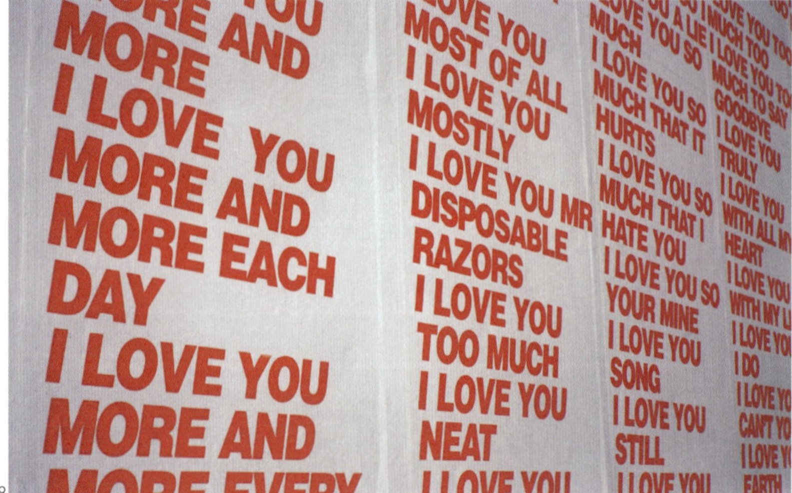

sites across the UK and Ireland. The project is initiated by Artangel and coincides with the broadcast of a Channel 4 television series about 1980s art

Start of on-going cultural exchange programme with Liverpool's sister city of Cologne, coordinated by Merseyside Arts. Bluecoat Gallery continues the exchange with Cologne's BBK Gallery over next ten years, after which it is superseded by *Eight Days A Week*

1988
Tate Gallery Liverpool opens on 24 May. Its first exhibition is *Starlit Waters: British Sculpture, an International Art 1968-1988*

Merseyside Moviola founded to commission and present work in galleries and other exhibition spaces by international artists working in film, video and new media

Photographer Edward Chambré-Hardman dies

Art transport company MOMART begin supporting an artist-in-residence programme at Tate Liverpool. Residency artists include Marion Coutts, Neville Gabie, Gary Perkins, James Rielly, Laura Godfrey Isaacs, Emma

Rushton, Maud Sulter and Paul Rooney. The scheme runs until 2002

1989
Bluecoat Arts Centre and ARK Records present *Pop Mechanica*: *Perestroika in the Avant-Garde*, bringing Soviet musicians and artists to Liverpool for a series of events

Sam Walsh dies aged 55; he has a memorial show at the Walker Art Gallery

Merseyside Moviola organises the first *Video Positive* biennial. Works are sited at Bluecoat Arts Centre, Williamson Art Gallery and Tate Gallery Liverpool

Jimmy McGovern's *Cracker* first broadcast on ITV

1992
Tracey Emin organises *The Phone Box* project, which involves placing artworks in telephone boxes in the red light districts of London and Liverpool

James Barton launches the Cream dance music night at Nation nightclub, Wolstenholme Square. One of the first

'superclubs', it spawns a record label, a residency in Ibiza and Creamfields, an annual dance music festival

The first Visionfest annual visual arts festival takes place

Trophies of Empire exhibition at the Bluecoat, includes works by Nina Edge, Sunil Gupta and Keith Piper

1994
Arthur Ballard dies

1995
Alan Dunn begins the Liverpool Billboard Project

1996
Artist group Common Culture form in Liverpool. Its members comprise David Campbell, Mark Durden, Paul Rooney and Anna Vickery

Liverpool Institute for Performing Arts (LIPA) is founded

1997
Mixing It, a season of live art performances commissioned by the Bluecoat Gallery includes the premiere of Jeremy Deller's

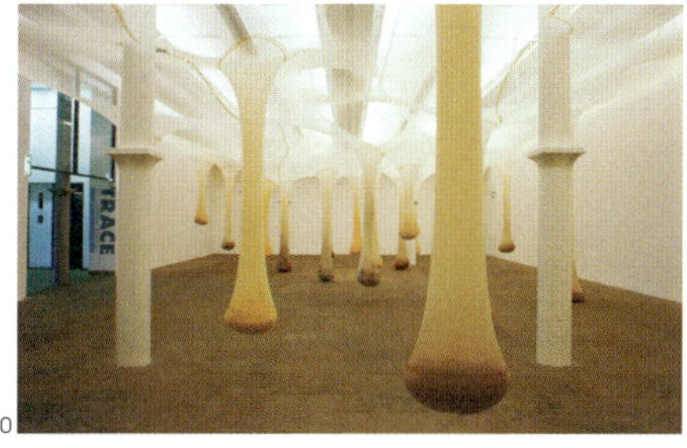

20

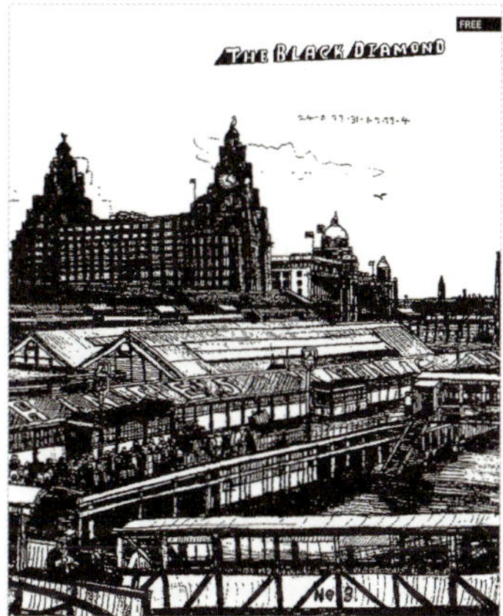

21

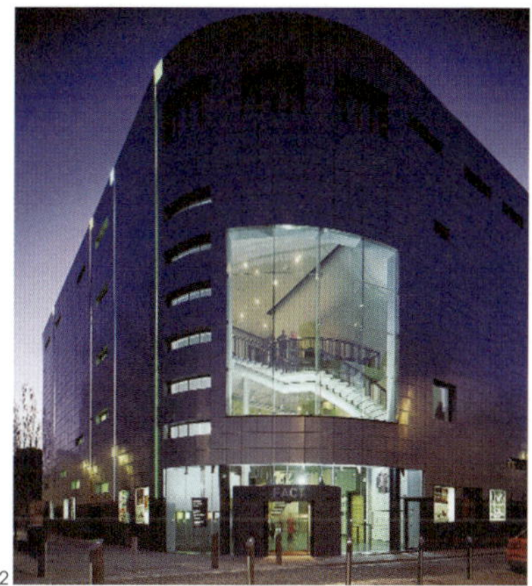

22

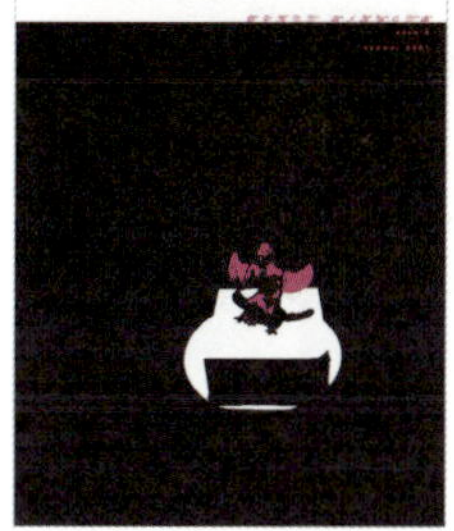

Acid Brass, 1997, which is performed by the Williams Fairey Brass Band at LIPA

1998
Continuing a family tradition of arts patronage, James Moores establishes the A Foundation to support the development and exhibition of contemporary art in Liverpool

Static, an arts organisation offering working and exhibition space to Liverpool-based artists and architects is established

Michael Wilford completes the second phase of Tate Liverpool's development. The scheme creates new galleries, more space for education activities and improved visitor facilities. The building reopens with *Artranspennine98*, a festival of international contemporary art staged at venues across the North of England. One of the commissions is Taro Chiezo's *Superlambanana*, 1998, which becomes an iconic piece of public sculpture in Liverpool

Tom Wood's *All Zones Off Peak* is exhibited at the Open Eye Gallery and Bluecoat Gallery

1999
The first Liverpool Biennial is presented at arts venues across Liverpool. Its international exhibition, *Trace,* curated by Tony Bond, includes Liverpool artists Susan Fitch and Amanda Ralph. The Biennial also opens up opportunities for grass-roots and artist-led initiatives through *Tracey,* the independent strand of the festival

Adrian Henri retrospective at the Walker Art Gallery

Black Diamond arts magazine is established by Liverpool artist Duncan Hamilton

2000
Adrian Henri dies

2002
Second Liverpool Biennial staged

2003
Foundation for Art and Creative Technology (FACT) established in a building on Wood Street having operated out of the Bluecoat since the mid-1980s as Merseyside Moviola, having changed its name in 1997. Dedicated to commissioning and developing the work of artists working in film, video and emerging media, this is the first purpose-built arts centre in Liverpool since the Philharmonic Hall opened in 1939

17
Tate Gallery Liverpool
1988

18
Tara Chiezo
Superlambanana 1998

19
Fiona Banner
Love Double 1999
commissioned by Alan Dunn & Godfrey Burke Liverpool Billboard Project. Digital print by Augustus Martin. Billboard courtesy of Maiden Outdoor located at Prescot Road, Liverpool, 1999. Photograph by Alan Dunn

20
Ernesto Neto
We Fishing the Time (densidades e buracos de minhoca) 1999
Trace: Liverpool Biennial of Contemporary Art at Tate Gallery Liverpool

21
Black Diamond
Issue 1, 1999
Issue 3, 2001
Arts magazine established in Liverpool by Duncan Hamilton

22
FACT
(Foundation for Art and Creative Technology), Liverpool, 2003

Campaigning under the slogan 'The World
in One City', Liverpool is awarded 2008
European Capital of Culture status

Tatler magazine describes Liverpool as
'Livercool… the jewel of the north… the
place where tradition meets cutting edge'

George Wallace Jardine, the Liverpool
surrealist, dies aged 82

2004
UNESCO inscripts the Liverpool Maritime
Mercantile City as a World Heritage Site

Liverpool Biennial 2004 takes place

2005
Liverpool artist Nicholas Horsfield dies.
Horsfield had been a member of the
Liverpool Academy of Arts from 1954,
and its president from 1960 to 1965

Antony Gormley's *Another Place* is installed
on Crosby Beach

2006
A Foundation launches its Greenland
Street arts venue in three former
industrial buildings

Liverpool Biennial 2006 staged

23
A Foundation,
View from the roof of
Greenland Street,
July 2006

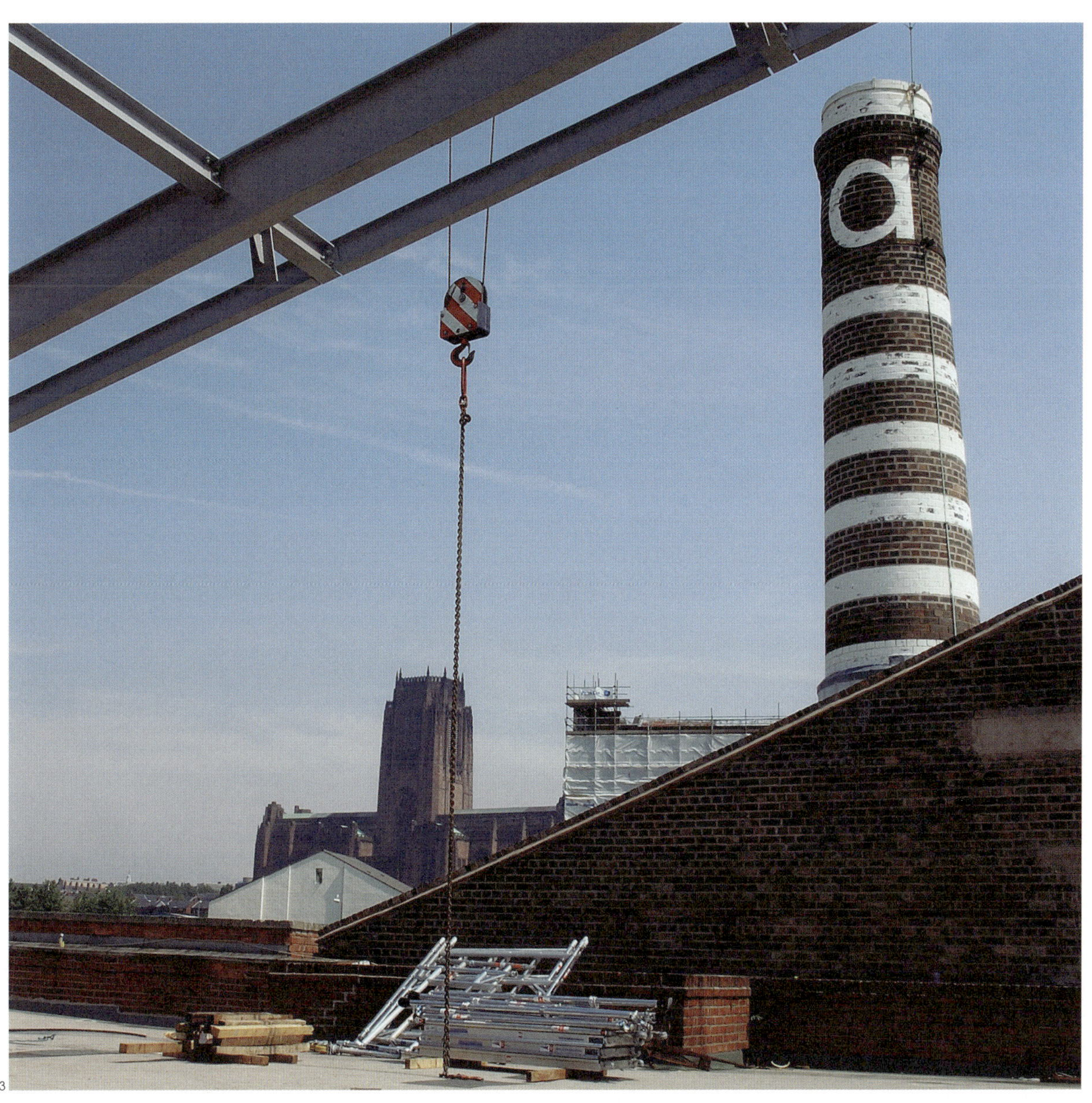

23

Christoph Grunenberg has been Director of Tate Liverpool since 2001. He previously held positions in the Collections Division of Tate, the Institute of Contemporary Art in Boston, the Kunsthalle Basel and the National Gallery of Art in Washington, D.C. He has curated numerous exhibition including *Rachel Whiteread* (1995); *Gothic: Transmutations of Horror in Late 20th Century Art* (1997); *Shopping: A Century of Art and Consumer Culture* (2002); *The Uncanny by Mike Kelley:* (2003); *Summer of Love: Art of the Psychedelic Era* (2005) and *Jake and Dinos Chapman: Bad Art for Bad People* (2006).

Robert Knifton is a PhD student on the AHRC-funded collaborative programme between Tate Liverpool and the Manchester Institute for Research in Art & Design at Manchester Metropolitan University. His museum experience includes work at The Victoria and Albert Museum, South Kensington, The Whitworth Art Gallery, Manchester, The Walker Art Gallery, Liverpool, and Cube, Manchester.

Bryan Biggs has been closely involved in the arts in Liverpool since he first came to the city in the early 1970s. He is an artistic administrator and curator, working in various roles at Bluecoat Arts Centre, where he is now Artistic Director. He has curated many exhibitions, including the 2002 Liverpool Biennial *International* and *Walk On*, an exhibition for the 2006 Shanghai Biennale. He has written about contemporary art and popular music for publications such as *Bidoun*, *Third Text* and *Strange Things Are Happening*, and is an artist known for his drawings.

Bill Drummond is an artist. He is best known as co-founder of The KLF, the avant-garde 'pop group' of the late 1980s, the K Foundation, its 1990s 'avant-art' media-manipulating successor, as the

original manager of Echo and the Bunnymen, and for burning a million quid. He has written several books – including *From the Shores of Lake Placid*, *45*, *How To Be An Artist*, *The Wild Highway* and *Scores 18 – 76* – and produced a variety of different conceptual art projects.

Sam Gathercole is an art historian, writer and curator living in London. Sam has held teaching posts at a number of institutions, including University of Essex and University of Liverpool. Recent publications include "'I'm sort of sliding around in place… ummm…": Art in the 1970s' in *A Companion to Contemporary Art since 1945* edited by Amelia Jones (2006) and 'Art and Construction in the 1950s,' in *Art History* (2006). Sam curated (with Steven Gartside) the exhibition *Concrete Thoughts* at Whitworth Art Gallery, Manchester in the autumn of 2006, and (with Claire Brown) he has curated *Good Riddance* at the MOT Gallery, London, in early 2007.

Jaki Florek is a ceramic artist, poet, musician and writer who played at Eric's Club in Liverpool; she is currently writing a history of the club. No longer able to perform (FMS), Jaki manages the experimental group Stig Sound System and art-ska band Zen Baseballbat, runs Loose Music Collective, and is editor of *Feedback* arts and music magazine.

Paul R. Jones is a Lecturer in Sociology at the University of Liverpool. His main research interests fall within the broad area of urban sociology, with a particular focus on culture, power and collective identities. He is currently addressing these themes in relation to regeneration in Liverpool, with specific reference to the tensions associated with rebranding the city as Capital of Culture 2008.

Richard Koeck is an architect, digital filmmaker, and postdoctoral researcher whose practical as well as theoretical work is dedicated to the correlation between architecture and the moving image. Alongside Les Roberts, he is currently working as a postdoctoral researcher at the University of Liverpool on the interdisciplinary project *City in Film: Liverpool's Urban Landscape and the Moving Image*, an AHRC-funded research project run by Dr Julia Hallam from the School of Politics & Communication Studies, and Professor Robert Kronenburg from the School of Architecture.

Paul Morley has written for numerous publications including the *New Musical Express*, *The Face*, *New Statesman* and *Esquire*. As a musician, he co-founded ZTT Records with producer Trevor Horn and was a member of Art of Noise. He currently records as a member of Infantjoy. His books include *Ask: Chatter of Pop*, *Nothing* and *Words and Music: A History of Pop in the Shape of a City*, and he is presently writing a book about the North. He appears regularly on BBC2's arts review programme *Newsnight Review*, is the rock critic for *The Sunday Telegraph* and critic-at-large for *The Observer Music Monthly*.

Darren Pih is an Assistant Curator at Tate Liverpool. He also wrote for *Summer of Love: Psychedelic Art, Social Crisis and Counterculture in the 1960s* published by Liverpool University Press, and previously worked at the Whitworth Art Gallery, Manchester and at Camden Arts Centre, London.

Lucy Reynolds is an artist, writer, independent film programmer and Content Manager for LuxOnline. Her current research as a PhD student at the University of East London explores the expanded cinema events of Gill Eatherley, Annabel Nicolson and Lis Rhodes. She has curated numerous screening of artists film and video since the late 1990s, her recent film programme, *Describing Form*, exploring the relationship between film and sculpture, has toured museums and galleries across Britain. Recent publications include 'Margaret Tait: The Marks of Time' in *Subjects and Sequences: A Margaret Tait Reader* and 'Found Footage Film: The World in Fragments' in *Ghostings: The Role of the Archive in Contemporary Artists Film and Video*. She teaches the history and theory of artists' moving image at the University of Westminster, the University of Derby and Birkbeck College.

Les Roberts is a cultural geographer and theorist whose work examines the broad intersection between ideas of space, place and mobility, particularly in relation to film. Alongside Richard Koeck, he is currently working as a postdoctoral researcher at the University of Liverpool on the interdisciplinary project *City in Film: Liverpool's Urban Landscape and the Moving Image*, an AHRC-funded research project run by Dr Julia Hallam from the School of Politics & Communication Studies, and Professor Robert Kronenburg from the School of Architecture.

Russell Roberts is Senior Research Fellow in Photography – Exhibitions, at Ffotogallery and University of Wales, Newport. He has curated numerous international exhibitions including: *Memory & The Archive – Photographs, Images, Documents* (1995); *In Visible Light: Photography & Classification in Art, Science & The Everyday* (1997); *Specimens & Marvels – The Art & Science of William Henry Fox Talbot* (2000); *Unknown Pleasures* (2003); and *A Gentle Madness: The Photographs of Tony Ray-Jones* (2004). He is currently researching a book and exhibition on the work of Mass Observation.

Simon Warner teaches popular music at the University of Leeds. A former rock journalist – he was a reviewer with *The Guardian* from 1992-5 – he is also director of PopuLUs, the University's centre for the study of the world's popular musics. Simon Warner's publications include *Rockspeak: The Language of Rock and Pop* (Blandford, 1996) and, as editor, *Howl for Now: A Celebration of Allen Ginsberg's Epic Protest Poem* (Route, 2005).

Stuart Wilks-Heeg has research interests in globalisation and world city governance and economy, society and politics in contemporary Liverpool. He also works in the area of urban regeneration, with particular reference to cultural policy, and (with Paul Jones) has published 'Capitalising Culture: Liverpool 2008' in *Local Economy* (2004).

Editors & Contributors

Photography Credits

p. 2 (1), p. 54 (8),
p. 55 (9), p. 76 (20),
p. 77 (21)
© Tom Wood

p. 4 (2)
© Maurice Cockrill

p. 16 (1), p. 110 (15),
p. 111 (16), p. 134 (1),
p. 137 (2), p. 138 (3),
p. 140 (4), p. 238 (2),
p. 238 (3), p. 242 (13)
© National Museums
Liverpool, Walker Art
Gallery

p. 8 (3), p. 11 (4),
p. 147 (7), p. 68 (15),
p. 239 (5)
© Candida Höfer,
DACS, London 2007

p. 12 (5), **p. 15 (6),**
p. 63 (8/9/10),
p. 85 (4), p. 218 (9)
© National Museums
Liverpool, Merseyside
Maritime Museum

p. 19 (2/3), p. 43 (2),
p. 43 (3)
**© Henri Cartier-Bresson/
Magnum Photos**

cover image,
p. 19 (4), p. 40 (1),
p. 44 (4), p. 56 (1),
p. 61 (7), p. 94 (1),
p. 238 (1)
© NT/E.Chambré
Hardman Collection

p. 20 (5)
© Sheridon Davies

p. 22 (6), p. 47 (5),
p. 48 (6), p. 51 (7),
p. 79 (22), p. 210 (4/5),
p. 214 (7)
© Martin Parr/Magnum
Photos

p. 26 (7), p. 32 (11),
p. 104 (12), p. 109 (14),
p. 122 (7), p.123 (8)
© Catherine Marcangeli

p. 29 (8), p. 30 (10),
p. 35 (13), p. 246 (17),
p. 246 (18), p. 247 (20)
© Tate

p. 29 (9)
© Melik Ohanian

p. 34 (12)
© Keith Arnatt

p. 38 (14/15/16/17/18)
© Gordon Fazakerley

p. 59 (3)
© National Media
Museum/Science and
Society Picture Library

p. 60 (4/5)
© John Dudley Johnston

p. 60 (6)
© Royal Photographic
Society/National Media
Museum/Science and
Society Picture Library

p. 64 (11/12/13/14),
back cover image
© Cunard Archives, the
University of Liverpool
Library

p. 70 (16)
© Bernd and Hilla Becher

p. 73 (17/18)
© Ken Grant

p. 74 (19), p. 180 (19),
p. 202 (1), p. 206 (3),
p. 213 (6), p. 245 (16)
© Vanley Burke

p. 80 (23), p. 81 (24),
p. 224 (2), p. 228 (4)
© Alec Soth/Magnum
Photos

p. 82 (1), p. 85 (2),
p. 93 (10)
© Les Roberts and
Richard Koeck

p. 85 (3)
© Production: British
Film Institute (BFI),
Channel Four Films.
VHS – Sony Pictures

p. 88 (5)
© Production: Ealing
Studios

p. 90 (6), p. 90 (7),
p. 92 (8), p. 92 (9),
p. 98 (6), p. 99 (7),
p. 99 (8), p. 101 (10),
p. 127 (10), p. 154 (11),
p. 168 (1), p. 171 (2),
p 171 (3), p. 172 (6),
p. 172 (7), p. 172 (8),
p. 172 (10), p. 174 (11),
p. 174 (12), p. 174 (13),
p. 175 (14), p. 176 (15),
p. 176 (16), p. 179 (18),
p. 241 (9), p. 241 (10),
p. 241 (11)
© Unable to trace
copyright holders

p. 97 (2), p. 97 (3),
p. 97 (4), p. 97 (5),
p. 171 (5), p. 238 (4)
© Max Scheler/K&K
(Liverpool 1964)

p. 99 (9)
© Wendy Harpe (cover)
Heather Holden (poem)

p. 102 (11)
© The Trustees of
The British Museum

p. 107 (13)
© Whitford Fine Art,
London

p. 112 (1)
© Estate of Sam Walsh

p. 115 (2), p. 116 (3)
© Telegraph Media Group
Limited

p. 119 (4)
© James MacRitchie,
Boulder, Colorado

p. 119 (5)
© Penguin

p. 120 (6)
© The University of
Manchester

p. 124 (9)
© ITV Archives

p. 128 (11)
© Gwyn Ritchards

p. 130 (12/13),
p. 132 (14/15)
© Jeremy Deller and
Paul Ryan

p. 142 (5)
© Victoria Miro Gallery

p. 144 (6)
© Stephen Willats

p. 148 (8), p. 149 (9),
p. 150 (10), p. 155 (12)
© Boyle Family

p. 156 (1), p. 159 (2),
p. 162 (6)
© David Crosswaite

p. 159 (3/4), p. 160 (5),
p. 166 (7)
© William Raban

p. 171 (4), p. 240 (7)
© Bettmann/CORBIS

p. 172 (9)
© Pete Fulwell

p. 176 (17)
© Geoff Roberts

p. 182 (1), p. 185 (2),
p. 185 (3), p. 186 (4),
p. 186 (5), p. 189 (7),
p. 190 (8), p. 192 (9),
p. 192 (10), p. 195 (11),
p. 196 (12), p. 196 (13),
p. 196 (14)
© Bluecoat Arts Centre

p. 189 (6)
© Will Curwen

p. 198 (15), p. 198 (16)
© Bob and Roberta Smith

p. 199 (17)
© Rineke Dijkstra

p. 200 (18)
© Anna Fox

p. 205 (2)
© Neville Gabie

p. 216 (8)
© Paul Ryan

p. 220 (1), p. 226 (3)
© Bill Drummond

p. 231, p. 233, p. 235,
p. 236-7
© CollinsBartholomew

p. 239 (6)
© Wendy Harpe

p. 240 (8)
© Neville Weston

p. 242 (12)
© Dave Clapham

p. 243 (14)
© Institute of
Contemporary Arts/
Estate of G. W. Jardine

p. 244 (15)
© Bob Letsche, 1977

p. 246 (19)
© Alan Dunn

p. 247 (21)
© Duncan Hamilton

p. 247 (22)
© FACT
(Foundation for Art and
Creative Technology)

p. 248 (23)
Courtesy of Rob Meighen
© A Foundation

Every effort has been made
to trace the holders of
copyright material reproduced
in this book, and it is noted
below where this has not
been possible. Liverpool
University Press would be
pleased to hear from the
owners of this material in
order to recognise the
copyright holders. They
would also be pleased to be
informed of any errors or
omissions for corrections in
future editions of this book.

Index

First published 2007 by

Liverpool University Press
4 Cambridge Street
Liverpool
L69 7ZU
www.liverpool-unipress.co.uk

in association with

Tate Liverpool
Albert Dock
Liverpool
L3 4BB
www.tate.org.uk/liverpool

Distributed in the Canada, Mexico and the USA
by University of Chicago Press

British Library Cataloguing-in-Publication Data
A British Library CIP record is available

ISBN 9781846310898 cased
     9781846310812 limp

Designed by Lawn Creative, Liverpool

Header text: ITC Avant-Garde Gothic 15pt
Body text: Times New Roman 8.5/11pt

Soft cover: 350gsm Chromomat, North West Paper
Text: 135gsm Cypher, Premier Paper

Printed in the European Union by
Synergy Fine Colour Printers, Wirral

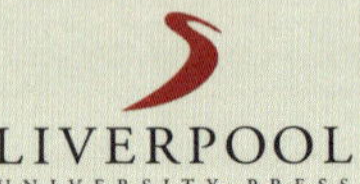
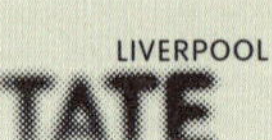

cover
**Edward
Chambré-Hardman**
*Liverpool's Two
Cathedrals* 1969
Black and white photograph
39.4 x 45 cm
The National Trust,
Edward Chambré-Hardman
Collection

back cover
Stewart Bale
Ivernia
Colour photograph
40.7 x 50.8 cm
The University of Liverpool
Special Collections
and Archives